International Series in Pure and Applied Mathematics

William Ted Martin, CONSULTING EDITOR

FOURIER TRANSFORMS

International Series in Pure and Applied Mathematics

WILLIAM TED MARTIN, *Consulting Editor*

FOURIER TRANSFORMS

IAN N. SNEDDON

Lecturer in Natural Philosophy
University of Glasgow

FIRST EDITION
SECOND IMPRESSION

New York   Toronto   London

McGRAW-HILL BOOK COMPANY, INC.

1951

FOURIER TRANSFORMS

C

THE MAPLE PRESS COMPANY, YORK, PA.

To

The University of Glasgow
on the occasion of
its fifth centenary

1451–1951

PREFACE

The aim of this book is to present the theory of Fourier transforms and related topics in a form suitable for the use of students and research workers interested in the boundary value problems of physics and engineering. It is based upon postgraduate lectures given, during the last few years, in the University of Glasgow to audiences drawn mainly from the research schools in mathematics, theoretical physics, and engineering. Some sections have also been used in lectures to "honours" undergraduates. The first three chapters contain the basic theory and the remaining seven are devoted to the illustration of the use of this theory in the solution of boundary and initial value problems in engineering and physics.

Since it has been written for those whose interest is primarily in the applications of the theory rather than in the theory itself, it makes no attempt to present the foundations in their most general form, as is done so elegantly, for instance, in the classical treatises of Titchmarsh and Widder. The main theorems are established for a certain class of functions which is sufficiently wide to embrace most of those which occur in problems in applied mathematics. In addition, in order that it may be read by undergraduates beginning the study of theoretical physics, no specialized knowledge of physics is assumed; each chapter begins with a discussion of the physical fundamentals and the derivation of the basic equations. Most of the book should, therefore, be accessible to a student well grounded in the methods of advanced calculus, but the material of the first three chapters is arranged in such a way that, if the reader wishes to use the results of the pure mathematical theory without entering into details of proof, he may readily pick out the results he needs. The chapters dealing with applications are quite independent and may be read in any order.

Books dealing with the applications of integral transforms to physical problems suffer, in the main, from two defects. They seldom attempt to cover the whole field of Fourier transform theory, restricting themselves to the theory of some special transform, such as the Mellin or Laplace transform, which forms but a corner of the entire field. Secondly, the applications discussed are often of a trivial nature—more suitable for illustrating the basic points of the theory than for helping the research worker to acquire a body of technique sufficient to enable him to handle the problems he encounters in the course of his researches.   An attempt has been made to overcome the first difficulty by including, in the chapters on basic theory, not only the common properties of the Fourier transforms but also those of the Mellin, Laplace, and Hankel transforms. Finite transforms, dual integral equations, the Wiener-Hopf procedure, and the properties of the Dirac delta function are also considered in some detail.   In an attempt to make the book more directly useful to students whose interest is in "applied" problems, the physical problems discussed have been chosen for their current interest and are seldom trivial. Most of them are taken from research papers written in the last ten years.

The use of the Dirac delta function is frowned upon by many pure mathematicians, and certainly its use is apt to lead to a kind of mathematics which, as Professor Titchmarsh remarks, is quite unlike anything to be found in Landau's "Handbuch" or Hardy's lectures.   It does, however, afford the applied mathematician a powerful tool with which to construct solutions whose validity may be verified by more orthodox methods.

The author wishes to extend his thanks to the Council of the Royal Society for permission to reproduce Figs. 84, 85, and 101 to 105 from one of his own papers in the *Proceedings* of the society, and to the Council of the Cambridge Philosophical Society for similar permission for the use of Figs. 14 to 18, 83, 92, 93, and 96 to 100.   He is also indebted to the editor of the *Physical Review* for permission to reproduce Fig. 46 from a paper by G. Placzek, to the editor of the *Philosophical Magazine* for permitting the reproduction of Fig. 55 and Figs. 106 to 108 from papers by W. R. Dean and C. J. Tranter, respectively, and to the Council of the Physical Society of London for Figs. 72 and 73 taken from a paper by C. A. Coulson in their *Proceedings*.

The critical comments of colleagues and students who attended the lectures upon which this book is based were of considerable value to the author and are most gratefully acknowledged.   In particular he wishes to thank Dr. Daniel Martin for reading the final manuscript with great thoroughness and for making suggestions for the removal of blemishes, Catherine Anderson for her assistance in the preparation of the manuscript for the press, and Robin Giles who devoted a great deal of time to a careful reading of the proof sheets.

The influence of Titchmarsh's book on the present one will be obvious to all who study both; the author would like to record not only his indebtedness but the keen pleasure he derived from the study of this work.

In conclusion, two debts of a more personal kind must be mentioned. The author would like to take this opportunity to express his indebtedness to Dr. J. W. Harding, who first aroused his interest in the theory of integral transforms and guided his first steps in research. Most of the problems discussed in Chapters 9 and 10 were first studied by the author when, during the Second World War, he worked under the supervision of Professor N. F. Mott. Like not a few men of his generation, the author is indebted to Mott not only for his valuable comments on the work in hand but also for the stimulus and encouragement he gave them not to lose sight of fundamental problems while engaged on day-to-day ones for the armed forces.

IAN N. SNEDDON

GLASGOW, SCOTLAND
December, 1950

CONTENTS

CHAPTER 8

Theory of radioactive transformations. Van der Waals attraction between spherical particles. Interaction of radiation with an electron. Cascade theory of cosmic ray showers. Distribution of momentum in atomic and molecular systems. Binding energies of the lightest nuclei

CHAPTER 9

Equations of motion. Infinite elastic solid with body forces. Application of pressure to the surfaces of a two-dimensional elastic solid. Distribution of stress due to a force in the interior of a semiinfinite elastic medium. Distribution of stress in the neighborhood of a Griffith crack. Indentation problems. Two-dimensional problems in polar coordinates. Dynamical problems

CHAPTER 10

Equations of equilibrium. Stresses produced by the indentation of the plane surface of a semiinfinite elastic medium by a rigid punch. Application of pressure to the faces of a thick plate. Distribution of stress in the neighborhood of a circular crack in an elastic body. Distribution of stress in a semiinfinite elastic medium due to a torsional displacement of the surface. Stress distribution in a long circular cylinder when a discontinuous pressure is applied to the curved surface.

APPENDIX A

Bessel's differential equation. Recurrence relations for Bessel functions of the first kind. Definite integrals involving Bessel functions. Infinite integrals involving Bessel functions. Relation between the Bessel functions and circular functions. Integral expression for the Bessel function $J_n(x)$

APPENDIX B

Method of steepest descents for contour integrals. Numerical calculations of Fourier integrals

APPENDIX C

Fourier transforms. Fourier cosine transforms. Fourier sine transforms. Laplace transforms. Mellin transforms. Hankel transforms. Finite Fourier cosine transforms. Finite Fourier sine transforms. Finite Hankel transforms

CHAPTER 1

FOURIER TRANSFORMS

1. Integral Transforms

For a considerable time it has been recognized that the operator calculus devised by Oliver Heaviside for the solution of transient problems in physics and electrical engineering was formally equivalent to a systematic use of the Laplace transform. This is the method of presentation adopted in most modern textbooks on operator calculus.[1] If, for instance, the function $f(x)$ is defined by a differential equation and certain boundary conditions, it is found simpler in certain circumstances to translate the boundary value problem for $f(x)$ into one for the function

$$\phi(p) = \int_0^\infty f(x)e^{-px}\,dx \tag{1}$$

obtained from $f(x)$ by multiplying by e^{-px} and integrating with respect to x from 0 to ∞. The function $\phi(p)$ defined in this way is obviously a function of the variable p. It is called the *Laplace transform* of the function $f(x)$.

This concept may be extended in an obvious way. When the function $K(\alpha,x)$ is a known function of the two variables α and x and the integral

$$I_f(\alpha) = \int_0^\infty f(x)K(\alpha,x)dx \tag{2}$$

is convergent, then the equation (2) defines a function of the variable α. This function is called the *integral transform* of the function $f(x)$ by the kernel $K(\alpha,x)$. The simplest example of such a kernel is

$$K(\alpha,x) = e^{-\alpha x}$$

leading to the Laplace transform (1). Another kernel which is commonly

---

[1] See, for example, H. Jeffreys, "Operational Methods in Mathematical Physics" (Cambridge, London, 1931); J. R. Carson, "Electric Circuit Theory and the Operational Calculus" (McGraw-Hill, New York, 1926); N. W. McLachlan, "Complex Variable and the Operator Calculus" (Cambridge, London, 1942); G. Doetsch, "Theorie und Anwendung der Laplace-Transformation" (Dover, New York, 1944); H. S. Carslaw and J. C. Jaeger, "Operational Methods in Applied Mathematics" (Oxford, New York, 1941); R. V. Churchill, "Modern Operational Mathematics in Engineering" (McGraw-Hill, New York, 1944).

used in this way is the kernel

$$K(\alpha,x) = x^{\alpha-1}$$

leading to the transform

$$\mathsf{F}(\alpha) = \int_0^\infty f(x)x^{\alpha-1}\,dx \tag{3}$$

Integral transforms of this type were investigated systematically for the first time by Mellin,[1] and, for that reason, the function $\mathsf{F}(\alpha)$ defined by equation (3) is called the *Mellin transform* of the function $f(x)$. Other special transforms arise when the kernel $K(\alpha,x)$ is a sine or a cosine and when it is a solution of Bessel's differential equation. We shall define these transforms and consider some of their properties later.

It will be observed immediately from the definition (2) that, if $f(x)$ and $g(x)$ are two functions which possess integral transforms by the kernel $K(\alpha,x)$, then the integral transform of their sum is

$$\int_0^\infty (f+g)K(\alpha,x)dx = \int_0^\infty f(x)K(\alpha,x)dx + \int_0^\infty g(x)K(\alpha,x)dx$$

that is, it is the sum of their integral transforms. Furthermore, if c is a scalar,

$$\int_0^\infty cf(x)K(\alpha,x)dx = c\int_0^\infty f(x)K(\alpha,x)dx$$

These equations express the fact that the operator transforming the function $f(x)$ into its integral transform $I_f(\alpha)$ is a linear operator.

We might then regard equation (2) as a transformation between the functions $f(x)$ and $I_f(\alpha)$ and build up an abstract theory of transformations of this type by means of the properties of Banach spaces. Such a program would be of great interest mathematically, but it is not very fruitful if our main interest lies in the direction of making applications to mathematical physics. Such a discussion will not, therefore, be given here. We shall confine our attention to the consideration of such properties of integral transforms as will be of use in the subsequent analysis of boundary value problems.

2. Fourier Kernels

2.1 Fourier kernels. We saw above that the operator transforming a function into its integral transform by the kernel $K(\alpha,x)$ is a linear operator which we may denote by L, say, so that

$$L(f) = I_f(\alpha)$$

If we now assume that for every function $B(\alpha)$, belonging to a certain

[1] H. Mellin, *Acta Soc. Sci. Fennicae*, **21**, 1–115 (1896); *Acta Math.*, **25**, 139 (1902).

class of functions of the variable α, the equation

$$L(f) = B(\alpha)$$

is satisfied by one, and only one, function $f(x)$, then it can readily be proved that there exists a linear operator L^{-1}, called the inverse of L, such that the equations

$$L(f) = B(\alpha), \qquad f(x) = L^{-1}(B)$$

are equivalent.[1] Our main problem is the determination of these inverse operators for some special cases of the operator L.

These considerations would seem to indicate that, under certain circumstances, it may be possible to determine a solution of the integral equation

$$I_f(\alpha) = \int_0^\infty f(x)K(\alpha,x)dx \tag{4}$$

in the form

$$f(x) = \int_a^b I_f(\alpha)H(\alpha,x)d\alpha \tag{5}$$

A formula of the type (5) which expresses the function $f(x)$ in terms of its integral transform (4) we shall call an *inversion theorem*. In the special case in which the solution (5) of equation (4) is of the type

$$f(x) = \int_0^\infty I_f(\alpha)K(\alpha,x)d\alpha \tag{6}$$

so that the relation between the function and its integral transform is symmetrical, the function $K(\alpha,x)$ is called a *Fourier kernel*.

Before proceeding to a discussion of inversion theorems for special forms of the kernel $K(\alpha,x)$ we shall attempt to establish a necessary condition for a given function to be a Fourier kernel. This, in turn, will help in suggesting possible forms of inversion theorem. We shall restrict our attention to the case in which the kernel $K(\alpha,x)$ is a function of αx alone,

$$K(\alpha,x) = K(x,\alpha) = K(\alpha x),$$

as this case has the widest applications. The main result is contained in:

Theorem 1. *A necessary condition for the function $K(\alpha x)$ to be a Fourier kernel is that the Mellin transform $\mathsf{K}(s)$ of the function $K(x)$ should satisfy the functional equation*

$$\mathsf{K}(s)\mathsf{K}(1 - s) = 1 \tag{7}$$

It will be noted from equation (3) that since $\mathsf{K}(s)$ is the Mellin transform of the function $K(x)$

$$\mathsf{K}(s) = \int_0^\infty K(x)x^{s-1}\,dx$$

---

[1] See, for example, E. B. Curry, *Am. Math. Monthly*, **50**, 365 (1943).

To prove the theorem we multiply both sides of equation (4) by α^{s-1} and integrate with respect to α from 0 to ∞ and obtain

$$\int_0^\infty I_f(\alpha)\alpha^{s-1}\,d\alpha = \int_0^\infty \alpha^{s-1}\,d\alpha \int_0^\infty f(x)K(\alpha x)dx$$
$$= \int_0^\infty f(x)dx \int_0^\infty K(\alpha x)\alpha^{s-1}\,d\alpha$$

the change in the order of integration being justified by Fubini's theorem under wide conditions. Changing the variable in the inner integral to $\eta = \alpha x$ we have

$$\int_0^\infty K(\alpha x)\alpha^{s-1}\,d\alpha = x^{-s}\int_0^\infty K(\eta)\eta^{s-1}\,d\eta = x^{-s}\mathsf{K}(s)$$

so that

$$\int_0^\infty I_f(\alpha)\alpha^{s-1}\,d\alpha = \int_0^\infty f(x)x^{-s}\,dx\,\mathsf{K}(s) \tag{8}$$

If we write

$$\mathsf{I}(s) = \int_0^\infty \overline{I_f(\alpha)\alpha^{s-1}}\,d\alpha, \qquad \mathsf{F}(s) = \int_0^\infty f(x)x^{s-1}\,dx$$

so that $\mathsf{I}(s)$ and $\mathsf{F}(s)$ are the Mellin transforms of $I_f(\alpha)$ and $f(x)$, respectively, then equation (8) becomes

$$\mathsf{I}(s) = \mathsf{K}(s)\mathsf{F}(1-s) \tag{9}$$

On the other hand, if we multiply both sides of equation (6) by x^{s-1} and integrate with respect to x from 0 to ∞, we obtain

$$\int_0^\infty f(x)x^{s-1}\,dx = \int_0^\infty x^{s-1}\,dx \int_0^\infty I_f(\alpha)K(\alpha x)d\alpha$$
$$= \int_0^\infty I_f(\alpha)d\alpha \int_0^\infty K(\alpha x)x^{s-1}\,dx$$
$$= \int_0^\infty I_f(\alpha)\alpha^{-s}\,d\alpha \int_0^\infty K(\eta)\eta^{s-1}\,d\eta$$

which may be written in the form

$$\mathsf{F}(s) = \mathsf{I}(1-s)\mathsf{K}(s)$$

Replacing s by $1 - s$ in this equation, we have

$$\mathsf{F}(1-s) = \mathsf{I}(s)\mathsf{K}(1-s) \tag{10}$$

Eliminating the ratio $\mathsf{F}(1-s)/\mathsf{I}(s)$ between the equations (9) and (10), we find that $\mathsf{K}(s)$ satisfies the functional equation

$$\mathsf{K}(s)\mathsf{K}(1-s) = 1 \tag{7}$$

as stated in the theorem.

It may be conjectured that the condition (7) is also in some sense a sufficient condition for the function to be a Fourier kernel, but the further investigation of this problem would involve the use of convolution theorems, discussion of which we postpone until later (see Sec. 6.2).

2.2 Examples of Fourier kernels

1. As an example of a function whose Mellin transform satisfies equation (7) consider $K(x) = A \cos(x)$, where A is a constant, unspecified for the moment. Then by the definition

$$\mathsf{K}(s) = A \int_0^\infty x^{s-1} \cos x\, dx = \frac{1}{2} A \left(\int_0^\infty e^{ix} x^{s-1}\, dx + \int_0^\infty e^{-ix} x^{s-1}\, dx \right)$$

Now we know that if p is real and positive

$$\int_0^\infty e^{-px} x^{s-1}\, dx = \frac{\Gamma(s)}{p^s}$$

so that *formally* we may write

$$\int_0^\infty e^{\pm ix} x^{s-1}\, dx = e^{\pm \frac{1}{2}\pi i s} \Gamma(s)$$

and obtain

$$\mathsf{K}(s) = A \cos\left(\frac{s\pi}{2}\right) \Gamma(s)$$

so that

$$\mathsf{K}(1 - s) = A \sin\left(\frac{s\pi}{2}\right) \Gamma(1 - s)$$

If the function $K(x)$ is a Fourier kernel, then we must have

$$1 = \mathsf{K}(s)\mathsf{K}(1 - s) = A^2 \sin\left(\frac{s\pi}{2}\right) \cos\left(\frac{s\pi}{2}\right) \Gamma(s)\Gamma(1 - s)$$

But

$$\Gamma(s)\Gamma(1 - s) = \pi \operatorname{cosec}(s\pi), \qquad \sin\left(\tfrac{1}{2}s\pi\right) \cos\left(\tfrac{1}{2}s\pi\right) = \tfrac{1}{2} \sin(s\pi)$$

so that the condition (7) reduces to $\frac{1}{2}\pi A^2 = 1$, giving $A = (2/\pi)^{\frac{1}{2}}$. This indicates that the solution of the integral equation

$$F_c(\alpha) = \sqrt{\frac{2}{\pi}} \int_0^\infty f(x) \cos(\alpha x) dx \qquad (11)$$

is probably

$$f(x) = \sqrt{\frac{2}{\pi}} \int_0^\infty F_c(\alpha) \cos(\alpha x) d\alpha \qquad (12)$$

The function $F_c(\alpha)$ defined by equation (11) is called the *Fourier cosine transform* of $f(x)$. If the relation (12) is true, then the relation between a function and its Fourier cosine transform is symmetrical; in other words, $f(\alpha)$ is the Fourier cosine transform of $F_c(x)$. It will be observed, however, that, since the calculation of $\mathsf{K}(s)$ was purely formal, we cannot yet assert that the inversion theorem (12) is true. The calculations given above provide us with an indication that this formula is valid, but not with a proof of its validity. This we consider independently a little later.

2. Calculations similar to those we have just given indicate that the function $K(x) = (2/\pi)^{\frac{1}{2}} \sin (x)$ is also a Fourier kernel. If this were so, it would mean that if

$$F_s(\alpha) = \sqrt{\frac{2}{\pi}} \int_0^\infty f(x) \sin (\alpha x) dx \qquad (13)$$

then

$$f(x) = \sqrt{\frac{2}{\pi}} \int_0^\infty F_s(\alpha) \sin (\alpha x) d\alpha \qquad (14)$$

3. Similarly if

$$K(x) = x^{\frac{1}{2}} J_\nu(x)$$

where $J_\nu(x)$ denotes a Bessel function of the first kind of order ν, then, putting $a = 1$ and $\mu = s - \frac{1}{2}$ in equation (18), Appendix A, we find that

$$\mathsf{K}(s) = 2^{s-\frac{1}{2}} \frac{\Gamma(\frac{1}{2}\nu + \frac{1}{2}s + \frac{1}{4})}{\Gamma(\frac{1}{2}\nu - \frac{1}{2}s + \frac{3}{4})}$$

and it is immediately obvious that $\mathsf{K}(s)$ satisfies the functional equation (7). We thus expect $x^{\frac{1}{2}} J_\nu(x)$ to be a Fourier kernel of the type defined above; *i.e.*, if we define a function $\bar{g}$ by the relation

$$\bar{g}(\alpha) = \int_0^\infty g(x)(\alpha x)^{\frac{1}{2}} J_\nu(\alpha x) dx \qquad (15)$$

then $g(x)$ is given in terms of $\bar{g}(\alpha)$ by the inversion formula

$$g(x) = \int_0^\infty \bar{g}(\alpha)(\alpha x)^{\frac{1}{2}} J_\nu(\alpha x) d\alpha \qquad (15a)$$

If we replace $g(x)$ by $x^{\frac{1}{2}} f(x)$, $\bar{g}(\alpha)$ by $\alpha^{\frac{1}{2}} \bar{f}(\alpha)$, then these formulas become

$$\bar{f}(\alpha) = \int_0^\infty x f(x) J_\nu(\alpha x) dx \qquad (16)$$

$$f(x) = \int_0^\infty \alpha \bar{f}(\alpha) J_\nu(\alpha x) d\alpha \qquad (17)$$

We say that the function $\bar{f}(\alpha)$ defined by equation (16) is the *Hankel transform of order* ν of the function $f(x)$.

2.3 Unsymmetrical inversion formulas. In a precisely similar fashion we can treat the unsymmetrical formulas (4) and (5); the result is expressed in the following theorem:

Theorem 2. *A necessary condition for the integral equation*

$$I_f(\alpha) = \int_0^\infty f(x)K(\alpha x)dx$$

to have a solution of the form

$$f(x) = \int_0^\infty I_f(\alpha)H(\alpha x)d\alpha$$

is that the Mellin transforms $\mathsf{K}(s)$, $\mathsf{H}(s)$ *of the functions* $K(x),H(x)$ *should satisfy the functional equation*

$$\mathsf{K}(s)\mathsf{H}(1 - s) = 1$$

For, by definition, we have

$$\mathsf{I}(s) = \int_0^\infty I_f(\alpha)\alpha^{s-1}\,d\alpha = \int_0^\infty \alpha^{s-1}\,d\alpha \int_0^\infty f(x)K(\alpha x)dx$$
$$= \int_0^\infty f(x)x^{-s}\,dx \int_0^\infty K(\eta)\eta^{s-1}\,d\eta$$

so that

$$\mathsf{I}(s) = \mathsf{F}(1 - s)\mathsf{K}(s) \tag{18}$$

and

$$\mathsf{F}(s) = \int_0^\infty f(x)x^{s-1}\,dx = \int_0^\infty x^{s-1}\,dx \int_0^\infty I_f(\alpha)H(\alpha x)d\alpha$$
$$= \int_0^\infty I_f(\alpha)\alpha^{-s}\,d\alpha \int_0^\infty H(\eta)\eta^{s-1}\,d\eta$$
$$= \mathsf{I}(1 - s)\mathsf{H}(s)$$

Putting $1 - s$ for s in this last equation, we obtain

$$\mathsf{F}(1 - s) = \mathsf{I}(s)\mathsf{H}(1 - s) \tag{19}$$

and eliminating the ratio $\mathsf{F}(1 - s)/\mathsf{I}(s)$ from equations (18) and (19), we get the necessary condition

$$\mathsf{K}(s)\mathsf{H}(1 - s) = 1 \tag{20}$$

which reduces to equation (7) in the case in which $H \equiv K$.

3. Fourier's Integral Theorem

We saw in equations (11) and (12) that under certain circumstances it may be possible to write a function $f(x)$ as a double integral of the form

$$f(x) = \frac{2}{\pi}\int_0^\infty d\alpha \int_0^\infty f(\eta)\cos{(\alpha\eta)}\cos{(\alpha x)}d\eta \tag{21}$$

Furthermore we know from the theory of Fourier series[1] that if $f(x)$ satisfies certain conditions in the closed interval $(0,l)$ it may be repre-

[1] R. V. Churchill, "Fourier Series and Boundary Value Problems" (McGraw-Hill, New York, 1941), p. 58.

sented by the Fourier series

$$f(x) = \frac{1}{l} \int_0^l f(\eta)d\eta + \frac{2}{l} \sum_{n=1}^{\infty} \cos \frac{n\pi x}{l} \int_0^l f(\eta) \cos \frac{n\pi\eta}{l} d\eta \qquad (22)$$

If we now choose l to be sufficiently large and assume that the integral $\int_0^{\infty} f(\eta)d\eta$ is convergent, the first term of the series (22) may be made as small as we please and we may therefore neglect it. In addition we may write

$$\frac{2}{l} \sum_{n=1}^{\infty} \cos \frac{n\pi x}{l} \int_0^l f(\eta) \cos \frac{n\pi\eta}{l} d\eta$$

$$= \frac{2\delta\alpha}{\pi} \sum_{n=1}^{\infty} \cos (nx\ \delta\alpha) \int_0^{\pi/\delta\alpha} f(\eta) \cos (n\eta\ \delta\alpha)d\eta$$

by the substitution $\delta\alpha = \pi/l$, and the term on the right may be written

$$\frac{2}{\pi} \int_0^{\pi/\delta\alpha} f(\eta)d\eta \sum_{n=1}^{\infty} \cos [x(n\ \delta\alpha)] \cos [\eta(n\ \delta\alpha)]\delta\alpha$$

Assuming that this series has a limit as $l \to \infty$, that is, as $\delta\alpha \to 0$, we may write for its limiting value

$$\frac{2}{\pi} \int_0^{\infty} d\eta \int_0^{\infty} f(\eta) \cos (x\alpha)\cdot \cos (\eta\alpha)d\alpha$$

Substituting this expression into the right-hand side of equation (22), we obtain the formula (21).

Similarly, if we had started from the Fourier series

$$f(x) = \frac{1}{2l} \int_{-l}^l f(\eta)d\eta + \frac{1}{l} \sum_{n=1}^{\infty} \int_{-l}^l f(\eta) \cos \left(n\pi\ \frac{\eta - x}{l}\right) d\eta$$

and then let $l \to \infty$, we should have arrived at the result

$$f(x) = \frac{1}{2\pi} \int_{-\infty}^{\infty} d\alpha \int_{-\infty}^{\infty} f(\eta) \cos \alpha(\eta - x)d\eta \qquad (23)$$

It will be observed that these considerations do not in any sense constitute a rigorous proof of the representation (23). Indeed, it is immediately apparent that the theorem is not valid for all functions. For instance, it breaks down in the case in which $f(x)$ is a constant, for then the integral with respect to η is indeterminate.

We shall now establish that provided $f(x)$ satisfies certain conditions the result (23) is valid. Fourier integral theorems of the type (23) with very general conditions on the behavior of $f(x)$ have been established.[1] Since the proofs of these theorems employ the techniques of the more modern theories of integration, we shall not aim at the greatest possible generality here, but shall confine our attention to establishing the theorem for a certain class of functions which is sufficiently wide to embrace most of those which arise in problems in applied mathematics.

3.1 Dirichlet's integrals. In order to set up conditions under which the result (23) is valid we must first establish one or two preliminary lemmas on the behavior of certain trigonometrical integrals when a parameter occurring in them tends to infinity. The functions occurring in these integrals all belong to the same class, which we shall now define. We say that the function $f(x)$ satisfies *Dirichlet's conditions* in the interval (a,b) if

1. $f(x)$ has only a finite number of maxima and minima in (a,b).

2. $f(x)$ has only a finite number of finite discontinuities in (a,b)—and no infinite discontinuities. .

It will be observed that any function which is continuous in (a,b) and has only a finite number of maxima or minima in that range satisfies Dirichlet's conditions in (a,b). For example, the function $x/(1 + x^2)$ satisfies Dirichlet's conditions in the range $(-\infty,\infty)$. On the other hand the function $(1 - x)^{-1}$ does *not* satisfy Dirichlet's conditions in any interval which includes the point $x = 1$ since the function has an infinite disconti-nuity there. The function $\sin(1/x)$ does *not* satisfy Dirichlet's conditions in any interval which includes the

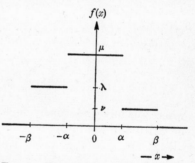

FIG. 1. Example of a function with a finite number of discontinuities.

origin since it has an infinite number of maxima and minima in the neigh-borhood of the origin.

Functions which do satisfy Dirichlet's conditions and which arise fre-quently in applications of the theory are "step functions" of the type shown in Fig. 1. The function shown in Fig. 1 is defined by the equations

---

[1] See, for example, E. C. Titchmarsh, "Introduction to the Theory of Fourier Integrals" (Oxford, New York, 1937), and D. V. Widder, "The Laplace Transform" (Princeton University Press, Princeton, N. J., 1940).

$$f(x) = \begin{cases} 0 & x < -\beta \\ \lambda & -\beta \leq x < -\alpha \\ \mu & -\alpha \leq x \leq \alpha \\ \nu & \alpha < x < \beta \\ 0 & x > \beta \end{cases}$$

It has finite discontinuities at the points $x = \pm\alpha, \pm\beta$, and hence it has only four in the range $(-\infty, \infty)$. Also, it has only a finite number of turning values in that range so that it satisfies Dirichlet's conditions in the entire range $(-\infty, \infty)$.

Before considering integrals involving functions which satisfy Dirichlet's conditions, we shall prove the following lemma in the theory of convergent integrals:

Theorem 3. *If the integral* $\int_0^\infty f(x)dx$ *is convergent then*

$$\left| \int_0^N f(x)dx \right|$$

is bounded for all positive values of N.

The proof of this result follows from the definition of the convergence of an infinite integral. Since the integral

$$\int_0^\infty f(x)dx$$

is convergent, then there must exist a number I and a positive number M such that when $N \geq M$

$$\left| \int_0^N f(x)dx - I \right| < \epsilon$$

where ϵ is any prescribed small positive quantity. This inequality may be written in the form

$$I - \epsilon < \int_0^N f(x)dx < I + \epsilon$$

which shows that when $N \geq M$ the quantity

$$\left| \int_0^N f(x)dx \right|$$

is less than the larger of the two quantities $|I - \epsilon|, |I + \epsilon|$. Also, when $0 \leq N \leq M$,

$$\left| \int_0^N f(x)dx \right|$$

has a maximum value, K, say. If we now let L be the largest of the three numbers K, $|I - \epsilon|$, and $|I + \epsilon|$, we shall have that, for all values of N,

$$\left| \int_0^N f(x)dx \right| < L$$

which is what we mean when we say that $\left| \int_0^N f(x)dx \right|$ is bounded.

The first of the theorems relating to functions which satisfy Dirichlet's conditions is as follows:

Theorem 4. *If $f(x)$ satisfies Dirichlet's conditions in the interval (a,b), then each of the integrals $\int_a^b f(x) \sin (\omega x)dx$, $\int_a^b f(x) \cos (\omega x)dx$ tends to zero as ω tends to infinity through any set of values.*

To prove this result suppose that $a_1, a_2, \ldots , a_p$ are the points in (a,b), taken in order, at which the function $f(x)$ has either a turning value or a finite discontinuity. If we replace a by a_0 and b by a_{p+1}, then we may write

$$\int_a^b f(x) \sin (\omega x)dx = \sum_{r=0}^p \int_{a_r}^{a_{r+1}} f(x) \sin (\omega x)dx \tag{24}$$

Now in each of the intervals $(a_r, a_{r+1})(r = 0,1,2, \ldots ,p)$, $f(x)$ is a continuous function and is either monotonic increasing or monotonic decreasing, so that, by the second mean value theorem of the integral calculus,[1]

$$\int_{a_r}^{a_{r+1}} f(x) \sin (\omega x)dx$$
$$= f(a_r + 0) \int_{a_r}^{\xi} \sin (\omega x)dx + f(a_{r+1} - 0) \int_{\xi}^{a_{r+1}} \sin (\omega x)dx$$

where ξ is some value of x in the range (a_r, a_{r+1}) and in the usual notation

$$f(a_r + 0) = \lim_{y \to 0} f(a_r + y), \qquad f(a_{r+1} - 0) = \lim_{y \to 0} f(a_{r+1} - y)$$

y being positive. The integrations may be performed immediately, and we obtain

$$\int_{a_r}^{a_{r+1}} f(x) \sin (\omega x)dx = f(a_r + 0) \frac{\cos (\omega a_r) - \cos (\omega \xi)}{\omega}$$
$$+ f(a_{r+1} - 0) \frac{\cos (\omega \xi) - \cos (\omega a_{r+1})}{\omega}$$

so that

$$\lim_{\omega \to \infty} \int_{a_r}^{a_{r+1}} f(x) \sin (\omega x)dx = 0$$

[1] L. M. Graves, "The Theory of Functions of Real Variables" (McGraw-Hill, New York, 1946), p. 96.

Now, since the number of terms on the right-hand side of equation (24) is finite, we have

$$\lim_{\omega \to \infty} \int_a^b f(x) \sin (\omega x) dx = \sum_{r=0}^p \lim_{\omega \to \infty} \int_{a_r}^{a_{r+1}} f(x) \sin (\omega x) dx = 0$$

A similar result is easily shown to hold for the case in which $\sin (\omega x)$ is replaced by $\cos (\omega x)$ so that, finally, we have

$$\lim_{\omega \to \infty} \int_a^b f(x) \sin (\omega x) dx = \lim_{\omega \to \infty} \int_a^b f(x) \cos (\omega x) dx = 0$$

which proves the theorem. It will be observed that the Dirichlet conditions, that the number of points a_r is finite, are necessary if we are to be permitted to interchange the processes of summing and proceeding to the limit in equation (24).

Another result of the same type is as follows:

Theorem 5. *If $f(x)$ satisfies Dirichlet's conditions in an interval (a,b) where $0 \leq a < b$, then, as ω tends to infinity through any set of positive values, the integral*

$$\int_a^b f(x) \frac{\sin (\omega x)}{x} dx$$

tends to zero if $a > 0$ and to $\frac{1}{2}\pi f(+0)$ if $a = 0$.

The cases $a = 0$, $a > 0$ require separate proofs:

Case 1: $a > 0$. As in the case of Theorem 4, divide the range (a,b) into a series of intervals (a_r, a_{r+1}), $r = 0,1,2,3, \ldots , p$ in each of which the function $f(x)$ is monotonic and continuous. Then by the second theorem of mean value

$$\int_{a_r}^{a_{r+1}} f(x) \frac{\sin \omega x}{x} dx = f(a_r + 0) \int_{a_r}^{\xi} \frac{\sin \omega x}{x} dx$$
$$+ f(a_{r+1} - 0) \int_{\xi}^{a_{r+1}} \frac{\sin \omega x}{x} dx = f(a_r + 0) \int_{\omega a_r}^{\omega \xi} \frac{\sin \zeta}{\zeta} d\zeta$$
$$+ f(a_{r+1} - 0) \int_{\omega \xi}^{a_{r+1}\omega} \frac{\sin \zeta}{\zeta} d\zeta$$

where $a_r \leq \xi \leq a_{r+1}$. Now by the definition of a convergent integral there exists a number M such that if $N_1 > M$, $N_2 > M$,

$$\left| \int_0^{N_1} \frac{\sin \zeta}{\zeta} d\zeta - \frac{1}{2}\pi \right| < \frac{1}{2}\epsilon, \qquad \left| \int_0^{N_2} \frac{\sin \zeta}{\zeta} d\zeta - \frac{1}{2}\pi \right| < \frac{1}{2}\epsilon$$

where ϵ is arbitrarily small, and we make use of the result

$$\int_0^\infty \frac{\sin \zeta}{\zeta} d\zeta = \frac{1}{2}\pi$$

Hence

$$\left| \int_{N_1}^{N_2} \frac{\sin \zeta}{\zeta} \, d\zeta \right| < \epsilon$$

in other words, if $N_2 > N_1$,

$$\lim_{N_1 \to \infty} \int_{N_1}^{N_2} \frac{\sin \zeta}{\zeta} \, d\zeta = 0$$

This gives

$$\lim_{\omega \to \infty} \int_{a_r}^{a_{r+1}} f(x) \frac{\sin \omega x}{x} \, dx = 0$$

whence it follows immediately that

$$\lim_{\omega \to \infty} \int_a^b f(x) \frac{\sin \omega x}{x} \, dx = \sum_{r=0}^p \lim_{\omega \to \infty} \int_{a_r}^{a_{r+1}} f(x) \frac{\sin \omega x}{x} \, dx = 0$$

which proves the desired result.

Case 2: $a = 0$. Divide the interval $(0,b)$ into a series of intervals as before, and let a_1 be the first maximum or minimum or point of discontinuity of the function $f(x)$ other than, possibly, the origin. Then, since the function $f(x)$ is continuous in the interval $0 < x < a_1$, we can find a value k of x in this range such that $|f(k) - f(0)|$ is arbitrarily small. We then have

$$\int_a^b f(x) \frac{\sin \omega x}{x} \, dx = \int_a^k f(x) \frac{\sin \omega x}{x} \, dx + \int_k^b f(x) \frac{\sin \omega x}{x} \, dx \quad (25)$$

and by case 1 the second integral on the right tends to zero as ω tends to infinity. By the second mean value theorem we have for the first integral

$$\int_0^k f(x) \frac{\sin \omega x}{x} \, dx = f(+0) \int_0^\xi \frac{\sin \omega x}{x} \, dx + f(k) \int_\xi^k \frac{\sin \omega x}{x} \, dx$$

$$= f(+0) \int_0^k \frac{\sin \omega x}{x} \, dx + [f(k) - f(0)] \int_\xi^k \frac{\sin \omega x}{x} \, dx$$

$$= f(+0) \int_0^{k\omega} \frac{\sin \zeta}{\zeta} \, d\zeta + [f(k) - f(0)] \int_{\xi\omega}^{k\omega} \frac{\sin \zeta}{\zeta} \, d\zeta$$

$$(26)$$

Let us now consider the behavior of the second term as $\omega \to \infty$. Since the integral $\int_0^\infty \sin \zeta \, d\zeta/\zeta$ is convergent, it follows from Theorem 3 that

$$\left| \int_0^{k\omega} \frac{\sin \zeta}{\zeta} \, d\zeta \right| < L, \qquad \left| \int_0^{\xi\omega} \frac{\sin \zeta}{\zeta} \, d\zeta \right| < L$$

so that

$$\left| \int_{\omega\xi}^{\omega k} \frac{\sin \zeta}{\zeta} \, d\zeta \right| < 2L$$

Now let us choose k so that

$$|f(k) - f(0)| < \frac{\epsilon}{2L}$$

where ϵ is arbitrarily small. Then

$$\left| [f(k) - f(0)] \int_{\omega\xi}^{\omega k} \frac{\sin \zeta}{\zeta} \, d\zeta \right| < \epsilon$$

in other words,

$$\lim_{\omega \to \infty} \left| [f(k) - f(0)] \int_{\omega\xi}^{\omega k} \frac{\sin \zeta}{\zeta} \, d\zeta \right| = 0 \qquad (27)$$

Substituting from equations (26) and (27) into equation (25), we have

$$\lim_{\omega \to \infty} \int_0^b f(x) \frac{\sin \omega x}{x} \, dx = \frac{1}{2} \pi f(+0) \qquad b > 0 \qquad (28)$$

since $\int_0^\infty \sin \zeta \, d\zeta/\zeta = \frac{1}{2}\pi$.

As a corollary to this result we have the following theorem:

Theorem 6. *If $f(x + u)$ satisfies Dirichlet's conditions in the interval $a < u < b$, then*

$$\lim_{\omega \to \infty} \frac{2}{\pi} \int_a^b f(x + u) \frac{\sin \omega u}{u} \, du$$

$$= \begin{cases} f(x + 0) + f(x - 0) & \text{if } a < 0 < b \\ f(x + 0) & \text{if } a = 0 < b \\ f(x - 0) & \text{if } a < 0 = b \\ 0 & \text{if } 0 < a < b, \, a < b < 0 \end{cases}$$

For, if $a < b \leq 0$,

$$\int_a^b f(u) \sin \omega u \, \frac{du}{u} = \int_{-b}^{-a} f(-u) \sin \omega u \, \frac{du}{u}$$

giving

$$\lim_{\omega \to \infty} \int_a^b f(u) \frac{\sin \omega u}{u} \, du = \begin{cases} 0 & \text{if } a < b < 0 \\ \frac{1}{2}\pi f(-0) & \text{if } a < b = 0 \end{cases} \qquad (29)$$

Also, if $a < 0 < b$,

$$\int_a^b f(u) \frac{\sin \omega u}{u} \, du = \int_0^{-a} f(-u) \frac{\sin \omega u}{u} \, du + \int_0^b f(u) \frac{\sin \omega u}{u} \, du$$

so that as a result of equations (29) and (28)

$$\lim_{\omega \to \infty} \int_a^b f(u) \, \frac{\sin \omega u}{u} \, du = \frac{1}{2} \pi [f(-0) + f(+0)] \quad \text{if } a < 0 < b \quad (30)$$

The theorem then follows from equations (28), (29), and (30) as a result of the substitution of $f(x + u)$ for $f(u)$.

3.2 A proof of Fourier's integral theorem. We shall now show that under certain circumstances the formula (23) is valid. The result is contained in the following theorem:

Theorem 7. *If $f(x)$ satisfies Dirichlet's conditions for $-\infty < x < \infty$ and if the integral $\int_{-\infty}^{\infty} f(x)dx$ is absolutely convergent, then*

$$\frac{1}{\pi} \int_{-\infty}^{\infty} d\alpha \int_{-\infty}^{\infty} f(\eta) \cos \alpha(\eta - x) d\eta = \frac{1}{2} [f(x + 0) + f(x - 0)]$$

If we assume that the integral $\int_{-\infty}^{\infty} f(x)dx$ is *absolutely* convergent, this means simply that the integral $\int_{-\infty}^{\infty} |f(x)|dx$ is convergent.

Now we can write

$$\int_0^{\infty} f(\eta)d\eta \int_0^m \cos \alpha(\eta - x)d\alpha - \int_0^m d\alpha \int_0^{\infty} f(\eta) \cos \alpha(\eta - x)d\eta$$

$$= \int_0^k f(\eta)d\eta \int_0^m \cos \alpha(\eta - x)d\alpha - \int_0^m d\alpha \int_0^k f(\eta) \cos \alpha(\eta - x)d\eta$$

$$+ \int_k^{\infty} f(\eta)d\eta \int_0^m \cos \alpha(\eta - x)d\alpha - \int_0^m d\alpha \int_k^{\infty} f(\eta) \cos \alpha(\eta - x)d\eta$$

The first two integrals are equal in value since both m and k are finite. Now since $\int_{-\infty}^{\infty} f(x)dx$ is absolutely convergent, there exists a number K such that

$$\left| \int_k^{\infty} |f(\eta)|d\eta \right| < \frac{\epsilon}{2m}$$

where ϵ is arbitrarily small and $k > K$. It follows then that

$$\left| \int_0^m d\alpha \int_k^{\infty} f(\eta) \cos \alpha(\eta - x)d\eta \right| \le \int_0^m d\alpha \int_k^{\infty} |f(\eta)|d\eta < \frac{1}{2}\epsilon, \quad k > K$$

Also,

$$\left| \int_k^{\infty} f(\eta)d\eta \int_0^m \cos \alpha(\eta - x)d\alpha \right| = \left| \int_{k+x}^{\infty} f(\eta + x) \frac{\sin m\eta}{\eta} d\eta \right|$$

$$< \frac{1}{k} \int_k^{\infty} |f(\eta + x)|d\eta < \frac{\epsilon}{2k}$$

Thus, no matter how large m is, K can be chosen so large that

$$\left| \int_0^\infty f(\eta)d\eta \int_0^m \cos \alpha(\eta - x)d\alpha - \int_0^m d\alpha \int_0^\infty f(\eta) \cos \alpha(\eta - x)d\eta \right|$$

$$< \frac{1}{2}\epsilon \left(\frac{1}{k} + 1 \right) < \epsilon$$

In other words,

$$\lim_{m \to \infty} \int_0^\infty f(\eta)d\eta \int_0^m \cos \alpha(\eta - x)d\alpha = \lim_{m \to \infty} \int_0^m d\alpha \int_0^\infty f(\eta) \cos \alpha(\eta - x)d\eta$$

Similarly, we can show that

$$\lim_{m \to \infty} \int_{-\infty}^0 f(\eta)d\eta \int_0^m \cos \alpha(\eta - x)d\alpha$$

$$= \lim_{m \to \infty} \int_0^m d\alpha \int_{-\infty}^0 f(\eta) \cos \alpha(\eta - x)d\eta$$

giving on addition

$$\lim_{m \to \infty} \int_{-\infty}^\infty f(\eta)d\eta \int_0^m \cos \alpha(\eta - x)d\alpha$$

$$= \lim_{m \to \infty} \int_0^m d\alpha \int_{-\infty}^\infty f(\eta) \cos \alpha(\eta - x)d\eta \quad (31)$$

Now by Theorem 6,

$$\frac{1}{2}[f(x + 0) + f(x - 0)] = \lim_{m \to \infty} \frac{1}{\pi} \int_{-\infty}^\infty f(x + u) \frac{\sin (mu)}{u} du$$

$$= \lim_{m \to \infty} \frac{1}{\pi} \int_{-\infty}^\infty f(\eta) \frac{\sin m(\eta - x)}{\eta - x} d\eta$$

$$= \lim_{m \to \infty} \frac{1}{\pi} \int_{-\infty}^\infty f(\eta)d\eta \int_0^m \cos \alpha(\eta - x)d\alpha$$

$$= \lim_{m \to \infty} \frac{1}{\pi} \int_0^m d\alpha \int_{-\infty}^\infty f(\eta) \cos \alpha(\eta - x)d\eta$$

by means of equation (31).   Hence we obtain the result

$$\frac{1}{2}[f(x + 0) + f(x - 0)] = \frac{1}{\pi} \int_0^\infty d\alpha \int_{-\infty}^\infty f(\eta) \cos \alpha(\eta - x)d\eta \quad (32)$$

which is known as Fourier's integral theorem. .

If the function $f(x)$ is continuous at the point x, then

$$f(x + 0) = f(x - 0) = f(x),$$

so that equation (32) reduces to the form

$$f(x) = \frac{1}{\pi} \int_0^\infty d\alpha \int_{-\infty}^\infty f(\eta) \cos \alpha(\eta - x)d\alpha \quad (33)$$

3.3 Inversion theorems for Fourier transforms. In the case in which the function $f(x)$ is defined only for positive values of the variable x there are two important special forms of the Fourier integral theorem (32). If $f(x)$ is defined in the range $0 \leq x < \infty$, then we may define it in the range $-\infty < x < \infty$ by the equation $f(x) = f(-x)$, when $-\infty < x < 0$. We then have

$$\frac{1}{\pi} \int_0^\infty d\alpha \int_{-\infty}^\infty f(\eta) \cos \alpha(\eta - x) d\eta$$

$$= \frac{1}{\pi} \int_0^\infty d\alpha \int_0^\infty f(\eta) \cos \alpha(\eta - x) d\eta + \frac{1}{\pi} \int_0^\infty d\alpha \int_{-\infty}^0 f(\eta) \cos \alpha(\eta - x) d\eta$$

Now

$$\int_{-\infty}^0 f(\eta) \cos \alpha(\eta - x) d\eta = \int_0^\infty f(-\eta) \cos \alpha(-\eta - x) d\eta$$

$$= \int_0^\infty f(\eta) \cos \alpha(\eta + x) d\eta$$

so that

$$\frac{1}{\pi} \int_0^\infty d\alpha \int_{-\infty}^\infty f(\eta) \cos \alpha(\eta - x) d\eta$$

$$= \frac{1}{\pi} \int_0^\infty d\alpha \int_0^\infty f(\eta)[\cos \alpha(\eta - x) + \cos \alpha(\eta + x)] d\eta$$

$$= \frac{2}{\pi} \int_0^\infty \cos (\alpha x) d\alpha \int_0^\infty f(\eta) \cos (\alpha \eta) d\eta$$

Equation (33) may therefore be written in the form

$$f(x) = \frac{2}{\pi} \int_0^\infty \cos (\alpha x) d\alpha \int_0^\infty f(\eta) \cos (\alpha \eta) d\eta \qquad (34)$$

which may be stated as follows:

Theorem 8.   *If F_c is the Fourier cosine transform of $f(x)$, that is, if*

$$F_c(\alpha) = \sqrt{\frac{2}{\pi}} \int_0^\infty f(\eta) \cos (\alpha \eta) d\eta \qquad (35)$$

then $f(x)$ is given by

$$f(x) = \sqrt{\frac{2}{\pi}} \int_0^\infty F_c(\alpha) \cos (\alpha x) d\alpha \qquad (35a)$$

The pair of formulas (35) and (35a) are known as the *Fourier cosine formulas*. The above considerations show that the equations (11) and (12), whose validity we conjectured earlier, are in fact true for a wide class of functions $f(x)$.

Alternatively, when we are extending the range of definition of $f(x)$ from

$0 < x < \infty$ to $-\infty < x < \infty$, we could define $f(x)$ in $-\infty < x < 0$ to be given by the equation

$$f(x) = -f(-x)$$

in which case we have

$$\frac{1}{\pi} \int_0^\infty d\alpha \int_{-\infty}^\infty f(\eta) \cos \alpha(\eta - x) d\eta$$

$$= \frac{1}{\pi} \int_0^\infty d\alpha \int_0^\infty f(\eta)[\cos \alpha(\eta - x) - \cos \alpha(\eta + x)] d\eta$$

which shows that equation (33) assumes the form

$$f(x) = \frac{2}{\pi} \int_0^\infty \sin (\alpha x) d\alpha \int_0^\infty f(\eta) \sin (\alpha\eta) d\eta$$

and hence gives the following theorem:

Theorem 9. *If $F_s(\alpha)$ is the Fourier sine transform of $f(x)$, that is, if*

$$F_s(\alpha) = \sqrt{\frac{2}{\pi}} \int_0^\infty f(\eta) \sin \alpha\eta \, d\eta \tag{36}$$

then $f(x)$ is given in terms of $F_s(\alpha)$ by the formula

$$f(x) = \sqrt{\frac{2}{\pi}} \int_0^\infty F_s(\alpha) \sin \alpha x \, d\alpha \tag{36a}$$

This theorem is usually referred to as *Fourier's sine formula.*

The Fourier integral theorem may be written in yet another form. If we make use of the results

$$\int_{-m}^m \cos \alpha(\eta - x) d\alpha = 2 \int_0^m \cos \alpha(\eta - x) d\alpha, \qquad \int_{-m}^m \sin \alpha(\eta - x) d\alpha = 0$$

which are a result of the fact that $\sin x$ and $\cos x$ are, respectively, odd and even functions of x, we may write

$$\int_0^m \cos \alpha(\eta - x) d\alpha = \frac{1}{2} \int_{-m}^m e^{i\alpha(\eta - x)} \, d\alpha$$

in the equation

$$f(x) = \lim_{m \to \infty} \frac{1}{\pi} \int_{-\infty}^\infty f(\eta) d\eta \int_0^m \cos \alpha(\eta - x) d\alpha$$

to obtain the result

$$f(x) = \frac{1}{2\pi} \int_{-\infty}^\infty e^{-i\alpha x} \, d\alpha \int_{-\infty}^\infty f(\eta) e^{i\eta\alpha} \, d\eta \tag{37}$$

We can express this result in another way, *viz.*:

Theorem 10.   *If $F(\alpha)$ is the Fourier transform of $f(x)$, that is, if*

$$F(\alpha) = \frac{1}{\sqrt{2\pi}} \int_{-\infty}^{\infty} f(x) e^{i\alpha x} \, dx \qquad (38)$$

then $f(x)$ is given in terms of $F(\alpha)$ by the relation

$$f(x) = \frac{1}{\sqrt{2\pi}} \int_{-\infty}^{\infty} F(\alpha) e^{-i\alpha x} \, d\alpha \qquad (38a)$$

It will be observed from these results that the relation between a function $f(x)$ and its Fourier transform $F(\alpha)$ is not a symmetrical one, whereas the relations between the functions and its sine and cosine transforms $F_s(\alpha)$, $F_c(\alpha)$ are symmetrical.   Often, too, these results are stated in a slightly different form.   For example, it is often convenient to write the equations (38) and (38a) in the following form: If

$$\bar{f}(\alpha) = \int_{-\infty}^{\infty} f(x) e^{i\alpha x} \, dx$$

then $\qquad\qquad\qquad\qquad\qquad\qquad\qquad\qquad\qquad\qquad\qquad\qquad (39)$

$$f(x) = \frac{1}{2\pi} \int_{-\infty}^{\infty} \bar{f}(\alpha) e^{-i\alpha x} \, d\alpha$$

the factor $(1/2\pi)^{\frac{1}{2}}$ being omitted in the definition of the transform. Although this form of the result is often useful, it does destroy the partial symmetry between the function $f(x)$ and the transform.

It should be noted that we are justified in using these theorems only in cases in which $f(x)$ satisfies Dirichlet's conditions in whichever of the ranges $(-\infty, \infty)$, $(0, \infty)$ is appropriate and in which the integral

$$\int_{-\infty}^{\infty} |f(x)| \, dx$$

is convergent.

3.4 Evaluation of integrals by means of the inversion theorems.   The inversion theorems we developed in the last section may be employed to obtain easily the values of certain integrals involving trigonometric functions.   Let us consider, first of all, the integrals

$$I_1 = \int_0^{\infty} e^{-bx} \cos \alpha x \, dx, \qquad I_2 = \int_0^{\infty} e^{-bx} \sin \alpha x \, dx$$

Integrating the former of these two integrals by parts, we obtain

$$I_1 = \left[-\frac{1}{b} e^{-bx} \cos \alpha x \right]_0^{\infty} - \frac{\alpha}{b} \int_0^{\infty} e^{-bx} \sin \alpha x \, dx$$

which may be written as

$$I_1 = \frac{1}{b} - \frac{\alpha}{b} I_2$$

In a similar way we obtain, by integrating I_2 by parts,

$$I_2 = \frac{\alpha}{b} I_1$$

Solving these equations for I_1 and I_2, we obtain

$$I_1 = \frac{b}{\alpha^2 + b^2}, \qquad I_2 = \frac{\alpha}{\alpha^2 + b^2}$$

This means that, if we write $f(x) = e^{-bx}$, then its cosine and sine transforms are, respectively,

$$F_c(\alpha) = \sqrt{\frac{2}{\pi}} \frac{b}{\alpha^2 + b^2}, \qquad F_s(\alpha) = \sqrt{\frac{2}{\pi}} \frac{\alpha}{\alpha^2 + b^2}$$

Substituting these expressions in Theorems 8 and 9, respectively, we obtain the integrals

$$\int_0^\infty \frac{\cos \alpha x}{\alpha^2 + b^2} \, d\alpha = \frac{\pi}{2b} e^{-bx}, \qquad \int_0^\infty \frac{\alpha \sin \alpha x}{\alpha^2 + b^2} \, d\alpha = \frac{\pi}{2} e^{-bx} \qquad (40)$$

Similarly if we take $f(x) = 1$ if $0 < x < a$, 0 if $x > a$, and hence

$$F_c(\alpha) = \sqrt{\frac{2}{\pi}} \int_0^a \cos \alpha x \, dx = \sqrt{\frac{2}{\pi}} \frac{\sin \alpha a}{\alpha}$$

in Theorem 8 we obtain the result

$$\frac{2}{\pi} \int_0^\infty \frac{\sin \alpha a \cos \alpha x}{\alpha} \, d\alpha = \begin{cases} 1 & \text{if } 0 \le x < a \\ 0 & \text{if } x \ge a \end{cases}$$

A more complicated integral results from taking

$$f(x) = \begin{cases} 0 & 0 < x < a \\ x & a \le x \le b \\ 0 & x > b \end{cases}$$

and hence

$$F_s(\alpha) = \sqrt{\frac{2}{\pi}} \int_a^b x \sin \alpha x \, dx$$

$$= \sqrt{\frac{2}{\pi}} \left(\frac{a \cos \alpha a - b \cos \alpha b}{\alpha} + \frac{\sin \alpha b - \sin \alpha a}{\alpha^2} \right)$$

in Theorem 9. In this way we obtain the integral

$$\frac{2}{\pi} \int_0^\infty \sin \alpha x \left(\frac{a \cos \alpha a - b \cos \alpha b}{\alpha} + \frac{\sin \alpha b - \sin \alpha a}{\alpha^2} \right) d\alpha$$

$$= \begin{cases} 0 & 0 < x < a \\ x & a < x < b \\ 0 & x > b \end{cases}$$

Similarly, putting $f(x) = 1 \; (0 < x < a)$, 0, $(x > a)$,

$$F_s(\alpha) = (1/\alpha)(1 - \cos a\alpha)$$

in equations (36) and (36a), we have that

$$\frac{2}{\pi} \int_0^\infty \sin \alpha x \left(\frac{1 - \cos \alpha a}{\alpha} \right) d\alpha = \begin{cases} 1 & 0 < x < a \\ 0 & x > a \end{cases}$$

and putting $f(x) = 1$ if $a < x < b$, 0 otherwise, we have

$$\frac{2}{\pi} \int_0^\infty \sin \alpha x \left(\frac{\cos \alpha a - \cos \alpha b}{\alpha} \right) d\alpha = \begin{cases} 0 & 0 < x < a \\ 1 & a < x < b \\ 0 & x > b \end{cases}$$

Combining these results, we obtain

$$\frac{2}{\pi} \int_0^\infty \sin \alpha x \left(\frac{a - b}{\alpha} + \frac{\cos \alpha a - \cos \alpha b}{\alpha^2} \right) d\alpha = \begin{cases} a - b & 0 < x < a \\ x - b & a < x < b \\ 0 & x > b \end{cases}$$

and making use of the result

$$\frac{2}{\pi} \int_0^\infty \frac{\sin \alpha x}{\alpha} d\alpha = 1 \qquad \text{if } x > 0$$

we have finally

$$\frac{2}{\pi} \int_0^\infty \sin \alpha x \left(\frac{h}{\alpha} + \frac{\cos \alpha a - \cos \alpha b}{\alpha^2} \tan \psi \right) d\alpha$$

$$= \begin{cases} h & 0 < x < a \\ h + (x - a) \tan \psi & a < x < b \\ h + (b - a) \tan \psi & x > b \end{cases}$$

so that the integral is the ordinate of a broken line running parallel to the x axis from 0 to a and from $x = b$ to infinity, and inclined to the x axis at an angle ψ between $x = a$ and $x = b$ (cf. Fig. 2).

These examples show how it is often possible to make use of Fourier's integral theorem to evaluate definite and infinite integrals of complicated types. Further instances of this procedure arise in the discussion of special problems later.

3.5 Fourier's theorem for holomorphic functions. It was shown by MacRobert[1] that certain formulas, of the type (40), for instance, which are usually obtained by means of

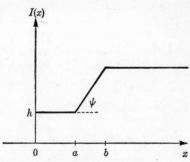

FIG. 2. Variation of the integral

$$\frac{2}{\pi} \int_0^\infty \sin (\alpha x) \left[\frac{h}{\alpha} + \frac{\cos (a\alpha) - \cos (b\alpha)}{\alpha^2} \tan \psi \right] d\alpha$$

for positive values of x.

[1] T. M. MacRobert, *Proc. Edinburgh Math. Soc.* (ii), **2**, 26 (1926).

Fourier's integral theorem, could also be evaluated by contour integration. This naturally suggested that Fourier's theorem itself could be established by the same method. The functions involved must be holomorphic so that the proof given by MacRobert[1] does not justify the application of the theorem to such wide classes of functions as the usual proofs by means of Dirichlet integrals (Sec. 3.1), but the proof is so simple that it warrants our attention here, the more so since a similar method gives other inversion theorems which we shall consider later. In what follows it will be assumed that all the integrals are convergent and that changes in the order of integration are justified. Under these circumstances we may prove Fourier's integral theorem in the following form:

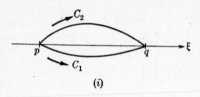

(i)

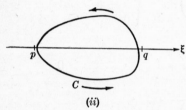

(ii)

Fig. 3. Contours in the ζ plane.

Theorem 11. *If, for all real values of λ,*

$$\int_p^q e^{i\lambda\rho}\phi(\rho)d\rho = f(\lambda)$$

where $-\infty \leq p < q \leq \infty$, *then*

$$\frac{1}{2\pi}\int_{-\infty}^{\infty} e^{-i\lambda r}f(\lambda)d\lambda = \begin{cases} \phi(r) & p < r < q \\ 0 & r < p \text{ or } r > q \end{cases}$$

For

$$I \equiv \int_{-\infty}^{\infty} e^{-i\lambda r}f(\lambda)d\lambda = \int_{-\infty}^{\infty} e^{-i\lambda r}\,d\lambda \int_p^q e^{i\lambda\rho}\phi(\rho)d\rho$$

$$= \int_{-\infty}^0 e^{-i\lambda r}\,d\lambda \int_{C_1} e^{i\lambda\zeta}\phi(\zeta)d\zeta + \int_0^{\infty} e^{-i\lambda r}\,d\lambda \int_{C_2} e^{i\lambda\zeta}\phi(\zeta)d\zeta$$

where C_1 and C_2 are contours from p to q in the ζ plane [Fig. 3(i)] below and above the ρ axis, respectively. In the cases $p = -\infty$ or $q = \infty$ the contours approach the ρ axis asymptotically. In both integrals

$$R(i\lambda\zeta) < 0$$

If, now, we change the order of integration, we find that

$$I = \int_{C_1} \phi(\zeta)d\zeta \int_{-\infty}^0 e^{i\lambda(\zeta-r)}\,d\lambda + \int_{C_2} \phi(\zeta)d\zeta \int_0^{\infty} e^{i\lambda(\zeta-r)}\,d\lambda$$

$$= \int_{C_1} \frac{\phi(\zeta)d\zeta}{i(\zeta - r)} - \int_{C_2} \frac{\phi(\zeta)d\zeta}{i(\zeta - r)}$$

$$= \int_c \frac{\phi(\zeta)d\zeta}{i(\zeta - r)}$$

[1] T. M. MacRobert, *Proc. Roy. Soc. Edinburgh*, **51**, 116 (1931).

where C is a closed contour between p and q [Fig. 3(ii)]. Hence, by Cauchy's theorem,

$$I = \begin{cases} 2\pi\phi(r) & \text{if } p < r < q \\ 0 & \text{if } r < p \text{ or } r > q \end{cases}$$

Conversely, if

$$\int_{-\infty}^{\infty} e^{-i\rho r} f(r)dr = \begin{cases} 2\pi\phi(\rho) & \text{if } p < \rho < q \\ 0 & \text{if } \rho < p \text{ or } \rho > q \end{cases}$$

then, for all real values of λ,

$$\int_p^q e^{i\lambda\rho}\phi(\rho)d\rho = f(\lambda)$$

for

$$J = \int_p^q e^{i\lambda\rho}\phi(\rho)d\rho = \frac{1}{2\pi} \int_{-\infty}^{\infty} e^{i\lambda\rho} \, d\rho \int_{-\infty}^{\infty} e^{-i\rho r} f(r)dr$$

$$= \frac{1}{2\pi} \int_0^{\infty} e^{i\lambda\rho} \, d\rho \int_{C_1} e^{-i\rho\zeta} f(\zeta)d\zeta + \frac{1}{2\pi} \int_{-\infty}^0 e^{i\lambda\rho} \, d\rho \int_{C_2} e^{-i\rho\zeta} f(\zeta)d\zeta$$

where C_1 and C_2 are the contours of Fig. 3(i) in the case $p = -\infty$, $q = \infty$.

Thus

$$J = \frac{1}{2\pi} \int_{C_1} f(\zeta)d\zeta \int_0^{\infty} e^{-i\rho(\zeta-\lambda)} \, d\rho + \frac{1}{2\pi} \int_{C_2} f(\zeta)d\zeta \int_{-\infty}^0 e^{-i\rho(\zeta-\lambda)} \, d\rho$$

$$= \frac{1}{2\pi i} \int_{C_1} \frac{f(\zeta)d\zeta}{\zeta - \lambda} - \frac{1}{2\pi i} \int_{C_2} \frac{f(\zeta)d\zeta}{\zeta - \lambda}$$

$$= \frac{1}{2\pi i} \int_C \frac{f(\zeta)d\zeta}{\zeta - \lambda} = f(\lambda)$$

by Cauchy's theorem, since C is a closed contour encircling the point $\zeta = \lambda$.

3.6 Convolution, or Faltung, theorems for Fourier transforms. The function

$$f*g = \frac{1}{\sqrt{2\pi}} \int_{-\infty}^{\infty} g(\eta)f(x - \eta)d\eta \tag{41}$$

is called the *convolution*, or *Faltung*, of the functions f and g over the interval $(-\infty, \infty)$. By means of the theorems established in Sec. **3.3**, we may write this integral in another way. For if we suppose f and g to be functions such that the inversion theorem 10 is valid and such that the required changes in the order of the integrations are justified, we may write

$$\int_{-\infty}^{\infty} g(\eta)f(x-\eta)d\eta = \frac{1}{\sqrt{2\pi}} \int_{-\infty}^{\infty} g(\eta)d\eta \int_{-\infty}^{\infty} F(t)e^{-it(x-\eta)}\,dt$$

$$= \frac{1}{\sqrt{2\pi}} \int_{-\infty}^{\infty} F(t)e^{-itx}\,dt \int_{-\infty}^{\infty} g(\eta)e^{it\eta}\,d\eta$$

$$= \int_{-\infty}^{\infty} F(t)G(t)e^{-itx}\,dt \tag{42}$$

where F and **G are the** Fourier transforms of f and g, respectively. In this way we obtain the *convolution*, or *Faltung, theorem*:

Theorem 12. *If $F(t)$ and $G(t)$ are the Fourier transforms of $f(x)$ and $g(x)$, respectively, then the Fourier transform of the product FG is the convolution $f*g$; in other words,*

$$\int_{-\infty}^{\infty} F(t)G(t)e^{-ixt}\,dt = \int_{-\infty}^{\infty} g(\eta)f(x-\eta)d\eta$$

Similar results may be established for the sine and cosine transforms of the functions f and g. For instance, if the Fourier cosine transforms of $f(x)$ and $g(x)$ are denoted by $F_c(t)$ and $G_c(t)$, respectively, then

$$\int_0^{\infty} F_c(t)G_c(t)\cos(xt)dt = \sqrt{\frac{2}{\pi}} \int_0^{\infty} F_c(t)\cos(xt)dt \int_0^{\infty} g(\eta)\cos(\eta t)d\eta$$

$$= \frac{1}{\sqrt{2\pi}} \int_0^{\infty} g(\eta)d\eta \int_0^{\infty} F_c(t)[\cos|x-\eta|t + \cos(x+\eta)t]dt$$

$$= \frac{1}{2} \int_0^{\infty} g(\eta)[f(|x-\eta|) + f(x+\eta)]d\eta \tag{43}$$

Similarly, if $F_s(t)$ and $G_s(t)$ are the Fourier sine transforms of $f(x)$ and $g(x)$, we have

$$\int_0^{\infty} F_c(t)G_s(t)\sin(xt)dt = \sqrt{\frac{2}{\pi}} \int_0^{\infty} F_c(t)\sin(xt)dt \int_0^{\infty} g(\eta)\sin(t\eta)d\eta$$

$$= \frac{1}{\sqrt{2\pi}} \int_0^{\infty} g(\eta)d\eta \int_0^{\infty} F_c(t)[\cos|x-\eta|t - \cos(x+\eta)t]dt$$

$$= \frac{1}{2} \int_0^{\infty} g(\eta)[f(|x-\eta|) - f(x+\eta)]d\eta \tag{44}$$

and

$$\int_0^{\infty} F_s(t)G_c(t)\sin(xt)dt = \frac{1}{2} \int_0^{\infty} f(\eta)[g(|x-\eta|) - g(x+\eta)]d\eta \tag{45}$$

If we take $x = 0$ in the left-hand side of equation (43), we obtain

$$\int_0^\infty F_c(t)G_c(t)dt = \int_0^\infty F_c(t)dt \sqrt{\frac{2}{\pi}} \int_0^\infty g(\eta) \cos(t\eta)d\eta$$

$$= \int_0^\infty g(\eta)d\eta \sqrt{\frac{2}{\pi}} \int_0^\infty F_c(t) \cos(t\eta)dt$$

$$= \int_0^\infty f(\eta)g(\eta)d\eta \quad (46)$$

and in the special case in which f is identical with g we obtain

$$\int_0^\infty [F_c(t)]^2 \, dt = \int_0^\infty [f(\eta)]^2 \, d\eta \quad (47)$$

Analogous formulas

$$\int_0^\infty F_s(t)G_s(t)dt = \int_0^\infty f(\eta)g(\eta)d\eta \quad (48)$$

$$\int_0^\infty [F_s(t)]^2 \, dt = \int_0^\infty [f(\eta)]^2 \, d\eta \quad (49)$$

can readily be established for the Fourier sine transforms. The formula for Fourier transforms is slightly different. We have

$$\int_{-\infty}^\infty F(t)G(t)dt = \int_{-\infty}^\infty F(t)dt \frac{1}{\sqrt{2\pi}} \int_{-\infty}^\infty g(\eta)e^{i\eta t} \, d\eta$$

$$= \int_{-\infty}^\infty g(\eta)d\eta \frac{1}{\sqrt{2\pi}} \int_{-\infty}^\infty F(t)e^{i\eta t} \, dt$$

$$= \int_{-\infty}^\infty f(-\eta)g(\eta)d\eta \quad (50)$$

It will be observed that we could have derived (50) from (42) by the substitution $x = 0$. Because of the similarity of the formulas (47) and (48) to Parseval's theorem

$$\frac{1}{\pi} \int_{-\pi}^\pi [f(x)]^2 \, dx = \frac{1}{2} a_0^2 + \sum_{n=1}^\infty (a_n^2 + b_n^2)$$

in the theory of Fourier series,[1] the formulas (46) to (50) are usually known as *Parseval's relations for Fourier transforms*.

These formulas may be used to obtain easily the values of certain integrals. For instance, in equations (40) we showed that the Fourier cosine transforms of the functions

$$f(x) = e^{-bx}, \qquad g(x) = e^{-ax}$$

were, respectively,

$$F_c(t) = \sqrt{\frac{2}{\pi}} \frac{b}{b^2 + t^2}, \qquad G_c(t) = \sqrt{\frac{2}{\pi}} \frac{a}{a^2 + t^2}$$

---

[1] R. V. Churchill, "Fourier Series and Boundary Value Problems" (McGraw-Hill, New York, 1941), p. 86.

Substituting these functions in equation (46), we find that

$$\frac{2ab}{\pi} \int_0^\infty \frac{dt}{(a^2 + t^2)(b^2 + t^2)} = \int_0^\infty e^{-(a+b)\eta}\, d\eta = \frac{1}{a+b}$$

from which we derive the integral

$$\int_0^\infty \frac{dt}{(a^2 + t^2)(b^2 + t^2)} = \frac{\pi}{2ab(a+b)} \tag{51}$$

As a further example, taking

$$f(x) = \begin{cases} 1 & 0 < x < \lambda \\ 0 & x > \lambda \end{cases}, \qquad g(x) = \begin{cases} 1 & 0 < x < \mu \\ 0 & x > \mu \end{cases}$$

and noting that

$$F_c(t) = \sqrt{\frac{2}{\pi}} \frac{\sin\,(\lambda t)}{t}, \qquad G_c(t) = \sqrt{\frac{2}{\pi}} \frac{\sin\,(\mu t)}{t}$$

we see from formula (46) that

$$\int_0^\infty \frac{\sin\,(\lambda t)\,\sin\,(\mu t)}{t^2}\, dt = \frac{\pi}{2} \int_0^{\min(\lambda,\mu)} d\eta = \frac{1}{2} \pi \min\,(\lambda,\mu) \tag{52}$$

where $\min(\lambda,\mu)$ denotes the lesser of the two positive numbers λ and μ.

Again, taking $g(x) = e^{-ax}$, $f(x) = 1(0 < x < \lambda)$, $0(x > \lambda)$ in equation (46), we obtain

$$\frac{2a}{\pi} \int_0^\infty \frac{\sin\,(\lambda t)dt}{t(a^2 + t^2)} = \int_0^\lambda e^{-a\eta}\, d\eta$$

which yields the result

$$\int_0^\infty \frac{\sin\,(\lambda t)dt}{t(a^2 + t^2)} = \frac{\pi}{2}\left(\frac{1 - e^{-\lambda a}}{a^2}\right) \tag{53}$$

The usefulness of this method of evaluating integrals may be extended if we observe that, if F, G, and H are the Fourier transforms of f, g, and h, then

$$\int_{-\infty}^\infty F(t)G(t)H(t)dt = \frac{1}{\sqrt{2\pi}} \int_{-\infty}^\infty F(t)G(t)dt \int_{-\infty}^\infty h(\xi)e^{i\xi t}\, d\xi$$

$$= \frac{1}{2\pi} \int_{-\infty}^\infty h(\xi)d\xi \int_{-\infty}^\infty F(t)e^{i\xi t}\, dt \int_{-\infty}^\infty g(\eta)e^{i\eta t}\, d\eta$$

$$= \frac{1}{\sqrt{2\pi}} \int_{-\infty}^\infty h(\xi)d\xi \int_{-\infty}^\infty g(\eta)d\eta \frac{1}{\sqrt{2\pi}} \int_{-\infty}^\infty F(t)e^{i(\xi+\eta)t}\, dt$$

But we may write

$$\frac{1}{\sqrt{2\pi}} \int_{-\infty}^{\infty} F(t)e^{i(\xi+\eta)t}\,dt = f(-\xi-\eta)$$

so that we obtain the result

$$\int_{-\infty}^{\infty} F(t)G(t)H(t)dt = \frac{1}{\sqrt{2\pi}} \int_{-\infty}^{\infty} h(\xi)d\xi \int_{-\infty}^{\infty} g(\eta)f(-\xi-\eta)d\eta \quad (54)$$

3.7 Relations between the Fourier transforms of the derivatives of a function. In many applications of the theory of Fourier transforms to boundary value problems in mathematical physics it is desirable to express the Fourier transform of the function $d^r f/dx^r$ in terms of F, the Fourier transform of $f(x)$. By definition the Fourier transform of $d^r f/dx^r$ is

$$\frac{1}{\sqrt{2\pi}} \int_{-\infty}^{\infty} \frac{d^r f}{dx^r} e^{i\alpha x}\,dx = F^{(r)}(\alpha), \text{ say}$$

Integrating the function on the left by parts, we obtain

$$F^{(r)} = \left[\frac{1}{\sqrt{2\pi}} \frac{d^{r-1}f}{dx^{r-1}} e^{i\alpha x} \right]_{-\infty}^{\infty} - \frac{1}{\sqrt{2\pi}} \int_{-\infty}^{\infty} \frac{d^{r-1}f}{dx^{r-1}} (i\alpha)e^{i\alpha x}\,dx$$

If we assume that $d^{r-1}f/dx^{r-1}$ tends to zero as $|x|$ tends to ∞, we may write this result in the form

$$F^{(r)} = -i\alpha F^{(r-1)}$$

By a repetition of this rule and by the assumption that

$$\lim_{|x|\to\infty} \left(\frac{d^s f}{dx^s} \right) = 0 \qquad s = 1,2,\ldots,r-1$$

we have finally

$$F^{(r)} = (-i\alpha)^r F \tag{55}$$

showing that in these circumstances we obtain the following:

Theorem 13. *The Fourier transform of the function $d^r f/dx^r$ is $(-i\alpha)^r$ times the Fourier transform of the function $f(x)$ provided that the first $(r-1)$ derivatives of $f(x)$ vanish as $x \to \pm\infty$.*

The results for the Fourier cosine and sine transforms are not quite so simple. Let us define $F_c^{(r)}$ and $F_s^{(r)}$ by the equations

$$F_c^{(r)} = \sqrt{\frac{2}{\pi}} \int_0^{\infty} \frac{d^r f}{dx^r} \cos(\alpha x)dx, \qquad F_s^{(r)} = \sqrt{\frac{2}{\pi}} \int_0^{\infty} \frac{d^r f}{dx^r} \sin(\alpha x)dx \tag{56}$$

then, integrating by parts, we obtain

$$F_c^{(r)} = \sqrt{\frac{2}{\pi}} \left[\frac{d^{r-1}f}{dx^{r-1}} \cos(\alpha x) \right]_0^{\infty} + \alpha \sqrt{\frac{2}{\pi}} \int_0^{\infty} \frac{d^{r-1}f}{dx^{r-1}} \sin(\alpha x)dx$$

If we assume that

$$\lim_{x \to \infty} \left(\frac{d^{r-1}f}{dx^{r-1}} \right) = 0, \qquad \lim_{x \to 0} \sqrt{\frac{2}{\pi}} \left(\frac{d^{r-1}f}{dx^{r-1}} \right) = a_{r-1}$$

we may write this equation as

$$F_c^{(r)} = -a_{r-1} + \alpha F_s^{(r-1)} \tag{57}$$

Similarly, from the second of equations (56) we derive as a result of an integration by parts

$$F_s^{(r)} = -\alpha F_c^{(r-1)} \tag{58}$$

It follows immediately from these equations that

$$F_c^{(r)} = -a_{r-1} - \alpha^2 F_c^{(r-2)} \tag{59}$$

By repeated applications of these results we can reduce $F_c^{(r)}$ to a sum of a's and either $F_c^{(1)}$ or F_c. The $F_c^{(1)}$ will arise if r is odd and may be replaced by $a_0 + \alpha F_s$. In this way we obtain the formulas

$$F_c^{(2r)} = -\sum_{n=0}^{r-1} (-1)^n a_{2r-2n-1} \alpha^{2n} + (-1)^r \alpha^{2r} F_c \tag{60}$$

$$F_c^{(2r+1)} = -\sum_{n=0}^{r} (-1)^n a_{2r-2n} \alpha^{2n} + (-1)^r \alpha^{2r+1} F_s \tag{61}$$

which give the Fourier cosine transforms of the derivatives of $f(x)$ in terms of the Fourier cosine and sine transforms of $f(x)$.

Similar results hold for sine transforms. If we eliminate $F_c^{(r)}$ from equations (57) and (58), we obtain

$$F_s^{(r)} = \alpha a_{r-2} - \alpha^2 F_s^{(r-2)}$$

from which follow the formulas

$$F_s^{(2r)} = -\sum_{n=1}^{r} (-1)^n \alpha^{2n-1} a_{2r-2n} + (-1)^{r+1} \alpha^{2r} F_s \tag{62}$$

$$F_s^{(2r+1)} = -\sum_{n=1}^{r} (-1)^n \alpha^{2n-1} a_{2r-2n+1} + (-1)^{r+1} \alpha^{2r+1} F_c \tag{63}$$

Certain special cases of these formulas arise frequently. For instance, if, when $x = 0$,

$$\frac{df}{dx} = \frac{d^3f}{dx^3} = 0$$

then

$$\sqrt{\frac{2}{\pi}} \int_0^\infty \frac{d^2f}{dx^2} \cos \alpha x \, dx = -\alpha^2 F_c$$

and

$$\sqrt{\frac{2}{\pi}} \int_0^\infty \frac{d^4 f}{dx^4} \cos \alpha x \, dx = \alpha^4 F_c$$

On the other hand if, when $x = 0$,

$$f = \frac{d^2 f}{dx^2} = 0$$

then

$$\sqrt{\frac{2}{\pi}} \int_0^\infty \frac{d^2 f}{dx^2} \sin (\alpha x) dx = -\alpha^2 F_s$$

and

$$\sqrt{\frac{2}{\pi}} \int_0^\infty \frac{d^4 f}{dx^4} \sin \alpha x \, dx = \alpha^4 F_s$$

4. Laplace Transform

4.1 Laplace inversion theorem. We saw in the proof of Theorem 7 that, if the integral

$$\int_{-\infty}^\infty |f(x)| dx \tag{64}$$

is not convergent, then the Fourier transform of the function $f(x)$ need not exist. This situation does in fact arise in many cases of interest. For example, a case of great interest is

$$f(x) = \sin \omega x$$

and this function is such that the integral (64) is divergent. In this case, then, equations (38) and (38a) do not define a Fourier transform $F(\alpha)$ of the function $f(x)$. In many problems of mathematical physics, especially where transient effects are of interest, we have a function $f(x)$ of this type but which may be taken to be zero for negative values of x. In other words, we may write $f(x) = 0$, if $-\infty < x < 0$. Since $f(x)$ does not make the integral (64) convergent, we consider instead the function

$$f_1(x) = e^{-\gamma x} f(x) \tag{65}$$

where γ is a positive constant. Since $f_1(x)$ now satisfies the conditions of Fourier's theorem and is of such a nature that $f_1 = 0$ if $-\infty < x < 0$, it follows that

$$f_1(x) = \frac{1}{2\pi} \int_{-\infty}^\infty e^{i\eta x} d\eta \int_0^\infty f_1(\xi) e^{-i\xi\eta} d\xi$$

Substituting from equation (65) into this equation, we obtain the result

$$f(x) = \frac{e^{\gamma x}}{2\pi} \int_{-\infty}^\infty e^{i\eta x} d\eta \int_0^\infty f(\xi) e^{-(\gamma+i\eta)\xi} d\xi$$

If we now set

$$p = \gamma + i\eta, \qquad \phi(p) = \int_0^\infty f(\xi)e^{-p\xi}\,d\xi, \qquad dp = i\,d\eta \qquad (66)$$

in this equation, we obtain the formula

$$f(x) = \frac{1}{2\pi i} \int_{\gamma-i\infty}^{\gamma+i\infty} \phi(p)e^{px}\,dp \qquad (67)$$

As we observed at the beginning of this chapter, the function $\phi(p)$ is called the *Laplace transform* of the function. The form (67) of Fourier's integral theorem therefore expresses $f(x)$ in terms of its Laplace transform. That is, it is an inversion theorem for the Laplace transform. If

$$\int_0^\infty |f(x)|\,dx$$

is not bounded but

$$\int_0^\infty e^{-cx}|f(x)|\,dx$$

is bounded for some positive value of c, then the inversion formula (67) holds with $\gamma > c$.

The following theorem gives conditions on the function $\phi(p)$ sufficient to ensure the validity of the inversion theorem (67). The conditions imposed on the function $f(x)$ as a result of those on $\phi(p)$ are also noted.

Theorem 14. *If $\phi(p)$ is an analytic function of the complex variable p and is of order $0(p^{-k})$ in some half plane $\mathsf{R}(p) \geq c$, where c,k are real and $k > 1$, then the integral*

$$\frac{1}{2\pi i} \lim_{\beta \to \infty} \int_{\gamma-i\beta}^{\gamma+i\beta} e^{px}\phi(p)dp$$

along any line $\mathsf{R}(p) = \gamma \geq c$ converges to a function $f(x)$ which is independent of γ and whose Laplace transform is $\phi(p)$, $\mathsf{R}(p) > c$. Furthermore, the function $f(x)$ is continuous for each $x \geq 0$, $f(0) = 0$, and $f(x)$ is of the order $0(e^{\gamma x})$ for all $x \geq 0$.

For a proof of the inversion formula (67) in this form the reader should consult Churchill's "Modern Operational Mathematics in Engineering" (Sec. 56). Other formulas expressing a function in terms of its Laplace transform are known, but the inversion formula (67) is the only one of which we shall make use in applications considered in this book.

4.2 Faltung theorem for the Laplace transform. Suppose that $\phi(p)$ and $\psi(p)$ are the Laplace transforms of the functions $f(x)$ and $g(x)$, then

$$\frac{1}{2\pi i} \int_{\gamma-i\infty}^{\gamma+i\infty} \phi(p)\psi(p)e^{px}\,dp = \frac{1}{2\pi i} \int_{\gamma-i\infty}^{\gamma+i\infty} e^{px}\phi(p)dp \int_0^\infty g(y)e^{-py}\,dy$$

$$= \int_0^\infty g(y)dy \frac{1}{2\pi i} \int_{\gamma-i\infty}^{\gamma+i\infty} e^{p(x-y)}\phi(p)dp$$

But

$$\frac{1}{2\pi i} \int_{\gamma-i\infty}^{\gamma+i\infty} \phi(p)e^{p(x-y)} \, dp = f(x-y)$$

so that

$$\frac{1}{2\pi i} \int_{\gamma-i\infty}^{\gamma+i\infty} \phi(p)\psi(p)e^{px} \, dp = \int_0^\infty g(y)f(x-y)dy$$

Now

$$f(x-y) = 0 \qquad \text{if } x-y < 0 \text{, that is, if } y > x$$

and hence the integrand vanishes if $y > x$, and we obtain finally

$$\frac{1}{2\pi i} \int_{\gamma-i\infty}^{\gamma+i\infty} \phi(p)\psi(p)e^{px} \, dp = \int_0^x g(y)f(x-y)dy \tag{68}$$

Changing the variable in the integral on the right-hand side of equation (68) from y to $\eta = x - y$, we obtain

$$\frac{1}{2\pi i} \int_{\gamma-i\infty}^{\gamma+i\infty} \phi(p)\psi(p)e^{px} \, dp = \int_0^x f(\eta)g(x-\eta)d\eta \tag{69}$$

This is the Faltung theorem for Laplace transforms. It can be established rigorously.

Similarly we can write

$$\frac{1}{2\pi i} \int_{\gamma-i\infty}^{\gamma+i\infty} \phi(p)\psi(-p)e^{px} \, dp = \frac{1}{2\pi i} \int_0^\infty f(y)dy \int_{\gamma-i\infty}^{\gamma+i\infty} \psi(-p)e^{p(x-y)} \, dp$$

$$= \int_m^\infty f(y)g(y-x)dy \tag{70}$$

where m is the greater of x and 0. Thus, if $x \geq 0$,

$$\frac{1}{2\pi i} \int_{\gamma-i\infty}^{\gamma+i\infty} \phi(p)\psi(-p)e^{px} \, dp = \int_x^\infty f(y)g(y-x)dy$$

4.3 Relations between the Laplace transforms of the derivatives of a function. As in the case of the Fourier transforms we may express the Laplace transform of the function $d^r f/dx^r$ in terms of the Laplace transform of the function $f(x)$. By definition the Laplace transform of $d^r f/dx^r$ is

$$\phi^{(r)}(p) = \int_0^\infty \frac{d^r f}{dx^r} \, e^{-px} \, dx$$

Integrating by parts, we obtain

$$\phi^{(r)}(p) = \left[\frac{d^{r-1}f}{dx^{r-1}} e^{-px} \right]_0^\infty + p \int_0^\infty \frac{d^{r-1}f}{dx^{r-1}} e^{-px} \, dx$$

The function in the brackets vanishes at the upper limit so that if we write

$$f_0^{(r-1)} = \lim_{x \to 0} \left(\frac{d^{r-1}f}{dx^{r-1}} \right)$$

we obtain the relation

$$\phi^{(r)}(p) = -f_0^{(r-1)} + p\phi^{(r-1)}(p)$$

from which it follows that

$$\phi^{(r)}(p) = -\sum_{n=0}^{r-1} p^n f_0^{(r-n-1)} + p^r \phi(p) \tag{71}$$

If the first $(r-1)$ derivatives of $f(x)$ vanish at $x = 0$, this reduces simply to

$$\phi^{(r)}(p) = p^r \phi(p) \tag{72}$$

4.4 Dirac delta function. A problem which arises in applications of the theory of the Laplace transform to the solutions of specific problems is that of determining a function $f(x)$ whose Laplace transform $\phi(p)$ is unity. To find such a function we introduce the Dirac δ function[1] $\delta(x)$, which is defined to be zero everywhere except at the point $x = 0$, that is,

$$\delta(x) = 0 \qquad\qquad x \neq 0 \tag{73}$$

but is such that

$$\int_{-\infty}^{\infty} \delta(x)dx = 1 \tag{74}$$

The function $\delta(x)$ defined in this way is not like the ordinary functions of mathematical analysis, which are defined to have a definite value at each point in a certain domain, and is called by Dirac an "improper function." It may be used in analysis only when it is obvious that no inconsistency will follow from its use. To emphasize that the work in this section and in Sec. 4.5 is entirely formal, the equations derived in these sections will have the letter f added to their number. This will indicate that they are formal equations, not necessarily holding rigorously.

The equations (73) and (74) defining the Dirac δ function do not give us a clear picture of $\delta(x)$. We may infer that it is a function which is very large in the neighborhood of the point $x = 0$ but is zero outside a very small interval surrounding the origin. The precise variation of $\delta(x)$ with x in this interval is not important provided that its oscillations, if any, are not unnecessarily violent.

---

[1] P. A. M. Dirac, "The Principles of Quantum Mechanics," 3d ed (Oxford, New York, 1947), p. 58.

For instance, if we define a function $\delta_\epsilon(x)$ by the relations

$$\delta_\epsilon(x) = \begin{cases} 0 & x < 0 \\ \dfrac{1}{\epsilon} & 0 < x < \epsilon \\ 0 & x > \epsilon \end{cases}$$

then, since

$$\int_{-\infty}^{\infty} \delta_\epsilon(x)dx = \int_0^\epsilon \frac{dx}{\epsilon} = 1$$

it follows that we may regard $\delta(x)$ as being the limiting form of $\delta_\epsilon(x)$ as ϵ becomes zero, that is,

$$\lim_{\epsilon \to 0} \delta_\epsilon(x) = \delta(x) \tag{75f}$$

Suppose now that the function $f(x)$ is continuous in a certain interval which includes the origin. Then

$$\int_{-\infty}^{\infty} \delta_\epsilon(x)f(x)dx = \int_0^\epsilon \delta_\epsilon(x)f(x)dx = \frac{1}{\epsilon}\int_0^\epsilon f(x)dx$$

Now by the mean value theorem of the integral calculus

$$\int_0^\epsilon f(x)dx = f(\xi\epsilon)\int_0^\epsilon dx = \epsilon f(\xi\epsilon)$$

where $0 \le \xi \le 1$. Thus

$$\int_{-\infty}^{\infty} f(x)\delta_\epsilon(x)dx = f(\xi\epsilon) \qquad 0 \le \xi \le 1$$

If we let ϵ tend to zero in this equation, we obtain

$$\int_{-\infty}^{\infty} f(x)\delta(x)dx = f(0) \tag{76f}$$

Changing the variable on the right to ξ where $\xi = x + a$, we obtain the relation

$$\int_{-\infty}^{\infty} f(\xi)\delta(\xi - a)d\xi = f(a) \tag{77f}$$

showing that the operation of multiplying a function of the real variable x by the delta function $\delta(x - a)$ and integrating over the range $(-\infty, \infty)$ of x is equivalent to the process of substituting a for x. It follows as a result of equation (77f) that

$$f(x)\delta(x - a) = f(a)\delta(x - a) \tag{78f}$$

the meaning of such an equation being that its two sides give equivalent results as factors in an integrand. With a similar interpretation we may write

$$x\delta(x) = 0 \tag{79f}$$

as a consequence of equation (76f) or (78f).

Furthermore

$$\int_{-\infty}^{\infty} \int_{-\infty}^{\infty} f(\eta)\delta(\eta - \xi)\delta(\xi - b)d\xi \, d\eta = \int_{-\infty}^{\infty} \delta(\xi - b)d\xi \int_{-\infty}^{\infty} f(\eta)\delta(\eta - \xi)d\eta$$

$$= \int_{-\infty}^{\infty} f(\xi)\delta(\xi - b)d\xi$$

$$\equiv \int_{-\infty}^{\infty} f(\eta)\delta(\eta - b)d\eta$$

a result which may be expressed in the form

$$\int_{-\infty}^{\infty} \delta(\eta - \xi)\delta(\xi - b)d\xi = \delta(\eta - b) \tag{80f}$$

In a similar way we may establish

$$\delta(x^2 - a^2) = \frac{1}{2a}[\delta(x - a) + \delta(x + a)] \quad a > 0 \tag{81f}$$

The equations (76f) to (81b) provide us with the essential rules of manipulation in the algebra of δ functions. They have been derived from the definition (75f) of the Dirac δ function, but it can readily be shown that they are independent of the precise mode of definition of $\delta(x)$, provided that equations (73) and (74) are satisfied.

If we now introduce the discontinuous function

$$\epsilon(x) = \begin{cases} 0 & -\infty < x < 0 \\ 1 & 0 < x < \infty \end{cases}$$

then, denoting the derivative of this function by $\epsilon'(x)$, we have, on integrating by parts,

$$\int_{-g_2}^{g_1} f(x)\epsilon'(x)dx = \left[f(x)\epsilon(x) \right]_{-g_2}^{g_1} - \int_{-g_2}^{g_1} f'(x)\epsilon(x)dx \tag{82f}$$

g_1 and g_2 being positive. Now

$$\left[f(x)\epsilon(x) \right]_{-g_2}^{g_1} = f(g_1)$$

$$\int_{-g_2}^{g_1} f'(x)\epsilon(x)dx = \int_{0}^{g_1} f'(x)dx = f(g_1) - f(0)$$

so that, substituting in equation (82f) and letting g_1 and g_2 both tend to infinity, we obtain

$$\int_{-\infty}^{\infty} f(x)\epsilon'(x)dx = f(0) \tag{83f}$$

Comparing equations (76f) and (83f), we see that

$$\delta(x) = \epsilon'(x) \tag{84f}$$

showing that the derivative of the discontinuous function $\epsilon(x)$ is the Dirac delta function.

4.5 Laplace transform of the Dirac delta function. By definition the Laplace transform of the Dirac delta function is

$$\int_0^\infty \delta(x)e^{-px}\,dx$$

Now

$$\int_0^\infty \delta_\epsilon(x)e^{-px}\,dx = \frac{1}{\epsilon}\int_0^\epsilon e^{-px}\,dx = \frac{1}{p\epsilon}(1 - e^{-p\epsilon})$$

$$= \frac{1}{p\epsilon}\left[1 - \left(1 - p\epsilon + \frac{1}{2}p^2\epsilon^2 - \cdots\right)\right]$$

$$= 1 + 0(\epsilon)$$

Letting ϵ tend to zero on both sides of this equation, we obtain

$$\int^\infty \delta(x)e^{-px}\,dx = 1 \tag{85f}$$

showing that $\delta(x)$ has the Laplace transform unity. By a formal application of the Laplace inversion formula (67) we write this result in the form

$$\delta(x) = \frac{1}{2\pi i}\int_{\gamma - i\infty}^{\gamma + i\infty} e^{px}\,dp$$

By similar arguments we see that the Fourier transform of $\delta(x)$ is

$$\frac{1}{\sqrt{2\pi}}\int_{-\infty}^\infty \delta(x)e^{i\alpha x}\,dx = \frac{1}{\sqrt{2\pi}}$$

Making use of the Fourier inversion formula, we may write formally

$$\int_{-\infty}^\infty e^{-i\alpha x}\,d\alpha = 2\pi\,\delta(x) \tag{86f}$$

a result which is used extensively in quantum mechanics.[1]

5. Foundations of Operator Calculus

5.1 General theory. To illustrate the application of the theory of Laplace transforms to specific problems, we shall now show how it may be used to justify the D method of solving ordinary linear differential equations with constant coefficients. An equation of this type may be written in the form

$$a_n\frac{d^n y}{dx^n} + a_{n-1}\frac{d^{n-1}y}{dx^{n-1}} + \cdots + a_1\frac{dy}{dx} + a_0 y = \phi(x)$$

where the quantities $a_0, a_1, \ldots, a_{n-1}, a_n$ are constants and $\phi(x)$ is a

---

[1] Cf., for instance, *ibid.*, p. 95.

known function of x. If we write D for the operator d/dx, we may write this equation in the form

$$f(D)y = \phi(x) \tag{87}$$

where we define $f(D)$ by the relation

$$f(D) = \sum_{s=0}^{n} a_s D^s \tag{88}$$

Suppose, further, that we wish a solution of equation (87) valid for $x \geq 0$.

The D method, or symbolic method, of solving equations of the type (87) is well known.[1] If the equation $f(D) = 0$ has no repeated roots so that we may write

$$f(D) = a_n \prod_{\mu=1}^{n} (D - \alpha_\mu) \tag{89}$$

where the α_μ's are all different, then the solution of equation (87) may be written symbolically as

$$y = \sum_{\mu=1}^{n} B_\mu e^{\alpha_\mu x} + \frac{1}{f(D)} \phi(x) \tag{90}$$

where the B_μ's are arbitrary. Rules are given for the interpretation of $f^{-1}(D)\phi(x)$. For instance, if $\phi(x) = e^{ax}$ and a is *not* a root of the equation $f(D) = 0$, then

$$\frac{1}{f(D)} \phi(x) \equiv \frac{1}{f(D)} e^{ax} = \frac{1}{f(a)} e^{ax} \tag{91}$$

and similarly

$$\frac{1}{f(D)} e^{ax}\chi(x) = e^{ax} \frac{1}{f(D+a)} \chi(x) \tag{92}$$

Solutions similar to (90) can also be constructed when the equation $f(D) = 0$ has multiple roots. We shall now show how these working rules may be established by means of the Laplace inversion theorem.

Multiply both sides of equation (87) by e^{-px}, where $\mathsf{R}(p) > 0$, and integrate with respect to x over the range $(0, \infty)$ to obtain

$$\sum_{s=0}^{n} a_s \int_0^\infty \frac{d^s y}{dx^s} e^{-px} \, dx = \int_0^\infty \phi(x)e^{-px} \, dx$$

If we denote the Laplace transform of $\phi(x)$ by $\bar{\phi}(p)$ and that of $y(x)$ by

---

[1] H. T. H. Piaggio, "An Elementary Treatise on Differential Equations and Their Applications" (G. Bell, London, 1940), pp. 30–48.

$\bar{y}(p)$, then, since, from equation (71),

$$\int_0^\infty \frac{d^s y}{dx^s} e^{-px}\, dx = -\sum_{\lambda=0}^{s-1} p^\lambda y_0{}^{(s-\lambda-1)} + p^s \bar{y}(p)$$

we have

$$\sum_{s=0}^n a_s \left[p^s \bar{y}(p) - \sum_{\lambda=1}^s p^{\lambda-1} y_0^{(s-\lambda)} \right] = \bar{\phi}(p)$$

where $y_0^{(s-\lambda)}$ denotes the value of $d^{s-\lambda}y/dx^{s-\lambda}$ at the point $x = 0$. Now by definition [equation (88)]

$$f(p) = \sum_{s=0}^n a_s p^s$$

so that

$$f(p)\bar{y}(p) - \sum_{s=0}^n \sum_{\lambda=1}^s a_s y_0^{(s-\lambda)} p^{\lambda-1} = \bar{\phi}(p)$$

Solving this equation for $\bar{y}(p)$, we find

$$\bar{y}(p) = \frac{\bar{\phi}(p) + \displaystyle\sum_{s=0}^n \sum_{\lambda=1}^s a_s y_0^{(s-\lambda)} p^{\lambda-1}}{f(p)}$$

Inverting this equation by means of the Laplace inversion formula (67), we find that the solution of equation (87) may be written

$$y(x) = \psi_1(x) + \psi_2(x)$$

where $\psi_1(x)$ denotes the *complementary function*

$$\psi_1(x) = \frac{1}{2\pi i} \int_{\gamma-i\infty}^{\gamma+i\infty} e^{px} \sum_{s=0}^n \sum_{\lambda=1}^s a_s y_0^{(s-\lambda)} p^{\lambda-1} \frac{dp}{f(p)} \qquad (93)$$

and $\psi_2(x)$ denotes the *particular integral*

$$\psi_2(x) = \frac{1}{2\pi i} \int_{\gamma-i\infty}^{\gamma+i\infty} \frac{\bar{\phi}(p)}{f(p)} e^{px}\, dp \qquad (94)$$

5.2 The complementary function. We shall begin by considering the complementary function $\psi_1(x)$. It will be observed that it is the solution of the homogeneous equation $f(D)y = 0$. There are two cases to be considered: that in which the roots of $f(D) = 0$ are simple, and then that in which $f(D) = 0$ has repeated roots.

Case $1: f(D) = 0$, *having no repeated roots, real or complex.* If the equation $f(D) = 0$ has no repeated roots, we can express $1/f(p)$ as the sum of partial fractions thus:

$$\frac{1}{f(p)} = \sum_{\mu=1}^{n} \frac{A_\mu}{p - \alpha_\mu} \tag{95}$$

where the α_μ's are all different and $f(\alpha_\mu) = 0$ $(\mu = 1, 2, \ldots, n)$. The quantities A_μ and α_μ will, of course, be complex in the general case. Thus we may write

$$\psi_1(x) = \sum_{\mu=1}^{n} \sum_{s=0}^{n} \sum_{\lambda=1}^{s} A_\mu a_s y_0^{(s-\lambda)} \left(\frac{1}{2\pi i} \int_{\gamma - i\infty}^{\gamma + i\infty} \frac{e^{px} p^{\lambda-1}}{p - \alpha_\mu} \, dp \right)$$

Since $\lambda \geq 1$, the only pole of the integrand of the integral in the large parentheses is at the point $p = \alpha_\mu$, where the residue is $e^{\alpha_\mu x}(\alpha_\mu)^{\lambda-1}$. Thus we have[1]

$$\psi_1(x) = \sum_{\mu=1}^{n} e^{\alpha_\mu x} \left(\sum_{s=0}^{n} \sum_{\lambda=1}^{s} A_\mu \alpha_\mu^{\lambda-1} a_s y_0^{(s-\lambda)} \right)$$

$$= \sum_{\mu=1}^{n} B_\mu e^{\alpha_\mu x} \tag{96}$$

where B_μ is a constant

$$\sum_{s=0}^{n} \sum_{\lambda=1}^{s} A_\mu \alpha_\mu^{\lambda-1} a_s y_0^{(s-\lambda)}$$

depending on the initial values of the $(n - 1)$ derivatives $d^r y/dx^r$ $(0 \leq r \leq n - 1)$. It will be observed that equation (96) is the first part of equation (90).

It is of interest to examine more closely the interpretation of complex roots of the equation $f(D) = 0$. Since, if the coefficients of this equation are real, complex roots occur in conjugate pairs, they give rise to factors of the form

$$\frac{A}{(p + \theta)^2 + \phi^2}$$

in $1/f(p)$. Suppose, as a simple case, that $1/f(p)$ is given by this expression; then

$$\psi_1(x) = \frac{1}{2\pi i} \int_{\gamma - i\infty}^{\gamma + i\infty} \frac{A e^{px} \Sigma \Sigma a_s y_0^{(s-\lambda)} p^{\lambda-1}}{(p + \theta)^2 + \phi^2} \, dp$$

$$= e^{-\theta x}(B_1 \cos \phi x + B_2 \sin \phi x)$$

---

[1] For the details of the method of evaluating contour integrals of this type, see R. V. Churchill, "Modern Operational Mathematics in Engineering" (McGraw-Hill, New York, 1944).

where, as before, the B's are constants of integration. The general case can be treated along similar lines.

Case 2: $f(D) = 0$, *having repeated roots.* If $f(D) = 0$ has repeated roots, then we must replace equation (95) by an equation of the form

$$\frac{1}{f(p)} = \sum_{(\mu+r) \leq n} \sum \frac{A_{\mu r}}{(p - \alpha_\mu)^r} \tag{97}$$

where, as before, $A_{\mu r}$ and α_μ are, in general, complex. For simplicity we shall consider only the case in which

$$\frac{1}{f(p)} = \frac{1}{(p - \alpha_\mu)^r} \tag{98}$$

There is, however, no loss of generality as the result for a more general form of $1/f(p)$ can be obtained by summation. The complementary function corresponding to the form (98) is

$$\psi_1(x) = \frac{1}{2\pi i} \int_{\gamma - i\infty}^{\gamma + i\infty} \frac{e^{px}\, dp}{(p - \alpha_\mu)^r} \sum_{s=0}^{r} \sum_{\lambda=1}^{s} a_s y_0^{(s-\lambda)} p^{\lambda-1}$$

$$= \sum_{s=0}^{r} \sum_{\lambda=1}^{s} a_s y_0^{(s-\lambda)} \frac{1}{2\pi i} \int_{\gamma - i\infty}^{\gamma + i\infty} \frac{e^{px} p^{\lambda-1}}{(p - \alpha_\mu)^r}\, dp$$

Now

$$\frac{1}{2\pi i} \int_{\gamma - i\infty}^{\gamma + i\infty} \frac{e^{px} p^{\lambda-1}\, dp}{(p - \alpha_\mu)^r} = \frac{1}{(r - 1)!} \left[\frac{d^{r-1}}{dp^{r-1}} \left(e^{px} p^{\lambda-1} \right) \right]_{p=\alpha_\mu}$$

$$= \frac{e^{\alpha_\mu x}}{(r - 1)!} [x^{r-1}\alpha_\mu^{\lambda-1} + x^{r-2}(r - 1)(\lambda - 1)\alpha_\mu^{\lambda-2} + \cdots$$

$$+ (\lambda - 1) \cdots (\lambda - r + 1)\alpha_\mu^{\lambda-r}]$$

whence

$$\psi_1(x) = e^{\alpha_\mu x}(B_{\mu,1} x^{r-1} + B_{\mu,2} x^{r-2} + \cdots + B_{\mu,r-1} x + B_{\mu,r})$$

where, once again, the coefficients $B_{\mu,m}$ are dependent on the initial values of the derivatives $d^i y/dx^i$ $(0 \leq i \leq r - 1)$.

5.3 The particular integral. We shall now derive some of the rules for the calculation of the particular integral

$$\psi_2(x) \equiv \frac{1}{f(D)}\, \phi(x) = \frac{1}{2\pi i} \int_{\gamma - i\infty}^{\gamma + i\infty} \frac{\bar{\phi}(p)}{f(p)}\, e^{px}\, dp$$

With this notation we then have the following lemmas:

Lemma 1. *If a is not a root of the equation $f(D) = 0$, then*

$$\frac{1}{f(D)}\, e^{ax} = \frac{1}{f(a)}\, e^{ax}$$

For, if we put $\phi(x) = e^{ax}$, $\bar{\phi}(p) = (p - a)^{-1}$, and

$$\frac{1}{f(D)} = \sum_{(\mu+r) \leq n} \sum \frac{A_{\mu r}}{(D - \alpha_\mu)^r}$$

then

$$\frac{1}{f(D)} e^{ax} = \sum_{(\mu+r) \leq n} \sum A_{\mu r} \left[\frac{1}{2\pi i} \int_{\gamma - i\infty}^{\gamma + i\infty} \frac{e^{px}\, dp}{(p - \alpha_\mu)^r (p - a)} \right]$$

$$= \sum_{(\mu+r) \leq n} \sum A_{\mu r} \frac{e^{ax}}{(a - \alpha_\mu)^r} + \sum_{(\mu+r) \leq n} \sum A_{\mu r} \left[\frac{d^{r-1}}{dp^{r-1}} \left(\frac{e^{px}}{p - a} \right) \right]_{p = \alpha_\mu}$$

However, the second term on the right has already been included in the complementary function; thus it can be left out of the discussion of the particular integral. Hence

$$\frac{1}{f(D)} e^{ax} = e^{ax} \sum_{(\mu+r) \leq n} \sum \frac{A_{\mu r}}{(a - \alpha_\mu)^r} = \frac{1}{f(a)} e^{ax}$$

which proves the lemma.

Lemma 2. *If a is not a root of the equation $f(D) = 0$, then*

$$\frac{1}{f(D)} [e^{ax}\chi(x)] = e^{ax} \frac{1}{f(D + a)} \chi(x)$$

If the Laplace transform of $\chi(x)$ is $\bar{\chi}(p)$, then that of $e^{ax}\chi(x)$ is

$$\int_0^\infty e^{-px} e^{ax} \chi(x)\, dx = \int_0^\infty e^{-(p-a)x} \chi(x)\, dx = \bar{\chi}(p - a)$$

so that

$$\frac{1}{f(D)} [e^{ax}\chi(x)] = \frac{1}{2\pi i} \int_{\gamma - i\infty}^{\gamma + i\infty} \frac{\bar{\chi}(p - a)}{f(p)} e^{px}\, dp$$

Changing the independent variable in this integration from p to $q = p - a$, we obtain the equation

$$\frac{1}{f(D)} [e^{ax}\chi(x)] = \frac{1}{2\pi i} e^{ax} \int_{-i\infty}^{\delta + i\infty} e^{qx} \frac{\bar{\chi}(q)}{f(q + a)}\, dq$$

Now, by definition,

$$\frac{1}{f(D + a)} \chi(x) = \frac{1}{2\pi i} \int_{\delta - i\infty}^{\delta + i\infty} \frac{\bar{\chi}(q)}{f(q + a)} e^{px}\, dq$$

so that

$$\frac{1}{f(D)} [e^{ax}\chi(x)] = e^{ax} \frac{1}{f(D + a)} \chi(x)$$

proving the lemma.

Lemma 3. *If r is a positive integer and k is a constant, then*

$$D^{-r}k = \frac{kx^r}{r!}$$

By definition, the Laplace transform of k is k/p so that

$$D^{-r}k = \frac{1}{2\pi i} \int_{\gamma-i\infty}^{\gamma+i\infty} \frac{ke^{px}}{p^{r+1}} \, dp$$

$$= \frac{k}{r!} \left[\frac{d^r}{dp^r} (e^{px}) \right]_{p=0} = \frac{kx^r}{r!}$$

giving the required result.

Lemma 4. *If $f(D) = (D - a)^r g(D)$ where $g(a) \neq 0$, then*

$$\frac{1}{f(D)} e^{ax} = \frac{e^{ax}x^r}{r!g(a)}$$

This lemma follows as a direct consequence of the last three, for

$$\frac{1}{f(D)} e^{ax} = \frac{1}{(D - a)^r} \frac{1}{g(D)} e^{ax} = \frac{1}{g(a)} \frac{1}{(D - a)^r} e^{ax}$$

by Lemma 1.   Applying Lemma 2 with $\chi(x) = 1$, we have

$$\frac{1}{f(D)} e^{ax} = \frac{1}{g(a)} e^{ax} \frac{1}{D^r} (1) = \frac{1}{g(a)} e^{ax} \frac{x^r}{r!}$$

taking $k = 1$ in Lemma 3.

By means of the theory of the Laplace transform we have thus been able to justify the procedure adopted in the solution of ordinary differential equations by the symbolic D method.   For examples of the use of the D method the reader should consult the treatise by Piaggio referred to above.   It is usually much simpler to use the expressions (93) and (94) for the determination of the complementary function and the particular integral.   This is the procedure adopted by most modern textbooks on operational calculus, *e.g.*, those by Churchill and by Carslaw and Jaeger referred to in Sec. 1.

6. Mellin Transform

6.1 Mellin transform theorem.   We saw above (Sec. 1) that the Mellin transform $\mathsf{F}(s)$ of the function $f(x)$ is defined by the equation

$$\mathsf{F}(s) = \int_0^\infty f(x)x^{s-1} \, dx \tag{99}$$

Now if we let $\xi = e^x$, $s = c + i\alpha$ in equation (38), we find that it becomes

$$F\left(\frac{s - c}{i}\right) = \frac{1}{\sqrt{2\pi}} \int_0^\infty \xi^{-c} f(\log \xi) \xi^{s-1} \, d\xi$$

and the same substitutions in (38b) give

$$f(\log \xi) = \frac{1}{i \sqrt{2\pi}} \int_{c-i\infty}^{c+i\infty} F\left(\frac{s-c}{i}\right) \xi^{c-s} \, ds$$

If therefore we write

$$g(\xi) = (2\pi)^{-\frac{1}{2}} \xi^{-c} f(\log \xi)$$

$$\mathsf{G}(s) = F\left(\frac{s-c}{i}\right)$$

we obtain the Mellin inversion formula, as follows:

Theorem 15. *If the integral $\int_0^\infty \xi^{k-1} |g(\xi)| \, d\xi$ is bounded for some $k > 0$ and if*

$$\mathsf{G}(s) = \int_0^\infty \xi^{s-1} g(\xi) d\xi$$

then

$$g(\xi) = \frac{1}{2\pi i} \int_{c-i\infty}^{c+i\infty} \mathsf{G}(s) \xi^{-s} \, ds$$

where $c > k$.

The relations between the Mellin transforms of the derivatives of a function are not of such a simple nature as those for Fourier and Laplace transforms. For instance,

$$\int_0^\infty \frac{d^r f}{dx^r} x^{s-1} \, dx = \left[\frac{d^{r-1} f}{dx^{r-1}} x^{s-1}\right]_0^\infty - (s-1) \int_0^\infty \frac{d^{r-1} f}{dx^{r-1}} x^{s-2} \, dx$$

so that, if we assume f to be of such a nature that the square bracket vanishes, we have the relation

$$\mathsf{F}^{(r)}(s) = -(s-1)\mathsf{F}^{(r-1)}(s-1)$$

where $\mathsf{F}^{(r)}(s)$ denotes the Mellin transform of the derivative $d^r f/dx^r$. Applying this rule until we reach $\mathsf{F}^{(0)}(s)$, we find that

$$\mathsf{F}^{(r)}(s) = (-1)^r \frac{\Gamma(s)}{\Gamma(s-r)} \mathsf{F}(s-r) \tag{100}$$

is the formula giving the Mellin transform of the derivative in terms of the Mellin transform of the function itself.

6.2 Faltung theorems for the Mellin transform. Let us suppose that $\mathsf{F}(s)$ and $\mathsf{G}(s)$ are the Mellin transforms of the functions $f(x)$ and $g(x)$; then the Mellin transform of the product $f(x)g(x)$ is defined to be

$$\int_0^\infty f(x)g(x)x^{s-1} \, dx = \int_0^\infty g(x)dx \, x^{s-1} \frac{1}{2\pi i} \int_{c-i\infty}^{c+i\infty} \mathsf{F}(\sigma)x^{-\sigma} \, d\sigma$$

$$= \frac{1}{2\pi i} \int_{c-i\infty}^{c+i\infty} \mathsf{F}(\sigma)d\sigma \int_0^\infty g(x)x^{s-\sigma-1} \, dx$$

$$= \frac{1}{2\pi i} \int_{c-i\infty}^{c+i\infty} \mathsf{F}(\sigma)\mathsf{G}(s-\sigma)d\sigma \tag{101}$$

A special case of this formula is

$$\int_0^\infty f(x)g(x)dx = \frac{1}{2\pi i} \int_0^\infty g(x)dx \int_{c-i\infty}^{c+i\infty} F(s)x^{-s}\,ds$$

$$= \frac{1}{2\pi i} \int_{c-i\infty}^{c+i\infty} F(s)G(1-s)ds \qquad (101a)$$

In a similar way the Mellin transform of the product $F(s)G(s)$ is

$$\frac{1}{2\pi i} \int_{c-i\infty}^{c+i\infty} F(s)G(s)x^{-s}\,ds = \frac{1}{2\pi i} \int_{c-i\infty}^{c+i\infty} F(s)x^{-s}\,ds \int_0^\infty g(u)u^{s-1}\,du$$

$$= \int_0^\infty g(u)\,\frac{du}{u}\,\frac{1}{2\pi i} \int_{c-i\infty}^{c+i\infty} F(s)\left(\frac{x}{u}\right)^{-s}\,ds$$

$$= \int_0^\infty f\left(\frac{x}{u}\right) g(u)\,\frac{du}{u} \qquad (102)$$

and, in particular,

$$\frac{1}{2\pi i} \int_{c-i\infty}^{c+i\infty} F(s)G(s)ds = \frac{1}{2\pi i} \int_{c-i\infty}^{c+i\infty} F(s)ds \int_0^\infty g(u)u^{s-1}\,du$$

$$= \int_0^\infty g(u)\,\frac{du}{u}\,\frac{1}{2\pi i} \int_{c-i\infty}^{c+i\infty} F(s)\left(\frac{1}{u}\right)^{-s}\,ds$$

$$= \int_0^\infty f\left(\frac{1}{u}\right) g(u)\,\frac{du}{u} \qquad (102a)$$

7. Multiple Fourier Transforms

7.1 Multiple Fourier transforms. The theory of Fourier transforms of functions of a single variable can be extended to functions of several variables. Suppose, for instance, that $f(x,y)$ is a function of the two independent variables x and y; then, regarded as a function of x, f has the Fourier transform

$$\bar{f}(\xi,y) = \frac{1}{\sqrt{2\pi}} \int_{-\infty}^\infty f(x,y)e^{i\xi x}\,dx \qquad (103)$$

and this function, regarded as a function of y, has the Fourier transform

$$F(\xi,\eta) = \frac{1}{\sqrt{2\pi}} \int_{-\infty}^\infty \bar{f}(\xi,y)e^{i\eta y}\,dy \qquad (104)$$

Combining equations (103) and (104), we see that the relation between the functions $f(x,y)$ and $F(\xi,\eta)$ is

$$F(\xi,\eta) = \frac{1}{2\pi} \int_{-\infty}^\infty \int_{-\infty}^\infty f(x,y)e^{i(\xi x+\eta y)}\,dx\,dy \qquad (105)$$

and we say that $F(\xi,\eta)$ is the two-dimensional Fourier transform of the function $f(x,y)$. Applying Theorem 10 to equation (103), we find that $f(x,y)$ may be expressed in terms of $\bar{f}(\xi,y)$ by the relation

$$f(x,y) = \frac{1}{\sqrt{2\pi}} \int_{-\infty}^{\infty} \bar{f}(\xi,y)e^{-i\xi x}\, d\xi \tag{106}$$

Similarly from equation (105) we find that

$$\bar{f}(\xi,y) = \frac{1}{\sqrt{2\pi}} \int_{-\infty}^{\infty} F(\xi,\eta)e^{-i\eta y}\, d\eta \tag{107}$$

and hence it follows from equations (106) and (107) that

$$f(x,y) = \frac{1}{2\pi} \int_{-\infty}^{\infty} \int_{-\infty}^{\infty} F(\xi,\eta)e^{-i(\xi x+\eta y)}\, d\xi\, d\eta \tag{108}$$

giving the inversion formula for the double Fourier transform (105).

If we now form the Fourier transforms of the functions $F(\xi,\eta)$ and $G(\xi,\eta)$, we have, for the Fourier transform of FG,

$$\frac{1}{2\pi} \int_{-\infty}^{\infty} \int_{-\infty}^{\infty} F(\xi,\eta)G(\xi,\eta)e^{-i(\xi x+\eta y)}\, d\xi\, d\eta$$

$$= \frac{1}{2\pi} \int_{-\infty}^{\infty} \int_{-\infty}^{\infty} G(\xi,\eta)e^{-i(\xi x+\eta y)}\, d\xi\, d\eta \left[\frac{1}{2\pi} \int_{-\infty}^{\infty} \int_{-\infty}^{\infty} f(u,v)e^{i(\xi u+\eta v)}\, du\, dv\right]$$

$$= \frac{1}{2\pi} \int_{-\infty}^{\infty} \int_{-\infty}^{\infty} f(u,v)\, du\, dv \left\{\frac{1}{2\pi} \int_{-\infty}^{\infty} \int_{-\infty}^{\infty} G(\xi,\eta)e^{-i[\xi(x-u)+\eta(y-v)]}\, d\xi\, d\eta\right\}$$

$$= \frac{1}{2\pi} \int_{-\infty}^{\infty} \int_{-\infty}^{\infty} f(u,v)g(x-u,y-v)\, du\, dv$$

since the expression in the braces is, by definition, the Fourier transform of $G(\xi,\eta)$. In this way we establish the Faltung theorem

$$\int_{-\infty}^{\infty} \int_{-\infty}^{\infty} F(\xi,\eta)G(\xi,\eta)e^{-i(\xi x+\eta y)}\, d\xi\, d\eta$$
$$= \int_{-\infty}^{\infty} \int_{-\infty}^{\infty} f(u,v)g(x-u,y-v)du\, dv \tag{109}$$

The generalization to a greater number of variables is obvious. Suppose $f(x_1,x_2, \ldots ,x_n)$ is a function of the n independent variables $x_1,x_2, \ldots ,x_n$; then the n-dimensional Fourier transform of the function f is defined to be

$$F(\xi_1,\xi_2, \ldots ,\xi_n)$$
$$= \left(\frac{1}{2\pi}\right)^{\frac{1}{2}n} \int_{-\infty}^{\infty} \cdots \int_{-\infty}^{\infty} f(x_1,x_2, \ldots ,x_n)e^{i(\xi \cdot x)}\, dx_1 \cdots dx_n \tag{110}$$

where $(\xi \cdot \mathbf{x})$ denotes the inner product

$$\xi_1 x_1 + \xi_2 x_2 \cdots + \xi_n x_n$$

The corresponding inversion formula can then be shown to be

$$f(x_1, \ldots, x_n)$$
$$= \left(\frac{1}{2\pi}\right)^{\frac{1}{2}n} \int_{-\infty}^{\infty} \cdots \int_{-\infty}^{\infty} F(\xi_1, \ldots, \xi_n) e^{-i(\xi \cdot \mathbf{x})} \, d\xi_1 \cdots d\xi_n \quad (111)$$

and the n-dimensional analogue of the result (109) to be

$$\int_{-\infty}^{\infty} \cdots \int_{-\infty}^{\infty} F(\xi_1, \xi_2, \ldots, \xi_n) G(\xi_1, \xi_2, \ldots, \xi_n) e^{-i(\xi \cdot \mathbf{x})} \, d\xi_1 \, d\xi_2 \cdots d\xi_n$$
$$= \int_{-\infty}^{\infty} \cdots \int_{-\infty}^{\infty} f(u_1, u_2, \ldots, u_n) g(x_1 - u_1, x_2 - u_2, \ldots, x_n - u_n)$$
$$\times du_1 \, du_2 \cdots du_n \quad (112)$$

7.2 Double Laplace transforms. Just as the theory of Fourier transforms may be easily extended to functions of more than one variable, we may set up a theory of multiple Laplace transforms. It was pointed out by Jaeger[1] that partial differential equations in which the range of two (or more) independent variables is $(0, \infty)$ may easily be handled by simultaneous Laplace transforms in these variables. The point of view adopted is that the Laplace transform method should be regarded as purely formal and the solution as subject to verification.

We consider a function $f(x,y)$ defined in the region $x \geq 0$, $y \geq 0$ and let

$$g_0(x) = f(x,0), \qquad g_1(x) = \left(\frac{\partial f}{\partial y}\right)_{y=0}$$
$$h_0(y) = f(0,y), \qquad h_1(y) = \left(\frac{\partial f}{\partial x}\right)_{x=0}$$

The Laplace transform of $f(x,y)$ with respect to y will be denoted by a "bar," thus,

$$\bar{f}(x,p) = \int_0^{\infty} e^{-py} f(x,y) \, dy$$

and the Laplace transform with respect to x by a capital letter, thus,

$$F(p',y) = \int_0^{\infty} e^{-p'x} f(x,y) \, dx$$

The double transform we denote by both:

$$\bar{F}(p',p) = \int_0^{\infty} \int_0^{\infty} e^{-p'x - py} f(x,y) \, dx \, dy$$

---

[1] J. C. Jaeger, *Bull. Am. Math. Soc.*, **46**, 687 (1940). See also V. R. Thiruvenkatachar, *Jour. Mysore Univ.* (**B**), **1**, 115 (1941).

The quantities p' and p are supposed to have real parts which are sufficiently large to ensure the convergence of the integrals. This notation indicates in a compact fashion the variables which occur in any expression. If there are other independent variables $z,t, \ldots$, they will occur throughout.

Then, subject to certain rather wide conditions on the function $f(x,y)$, we have the relations

$$\int_0^\infty \int_0^\infty e^{-p'x-py} \frac{\partial f}{\partial y} \, dx \, dy = p\bar{F}(p',p) - G_0(p') \tag{113}$$

$$\int_0^\infty \int_0^\infty e^{-p'x-py} \frac{\partial^2 f}{\partial y^2} \, dx \, dy = p^2\bar{F}(p',p) - pG_0(p') - G_1(p') \tag{114}$$

$$\int_0^\infty \int_0^\infty e^{-p'x-py} \frac{\partial f}{\partial x} \, dx \, dy = p'\bar{F}(p',p) - \bar{h}_0(p) \tag{115}$$

$$\int_0^\infty \int_0^\infty e^{-p'x-py} \frac{\partial^2 f}{\partial x^2} \, dx \, dy = p'^2\bar{F}(p',p) - p'\bar{h}_0(p) - \bar{h}_1(p) \tag{116}$$

To derive the expression for the function $f(x,y)$ when its double Laplace transform $F(p',p)$ is known, we assume an inversion theorem which may be derived formally from Fourier's integral theorem in several variables:

$$f(x,y) = \frac{-1}{4\pi^2} \int_{\gamma-i\infty}^{\gamma+i\infty} dp \int_{\gamma'-i\infty}^{\gamma'+i\infty} e^{p'x+py}\bar{F}(p',p)dp' \tag{117}$$

where $-\pi < \arg(p) < \pi$ and $-\pi < \arg(p') < \pi$, provided that $\bar{F}(p',p)$ is bounded in some half planes $R(p') > \alpha'$, $R(p) > \alpha$ and $\gamma' > \alpha'$, $\gamma > \alpha$. In addition to this last condition there will be other conditions necessary for the validity of the theorem (117), but neither these nor the assumptions involved in the derivation of equations (113) to (116) need be discussed since the whole process of determining $f(x,y)$ as a double contour integral of type (117) is regarded as purely formal. It only remains to verify that the solution derived in this way does in fact satisfy the differential equation and the boundary conditions of the problem.

In an analogous manner we may define an *iterated Laplace transform* of the function $f(x,y)$ by the equation

$$\bar{F}(s) = \int_0^\infty e^{-sy} \, dy \int_0^\infty e^{-sx}f(x,y)dx \tag{118}$$

$$\bar{F}(s) = \int_0^\infty \int_0^\infty e^{-s(x+y)}f(x,y)dx \, dy \tag{118a}$$

We shall make use of a transform of this type in the establishment of an important theorem in the theory of the conduction of heat in solids (Sec. 22.3). In the proof of that theorem we consider the generalized convolution of Bartels and Churchill[1] defined by the relation

$$f^*(x) = \int_0^x f(x - y, y) dy \tag{119}$$

If we denote the Laplace transform of this function by $\theta(s)$, then by definition

$$\theta(s) \equiv L[f^*(x)] = \int_0^\infty e^{-sx} f^*(x) dx \tag{120}$$

Consider now the integral

$$\theta(R,s) = \int_0^R e^{-sx} dx \int_0^x f(x - y, y) dy \tag{121}$$

Then

$$\theta(s) = \lim_{R \to \infty} \theta(R,s) \tag{122}$$

Changing the variables in the double integral on the right-hand side of equation (121) from x and y to u and v where $u = x - y$ and $v = y$, we see that

$$\theta(R,s) = \int \int_\Delta e^{-su-sv} f(u,v) du\, dv \tag{123}$$

where the area of integration Δ is the triangle enclosed by the lines $u = 0$, $v = 0$, $u + v = R$. As $R \to \infty$, the region Δ becomes the whole of the positive quadrant of the uv plane, and it follows from equations (122) and (123) that

$$\theta(s) = \int_0^\infty \int_0^\infty e^{-s(u+v)} f(u,v) du\, dv$$

and hence from equation (118) that

$$\theta(s) = \bar{F}(s) \tag{124}$$

so that the Laplace transform of the generalized convolution $f^*(x)$ is the iterated Laplace transform of the function $f(x,y)$.

[1] R. C. F. Bartels and R. V. Churchill, *Bull. Am. Math. Soc.*, **48**, 276 (1942).

CHAPTER 2

HANKEL TRANSFORMS

8. Hankel Inversion Theorem

8.1 Hankel inversion theorem. An example we considered above (case 3, Sec. 2.2) suggests that there is reason to believe that the function $x^{\frac{1}{2}}J_\nu(x)$ is a Fourier kernel, *i.e.*, that in some sense

$$\int_0^\infty (x\alpha)^{\frac{1}{2}}J_\nu(x\alpha)d\alpha \int_0^\infty (\alpha\beta)^{\frac{1}{2}}J_\nu(\alpha\beta)f(\beta)d\beta = f(x) \tag{1}$$

We shall now proceed to investigate this result in more detail. The main theorem establishing a result of this kind is proved as a result of a series of lemmas.[1] The first of these is as follows:

Theorem 16. *If λ is positive and finite,*

$$\int_0^\lambda xJ_\nu(ax)J_\nu(bx)dx = \frac{\lambda}{a^2 - b^2}[aJ_{\nu+1}(\lambda a)J_\nu(\lambda b) - bJ_{\nu+1}(\lambda b)J_\nu(\lambda a)]$$

If we write

$$I_\nu(\epsilon) = \int_\epsilon^\lambda xJ_\nu(ax)J_\nu(bx)dx$$

then from the theory of Bessel functions [equations (8) and (9), Appendix A] we obtain

$$\frac{d}{dx}[x^\nu J_\nu(x)] = x^\nu J_{\nu-1}(x), \qquad \frac{d}{dx}[x^{-\nu}J_\nu(x)] = -x^{-\nu}J_{\nu+1}(x)$$

from which it follows by writing

$$I_\nu(\epsilon) = \int_\epsilon^\lambda x^{\nu+1}J_\nu(ax)x^{-\nu}J_\nu(bx)dx$$

and then integrating by parts that

$$I_\nu(\epsilon) = \left[\frac{1}{a}x^{\nu+1}J_{\nu+1}(ax)x^{-\nu}J_\nu(bx)\right]_\epsilon^\lambda + \frac{b}{a}\int_\epsilon^\lambda x^{\nu+1}J_{\nu+1}(ax)x^{-\nu}J_{\nu+1}(bx)dx$$

$$= \left[\frac{x}{a}J_{\nu+1}(ax)J_\nu(bx)\right]_\epsilon^\lambda + \frac{b}{a}\int_\epsilon^\lambda xJ_{\nu+1}(ax)J_{\nu+1}(bx)dx$$

[1] Cf. G. N. Watson, "The Theory of Bessel Functions" (Cambridge, London, 1922), pp. 453–468.

If we now let ϵ tend to zero, we obtain

$$I_\nu = \frac{\lambda}{a} J_{\nu+1}(a\lambda) J_\nu(b\lambda) + \frac{b}{a} I_{\nu+1} \tag{2}$$

where we have put

$$I_\nu = \lim_{\epsilon \to 0} I_\epsilon(\nu)$$

Now both I_ν and $I_{\nu+1}$ are symmetrical in a and b. Interchanging a and b in equation (2), we are led to the result

$$I_\nu = \frac{\lambda}{b} J_{\nu+1}(b\lambda) J_\nu(a\lambda) + \frac{a}{b} I_{\nu+1} \tag{3}$$

Eliminating $I_{\nu+1}$ between the two equations (2) and (3) we obtain the relation

$$I_\nu = \frac{\lambda}{a^2 - b^2} [a J_{\nu+1}(\lambda a) J_\nu(\lambda b) - b J_{\nu+1}(\lambda b) J_\nu(\lambda a)] \tag{4}$$

proving the theorem.

If now we write

$$H_\nu(\alpha,\beta) = \int_0^\lambda J_\nu(xu)(xu)^{\frac{1}{2}} \, du \int_\beta^\alpha J_\nu(uy)(uy)^{\frac{1}{2}} f(y) dy \tag{5}$$

then

$$\int_0^\lambda J(xu)(ux)^{\frac{1}{2}} \, du \int_0^\infty J(uy)(uy)^{\frac{1}{2}} f(y) dy$$
$$= H_\nu(\infty, x + \delta) + H_\nu(x + \delta, x) + H_\nu(x, x - \delta) + H_\nu(x - \delta, 0) \tag{6}$$

and we proceed to examine the behavior of $H_\nu(\alpha,\beta)$ as λ tends to infinity.

Theorem 17. *If δ is a small positive number, then $H_\nu(x - \delta, 0) \to 0$, $H_\nu(\infty, x + \delta) \to 0$, as $\lambda \to \infty$, provided that the integral $\int_0^\infty f(y) dy$ is absolutely convergent.*

By definition

$$H_\nu(x - \delta, 0) = \int_0^\lambda J_\nu(xu)(xu)^{\frac{1}{2}} \, du \int_0^{x-\delta} J_\nu(uy)(uy)^{\frac{1}{2}} f(y) dy$$
$$= x^{\frac{1}{2}} \int_0^{x-\delta} y^{\frac{1}{2}} f(y) dy \int_0^\lambda J_\nu(xu) J_\nu(yu) u \, du$$

The integral on the right-hand side of this equation may be evaluated by Theorem 16, and we obtain

$$H_\nu(x - \delta, 0) = x^{\frac{1}{2}} \lambda \int_0^{x-\delta} \frac{x J_{\nu+1}(\lambda x) J_\nu(\lambda y) - y J_{\nu+1}(\lambda y) J_\nu(\lambda x)}{x^2 - y^2} y^{\frac{1}{2}} f(y) dy$$

Now for $z \gg 1$ we can write

$$J_\nu(z) = \frac{A \cos z - B \sin z}{z^{\frac{1}{2}}} + 0(z^{-\frac{3}{2}}) \tag{7}$$

so that

$$H_\nu(x - \delta, 0) = 0(\lambda^{\frac{1}{2}}) \int_0^{x-\delta} J_\nu(\lambda y) y^{\frac{1}{2}}(x^2 - y^2)^{-1} f(y) dy$$
$$+ 0(\lambda^{\frac{1}{2}}) \int_0^{x-\delta} J_{\nu+1}(\lambda y) y^{\frac{3}{2}}(x^2 - y^2)^{-1} f(y) dy$$

for any fixed x and δ. Now

$$\int_0^{x-\delta} y^{\frac{1}{2}} J_\nu(\lambda y) \frac{f(y)}{x^2 - y^2} dy = \int_{1/\lambda}^{x-\delta} y^{\frac{1}{2}} J_\nu(\lambda y) \frac{f(y)}{x^2 - y^2} dy$$
$$+ \int_0^{1/\lambda} y^{\frac{1}{2}} J_\nu(\lambda y) \frac{f(y)}{x^2 - y^2}$$

and

$$\int_0^{1/\lambda} y^{\frac{1}{2}} J_\nu(\lambda y) \frac{f(y)}{x^2 - y^2} dy = 0\left[\int_0^{1/\lambda} (\lambda y)^\nu y^{\frac{1}{2}} |f(y)| dy \right]$$
$$= 0\left[\lambda^\nu \int_0^{1/\lambda} y^{\nu + \frac{1}{2}} |f(y)| dy \right]$$
$$= 0\left[\lambda^{-\frac{1}{2}} \int_0^{1/\lambda} |f(y)| dy \right]$$
$$= 0(\lambda^{-\frac{1}{2}})$$

if the integral $\int_0^\infty |f(y)| dy$ is convergent, *i.e.*, if the integral $\int_0^\infty f(y) dy$ is absolutely convergent. Applying equation (7), we find

$$\int_{1/\lambda}^{x-\delta} J_\nu(\lambda y) \frac{y^{\frac{1}{2}} f(y)}{x^2 - y^2} dy$$
$$= \lambda^{-\frac{1}{2}} \int_{1/\lambda}^{x-\delta} (A \cos \lambda y + B \sin \lambda y) \frac{f(y) dy}{x^2 - y^2} = 0(\lambda^{-\frac{1}{2}})$$

In other words,
$$H_\nu(x - \delta, 0) = 0(\lambda^{-\frac{1}{2}})$$
so that
$$H_\nu(x - \delta, 0) \to 0 \tag{8}$$

as $\lambda \to \infty$.

The proof that
$$H_\nu(\infty, x + \delta) \to 0 \tag{9}$$

as $\lambda \to \infty$ is similar, but simpler, since in this case y is not small.

Theorem 18. *If the function $f(y)$ is of bounded variation over the interval $(x - \delta, x + \delta)$, δ being small, then if $\nu \geq -\frac{1}{2}$*

$$H_\nu(x + \delta, x) \to \tfrac{1}{2} f(x + 0), \qquad H_\nu(x, x - \delta) \to \tfrac{1}{2} f(x - 0)$$

as $\lambda \to \infty$ and $\delta \to 0$.

For, if $f(y)$ is of bounded variation over $(x - \delta, x + \delta)$, then so also is the function $y^{-\nu - \frac{1}{2}} f(y)$ $(x < y \leq x + \delta)$ and we can write

$$y^{-\nu - \frac{1}{2}} f(y) = x^{-\nu - \frac{1}{2}} f(x + 0) + \chi_1(y) - \chi_2(y)$$

where $\chi_1(y)$ and $\chi_2(y)$ are positive increasing functions of y, each less than a positive number ϵ which is dependent on δ.   Then

$$H_\nu(x + \delta, x) = x^{-\nu - \frac{1}{2}} f(x + 0) \int_0^\lambda J_\nu(xu) u \, du \int_x^{x+\delta} J_\nu(yu) y^{\nu+1} \, dy$$
$$+ x^{\frac{1}{2}} \int_0^\lambda u J_\nu(xu) du \int_x^{x+\delta} J_\nu(yu) y^{\nu+1} [\chi_1(y) - \chi_2(y)] dy$$

By Theorem 16 the first term contributes

$$x^{-\nu} f(x + 0) \int_0^\lambda J_\nu(xu) [J_{\nu+1}(xu + \delta u)(x + \delta)^{\nu+1} - J_{\nu+1}(xu) x^{\nu+1}] du$$
$$= x^{-\nu} f(x + 0) \left[(x + \delta)^{\nu+1} \int_0^\lambda J_\nu(xu) J_{\nu+1}(xu + \delta u) du \right.$$
$$\left. - x^{\nu+1} \int_0^\lambda J_\nu(xu) J_{\nu+1}(xu) du \right]$$

Now

$$\int_0^\infty J_\nu(ax) J_{\nu+1}(x) dx = \begin{cases} a^\nu & 0 < a < 1 \\ \dfrac{1}{2} & a = 1 \\ 0 & a > 1 \end{cases}$$

so that as $\lambda \to \infty$ this term tends to the value

$$x^{-\nu} f(x + 0)(x^\nu - \tfrac{1}{2} x^\nu) = \tfrac{1}{2} f(x + 0) \tag{10}$$

The term involving the function $\chi_1(y)$ gives

$$x^{\frac{1}{2}} \int_0^\lambda J_\nu(xu) u \, du \int_x^{x+\delta} J_\nu(uy) y^{\nu+1} \chi_1(y) dy$$
$$= x^{\frac{1}{2}} \chi_1(x + \delta) \int_\xi^{x+\delta} y^{\nu+1} \, dy \int_0^\lambda J_\nu(xu) J_\nu(yu) u \, du \qquad x < \xi < x + \delta$$
$$= x^{\frac{1}{2}} \chi_1(x + \delta) \int_0^\lambda J_\nu(xu) u \, du \int_\xi^{x+\delta} y^{\nu+1} J_\nu(yu) dy$$

Now, by equation (10), Appendix A,

$$\int_\xi^{x+\delta} y^{\nu+1} J_\nu(yu) dy = \frac{1}{u} [(x + \delta)^{\nu+1} J_{\nu+1}(xu + \delta u) - \xi^{\nu+1} J_{\nu+1}(\xi u)]$$

so that

$$x^{\frac{1}{2}} \int_0^\lambda u J_\nu(xu) du \int_x^{x+\delta} y^{\nu+1} \chi_1(y) J_\nu(uy) dy$$
$$= x^{\frac{1}{2}} \chi_1(x + \delta) \int_0^\lambda J_\nu(xu) du [(x + \delta)^{\nu+1} J_{\nu+1}(xu + \delta u) - \xi^{\nu+1} J_{\nu+1}(\xi u)]$$
$$= x^{\frac{1}{2}} (x + \delta)^{\nu+1} \chi_1(x + \delta) \int_0^\lambda J_\nu(xu) J_{\nu+1}(xu + \delta u) du$$
$$- x^{\frac{1}{2}} \xi^{\nu+1} \chi_1(x + \delta) \int_0^\lambda J_\nu(xu) J_{\nu+1}(\xi u) du$$

Now if $x \geq x_0 > 0$, $y \geq x_0$, $\nu \geq -\frac{1}{2}$,

$$\int_0^\lambda J_\nu(xu) J_{\nu+1}(yu) du = 0(1)$$

for all values of λ. The contribution from the term involving $\chi_1(y)$ is therefore of order ϵ and so tends to zero as $\delta \to 0$ whatever the value of λ. Similarly the contribution from the integral involving the function $\chi_2(y)$ tends to zero as $\delta \to 0$ and $\lambda \to \infty$. Hence from equation (10) we have

$$H_\nu(x + \delta, x) \to \tfrac{1}{2}f(x + 0) \tag{11}$$

as $\delta \to 0$ and $\lambda \to \infty$.

The second part of the theorem, that

$$H_\nu(x, x - \delta) \to \tfrac{1}{2}f(x - 0) \tag{12}$$

as $\delta \to 0$ and $\lambda \to \infty$ can be established in a similar way.

We are now in a position to prove the main theorem:

Theorem 19. *If the integral* $\int_0^\infty f(y)dy$ *is absolutely convergent, and if the function $f(y)$ is of bounded variation in the neighborhood of the point x, then, for $\nu \geq -\tfrac{1}{2}$,*

$$\int_0^\infty J_\nu(xu)(xu)^{\frac{1}{2}}\, du \int_0^\infty J_\nu(uy)(uy)^{\frac{1}{2}}f(y)dy = \frac{1}{2}[f(x + 0) + f(x - 0)]$$

The proof follows by a direct application of the last two lemmas. If we write

$$\int_0^\lambda J_\nu(xu)(xu)^{\frac{1}{2}}\, du \int_0^\infty J_\nu(uy)(uy)^{\frac{1}{2}}f(y)dy$$
$$= H_\nu(\infty, x + \delta) + H_\nu(x + \delta, x) + H_\nu(x, x - \delta) + H_\nu(x - \delta, 0)$$

and then choose δ so small that the function $f(y)$ is of bounded variation over the interval $x - \delta \leq y \leq x + \delta$, all the conditions of Theorems 17 and 18 are satisfied if $\nu \geq -\tfrac{1}{2}$. The theorem follows at once by letting λ tend to infinity and δ tend to zero and making use of equations (8), (9), (11), and (12).

If the function $f(x)$ is continuous at the point x,

$$f(x + 0) = f(x - 0) = f(x)$$

so that the theorem gives simply

$$\int_0^\infty J_\nu(xu)(xu)^{\frac{1}{2}}\, du \int_0^\infty J_\nu(uy)(uy)^{\frac{1}{2}}f(y)dy = f(x) \tag{13}$$

If we now replace $f(x)$ by $x^{\frac{1}{2}}f(x)$ and write

$$\bar{f}(u) = \int_0^\infty yf(y)J_\nu(uy)dy \tag{14}$$

we may put equation (13) in the form

$$f(x) = \int_0^\infty u\bar{f}(u)J_\nu(xu)du \tag{15}$$

The function $f(u)$ is called the *Hankel transform* of *order ν* of the function $f(x)$. In subsequent chapters we shall often refer to Theorem 19 as the *Hankel inversion theorem.*

8.2 MacRobert's proof of the Hankel inversion theorem. It has been shown by MacRobert[1] that the Hankel inversion theorem can also be established by means of contour integration. In the form proved by MacRobert the theorem may be stated as follows:

Theorem 20. *If the real part of n exceeds -1 and if*

$$f(\lambda) = \int_p^q \phi(\rho) J_n(\lambda \rho) \rho \, d\rho \qquad 0 \le p < q \le \infty$$

then

$$\int_0^\infty f(\lambda) J_n(\lambda r) \lambda \, d\lambda = \begin{cases} \phi(r) & p < r < q, \\ 0 & 0 < r < p, q < r < \infty \end{cases}$$

As in the proof of Fourier's theorem for holomorphic functions (Sec. 3.5) the functions involved must be holomorphic, so that the proof is not so general as that given in the last section. The proof is based on Lommel's integral[2]

$$(\lambda^2 - \mu^2) \int_a^b x U_n(\lambda x) V_n(\mu x) dx$$
$$= [U_n(\lambda x)\mu x V_n'(\mu x) - V_n(\mu x)\lambda x U_n'(\lambda x)]_a^b \quad (16)$$

in which U_n and V_n are solutions of Bessel's differential equation. It will be observed that equation (16) is a generalization of the integral evaluated in Theorem 16; it may be established in precisely the same way. From equation (16) with U_n and V_n replaced by the Bessel functions J_n and G_n of the first and second kinds, respectively [defined by equations (2) and (3), Appendix A], and from the asymptotic expansions

$$G_n(z) \sim \sqrt{\frac{\pi}{2z}} \exp\left[i\left(z + \frac{1}{4}\pi\right) - \frac{1}{2}n\pi i\right] \qquad -\pi < \text{amp}(z) < \pi \quad (17)$$

and

$$J_n(z) \sim \sqrt{\frac{2}{\pi z}} \cos\left(z - \frac{1}{4}\pi - \frac{1}{2}n\pi\right) \qquad -\pi < \text{amp}(z) < \pi \quad (18)$$

we find that, if λ is real and $I(\mu) > 0$,

$$(\lambda^2 - \mu^2) \int_0^\infty x J_n(\lambda x) G_n(\mu x) dx = \left(\frac{\lambda}{\mu}\right)^n \qquad (19)$$

[1] T. M. MacRobert, *Proc. Roy. Soc. Edinburgh*, **51**, 116 (1931).
[2] A. Gray, G. B. Matthews, and T. M. MacRobert, "Bessel Functions" (Macmillan, London, 1922), p. 69.

while if $I(\mu) < 0$,

$$(\lambda^2 - \mu^2) \int_0^\infty x J_n(\lambda x) G_n(\mu x e^{i\pi}) dx = \left(\frac{\lambda}{\mu}\right)^n e^{-in\pi} \qquad (20)$$

We now consider the integral

$$I(r) = \int_0^\infty \lambda f(\lambda) J_n(\lambda r) d\lambda \qquad (21)$$

where $f(\lambda)$ is defined by the equation

$$f(\lambda) = \int_p^q \rho\phi(\rho) J_n(\rho\lambda) d\rho \quad 0 \le p < q \le \infty \qquad (22)$$

Substituting from equation (22) into equation (21), we find that

$$I(r) = \int_0^\infty \lambda J_n(\lambda r) d\lambda \int_p^q \rho\phi(\rho) J_n(\lambda\rho) d\rho$$

$$= \int_0^\infty \lambda Jn(\lambda r) d\lambda \int_p^q \rho\phi(\rho) \frac{1}{\pi i} [G_n(\lambda\rho) - e^{in\pi} G_n(\lambda\rho e^{i\pi})] d\rho$$

since the relation between J_n and G_n may be put in the form

$$\pi i J_n(z) = G_n(z) - e^{in\pi} G_n(z e^{i\pi})$$

We therefore have

$$I(r) = \frac{1}{\pi i} \int_0^\infty \lambda J_n(\lambda r) d\lambda \int_p^q \rho\phi(\rho) G_n(\lambda\rho) d\rho$$

$$- \frac{e^{in\pi}}{\pi i} \int_0^\infty \lambda J_n(\lambda r) d\lambda \int_p^q \rho\phi(\rho) G(\lambda\rho e^{i\pi}) d\rho$$

$$= \frac{1}{\pi i} \int_{C_2} \zeta\phi(\zeta) d\zeta \int_0^\infty \lambda Jn_n(\lambda r) G_n(\lambda\zeta) d\lambda$$

$$- \frac{e^{in}}{\pi i} \int_{C_1} \zeta\phi(\zeta) d\zeta \int_0^\infty \lambda J_n(\lambda r) G_n(\lambda\zeta e^{i\pi}) d\lambda$$

where C_1 and C_2 are the contours shown in Fig. 3 (page 22). The inner integrals can now be evaluated by means of equations (20) and (21). These formulas do not hold at the end points of C_1 and C_2, but this difficulty can be overcome in the following way. Let C_1' and C_2' be contours obtained from C_1 and C_2 by cutting off small parts at both ends. Then the integrals along C_1 and C_2 may be defined as the limits of the corresponding integrals along C_1' and C_2' when the parts cut off tend to zero.

In this way we obtain

$$I(r) = \frac{1}{\pi i} \int_{C_2} \frac{\phi(\zeta)}{r^2 - \zeta^2} \left(\frac{r}{\zeta}\right)^n \zeta \, d\zeta - \frac{1}{\pi i} \int_{C_1} \frac{\phi(\zeta)}{r^2 - \zeta^2} \left(\frac{r}{\zeta}\right)^n \zeta \, d\zeta$$

$$= \frac{1}{2\pi i} \int_C \phi(\zeta) \left(\frac{r}{\zeta}\right)^n \frac{2\zeta}{\zeta + r} \frac{d\zeta}{\zeta - r}$$

where (cf. Fig. 3) C is a closed contour between p and q. If $\phi(\zeta)$ is a holomorphic function of ζ in the region of the ζ plane enclosed by the contour C, then if $p < r < q$, the only pole within C of the integrand is at the point $\zeta = r$ and if $0 < r < p$ or $r > q$ the integrand has no poles within the contour C. Thus, applying Cauchy's theorem, we have

$$I(r) = \begin{cases} \phi(r) & \text{if } p < r < q \\ 0 & \text{if } 0 < r < p \text{ or } r > q \end{cases}$$

As an example of the use of the Hankel inversion theorem in this form for the evaluation of definite integrals we shall evaluate Sonine's integral

$$\int_0^\infty \frac{J_n(\lambda r) J_m(\lambda)}{\lambda^{m-n-1}} \, d\lambda$$

Let

$$\phi(\rho) = \frac{2^{1+n-m}}{\Gamma(m-n)} \rho^n (1 - \rho^2)^{m-n-1}$$

Then, by the definition (22), with $p = 0$, $q = 1$, we have

$$f(\lambda) = \frac{2^{1+n-m}}{\Gamma(m-n)} \int_0^1 \rho^{n+1}(1 - \rho^2)^{m-n-1} J_n(\lambda\rho) d\rho$$

Expanding the Bessel function $J_n(\lambda\rho)$ in ascending powers of $\lambda\rho$ and integrating term by term, we obtain

$$f(\lambda) \frac{2^{1+n-m}}{\Gamma(m-n)} \sum_{s=0}^\infty \int_0^1 \rho^{n+1}(1 - \rho^2)^{m-n-1} \frac{(-1)^s (\lambda\rho)^{n+2s} \, d\rho}{2^{n+2s} s! \Gamma(n+s+1)},$$

which reduces by the substitution $\xi = \rho^2$ to the form

$$f(\lambda) = \frac{1}{\Gamma(m-n)} \sum_{s=0}^\infty \frac{\lambda^{n+2s}}{2^{m+2s}} \int_0^1 \xi^{n+s}(1 - \xi)^{m-n-1} \frac{(-1)^s \, d\xi}{s! \Gamma(n+s+1)}$$

$$= \sum_{s=0}^\infty \frac{(-1)^s \lambda^{m+2s}}{2^{m+2s} \Gamma(m+s+1)} \frac{\lambda^{n-m}}{s!}$$

$$= \lambda^{n-m} J_m(\lambda) \tag{23}$$

Substituting from equations (22) and (23) into Theorem 20, we obtain Sonine's result

$$\int_0^\infty \frac{J_m(\lambda) J_n(\lambda r)}{\lambda^{m-n-1}} \, d\lambda = \begin{cases} \dfrac{r^n (1 - r^2)^{m-n-1}}{2^{m-n-1} \Gamma(m-n)} & \text{if } 0 < r < 1 \\ 0 & \text{if } r > 1 \end{cases}$$

provided that the real part of n is greater than -1.

8.3 Other forms of Fourier-Bessel integral theorem. The inversion theorem considered in the previous section corresponds to the ordinary Fourier-Bessel expansion theorem in the theory of Bessel functions.[1] There is a second Fourier-Bessel expansion of the form

$$f(\lambda) = \sum_s A_s T_n(r_s, \lambda) \tag{24}$$

where

$$T_n(r,\lambda) = J_n(r\lambda)G_n(ra) - G_n(r\lambda)J_n(ra) \tag{24a}$$

and r_s is a positive root of the transcendental equation

$$T_n(r,b) = 0 \tag{24b}$$

The coefficient A_s is given by

$$A_s = \frac{2r_s^2 J_n^2(r_s b)}{J_n^2(ar_s) - J_n^2(br_s)} \int_a^b u f(u) T_n(r_s, u) du$$

The series vanishes for $\lambda = a$ and $\lambda = b$ and is equal to

$$\tfrac{1}{2}[f(\lambda + 0) + f(\lambda - 0)] \text{ for } a < \lambda < b.[2]$$

The corresponding integral theorem may be stated as follows:

Theorem 21. *If* $f(\lambda) = \displaystyle\int_p^q \rho\phi(\rho)T_n(\rho,\lambda)d\rho$, *then*

$$\int_a^\infty \lambda f(\lambda)T_n(r,\lambda)d\lambda = \begin{cases} \dfrac{1}{2} B_n(ra)[\phi(r+0) + \phi(r-0)] & p < r < q \\ 0 & 0 < r < p \text{ or } r > q \end{cases}$$

where the function $B_n(z)$ *is defined to be*

$$B_n(z) = (\tfrac{1}{2}\pi \text{ cosec } n\pi)^2 [J_n^2(z) - 2J_n(z)J_{-n}(z) \cos(n\pi) + J_{-n}^2(z)]$$

This result may be established by the method of contour integration employed in the last section. In this instance, however, it is just as simple to employ the method of Dirichlet integrals. Since we need only then assume that the function $\phi(\rho)$ satisfies the Dirichlet conditions, the results will be more general than those established by contour integration.

If we write

$$I = (r^2 - \rho^2) \int_a^h T_n(r,\lambda)T_n(\rho,\lambda)\lambda \, d\lambda$$

then it follows from equation (16) and the recurrence relations

$$xJ_n'(x) = nJ_n(x) - xJ_{n+1}(x), \qquad xG_n'(x) = nG_n(x) - xG_{n+1}(x)$$

[1] Watson, *op. cit.*, p. 576.
[2] T. M. MacRobert, *Proc. Roy. Soc. Edinburgh*, **42**, 90 (1922).

that

$$I = rhT_n(\rho,h)[J_{n+1}(rh)G_n(ra) - G_{n+1}(rh)J_n(ra)]$$
$$- \rho h T_n(r,h)[J_{n+1}(\rho h)G_n(\rho a) - G_{n+1}(\rho h)J_n(\rho a)]$$

If we now replace all the Bessel functions involving h on the right-hand side by their asymptotic expansions, we obtain

$$I = \frac{\rho - r}{2\pi(r\rho)^{\frac{1}{2}}} e^{in\pi}[e^{i(\rho+r)h}G_n(rae^{i\pi})G_n(\rho ae^{i\pi}) + e^{-i(\rho+r)h}G_n(ra)G_n(\rho a)]$$
$$+ \frac{\rho + r}{2\pi(r\rho)^{\frac{1}{2}}} e^{in\pi}[ie^{i(\rho-r)h}G_n(ra)G_n(\rho ae^{i\pi}) - ie^{-i(\rho-r)h}G_n(rae^{i\pi})G_n(\rho a)] + \frac{P}{h}$$

where P is finite for all values of h and contains $(\rho - r)$ as a factor. Hence

$$\lim_{h\to\infty} \int_p^q \rho\phi(\rho)d\rho \int_a^h T_n(r,\lambda)T_n(\rho,\lambda)d\lambda$$
$$= \lim_{h\to\infty} \left\{ \int_p^q \frac{\rho\phi(\rho)}{2\pi(r\rho)^{\frac{1}{2}}} \frac{\sin(\rho - r)h}{\rho - r} e^{in\pi}[G_n(ra)G_n(\rho ae^{i\pi}) \right.$$
$$\left. + G_n(rae^{i\pi})G_n(\rho a)]d\rho + J \right\}$$

in which J denotes integrals which tend to zero as h tends to infinity. Applying Dirichlet's theorem 6, we then obtain

$$\lim_{h\to\infty} \int_p^q \rho\phi(\rho)d\rho \int_a^h T_n(r,\lambda)T_n(\rho,\lambda)d\lambda$$
$$= \begin{cases} \frac{1}{2}[\phi(r+0) + \phi(r-0)]e^{in\pi}G_n(ra)G_n(rae^{i\pi}) & \text{if } p < r < q \\ 0 & \text{if } 0 < r < p \text{ or } r > q \end{cases}$$

Changing the order of integration and noting that

$$e^{in\pi}G_n(ra)G_n(rae^{i\pi}) = B_n(ra)$$

we see that the theorem follows.

Another integral theorem, this time associated with the Kapetyn series of Bessel functions, has also been established by MacRobert. It may be stated in the following form:

Theorem 22. *If* $f(\lambda) = \int_p^q \rho\phi(\rho)J_\rho(\rho\lambda)d\rho$, $0 \le p \le q$, *then*

$$\int_0^\infty \left(\lambda - \frac{1}{\lambda}\right)f(\lambda)J_m(m\lambda)d\lambda = \begin{cases} \frac{1}{2}[\phi(m+0) + \phi(m-0)] & \text{if } p < m < q \\ 0 & \text{if } 0 < m < p \text{ or } m > q \end{cases}$$

We shall establish this result by means of Dirichlet integrals. The proof by contour integration is left as an exercise to the reader. From the Lommel integral[1]

$$(m^2 - \rho^2) \int_a^b \left(\lambda - \frac{1}{\lambda}\right) U_m(m\lambda) V_\rho(\rho\lambda) d\lambda$$

$$= \left\{\lambda \left[U_m(m\lambda) \frac{\partial}{\partial \lambda} V_\rho(\rho\lambda) - V_\rho(\rho\lambda) \frac{\partial}{\partial \lambda} U_m(m\lambda) \right]\right\}_a^b$$

we obtain

$$\int_0^h \left(\lambda - \frac{1}{\lambda}\right) J_m(m\lambda) J_\rho(\rho\lambda) d\lambda$$

$$= \frac{h}{\rho^2 - m^2} \left[\rho J_m(mh) J_{\rho+1}(\rho h) - m J_\rho(\rho h) J_{m+1}(mh)\right]$$

$$- \frac{1}{\rho + m} J_m(mh) J_\rho(\rho h) \quad (25)$$

by means of the recurrence relation

$$\frac{d}{dx} J_n(x) = \frac{n}{x} J_n(x) - J_{n+1}(x)$$

When the Bessel functions on the right-hand side of this equation are replaced by their asymptotic expansions [cf. equation (18)], it is found that

$$I = \frac{2}{\pi(\rho^2 - m^2)(\rho m)^{\frac{1}{2}}}\left\{(\rho + m) \sin \left[(\rho - m) \left(h - \frac{1}{2}\pi\right)\right] \right.$$

$$\left. - (\rho - m) \sin \left[(\rho + m) \left(h - \frac{1}{2}\pi\right)\right]\right\} + \frac{P}{h}$$

in which P remains finite as h tends to infinity. Therefore

$$\lim_{h\to\infty} \int_p^q \rho\phi(\rho)d\rho \int_0^h \left(\lambda - \frac{1}{\lambda}\right) J_m(m\lambda) J_\rho(\rho\lambda) d\lambda$$

$$= \frac{2}{\pi} \lim_{h\to\infty} \int_p^q \left(\frac{\rho}{m}\right)^{\frac{1}{2}} \phi(\rho) \frac{\sin\left[(\rho - m)(h - \frac{1}{2}\pi)\right]}{\rho - m} d\rho$$

$$- \frac{2}{\pi} \lim_{h\to\infty} \int_p^q \left(\frac{\rho}{m}\right)^{\frac{1}{2}} \phi(\rho) \frac{\sin\left[(\rho + m)(h - \frac{1}{2}\pi)\right]}{\rho + m} d\rho$$

$$= \begin{cases} \frac{1}{2}[\phi(m + 0) + \phi(m - 0)] & \text{if } p < m < q \\ 0 & \text{if } 0 < m < p \text{ or } m > q \end{cases}$$

by Theorem 6. Changing the order of integration, we then obtain the theorem.

Various new integrals can be evaluated by assuming the converse of this theorem. For instance, from the integral [cf. equation (19),

[1] Gray, Matthews, and MacRobert, *op. cit.*, p. 69.

Appendix A]

$$\int_0^\infty u^n e^{-\lambda u} J_m(\rho u) du = \frac{(n+m)!}{(\lambda^2+\rho^2)^{\frac{1}{2}n+\frac{1}{2}}} P_n^{-m}\left(\frac{\lambda}{\sqrt{\lambda^2+\rho^2}}\right) \quad m \geq n$$

we have, on letting $\lambda = a$, $\rho = m$, $n = 0$,

$$\int_0^\infty e^{-a\lambda} J_m(m\lambda) d\lambda = \frac{m!}{(a^2+m^2)^{\frac{1}{2}}} P_0^{-m}\left(\frac{a}{\sqrt{m^2+a^2}}\right) \quad m \geq 0$$

From the definition of $P_n^{-m}(z)$ we see that this may be written in the form

$$\int_0^\infty e^{-a\lambda} J_m(m\lambda) d\lambda = \frac{1}{\sqrt{a^2+m^2}}\left(\frac{\sqrt{a^2+m^2}-a}{m}\right)^m$$

with $a > 0$, $m \geq 0$. From the converse of Theorem 22 it then follows that

$$\int_0^\infty \frac{\rho J_\rho(\rho\lambda)}{\sqrt{a^2+\rho^2}}\left(\frac{\sqrt{a^2+\rho^2}-a}{\rho}\right)^\rho d\rho = \frac{\lambda}{\lambda^2-1} e^{-a\lambda} \quad \lambda \geq 0$$

In particular, if we let a tend to zero, these formulas reduce to the simple forms

$$\int_0^\infty J_m(m\lambda) d\lambda = \frac{1}{m} \qquad m > 0,$$

and

$$\int_0^\infty J_\rho(\rho\lambda) d\rho = \frac{\lambda}{\lambda^2-1} \qquad \lambda \geq 0$$

9. Parseval's Theorem for Hankel Transforms

The fact that there is no simple expression for the product $J_\nu(\alpha x) J_\nu(\alpha\beta)$ in the sense that there is a simple expression $\exp i(\alpha x + \alpha\beta)$ for the product $\exp(i\alpha x) \exp(i\alpha\beta)$ means that there is no simple Faltung theorem for the Hankel transform corresponding to Theorem 12. A simple theorem of Parseval type can, however, be derived.

Suppose that $\bar{f}(u)$ and $\bar{g}(u)$ are the Hankel transforms of the functions $f(x)$ and $g(x)$; then

$$\int_0^\infty u\bar{f}(u)\bar{g}(u) du = \int_0^\infty u\bar{f}(u) du \int_0^\infty xg(x)J_\nu(ux) dx$$

by the definition of $\bar{g}(u)$. Interchanging the order of the integrations, we have

$$\int_0^\infty u\bar{f}(u)\bar{g}(u) du = \int_0^\infty xg(x) dx \int_0^\infty u\bar{f}(u)J_\nu(ux) du$$

$$= \int_0^\infty xf(x)g(x) dx$$

A systematic discussion of this formula has been given by Macauley-Owen,[1] who proves the following:

Theorem 23. *If the functions $f(x)$ and $g(x)$ satisfy the conditions of Theorem 19 and if $\bar{f}(u)$ and $\bar{g}(u)$ denote their Hankel transforms of order $\nu \geq -\frac{1}{2}$, then*

$$\int_0^\infty xf(x)g(x)dx = \int_0^\infty u\bar{f}(u)\bar{g}(u)du$$

10. Hankel Transforms of the Derivatives of a Function

Suppose that $\bar{f}_\nu(\xi)$ is the Hankel transform of order ν of the function $f(r)$, so that

$$\bar{f}_\nu(\xi) = \int_0^\infty rf(r)J_\nu(\xi r)dr$$

then the Hankel transform of the function df/dr is, by definition,

$$\bar{f}_\nu'(\xi) = \int_0^\infty r\frac{df}{dr}J_\nu(\xi r)dr$$

Integration by parts of the integral on the right yields

$$\bar{f}_\nu'(\xi) = [rf(r)J_\nu(\xi r)]_0^\infty - \int_0^\infty f(r)\frac{d}{dr}[rJ_\nu(\xi r)]dr \qquad (26)$$

Now

$$\frac{d}{dr}[rJ_\nu(\xi r)] = J_\nu(\xi r) + rJ_\nu'(\xi r)$$

and the second term on the right becomes

$$\xi rJ_{\nu-1}(\xi r) - \nu J_\nu(\xi r)$$

as a result of equation (5), Appendix A, so that

$$\frac{d}{dr}[rJ_\nu(\xi r)] = (1 - \nu)J_\nu(\xi r) + \xi rJ_{\nu-1}(\xi r)$$

Substituting this expression into equation (26) and making the assumption that $rf(r)$ tends to zero as r tends either to zero or to infinity, we find that

$$\bar{f}_\nu'(\xi) = (\nu - 1)\int_0^\infty f(r)J_\nu(\xi r)dr - \xi\bar{f}_{\nu-1}(\xi) \qquad (27)$$

The first term on the right is the Hankel transform of order ν of the function $f(r)/r$, but a simple expression can be found for it in terms of the Hankel transforms of $f(r)$ of orders $\nu \pm 1$. For, by equation (7), Appendix A,

---

[1] P. Macauley-Owen, *Proc. London Math. Soc.*, **45**, 458 (1939).

$$2\nu \int_0^\infty f(r)J_\nu(\xi r)dr = \xi\left[\int_0^\infty rf(r)J_{\nu-1}(\xi r)dr + \int_0^\infty rf(r)J_{\nu+1}(\xi r)dr\right]$$

$$= \xi\bar{f}_{\nu-1}(\xi) + \xi\bar{f}_{\nu+1}(\xi) \quad (28)$$

Eliminating the integral $\int_0^\infty f(r)J_\nu(\xi r)dr$ between equations (27) and (28), we have

$$\bar{f}_\nu'(\xi) = -\xi\left[\frac{\nu+1}{2\nu}\bar{f}_{\nu-1}(\xi) - \frac{\nu-1}{2\nu}\bar{f}_{\nu+1}(\xi)\right] \quad (29)$$

The formulas for the Hankel transforms of higher derivatives of the function $f(r)$ may be obtained by repeated applications of equation (29). For instance

$$\bar{f}_\nu''(\xi) = -\xi\left[\frac{\nu+1}{2\nu}\bar{f}_{\nu-1}'(\xi) - \frac{\nu-1}{2\nu}\bar{f}_{\nu+1}'(\xi)\right] \quad (30)$$

so that inserting the values for $\bar{f}_{\nu-1}'(\xi)$ and $\bar{f}_{\nu+1}'(\xi)$ obtained from equation (29) we have

$$\bar{f}_\nu''(\xi) = \frac{1}{4}\xi^2\left[\frac{\nu+1}{\nu-1}\bar{f}_{\nu-2}(\xi) - 2\frac{\nu^2-3}{\nu^2-1}\bar{f}_\nu(\xi) + \frac{\nu-1}{\nu+1}\bar{f}_{\nu+2}(\xi)\right] \quad (31)$$

Also, integrating by parts, we see that

$$\int_0^\infty r\frac{d^2f}{dr^2}J_\nu(\xi r)dr = -\xi\int_0^\infty \frac{df}{dr}\frac{d}{dr}[rJ_\nu(\xi r)]dr$$

if $rf'(r)$ tends to zero as r tends to zero or to infinity, so that

$$\int_0^\infty r\left(\frac{d^2f}{dr^2} + \frac{1}{r}\frac{df}{dr}\right)J_\nu(\xi r)dr = -\xi\int_0^\infty \frac{df}{dr}rJ_\nu'(\xi r)dr$$

$$= \xi\int_0^\infty f(r)\frac{d}{dr}[rJ'(r)]dr$$

provided that $rf(r)$ vanishes at $r = 0$ and $r = \infty$. Now it follows from equation (1), Appendix A, that the function $J_\nu(\xi r)$ satisfies the differential equation

$$\frac{d}{dr}[rJ_\nu'(\xi r)] = -\left(\xi^2 - \frac{\nu^2}{r^2}\right)rJ_\nu(\xi r)$$

so that

$$\int_0^\infty r\left(\frac{d^2f}{dr^2} + \frac{1}{r}\frac{df}{dr} - \frac{\nu^2}{r^2}f\right)J_\nu(\xi r)dr = -\xi^2\bar{f}_\nu(\xi) \quad (32)$$

where, as before, $\bar{f}_\nu(\xi)$ denotes the Hankel transform of order ν of the function $f(r)$.

Special cases of these general results arise with such frequency that they will be cited here. Putting $\nu = 1$ in equation (29) we obtain the equation

$$\int_0^\infty r \frac{df}{dr} J_1(\xi r) dr = -\xi \bar{f}(\xi) \tag{33}$$

where $\bar{f}(\xi)$ is defined to be the zero-order transform

$$\bar{f}(\xi) = \int_0^\infty r f(r) J_0(\xi r) dr \tag{34}$$

Similarly, putting $\nu = 0$ in equation (32), we arrive at the equation

$$\int_0^\infty r \left(\frac{d^2f}{dr^2} + \frac{1}{r} \frac{df}{dr} \right) J_0(\xi r) dr = -\xi^2 \bar{f}(\xi) \tag{35}$$

$\bar{f}(\xi)$ again being defined by equation (34).

11. Relation between Hankel Transforms and Fourier Transforms

Let us now consider the Fourier transform $F(\xi_1, \xi_2)$ of a function $f(x_1, x_2)$ which is a function of the variable $r = (x_1^2 + x_2^2)^{\frac{1}{2}}$ only. We have from the definition (105), Chap. 1, that

$$F(\xi_1, \xi_2) = \frac{1}{2\pi} \int_{-\infty}^\infty \int_{-\infty}^\infty f(\sqrt{x_1^2 + x_2^2}) e^{i(\xi_1 x_1 + \xi_1 x_2)} \, dx_1 \, dx_2$$

If in this integral we make the substitutions

$$x_1 = r \cos\theta, \quad x_2 = r \sin\theta, \quad \xi_1 = \rho \cos\varphi, \quad \xi_2 = \rho \sin\varphi$$

then, since

$$dx_1 \, dx_2 = r \, dr \, d\theta$$

and

$$\xi_1 x_1 + \xi_2 x_2 = r\rho \cos(\theta - \varphi)$$

we find that the integral becomes

$$F(\xi_1, \xi_2) = \frac{1}{2\pi} \int_0^\infty r f(r) dr \int_0^{2\pi} e^{i\rho r \cos(\theta - \varphi)} \, d\theta \tag{36}$$

Now because of the periodic nature of the integrand

$$\int_0^{2\pi} e^{ir\rho \cos(\theta - \varphi)} \, d\theta \equiv \int_0^{2\pi} e^{ir\rho \cos\theta} \, d\theta$$

and the integral on the right is known by equation (24), Appendix A, to have the value $2\pi J_0(\rho r)$. If, therefore, we let $\rho = (\xi_1^2 + \xi_2^2)^{\frac{1}{2}}$, we see that $F(\xi_1, \xi_2)$ is a function of ρ only and may be written

$$F(\rho) = \int_0^\infty r f(r) J_0(\rho r) dr \tag{37}$$

so that it is the zero-order Hankel transform of the function $f(r)$.   Now by the Fourier inversion theorem for multiple transforms we know that

$$f(x_1,x_2) = \frac{1}{2\pi} \int_{-\infty}^{\infty} \int_{-\infty}^{\infty} F(\xi_1,\xi_2)e^{-i(\xi_1 x_1 + \xi_2 x_2)}\, d\xi_1\, d\xi_2$$

which with the previous substitutions may be written in the form

$$f(r) = \frac{1}{2\pi} \int_0^{\infty} \rho F(\rho)d\rho \int_0^{2\pi} e^{-ir\rho \cos(\theta - \varphi)}\, d\varphi$$

The integrations proceed as before, and we obtain

$$f(r) = \int_0^{\infty} \rho F(\rho)J_0(\rho r)d\rho \tag{38}$$

Equations (37) and (38) merely express the Hankel inversion theorem in the special case $\nu = 0$, so that this particular case of the theorem may be deduced from the theory of two-dimensional Fourier transforms.

The result is readily generalized.   If the function $f(x_1,x_2, \ldots ,x_n)$ is a function only of $r = (x_1^2 + x_2^2 + \cdots + x_n^2)^{\frac{1}{2}}$, then its Fourier transform is, by definition,

$$F(\xi_1,\xi_2, \ldots ,\xi_n) = \left(\frac{1}{2\pi}\right)^{\frac{1}{2}n} \int_{-\infty}^{\infty} \cdots \int_{-\infty}^{\infty} f(r)e^{i(\xi \cdot x)}\, dx_1\, dx_2 \cdots dx_n$$

$(\xi \cdot x)$ denoting the inner product $\xi_1 x_1 + \xi_2 x_2 + \cdots + \xi_n x_n$.   If, now, we write

$$\rho^2 = \xi_1^2 + \xi_2^2 + \cdots + \xi_n^2$$

and make the transformations

$$\xi_i = \rho\alpha_i \qquad i = 1,2, \ldots ,n$$

$$y_1 = \sum_{i=1}^{n} \alpha_i x_i, \qquad y_j = \sum_{i=1}^{n} \alpha_{ij}x_i \quad j = 2,3, \ldots ,n$$

the coefficients α_{ij} being chosen so as to make the transformation orthogonal, we obtain

$$r = (y_1^2 + y_2^2 + \cdots + y_n^2)^{\frac{1}{2}}$$
$$dx_1\, dx_2\, dx_3 \cdots dx_n = dy_1\, dy_2 \cdots dy_n$$

and

$$\xi \cdot x = \sum_{i=1}^{n} \xi_i x_i = \rho \sum_{i=1}^{n} \alpha_i x_i = \rho y_1$$

If we put

$$\lambda^2 = y_2^2 + y_3^2 + \cdots + y_n^2$$
$$\int_{-\infty}^{\infty} \int_{-\infty}^{\infty} \cdots \int_{-\infty}^{\infty} dy_2\, dy_3 \cdots dy_n = \int_0^{\infty} \Omega\, d\lambda$$

we find that the expression for the Fourier transform F reduces to

$$F(\xi_1, \ldots, \xi_n) = \left(\frac{1}{2\pi}\right)^{\frac{1}{2}n} \int_{-\infty}^{\infty} dy_1 \int_0^{\infty} \Omega \, d\lambda \, f(\sqrt{y_1^2 + \lambda^2}) e^{i\rho y_1} \quad (39)$$

In this notation, we have, for any arbitrary function $\Phi(\lambda)$,

$$\int_{-\infty}^{\infty} \cdots \int_{-\infty}^{\infty} \Phi(\sqrt{y_2^2 \cdots y_n^2}) dy_2 \cdots dy_n = \int_0^{\infty} \Omega \Phi(\lambda) d\lambda \quad (40)$$

To determine the form of the quantity Ω, we note that since it is a volume element in $(n-1)$ space it is of the form

$$\Omega = \omega \lambda^{n-2} \quad (41)$$

where ω is a function of n but not of λ. To determine the form of this quantity, we consider the special case

$$\Phi(\lambda) = e^{-\lambda^2}$$

Making this substitution in equation (40) and replacing Ω by its expression (41) we obtain the relation

$$\left(\int_{-\infty}^{\infty} e^{-y^2} dy\right)^{n-1} = \omega \int_0^{\infty} \lambda^{n-2} e^{-\lambda^2} d\lambda$$

for the determination of the constant ω. Making use of the definite integrals

$$\int_{-\infty}^{\infty} e^{-y^2} dy = \pi^{\frac{1}{2}}, \qquad \int_0^{\infty} \lambda^{n-2} e^{-\lambda^2} d\lambda = \frac{1}{2} \Gamma\left(\frac{n-1}{2}\right)$$

we see at once that ω is given by the equation

$$\omega = \frac{2\pi^{(n-1)/2}}{\Gamma\left(\dfrac{n-1}{2}\right)} \quad (42)$$

Substituting from equations (41) and (42) into equation (39), we obtain

$$F(\xi_1, \ldots, \xi_n) = \frac{1}{2^{\frac{1}{2}n-1}\Gamma(\frac{1}{2})\Gamma(\frac{1}{2}n - \frac{1}{2})} \int_{-\infty}^{\infty} dy_1 \int_0^{\infty} f(\sqrt{y_1^2 + \lambda^2})$$
$$\times e^{i\rho y_1} \lambda^{n-2} d\lambda$$

To evaluate this integral we make the substitutions

$$\lambda = r \sin \phi \qquad y_1 = r \cos \phi$$

We then find

$$F(\xi_1, \ldots, \xi_n) = \frac{1}{2^{\frac{1}{2}n-1}\Gamma(\frac{1}{2})\Gamma(\frac{1}{2}n - \frac{1}{2})} \int_0^{\infty} r^{n-1} f(r) dr \int_0^{\pi} \sin^{n-2} \phi$$
$$\times e^{i\rho r \cos \phi} \, d\phi$$

Now, by equation (25), Appendix A,

$$\int_0^\pi \sin^{n-2}\phi\, e^{ir\rho\cos\phi}\, d\phi = \frac{2^{\frac{1}{2}n-1}\Gamma(\frac{1}{2})\Gamma(\frac{1}{2}n - \frac{1}{2})}{(\rho r)^{\frac{1}{2}n-1}} J_{\frac{1}{2}n-1}(\rho r)$$

Making this substitution in the equation for $F(\xi_1,\xi_2, \ldots ,\xi_n)$, we see that this function is a function only of the variable ρ and so may be written $F(\rho)$. We then obtain the equation

$$\rho^{\frac{1}{2}n-1}F(\rho) = \int_0^\infty r[r^{\frac{1}{2}n-1}f(r)]J_{\frac{1}{2}n-1}(\rho r)dr$$

showing that the function $\rho^{\frac{1}{2}n-1}F(\rho)$ is the Hankel transform of order $\frac{1}{2}n - 1$ of the function $r^{\frac{1}{2}n-1}f(r)$. A Fourier transform in n-dimensional space can, therefore, in certain circumstances, be reduced to a Hankel transform in one-dimensional space. Any theorem that can be proved for a Fourier transform of a function of several variables therefore yields a corresponding theorem for Hankel transforms. In particular we know by a similar analysis applied to the formula

$$f(x_1, \ldots ,x_n) = \left(\frac{1}{2\pi}\right)^{\frac{1}{2}n} \int_{-\infty}^\infty \cdots \int_{-\infty}^\infty F(\xi_1, \ldots ,\xi_n)e^{-i(\xi\cdot x)}$$
$$\times d\xi_1\, d\xi_2 \cdots d\xi_n$$

that

$$r^{\frac{1}{2}n-1}f(r) = \int_0^\infty \rho[\rho^{\frac{1}{2}n-1}F(\rho)]J_{\frac{1}{2}n-1}(\rho r)d\rho$$

Writing

$$\phi(r) = r^{\frac{1}{2}n-1}f(r), \qquad \bar\phi(\rho) = \rho^{\frac{1}{2}n-1}F(\rho), \qquad \nu = \tfrac{1}{2}n - 1$$

we obtain finally the reciprocal formulas

$$\bar\phi(\rho) = \int_0^\infty r\phi(r)J_\nu(\rho r)dr, \qquad \phi(r) = \int_0^\infty \rho\bar\phi(\rho)J_\nu(\rho r)dr$$

yielding a proof of the Hankel inversion theorem.

12. Dual Integral Equations

In the application of the theory of Hankel transforms to the solution of boundary value problems in mathematical physics it often happens that the problem may be reduced to the solution of the pair of simultaneous equations

$$\left.\begin{aligned}\int_0^\infty y^\alpha f(y)J_\nu(xy)dy &= g(x) \qquad 0 < x < 1 \\ \int_0^\infty f(y)J_\nu(xy)dy &= 0 \qquad\quad x > 1\end{aligned}\right\} \tag{43}$$

in which the function $g(x)$ is known and the function $f(y)$ has to be determined. The formal solution of these equations by the use of the theory of

Mellin transforms was first given by Titchmarsh in his book on Fourier integrals.[1] Equations of the type (43) are called *dual integral equations* and may be solved as follows:

The Mellin transform of the function $y^\alpha J_\nu(xy)$ is

$$\mathbf{J}_\alpha(s) = \int_0^\infty y^{\alpha+s-1} J_\nu(xy)dy = \frac{2^{\alpha+s-1}}{x^{\alpha+s}} \frac{\Gamma\left(\dfrac{\alpha + \nu + s}{2}\right)}{\Gamma\left(\dfrac{2 - \alpha - s + \nu}{2}\right)}$$

as is readily seen by applying equation (18), Appendix A. Putting $\alpha = 0$ in this expression, we see that the Mellin transform of the Bessel function $J_\nu(xy)$ is the function

$$\mathbf{J}_\nu(s) = \frac{2^{s-1}}{x^s} \frac{\Gamma(\tfrac{1}{2}\nu + \tfrac{1}{2}s)}{\Gamma(1 + \tfrac{1}{2}\nu - \tfrac{1}{2}s)}$$

Now by the Faltung theorem for Mellin transforms [equation (101a), Chap. 1] we have

$$\int_0^\infty y^\alpha f(y) J_\nu(xy)dy = \frac{1}{2\pi i} \int_{c-i\infty}^{c+i\infty} \mathbf{F}(s)\mathbf{J}_\alpha(1 - s)ds$$

$$\int_0^\infty f(y) J_\nu(xy)dy = \frac{1}{2\pi i} \int_{c-i\infty}^{c+i\infty} \mathbf{F}(s)\mathbf{J}_0(1 - s)ds$$

where $\mathbf{F}(s)$ is the Mellin transform of the function $f(y)$.

The dual integral equations (43) are therefore equivalent to the pair of equations

$$\frac{1}{2\pi i} \int_{c-i\infty}^{c+i\infty} \mathbf{F}(s) \frac{2^{\alpha-s}\Gamma\left(\dfrac{\alpha + \nu + 1 - s}{2}\right)}{x^{1+\alpha-s}\Gamma\left(\dfrac{1 - \alpha + s + \nu}{2}\right)} ds = g(x) \qquad 0 < x < 1$$

$$\frac{1}{2\pi i} \int_{c-i\infty}^{c+i\infty} \mathbf{F}(s) \frac{2^{-s}\Gamma\left(\dfrac{\nu + 1 - s}{2}\right)}{x^{1-s}\Gamma\left(\dfrac{\nu + 1 + s}{2}\right)} ds = 0 \qquad x > 1$$

If we now put

$$\mathbf{F}(s) = 2^{s-\alpha} \frac{\Gamma\left(\dfrac{1 + \nu + s}{2}\right)}{\Gamma\left(\dfrac{1 + \nu + \alpha - s}{2}\right)} \chi(s)$$

[1] E. C. Titchmarsh, "Introduction to the Theory of Fourier Integrals" (Oxford, New York, 1937), p. 337.

these equations reduce to

$$\frac{1}{2\pi i}\int_{c-i\infty}^{c+i\infty}\frac{\Gamma\left(\dfrac{1+\nu+s}{2}\right)}{\Gamma\left(\dfrac{1+\nu-\alpha+s}{2}\right)}\chi(s)x^{s-1-\alpha}\,ds = g(x) \quad 0 < x < 1 \quad (44)$$

$$\frac{1}{2\pi i}\int_{c-i\infty}^{c+i\infty}\frac{\Gamma\left(\dfrac{1+\nu-s}{2}\right)}{\Gamma\left(\dfrac{1+\nu+\alpha-s}{2}\right)}\chi(s)x^{s-1}\,ds = 0 \quad\quad x > 1 \quad (45)$$

Multiplying the first of these equations by $x^{\alpha-w}$ where $\mathsf{R}(s) - \mathsf{R}(w) > 0$ (R denoting "the real part of"), and integrating with respect to x from 0 to 1, we obtain the relation

$$\frac{1}{2\pi i}\int_{c-i\infty}^{c+i\infty}\frac{\Gamma\left(\dfrac{1+\nu+s}{2}\right)}{\Gamma\left(\dfrac{1+\nu-\alpha+s}{2}\right)}$$

$$\times\frac{\chi(s)ds}{s-w} = \mathsf{G}(\alpha - w + 1)$$

where

$$\mathsf{G}(s) = \int_0^1 g(x)x^{s-1}\,dx$$

is the Mellin transform of the function

$$y(x) = \begin{cases} g(x) & 0 \le x \le 1 \\ 0 & x > 1 \end{cases}$$

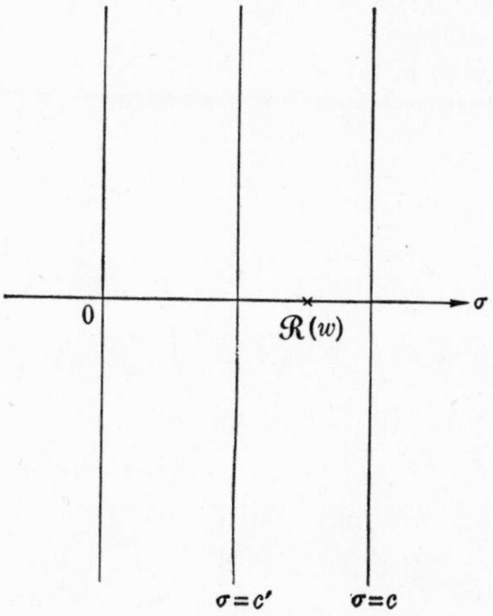

Moving the line of integration from $\mathsf{R}(s) = c$ to $\mathsf{R}(s) = c' < \mathsf{R}(w)$ (cf. Fig. 4), we obtain

Fig. 4. Lines of integration in the s plane.

$$\frac{1}{2\pi i}\int_{c'-i\infty}^{c'+i\infty}\frac{\Gamma\left(\dfrac{1+\nu+s}{2}\right)}{\Gamma\left(\dfrac{1+\nu-\alpha+s}{2}\right)}\frac{\chi(s)}{s-w}\,ds + \frac{\Gamma\left(\dfrac{1+\nu+w}{2}\right)\chi(w)}{\Gamma\left(\dfrac{1+\nu-\alpha+w}{2}\right)}$$

$$= \mathsf{G}(\alpha - w + 1)$$

Now the integral occurring on the left-hand side of this equation is a regular function of w for $\mathsf{R}(w) > c'$. Therefore so also is the function

$$G(\alpha - w + 1) - \frac{\Gamma\left(\dfrac{1 + \nu + w}{2}\right) \chi(w)}{\Gamma\left(\dfrac{1 + \nu - \alpha + w}{2}\right)}$$

a regular function of w for $R(w) > c'$.   Hence so also is

$$\chi(w) - \frac{\Gamma\left(\dfrac{1 + \nu - \alpha + w}{2}\right)}{\Gamma\left(\dfrac{1 + \nu + w}{2}\right)} G(\alpha - w + 1)$$

so that

$$\frac{1}{2\pi i} \int_{c - i\infty}^{c + i\infty} \left[\chi(s) - \frac{\Gamma\left(\dfrac{1 + \nu - \alpha + s}{2}\right)}{\Gamma\left(\dfrac{1 + \nu + s}{2}\right)} G(\alpha + 1 - s) \right] \frac{ds}{s - w} = 0$$

with $R(w) < c$.   Similarly from equation (45) we can show that

$$\frac{1}{2\pi i} \int_{c - i\infty}^{c + i\infty} \chi(s) \frac{ds}{s - w} = \chi(w) \qquad R(w) < c$$

Thus

$$\chi(w) = \frac{1}{2\pi i} \int_{c - i\infty}^{c + i\infty} \frac{\Gamma\left(\dfrac{1 + \nu - \alpha + s}{2}\right)}{\Gamma\left(\dfrac{1 + \nu + s}{2}\right)} \frac{G(\alpha - s + 1)}{s - w} \, ds$$

Now, by definition,

$$G(\alpha - s + 1) = \int_0^1 g(\xi) \xi^{\alpha - s} \, d\xi$$

and we may write

$$\frac{1}{s - w} = \int_0^1 \eta^{s - w - 1} \, d\eta$$

so that, interchanging the orders of the integrations, we obtain
$\chi(w) =$

$$\int_0^1 g(\xi) \xi^\alpha \, d\xi \int_0^1 \eta^{-w-1} \, d\eta \, \frac{1}{2\pi i} \int_{c - i\infty}^{c + i\infty} \frac{\Gamma\left(\dfrac{1 + \nu + s - \alpha}{2}\right)}{\Gamma\left(\dfrac{1 + \nu + s}{2}\right)} \left(\frac{\xi}{\eta}\right)^{-s} ds$$

Consider now the integral

$$\int_0^1 x^{2\beta}(1 - x^2)^{\gamma - 1} x^{s - 1} \, dx$$

Changing the variable of integration from x to ξ where $\xi = x^2$, we find that the integral has the value

$$\frac{1}{2} \int_0^1 \xi^{\beta + \frac{1}{2}s - 1}(1 - \xi)^{\gamma - 1} \, d\xi = \frac{\Gamma(\gamma)\Gamma(\beta + \frac{1}{2}s)}{2\Gamma(\gamma + \beta + \frac{1}{2}s)}$$

It then follows as a result of applying the Mellin inversion theorem 15 that

$$\frac{1}{2\pi i}\int_{c-i\infty}^{c+i\infty}\frac{\Gamma(\beta+\tfrac{1}{2}s)}{\Gamma(\gamma+\beta+\tfrac{1}{2}s)}\,x^{-s}\,ds=\begin{cases}\dfrac{2x^{2\beta}(1-x^2)^{\nu-1}}{\Gamma(\gamma)} & 0\le x\le 1\\[2mm] 0 & x>1\end{cases}$$

Putting $x=(\xi/\eta)$, $\beta=\tfrac{1}{2}(1+\nu-\alpha)$, $\gamma=\tfrac{1}{2}\alpha$ in this result, we obtain the integral

$$\frac{1}{2\pi i}\int_{c-i\infty}^{c+i\infty}\frac{\Gamma\left(\dfrac{1+\nu+s-\alpha}{2}\right)}{\Gamma\left(\dfrac{1+\nu+s}{2}\right)}\left(\frac{\xi}{\eta}\right)^{-s}ds$$

$$=\begin{cases}\dfrac{2}{\Gamma(\tfrac{1}{2}\alpha)}\,\xi^{1+\nu-\alpha}(\eta^2-\xi^2)^{\tfrac{1}{2}\alpha-1}\eta^{1-\nu} & \eta\ge\xi\\[2mm] 0 & 0<\eta<\xi\end{cases}$$

so that

$$\chi(w)=\frac{2}{\Gamma(\tfrac{1}{2}\alpha)}\int_0^1 g(\xi)\xi^{1+\nu}\,d\xi\int_\xi^1\eta^{-w-\nu}(\eta^2-\xi^2)^{\tfrac{1}{2}\alpha-1}\,d\eta$$

Changing the order of integration (cf. Fig. 5), we find that

$$\chi(w)=\frac{2}{\Gamma(\tfrac{1}{2}\alpha)}\int_0^1\eta^{-w-\nu}\,d\eta$$

$$\times\int_0^\eta g(\xi)\xi^{1+\nu}(\eta^2-\xi^2)^{\tfrac{1}{2}\alpha-1}\,d\xi$$

$$=\frac{2}{\Gamma(\tfrac{1}{2}\alpha)}\int_0^1\eta^{\alpha-w}\,d\eta$$

$$\times\int_0^1 g(\eta\zeta)\zeta^{\nu+1}(1-\zeta^2)^{\tfrac{1}{2}\alpha-1}\,d\zeta$$

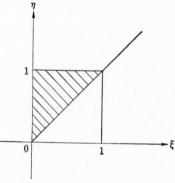

Now by the definition of $\chi(s)$ and the Mellin inversion formula

$$f(x)=\frac{1}{2\pi i}\int_{c-i\infty}^{c+i\infty}F(s)x^{-s}\,ds$$

Fig. 5.   The field of integration in the $\xi\eta$ plane.

we find, for the function $f(x)$,

$$f(x)=\frac{2}{\Gamma(\tfrac{1}{2}\alpha)}\int_0^1\eta^\alpha\,d\eta\int_0^1 g(\eta\zeta)\zeta^{\nu+1}(1-\zeta^2)^{\tfrac{1}{2}\alpha-1}\,d\zeta$$

$$\times\frac{1}{2\pi i}\int_{c-i\infty}^{c+i\infty}2^{s-\alpha}(x\eta)^{-s}\frac{\Gamma\left(\dfrac{1+\nu+s}{2}\right)}{\left(\dfrac{1+\nu+\alpha-s}{2}\right)}\,ds$$

If we replace μ by $s - \frac{1}{2}$, ν by $\nu + \frac{1}{2}\alpha$ in equation (18), Appendix A, we find that

$$\int_0^\infty J_{\nu+\frac{1}{2}\alpha}(at)t^{1-\frac{1}{2}}t^{s-1}\,dt = \frac{2^{s-\frac{1}{2}}\,\Gamma\left(\dfrac{1+\nu+s}{2}\right)}{a^{s-\frac{1}{2}+1}\,\Gamma\left(\dfrac{1+\nu+\alpha-s}{2}\right)}$$

and so by Theorem 15

$$\frac{1}{2\pi i}\int_{c-i\infty}^{c+i\infty} 2^{s-\alpha}\frac{\Gamma\left(\dfrac{1+\nu+s}{2}\right)}{\Gamma\left(\dfrac{1+\nu+\alpha-s}{2}\right)}(at)^{-s}\,ds = 2^{-\frac{1}{2}\alpha}(at)^{1-\frac{1}{2}\alpha}J_{\nu+\frac{1}{2}\alpha}(at)$$

giving finally

$$f(x) = \frac{(2x)^{1-\frac{1}{2}\alpha}}{\Gamma(\frac{1}{2}\alpha)}\int_0^1 \eta^{1+\frac{1}{2}\alpha}J_{\nu+\frac{1}{2}\alpha}(\eta x)d\eta \int_0^1 g(\eta\zeta)\zeta^{\nu+1}(1-\zeta^2)^{\frac{1}{2}\alpha-1}\,d\zeta \quad (46)$$

This solution is valid for $\alpha > 0$. It breaks down when $\alpha \leq 0$, but another form of solution which is valid when $\alpha > -2$ and is equivalent to the solution (46) when $\alpha > 0$ has been derived by Busbridge.[1] If $g(y)$ is integrable over the interval $(0,1)$, the solution obtained by Busbridge is

$$f(x) = \frac{2^{-\frac{1}{2}\alpha}x^{-\alpha}}{\Gamma(1+\frac{1}{2}\alpha)}\left[x^{1+\frac{1}{2}\alpha}J_{\nu+\frac{1}{2}\alpha}(x)\int_0^1 y^{\nu+1}(1-y^2)^{\frac{1}{2}\alpha}g(y)dy\right.$$
$$\left. + \int_0^1 u^{\nu+1}(1-u^2)^{\frac{1}{2}\alpha}\,du\int_0^1 g(yu)(xy)^{2+\frac{1}{2}\alpha}J_{\nu+1+\frac{1}{2}\alpha}(xy)dy\right] \quad (47)$$

valid for $\alpha > -2$ and $-\nu - 1 < \alpha - \frac{1}{2} < \nu + 1$. When $\alpha > 0$, it can be shown that the solution (47) can be reduced to the form (46) but the reduction is tedious and will not be reproduced here. For details the reader is referred to the paper cited above.

[1] I. W. Busbridge, *Proc. London Math. Soc.*, **44**, 115 (1938).

CHAPTER 3

FINITE TRANSFORMS

13. Finite Fourier Transforms

13.1 Introduction. The method of integral transforms outlined in the last two chapters may, under certain circumstances, be applied to the solution of boundary value and initial value problems in mathematical physics. In problems in which the range of values which can be assumed by one of the independent variables, x say, is $(0, \infty)$ the use of an integral transform of the type

$$\int_0^\infty f(x)K(\xi_i,x)dx \tag{1}$$

will often reduce a partial differential equation in n independent variables to one in $n - 1$ independent variables, thus reducing the complexity of the problem under discussion. In some instances successive operations of this type will ultimately reduce the problem to a boundary value problem for an ordinary differential equation, the theory of which has been much more extensively developed.

There are two obvious ways in which this method can be extended. In the first place, by extending the types of kernel $K(\xi_i,x)$ beyond those at present in common use it may be possible to deal with boundary value problems not hitherto tractable to this method. However, the choice of kernel is largely determined by the form of the differential equation whose solution is sought. The other alternative is to extend the method to *finite* intervals, *i.e.*, to employ integral transforms suitable to problems in which the field of variation of the independent variable x is now (a,b) where both a and b are real and finite. One, of course, may be zero. This extension was first suggested by Doetsch[1] in the case of trigonometric kernels. Defining the finite Fourier sine transform of a function $f(x)$ by the equation

$$\bar{f}(n) = \int_0^\pi f(x) \sin (nx)dx \tag{2}$$

Doetsch pointed out that the inversion formula

$$f(x) = \frac{2}{\pi} \sum_n \bar{f}(n) \sin (nx) \tag{3}$$

[1] G. Doetsch, *Math. Ann.*, **62**, 52 (1935).

71

is an immediate consequence of a well-known theorem in the theory of Fourier series.

This method has been developed and generalized by Kneiss,[1] Koschmieder,[2] Roettinger,[3] and others and applied by Brown[4] to the discussion of the classical boundary value problems of mathematical physics. The use of finite Fourier transforms does not, of course, solve problems which are incapable of solution by the direct application of the theory of Fourier series, but it does facilitate the resolution of boundary value problems.

13.2 Finite sine and cosine transforms. It is a well-known result of the theory of Fourier series[5] that, if the function $f(x)$ satisfies Dirichlet's conditions in the interval $0 \leq x \leq \pi$, then the series

$$\frac{1}{\pi} a_0 + \frac{2}{\pi} \sum_{n=1}^{\infty} a_n \cos(nx)$$

in which

$$a_n = \int_0^\pi f(x) \cos(nx) dx \tag{4}$$

converges to the value $\frac{1}{2}[f(x + 0) + f(x - 0)]$ at each point x in the interval $(0,\pi)$ and to the value $f(x)$ at each point x of that interval at which the function $f(x)$ is continuous.

If, instead of the coefficient a_n, we introduce the finite cosine transform of the function $f(x)$, denoted by $\bar{f}_c(n)$, and defined by the equation

$$\bar{f}_c(n) = \int_0^\pi f(x) \cos(nx) dx$$

we may state the above theorem on Fourier series as the following theorem on finite cosine transforms:

Theorem 24. *If $f(x)$ satisfies Dirichlet's conditions in the interval* $0 \leq x \leq \pi$ *and if*

$$\bar{f}_c(n) = \int_0^\pi f(x) \cos(nx) dx$$

is its finite cosine transform, then

$$f(x) = \frac{\bar{f}_c(0)}{\pi} + \frac{2}{\pi} \sum_{n=1}^{\infty} \bar{f}_c(n) \cos(nx) \tag{5}$$

[1] H. Kneiss, *Math. Z.*, **44**, 226 (1938).

[2] L. Koschmieder, *Deut. Math.*, **5**, 521 (1945).

[3] I. Roettinger, *Bull. Am. Math. Soc.*, **51**, 67 (1945); *Quart. Applied Math.*, **5**, 298 (1947).

[4] H. K. Brown, *Bull. Am. Math. Soc.*, **50**, 376 (1944); *Jour. Applied Phys.*, **14**, 609 (1943), **15**, 410 (1944).

[5] R. V. Churchill, "Fourier Series and Boundary Value Problems" (McGraw-Hill, New York, 1941), p. 74.

at each point in the interval $(0,\pi)$ *at which* $f(x)$ *is continuous.* At any point of the interval at which $f(x)$ has a finite discontinuity the left-hand side of equation (5) is replaced by $\frac{1}{2}[f(x+0)+f(x-0)]$. We shall often in the sequel refer to Theorem 24 as the Fourier inversion theorem for finite cosine transforms.

A similar theorem holds when the independent variable x lies in the range $(0,a)$. If we now define the finite cosine transform to be

$$\bar{f}_c(n) = \int_0^a f(x) \cos (\xi_n x) dx$$

where ξ_n is as yet unspecified, then, writing $y = \pi x/a$, we find that

$$\bar{f}_c(n) = \frac{a}{\pi} \int_0^\pi F(y) \cos \left(\xi_n \frac{ay}{\pi} \right) dy$$

in which $F(y)$ denotes $f(ay/\pi)$. It follows at once from Theorem 24 that if $a\xi_n/\pi = n$, that is, if $\xi_n = n\pi/a$, then

$$\frac{a}{\pi} F(y) = \frac{1}{\pi}\bar{f}_c(0) + \frac{2}{\pi} \sum_{n=1}^{\infty} \bar{f}_c(n) \cos (ny)$$

Returning to the original variable x, we see that this result may be stated as follows:

Theorem 25. *If* $f(x)$ *satisfies Dirichlet's conditions in the interval* $(0,a)$ *and if*

$$\bar{f}_c(n) = \int_0^a f(x) \cos \frac{n\pi x}{a} dx \tag{6}$$

denotes its finite cosine transform, then $f(x)$ *is given at each point of continuity in the interval* $(0,a)$ *by the series*

$$f(x) = \frac{1}{a}\bar{f}_c(0) + \frac{2}{a} \sum_{n=1}^{\infty} \bar{f}_c(n) \cos \frac{n\pi x}{a} \tag{7}$$

Similar results hold for finite sine transforms defined by the equation

$$\bar{f}_s(n) = \int_0^\pi f(x) \sin (nx) dx \tag{8}$$

Translated into the language of finite transform theory, the well-known theorem in the theory of Fourier series,[1] that, if the function $f(x)$ satisfies Dirichlet's conditions in the interval $0 \leq x \leq \pi$ the series

$$\frac{2}{\pi} \sum_{n=1}^{\infty} b_n \sin (nx)$$

[1] *Ibid.*, p. 73.

in which

$$b_n = \int_0^\pi f(x) \sin (nx)dx$$

converges to $f(x)$ at each point of continuity, becomes as follows:

Theorem 26. *If $f(x)$ satisfies Dirichlet's conditions in the interval $(0,\pi)$ and if*

$$\bar{f}_s(n) = \int_0^\pi f(x) \sin (nx)dx$$

is defined to be its finite sine transform, then

$$f(x) = \frac{2}{\pi} \sum_{n=1}^{\infty} \bar{f}_s(n) \sin (nx) \tag{9}$$

at each point of continuity in the interval $(0,\pi)$.

The simple substitution $y = \pi x/a$ in this result gives, by a process similar to that used in the establishment of Theorem 25 from Theorem 24, the following theorem for functions defined in the range $0 \leq x \leq a$:

Theorem 27. *If $f(x)$ satisfies Dirichlet's conditions in the interval $(0,a)$ and if for that range its finite sine transform is defined to be*

$$\bar{f}_s(n) = \int_0^a f(x) \sin \frac{n\pi x}{a} dx \tag{10}$$

then, at each point of $(0,a)$ at which $f(x)$ is continuous,

$$f(x) = \frac{2}{a} \sum_{n=1}^{\infty} \bar{f}_s(n) \sin \frac{n\pi x}{a} \tag{11}$$

13.3 Relations between the finite Fourier transforms of the derivatives of a function. In the application of these theorems on finite Fourier transforms to the solution of boundary value problems it is often necessary to express an integral of the type

$$\int_0^a \frac{\partial^r f}{\partial x^r} \sin \frac{n\pi x}{a} dx, \qquad \int_0^a \frac{\partial^r f}{\partial x^r} \cos \frac{n\pi x}{a} dx$$

in terms of the finite Fourier transforms of the function $f(x)$.

The fundamental results are those involving the first derivative of the function $f(x)$. For example, we have, as a result of an integration by parts, that

$$\int_0^a \frac{\partial f}{\partial x} \sin \frac{n\pi x}{a} dx = \left[f(x) \sin \frac{n\pi x}{a} \right]_0^a - \frac{n\pi}{a} \int_0^a f(x) \cos \frac{n\pi x}{a} dx$$

Now, since n is an integer, $\sin(n\pi x/a)$ vanishes both at $x = 0$ and at $x = a$ so that if we define $\bar{f}_c(n)$ by equation (6) we have that

$$\int_0^a \frac{\partial f}{\partial x} \sin \frac{n\pi x}{a} \, dx = -\frac{n\pi}{a} \bar{f}_c(n) \tag{12}$$

whatever the values of $f(0)$ and $f(a)$, provided, of course, that they are not infinite. Similarly, integrating by parts, we find that

$$\int_0^a \frac{\partial f}{\partial x} \cos \frac{n\pi x}{a} \, dx = \left[f(x) \cos \frac{n\pi x}{a} \right]_0^a + \frac{n\pi}{a} \int_0^a f(x) \sin \frac{n\pi x}{a} \, dx$$

Since $\cos(n\pi) = (-1)^n$, when n is an integer we may write this result in the form

$$\int_0^a \frac{\partial f}{\partial x} \cos \frac{n\pi x}{a} \, dx = (-1)^n f(a) - f(0) + \frac{n\pi}{a} \bar{f}_s(n) \tag{13}$$

in which $\bar{f}_s(n)$ denotes the finite sine transform defined by equation (8). As a special case of this result we see that if $f(x)$ vanishes both at $x = a$ and at $x = 0$ then

$$\int_0^a \frac{\partial f}{\partial x} \cos \frac{n\pi x}{a} \, dx = \frac{n\pi}{a} \bar{f}_s(n) \tag{14}$$

The results for higher derivatives may be established by the repeated use of the fundamental results (12) and (13). For instance, it follows from (12) that

$$\int_0^a \frac{\partial^2 f}{\partial x^2} \sin \frac{n\pi x}{a} \, dx = -\frac{n\pi}{a} \int_0^a \frac{\partial f}{\partial x} \cos \frac{n\pi x}{a} \, dx$$

and hence by the application of (13) that

$$\int_0^a \frac{\partial^2 f}{\partial x^2} \sin \frac{n\pi x}{a} \, dx = \frac{n\pi}{a} [(-1)^{n+1} f(a) + f(0)] - \frac{n^2\pi^2}{a^2} \bar{f}_s(n) \tag{15}$$

In the particular case in which $f(0) = f(a) = 0$ this reduces to the simple form

$$\int_0^a \frac{\partial^2 f}{\partial x^2} \sin \frac{n\pi x}{a} \, dx = -\frac{n^2\pi^2}{a^2} \bar{f}_s(n) \tag{16}$$

Similarly it follows from equation (13) that

$$\int_0^a \frac{\partial^2 f}{\partial x^2} \cos \frac{n\pi x}{a} \, dx = (-1)^n f'(a) - f'(0) - \frac{n^2\pi^2}{a^2} \bar{f}_c(n) \tag{17}$$

If $\partial f/\partial x$ vanishes at the end points $x = 0$ and $x = a$, then this equation becomes simply

$$\int_0^a \frac{\partial^2 f}{\partial x^2} \cos \frac{n\pi x}{a} \, dx = -\frac{n^2\pi^2}{a^2} \bar{f}_c(n) \tag{18}$$

For derivatives of order greater than 2 the results may be obtained by induction. In the analysis of boundary value problems we often need to know the results for fourth-order derivatives. It follows from equation (16) that if $\partial^2 f/\partial x^2$ is zero at the end points $x = 0$ and $x = a$ then

$$\int_0^a \frac{\partial^4 f}{\partial x^4} \sin \frac{n\pi x}{a} \, dx = -\frac{n^2 \pi^2}{a^2} \int_0^a \frac{\partial^2 f}{\partial x^2} \sin \frac{n\pi x}{a} \, dx = \frac{n^4 \pi^4}{a^4} \bar{f}_s(n) \qquad (19)$$

Similarly if $\partial^3 f/\partial x^3 = \partial f/\partial x = 0$ when $x = 0$ and when $x = a$, it is easily seen by two applications of equation (18) that

$$\int_0^a \frac{\partial^4 f}{\partial x^4} \cos \frac{n\pi x}{a} \, dx = \frac{n^4 \pi^4}{a^4} \bar{f}_c(n) \qquad (20)$$

13.4 Faltung theorems for finite Fourier transforms. The Faltung theorems for finite Fourier transforms cannot be put into simple, elegant forms such as hold for ordinary Fourier transforms. To present the results in a neat form, we introduce two functions $F_1(u)$ and $F_2(u)$, which we call the *odd* and *even* periodic extensions of the function $f(u)$ which is defined in the interval $0 \le u \le \pi$. Thus in the interval $-\pi \le u \le \pi$ we define $F_1(u)$, the odd periodic extension with period 2π, of the function $f(u)$ by the equations

$$F_1(u) = \begin{cases} f(u) & 0 \le u \le \pi \\ -f(-u) & -\pi \le u < 0 \end{cases}$$

Similarly the even periodic extension $F_2(u)$ is defined in $-\pi \le u \le \pi$ by the equations

$$F_2(u) = \begin{cases} f(u) & 0 \le u \le \pi \\ f(-u) & -\pi \le u < 0 \end{cases}$$

It follows immediately from this definition of $F_1(u)$ that if $F_1(u)$ and $G_1(u)$ are the odd periodic extensions of $f(u)$ and $g(u)$, respectively, then

$$\int_{-\pi}^{\pi} F_1(x - u)G_1(u)du = \int_0^{\pi} f(x - u)g(u)du - \int_0^{\pi} f(u - x)g(u)du \qquad (21)$$

and also, because F_1 is periodic,

$$\int_{-\pi}^{\pi} F_1(x - u)G_1(u)du = \int_0^{\pi} f(-x - u)g(u)du - \int_0^{\pi} f(x + u)g(u)du \qquad (22)$$

With the notation introduced by Churchill[1] we write $F_1(x) * G_1(x)$ for the integral

$$\int_{-\pi}^{\pi} F_1(x - u)G_1(u)du$$

and call it the *Faltung*, or *convolution*, of the functions F_1 and G_1.

[1] R. V. Churchill, "Modern Operational Mathematics in Engineering" (McGraw-Hill, New York, 1944), p. 274.

If we denote the finite Fourier sine transforms of the functions $f(x)$ and $g(x)$ by $\bar{f}_s(n)$ and $\bar{g}_s(n)$, respectively, then we may write

$$\bar{f}_s(n) = \int_0^\pi f(\xi) \sin (n\xi) d\xi, \qquad \bar{g}_s(n) = \int_0^\pi g(\eta) \sin (n\eta) d\eta$$

so that

$$\frac{2}{\pi} \sum_{n=1}^m \bar{f}_s(n) \bar{g}_s(n) \cos (nx)$$

$$= \frac{2}{\pi} \int_0^\pi d\xi \int_0^\pi d\eta f(\xi) g(\eta) \sum_{n=1}^m \cos (nx) \sin (n\xi) \sin (n\eta)$$

on interchanging the orders of summation and integration.   Making use of the results

$$4 \sin (n\xi) \sin (n\eta) \cos (nx) = \cos (\xi - \eta + x)n + \cos (\xi - \eta - x)n$$
$$- \cos (\xi + \eta + x)n - \cos (\xi + \eta - x)n$$

and

$$\sum_{r=1}^m \cos (r\alpha) = -\frac{1}{2} + \frac{\sin (m - \frac{1}{2})\alpha}{2 \sin \frac{1}{2}\alpha}$$

we find that

$$\frac{2}{\pi} \sum_{n=1}^m \bar{f}_s(n) \bar{g}_s(n) \cos (nx) = \frac{1}{4\pi} \int_0^\pi f(\xi) d\xi \int_0^\pi g(\eta) d\eta$$

$$\left[\frac{\sin (m - \frac{1}{2})(\xi - \eta + x)}{\sin \frac{1}{2}(\xi - \eta + x)} + \frac{\sin (m - \frac{1}{2})(\xi - \eta - x)}{\sin \frac{1}{2}(\xi - \eta - x)} \right.$$
$$\left. - \frac{\sin (m - \frac{1}{2})(\xi + \eta + x)}{\sin \frac{1}{2}(\xi + \eta + x)} - \frac{\sin (m - \frac{1}{2})(\xi + \eta - x)}{\sin \frac{1}{2}(\xi + \eta - x)} \right]$$

If in the first of these four integrals we change the variables of integration from ξ and η to λ and μ where

$$\lambda = \xi - \eta + x, \qquad \mu = \eta$$

we find that

$$\frac{1}{4\pi} \int_0^\pi f(\xi) d\xi \int_0^\pi g(\eta) \frac{\sin (m - \frac{1}{2})(\xi - \eta + x)}{\sin \frac{1}{2}(\xi - \eta + x)} d\eta$$

$$= \frac{1}{2\pi} \int_0^\pi g(\mu) d\mu \int_{x-\mu}^{x+\pi-\mu} f(\lambda + \mu - x) \frac{\sin (m - \frac{1}{2})\lambda}{\lambda} \frac{\frac{1}{2}\lambda}{\sin \frac{1}{2}\lambda} d\lambda$$

which tends to

$$\frac{1}{4} \int_0^\pi g(\mu) f(\mu - x) d\mu$$

as m tends to infinity, as is easily seen by a direct application of Theorem 5. The other three terms can be evaluated in a similar fashion to give

$$\frac{2}{\pi} \sum_{n=1}^{\infty} \bar{f}_s(n) \bar{g}_s(n) \sin (nx)$$

$$= -\frac{1}{4} \int_0^\pi g(\mu)[f(x - \mu) + f(-x - \mu) - f(\mu - x) - f(\mu + x)]d\mu$$

Hence by equations (21) and (22) we have

$$\frac{2}{\pi} \sum_{n=1}^{\infty} \bar{f}_s(n) \bar{g}_s(n) \cos (nx) = -\frac{1}{2} \int_{-\pi}^{\pi} F_1(x - \mu)G_1(\mu)d\mu$$

$$= -\frac{1}{2} F_1(x) * G_1(x) \tag{23}$$

or, making use of the inversion theorem 26,

$$\int_0^\pi F_1(x) * G_1(x) \cos (nx)dx = -2\bar{f}_s(n)\bar{g}_s(n) \tag{24}$$

Doetsch introduced a notation for finite Fourier transforms which is useful in cases, such as the one we have just been considering, in which the function being transformed is of a complicated nature. We write

$$\mathsf{C}(f) = \int_0^\pi f(x) \cos (nx)dx, \qquad \mathsf{S}(f) = \int_0^\pi f(x) \sin (nx)dx$$

With this notation we may write equation (24) finally in the form

$$\mathsf{C}(F_1 * G_1) = -2\bar{f}_s(n)\bar{g}_s(n) \tag{25}$$

Similarly by considering the value of the sum

$$\frac{2}{\pi} \sum_{n=1}^{m} \bar{f}_s(n) \bar{g}_c(n) \sin (nx)$$

as m tends to infinity we can show that

$$\mathsf{S}(F_1 * G_2) = 2\bar{f}_s(n)\bar{g}_c(n) \tag{26}$$

For an alternative proof of equation (26) the reader is referred to pages 274 to 276 of R. V. Churchill's "Modern Operational Mathematics in Engineering" (McGraw-Hill, New York, 1944).

By either of these methods we can show further that

$$\mathsf{C}(F_2 * G_2) = 2\bar{f}_c(n)\bar{g}_c(n) \tag{27}$$

and that

$$\mathsf{S}(F_2 * G_1) = 2\bar{f}_c(n)\bar{g}_s(n) \tag{28}$$

Since, in the derivation of these formulas, we have been making use of Theorems 24 and 26, it follows that they are valid only for functions $f(x)$ and $g(x)$ which satisfy Dirichlet's conditions in the interval $0 \leq x \leq \pi$.

13.5 Multiple finite transforms. Suppose that $f(x,y)$ is a function of the two independent variables x and y, defined in the square $0 \leq x \leq \pi$, $0 \leq y \leq \pi$. Then, regarded as a function of x, $f(x,y)$ will, if it satisfies certain wide conditions, possess a finite sine transform. If we denote this transform by $F(m,y)$ then

$$F(m,y) = \int_0^\pi f(x,y) \sin (mx) dx \tag{29}$$

This function will itself have a finite Fourier sine transform, which we may denote by $\bar{f}_s(m,n)$, defined by the equation

$$\bar{f}_s(m,n) = \int_0^\pi F(m,y) \sin (ny) dy \tag{30}$$

If we substitute from equation (30) into equation (29), we find that the relation between $f(x,y)$ and $\bar{f}_s(m,n)$ is

$$\bar{f}_s(m,n) = \int_0^\pi \int_0^\pi f(x,y) \sin (mx) \sin (ny) dx \, dy \tag{31}$$

We shall regard this equation as defining the double finite sine transform of the function $f(x,y)$ for the region $0 \leq x \leq \pi$, $0 \leq y \leq \pi$. To obtain a formula giving $f(x,y)$ in terms of its double finite sine transform $\bar{f}_s(m,n)$, we note that if we apply Theorem 26 to equations (29) and (30) we obtain

$$F(m,y) = \frac{2}{\pi} \sum_{n=1}^\infty \bar{f}_s(m,n) \sin (ny) \tag{32}$$

and

$$f(x,y) = \frac{2}{\pi} \sum_{m=1}^\infty F(m,y) \sin (mx) \tag{33}$$

Substituting for $F(m,y)$ from equation (32) into equation (33), we have finally

$$f(x,y) = \frac{4}{\pi^2} \sum_{m=1}^\infty \sum_{n=1}^\infty \bar{f}_s(m,n) \sin (mx) \sin (ny) \tag{34}$$

The inversion theorem contained in equations (31) and (34) is applicable when $0 \leq x \leq \pi$ and $0 \leq y \leq \pi$. When the function $f(x,y)$ is defined in the rectangle $0 \leq x \leq a$, $0 \leq y \leq b$, by applying Theorem 27 twice we establish in a similar way the following theorem:

Theorem 28. *If $f(x,y)$ is a function of two variables satisfying Dirichlet's conditions in the rectangle $0 \le x \le a$, $0 \le y \le b$, and if its finite sine transform is defined to be*

$$\bar{f}_s(m,n) = \int_0^a dx \int_0^b f(x,y) \sin \frac{m\pi x}{a} \sin \frac{n\pi y}{b} dy \qquad (35)$$

then at points of the rectangle at which the function $f(x,y)$ is continuous

$$f(x,y) = \frac{4}{ab} \sum_{m=1}^{\infty} \sum_{n=1}^{\infty} \bar{f}_s(m,n) \sin \frac{m\pi x}{a} \sin \frac{n\pi y}{b} \qquad (36)$$

The double transforms of the partial derivatives of a function satisfying these conditions may readily be written down. For instance, it follows from equation (15) that

$$\int_0^a \frac{\partial^2 f}{\partial x^2} \sin \frac{m\pi x}{a} dx = -\frac{m\pi}{a} \left[\cos \frac{m\pi x}{a} f(x,y) \right]_0^a$$
$$- \frac{m^2 \pi^2}{a^2} \int_0^a f(x,y) \sin \frac{m\pi x}{a} dx$$

Thus, if we are given that

$$f(0,y) = \lambda(y), \qquad f(a,y) = \mu(y)$$

we see that

$$\int_0^a \frac{\partial^2 f}{\partial x^2} \sin \frac{m\pi x}{a} dx = \frac{m\pi}{a} [\lambda(y) + (-1)^{m+1}\mu(y)]$$
$$- \frac{m^2 \pi^2}{a^2} \int_0^a f(x,y) \sin \frac{m\pi x}{a} dx$$

Multiplying both sides of this equation by $\sin (n\pi y/b)$ and integrating with respect to y from 0 to b, we obtain the relation

$$\int_0^a dx \int_0^b \frac{\partial^2 f}{\partial x^2} \sin \frac{m\pi x}{a} \sin \frac{n\pi y}{b} dy$$
$$= \frac{m\pi}{a} [\bar{\lambda}_s(n) + (-1)^{m+1}\bar{\mu}_s(n)] - \frac{m^2 \pi^2}{a^2} \bar{f}_s(m,n)$$

where $\bar{\lambda}_s(n)$ and $\bar{\mu}_s(n)$ denote the finite Fourier sine transforms of the functions $\lambda(y)$ and $\mu(y)$, respectively. In particular, if $f(x,y)$ vanishes along the lines $x = 0$, $x = a$ $(0 \le y \le b)$, then $\lambda(y)$ and $\mu(x)$ are identically zero and we have simply

$$\int_0^a \int_0^b \frac{\partial^2 f}{\partial x^2} \sin \frac{m\pi x}{a} \sin \frac{n\pi y}{b} dx\, dy = -\frac{\pi^2 m^2}{a^2} \bar{f}_s(m,n) \qquad (37)$$

A similar result holds for the double finite sine transform of the partial derivative $\partial^2 f/\partial y^2$. Adding the two results, we find that, if the function $f(x,y)$ vanishes along the perimeter of the rectangle $0 \leq x \leq a, 0 \leq y \leq b$, then

$$\int_0^a \int_0^b \left(\frac{\partial^2 f}{\partial x^2} + \frac{\partial^2 f}{\partial y^2} \right) \sin \frac{m\pi x}{a} \sin \frac{n\pi y}{b} \, dx \, dy$$

$$= -\pi^2 \left(\frac{m^2}{a^2} + \frac{n^2}{b^2} \right) \bar{f}_s(m,n) \quad (38)$$

where $\bar{f}_s(m,n)$ is defined by equation (35).

A theory of double finite cosine transforms can be built up in a similar way. This will not be attempted here since only double sine transforms will be used in the applications of the theory to the solution of boundary value problems in a rectangular region.

The theory outlined above can be extended in another way, by considering functions of many variables $x_1, x_2, \ldots, x_p$. The inversion theorem is easily established by the method sketched above for Theorem 28. It comes out to be as follows:

Theorem 29. *If* $f(x_1, x_2, \ldots, x_p)$ *is a function of the* p *variables* $x_1, x_2, \ldots, x_p$ *and satisfies Dirichlet's conditions in the region defined by the equations* $0 \leq x_i \leq a_i$ $(i = 1, 2, \ldots, p)$, *and if its multiple sine transform is taken to be defined by*

$$\bar{f}_s(n_1, n_2, \ldots, n_p)$$

$$= \int_0^{a_1} \cdots \int_0^{a_p} f(x_1, x_2, \ldots, x_p) \sin \frac{n_1 \pi x_1}{a_1} \cdots \sin \frac{n_p \pi x_p}{a_p} \, dx_1 \cdots dx_p$$

then at any point of the region at which the function is continuous

$$f(x_1, x_2, \ldots, x_p)$$

$$= 2^p (a_1 a_2 \cdots a_p)^{-1} \sum_{n_1=1}^{\infty} \cdots \sum_{n_p=1}^{\infty} \bar{f}_s(n_1, \ldots, n_p) \sin \frac{n_1 \pi x_1}{a_1}$$

$$\cdots \sin \frac{n_p \pi x_p}{a_p}$$

The extension of the result (37) is also obvious. It is that, if the function $f(x_1, x_2, \ldots, x_p)$ satisfies the conditions of Theorem 28 and if it vanishes when $x_1 = 0$ and when $x_1 = a_1$, then

$$\int_0^{a_1} \cdots \int_0^{a_p} \frac{\partial^2 f}{\partial x_1^2} \sin \frac{n_1 \pi x_1}{a_1} \cdots \sin \frac{n_p \pi x_p}{a_p} \, dx_1 \cdots dx_p$$

$$= -\frac{n_1^2 \pi^2}{a_1^2} \bar{f}_s(n_1, n_2, \ldots, n_p) \quad (39)$$

Similarly if the function f vanishes at every point of the boundary of the region in which it is defined,

$$\int_0^{a_1} \cdots \int_0^{a_p} \sum_{i=1}^{p} \frac{\partial^2 f}{\partial x_i^2} \sin \frac{n_1 \pi x_1}{a_1} \cdots \sin \frac{n_p \pi x_p}{a_p} dx_1 \cdots dx_p$$

$$= -\pi^2 \bar{f}_s(n_1, \ldots, n_p) \sum_{i=1}^{p} \frac{n_i^2}{a_i^2} \quad (40)$$

$\bar{f}_s(n_1, \ldots, n_p)$ being defined in the enunciation of Theorem 29.

14. Finite Hankel Transforms[1]

14.1 Inversion theorems for finite Hankel transforms. The method of finite transforms can similarly be extended in the case of Hankel transforms—in which the kernel $K(\xi_i, x)$ of equation (1) is a solution of Bessel's differential equation. A finite transform of simple type (there are several, depending on the choice of the function K of the parameter ξ_i) was introduced to facilitate the solution of certain initial and boundary value problems in the theory of elastic vibrations.[2] We shall now give an account of some of the simpler properties of finite Hankel transforms with a view to using them later to solve boundary value problems relating to systems possessing axial symmetry. The usual method[3] of attacking problems of this type is to eliminate one of the variables, say the time, by means of a Laplace transform. This method is long and often involves the evaluation of intricate contour integrals, whereas the method of finite Hankel transforms, which we shall now outline, is quick and simple to use, avoiding the use of the calculus of residues to evaluate the integrals.

It is a well-known result of the theory of Bessel functions that, if the function $f(x)$ satisfies Dirichlet's conditions in the interval $0 \leq x \leq a$, then the series

$$\frac{2}{a^2} \sum_i a_i \frac{J_\mu(x\xi_i)}{[J'_\mu(a\xi_i)]^2}$$

in which a_i denotes the definite integral

$$a_i = \int_0^a x f(x) J_\mu(x\xi_i) dx \quad (41)$$

and the sum is taken over all the *positive* zeros of the function $J_\mu(a\xi_i)$, converges to the sum $\frac{1}{2}[f(x + 0) + f(x - 0)]$. This may be written in

[1] I. N. Sneddon, *Phil. Mag.*, **37**, 17 (1946).

[2] I. N. Sneddon, *Proc. Cambridge Phil. Soc.*, **41**, 29 (1945). See also Sec. 20.5.

[3] See, *e.g.*, numerous examples in H. S. Carslaw and J. C. Jaeger, "Operationa Methods in Applied Mathematics" (Oxford, New York, 1941).

the form of an inversion theorem for the finite Hankel transform defined by the linear functional operator

$$J[f(x)] = \int_0^a xf(x)J_\mu(x\xi_i)dx = \bar{f}_J(\xi_i) \tag{42}$$

valid for all functions $f(x)$ satisfying Dirichlet's conditions in the closed interval $(0,a)$. With this interpretation the result quoted above assumes the following form:

Theorem 30. *If $f(x)$ satisfies Dirichlet's conditions in the interval $(0,a)$ and if its finite Hankel transform in that range is defined to be*

$$\bar{f}_J(\xi_i) = \int_0^a xf(x)J_\mu(x\xi_i)dx$$

where ξ_i is a root of the transcendental equation

$$J_\mu(a\xi_i) = 0 \tag{43}$$

then at any point of $(0,a)$ at which the function $f(x)$ is continuous

$$f(x) = \frac{2}{a^2} \sum_i \bar{f}_J(\xi_i) \frac{J_\mu(x\xi_i)}{[J_\mu'(a\xi_i)]^2} \tag{44}$$

where the sum is taken over all the positive roots of equation (43).

A particular case of this theorem which is of great importance is that corresponding to $\mu = 0$. Putting $n = 0$ in the recurrence relation [equation (9), Appendix A], we have

$$J_0'(x) = -J_1(x)$$

so that in the case $\mu = 0$ the series (44) reduces to

$$f(x) = \frac{2}{a^2} \sum_i \bar{f}_J(\xi_i) \frac{J_0(x\xi_i)}{[J_1(a\xi_i)]^2} \tag{45}$$

In the inversion theorem 30 the parameter ξ_i occurring in the definition (42) of the finite Hankel transform $\bar{f}_J(\xi_i)$ is a root of the transcendental equation (43). We get another form of finite Hankel transform if in the definition (42) we take ξ_i to be a root of the transcendental equation

$$\xi_i J_\mu'(\xi_i a) + hJ_\mu(\xi_i a) = 0$$

For this type of transform the classical theorems relating to Fourier-Bessel series (see Watson's treatise) give the following inversion theorem:

Theorem 31. *If $f(x)$ satisfies Dirichlet's conditions in the closed interval $(0,a)$ and if its finite Hankel transform is defined to be*

$$\bar{f}_J(\xi_i) = \int_0^a xf(x)J_\mu(x\xi_i)dx$$

in which ξ_i is a root of the transcendental equation

$$\xi_i J_\mu'(\xi_i a) + h J_\mu(\xi_i a) = 0 \qquad (46)$$

then, at each point of the interval at which $f(x)$ is continuous,

$$f(x) = \frac{2}{a^2} \sum_i \frac{\xi_i^2 \bar{f}_J(\xi_i)}{h^2 + \left(\xi_i^2 - \dfrac{\mu^2}{a^2}\right)} \frac{J_\mu(x\xi_i)}{[J_\mu(a\xi_i)]^2} \qquad (47)$$

where the sum is taken over all the positive roots of equation (46). In the case $\mu = 0$ the series (47) reduces to

$$f(x) = \frac{2}{a^2} \sum_i \frac{\xi_i^2 \bar{f}_J(\xi_i)}{h^2 + \xi_i^2} \frac{J_0(x\xi_i)}{[J_0(a\xi_i)]^2}$$

the sum being taken over all the positive roots of the equation

$$h J_0(\xi_i a) = \xi_i J_1(\xi_i a)$$

In the general case the series (47) may be written in the form

$$f(x) = \frac{2}{a^2} \sum_i \frac{\bar{f}_J(\xi_i)}{1 + \left(\xi_i^2 - \dfrac{\mu^2}{a^2}\right) \Big/ h^2} \frac{J_\mu(x\xi_i)}{\left[\dfrac{h J_\mu(\xi_i a)}{\xi_i}\right]^2}$$

which, by equation (46), becomes

$$f(x) = \frac{2}{a^2} \sum_i \frac{\bar{f}_J(\xi_i)}{1 + \left(\xi_i^2 - \dfrac{\mu^2}{a^2}\right) \Big/ h^2} \frac{J_\mu(x\xi_i)}{[J_\mu'(a\xi_i)]^2} \qquad (48)$$

where the sum is taken over all the positive roots of the equation

$$J_\mu(\xi_i a) = -\frac{\xi_i J_\mu'(\xi_i a)}{h} \qquad (49)$$

Letting h tend to infinity in equations (48) and (49), we see that they then reduce to equations (44) and (43), respectively, showing that Theorem 30 is a limiting case of Theorem 31.

The two finite Hankel transforms which are involved in Theorems 30 and 31 are of use when the variable x lies in the interval $(0,a)$. When the range of variation of x does *not* include the origin, *i.e.*, when x lies in the interval $0 < b \le x \le a$, we make use of a second type of transform defined by the equation

$$\bar{f}_H(\xi_i) = \int_b^a x f(x) [J_\mu(x\xi_i) G_\mu(a\xi_i) - G_\mu(x\xi_i) J_\mu(a\xi_i)] dx \qquad (50)$$

In this equation $G_\mu(z)$ is the Bessel function of order μ of the second kind defined by equation (3), Appendix A. For this type of transform the theory of Fourier-Bessel series gives the following inversion theorem:

Theorem 32. *If $f(x)$ satisfies Dirichlet's conditions in the range $b \leq x \leq a$ and if its finite Hankel transform in that range is defined to be*

$$\mathsf{H}[f(x)] \equiv \bar{f}_H(\xi_i) = \int_b^a xf(x)[J_\mu(x\xi_i)G_\mu(a\xi_i) - J_\mu(a\xi_i)G_\mu(x\xi_i)]dx \quad (51)$$

in which ξ_i is a root of the transcendental equation

$$J_\mu(\xi_i b)G_\mu(\xi_i a) - J_\mu(\xi_i a)G_\mu(\xi_i b) = 0 \quad (52)$$

then at each point in the interval (b,a) at which the function $f(x)$ is continuous

$$f(x) = \sum_i \frac{2\xi_i^2 J_\mu^2(\xi_i b)\bar{f}_H(\xi_i)}{J_\mu^2(a\xi_i) - J_\mu^2(b\xi_i)} [J_\mu(x\xi_i)G_\mu(a\xi_i) - J_\mu(a\xi_i)G_\mu(x\xi_i)] \quad (53)$$

the summation extending over all the positive roots of equation (52).

It is clear that, just as in the case of finite Fourier transforms, no result can be obtained by the use of finite Hankel transforms, of the types defined above, which could not have been established by applying directly the well-known properties of Fourier-Bessel expansions. The sole advantage to be derived from the use of these forms of the Fourier-Bessel expansion theorems is, as is seen from the examples we shall consider later, that it greatly reduces the amount of *formal* calculation involved in the solution of certain types of initial value and boundary value problems.

14.2 Properties of finite Hankel transforms. In the application of the theory of finite Hankel transforms to the solution of special problems we shall require some simple properties of the finite Hankel transform defined by equation (42).

Case 1: ξ_i *is a root of equation* (43). The case which arises most frequently is that in which the parameter ξ_i occurring in the definition (42) of the Hankel transform $\mathsf{J}_\mu[f(x)]$ is a root of the transcendental equation (43). We shall begin by considering the properties of such transforms.

Integrating by parts, we see that

$$\int_0^a x\frac{df}{dx}J_\mu(\xi_i x)dx = [xf(x)J_\mu(\xi_i x)]_0^a - \int_0^a f(x)\frac{d}{dx}[xJ_\mu(x\xi_i)]dx \quad (54)$$

If we suppose $\mu \geq 0$, then $xJ_\mu(x\xi_i)$ will vanish when $x = 0$ and since ξ_i is a root of equation (43) it will vanish when $x = a$. The quantity in the first brackets on the right-hand side of equation (54) is therefore zero. Furthermore

$$\frac{d}{dx}[xJ_\mu(x\xi_i)] = J_\mu(x\xi_i) + \xi_i x J_\mu'(x\xi_i)$$

Adding equations (5) and (6), Appendix A, we find

$$2\xi_i x J_\mu'(x\xi_i) = x\xi_i J_{\mu-1}(x\xi_i) - x\xi_i J_{\mu+1}(x\xi_i)$$

and from equation (7), Appendix A,

$$2\mu J_\mu(\xi_i x) = x\xi_i J_{\mu-1}(x\xi_i) + x\xi_i J_{\mu+1}(x\xi_i)$$

so that

$$\frac{d}{dx}[xJ_\mu(x\xi_i)] = \frac{\xi_i}{2\mu}(\mu+1)xJ_{\mu-1}(x\xi_i) - \frac{\xi_i}{2\mu}(\mu-1)xJ_{\mu+1}(x\xi_i) \quad (55)$$

Substituting from equation (55) into equation (54), we see that, when $\mu > 0$,

$$\mathsf{J}_\mu\left(\frac{df}{dx}\right) = \frac{\xi_i}{2\mu}[(\mu-1)\mathsf{J}_{\mu+1}(f) - (\mu+1)\mathsf{J}_{\mu-1}(f)] \quad (56)$$

Similarly from the recurrence relation (7), Appendix A, we have

$$2\mu\int_0^a f(x)J_\mu(x\xi_i)dx = \xi_i\int_0^a xf(x)J_{\mu-1}(x\xi_i)dx + \xi_i\int_0^a xf(x)J_{\mu+1}(x\xi_i)dx$$

which, in the notation of equation (56), may be written as

$$\mu\mathsf{J}_\mu\left(\frac{f}{x}\right) = \frac{\xi_i}{2}[\mathsf{J}_{\mu+1}(f) + \mathsf{J}_{\mu-1}(f)] \quad (57)$$

If in equations (56) and (57) we replace f by df/dx and then add, we obtain the relation

$$\mathsf{J}_\mu\left(\frac{d^2f}{dx^2} + \frac{1}{x}\frac{df}{dx}\right) = \frac{1}{2}\xi_i\left[\mathsf{J}_{\mu+1}\left(\frac{df}{dx}\right) + \mathsf{J}_{\mu-1}\left(\frac{df}{dx}\right)\right] \quad (58)$$

We may obtain an expression for the quantity on the left-hand side of this last equation in another way. Integrating the first term by parts and leaving the second unaltered, we see that

$$\int_0^a x\left(\frac{d^2f}{dx^2} + \frac{1}{x}\frac{df}{dx}\right)J_\mu(x\xi_i)dx$$

$$= \left[x\frac{df}{dx}J_\mu(x\xi_i)\right]_0^a - \int_0^a \frac{df}{dx}\left\{\frac{d}{dx}[xJ_\mu(x\xi_i)] - J_\mu(x\xi_i)\right\}dx$$

The first term vanishes, and the second becomes

$$-\xi_i\int_0^a x\frac{df}{dx}J_\mu'(x\xi_i)dx$$

which may be integrated by parts to give

$$-\xi_i a f(a) J'_\mu(a\xi_i) + \xi_i \int_0^a f(x)[x\xi_i J''_\mu(x\xi_i) + J'_\mu(x\xi_i)]dx$$

Now making use of the fact that the Bessel function $J_\mu(x\xi_i)$ satisfies the differential equation

$$J''_\mu(x\xi_i) + \frac{1}{x\xi_i} J'_\mu(x\xi_i) + \left(1 - \frac{\mu^2}{x^2\xi_i^2}\right) J_\mu(x\xi_i) = 0$$

we see that

$$\int_0^a \left(\frac{d^2f}{dx^2} + \frac{1}{x}\frac{df}{dx} - \frac{\mu^2 f}{x^2}\right) x J_\mu(x\xi_i)dx$$

$$= -a\xi_i f(a) J'_\mu(a\xi_i) - \xi_i^2 \int_0^a x f(x) J_\mu(x\xi_i)dx$$

In other words,

$$\mathsf{J}_\mu\left(\frac{d^2f}{dx^2} + \frac{1}{x}\frac{df}{dx} - \frac{\mu^2 f}{x^2}\right) = -a\xi_i f(a) J'_\mu(a\xi_i) - \xi_i^2 \mathsf{J}_\mu(f) \tag{59}$$

The results in the case $\mu = 0$ are of special interest. Putting $\mu = 1$ in equation (56), we see that

$$\mathsf{J}_1\left(\frac{df}{dx}\right) = -\xi_i \mathsf{J}_0(f) \tag{60}$$

Similarly putting $\mu = 0$ in equation (59) and making use of the fact that

$$J'_0(z) = -J_1(z)$$

we find that

$$\mathsf{J}_0\left(\frac{d^2f}{dx^2} + \frac{1}{x}\frac{df}{dx}\right) = a\xi_i f(a) J_1(a\xi_i) - \xi_i^2 \mathsf{J}_0(f) \tag{61}$$

so that if we know from the conditions of the problem that $f(a)$ is zero we have

$$\mathsf{J}_0\left(\frac{d^2f}{dx^2} + \frac{1}{x}\frac{df}{dx}\right) = -\xi_i^2 \mathsf{J}_0(f) \tag{62}$$

In the interpretation of results obtained by the use of finite Hankel transforms of this type it is useful to know the finite transforms of some simple functions. For example, from equation (10), Appendix A, we have

$$\int_0^\alpha x^{\mu+1} J_\mu(x)dx = \alpha^{\mu+1} J_{\mu+1}(\alpha)$$

so that, writing $x = \xi_i r$, $\alpha = \xi_i a$ in the integral on the left, we find

$$\int_0^a (r^\mu) r J_\mu(\xi_i r)dr = \frac{a^{\mu+1}}{\xi_i} J_{\mu+1}(a\xi_i)$$

which shows that

$$J_\mu(x^\mu) = \frac{a^{\mu+1}}{\xi_i} J_{\mu+1}(a\xi_i) \tag{63}$$

and in particular that

$$J_0(c) = \frac{ac}{\xi_i} J_1(a\xi_i) \tag{64}$$

where c is a constant. Similarly from equation (13), Appendix A, we have

$$\int_0^a (a^2 - x^2)xJ_0(\xi_i x)dx = \frac{4a}{\xi_i^3} J_1(\xi_i a) - \frac{2a^2}{\xi_i^2} J_0(\xi_i a)$$

Now, since ξ_i is a root of equation (43), the second term on the right-hand side is zero and we have

$$J_0(a^2 - x^2) = \frac{4a}{\xi_i^3} J_1(a\xi_i) \tag{65}$$

Furthermore since

$$x^2 \frac{d^2}{dx^2} J_\mu(\alpha x) + x \frac{d}{dx} J_\mu(\alpha x) + (\alpha^2 x^2 - \mu^2)J_\mu(\alpha x) = 0$$

and

$$x^2 \frac{d^2}{dx^2} J_\mu(\xi_i x) + x \frac{d}{dx} J_\mu(\xi_i x) + (\xi_i^2 x^2 - \mu^2)J_\mu(\xi_i x) = 0$$

we find on multiplying the first equation by $J_\mu(\xi_i x)$ and the second by $J_\mu(\alpha x)$ and subtracting that

$$(\alpha^2 - \xi_i^2)xJ_\mu(\alpha x)J_\mu(\xi_i x)$$
$$= \frac{d}{dx} \left\{ x \left[J_\mu(\alpha x) \frac{d}{dx} J(\xi_i x) - J_\mu(\xi_i x) \frac{d}{dx} J_\mu(\alpha x) \right] \right\}$$

Integrating with respect to x from 0 to a and remembering that $J_\mu(\xi_i a)$ is zero, we have

$$(\alpha^2 - \xi_i^2) \int_0^a xJ_\mu(\alpha x)J_\mu(\xi_i x)dx = \xi_i aJ_\mu(\alpha a)J_\mu'(\xi_i a)$$

whence

$$\int_0^a \frac{J_\mu(\alpha x)}{J_\mu(\alpha a)} xJ_\mu(\xi_i x)dx = \frac{\xi_i a}{\alpha^2 - \xi_i^2} J_\mu'(\xi_i a)$$

In other words, we have shown that

$$J_\mu \left[\frac{J_\mu(\alpha x)}{J_\mu(\alpha a)} \right] = \frac{\xi_i a}{\alpha^2 - \xi_i^2} J_\mu'(\xi_i a) \tag{66}$$

and in particular that

$$J_0 \left[\frac{J_0(\alpha x)}{J_0(\alpha a)} \right] = - \frac{\xi_i a}{\alpha^2 - \xi_i^2} J_1(\xi_i a) \tag{67}$$

If we make the substitution $c = 1$ in equation (64) and subtract from equation (67), we have finally

$$\mathbf{J}_0 \left[\frac{J_0(\alpha x)}{J_0(\alpha a)} - 1 \right] = - \frac{J_1(\xi_i a) a}{\xi_i (1 - \xi_i^2/\alpha^2)} \qquad (68)$$

Case 2: ξ_i is a root of equation (46). Similar results to those derived above hold for the finite Hankel transform (42) when the parameter ξ_i appearing in the definition is a root of equation (46). We shall consider only one such property as it is the only one we require in the subsequent application to particular problems.

Proceeding as in the derivation of equation (59), we see that

$$\int_0^a x \left(\frac{d^2f}{dx^2} + \frac{1}{x} \frac{df}{dx} \right) J_0(\xi_i x) dx$$

$$= \left[x \frac{df}{dx} J_0(x \xi_i) - x \xi_i f J_0'(\xi_i x) \right]_0^a - \xi_i^2 \int_0^a x f(x) J_0(x \xi_i) dx$$

The expression in the brackets vanishes at the lower limit. At the upper limit we may write

$$- \xi_i J_0'(a \xi_i) = h J_0(a \xi_i)$$

since ξ_i is a root of equation (46). We therefore have shown that if ξ_i is a root of equation (46)

$$\mathbf{J}_0 \left(\frac{d^2f}{dx^2} + \frac{1}{x} \frac{df}{dx} \right) = a J_0(a \xi_i) \left(\frac{df}{dx} + hf \right)_{x=a} - \xi_i^2 \mathbf{J}_0(f) \qquad (69)$$

This equation shows us the circumstances under which the finite Hankel transform defined by equations (42) and (46) is used; for if $f(x)$ is defined in the region $0 \leq x \leq a$, and if

$$\frac{df}{dx} + hf = 0 \qquad \text{when } x = a \qquad (70)$$

then

$$\mathbf{J}_0 \left(\frac{d^2f}{dx^2} + \frac{1}{x} \frac{df}{dx} \right) = - \xi_i^2 \mathbf{J}_0(f) \qquad (71)$$

Boundary conditions of the type (70) arise in the discussion of diffusion phenomena, and the boundary value problems to which they give rise may then be solved by employing a finite Hankel transform of this type (cf. Sec. 23.5, case 3).

Case 3: ξ_i is a root of equation (52). In the application of Theorem 32 to boundary value problems we require the analogue of equation (59). Integrating by parts, we find that

$$\int_b^a x[J_\mu(x\xi_i)G_\mu(a\xi_i) - J_\mu(a\xi_i)G_\mu(x\xi_i)]\left(\frac{d^2f}{dx^2} + \frac{1}{x}\frac{df}{dx}\right)dx$$
$$= -\xi_i\{xf(x)[J_\mu'(x\xi_i)G_\mu(a\xi_i) - J_\mu(a\xi_i)G_\mu'(x\xi_i)]\}$$
$$+ \xi_i\int_b^a \left\{xf(x)\frac{d}{dx}[J_\mu'(x\xi_i)G_\mu(a\xi_i) - J_\mu(a\xi_i)G_\mu'(x\xi_i)]\right.$$
$$\left. + f(x)[J_\mu'(x\xi_i)G_\mu(a\xi_i) - J_\mu(a\xi_i)G_\mu'(x\xi_i)]\right\}dx$$

Now it can be shown that

$$J_\mu'(\xi_ib)G_\mu(\xi_ia) - G_\mu'(\xi_ib)J_\mu(\xi_ia) = \frac{1}{\xi_ib}\frac{J_\mu(\xi_ia)}{J_\mu(\xi_ib)} \tag{72}$$

and since both J_μ and G_μ are solutions of Bessel's equation, we find that

$$\int_0^a x\left(\frac{d^2f}{dx^2} + \frac{1}{x}\frac{df}{dx}\right)[J_\mu(x\xi_i)G_\mu(a\xi_i) - J_\mu(a\xi_i)G_\mu(x\xi_i)]dx$$
$$= \int_0^a \left(\frac{\mu^2}{x^2} - \xi_i^2\right)xf(x)[J_\mu(x\xi_i)G_\mu(a\xi_i) - J_\mu(a\xi_i)G_\mu(x\xi_i)]dx$$

In the notation of equation (51) we have therefore

$$\mathsf{H}_\mu\left(\frac{d^2f}{dx^2} + \frac{1}{x}\frac{df}{dx} - \frac{\mu^2}{x^2}\right) = \frac{J_\mu(\xi_ia)}{J_\mu(\xi_ib)}f(b) - f(a) - \xi_i^2\mathsf{H}_\mu(f) \tag{73}$$

In particular if $f(x)$ vanishes when $x = a$ and when $x = b$, then

$$\mathsf{H}_\mu\left(\frac{d^2f}{dx^2} + \frac{1}{x}\frac{df}{dx} - \frac{\mu^2}{x^2}\right) = -\xi_i^2\mathsf{H}_\mu(f) \tag{74}$$

A special transform of this type which we shall employ later is that of the function $(x^2 - a^2)/x$. It is readily deduced from equations (9) and (10), Appendix A, that

$$\int_b^a (x^2 - a^2)J_1(\xi_ix)dx = \frac{1}{\xi_i^2}[2xJ_1(\xi_ix) - \xi_i(x^2 - a^2)J_0(\xi_ix)]_b^a \tag{75}$$

Now the Bessel function G_1 satisfies precisely the same recurrence relations as the function J_1, so that we have similarly

$$\int_b^a (x^2 - a^2)G_1(\xi_ix)dx = \frac{1}{\xi_i^2}[2xG_1(\xi_ix) - \xi_i(x^2 - a^2)G_0(\xi_ix)]_b^a \tag{76}$$

Multiplying equation (75) by $G_1(\xi_ia)$, equation (76) by $J_1(\xi_ia)$, and subtracting, we find that

$$\int_b^a (x^2 - a^2)[J_1(\xi_ix)G_1(\xi_ia) - G_1(\xi_ix)J_1(\xi_ia)]dx$$
$$= -\frac{b^2 - a^2}{\xi_i}[J_0(\xi_ib)G_1(\xi_ia) - G_0(\xi_ib)J_1(\xi_ia)]$$

Making use of the recurrence relations

$$J_0(\xi_i b) = J_1'(\xi_i b) + \frac{1}{\xi_i b} J_1(\xi_i b), \qquad G_0(\xi_i b) = G_1'(\xi_i b) + \frac{1}{\xi_i b} G_1(\xi_i b)$$

and the fact that the functions $J_1(\xi_i a)$, $J_1(\xi_i b)$, $G_1(\xi_i a)$, and $G_1(\xi_i b)$ satisfy the relations (52) and (72), we obtain the integral

$$\int_b^a (x^2 - a^2) [J_1(\xi_i x) G_1(\xi_i a) - G_1(\xi_i x) J_1(\xi_i a)] dx = \frac{a^2 - b^2}{b \xi_i^2} \frac{J_1(\xi_i a)}{J_1(\xi_i b)}$$

which, in the notation of equation (51), is equivalent to

$$H_1\left(\frac{x^2 - a^2}{x}\right) = \frac{a^2 - b^2}{b \xi_i^2} \frac{J_1(\xi_i a)}{J_1(\xi_i b)} \tag{77}$$

CHAPTER 4

THE THEORY OF VIBRATIONS

Having sketched the main properties of Fourier and Hankel transforms, we shall, in the following chapters, show how we make use of these properties in deriving the solutions of certain classical problems in mathematical physics.

15. Electrical Oscillations in Simple Circuits

Before passing on to the consideration of the theory of vibrations which are governed by partial differential equations we shall consider briefly oscillations which are governed by an ordinary linear differential equation. The treatment given here is brief because the subject is treated extensively in the books on operational calculus by Churchill and by Carslaw and Jaeger. Here we shall consider the electrical oscillations in a simple circuit mainly because we shall often make use of the solution of the differential equation involved. The mathematical problem for an electrical circuit of this type is substantially the same as that for the forced vibrations of a pendulum suspended in a medium which is damping the vibrations. A simple change of notation and terminology enables us to pass from one problem to the other.

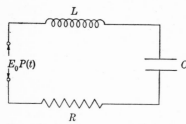

FIG. 6. Circuit containing a resistance R, a capacity C, and an inductance L.

Consider the electrical oscillations in a circuit containing a resistance R, an inductance L, a condenser of capacity C, and a source of electromotive force $E_0P(t)$, where E_0 is a constant and $P(t)$ is a known function of the time t. If the charge on the plates of the condenser is q, then the potential difference across the plates is q/C. Similarly if i is the current flowing through the resistance and the inductance, the differences of potential between their ends are Ri and $L(di/dt)$, respectively. By the equation of continuity

$$i = \frac{dq}{dt} \tag{1}$$

so that these potential differences may be written as $R\dot{q}$ and $L\ddot{q}$, respectively (dots denoting differentiation with respect to the time variable t). Thus we obtain the ordinary differential equation

$$L \frac{d^2q}{dt^2} + R \frac{dq}{dt} + \frac{q}{C} = E_0 P(t) \tag{2}$$

for the determination of the charge q which accumulates on the plates of the condenser. If we assume that initially this charge is Q and that a current I is flowing in the circuit, then we obtain the initial conditions

$$q = Q, \qquad \frac{dq}{dt} = i = I \qquad \text{when } t = 0 \tag{3}$$

Our problem is then that of solving the ordinary differential equation (2) subject to the initial conditions (3).

If we write

$$\theta(p) = \int_0^\infty e^{-pt} q(t) dt, \qquad \phi(p) = \int_0^\infty e^{-pt} P(t) dt \tag{4}$$

then it follows from Sec. 6.2 that

$$\int_0^\infty e^{-pt} \frac{dq}{dt} dt = -Q + p\theta(p)$$

$$\int_0^\infty e^{-pt} \frac{d^2q}{dt^2} dt = -I - pQ + p^2\theta(p)$$

so that if we multiply both sides of equation (2) by e^{-pt} and integrate with respect to t from 0 to ∞ we have

$$L(-I - pQ + p^2\theta) + R(-Q + p\theta) + \frac{\theta}{C} = E_0\phi(p)$$

that is,

$$(Lp^2 + Rp + \gamma)\theta(p) = E_0\phi(p) + LI + QR + LQp \tag{5}$$

where, for convenience, we have written $\gamma = 1/C$. It follows from equation (5) that

$$\theta = \theta_1 + \theta_2$$

where

$$\theta_1 = \frac{E_0}{Lp^2 + Rp + \gamma} \phi(p)$$

and

$$\theta_2 = \frac{LI + QR + LQp}{Lp^2 + Rp + \gamma}$$

If we suppose that $R < 2(L/C)^{\frac{1}{2}}$, we may write

$$Lp^2 + Rp + \gamma = L \left[\left(p + \frac{R}{2L} \right)^2 + \omega^2 \right]$$

where

$$\omega^2 = \frac{1}{LC} - \frac{R^2}{4L^2} > 0 \tag{6}$$

Using the inversion formula for the Laplace transform, we have

$$q_1(t) = \frac{1}{2\pi i} \int_{\gamma' - i\infty}^{\gamma' + i\infty} \theta_1(p)e^{pt}\, dp$$

$$= \frac{E_0}{L} \left[\frac{1}{2\pi i} \int_{\gamma' - i\infty}^{\gamma' + i\infty} \frac{\phi(p)e^{pt}\, dp}{\left(p + \dfrac{R}{2L}\right)^2 + \omega^2} \right] \tag{7}$$

Now since

$$\int_0^\infty e^{-\Omega t} \sin \omega t\, dt = \frac{\omega}{\omega^2 + \Omega^2}$$

it follows that

$$\int_0^\infty e^{-pt}e^{-Rt/2L} \sin \omega t\, dt = \frac{\omega}{\left(p + \dfrac{R}{2L}\right)^2 + \omega^2} \tag{8}$$

showing that

$$\frac{1}{\omega} e^{-Rt/2L} \sin \omega t$$

has the Laplace transform

$$\frac{1}{\left(p + \dfrac{R}{2L}\right)^2 + \omega^2}$$

In addition the function $P(t)$ has the Laplace transform $\phi(p)$ so that by the Faltung theorem for the Laplace transform [equation (69), Chap. 1] we obtain

$$\frac{1}{2\pi i} \int_{\gamma' - i\infty}^{\gamma' + i\infty} \frac{\phi(p)e^{pt}\, dp}{\left(p + \dfrac{R}{2L}\right)^2 + \omega^2} = \frac{1}{\omega} \int_0^t P(\eta)e^{-R(t-\eta)/2L} \sin \omega(t - \eta)d\eta$$

and thus, substituting from this result in equation (7), we find that

$$q_1(t) = \frac{E_0}{\omega L} e^{-Rt/2L} \int_0^t P(\eta)e^{R\eta/2L} \sin \omega(t - \eta)d\eta \tag{9}$$

Similarly the expression for the second term of q is

$$q_2(t) = \frac{1}{2\pi i} \int_{\gamma' - i\infty}^{\gamma' + i\infty} \theta_2(p)e^{pt}\, dp$$

$$= \frac{1}{2\pi i} \int_{\gamma' - i\infty}^{\gamma' + i\infty} \frac{LI + QR + LQp}{Lp^2 + Rp + \gamma} e^{pt}\, dp$$

which may be written in the form

$$q_2(t) = \frac{Q}{2\pi i} \int_{\gamma'-i\infty}^{\gamma'+i\infty} \frac{(p + R/2L)e^{pt}\,dp}{(p + R/2L)^2 + \omega^2}$$
$$+ \left(I + \frac{RQ}{2L}\right) \frac{1}{2\pi i} \int_{\gamma'-i\infty}^{\gamma'+i\infty} \frac{e^{pt}\,dp}{(p + R/2L)^2 + \omega^2}$$

It follows from equation (8) that

$$\frac{1}{2\pi i} \int_{\gamma'-i\infty}^{\gamma'+i\infty} \frac{e^{pt}\,dp}{(p + R/2L)^2 + \omega^2} = \frac{1}{\omega} e^{-Rt/2L} \sin \omega t$$

and from the result

$$\int_0^\infty e^{-pt}e^{-Rt/2L} \cos \omega t\,dt = \frac{p + R/2L}{(p + R/2L)^2 + \omega^2}$$

that

$$\frac{1}{2\pi i} \int_{\gamma'-i\infty}^{\gamma'+i\infty} \frac{(p + R/2L)e^{pt}\,dp}{(p + R/2L)^2 + \omega^2} = e^{-Rt/2L} \cos \omega t$$

so that we have

$$q_2(t) = e^{-Rt/2L}\left[Q \cos \omega t + \frac{1}{\omega}\left(I + \frac{RQ}{2L}\right) \sin \omega t \right] \tag{10}$$

Adding equations (9) and (10), we obtain finally for the solution of our problem

$$q(t) = e^{-Rt/2L}\left[Q \cos \omega t + \frac{1}{\omega}\left(I + \frac{RQ}{2L}\right) \sin \omega t \right]$$
$$+ \frac{E_0}{\omega L} e^{-Rt/2L} \int_0^t P(\eta)e^{R\eta/2L} \sin \omega(t - \eta)d\eta \tag{11}$$

In particular if the resistance of the circuit is zero, *i.e.*, if $R = 0$, we obtain

$$q(t) = Q \cos \omega t + \frac{I}{\omega} \sin \omega t + \frac{E_0}{\omega L} \int_0^t P(\eta) \sin \omega(t - \eta)d\eta \tag{12}$$

The form of this solution which we shall use most frequently is that the solution of the equation

$$\frac{d^2q}{dt^2} + \omega^2 q = P(t)$$

for which $q = (dq/dt) = 0$ when $t = 0$ is

$$q(t) = \frac{1}{\omega} \int_0^t P(\eta) \sin \omega(t - \eta)d\eta \tag{13}$$

16. Transverse Vibrations of a Continuous String

16.1 Equation of motion. We shall begin by establishing the partial differential equation governing the transverse oscillations of a heavy string of mass ρ per unit length, *i.e.*, the vibrations in which every particle of the string is given a displacement perpendicular to the original direction of the string. We suppose that the string is stretched to a tension T between two points which may be considered as defining the x axis of coordinates and that there is an external force F per unit length acting normal to this direction. Let us now consider the motion of an element P_1P_2 of the string of length δs. Then resolving the tensions at P_1 and P_2 normal to the x axis, we obtain as our equation of motion

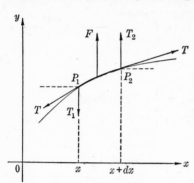

FIG. 7. The forces acting on an element of a continuous string.

$$\rho \, \delta s \, \frac{\partial^2 y}{\partial t^2} = F \, \delta s + T_2 - T_1$$

Now

$$T_2 = T_1 + \frac{\partial T_1}{\partial x} \, dx$$

so that

$$\rho \frac{ds}{dx} \frac{\partial^2 y}{\partial t^2} = F \frac{ds}{dx} + \frac{\partial T_1}{\partial x}$$

In terms of the tension T we have

$$T_1 = T \frac{\partial y}{\partial s} = T \frac{\partial y}{\partial x} \frac{dx}{ds}$$

If the transverse vibrations are small, we may neglect $(\partial y/\partial x)^2$ in comparison with unity, *i.e.*, we may take ds/dx to be unity and hence obtain as our equation of motion

$$\rho \, \frac{\partial^2 y}{\partial t^2} = F(x,t) + T \frac{\partial^2 y}{\partial x^2}$$

If we write $c^2 = T/\rho$, $F(x,t) = T\theta(x,t)$, then small transverse vibrations are governed by the partial differential equation

$$\frac{1}{c^2} \frac{\partial^2 y}{\partial t^2} = \theta(x,t) + \frac{\partial^2 y}{\partial x^2} \tag{14}$$

16.2 Free vibrations of an infinite string. As a first example of the solution of equation (14) by the use of the theory of integral transforms, we consider the motion of the infinite string $-\infty \le x \le \infty$ when it is free from external force, *i.e.*, the function $\theta(x,t)$ is identically zero. The motion is produced by the string being drawn aside from its equilibrium position and being given a prescribed velocity. In other words, we have to solve the partial differential equation (14) subject to the initial conditions

$$y = f(x), \quad \frac{\partial y}{\partial t} = g(x) \qquad \text{at } t = 0$$

where the functions $f(x)$ and $g(x)$ are prescribed.

To solve equation (14), we multiply it (after putting $\theta \equiv 0$) by $\exp(i\xi x)$ and integrate over x from $-\infty$ to ∞ to obtain

$$\frac{1}{c^2} \frac{\partial^2}{\partial t^2} \int_{-\infty}^{\infty} y(x,t)e^{i\xi x}\,dx = \int_{-\infty}^{\infty} \frac{\partial^2 y}{\partial x^2} e^{i\xi x}\,dx \tag{15}$$

Integrating by parts, we see that

$$\int_{-\infty}^{\infty} \frac{\partial^2 y}{\partial x^2} e^{i\xi x}\,dx = \left[\left(\frac{\partial y}{\partial x} - i\xi y\right)e^{i\xi x}\right]_{-\infty}^{\infty} - \xi^2 \int_{-\infty}^{\infty} y e^{i\xi x}\,dx$$

If we assume that y and $\partial y/\partial x$ both tend to zero as $|x| \to \infty$, the expression in the brackets vanishes. Thus if we write

$$Y = \left(\frac{1}{2\pi}\right)^{\frac{1}{2}} \int_{-\infty}^{\infty} y(x,t)e^{i\xi x}\,dx \tag{16}$$

equation (15) may be written in the form

$$\frac{1}{c^2} \frac{d^2 Y}{dt^2} + \xi^2 Y = 0 \tag{17}$$

With the transformation (16) we have therefore reduced the problem of solving a partial differential equation to that of solving the ordinary differential equation (17). We must now examine the initial conditions to be satisfied at $t = 0$. Since, at $t = 0$, $y = f(x)$, it follows that

$$Y = \left(\frac{1}{2\pi}\right)^{\frac{1}{2}} \int_{-\infty}^{\infty} f(x)e^{i\xi x}\,dx \equiv F(\xi) \qquad t = 0$$

and similarly that

$$\frac{dY}{dt} = \left(\frac{1}{2\pi}\right)^{\frac{1}{2}} \int_{-\infty}^{\infty} g(x)e^{i\xi x}\,dx \equiv G(\xi) \qquad t = 0$$

The solution of equation (17) satisfying these initial conditions is

$$Y = \frac{1}{2} F(\xi)(e^{ict\xi} + e^{-ict\xi}) + \frac{G(\xi)}{2ic\xi} (e^{ict\xi} - e^{-ict\xi})$$

The relation between y and Y is simply the Fourier inversion formula

$$y(x,t) = \left(\frac{1}{2\pi}\right)^{\frac{1}{2}} \int_{-\infty}^{\infty} Y(\xi,t)e^{-i\xi x} d\xi$$

so that substituting for $Y(\xi,t)$ we obtain the solution

$$y(x,t) = \frac{1}{2}\left\{\left(\frac{1}{2\pi}\right)^{\frac{1}{2}} \int_{-\infty}^{\infty} F(\xi)[e^{-i\xi(x-ct)} + e^{-i\xi(x+ct)}]d\xi\right\}$$

$$+ \frac{1}{2c}\left\{\left(\frac{1}{2\pi}\right)^{\frac{1}{2}} \int_{-\infty}^{\infty} \frac{G(\xi)}{i\xi}[e^{-i\xi(x-ct)} - e^{-i\xi(x+ct)}]d\xi\right\} \quad (18)$$

Now since $f(x)$ and $F(\xi)$ are Fourier transforms, we have

$$f(x) = \left(\frac{1}{2\pi}\right)^{\frac{1}{2}} \int_{-\infty}^{\infty} F(\xi)e^{-i\xi x} d\xi$$

so that

$$f(x \pm ct) = \left(\frac{1}{2\pi}\right)^{\frac{1}{2}} \int_{-\infty}^{\infty} F(\xi)e^{-i\xi(x\pm ct)} d\xi \quad (19)$$

Also, for a similar reason,

$$g(u) = \left(\frac{1}{2\pi}\right)^{\frac{1}{2}} \int_{-\infty}^{\infty} G(\xi)e^{-i\xi u} d\xi$$

Integrating both sides of this equation with respect to u from $x - ct$ to $x + ct$, we obtain

$$\int_{x-ct}^{x+ct} g(u)du = \left(\frac{1}{2\pi}\right)^{\frac{1}{2}} \int_{-\infty}^{\infty} \frac{G(\xi)}{i\xi}[e^{-i\xi(x-ct)} - e^{-i\xi(x+ct)}]d\xi \quad (20)$$

Substituting from equations (19) and (20) into equation (18), we obtain finally

$$y(x,t) = \frac{1}{2}[f(x + ct) + f(x - ct)] + \frac{1}{2c}\int_{x-ct}^{x+ct} g(u)du \quad (21)$$

16.3 Free vibrations of a semiinfinite string. We consider now the case of a string which is fixed at the origin $(0,0)$ and is stretched along the positive x axis to a tension T. The free transverse vibrations are governed by the equation

$$\frac{1}{c^2}\frac{\partial^2 y}{\partial t^2} = \frac{\partial^2 y}{\partial x^2} \qquad x \geq 0 \quad (22)$$

where we shall suppose that $y = f(x)$ and $\partial y/\partial t = g(x)$ when $t = 0$. To solve this boundary value problem we multiply both sides of equation (22) by $\sin(\xi x)$, integrate with respect to x over the range $(0,\infty)$, and note that

$$\int_0^{\infty} \frac{\partial^2 y}{\partial x^2}\sin \xi x \, dx = \left[\frac{\partial y}{\partial x}\sin \xi x - \xi y \cos \xi x\right]_0^{\infty} - \xi^2 \int_0^{\infty} y \sin \xi x \, dx$$

Now since the string is fixed at the origin, we shall have $y = 0$ at $x = 0$ for all values of t, and we assume that y and $\partial y / \partial x$ both tend to zero as x tends to infinity so that

$$\left(\frac{2}{\pi}\right)^{\frac{1}{2}} \int_0^\infty \frac{\partial^2 y}{\partial x^2} \sin (\xi x) dx = -\xi^2 Y_s(\xi)$$

where

$$Y_s(\xi,t) = \left(\frac{2}{\pi}\right)^{\frac{1}{2}} \int_0^\infty y(x,t) \sin (\xi x) dx \qquad (23)$$

Thus equation (22) is equivalent to

$$\frac{1}{c^2} \frac{d^2 Y_s}{dt^2} + \xi^2 Y_s = 0 \qquad (24)$$

The appropriate solution of equation (24) is then

$$Y_s(\xi,t) = F_s(\xi) \cos (c\xi t) + \frac{G_s(\xi)}{c\xi} \sin (c\xi t)$$

where

$$F_s(\xi) = \left(\frac{2}{\pi}\right)^{\frac{1}{2}} \int_0^\infty f(x) \sin (\xi x) dx$$

and $G_s(\xi)$ is defined similarly.

Inverting equation (23) by the Fourier sine formula (36), Chap. 1, we have

$$y(x,t) = \left(\frac{2}{\pi}\right)^{\frac{1}{2}} \int_0^\infty Y_s(\xi,t) \sin (\xi x) d\xi$$

$$= \left(\frac{2}{\pi}\right)^{\frac{1}{2}} \int_0^\infty \left[F_s \cos (ct\xi) \sin (\xi x) + \frac{1}{c\xi} G_s \sin (\xi ct) \sin (\xi x) \right] d\xi$$

$$= \frac{1}{2} \left(\frac{2}{\pi}\right)^{\frac{1}{2}} \int_0^\infty F_s(\xi)[\sin \xi(x + ct) + \sin \xi(x - ct)] d\xi$$

$$+ \frac{1}{2c} \left(\frac{2}{\pi}\right)^{\frac{1}{2}} \int_0^\infty G_s(\xi)[\cos \xi(x - ct) - \cos \xi(x + ct)] \frac{d\xi}{\xi}$$

If $x > 0$, $f(x)$ is defined by the formula

$$f(x) = \left(\frac{2}{\pi}\right)^{\frac{1}{2}} \int_0^\infty F_s(\xi) \sin (\xi x) d\xi \qquad x > 0$$

and $g(x)$ by a similar formula. It follows immediately then by reasoning similar to that employed at the end of the last section that, if $x > ct$,

$$y(x,t) = \frac{1}{2} [f(x + ct) + f(x - ct)] + \frac{1}{2c} \int_{x-ct}^{x+ct} g(u) du \qquad (25)$$

The corresponding formula when $x < ct$ may be derived in a similar way.

16.4 Free vibrations of a string of finite length. We shall next consider the case in which the string is stretched to a tension T between two points $(0,0)$ and $(L,0)$ which are a finite distance L apart and lie on the x axis. The equation of motion is once again equation (22), but now x is restricted to the closed interval $0 \leq x \leq L$. If we change the independent variable from x to z by the substitution $z = \pi x/L$, then z lies in the range $0 \leq z \leq \pi$ and the differential equation (22) becomes

$$\frac{L^2}{\pi^2 c^2} \frac{\partial^2 y}{\partial t^2} = \frac{\partial^2 y}{\partial z^2} \qquad 0 \leq z \leq \pi \qquad (26)$$

Furthermore since the string is fixed at the points $x = 0$ and $x = L$, it follows that, for all values of t, $y = 0$ when $z = 0$ or π. Now

$$\int_0^\pi \frac{\partial^2 y}{\partial z^2} \sin (nz) dz = \left[\frac{\partial y}{\partial z} \sin (nz) - ny \cos (nz) \right]_0^\pi - n^2 \int_0^\pi y \sin (nz) dz$$

and the term in the brackets vanishes if n is an integer. Therefore if we multiply equation (26) by $\sin (nz)$ and integrate with respect to z from 0 to π, we obtain the ordinary differential equation

$$\frac{d^2 \bar{y}_s(n)}{dt^2} + \frac{\pi^2 c^2 n^2}{L^2} \bar{y}_s(n) = 0 \qquad (27)$$

for the determination of the finite sine transform

$$\bar{y}_s(n,t) = \int_0^\pi y(z,t) \sin (nz) dz \qquad (28)$$

If initially, *i.e.*, at time $t = 0$,

$$y = f(x), \qquad \frac{\partial y}{\partial t} = g(x)$$

then the initial conditions on $\bar{y}_s(n)$ are

$$\bar{y}_s(n) = \bar{f}_s(n), \qquad \frac{d\bar{y}_s}{dt} = \bar{g}_s(n)$$

where $\bar{f}_s(n)$ and $\bar{g}_s(n)$ are the finite sine transforms of the functions $f(x)$ and $g(x)$ defined by formulas similar to equation (28). The solution of the ordinary differential equation (27) subject to these initial conditions is readily seen to be

$$\bar{y}_s(n,t) = \bar{f}_s(n) \cos \left(\frac{\pi n c t}{L} \right) + \bar{g}_s(n) \frac{L}{\pi n c} \sin \left(\frac{\pi n c t}{L} \right)$$

The relation between the functions $y(x,t)$ and $\bar{y}_s(n)$ is given by equation (11), Chap. 3, which in this case leads to the result

$$y(z,t) = \frac{2}{\pi} \sum_{n=1}^{\infty} \bar{y}_s(n) \sin(nz)$$

$$= \frac{2}{\pi} \sum_{n=1}^{\infty} \bar{f}_s(n) \sin(nz) \cos\left(\frac{n\pi ct}{L}\right) + \frac{2L}{\pi^2 c} \sum_{n=1}^{\infty} \frac{\bar{g}_s(n)}{n} \sin(nz) \sin\left(\frac{n\pi ct}{L}\right)$$

Reverting to the original variable x and noting that

$$\bar{f}_s(n) = \int_0^{\pi} f(z) \sin(nz)dz = \frac{\pi}{L} \int_0^{L} f(u) \sin\left(\frac{n\pi u}{L}\right) du$$

we obtain finally as our solution

$$y(x,t) = \frac{2}{L} \sum_{n=1}^{\infty} \sin\frac{n\pi x}{L} \cos\frac{n\pi ct}{L} \int_0^{L} f(u) \sin\frac{n\pi u}{L} du$$

$$+ \frac{2}{\pi c} \sum_{n=1}^{\infty} \frac{1}{n} \sin\frac{n\pi x}{L} \sin\frac{n\pi ct}{L} \int_0^{L} g(u) \sin\frac{n\pi u}{L} du \quad (29)$$

As an example of the use of this formula and of the Dirac delta function we shall consider the free vibrations of a string of finite length resulting from the application of an impulse to one point of the string. If the string is initially at rest in its equilibrium position, we have

$$f(x) = 0 \quad (30)$$

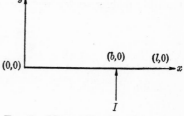

FIG. 8. The application of a normal impulse to a string of finite length.

Let us suppose that at the instant $t = 0$ the velocity of the point of the string whose abscissa is x is $g(x)$. Then the momentum imparted to an element of length dx is $\rho\, dx\, g(x)$, where ρ is the linear density. Thus the total impulse given to the string is

$$I = \rho \int_0^{L} g(x)dx$$

If the impulse is applied to the single point $x = b$ of the string (cf. Fig. 8), then the function $g(x)$ will be zero when $x \neq b$ and thus we may write $g(x) = \lambda\, \delta(x - b)$ where $\delta(x - b)$ is a Dirac δ function. The constant λ must then be chosen to satisfy the relation

$$I = \rho\lambda \int_0^{L} \delta(x - b)dx = \rho\lambda$$

In other words, $\lambda = I/\rho$, and we may write

$$g(x) = \frac{I}{\rho} \delta(x - b) \tag{31}$$

It follows at once from this equation that

$$\int_0^L g(u) \sin \frac{n\pi u}{L}\, du = \frac{I}{\rho} \int_0^L \delta(u - b) \sin \frac{n\pi u}{L}\, du = \frac{I}{\rho} \sin \frac{n\pi b}{L}$$

so that substituting from equations (30) and (31) into equation (29) we obtain for the subsequent displacement of the string from its equilibrium position

$$y(x,t) = \frac{2I}{\pi \rho c} \sum_{n=1}^{\infty} \frac{1}{n} \sin \frac{n\pi x}{L} \sin \frac{n\pi b}{L} \sin \frac{n\pi c t}{L} \tag{32}$$

with $0 \leq x \leq L$, $0 \leq b \leq L$, and $t > 0$.

16.5 Forced vibrations. The forced vibrations of a light string are governed by equation (14). If we assume that the string is stretched to a tension T between the two points $(0,0)$ and $(L,0)$ on the x axis, the motion will be described by equation (14) with the variable x restricted to the closed interval $0 \leq x \leq L$. Once again changing the independent variable from x to z where $z = \pi x/L$, we see that equation (14) becomes

$$\frac{1}{c^2} \frac{\partial^2 y}{\partial t^2} = \theta\left(\frac{Lz}{\pi}, t\right) + \frac{\pi^2}{L^2} \frac{\partial^2 y}{\partial z^2}$$

with $0 \leq z \leq \pi$. As in the last section we obtain the differential equation

$$\frac{d^2 \bar{y}_s(n)}{dt^2} + \frac{c^2 \pi^2 n^2}{L^2} \bar{y}_s(n) = c^2 \bar{\theta}_s(n,t)$$

where $\bar{y}_s(n)$ is defined by equation (28) and $\theta_s(n,t)$ by

$$\bar{\theta}_s(n,t) = \int_0^{\pi} \theta\left(\frac{Lz}{\pi}, t\right) \sin (nz)\, dz$$

It follows directly from equation (13) that, if $\theta = 0$ when $t < 0$ and if the string is set in motion from rest in its equilibrium position,

$$\bar{y}_s(n) = \frac{cL}{\pi n} \int_0^t \bar{\theta}_s(n,\tau) \sin \left[\frac{n\pi c}{L} (t - \tau)\right] d\tau \tag{33}$$

Inverting this equation by the Fourier sine formula (11), Chap. 3, we obtain

$$y(x,t) = \frac{2}{\pi} \sum_{n=1}^{\infty} \bar{y}_s(n) \sin \frac{n\pi x}{L}$$

$$= \frac{2cL}{\pi^2} \sum_{n=1}^{\infty} \frac{1}{n} \sin \frac{n\pi x}{L} \int_0^t \bar{\theta}_s(n,\tau) \sin \left[\frac{n\pi c(t - \tau)}{L} \right] d\tau$$

If the applied force is concentrated at a point $x = b$, where, of course, $0 \leq b \leq L$, then we may write

$$\theta(x,t) = \frac{F(t)}{T} \delta(x - b)$$

which leads to

$$\bar{\theta}_s(n,t) = \frac{F(t)}{T} \int_0^{\pi} \delta\left(\frac{Lz}{\pi} - b \right) \sin (nz) dz = \frac{F(t)}{T} \sin \left(\frac{n\pi b}{L} \right)$$

and we obtain for the forced vibration

$$y(x,t) = \frac{2cL}{\pi^2 T} \sum_{n=1}^{\infty} \frac{1}{n} \sin \left(\frac{n\pi x}{L} \right) \sin \left(\frac{n\pi b}{L} \right) \int_0^t F(\tau) \sin \left[\frac{n\pi c(t - \tau)}{L} \right] d\tau$$

A similar analysis can be carried out easily for infinite and semiinfinite strings and is left as an exercise to the reader.

17. Oscillations of a Heavy Chain[1]

17.1 Introduction. The problem of solving the differential equation governing the oscillations of a heavy chain suspended from one end, first treated by Daniel Bernoulli,[2] is of some significance since it was in Bernoulli's analysis that the Bessel function of zero order appeared for the first time. We shall consider here the small transverse oscillations of a heavy chain of uniform line density ρ, suspended vertically from one end. Taking the origin of coordinates at the position of equilibrium of the lower end and the x axis along the equilibrium position of the chain, pointing vertically *upward* so that the fixed end of a chain of length L has coordinates $(L,0)$, we find that the tension T at the point with abscissa x is given by $T = g\rho x$. If we denote by y the small horizontal deflection of the chain from its equilibrium position, then the equation of motion of an element of the chain of length Δx is

$$\rho \Delta x \frac{\partial^2 y}{\partial t^2} = p(x,t)\Delta x + \frac{\partial}{\partial x} \left(T \frac{\partial y}{\partial x} \right) \Delta x \tag{34}$$

where $p(x,t)$ denotes the intensity of the external transverse force. If we

---

[1] I. N. Sneddon, *Phil. Mag.*, **39**, 229 (1948).

[2] For references see G. N. Watson, "The Theory of Bessel Functions" (Cambridge, London, 1922), p. 3.

divide both sides of this equation by Δx and then change the independent variable to z where $4x = gz^2$, we find that equation (34) reduces to the form

$$\left(\frac{\partial^2}{\partial z^2} + \frac{1}{z}\frac{\partial}{\partial z} - \frac{\partial^2}{\partial t^2}\right) y(z,t) + \frac{1}{\rho} p\left(\frac{1}{4} gz^2, t\right) = 0 \tag{35}$$

To solve the partial differential equation (35), we introduce the finite Hankel transforms

$$\bar{y}_\beta = \int_0^\beta zy(z,t)J_0(\xi_i z)dz, \qquad \bar{p}_\beta = \int_0^\beta zp\left(\frac{1}{4} gz^2, t\right)J_0(\xi_i z)dz \tag{36}$$

where, for convenience, we have written $\beta^2 = 4L/g$. The quantity ξ_i remains, for the moment, undefined. Then integrating by parts we obtain the relation

$$\int_0^\beta z\left(\frac{\partial^2 y}{\partial z^2} + \frac{1}{z}\frac{\partial y}{\partial z}\right)J_0(\xi_i z)dz = \left[z\frac{\partial y}{\partial z}J_0(\xi_i z)\right]_0^\beta - \xi_i[zyJ_0'(\xi_i z)]_0^\beta - \xi_i^2\bar{y}_\beta$$

Since the chain is fixed at the upper end, $y = 0$ when $z = \beta$ and it is obvious physically that for small oscillations $z(\partial y/\partial z) = 0$ at $z = 0$ so that if we choose ξ_i to be a root of the transcendental equation

$$J_0(\xi_i\beta) = 0 \tag{37}$$

we have

$$\int_0^\beta z\left(\frac{\partial^2 y}{\partial z^2} + \frac{1}{z}\frac{\partial y}{\partial z}\right)J_0(\xi_i z)dz = -\xi_i^2\bar{y}_\beta$$

Hence, multiplying equation (35) throughout by $zJ_0(\xi_i z)$ and integrating with respect to z from 0 to β, we obtain

$$\left(\frac{d^2}{dt^2} + \xi_i^2\right)\bar{y}_\beta = \frac{1}{\rho}\bar{p}_\beta(\xi_i) \tag{38}$$

The solution of this ordinary linear differential equation subject to the correct initial conditions gives the value of $\bar{y}_\beta$, whence, by equation (45), Chap. 3, we derive

$$y(x,t) = \frac{2}{\beta^2}\sum_i \bar{y}_\beta \frac{J_0(\xi_i z)}{[J_1(\xi_i\beta)]^2} \tag{39}$$

the sum being taken over all the positive roots of equation (37).

If the chain is very long so that L may be taken to be infinite, we replace equations (36) by

$$\bar{y} = \int_0^\infty zy(z)J_0(\xi z)dz, \qquad \bar{p} = \int_0^\infty zp\left(\frac{1}{4} gz^2, t\right)J_0(\xi z)dz \tag{40}$$

Proceeding as before we find that $\bar{y}$ satisfies the differential equation (38) but with ξ_i replaced by ξ. In this case equation (15), Chap. 2, gives for the relation between y and $\bar{y}$

$$y(z) = \int_0^\infty \xi \bar{y}(\xi) J_0(\xi z) d\xi \tag{41}$$

17.2 Free vibrations of a chain of finite length. If the vibrations are free we may take

$$p(x,t) = \bar{p}_\beta(\xi_i,t) = 0$$

so that the appropriate solution of equation (38) is

$$\bar{y}_\beta = A(\xi_i) \cos (\xi_i t) + B(\xi_i) \sin (\xi_i t)$$

where the constants of integration are to be determined from the prescribed initial conditions. For example, suppose that

$$y = f(x), \qquad \frac{\partial y}{\partial t} = h(x)$$

when $t = 0$. Then the initial values of $\bar{y}_\beta$ and $d\bar{y}_\beta/dt$ at $t = 0$ are

$$\bar{y}_\beta = \int_0^\beta zf\left(\frac{1}{4} gz^2\right) J_0(\xi_i z) dz, \qquad \frac{d\bar{y}_\beta}{dt} = \int_0^\beta zh\left(\frac{1}{4} gz^2\right) J_0(\xi_i z) dz$$

whence we find that

$$\bar{y}_\beta = \int_0^\beta z\left[f\left(\frac{1}{4} gz^2\right) \cos (\xi_i t) + \xi_i^{-1} h\left(\frac{1}{4} gz^2\right) \sin (\xi_i t)\right] J_0(\xi_i z) dz$$

Inverting by the formula (39), we find that the subsequent transverse displacement is given by

$$y(z,t) = \frac{2}{\beta^2} \sum_i^\infty \frac{J_0(\xi_i z)}{[J_1(\xi_i \beta)]^2} \cos (\xi_i t) \int_0^\beta zf\left(\frac{1}{4} gz^2\right) J_0(\xi_i z) dz$$

$$+ \frac{2}{\beta^2} \sum_i^\infty \frac{J_0(\xi_i z)}{[J_1(\xi_i \beta)]^2} \frac{\sin (\xi_i t)}{\xi_i} \int_0^\beta zh\left(\frac{1}{4} gz^2\right) J_0(\xi_i z) dz$$

where the sums are taken over all the positive roots of equation (37). Reverting to the original variables, we have finally

$$y(x,t) = \frac{1}{L} \sum_i \cos\left(\frac{\alpha_i t g^{\frac{1}{2}}}{2L^{\frac{1}{4}}}\right) \frac{J_0(\alpha_i x^{\frac{1}{2}}/L^{\frac{1}{2}})}{[J_1(\alpha_i)]^2} \int_0^L f(u) J_0\left(\frac{\alpha_i u^{\frac{1}{2}}}{L^{\frac{1}{2}}}\right) du$$

$$+ \frac{2}{(Lg)^{\frac{1}{2}}} \sum_i \frac{1}{\alpha_i} \sin\left(\frac{\alpha_i t g^{\frac{1}{2}}}{2L^{\frac{1}{4}}}\right) \frac{J_0(\alpha_i x^{\frac{1}{2}}/L^{\frac{1}{2}})}{[J_1(\alpha_i)]^2} \int_0^L h(u) J_0\left(\frac{\alpha_i u^{\frac{1}{2}}}{L^{\frac{1}{2}}}\right) du \tag{42}$$

the summations now extending over all the positive roots of the equation

$$J_0(\alpha_i) = 0 \tag{43}$$

For example, if we take the initial velocity of the chain to be zero and assume that it is released from the position

$$y = f(x) = \epsilon\left(1 - \frac{x}{L}\right) \qquad 0 \le x \le L$$

then we find

$$\frac{1}{L}\int_0^L f(u)J_0\left(\frac{\alpha_i u^{\frac{1}{2}}}{L^{\frac{1}{2}}}\right)du = 2\epsilon\int_0^1 v(1 - v^2)J_0(\alpha_i v)dv = \frac{4\epsilon}{\alpha_i^2}J_2(\alpha_i)$$

If we now put $x = \alpha_i$, $n = 1$ into the recurrence relation

$$\frac{2n}{x}J_n(x) = J_{n-1}(x) + J_{n+1}(x)$$

we find, by virtue of the fact that α_i is a root of the equation (43), that

$$J_2(\alpha_i) = \frac{2}{\alpha_i}J_1(\alpha_i)$$

Hence, in this instance, we obtain finally for the transverse displacement of the chain

$$y(x,t) = 8\epsilon \sum_i \frac{J_0(\alpha_i x^{\frac{1}{2}}/L^{\frac{1}{2}})}{\alpha_i^3 J_1(\alpha_i)}\cos\left(\frac{\alpha_i t g^{\frac{1}{2}}}{2L^{\frac{1}{2}}}\right)$$

where the sum is taken over all the positive roots of equation (43).

It should be observed that the solution (42) may also be obtained by making use of the theory of the Laplace transform. If we put $p \equiv 0$ in equation (35) and multiply both sides by $\exp(-\lambda t)$, we have

$$\left(\frac{d^2}{dz^2} + \frac{1}{z}\frac{d}{dz}\right)\bar{y}_\lambda - \int_0^\infty \frac{\partial^2 y}{\partial t^2}e^{-\lambda t}\,dt = 0$$

where

$$\bar{y}_\lambda = \int_0^\infty y(z,t)e^{-\lambda t}\,dt$$

Now, integrating by parts,

$$\int_0^\infty \frac{\partial^2 y}{\partial t^2}e^{-\lambda t}\,dt = \left[\left(\frac{\partial y}{\partial t} + \lambda y\right)e^{-\lambda t}\right]_0^\infty + \lambda^2\bar{y}_\lambda$$

But when t tends to infinity, we assume that y and $\partial y/\partial t$ do not become infinite, and when $t = 0$, $y = f(x)$ and $\partial y/\partial t = h(x)$ so that

$$\int_0^\infty \frac{\partial^2 y}{\partial t^2}e^{-\lambda t}\,dt = -[h(x) + \lambda f(x)] + \lambda^2\bar{y}_\lambda$$

so that the differential equation for the determination of $\bar{y}_\lambda$ is

$$\left(\frac{d^2}{dz^2} + \frac{1}{z}\frac{d}{dz} - \lambda^2\right)\bar{y}_\lambda = -h\left(\frac{1}{4}gz^2\right) - \lambda f\left(\frac{1}{4}gz^2\right)$$

Furthermore we know that $\bar{y}$ is zero for $z = \beta$ and finite when $z = 0$. If $\bar{y}_\lambda$ is the appropriate solution of this equation, y can be determined from the Laplace inversion theorem as the integral

$$y = \frac{1}{2\pi i}\int_{c-i\infty}^{c+i\infty}\bar{y}_\lambda e^{\lambda t}\,d\lambda$$

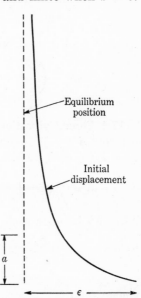

The contour integrations involved in the evaluation of this expression are rather complicated, but it can be shown that they lead to equation (42).

17.3 Free vibrations of a very long chain. As an example of the solution of the equation for the free vibrations of a very long chain we shall consider the motion of the semiinfinite chain $0 \le x \le \infty$, which is initially drawn aside to the form

$$y = f(x) = \frac{\epsilon}{1 + (x/a)} \qquad (44)$$

Fig. 9.   The initial displacement of a very long chain which is vibrating freely under gravity.

(cf. Fig. 9) and then released from rest at the instant $t = 0$. The problem is to determine the form of the chain at any subsequent time. As in the last section we may take the function $\bar{p}(\xi,t)$ occurring in equation (38) to be identically zero and obtain the solution

$$\bar{y}(\xi,t) = f(\xi)\cos \xi t \qquad (45)$$

where

$$\bar{f}(\xi) = \int_0^\infty zf\left(\frac{1}{4}gz^2\right)J_0(\xi z)dz = \epsilon\alpha\int_0^\infty\frac{zJ_0(\xi z)dz}{(\alpha^2 + z^2)^{\frac{1}{2}}} = \epsilon\alpha\frac{e^{-\alpha\xi}}{\xi}$$

and we have written $\alpha^2 = 4a/g$.   Inserting this value of $\bar{f}(\xi)$ into equation (45) and inverting by means of the Hankel formula (41), we obtain

$$y = \epsilon\alpha\int_0^\infty e^{-\alpha\xi}\cos \xi tJ_0(\xi z)d\xi$$

The integral on the right-hand side of this equation is the real part of the integral

$$\epsilon\int_0^\infty\exp\left[-\left(1 + \frac{it}{\alpha}\right)\xi\right]J_0\left(\frac{\xi z}{\alpha}\right)d\xi$$

so that, making use of the well-known result [cf. equation (20) Appendix A],

$$\int_0^\infty e^{-wx}J_0(\rho x)dx = (\rho^2 + w^2)^{-\frac{1}{2}}$$

and, equating real parts, we obtain finally

$$y = \epsilon R^{-\frac{1}{2}} \cos \tfrac{1}{2}\,\varphi \tag{46}$$

where R and φ are defined by the relations

$$R^2 = \left(\frac{x}{a} + 1 - \frac{gt^2}{4a}\right)^2 - \frac{gt^2}{a}, \qquad \tan \varphi = \frac{(gt^2/a)^{\frac{1}{2}}}{\dfrac{x}{a} + 1 - \dfrac{gt^2}{4a}}$$

17.4 Forced vibrations of a chain of finite length. Suppose that an external force of magnitude $\rho\psi(t)$ acts uniformly over the segment $(a - \epsilon, a + \epsilon)$ of the chain. Then, in obvious notation

$$\bar{p}_\beta = \frac{\rho}{2\epsilon}\,\psi(t)\int_{\alpha_1}^{\alpha_2} zJ_0(\xi_i z)dz = \frac{\rho\psi(t)}{2\epsilon}\left[\alpha_2 J_1(\xi_i\alpha_2) - \alpha_1 J_1(\xi_i\alpha_1)\right]$$

Now, if ϵ is small, $\alpha_1/\alpha_2 = 1 - \epsilon/a$ and hence

$$\alpha_2 J_1(\xi_i\alpha_2) - \alpha_1 J_1(\xi_i\alpha_1) = \alpha_2 J_1(\xi_i\alpha_2)$$
$$\times \left\{1 - \left(1 - \frac{\epsilon}{a}\right)\frac{J_1[\xi_i\alpha_2(1 - \epsilon/a)]}{J_1(\xi_i\alpha_2)}\right\} = \frac{\epsilon\xi_i\alpha_2^2 J_0(\xi_i\alpha_2)}{a}$$

since

$$J_1'(z) = J_0(z) - \frac{1}{z}J_1(z)$$

and therefore

$$J_1\left[\xi_i\alpha_2\left(1 - \frac{\epsilon}{a}\right)\right] = J_1(\xi_i\alpha_2) - \frac{\epsilon}{a}\,\xi_i\alpha_2\left[J_0(\xi_i\alpha_2) - \frac{J_1(\xi_i\alpha_2)}{\xi_i\alpha_2}\right]$$

Thus if ϵ tends to zero, *i.e.*, if the force is concentrated at the point $x = a$, we obtain

$$\bar{p}_\beta = \frac{2\rho}{g}\,\psi(t)J_0\left(\frac{2\xi_i a^{\frac{1}{2}}}{g^{\frac{1}{2}}}\right) \tag{47}$$

and the appropriate solution of equation (38) is

$$\bar{y}_\beta = \frac{2}{g}\,J_0\left(\frac{2\xi_i a^{\frac{1}{2}}}{g^{\frac{1}{2}}}\right)\frac{1}{\xi_i}\int_{-\infty}^{t}\psi(u)\,\sin\,[\xi_i(t - u)]du$$

Hence, by equation (39),

$$y = \frac{2}{g\beta^2}\sum_i \frac{J_0(2\xi_i a^{\frac{1}{2}}/g^{\frac{1}{2}})J_0(\xi_i z)}{\xi_i[J_1(\xi_i\beta)]^2}\int_{-\infty}^{t}\psi(u)\,\sin\,[\xi_i(t - u)]du$$

In terms of the original variables x and t we have finally

$$y(x,t) = \frac{1}{(Lg)^{\frac{1}{2}}} \sum_i \frac{J_0(\alpha_i a^{\frac{1}{2}}/L^{\frac{1}{2}})J_0(\alpha_i x^{\frac{1}{2}}/L^{\frac{1}{2}})}{\alpha_i[J_1(\alpha_i)]^2} \int_{-\infty}^{t} \psi(u) \sin\left[\frac{g^{\frac{1}{2}}\alpha_i(t-u)}{2L^{\frac{1}{2}}}\right] du$$

the sum being taken over all the positive roots of equation (43).

On the other hand, if the transverse force acts over the whole length of the chain,

$$\bar{p}_\beta = \rho\psi(t)\frac{1}{L}\int_0^\beta z J_0(\xi_i z)dz = \frac{2\rho\psi(t)}{(Lg)^{\frac{1}{2}}}\frac{J_1(\xi_i\beta)}{\xi_i}$$

The analysis proceeds as before, and we obtain

$$y(x,t) = \frac{4}{(Lg)^{\frac{1}{2}}} \sum_i \frac{J_0(\alpha_i x^{\frac{1}{2}}/L^{\frac{1}{2}})}{\alpha_i^2 J_1(\alpha_i)} \int_{-\infty}^{t} \psi(u) \sin\left[\frac{g^{\frac{1}{2}}\alpha_i(t-u)}{2L^{\frac{1}{2}}}\right] du$$

As an example, suppose that an external force of magnitude $P\rho \sin \omega t$ is applied to the lower end of the chain, which is initially at rest in its equilibrium position. In this case we may take $a = 0$ so that equation (47) reduces to

$$\bar{p}_\beta = \frac{2P\rho}{g} \sin (\omega t)$$

and the corresponding solution of equation (38) is

$$\bar{y}_\beta = \frac{2P}{g}\left[\frac{\omega \sin \xi_i t - \xi_i \sin \omega t}{\xi_i(\omega^2 - \xi_i^2)}\right]$$

It follows immediately from equation (39) that on reverting to the original variables

$$y(x,t) = \frac{8P\omega L^{\frac{1}{2}}}{g^{\frac{3}{2}}} \sum_i \frac{\sin(\frac{1}{2}\alpha_i t g^{\frac{1}{2}}/L^{\frac{1}{2}})J_0(\alpha_i x^{\frac{1}{2}}/L^{\frac{1}{2}})}{\alpha_i(4L\omega^2/g - \alpha_i^2)[J_1(\alpha_i)]^2}$$

$$- \frac{4P}{g}\sin \omega t \sum_i \frac{J_0(\alpha_i x^{\frac{1}{2}}/L^{\frac{1}{2}})}{(4L\omega^2/g - \alpha_i^2)[J_1(\alpha_i)]^2}$$

where the summations extend over all the positive roots of equation (43).

17.5 Forced vibrations of a very long chain. If the chain is of infinite length, the analysis proceeds exactly as in the last section as far as equation (47). Then

$$\bar{y}(\xi,t) = \frac{2J_0(2\xi a^{\frac{1}{2}}/g^{\frac{1}{2}})}{g\xi} \int_{-\infty}^{t} \psi(u) \sin [\xi(t-u)]du$$

and thus by equation (41) we have, on interchanging the order of the

u and ξ integrations,

$$y(x,t) = \frac{2}{g} \int_{-\infty}^{t} \psi(u)du \int_{0}^{\infty} J_0\left(\frac{2\xi a^{\frac{1}{2}}}{g^{\frac{1}{2}}}\right) J_0\left(\frac{2\xi x^{\frac{1}{2}}}{g^{\frac{1}{2}}}\right) \sin \xi(t-u)du$$

If the force is applied at the lower end of the chain, we may take $a = 0$ and the result

$$\int_0^\infty \sin (bt) J_0(at)dt = \begin{cases} 0 & b < a \\ (b^2 - a^2)^{-\frac{1}{2}} & b > a \end{cases}$$

then leads to the expression

$$y(x,t) = \frac{2}{g} \int_{t-2(x/g)^{\frac{1}{2}}}^{t} \frac{\psi(u)du}{[(t-u)^2 - (4x/g)]^{\frac{1}{2}}}$$

for the transverse displacement produced by the application of a point force of magnitude $\rho\psi(t)$ to the free end of a very long chain.

18. Transverse Oscillations of an Elastic Beam

18.1 Equation of motion. We consider a uniform beam which in its equilibrium position lies along the x axis. If we measure the transverse deflection of the beam at any point x in the downward direction, then it may readily be shown[1] that the load per unit length of the beam, $P(x,t)$, is given by the equation

$$P(x,t) = EI \frac{\partial^4 y}{\partial t^4} \tag{48}$$

where E is the Young's modulus of the material forming the beam and I is the moment of inertia of the cross section of the beam with respect to a line which is normal to both the x and y axes and passes through the center of mass of the cross-sectional area S.

The equation (48) is the condition of equilibrium in the static case if the function $P(x,t)$ is replaced by the static load, $w(x)$ say. To derive the equation of motion in the dynamical case we employ d'Alembert's principle, which states that any dynamical problem may be reduced to a statical problem by the addition of appropriate inertia forces. In this case the inertia force to be added to $P(x,t)$ is $-\rho S(\partial^2 y/\partial t^2)$, where ρ is the mass per unit length of the beam. The equation of motion then assumes the form

$$P(x,t) - \rho S \frac{\partial^2 y}{\partial t^2} = EI \frac{\partial^4 y}{\partial x^4}$$

If we write

$$a^2 = \frac{EI}{\rho S} \tag{49}$$

[1] See, for example, P. M. Morse, "Vibration and Sound," 2d ed. (McGraw-Hill, New York, 1948), p. 151.

we see that this equation may be put into the form

$$\frac{\partial^4 y}{\partial x^4} + \frac{1}{a^2}\frac{\partial^2 y}{\partial t^2} = \frac{P(x,t)}{EI} \tag{50}$$

It may also be shown that the bending moment $M(x)$ required to stretch and compress all the fibers in the bar is given by

$$M(x) = -EI\frac{\partial^2 y}{\partial x^2}$$

It follows immediately from this equation that, if the end of the elastic bar is at the point $x = 0$ and that if that end is freely hinged, then

$$y = \frac{\partial^2 y}{\partial x^2} = 0 \qquad\qquad \text{at } x = 0 \tag{51}$$

are the required boundary conditions at $x = 0$.

18.2 Free vibrations of an infinite beam. We shall begin by considering the free vibrations of a beam of infinite length $-\infty \le x \le \infty$. We shall suppose that the motion is produced by distorting the beam and then giving each point a known transverse velocity. In other words we shall assume that, when $t = 0$,

$$y = f(x), \qquad \frac{\partial y}{\partial t} = ag''(x) \tag{52}$$

where the functions $f(x)$ and $g(x)$ are prescribed and, as is usual, $g''(x)$ denotes the second derivative of $g(x)$ with respect to x.

To solve equation (50) subject to the initial conditions (52) and the boundary conditions that y and its derivatives with respect to x vanish when $x = \pm\infty$, we multiply equation (50) by $e^{i\xi x}$ and integrate from $-\infty$ to ∞ with respect to x. Since the vibrations are free, $P(x,t)$ is identically zero and we obtain

$$\left(\frac{1}{2\pi}\right)^{\frac{1}{2}}\int_{-\infty}^{\infty}\frac{\partial^4 y}{\partial x^4}e^{i\xi x}\,dx + \frac{1}{a^2}\frac{d^2 Y}{dt^2} = 0$$

where we have written

$$Y(\xi,t) = \left(\frac{1}{2\pi}\right)^{\frac{1}{2}}\int_{-\infty}^{\infty} y(x,t)e^{i\xi x}\,dx \tag{53}$$

It follows at once from Sec. 5 that

$$\left(\frac{1}{2\pi}\right)^{\frac{1}{2}}\int_{-\infty}^{\infty}\frac{\partial^4 y}{\partial x^4}e^{i\xi x}\,dx = \xi^4 Y$$

so that the ordinary differential equation for the determination of the

Fourier transform Y is

$$\frac{d^2Y}{dt^2} + a^2\xi^4 Y = 0$$

From the equations (52) we see that the initial conditions on Y and dY/dt are that

$$Y = F(\xi), \qquad \frac{dY}{dt} = -a\xi^2 G(\xi) \tag{54}$$

where $F(\xi)$ and $G(\xi)$ are the Fourier transforms of $f(x)$ and $g(x)$, respectively. The form of the Fourier transform Y is therefore

$$Y(\xi,t) = F(\xi) \cos (a\xi^2 t) - G(\xi) \sin (a\xi^2 t)$$

Inverting equation (53) by means of the Fourier inversion theorem (Theorem 10), we find that

$$y(x,t) = \left(\frac{1}{2\pi}\right)^{\frac{1}{2}} \int_{-\infty}^{\infty} F(\xi) \cos (a\xi^2 t) e^{-i\xi x}\, d\xi$$
$$- \left(\frac{1}{2\pi}\right)^{\frac{1}{2}} \int_{-\infty}^{\infty} G(\xi) \sin (a\xi^2 t) e^{-i\xi x}\, d\xi \tag{55}$$

Now if a is real, it is readily shown that

$$\left(\frac{1}{2\pi}\right)^{\frac{1}{2}} \int_{-\infty}^{\infty} e^{-\xi^2 a - i\xi x}\, d\xi = \left(\frac{1}{2a}\right)^{\frac{1}{2}} e^{-x^2/4a} \tag{56}$$

Furthermore

$$\frac{1}{(2ai)^{\frac{1}{2}}} = \frac{1}{(2a)^{\frac{1}{2}}} e^{-\frac{1}{4}\pi i} = \frac{1}{2a^{\frac{1}{2}}} (1 - i)$$

so that if we put ai in place of a in equation (56) we find that

$$\left(\frac{1}{2\pi}\right)^{\frac{1}{2}} \int_{-\infty}^{\infty} (\cos \xi^2 a - i \sin \xi^2 a) e^{-i\xi x}\, d\xi = \frac{1}{2a^{\frac{1}{2}}} (1 - i) e^{ix^2/4a}$$

Equating real and imaginary parts, we obtain the Fourier transforms

$$\left.\begin{array}{l}
\left(\dfrac{1}{2\pi}\right)^{\frac{1}{2}} \displaystyle\int_{-\infty}^{\infty} \cos (a\xi^2) e^{-i\xi x}\, d\xi = \dfrac{1}{2a^{\frac{1}{2}}} \left(\cos \dfrac{x^2}{4a} + \sin \dfrac{x^2}{4a}\right) \\[3mm]
\left(\dfrac{1}{2\pi}\right)^{\frac{1}{2}} \displaystyle\int_{-\infty}^{\infty} \sin (a\xi^2) e^{-i\xi x}\, d\xi = \dfrac{1}{2a^{\frac{1}{2}}} \left(\cos \dfrac{x^2}{4a} - \sin \dfrac{x^2}{4a}\right)
\end{array}\right\} \tag{57}$$

If therefore we make use of the first of these relations in the Faltung theorem 12, we find that

$$\int_{-\infty}^{\infty} \cos (at\xi^2) F(\xi) e^{-i\xi x}\, d\xi = \frac{1}{2(at)^{\frac{1}{2}}} \int_{-\infty}^{\infty} f(x - \eta) \left(\cos \frac{\eta^2}{4at} + \sin \frac{\eta^2}{4at}\right) d\eta$$

The integral involving $G(\xi)$ in equation (55) can be evaluated in a similar way.   Inserting these results in equation (55), we have

$$y(x,t) = \frac{1}{2(2\pi at)^{\frac{1}{2}}} \int_{-\infty}^{\infty} f(x - \eta) \left(\cos \frac{\eta^2}{4at} + \sin \frac{\eta^2}{4at} \right) d\eta$$

$$- \frac{1}{2(2\pi at)^{\frac{1}{2}}} \int_{-\infty}^{\infty} g(x - \eta) \left(\cos \frac{\eta^2}{4at} - \sin \frac{\eta^2}{4at} \right) d\eta$$

Writing $u^2 = \eta^2/4at$ and changing the variable of integration from η to u, we obtain finally for the general solution

$$y(x,t) = \left(\frac{1}{2\pi} \right)^{\frac{1}{2}} \int_{-\infty}^{\infty} f(x - 2ua^{\frac{1}{2}}t^{\frac{1}{2}})(\cos u^2 + \sin u^2)du$$

$$- \left(\frac{1}{2\pi} \right)^{\frac{1}{2}} \int_{-\infty}^{\infty} g(x - 2ua^{\frac{1}{2}}t^{\frac{1}{2}})(\sin u^2 - \cos u^2)du \quad (58)$$

a result established by Boussinesq.[1]

In any given problem it may be simpler to use the solution in the form (55) instead of the general solution (58).   For example, if

$$f(x) = \epsilon e^{-x^2/4r_0^2}, \qquad g(x) = 0$$

we have $G(\xi) = 0$ and

$$F(\xi) = \frac{\epsilon}{(2\pi)^{\frac{1}{2}}} \int_{-\infty}^{\infty} e^{-x^2/4r_0^2+i\xi x} \, dx = 2^{\frac{1}{2}}r_0\epsilon e^{-\xi^2 r_0^2}$$

so that from equation (55)

$$y = \frac{r_0\epsilon}{\pi^{\frac{1}{2}}} \int_{-\infty}^{\infty} e^{-\xi^2 r_0^2} \cos (at\xi^2)e^{-i\xi x} \, d\xi \qquad (59)$$

Writing the cosine factor in exponential form and then making use of equation (56), we have

$$y = \frac{1}{2} r_0\epsilon\pi^{-\frac{1}{2}} \int_{-\infty}^{\infty} [e^{-\xi^2(r_0^2+iat)-i\xi x} + e^{-\xi^2(r_0^2-iat)-i\xi x}]d\xi$$

$$= \frac{1}{2} r_0\epsilon \left[\frac{e^{-x^2/4(r_0^2+iat)}}{(r_0^2 + iat)^{\frac{1}{2}}} + \frac{e^{-x^2/4(r_0^2-iat)}}{(r_0^2 - iat)^{\frac{1}{2}}} \right]$$

If we now write

$$r_0^2 + iat = Re^{i\varphi}$$

it follows at once that

$$y = \frac{r_0\epsilon}{R^{\frac{1}{2}}} e^{-x^2 \cos \varphi/4R} \cos \left(\frac{x^2 \sin \varphi}{4R} - \frac{1}{2} \varphi \right)$$

[1] I. Todhunter and K. Pearson, "A History of the Theory of Elasticity" (Cambridge, London, 1893), Vol. II, Part II, p. 282.

Now by the definitions of R and φ it follows immediately that $R \cos \varphi = r_0^2$, $R \sin \varphi = at$, $R^2 = r_0^4 + a^2 t^2$, $\varphi = \tan^{-1}(at/r_0^2)$, so that finally

$$y(x,t) = \frac{\epsilon}{(1 + a^2 t^2/r_0^4)^{\frac{1}{4}}} \exp\left[\frac{-x^2 r_0^2}{4(r_0^4 + a^2 t^2)}\right] \cos\left[\frac{atx^2}{4(r_0^4 + a^2 t^2)} - \frac{1}{2}\tan^{-1}\left(\frac{at}{r_0^2}\right)\right]$$

This result, which is in agreement with that found by Morse,[1] may also be obtained directly by substituting $f(x) = e^{-x^2/4r_0^2}$, $g(x) = 0$ in the general solution (58).

18.3 Motion of a semiinfinite beam when its end has a prescribed motion. We shall now consider the motion of the semiinfinite elastic beam $0 \leq x \leq \infty$ when the end $x = 0$ is given a prescribed displacement. If we suppose that the end of the beam is freely hinged but that the hinge is in motion, our boundary conditions become

$$y = f(t), \qquad \frac{\partial^2 y}{\partial x^2} = 0 \quad \text{at } x = 0 \text{ for } t > 0 \quad (60)$$

and if we assume that the beam is originally at rest in its equilibrium position before the hinge is set in motion, we have

$$y = 0, \qquad \frac{\partial y}{\partial t} = 0 \quad \text{when } t = 0, x \geq 0 \quad (61)$$

as our initial conditions.

The transverse displacement $y(x,t)$ of the beam is again determined by equation (50) with the forcing term $P(x,t)$ identically zero. Now

$$\int_0^\infty \frac{\partial^4 y}{\partial x^4} \sin (\xi x)dx = -\xi^2 \int_0^\infty \frac{\partial^2 y}{\partial x^2} \sin (\xi x)dx$$

if, as is required by the second of equations (60), $\partial^2 y/\partial x^2$ vanishes at $x = 0$. Integrating the right-hand side of this equation by parts, we have

$$\int_0^\infty \frac{\partial^2 y}{\partial x^2} \sin (\xi x)dx = \left[\frac{\partial y}{\partial x} \sin (\xi x) - \xi y \cos (\xi x)\right]_0^\infty - \xi^2 \int_0^\infty y \sin (\xi x)dx$$

$$= \xi f(t) - \xi^2 \int_0^\infty y(x,t) \sin (\xi x)dx$$

by the first of the conditions (60). Thus if we multiply both sides of equation (50) by $(2/\pi)^{\frac{1}{2}} \sin (\xi x)$ and integrate from 0 to ∞ with respect to x, we find that the Fourier sine transform

$$Y_s(\xi) = \left(\frac{2}{\pi}\right)^{\frac{1}{2}} \int_0^\infty y(x,t) \sin (\xi x)dx$$

[1] Morse, *op. cit.*, p. 155, equation (14.9).

satisfies the second-order differential equation

$$\frac{d^2Y_s}{dt^2} + a^2\xi^4Y_s = \left(\frac{2}{\pi}\right)^{\frac{1}{2}} a^2\xi^3 f(t)$$

By equations (61)

$$Y = \frac{dY_s}{dt} = 0 \qquad \text{when } t = 0$$

so that the appropriate solution of this equation is found, from equation (13), to be

$$Y_s(\xi,t) = \left(\frac{2}{\pi}\right)^{\frac{1}{2}} a\xi \int_0^t f(u) \sin (a\xi^2 t - a\xi^2 u)du$$

Now, by the inversion theorem 9, the displacement $y(x,t)$ is given by the relation

$$y(x,t) = \left(\frac{2}{\pi}\right)^{\frac{1}{2}} \int_0^\infty Y_s(\xi,t) \sin (\xi x)d\xi$$

so that by inverting the order of the integrations we obtain

$$y(x,t) = \frac{2a}{\pi} \int_0^t f(u)du \int_0^\infty \xi \sin [a\xi^2(t - u)] \sin (\xi x)d\xi \qquad (62)$$

From the second of the equations (57) we find that

$$\int_0^\infty \sin (a\xi^2) \cos (\xi x)d\xi = \frac{1}{4}\left(\frac{2\pi}{a}\right)^{\frac{1}{2}} \left(\cos \frac{x^2}{4a} - \sin \frac{x^2}{4a}\right)$$

so that, differentiating both sides with respect to x, we have

$$\int_0^\infty \xi \sin (a\xi^2) \sin (\xi x)d\xi = \frac{x}{8a}\left(\frac{2\pi}{a}\right)^{\frac{1}{2}} \left(\sin \frac{x^2}{4a} + \cos \frac{x^2}{4a}\right)$$

Replacing a by $a(t - u)$ and substituting the result in equation (62), we have

$$y(x,t) = \frac{x}{4\pi}\left(\frac{2\pi}{a}\right)^{\frac{1}{2}} \int_0^t \frac{f(u)}{(t - u)^{\frac{3}{2}}}\left[\sin \frac{x^2}{4a(t - u)} + \cos \frac{x^2}{4a(t - u)}\right] du$$

Changing the variable of integration from u to v where $v^2 = x^2/2a(t - u)$, we obtain finally

$$y(x,t) = \frac{1}{\sqrt{\pi}} \int_{x/(2at)^{\frac{1}{2}}}^\infty f\left(\frac{t - x^2}{2av^2}\right)\left[\sin \left(\frac{1}{2} v^2\right) + \cos \left(\frac{1}{2} v^2\right)\right] dv$$

a result first established by Boussinesq.[1]

[1] Todhunter and Pearson, *op. cit.*, p. 280.

18.4 Vibrations of a beam of finite length.   We shall now consider the vibrations of a beam of finite length L which is freely hinged at its ends so that we may take

$$y = \frac{\partial^2 y}{\partial x^2} = 0 \quad \text{at } x = 0 \text{ and at } x = L \quad (63)$$

for all values of t.   Now if $\partial y^2/\partial x^2$ vanishes when $x = 0$ and $x = L$, it follows from equation (19), Chap. 3, that

$$\int_0^L \frac{\partial^4 y}{\partial x^4} \sin \frac{n\pi x}{L}\, dx = -\frac{n^2\pi^2}{L^2} \int_0^L \frac{\partial^2 y}{\partial x^2} \sin \frac{n\pi x}{L}\, dx$$

In a similar way, if $y = 0$ at $x = 0$ and $x = L$, it follows that the right-hand side of this last equation reduces to

$$\frac{n^4\pi^4}{L^4}\, \bar{y}_s(n)$$

where $\bar{y}_s(n)$ denotes the finite Fourier sine transform

$$\bar{y}_s(n) = \int_0^L y(x,t) \sin\left(\frac{n\pi x}{L}\right) dx$$

Therefore, if we multiply both sides of equation (50) by $\sin (n\pi x/L)$ and integrate with respect to x from 0 to L, we obtain the ordinary differential equation

$$\frac{d^2\bar{y}_s}{dt^2} + \frac{a^2 n^4 \pi^4}{L^4}\, \bar{y}_s = \frac{a^2}{EI}\, \bar{P}_s(n,t) \quad (64)$$

in which we have written

$$\bar{P}_s(n,t) = \int_0^L P(x,t) \sin\left(\frac{n\pi x}{L}\right) dx \quad (65)$$

If the initial values of $\bar{y}_s(n)$ and $d\bar{y}_s/dt$ are, respectively, denoted by $\bar{y}_0$ and $\bar{y}_1$, it follows from equation (12) that the solution of (64) is

$$\bar{y}_s(n,t) = \bar{y}_0 \cos\left(\frac{an^2\pi^2 t}{L^2}\right) + \frac{L\bar{y}_1}{an^2\pi^2} \sin\left(\frac{an^2\pi^2 t}{L^2}\right)$$
$$+ \frac{L^2 a}{EI n^2 \pi^2} \int_0^t \bar{P}_s(n,u) \sin\left(\frac{an^2\pi^2 (t-u)}{L^2}\right) du \quad (66)$$

Once $\bar{y}_s(n,t)$ has been determined by means of this equation, the transverse displacement $y(x,t)$ is found, from the finite Fourier inversion theorem 27, to be given by

$$y(x,t) = \frac{2}{L} \sum_{n=1}^{\infty} \bar{y}_s(n,t) \sin \frac{n\pi x}{L} \quad (67)$$

We shall now illustrate the use of these formulas by considering certain special cases.

Free Vibrations.   If the vibrations are free, $P(x,t)$, and hence $\bar{P}_s(n,t)$, is identically zero.   Furthermore if, initially,

$$y = f(x), \qquad \frac{\partial y}{\partial x} = g(x)$$

then

$$\bar{y}_0 = \int_0^L f(u) \sin\left(\frac{n\pi u}{L}\right) du, \qquad \bar{y}_1 = \int_0^L g(u) \sin\left(\frac{n\pi u}{L}\right) du \qquad (68)$$

Substituting from equations (68) into equations (66) and (67)—with $\bar{P}_s(n,t)$ put equal to zero—we obtain for the transverse displacement

$$y(x,t) = \frac{2}{L} \sum_{n=1}^{\infty} \sin\left(\frac{n\pi x}{L}\right) \cos\left(\frac{n^2\pi^2 at}{L^2}\right) \int_0^L f(u) \sin\left(\frac{n\pi u}{L}\right) du$$

$$+ \frac{2L}{\pi^2 a} \sum_{n=1}^{\infty} \frac{1}{n^2} \sin\left(\frac{n\pi x}{L}\right) \sin\left(\frac{n^2\pi^2 at}{L^2}\right) \int_0^L g(u) \sin\left(\frac{n\pi u}{L}\right) du$$

Suppose, for example, that the beam is at rest in its equilibrium position at time $t = 0$ when an impulse I is applied at the point $x = x'$ ($0 < x' < L$), then, just as in the case of a thin elastic string (Sec. 16.4), we have

$$f(u) = 0, \qquad g(u) = \frac{I}{\rho S} \delta(u - x')$$

where $\delta(x)$ denotes the Dirac delta function of argument x.   By equation (77), Chap. 1, we have

$$\int_0^L g(u) \sin\left(\frac{n\pi u}{L}\right) du = \frac{I}{\rho S} \sin\left(\frac{n\pi x'}{L}\right)$$

so that from equation (69) we find that

$$y(x,t) = \frac{2IL}{\pi^2 a \rho S} \sum_{n=1}^{\infty} \frac{1}{n^2} \sin\left(\frac{n\pi x}{L}\right) \sin\left(\frac{n\pi x'}{L}\right) \sin\left(\frac{n^2\pi^2 at}{L^2}\right) \qquad (69)$$

provided, of course, that $0 \leq x' \leq L$.

Forced Vibrations.   We shall next consider two simple types of applied force $P(x,t)$.   In both cases we shall assume that the beam is set in motion from rest in its equilibrium position so that both $\bar{y}_0$ and $\bar{y}_1$ are zero.   Inserting these values in equation (66) and then substituting for

$\bar{y}_s(n,t)$ in equation (67), we obtain, for the transverse displacement, the expression

$$y(x,t) = \frac{2La}{\pi^2 EI} \sum_{n=1}^{\infty} \frac{1}{n^2} \sin\left(\frac{n\pi x}{L}\right) \int_0^t \bar{P}_s(n,u) \sin\left[\frac{\pi^2 n^2 a(t-u)}{L^2}\right] du \quad (70)$$

For example, suppose that a variable force $\psi(t)$ is applied at the fixed point $x = x'$, then

$$P(x,t) = \psi(t)\, \delta(x - x'), \qquad (0 < x' < L)$$

so that

$$\bar{P}_s(n,t) = \psi(t) \int_0^L \delta(x - x') \sin\left(\frac{n\pi x}{L}\right) dx = \psi(t) \sin\left(\frac{n\pi x'}{L}\right)$$

Inserting this value for the function $\bar{P}_s$ in equation (70), we obtain the expression

$$y(x,t) = \frac{2La}{\pi^2 EI} \sum_{n=1}^{\infty} \sin\left(\frac{n\pi x}{L}\right) \sin\left(\frac{n\pi x'}{L}\right) \frac{1}{n^2} \int_0^t \psi(u) \sin\left[\frac{n^2 \pi^2 a(t-u)}{L^2}\right] du$$

for determining the transverse displacement at any time $t > 0$.

On the other hand, if the applied force is a point force whose point of application is moving uniformly along the beam with velocity V, we may take

$$P(x,t) = \begin{cases} \psi(t)\, \delta(x - Vt) & 0 \le Vt \le L \\ 0 & Vt > L \end{cases}$$

We then have

$$\bar{P}_s(n,t) = \psi(t) \int_0^L \sin\left(\frac{n\pi x}{L}\right) \delta(x - Vt)\, dx$$

$$= \begin{cases} \psi(t) \sin\left(\frac{n\pi Vt}{L}\right) & 0 \le t \le \dfrac{L}{V}, \\ 0 & t > \dfrac{L}{V} \end{cases}$$

so that if $0 \le t \le L/V$ we have

$$y(x,t) = \frac{2La}{\pi^2 EI} \sum_{n=1}^{\infty} \frac{1}{n^2} \sin\left(\frac{n\pi x}{L}\right) \int_0^t \psi(u) \sin\left(\frac{n\pi Vu}{L}\right) \sin\left[\frac{n^2 \pi^2 a(t-u)}{L^2}\right] du$$

In particular, if $\psi(t)$ is a constant, P_0 say, then using the result

$$\int_0^t \sin\left(\frac{n\pi Vu}{L}\right) \sin\left[\frac{n^2 \pi^2 a(t-u)}{L^2}\right] du$$

$$= \frac{L^3 V}{n\pi(L^2 V^2 - n^2 \pi^2 a^2)} \sin\left(\frac{n^2 \pi^2 a t}{L^2}\right) - \frac{L^2 V^2 a}{L^2 V^2 - n^2 \pi^2 a^2} \sin\left(\frac{n\pi Vt}{L}\right)$$

(where it is assumed that V is not an integral multiple of $a\pi/L$), we find that, when $0 \leq t \leq L/V$,

$$y(x,t) = \frac{2L^4 aV}{\pi^3 EI} \sum_{n=1}^{\infty} \frac{1}{n^3(L^2V^2 - n^2\pi^2a^2)} \sin\left(\frac{n^2\pi^2 at}{L^2}\right) \sin\left(\frac{n\pi x}{L}\right)$$

$$- \frac{2L^3 a^2 V^2}{\pi^2 EI} \sum_{n=1}^{\infty} \frac{1}{n^2(L^2V^2 - n^2\pi^2a^2)} \sin\left(\frac{n\pi Vt}{L}\right) \sin\left(\frac{n\pi x}{L}\right)$$

This result may also be obtained by using a Laplace transform[1] to reduce the equation (50) to a fourth-order ordinary differential equation in x, but this method is more cumbersome than that outlined above since it involves the solution of a differential equation of a higher order and the evaluation of a complicated contour integral.

Statical Problems. In the discussion of the static deflection of beams we may take $P(x,t)$ to be a function of x alone, $P(x)$ say. The finite Fourier sine transform of this function will therefore be a function of n alone, $\bar{P}_s(n)$ say. Furthermore in the statical case the term $d^2\bar{y}_s/dt^2$ is omitted from equation (64) so that it reduces to the simple form

$$\bar{y}_s(n) = \left(\frac{L^4}{\pi^4 EI}\right)\frac{\bar{P}_s(n)}{n^4} \tag{71}$$

If we recall that, by its definition,

$$\bar{P}_s(n) = \int_0^L P(u) \sin\left(\frac{n\pi u}{L}\right) du$$

and then substitute from equation (71) into equation (67), we find for the solution of the statical problem

$$y(x,t) = \frac{2L^3}{\pi^4 EI} \sum_{n=1}^{\infty} \frac{1}{n^4} \sin\left(\frac{n\pi x}{L}\right) \int_0^L P(u) \sin\left(\frac{n\pi u}{L}\right) du$$

In particular, if the applied load P is concentrated at the point $x = x'$ ($0 \leq x' \leq L$), then

$$P(u) = P \, \delta(u - x')$$

where P is a constant, and the static deflection is

$$y(x,t) = \frac{2PL^3}{\pi^4 EI} \sum_{n=1}^{\infty} \frac{1}{n^4} \sin\left(\frac{n\pi x}{L}\right) \sin\left(\frac{n\pi x'}{L}\right)$$

[1] Cf. H. S. Carslaw and J. C. Jaeger, "Operational Methods in Applied Mathematics" (Oxford, New York, 1941), pp. 150–152.

It must be kept in mind that these solutions are applicable only to a beam of finite length which is hinged freely at both ends. The solutions corresponding to other types of support may be obtained by similar methods, and their derivation is left to the reader.

19. Transverse Vibrations of a Thin Membrane

19.1 Equation of motion. The transverse vibrations of a thin plane membrane stretched to a uniform tension may be investigated in a similar manner to those of light strings, with the additional complication that the number of independent variables occurring in the differential equation is now three instead of two.

We shall discuss the transverse vibrations of a membrane of uniform surface density, whose mass per unit area is σ, and which in the equilibrium position lies in the plane $z = 0$. Further we shall suppose that the membrane is stretched to a uniform tension T—in other words, that if a line of unit length is drawn in any direction on the surface of the membrane the material on one side of the line exerts a force T on the material on the other side, the force acting normal to the line itself. We consider

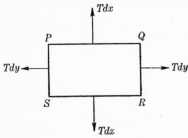

now an element of the membrane in the form of a rectangle of sides dx and dy (cf. Fig. 10). Then during the motion the two sides PQ and RS will be subjected to forces of amount $T\,dx$, while the other two sides QR and SP will be subjected to forces of magnitude $T\,dy$. These forces will act in the four tangent planes to the membrane passing through the edges of the element. If we denote the transverse displacement of the point (x,y)

FIG. 10. The forces acting on a rectangular element of a thin membrane stretched to a tension T.

of the membrane by z, we see that the net force acting normal to the surface of the membrane due to the pair of tensions $T\,dx$ will be

$$T\,dx\left[\left(\frac{\partial z}{\partial y}\right)_{y+dy} - \left(\frac{\partial z}{\partial y}\right)_{y}\right] = T\,\frac{\partial^2 z}{\partial y^2}\,dx\,dy$$

Similarly the net force produced by the pair of tensions $T\,dy$ will be $T\,dx\,dy(\partial^2 z/\partial x^2)$. If, in addition, there is an external force $p(x,y,t)$ per unit area acting on the membrane, normal to the plane $z = 0$, then the total force acting on the element in the z direction will be

$$\left[T\left(\frac{\partial^2 z}{\partial x^2} + \frac{\partial^2 z}{\partial y^2}\right) + p(x,y,t)\right]dx\,dy$$

This will, in turn, be equal to the rate of change of momentum of the element, namely, $\sigma(\partial^2 z/\partial t^2)dx\,dy$ so that we obtain as our equation of motion

$$T\left(\frac{\partial^2 z}{\partial x^2} + \frac{\partial^2 z}{\partial y^2}\right) + p(x,y,t) = \sigma\,\frac{\partial^2 z}{\partial t^2}$$

If we now put $c^2 = T/\sigma$, we find that the transverse displacement z is governed by the second-order inhomogeneous partial differential equation

$$\frac{1}{c^2}\frac{\partial^2 z}{\partial t^2} = \nabla_1^2 z + \frac{p(x,y,t)}{T} \tag{72}$$

in which ∇_1^2 denotes the two-dimensional Laplacian operator

$$\nabla_1^2 = \frac{\partial^2}{\partial x^2} + \frac{\partial^2}{\partial y^2}$$

19.2 Free vibrations of a very large membrane. To illustrate the application of the theory of Fourier transforms to the solution of the wave equation (72), we begin by considering the free vibrations of a membrane of infinite extent, when its displacement and velocity are prescribed initially. Since the vibrations are free we may take $p(x,y,t)$ to be zero in equation (72) and obtain the homogeneous wave equation

$$\frac{1}{c^2}\frac{\partial^2 z}{\partial t^2} = \nabla_1^2 z \tag{73}$$

The problem then resolves itself into the solution of this second-order equation subject to the initial conditions

$$z = f(x,y), \qquad \frac{\partial z}{\partial t} = g(x,y) \qquad t = 0 \tag{74}$$

where $f(x,y)$ and $g(x,y)$ are known functions of x and y. To solve the partial differential equation (73), we introduce the double Fourier transform

$$Z(\xi,\eta,t) = \frac{1}{2\pi}\int_{-\infty}^{\infty}\int_{-\infty}^{\infty} z(x,y,t)e^{i(\xi x + \eta y)}\,dx\,dy \tag{75}$$

of the transverse displacement $z(x,y,t)$. If we multiply both sides of equation (73) by $\exp[i(\xi x + \eta y)]$ and integrate with respect to x and y throughout the whole xy plane, then, making use of the results

$$\frac{1}{2\pi}\int_{-\infty}^{\infty}\int_{-\infty}^{\infty}\left(\frac{\partial^2 z}{\partial x^2}, \frac{\partial^2 z}{\partial y^2}\right)e^{i(\xi x + \eta y)}\,dx\,dy = -(\xi^2,\eta^2)Z(\xi,\eta,t)$$

which suppose that z, $\partial z/\partial x$, and $\partial z/\partial y$ all tend to zero as $(x^2 + y^2)$ tends to infinity, we find that the transform Z satisfies the ordinary differential equation

$$\frac{d^2Z}{dt^2} + c^2(\xi^2 + \eta^2)Z = 0 \qquad (76)$$

which has solution

$$Z = A \cos (\mu t) + B \sin (\mu t)$$

where μ is related to ξ and η by the equation

$$\mu^2 = c^2(\xi^2 + \eta^2) \qquad (77)$$

and A and B are arbitrary constants which will be, in general, functions of ξ and η. Now it follows from equations (74) that the initial conditions on $Z(\xi,\eta,t)$ are

$$Z = F(\xi,\eta), \qquad \frac{dZ}{dt} = G(\xi,\eta) \qquad t = 0$$

where $F(\xi,\eta)$ and $G(\xi,\eta)$ are the corresponding double Fourier transforms of the functions $f(x,y)$ and $g(x,y)$. The required solution of equation (76) is therefore

$$Z = F(\xi,\eta) \cos (\mu t) + \frac{G(\xi,\eta)}{\mu} \sin (\mu t) \qquad (78)$$

where, it will be remembered, μ is a function of ξ and η defined by equation (77).

Now by equation (108), Chap. 1, we know that z is related to Z by the equation

$$z(x,y,t) = \frac{1}{2\pi} \int_{-\infty}^{\infty} \int_{-\infty}^{\infty} Z(\xi,\eta,t)e^{-i(\xi x+\eta y)} \, d\xi \, d\eta \qquad (79)$$

so that substituting from equation (78) we have

$$z(x,y,t) = \frac{1}{2\pi} \int_{-\infty}^{\infty} \int_{-\infty}^{\infty} F(\xi,\eta) \cos (ct \sqrt{\xi^2 + \eta^2})e^{-i(\xi x+\eta y)} \, d\xi \, d\eta$$

$$+ \frac{1}{2\pi} \int_{-\infty}^{\infty} \int_{-\infty}^{\infty} \frac{G(\xi,\eta)}{c(\xi^2 + \eta^2)^{\frac{1}{2}}} \sin (ct \sqrt{\xi^2 + \eta^2})e^{-i(\xi x+\eta y)} \, d\xi \, d\eta \quad (80)$$

In any particular problem $F(\xi,\eta)$ and $G(\xi,\eta)$ could be evaluated by a double integration of the type (75) and the final result for $z(x,y,t)$ obtained from equation (80). If, however, we use the Faltung theorem (112), Chap. 1, we may write the general solution (80) explicitly in terms of $f(x,y)$ and $g(x,y)$. To use the Faltung theorem we need to know the Fourier transforms of the functions

$$\cos (ct \sqrt{\xi^2 + \eta^2}), \qquad \frac{\sin (ct \sqrt{\xi^2 + \eta^2})}{c \sqrt{\xi^2 + \eta^2}}$$

If we try to calculate these transforms by a formula of the type (79), we obtain divergent integrals. In other words, neither of these functions belongs to the class of functions considered in the proof of Fourier's integral theorem for functions of two variables. On the other hand, the functions

$$\Theta_\epsilon(\xi,\eta) = e^{-\epsilon\mu}\cos{(\mu t)}, \qquad \Phi_\epsilon(\xi,\eta) = e^{-\epsilon\mu}\frac{\sin{(\mu t)}}{\mu}$$

lead to convergent integrals and do therefore belong to the class of functions to which the general theory is applicable. The Fourier transform of the function $\Theta_\epsilon(\xi,\eta)$ is defined to be

$$\theta_\epsilon(x,y) = \frac{1}{2\pi}\int_{-\infty}^{\infty}\int_{-\infty}^{\infty} e^{-\epsilon\mu}\cos{(\mu t)}e^{-i(\xi x+\eta y)}\,d\xi\,d\eta$$

where $\mu^2 = c^2(\xi^2 + \eta^2)$. If we let the distance of the point (x,y) from the origin in the xy plane be r and that of (ξ,η) from the origin in the $\xi\eta$ plane be ρ, then if θ is the angle between the corresponding position vectors we have

$$\xi x + \eta y = r\rho\cos\theta, \qquad d\xi\,d\eta = \rho\,d\rho\,d\theta$$

so that

$$\theta_\epsilon(x,y) = \frac{1}{2\pi}\int_0^{2\pi}d\theta\int_0^{\infty} e^{-\epsilon c\rho}\cos{(c\rho t)}e^{-i\rho r\cos\theta}\,d\rho$$

Integrating with respect to ρ, we obtain

$$\theta_\epsilon(x,y) = \frac{1}{4\pi}\int_0^{2\pi}d\theta\left\{\frac{\rho e^{-\epsilon c\rho+i\rho(ct-r\cos\theta)}}{-\epsilon c+i(ct-r\cos\theta)} - \frac{e^{-\epsilon c\rho+i\rho(ct-r\cos\theta)}}{[-\epsilon c+i(ct-r\cos\theta)]^2}\right.$$

$$\left.+ \frac{\rho e^{-\epsilon c\rho+i\rho(-ct-r\cos\theta)}}{-c\epsilon-i(ct+r\cos\theta)} - \frac{e^{-\epsilon c\rho+i\rho(-ct-r\cos\theta)}}{[\epsilon c+i(ct+r\cos\theta)]^2}\right\}\Big|_0^{\infty}$$

$$= \frac{1}{4\pi}\int_0^{2\pi}d\theta\left\{\frac{-1}{[-\epsilon c+i(ct-r\cos\theta)]^2} - \frac{1}{[\epsilon c+i(ct+r\cos\theta)]^2}\right\}$$

As ϵ tends to zero, this becomes

$$\theta(x,y) = \frac{1}{4\pi}\int_0^{2\pi}\left[\frac{1}{(ct-r\cos\theta)^2} + \frac{1}{(ct+r\cos\theta)^2}\right]d\theta$$

$$= \frac{ct}{(c^2t^2-x^2-y^2)^{\frac{3}{2}}} = \frac{-1}{c}\frac{\partial}{\partial t}\frac{1}{(c^2t^2-x^2-y^2)^{\frac{1}{2}}}$$

Thus, applying the Faltung theorem in the form (112), Chap. 1,

$$\int_{-\infty}^{\infty}\int_{-\infty}^{\infty} F(\xi,\eta)\Theta(\xi,\eta)e^{-i(\xi x+\eta y)}\,d\xi\,d\eta$$

$$= \int_{-\infty}^{\infty}\int_{-\infty}^{\infty} f(\alpha,\beta)\theta(x-\alpha,y-\beta)d\alpha\,d\beta \quad (81)$$

to the functions

$$\theta(x,y) = -\frac{1}{c}\frac{\partial}{\partial t}(c^2t^2 - x^2 - y^2)^{-\frac{1}{2}}, \qquad \Theta(\xi,\eta) = \cos(\mu t)$$

we find that

$$\int_{-\infty}^{\infty}\int_{-\infty}^{\infty} F(\xi,\eta)\cos(\mu t)e^{-i(\xi x+\eta y)}\,d\xi\,d\eta$$

$$= -\frac{1}{c}\frac{\partial}{\partial t}\int_{-\infty}^{\infty}\int_{-\infty}^{\infty}\frac{f(\alpha,\beta)d\alpha\,d\beta}{[c^2t^2 - (x-\alpha)^2 - (y-\beta)^2]^{\frac{1}{2}}} \qquad (82)$$

Similarly the Fourier transform of $\Phi_\epsilon(\xi,\eta)$ is

$$\phi_\epsilon(x,y) = \frac{1}{2\pi}\int_0^{2\pi} d\theta \int_0^{\infty} \frac{e^{-\epsilon c\rho}\sin(c\rho t)e^{-i\rho r\cos\theta}}{c\rho}\,\rho\,d\rho$$

$$= \frac{1}{4\pi ic}\int_0^{2\pi}\left[\frac{1}{-\epsilon c + i(ct - r\cos\theta)} - \frac{1}{-\epsilon c - i(ct + r\cos\theta)}\right]d\theta$$

Letting ϵ tend to zero and integrating over θ, we obtain

$$\phi(x,y) = -\frac{1}{c(c^2t^2 - x^2 - y^2)^{\frac{1}{2}}}$$

Again applying the Faltung theorem in the form (81), we obtain

$$\int_{-\infty}^{\infty}\int_{-\infty}^{\infty} G(\xi,\eta)\frac{\sin(\mu t)}{\mu}e^{-i(\xi x+\eta y)}\,d\xi\,d\eta$$

$$= -\frac{1}{c}\int_{-\infty}^{\infty}\int_{-\infty}^{\infty}\frac{g(\alpha,\beta)d\alpha\,d\beta}{[c^2t^2 - (x-\alpha)^2 - (y-\beta)^2]^{\frac{1}{2}}} \qquad (83)$$

Substituting from equations (82) and (83) into equation (80), we obtain finally the solution

$$z(x,y,t) = -\frac{1}{2\pi c}\int_{-\infty}^{\infty}\int_{-\infty}^{\infty}\frac{\partial}{\partial t}\frac{f(\alpha,\beta)d\alpha\,d\beta}{[c^2t^2 - (x-\alpha)^2 - (y-\beta)^2]^{\frac{1}{2}}}$$

$$- \frac{1}{2\pi c}\int_{-\infty}^{\infty}\int_{-\infty}^{\infty}\frac{g(\alpha,\beta)d\alpha\,d\beta}{[c^2t^2 - (x-\alpha)^2 - (y-\beta)^2]^{\frac{1}{2}}} \qquad (84)$$

The solution (84) was first obtained by Poisson[1] by much less direct means. The derivation given above is due to Heins.[2] It is of interest to observe here that if the integrations had first been carried out with respect to θ then the problem would reduce to the evaluation of integrals of the form

$$\int_0^{\infty} \rho J_0(r\rho)e^{-\epsilon\rho}\cos(\rho ct)d\rho, \qquad \int_0^{\infty} \rho J_0(r\rho)\sin(\rho ct)e^{-\epsilon\rho}\,d\rho$$

This, however, makes the calculations a little longer.

[1] E. Goursat, "Cours d'analyse" (Paris, 1927), Vol. III, p. 103.
[2] A. E. Heins, *Jour. Math. Phys.*, **14**, 137 (1935).

19.3 Free symmetrical vibrations. In the case where the vibrations are symmetrical with regard to an axis through the origin normal to the equilibrium position of the membrane we may transform to polar coordinates r and θ defined by $x = r \cos \theta$, $y = r \sin \theta$, and then, since the displacement z will be a function of r alone, put $\partial/\partial\theta$ identically equal to zero. Equation (73) then becomes

$$\frac{\partial^2 z}{\partial r^2} + \frac{1}{r}\frac{\partial z}{\partial r} = \frac{1}{c^2}\frac{\partial^2 z}{\partial t^2} \tag{85}$$

This is the equation governing the free symmetrical vibrations. The forced symmetrical vibrations satisfy the equation

$$\frac{\partial^2 z}{\partial r^2} + \frac{1}{r}\frac{\partial z}{\partial r} = \frac{1}{c^2}\frac{\partial^2 z}{\partial t^2} - \frac{p(r,t)}{T} \tag{86}$$

$p(r,t)$ being the symmetrical applied pressure which is producing the vibrations.

To solve the equation (85), we introduce the Hankel transform

$$\bar{z}(\xi,t) = \int_0^\infty rz(r,t)J_0(\xi r)dr \tag{87}$$

of the displacement $z(r,t)$.

Now by equation (35), Chap. 2, we have

$$\int_0^\infty r\left(\frac{\partial^2 z}{\partial r^2} + \frac{1}{r}\frac{\partial z}{\partial r}\right)J_0(\xi r)dr = -\xi^2\bar{z}(\xi,t) \tag{88}$$

provided that $r(\partial z/\partial r)$ tends to zero at $r = 0$ and $r = \infty$.

If, therefore, we multiply both sides of equation (85) by $rJ_0(\xi r)$ and integrate with respect to r from 0 to ∞, we find that the Hankel transform of the displacement satisfies the ordinary differential equation

$$\frac{d^2\bar{z}}{dt^2} + c^2\xi^2\bar{z} = 0$$

which has the solution

$$\bar{z}(\xi,t) = A(\xi)\cos(c\xi t) + B(\xi)\sin(c\xi t) \tag{89}$$

Now if, initially at $t = 0$,

$$z = f(r), \qquad \frac{\partial z}{\partial t} = g(r)$$

then, at $t = 0$,

$$\bar{z} = \bar{f}(\xi), \qquad \frac{d\bar{z}}{dt} = \bar{g}(\xi)$$

where $\bar{f}$ and $\bar{g}$ denote the Hankel transforms of order zero of f and g, respectively. Thus we have

$$A = \bar{f}(\xi), \qquad B = \frac{\bar{g}(\xi)}{c\xi}$$

so that, substituting in equation (89) and forming z by means of the Hankel inversion formula (15), Chap. 2, we have

$$z(r,t) = \int_0^\infty \xi \bar{f}(\xi) \cos (c\xi t) J_0(\xi r) d\xi + \frac{1}{c} \int_0^\infty \bar{g}(\xi) \sin (c\xi t) J_0(\xi r) d\xi \qquad (90)$$

The evaluation of these integrals in the general case is difficult. If we wish to make use of the Parseval theorem for Hankel transforms (Theorem 23) to give an expression for $z(r,t)$ in terms of the functions $f(r)$ and $g(r)$, we shall have to evaluate integrals of the type

$$\int_0^\infty \xi J_0(\xi\eta) J_0(\xi r) \cos (c\xi t) d\xi$$

which are exceedingly complicated. We can however arrive at the general solution by making use of a procedure similar to that adopted in Sec. 11. We put $g(\alpha,\beta) = g(\rho), f(\alpha,\beta) = f(\rho), \alpha = \rho \cos \varphi, \beta = \rho \sin \varphi$, $x = r, y = 0$ in equation (84) to obtain

$$z(r,t) = -\frac{1}{2\pi c} \int_0^\infty \rho \, d\rho \int_0^{2\pi} d\varphi \left[f(\rho) \frac{\partial}{\partial t} + g(\rho) \right] (c^2 t^2 - r^2 - \rho^2$$
$$+ 2r\rho \cos \varphi)^{-\frac{1}{2}}$$

Now

$$\int_0^{2\pi} \frac{d\varphi}{(c^2 t^2 - r^2 - \rho^2 + 2r\rho \cos \varphi)^{\frac{1}{2}}}$$
$$= \frac{1}{(c^2 t^2 - r^2 - \rho^2)^{\frac{1}{2}}} \int_0^{2\pi} \frac{d\varphi}{\left[1 - \dfrac{4r\rho}{c^2 t^2 - (r - \rho)^2} \sin^2 \dfrac{1}{2} \varphi \right]^{\frac{1}{2}}}$$
$$= \frac{4F(k, \frac{1}{2}\pi)}{(c^2 t^2 - r^2 - \rho^2)^{\frac{1}{2}}}$$

in which we have written

$$k^2 = \frac{4r\rho}{c^2 t^2 - (r - \rho)^2}, \qquad F\left(k, \frac{1}{2}\pi\right) = \int_0^{\frac{1}{2}\pi} \frac{d\theta}{\sqrt{1 - k^2 \sin^2 \theta}}$$

In other words, equation (90) is equivalent to the solution

$$z(r,t) = \frac{-1}{2\pi c} \int_0^\infty \rho \left[f(\rho) \frac{\partial}{\partial t} + g(\rho) \right] \frac{F(k, \frac{1}{2}\pi) d\rho}{(c^2 t^2 - r^2 - \rho^2)^{\frac{1}{2}}} \qquad (91)$$

with $k^2 = [c^2 t^2 - (r - \rho)^2]^{-1} \cdot 4r\rho$.

Because of the complicated nature of this general result it is often easier to make use of the solution in the form (90). Suppose, for example, that initially (cf. Fig. 11)

$$z = \frac{\epsilon}{(1 + r^2/a^2)^{\frac{3}{2}}}, \qquad \frac{\partial z}{\partial t} = 0$$

Then $\bar{g}(\xi)$ is identically zero, and

$$\bar{f}(\xi) = \epsilon \int_0^\infty \frac{rJ_0(\xi r)dr}{(1 + r^2/a^2)^{\frac{3}{2}}} = \epsilon a^2 \int_0^\infty \frac{uJ_0(\xi au)du}{(1 + u^2)^{\frac{3}{2}}}$$

Now, by equation (20), Appendix A, we have

$$\int_0^\infty e^{-wx}J_0(\rho x)dx = \frac{1}{\sqrt{\rho^2 + w^2}} \tag{92}$$

so that by the Hankel inversion theorem

$$\int_0^\infty \frac{\rho J_0(\rho x)d\rho}{(\rho^2 + w^2)^{\frac{3}{2}}} = \frac{e^{-wx}}{x}$$

giving

$$\bar{f}(\xi) = \frac{\epsilon a}{\xi} e^{-\xi a}$$

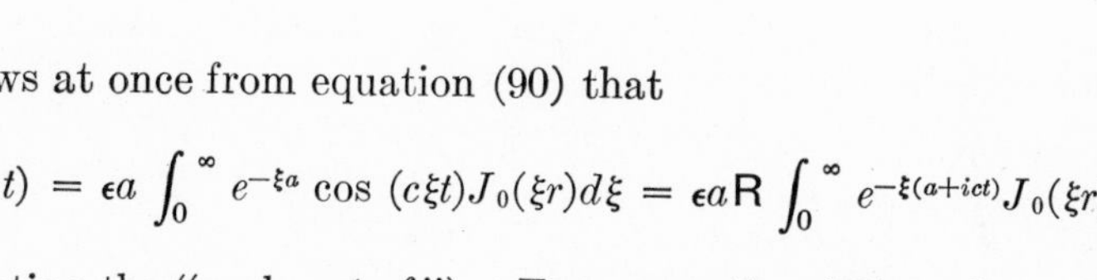

FIG. 11. The initial displacement of a thin membrane which is allowed to vibrate freely.

It follows at once from equation (90) that

$$z(r,t) = \epsilon a \int_0^\infty e^{-\xi a} \cos (c\xi t)J_0(\xi r)d\xi = \epsilon a \mathsf{R} \int_0^\infty e^{-\xi(a+ict)}J_0(\xi r)d\xi$$

(R denoting the "real part of"). From equation (92) we have therefore

$$z(r,t) = \frac{\epsilon a \cos \varphi}{R} = \epsilon a \left(\frac{1}{2R^2} + \frac{R^2 \cos 2\varphi}{2R^4} \right)^{\frac{1}{2}}$$

where

$$R^2 e^{2i\varphi} = a^2 + r^2 - c^2t^2 + 2iact$$

Hence

$$z = \frac{\epsilon}{\sqrt{2}} \left\{ \frac{1}{\left[\left(1 + \dfrac{r^2 - c^2 t^2}{a^2} \right)^2 + 4\left(\dfrac{ct}{a} \right)^2 \right]^{\frac{1}{2}}} \right.$$

$$\left. + \frac{1 + \dfrac{r^2 - c^2 t^2}{a^2}}{\left[\left(1 + \dfrac{r^2 - c^2 t^2}{a^2} \right)^2 + 4\left(\dfrac{ct}{a} \right)^2 \right]^{\frac{1}{2}}} \right\}^{\frac{1}{2}}$$

is the required solution.

19.4 Forced vibrations of a very large membrane. The solution of the equation of forced vibrations, (72), can be obtained by a method similar to that employed in Sec. 19.2. If we write

$$P(\xi,\eta,t) = \frac{1}{2\pi} \int_{-\infty}^{\infty} \int_{-\infty}^{\infty} p(x,y,t) e^{i(\xi x + \eta y)} \, dx \, dy$$

then equation (76) becomes in the case of forced vibrations

$$\frac{d^2 Z}{dt^2} + \mu^2 Z = \frac{1}{T} P(\xi,\eta,t) \tag{93}$$

where μ is defined by equation (77). The solution of this equation was derived previously—equation (13). It is

$$Z(\xi,\eta,t) = \frac{-1}{T\mu} \int_0^t P(\xi,\eta,\tau) \sin \mu(\tau - t) d\tau$$

in the case where $Z = dZ/dt = 0$ when $t = 0$, that is, if the plate is initially at rest in the equilibrium position. Thus

$$z(x,y,t) = -\frac{1}{T} \int_0^t d\tau \int_{-\infty}^{\infty} \int_{-\infty}^{\infty} P(\xi,\eta,\tau) \frac{\sin \mu(\tau - t)}{\mu} e^{-i(\xi x + \eta y)} \, d\xi \, d\eta$$

The infinite double integral on the right may then be evaluated by means of equation (83) to give for the displacement

$$z(x,y,t) = \frac{1}{cT} \int_{-\infty}^{\infty} d\alpha \int_{-\infty}^{\infty} d\beta \int_0^t \frac{p(\alpha,\beta,\tau) d\tau}{[c^2(\tau - t)^2 - (x - \alpha)^2 - (y - \beta)^2]^{\frac{1}{2}}} \tag{94}$$

19.5 Vibrations of a circular membrane.[1] In the problems considered above we assumed that the membrane was very large so that it was possible to employ double Fourier transforms and Hankel transforms to obtain solutions of the fundamental equation (72). As an example of

[1] Cf. I. N. Sneddon, *Phil. Mag.*, **37**, 17 (1946).

the use of the finite Hankel transform (42), Chap. 3, we shall consider the symmetrical vibrations of a thin membrane in the form of a circle of radius a. The equation governing the motion is therefore equation (86). Multiplying equation (86) throughout by $rJ_0(\xi_i r)$, integrating with respect to r from 0 to a, and making use of the boundary condition $z = 0$ when $r = a$, we find that the finite Hankel transform of order zero

$$\bar{z}_J = \int_0^a rz(r,t)J_0(\xi_i r)dr \tag{95}$$

satisfies the ordinary linear differential equation

$$\left(\frac{d^2}{dt^2} + c^2\xi_i^2\right)\bar{z}_J = \frac{1}{\sigma}\,\bar{p}_J(\xi_i,t) \tag{96}$$

where ξ_i is a zero of $J_0(\xi_i a)$, σ is the areal density of the membrane, and $p_J(\xi,t)$ denotes the finite Hankel transform of $p(r,t)$ defined by an equation similar to (95).

When the function $p(r,t)$ is known, we can find the solution of equation (96) and obtain z by means of the inversion formula (44), Chap. 3.

If the vibrations of the membrane are free, we may take $\bar{p}_J$ in equation (96) to be zero. Consider the membrane to be set in motion from the position $z = f(r)$ with a velocity $\partial z/\partial t = g(r)$. Then at $t = 0$ we have the initial values

$$\bar{z}_J = \int_0^a uf(u)J_0(\xi_i u)du, \qquad \frac{d\bar{z}_J}{dt} = \int_0^a ug(u)J_0(\xi_i u)du$$

so that the appropriate solution of equation (96) is

$$\bar{z}_J = \cos\,(c\xi_i t)\int_0^a uf(u)J_0(\xi_i u)du + \frac{\sin\,(c\xi_i t)}{c\xi_i}\int_0^a ug(u)J_0(\xi_i u)du$$

Inverting by equation (44), Chap. 3, we obtain finally for the displacement of the membrane

$$z = \frac{2}{a^2}\sum_i \frac{J_0(\xi_i r)}{[J_1(\xi_i a)]^2}\cos\,(c\xi_i t)\int_0^a uf(u)J_0(\xi_i u)du$$

$$+ \frac{2}{ca^2}\sum_i \frac{J_0(\xi_i r)}{[J_1(\xi_i a)]^2}\frac{\sin\,(c\xi_i t)}{\xi_i}\int_0^a ug(u)J_0(\xi_i u)du \tag{97}$$

where the summation with respect to i extends over all the positive roots of the equation $J_0(\xi_i a) = 0$.

The solution (97) may be obtained by eliminating the time variable from equation (86) by means of a Laplace transform. This method is longer than that involving the use of the finite Hankel transform and reduces to the evaluation of quite complicated contour integrals. If the motion is started from the equilibrium position, we may put $f(u) = 0$ in equation (97) to obtain a result which has been established by the use of the Laplace transform.[1] A comparison of the two methods of analysis reveals the economy of the finite Hankel transform method.

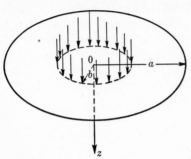

FIG. 12. Circular membrane distorted by the application of pressure which is uniformly distributed over a circular area.

To illustrate the use of the method of finite Hankel transforms in the discussion of the forced vibrations of a circular membrane, we consider forced vibrations of a simple type: Suppose a membrane of radius a, stretched by a tension T, is at rest in its equilibrium position. At time $t = 0$ a pressure $P_0\psi(t)$ is applied uniformly to the part of the surface bounded by the circle $r \leq b \leq a$ (cf. Fig. 12). Then, since

$$\int_0^b rJ_0(\xi_i r)dr = \frac{b}{\xi_i} J_1(b\xi_i)$$

we have

$$\bar{p}_J(\xi_i,t) = \frac{bP_0}{\xi_i} \psi(t)J_1(b\xi_i)$$

and equation (96) becomes

$$\left(\frac{d^2}{dt^2} + c^2\xi_i^2\right) \bar{z}_J = \frac{P_0 bJ_1(b\xi_i)}{\sigma\xi_i} \psi(t) \tag{98}$$

If the membrane is set in motion from rest in its equilibrium position, $\bar{z}_J = d\bar{z}_J/dt = 0$, when $t = 0$, so that the solution of equation (98) is

$$\bar{z}_J(\xi_i,t) = \frac{P_0 bJ_1(b\xi_i)}{\sigma\xi_i} \int_0^t \psi(u) \sin [c\xi_i(t - u)]du$$

whence by the inversion theorem (44), Chap. 3, we obtain for the transverse displacement of the membrane

$$z(r,t) = \frac{2P_0 b}{c\sigma a^2} \sum_i \frac{J_1(b\xi_i)J_0(r\xi_i)}{\xi_i^2[J_1(\xi_i a)]^2} \int_0^t \psi(u) \sin [c\xi_i(t - u)]du \tag{99}$$

where the sum is taken over all the positive roots of the equation

$$J_0(\xi_i a) = 0$$

[1] Carslaw and Jaeger, op. cit., pp. 160–161.

Since the roots of the equation

$$J_0(\lambda_i) = 0 \tag{100}$$

have been calculated,[1] it is more suitable to take the sum over all the positive roots λ_i. This may readily be effected by making the transformation $\xi_i = \lambda_i/a$ in equation (99).

There are two cases of special interest: when $a = b$, the force acting over the entire surface of the membrane, and when $b = 0$, the force being concentrated at the center of the membrane. If $a = b$, then equation (99) reduces to

$$z(r,t) = \frac{2P_0 a}{c\sigma} \sum_i \frac{J_0(r\lambda_i/a)}{\lambda_i^2 J_1(\lambda_i)} \int_0^t \psi(u) \sin\left[\frac{c\lambda_i(t - u)}{a}\right] du \tag{101}$$

where now the sum extends to all the positive roots of the transcendental equation (100). Similarly if we let b tend to zero and P_0 tend to infinity in such a way that the total load $\pi b^2 P_0$ tends to a finite limit F, then, since

$$J_1(b\xi) \simeq \tfrac{1}{2}b\xi$$

we find that equation (99) reduces to

$$z = \frac{Fa}{\pi c\sigma} \sum_i \frac{J_0(r\lambda_i/a)}{\lambda_i^2 [J_1(\lambda_i)]^2} \int_0^t \psi(u) \sin\left[\frac{c\lambda_i(t - u)}{a}\right] du \tag{102}$$

the sum being taken over the positive roots of equation (100).

For example, if we take $\psi(t) = 1$, for $t > 0$, then, in the general case $b \le a$,

$$z(r,t) = \frac{2P_0 ab}{T} \sum_i \frac{J_1(b\lambda_i/a)J_0(r\lambda_i/a)}{\lambda_i^3 [J_1(\lambda_i)]^2} \left(1 - \cos\frac{\lambda_i ct}{a}\right)$$

so that, if $a = b$,

$$z = \frac{P_0}{T}\left[2a^2 \sum_i \frac{J_0(r\lambda_i/a)}{\lambda_i^3 J_1(\lambda_i)} - 2a^2 \sum_i \frac{J_0(r\lambda_i/a)}{\lambda_i^3 J_1(\lambda_i)} \cos\frac{\lambda_i ct}{a}\right]$$

Now using the result (65), Chap. 3, in the formula (45), Chap. 3, we see that

$$2a^2 \sum_i \frac{J_0(r\lambda_i/a)}{\lambda_i^3 J_1(\lambda_i)} = \frac{1}{4}(a^2 - r^2)$$

giving finally

$$z = \frac{P_0}{T}\left[\frac{1}{4}(a^2 - r^2) - 2a^2 \sum_i \frac{J_0(r\lambda_i/a)}{\lambda_i^3 J_1(\lambda_i)} \cos\left(\frac{\lambda_i ct}{a}\right)\right]$$

the sum being taken over all the positive roots of equation (100).

[1] See, for instance, E. Jahnke and F. Emde, "Funktionentafeln mit Formeln und Kurven" (B. G. Teubner, Leipzig, 1933), p. 237.

Similarly, if $\psi(t) = \sin \omega t$, the appropriate solution of equation (98) is

$$\bar{z}_J = -\frac{P_0 b J_1(b\xi_i)}{\sigma c \xi_i^2} \frac{\omega \sin (c\xi_i t) - c\xi_i \sin (\omega t)}{c^2 \xi_i^2 - \omega^2}$$

whence

$$z = \frac{P_0 c^2}{T\omega^2} \sin (\omega t) \left\{ -\frac{2b}{a^2} \sum_i \frac{1}{\xi_i(1 - c^2\xi_i^2/\omega^2)} \frac{J_0(r\xi_i)J_1(b\xi_i)}{[J_1(a\xi_i)]^2} \right\}$$

$$+ \frac{2P_0\omega b c}{Ta^2} \sum_i \frac{\sin (c\xi_i t) J_0(r\xi_i)J_1(b\xi_i)}{\xi_i^2(\omega^2 - c^2\xi_i^2)[J_1(a\xi_i)]^2} \quad (103)$$

Substituting from equation (68), Chap. 3, into the inversion formula (45), Chap. 3, we obtain the expression

$$-\frac{2}{a} \sum_i \frac{J_0(r\xi_i)}{\xi_i(1 - c^2\xi_i^2/\omega^2)J_1(a\xi_i)} = \frac{J_0(r\omega/c)}{J_0(a\omega/c)} - 1$$

so that, if $b = a$, equation (103) reduces to

$$z = \frac{P_0 c^2}{T^2} \sin (\omega t) \left[\frac{J_0(r\omega/c)}{J_0(a\omega/c)} - 1 \right] + \frac{2P_0\omega c}{Ta} \sum_i \frac{\sin (c\xi_i t) J_0(r\xi_i)}{\xi_i^2(\omega^2 - c^2\xi_i^2)J_1(a\xi_i)}$$

the summation extending to all the positive roots of the equation

$$J_0(\xi_i a) = 0$$

19.6 Vibrations of a rectangular membrane. The theory of finite Fourier transforms can similarly be applied to give expressions for the transverse displacement of a rectangular membrane. We shall consider the membrane which in its equilibrium position occupies the rectangle

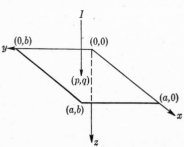

$$0 \le x \le a, \qquad 0 \le y \le b \quad (104)$$

lying in the plane $z = 0$ (cf. Fig. 13). If we assume that the edge of the membrane is fixed throughout the motion, then z will be zero, at all times,

Fig. 13. The application of a normal impulse to a rectangular membrane.

for each point lying on the bounding lines of the rectangle (104). Now by equation (12), Chap. 3,

$$\int_0^a \frac{\partial^2 z}{\partial x^2} \sin \left(\frac{m\pi x}{a}\right) dx = -\frac{m^2\pi^2}{a^2} \int_0^a z(x,y) \sin \left(\frac{m\pi x}{a}\right) dx$$

provided that z is zero (as we have assumed it to be) when $x = 0$ or a. Thus if we write

$$\bar{z}_s(m,n) = \int_0^a \int_0^b z(x,y) \sin\left(\frac{m\pi x}{a}\right) \sin\left(\frac{n\pi y}{b}\right) dx\, dy$$

it follows that

$$\int_0^a \int_0^b \frac{\partial^2 z}{\partial x^2} \sin\left(\frac{m\pi x}{a}\right) \sin\left(\frac{n\pi y}{b}\right) dx\, dy = -\frac{m^2\pi^2}{a^2} \bar{z}_s(m,n)$$

and similarly that

$$\int_0^a \int_0^b \frac{\partial^2 z}{\partial y^2} \sin\left(\frac{m\pi x}{a}\right) \sin\left(\frac{n\pi y}{b}\right) dx\, dy = -\frac{n^2\pi^2}{b^2} \bar{z}_s(m,n)$$

If we now introduce the transform

$$\bar{p}_s(m,n,t) = \int_0^a \int_0^b p(x,y,t) \sin\left(\frac{m\pi x}{a}\right) \sin\left(\frac{n\pi y}{b}\right) dx\, dy$$

and multiply both sides of equation (72) by $\sin(m\pi x/a) \sin(n\pi y/b)$, we obtain, on integrating over the rectangle (104),

$$\frac{1}{c^2} \frac{d^2\bar{z}_s}{dt^2} + \pi^2\left(\frac{m^2}{a^2} + \frac{n^2}{b^2}\right) \bar{z}_s = \frac{1}{T} \bar{p}_s(m,n,t)$$

Denoting the initial values of $\bar{z}_s$ and $d\bar{z}_s/dt$ by $\bar{z}_0$ and $\bar{z}_1$, respectively, and writing

$$\mu_{mn} = \left(\frac{m^2}{a^2} + \frac{n^2}{b^2}\right)^{\frac{1}{2}}$$

we find from equation (12) that

$$\bar{z}_s = \bar{z}_0 \cos(c\pi\mu_{mn}t) + \frac{\bar{z}_1}{c\pi\mu_{mn}} \sin(c\pi\mu_{mn}t)$$

$$+ \frac{c}{\pi T \mu_{mn}} \int_0^t \bar{p}_s(m,n,u) \sin[c\pi\mu_{mn}(t-u)]du \quad (105)$$

For the *free* vibrations resulting from the initial conditions

$$z = f(x,y), \qquad \frac{\partial z}{\partial t} = g(x,y) \qquad t = 0$$

we have, on putting $\bar{p}_s$ identically zero in equation (105),

$$\bar{z}_s = \cos(c\pi\mu_{mn}t) \int_0^a \int_0^b f(\xi,\eta) \sin\left(\frac{m\pi\xi}{a}\right) \sin\left(\frac{n\pi\eta}{b}\right) d\xi\, d\eta$$

$$+ \frac{\sin(c\pi\mu_{mn}t)}{c\pi\mu_{mn}} \int_0^a \int_0^b g(\xi,\eta) \sin\left(\frac{m\pi\xi}{a}\right) \sin\left(\frac{n\pi\eta}{b}\right) d\xi\, d\eta$$

so that, by equation (36), Chap. 3, the transverse displacement is given by

$$
z(x,y,t) = \frac{4}{ab} \sum_{m=1}^{\infty} \sum_{n=1}^{\infty} \sin \frac{m\pi x}{a} \sin \frac{n\pi y}{b} \cos (\pi \mu_{mn} ct) \int_0^a \int_0^b f(\xi,\eta) \sin \frac{m\pi \xi}{a}
$$

$$
\times \sin \frac{n\pi \eta}{b} d\xi \, d\eta + \frac{4}{\pi c} \sum_{m=1}^{\infty} \sum_{n=1}^{\infty} \sin \frac{m\pi x}{a} \sin \frac{n\pi y}{b}
$$

$$
\times \frac{\sin (\pi \mu_{mn} ct)}{(m^2 b^2 + n^2 a^2)^{\frac{1}{2}}} \int_0^a \int_0^b g(\xi,\eta) \sin \frac{m\pi \xi}{a} \sin \frac{n\pi \eta}{b} d\xi \, d\eta
$$

For example, if an impulse I is applied normal to the membrane at the point (p,q) in the equilibrium configuration $z = 0$ (cf. Fig. 13), then we may take

$$
f(x,y) = 0, \qquad g(x,y) = \frac{I}{\sigma} \delta(x - p) \delta(y - q)
$$

where $0 \leq p \leq a$, $0 \leq q \leq b$, and σ is the surface density of the membrane. Then, since

$$
\int_0^a \int_0^b g(\xi,\eta) \sin \left(\frac{m\pi \xi}{a} \right) \sin \left(\frac{n\pi \eta}{b} \right) d\xi \, d\eta = \frac{I}{\sigma} \sin \left(\frac{m\pi p}{a} \right) \sin \left(\frac{n\pi q}{b} \right)
$$

we find for the transverse displacement

$$
z(x,y,t) = \frac{4I}{\pi \sigma c} \sum_{m=1}^{\infty} \sum_{n=1}^{\infty} \frac{1}{(m^2 b^2 + n^2 a^2)^{\frac{1}{2}}} \sin \left[\pi ct \left(\frac{m^2}{a^2} + \frac{n^2}{b^2} \right)^{\frac{1}{2}} \right]
$$

$$
\times \sin \left(\frac{m\pi p}{a} \right) \sin \left(\frac{n\pi q}{b} \right) \sin \left(\frac{m\pi x}{a} \right) \sin \left(\frac{n\pi y}{b} \right)
$$

The forced vibrations of a rectangular membrane can be treated in the same way, but since no new principle is involved, such a discussion is left to the reader.

20. Vibrations of a Thin Elastic Plate

20.1 Introduction. We shall consider now the small transverse vibrations of the thin elastic plate which is bounded by the two parallel planes $z = \pm h$ but which is otherwise of unlimited extent. If the material of the plate is of uniform density ρ, the differential equation governing the displacement w of the point (x,y) of the central plane, $z = 0$, of the plate may be written in the form[1]

[1] A. E. H. Love, "The Mathematical Theory of Elasticity," 4th ed. (Cambridge, London, 1934), p. 496.

$$D \left(\frac{\partial^2}{\partial x^2} + \frac{\partial^2}{\partial y^2} \right)^2 w + 2\rho h \frac{\partial^2 w}{\partial t^2} = Z(x,y,t) \qquad (106)$$

where it is assumed that the plate is subjected to a transverse force of intensity $Z(x,y,t)$. In equation (106) the effects of the "rotatory inertia" and of the additional deflection caused by shear are neglected. The constant D denotes the flexural rigidity of the plate defined, in terms of Young's modulus E, and the Poisson ratio σ of the material of the plate, by the equation

$$D = \frac{2Eh^3}{3(1 - \sigma^2)} \qquad (107)$$

We shall make the simplifying assumption that the function $Z(x,y,t)$ can be split into the product of a space-dependent function and a time-dependent function. This is the case which arises most frequently in practice. Thus we write

$$Z(x,y,t) = 16\rho h b p(x,y)\psi'(t)$$

where

$$b^2 = \frac{D}{2\rho h} \qquad (108)$$

and p and ψ are functions of (x,y) and of t, respectively. The prime denotes, in this instance, differentiation with respect to time. With this notation equation (106) reduces to

$$b^2 \left(\frac{\partial^2}{\partial x^2} + \frac{\partial^2}{\partial y^2} \right)^2 w + \frac{\partial^2 w}{\partial t^2} = 8bp(x,y)\psi'(t) \qquad (106a)$$

An important special case is that in which the vibrations are symmetrical. If we transform the Laplace operator to polar coordinates (r,θ), then, in the case where the vibrations are symmetrical about the z axis, w and Z are functions of r and t only and the operator $\partial/\partial\theta$ is identically zero. Equation (106) therefore assumes the form

$$b^2 \left(\frac{\partial^2}{\partial r^2} + \frac{1}{r} \frac{\partial}{\partial r} \right)^2 w + \frac{\partial^2 w}{\partial t^2} = \frac{Z(r,t)}{2\rho h} \qquad (109)$$

for the case of forced vibrations. In the case of free vibrations we take the function $Z(x,y,t)$ of equation (106)—or $Z(r,t)$ of equation (109)—to be identically zero.

20.2 Free symmetrical vibrations of a very large plate.[1] As a first example of the solution of the fourth-order partial differential equation (109) by the method of integral transforms we shall consider the *free*

---

[1] I. N. Sneddon, *Proc. Cambridge Phil. Soc.*, **41**, 27 (1945).

vibrations of a thin elastic plate of infinite radius. We shall suppose that the vibrations result from the initial conditions

$$w = f(r), \qquad \frac{\partial w}{\partial t} = 0 \tag{110}$$

at $t = 0$. Since the vibrations are free, we may take the function $Z(r,t)$ occurring in equation (109) to be identically zero. To solve the resulting equation, we multiply both sides by $rJ_0(\xi r)$, integrate over r from 0 to ∞, and write

$$\int_0^\infty rw(r,t)J_0(\xi r)dr = \bar{w}(\xi,t) \tag{111}$$

Proceeding as in the establishment of equation (88), we see that, if F is any function of r,

$$\int_0^\infty r\left(\frac{\partial^2}{\partial r^2} + \frac{1}{r}\frac{\partial}{\partial r}\right)F(r)J_0(\xi r)dr = -\xi^2\bar{F}(\xi) \tag{88a}$$

where

$$\bar{F}(\xi) = \int_0^\infty rF(r)J_0(\xi r)dr$$

Putting

$$F(r) = \left(\frac{\partial^2}{\partial r^2} + \frac{1}{r}\frac{\partial}{\partial r}\right)w$$

in equation (88a), we find that

$$\int_0^\infty r\left(\frac{\partial^2}{\partial r^2} + \frac{1}{r}\frac{\partial}{\partial r}\right)^2 wJ_0(\xi r)dr = -\xi^2\int_0^\infty r\left(\frac{\partial^2}{\partial r^2} + \frac{1}{r}\frac{\partial}{\partial r}\right)wJ_0(\xi r)dr$$
$$= \xi^4\bar{w}(\xi,t)$$

by applying equation (88a) with $\bar{F} = \bar{w}$. It follows immediately from this result that if $w(r,t)$ is a solution of equation (109) with $Z(r,t) \equiv 0$ then the Hankel transform $\bar{w}(\xi,t)$ satisfies the ordinary differential equation

$$\frac{1}{b^2}\frac{d^2\bar{w}}{dt^2} + \xi^4\bar{w} = 0 \tag{112}$$

We may therefore write

$$\bar{w}(\xi,t) = A(\xi)\cos(b\xi^2 t) + B(\xi)\sin(b\xi^2 t) \tag{113}$$

For the initial conditions (110) it follows at once from the definition (111) that

$$A(\xi) = [\bar{w}]_{t=0} = \int_0^\infty uf(u)J_0(\xi u)du, \qquad B(\xi) = \left[\frac{d\bar{w}}{dt}\right]_{t=0} = 0$$

Substituting into equation (113), we have

$$\bar{w}(\xi,t) = \cos(b\xi^2 t)\int_0^\infty uf(u)J_0(\xi u)du$$

so that from the Hankel inversion theorem (Theorem 19) we have

$$w(r,t) = \int_0^\infty \xi \bar{w}(\xi) J_0(\xi r) d\xi = \int_0^\infty \xi J_0(\xi r) \cos (b\xi^2 t) d\xi \int_0^\infty u f(u) J_0(u\xi) du$$

or, changing the order of the integrations,

$$w(r,t) = \int_0^\infty u f(u) du \int_0^\infty \xi J_0(\xi r) J_0(\xi u) \cos (b\xi^2 t) d\xi$$

Now, by Weber's second exponential integral,[1]

$$\int_0^\infty \xi J_0(\xi u) J_0(\xi r) e^{-p\xi^2} d\xi = \frac{1}{2p} \exp \left(- \frac{u^2 + r^2}{4p} \right) I_0 \left(\frac{ur}{2p} \right)$$

where $I_0(z) = J_0(iz)$, so that, substituting $p = -ibt$ and equating real parts, we obtain

$$\int_0^\infty \xi J_0(\xi u) J_0(\xi r) \cos (b\xi^2 t) d\xi = \frac{1}{2bt} J_0 \left(\frac{ur}{2bt} \right) \sin \left(\frac{u^2 + r^2}{4bt} \right) \quad (114)$$

giving finally

$$w(r,t) = \frac{1}{2bt} \int_0^\infty u f(u) J_0 \left(\frac{ur}{2bt} \right) \sin \left(\frac{u^2 + r^2}{4bt} \right) du \quad (115)$$

for the displacement of any point of the central surface of the plate at any time.

For example, if the initial displacement of the central surface is given by

$$w = f(r) = \epsilon e^{-r^2/a^2}$$

where ϵ is small, then

$$\bar{w} = \epsilon \cos (bt\xi^2) \int_0^\infty r e^{-r^2/a^2} J_0(\xi r) dr$$

Putting $\nu = 0$, $p = 1/a^2$, $\mu = 2$, $a = \xi$ in Hankel's well-known result[2]

$$\int_0^\infty J_\nu(at) e^{-p t^2} t^{\mu-1} dt = \frac{a^\nu \Gamma(\frac{1}{2}\mu + \frac{1}{2}\nu)}{2^{\nu+1} p^{\frac{1}{2}\mu+\frac{1}{2}\nu} \Gamma(1 + \nu)} {}_1F_1 \left(\frac{1}{2} \mu + \frac{1}{2} \nu; \nu + 1; - \frac{a^2}{4p} \right)$$

$$(116)$$

we obtain

$$\bar{w}(\xi,t) = \tfrac{1}{2}\epsilon a^2 e^{-\frac{1}{4}\xi^2 a^2} \cos (bt\xi^2)$$

so that, by the inversion theorem (15), Chap. 2,

$$w(r,t) = \frac{1}{2} \epsilon a^2 \int_0^\infty d\xi e^{-\frac{1}{4}\xi^2 a^2} \cos (bt\xi^2) J_0(\xi r) d\xi$$

---

[1] Watson, *op. cit.*, p. 393.

[2] Watson, *op. cit.*, p. 393, or equation (15), Appendix A.

We can evaluate the integral on the right-hand side by putting $\mu = 2$, $\nu = 0$, $a = r$, and

$$p = \frac{a^2}{4}\left(1 + \frac{4ibt}{a^2}\right)$$

into equation (116) and then equating real parts. In this way we obtain the equation

$$w(r,t) = \frac{\epsilon \exp\left(-\dfrac{\rho^2}{1 + \tau^2}\right)}{1 + \tau^2}\left(\cos\frac{\rho^2\tau}{1 + \tau^2} + \tau\sin\frac{\rho^2\tau}{1 + \tau^2}\right) \qquad (117)$$

where $\tau = 4bt/a^2$ and $\rho = r/a$. The values of w for various values of ρ and τ can be calculated easily from tables of elementary functions and the form of the plate at subsequent times determined. Some of the results of calculations of this kind are shown in Fig. 14.

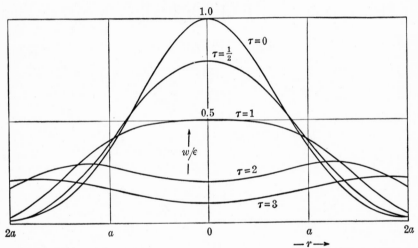

FIG. 14.   The form, at various times, of a plate which is vibrating freely ($\tau = 4bt/a^2$).

If we wish to determine what initial displacement of the plate will produce a given motion

$$w(0,t) = \psi(t)$$

of the center of the plate, then, putting $r = 0$ in equation (115), we see that the required initial displacement is $w = f(r)$ where $f(u)$ is a solution of the integral equation

$$\psi(t) = \frac{1}{2bt}\int_0^\infty uf(u)\sin\left(\frac{u^2}{4bt}\right)du \qquad (118)$$

To solve this equation, we note that it can be written in the form

$$\frac{1}{\alpha} \psi \left(\frac{1}{4b\alpha} \right) = \int_0^\infty f(v^{\frac{1}{2}}) \sin (\alpha v) dv$$

by putting $\alpha = 1/4bt$, $u^2 = v$. Inverting this last equation by Fourier's sine formula (36), Chap. 1, we have

$$f(v^{\frac{1}{2}}) = \frac{2}{\pi} \int_0^\infty \psi \left(\frac{1}{4b\alpha} \right) \frac{\sin (\alpha v)}{\alpha} d\alpha$$

which is equivalent to

$$f(r) = \frac{2}{\pi} \int_0^\infty \frac{\psi(t)}{t} \sin \left(\frac{r^2}{4bt} \right) dt \tag{119}$$

Therefore, if we give the plate the initial displacement defined by equation (119) and then release it from rest, the subsequent motion of the plate will be such that its center will move with a velocity $d\psi(t)/dt$.

For example, if we wish to ensure that the center of the plate will have the displacement

$$w(0,t) = \begin{cases} VT \left(1 - \dfrac{t}{T} \right) & 0 \leq t \leq T \\ 0 & t > T \end{cases}$$

then we must give the plate an initial displacement

$$w(r,0) = \frac{2V}{\pi} \int_0^T \frac{T - t}{t} \sin \left(\frac{r^2}{4bt} \right) dt = \frac{2VT}{\pi} F \left(\frac{r^2}{4bT} \right)$$

where the function $F(x)$ is defined by the equation

$$F(x) = \tfrac{1}{2}\pi - \text{Si } (x) + x \text{ Ci } (x) \tag{120}$$

with the usual definitions

$$\text{Si } (x) = \int_0^x \frac{\sin (u)}{u} du, \qquad \text{Ci } (x) = - \int_x^\infty \frac{\cos (u)}{u} du$$

for the sine and cosine integrals.

20.3 Forced symmetrical vibrations of a large plate. We now proceed to the consideration of certain types of forced vibrations of a large, thin elastic plate. We shall assume that the intensity of the transverse force applied to the plate is

$$Z(r,t) = 16\rho h b f(r)\psi'(t) \tag{121}$$

where $f(r)$ is a function of r alone and $\psi'(t) = d\psi/dt$ is a function of t alone. Equation (109) reduces then to

$$b^2 \left(\frac{\partial^2}{\partial r^2} + \frac{1}{r} \frac{\partial}{\partial r} \right)^2 w + \frac{\partial^2 w}{\partial t^2} = 8bf(r)\psi'(t)$$

If we multiply both sides of this equation by $rJ_0(\xi r)$ and integrate with respect to r from 0 to ∞, then we obtain the relation

$$\frac{d^2\bar{w}}{dt^2} + b^2\xi^4\bar{w} = 8b\bar{f}(\xi)\psi'(t) \tag{122}$$

between the function $\bar{w}(\xi,t)$ defined by equation (111) and the function $\bar{f}(\xi)$ defined by

$$\bar{f}(\xi) = \int_0^\infty rf(r)J_0(\xi r)dr$$

The ordinary differential equation (122) has the solution

$$\bar{w}(\xi,t) = 8b\bar{f}(\xi)\int_{-\infty}^t \psi(u)\cos[b(t-u)\xi^2]du$$

so that, by the Hankel inversion theorem,

$$w(r,t) = 8b\int_{-\infty}^t \psi(u)du\int_0^\infty \xi\bar{f}(\xi)J_0(\xi r)\cos[b(t-u)\xi^2]d\xi \tag{123}$$

Now

$$\int_0^\infty \xi\bar{f}(\xi)J_0(\xi r)\cos[b(t-u)\xi^2]d\xi$$

$$= \int_0^\infty vf(v)dv\int_0^\infty \xi J_0(\xi v)J_0(\xi r)\cos[b(t-u)\xi^2]d\xi$$

and the ξ integration is simply equation (114) so that we obtain finally the formula

$$w(r,t) = 4\int_{-\infty}^t \frac{\psi(u)du}{t-u}\int_0^\infty vf(v)\sin\left[\frac{v^2+r^2}{4b(t-u)}\right]J_0\left(\frac{vr}{2b(t-u)}\right)dv \tag{124}$$

If we have a force of total magnitude $16\rho hb\psi'(t)$ acting at the origin, then the function $f(r)$ must be such that it vanishes when $r \neq 0$ and satisfies

$$\int_0^\infty 2\pi rf(r)dr = 1$$

In other words, for a concentrated force we must take

$$f(r) = \frac{\delta(r)}{2\pi r}$$

where $\delta(r)$ denotes the Dirac delta function. Substituting $\delta(v)/2\pi v$ for $f(v)$ in equation (124), we obtain

$$w(r,t) = \frac{2}{\pi}\int_{-\infty}^t \psi(u)\sin\left[\frac{r^2}{4b(t-u)}\right]\frac{du}{t-u}$$

as the solution for a point force acting at the origin. Changing the variable of integration to

$$\xi = \frac{r^2}{4b(t-u)}$$

we see that this equation may be written in the form

$$w(r,t) = \frac{2}{\pi} \int_0^\infty \psi\left(t - \frac{r^2}{4b\xi}\right) \frac{\sin \xi}{\xi} d\xi \tag{125}$$

which is Boussinesq's solution for the case of a concentrated force.[1]

In dealing with special problems it is often simpler to make use of the solution in the form (123) instead of the more elegant result (124). For example, if the total force $16\rho hb\psi'(t)$ is distributed uniformly over a circle of radius a, then we may take

$$f(r) = \begin{cases} \dfrac{1}{\pi a^2} & 0 \le r \le a \\ 0 & r > a \end{cases}$$

so that

$$\bar{f}(\xi) = \frac{1}{\pi a^2} \int_0^a r J_0(\xi r) dr = \frac{J_1(\xi a)}{\pi a \xi}$$

and equation (123) reduces to

$$w(r,t) = \frac{8b}{\pi a} \int_{-\infty}^t \psi(u) du \int_0^\infty J_0(\xi r) J_1(\xi a) \cos\left[b(t-u)\xi^2\right] d\xi$$

If we let r tend to zero in this equation, we get the equation

$$w(0,t) = \frac{8b}{\pi a} \int_{-\infty}^t \psi(u) du \int_0^\infty J_1(\xi a) \cos\left[b(t-u)\xi^2\right] d\xi$$

Using the result

$$\int_0^\infty J_1(x) \cos(bx^2) dx = 1 - \cos\left(\frac{1}{4b}\right) \tag{126}$$

we find, on changing the variable of integration to

$$v = \frac{a^2}{4b(t-u)}$$

that

$$w(0,t) = \frac{2}{\pi} \int_0^\infty \psi\left(t - \frac{a^2}{4bv}\right) \frac{1 - \cos(v)}{v^2} dv$$

---

[1] J. Boussinesq, "Application des potentials" (Paris, 1885), p. 470. A more recent derivation is due to C. Zener, *Phys. Rev.*, **59**, 669 (1941).

Thus, in the general case in which the force is *not* concentrated, there is no simple relation between the velocity of the center of the plate and the magnitude of the applied force.

We shall now consider the application of these results to two special problems.

Bending of a Large Plate Deformed by Normal Impact.   As an example of the forced vibrations of a plate we now consider the bending of a large plate deformed by normal impact, by a force of magnitude $16\rho hbV$ uniformly distributed over a circle of radius a and acting for a time T.   In this instance the appropriate solution of equation (122) is

$$\bar{w}(\xi,t) = \frac{8bJ_1(a\xi)}{\pi a\xi} \frac{1}{b\xi^2} \int_{-\infty}^{t} \psi'(u) \sin [b\xi^2(t-u)]du$$

where

$$\psi'(u) = \begin{cases} 0 & \text{if } u < 0 \\ V & \text{if } 0 \leq u \leq T \\ 0 & \text{if } u > T \end{cases}$$

It follows at once that

$$\bar{w}(\xi,t) = \begin{cases} \dfrac{8VbJ_1(a\xi)}{\pi a\xi} \dfrac{1-\cos (bt\xi^2)}{b^2\xi^4} & 0 \leq t \leq T \\[3mm] \dfrac{8VbJ_1(a\xi)}{\pi a\xi} \dfrac{\cos [b(t-T)\xi^2] - \cos (bt\xi^2)}{b^2\xi^4} & t > T \end{cases}$$

Considering the first case $0 \leq t \leq T$, we have, on inverting by means of the Hankel inversion theorem (15), Chap. 2,

$$w(r,t) = \frac{8V}{\pi ab} \int_0^\infty J_0(\xi r)J_1(\xi a) \frac{1-\cos (bt\xi^2)}{\xi^4} d\xi \qquad (127)$$

If r is very much smaller than a, we can make use of the approximate result

$$J_0\left(\frac{r\xi}{a}\right) = 1 - \frac{1}{4}\left(\frac{r}{a}\right)^2 \xi^2 + O\left(\frac{r^4}{a^4}\right)$$

to obtain the approximate solution

$$w(r,t) = \frac{8Va^2}{\pi b} \int_0^\infty J_1(\xi) \frac{1-\cos (bt\xi^2/a^2)}{\xi^4} d\xi - \frac{2Va^2}{\pi b}\left(\frac{r}{a}\right)^2 \int_0^\infty J_1(\xi)$$
$$\times \frac{1-\cos (bt\xi^2/a^2)}{\xi^2} d\xi$$

Integrating both sides of equation (126) with respect to b from 0 to β, we obtain

$$\int_0^\infty J_1(\xi) \, \frac{1 - \cos{(\beta\xi^2)}}{\xi^4} \, d\xi = \frac{1}{2} \beta^2 \left[1 - \cos\left(\frac{1}{4\beta}\right) \right] + \frac{1}{4} \beta F\left(\frac{1}{4\beta}\right)$$
$$+ \frac{1}{32} G\left(\frac{1}{4\beta}\right) \quad (128)$$

where $F(x)$ is defined by equation (120) and $G(x)$ is defined by the relation

$$G(x) = \frac{\sin{(x)}}{x} - \text{Ci}\,(x) \quad (129)$$

Similarly integrating the result

$$\int_0^\infty J_1(\xi) \sin{(b\xi^2)} d\xi = \sin\left(\frac{1}{4b}\right)$$

with respect to b from 0 to β, we have

$$\int_0^\infty J_1(\xi) \, \frac{1 - \cos{(\beta\xi^2)}}{\xi^2} \, d\xi = \frac{1}{4} G\left(\frac{1}{4\beta}\right) \quad (130)$$

Substituting from equations (128) and (130) into the expression for $w(r,t)$, we obtain, for $0 \leq t \leq T$, $r \ll a$,

$$w(r,t) = \frac{2Vt}{\pi} \left\{ \frac{2bt}{a^2} \left[1 - \cos\left(\frac{a^2}{4bt}\right) \right] + F\left(\frac{a^2}{4bt}\right) + \frac{a^2}{8bt} G\left(\frac{a^2}{4bt}\right) \right.$$
$$\left. - \frac{r^2}{4bt} G\left(\frac{a^2}{4bt}\right) \right\} \quad (131)$$

A similar result can be derived easily for $t > T$.

When r is very much greater than a, we may assume that the Bessel function $J_1(\xi a/r)$ is replaced by the expression

$$\frac{1}{2} \xi \frac{a}{r} - \frac{1}{16} \xi^3 \left(\frac{a}{r}\right)^3$$

Substituting this value in equation (127), we have

$$w = \frac{4Vr^2}{\pi b} \int_0^\infty J_0(\xi) \, \frac{1 - \cos{(bt\xi^2/r^2)}}{\xi^3} \, d\xi$$
$$- \frac{Va^2}{2\pi b} \int_0^\infty J_0(\xi) \, \frac{1 - \cos{(bt\xi^2/r^2)}}{\xi} \, d\xi \quad (132)$$

Now, from equation (116) we can deduce the integrals

$$\int_0^\infty \xi J_0(\xi) \cos{(b\xi^2)} d\xi = \frac{1}{2b} \sin\left(\frac{1}{4b}\right),$$
$$\int_0^\infty \xi J_0(\xi) \sin{(b\xi^2)} d\xi = \frac{1}{2b} \cos\left(\frac{1}{4b}\right)$$

Integrating the former of these results twice with respect to b from 0 to β, we obtain

$$\int_0^\infty J_0(\xi)\,\frac{1 - \cos{(\beta\xi^2)}}{\xi^3}\,d\xi = \frac{1}{2}\,\beta F\left(\frac{1}{4\beta}\right)$$

and integrating the latter once with respect to b,

$$\int_0^\infty J_0(\xi)\,\frac{1 - \cos{(\beta\xi^2)}}{\xi}\,d\xi = -\frac{1}{2}\,\mathrm{Ci}\left(\frac{1}{4\beta}\right)$$

Using these results in equation (132), we finally have, for the case $r \gg a$,

$$w(r,t) = \frac{2Vt}{\pi}\left[\,F\left(\frac{r^2}{4bt}\right) + \frac{a^2}{8bt}\,\mathrm{Ci}\left(\frac{r^2}{4bt}\right)\right]\quad 0 \le t \le T \quad (133)$$

The result for $t > T$ follows immediately; it is

$$w(r,t) = \frac{2V}{\pi}\left(tF\left(\frac{r^2}{4bt}\right) - {}^\cdot(t - T)F\left[\frac{r^2}{4b(t - T)}\right]\right.$$
$$\left. + \frac{a^2}{8b}\left\{\mathrm{Ci}\left(\frac{r^2}{4bt}\right) - \mathrm{Ci}\left[\frac{r^2}{4b(t - T)}\right]\right\}\right) \quad (134)$$

The values of the displacement w for various values of r and t can be found easily from tables of the functions Ci, Si, F, and G†. In the case

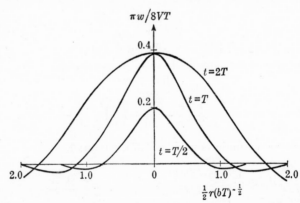

Fig. 15. The form of a large plate deformed by normal impact.

$a = 0$, the values of w for various values of r and t can be derived from a table of the function $F(x)$ by means of equations (133) and (134), and the form of the plate at various times determined. The results of a set of calculations of this kind are shown graphically in Fig. 15.

† Tables of Ci and Si are given in A. N. Lowan, "Tables of Sine, Cosine and Exponential Integrals" (W.P.A. Tables, New York, 1940), and of the functions F and G in I. N. Sneddon, *Proc. Cambridge Phil. Soc.*, **41**, 27 (1945).

Elastic Response of a Large Plate to a Gaussian Distribution of Pressure.[1]
In certain physical problems such as arise in the theory of armor penetration it is of advantage to consider the motion to be produced not by a uniformly distributed force but by a nonuniform distribution of pressure over one of the free surfaces of the plate. As an example of this kind of motion an account will now be given of the vibrations produced in a thin elastic plate by a Gaussian distribution of pressure,

$$Z(r,t) = \frac{4\rho h A}{s^2} e^{-r^2/s^2} f'(t) \tag{135}$$

For this function the Hankel transform is

$$\bar{Z}(\xi,t) = \frac{4\rho h A}{s^2} f'(t) \int_0^\infty r e^{-r^2/s^2} J_0(\xi r) dr = 2\rho h A f'(t) e^{-\frac{1}{4}\xi^2 s^2}$$

as a result of using equation (116). Substituting from equation (135) into equation (109), multiplying both sides by $rJ_0(\xi r)$, and integrating with respect to r from 0 to ∞, we obtain

$$\frac{d^2\bar{w}}{dt^2} + b^2\xi^4\bar{w} = A e^{-\frac{1}{4}s^2\xi^2} f'(t) \tag{136}$$

If the plate is set in motion from rest in its equilibrium position, we may take the solution of equation (136) to be

$$\bar{w}(\xi,t) = A e^{-\frac{1}{4}s^2\xi^2} \int_{-\infty}^t f(\tau) \cos [b\xi^2(t - \tau)] d\tau \tag{137}$$

or, alternatively, in the form

$$\bar{w}(\xi,t) = \frac{A}{b\xi^2} e^{-\frac{1}{4}s^2\xi^2} \int_{-\infty}^t f'(\tau) \sin [b\xi^2(t - \tau)] d\tau \tag{138}$$

For the solution (137) we have from the Hankel inversion theorem

$$w(r,t) = A \int_{-\infty}^t f(\tau) d\tau \int_0^\infty e^{-\frac{1}{4}s^2\xi^2} \cos [b\xi^2(t - \tau)] J_0(\xi r) d\xi$$

Now it can readily be shown from equation (116) that

$$\int_0^\infty \xi e^{-\frac{1}{4}s^2\xi^2} \cos [b\xi^2(t - \tau)] J_0(\xi r) d\xi = \frac{2e^{-\rho^2/(1+\eta^2)}}{s^2(1 + \eta^2)} \left(\cos \frac{\eta\rho^2}{1 + \eta^2} \right.$$
$$\left. + \eta \sin \frac{\eta\rho^2}{1 + \eta^2} \right)$$

where $\rho = r/s$ and $\eta = 4b(t - \tau)/s$. It follows immediately from the last two results that the displacement of any point on the plate at a

[1] I. N. Sneddon, *Proc. Cambridge Phil. Soc.*, **42**, 330 (1946).

distance r from the center is given, for any instant t, by the formula

$$w = A \int_{-\infty}^{t} f(\tau)H(t - \tau)d\tau \tag{139}$$

where the function $H(x)$ is defined by the equation

$$H(x) = \frac{2p^2 e^{-p\,q/(p^2+x^2)}}{s^2(p^2 + x^2)} \left[\cos\left(\frac{qx}{p^2 + x^2}\right) + \frac{x}{p} \sin\left(\frac{qx}{p^2 + x^2}\right) \right] \tag{140}$$

and $p = s/4b$, $q = r/4b$.

In particular, if we wish to determine the displacement w_0 of the center of the plate, we put $r = q = 0$ in the last two equations. We then obtain

$$\begin{aligned}
w_0 &= \frac{2pA}{s^2} \int_{-\infty}^{t} \frac{pf(\tau)d\tau}{p^2 + (t - \tau)^2} \\
&= \frac{A}{2b} \left\{ \left[f(\tau) \tan^{-1}\left(\frac{p}{t - \tau}\right) \right]_{-\infty}^{t} - \int_{-\infty}^{t} f'(\tau) \tan^{-1}\left(\frac{p}{t - \tau}\right) d\tau \right\}
\end{aligned}$$

as a result of integrating by parts. Thus the relation between the displacement of the center of the plate at any instant and the intensity of the applied force is given by the equations

$$w_0 = \frac{\pi A}{b} \int_{-\infty}^{t} f'(\tau)h(t - \tau)d\tau \tag{141}$$

and

$$h(x) = 1 - \frac{2}{\pi} \tan^{-1}\left(\frac{p}{x}\right) \tag{142}$$

Similarly from the solution (138) we obtain

$$\frac{d\bar{w}}{dt} = A e^{-\frac{1}{4}s^2\xi^2} \int_{-\infty}^{t} f'(\tau) \cos\left[b\xi^2(t - \tau)\right]d\tau$$

and inverting this equation by means of the Hankel inversion theorem we have

$$\frac{\partial w}{\partial t} = A \int_{-\infty}^{t} f'(\tau)H(t - \tau)d\tau \tag{143}$$

where H is defined by equation (140).

If the motion is due to an impulse of very short duration, we may take $f'(\tau)$ to be the Dirac delta function $\delta(\tau)$, and equation (143) gives

$$\frac{\partial w}{\partial t} = AH(t) = \frac{2Ap^2 e^{-p\,q/(p^2+t^2)}}{s^2(p^2 + t^2)} \left[\cos\left(\frac{qt}{p^2 + t^2}\right) + \frac{t}{p} \sin\left(\frac{qt}{p^2 + t^2}\right) \right] \tag{144}$$

The total impulse I is related to the constant A by the equation

$$I = \int_{0}^{\infty} 2\pi r\, dr\, \frac{4\rho hA}{s^2} e^{-r^2/s^2} = 4\pi\rho hA$$

The variation of velocity with time at various points of the plate, as calculated from equation (144), is shown in Fig. 16.

20.4 Nonsymmetrical vibrations of a large plate.[1]   In the last section the partial differential equation governing the symmetrical vibrations of a thin elastic plate was reduced to an ordinary differential equation by use of the Hankel transform method.   The purpose of this section is to extend the analysis to the general case, in which no such symmetry exists, by the use of a double Fourier transform.

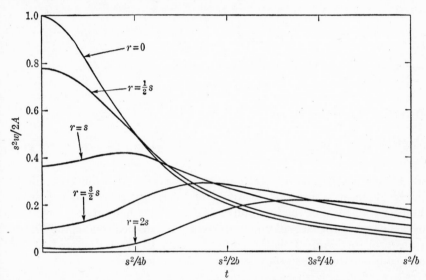

FIG. 16.   The elastic response of a large plate to a Gaussian distribution of impulse.

To solve equation (106a), we introduce the Fourier transform

$$W(\xi,\eta,t) = \frac{1}{2\pi} \int_{-\infty}^{\infty} \int_{-\infty}^{\infty} w(x,y,t)e^{i(\xi x + \eta y)} \, dx \, dy \qquad (145)$$

of the function $w(x,y,t)$.   If we denote the corresponding Fourier transform of $p(x,y)$ by $P(\xi,\eta)$ then, multiplying both sides of equation (106a) by $\exp[i(\xi x + \eta y)]$ and integrating with respect to x and y over the entire xy plane, we have, after a little reduction,

$$\frac{d^2W}{dt^2} + \lambda^2 W = 8bP(\xi,\eta)\psi'(t) \qquad (146)$$

where

$$\lambda^2 = b^2(\xi^2 + \eta^2)^2 \qquad (147)$$

When the initial conditions are known, equation (146) can be solved for

[1] I. N. Sneddon, *Proc. Cambridge Phil. Soc.*, **41**, 229 (1945).

W and the corresponding expression for w obtained from the inversion theorem contained in equation (108), Chap. 1.

We first of all consider the free vibrations of a thin elastic plate of infinite extent. It will be assumed that the motion results from the plate being deformed to the position $w = f(x,y)$ and then released from rest at the instant $t = 0$, that is, $\partial w / \partial t$ is initially zero for all values of x and y. Since the vibrations are free, we may take $P(\xi,\eta)$ to be identically equal to zero, and since, when $t = 0$,

$$W = F(\xi,\eta) = \frac{1}{2\pi} \int_{-\infty}^{\infty} \int_{-\infty}^{\infty} f(x,y)e^{i(\xi x+\eta y)}\, dx\, dy, \quad \frac{dW}{dt} = 0$$

the appropriate solution of equation (146) is

$$W = F(\xi,\eta) \cos (\lambda t)$$

Inverting this result by equation (108), Chap. 1, we have

$$w(x,y,t) = \frac{1}{2\pi} \int_{-\infty}^{\infty} \int_{-\infty}^{\infty} F(\xi,\eta) \cos (\lambda t)e^{-i(\xi x+\eta y)}\, d\xi\, d\eta \qquad (148)$$

To evaluate the integral (148) by means of the Faltung theorem for double Fourier transforms, it would be necessary to consider first the Fourier transform of the function $\cos (\lambda t)$. This function does not, however, belong to the class of functions considered in the proof of the Fourier transform theorem. It is therefore necessary to proceed as in Sec. 19.2 and consider the transform of some such function as

$$\Phi_\epsilon(\xi,\eta) = e^{-\epsilon\lambda} \cos (\lambda t)$$

which does belong to the required class of functions, and then to examine its behavior as ϵ tends to zero. Substituting the expression for $\Phi_\epsilon(\xi,\eta)$ into equation (108), Chap. 1, we find that it is the double Fourier transform of the function

$$\phi_\epsilon(x,y) = \frac{1}{4\pi} \int_{-\infty}^{\infty} \int_{-\infty}^{\infty} \{\exp\,[-\epsilon b(\xi^2 + \eta^2) + ibt(\xi^2 + \eta^2) - i(\xi x + \eta y)]$$
$$+ \exp\,[-\epsilon b(\xi^2 + \eta^2) - ibt(\xi^2 + \eta^2) - i(\xi x + \eta y)]\}d\xi\, d\eta$$

The integrations are elementary and give

$$\phi_\epsilon(x,y) = \frac{1}{2b(t^2 + \epsilon^2)} \exp\left[\frac{-\epsilon(x^2 + y^2)}{4b(t^2 + \epsilon^2)}\right]\left\{\epsilon \cos\left[\frac{(x^2 + y^2)t}{4b(t^2 + \epsilon^2)}\right]\right.$$
$$\left. + t \sin\left[\frac{(x^2 + y^2)t}{4b(t^2 + \epsilon^2)}\right]\right\} \qquad (149)$$

Applying the Faltung theorem, we find that

$$\frac{1}{2\pi} \int_{-\infty}^{\infty} \int_{-\infty}^{\infty} F(\xi,\eta)\Phi_\epsilon(\xi,\eta)e^{-i(\xi x+\eta y)} \, d\xi \, d\eta$$

$$= \frac{\epsilon}{4b\pi(t^2+\epsilon^2)} \int_{-\infty}^{\infty} \int_{-\infty}^{\infty} f(\alpha,\beta) \exp\left[\frac{-\epsilon(x-\alpha)^2 - \epsilon(y-\beta)^2}{4b(t^2+\epsilon^2)}\right]$$

$$\cos\left\{\frac{[(x-\alpha)^2+(y-\beta)^2]t}{4b(t^2+\epsilon^2)}\right\} \, d\alpha \, d\beta + \frac{t}{4b\pi(t^2+\epsilon^2)} \int_{-\infty}^{\infty} \int_{-\infty}^{\infty}$$

$$\times f(\alpha,\beta) \exp\left[\frac{-\epsilon(x-\alpha)^2 - \epsilon(y-\beta)^2}{4b(t^2+\epsilon^2)}\right] \sin\left\{\frac{[(x-\alpha)^2+(y-\beta)^2]t}{4b(t^2+\epsilon^2)}\right\}$$

$$\times \, d\alpha \, d\beta$$

Letting ϵ tend to zero, we obtain from equation (148),

$$w(x,y,t) = \frac{1}{4\pi bt} \int_{-\infty}^{\infty} \int_{-\infty}^{\infty} f(\alpha,\beta) \sin\left[\frac{(x-\alpha)^2+(y-\beta)^2}{4bt}\right] d\alpha \, d\beta \quad (150)$$

The corresponding result for symmetrical free vibrations can be deduced readily from the nonsymmetrical result (150). If the initial displacement is symmetrical about the z axis, we may take $f(x,y) = f(r)$, where $r^2 = x^2 + y^2$. We obtain the expression for the subsequent displacement by substituting the values $\alpha = \rho \cos \varphi$, $\beta = \rho \sin \varphi$, $f(\alpha,\beta) = f(\rho)$, $d\alpha \, d\beta = \rho \, d\rho \, d\varphi$ into equation (150). Because of the symmetry there is no loss of generality incurred by assuming $x = r$, $y = 0$ in this equation. We then have

$$w(r,t) = \frac{1}{4\pi bt} \int_0^{\infty} \rho f(\rho) d\rho \int_0^{2\pi} \sin\left(\frac{r^2+\rho^2}{4bt} - \frac{r\rho}{2bt} \cos \varphi\right) d\varphi$$

Expanding the integrand by the rule for the sine of the difference of two angles and using the results (23) and (24), Appendix A, namely,

$$\int_0^{2\pi} \cos(z \cos \varphi) d\varphi = 2\pi J_0(z), \qquad \int_0^{2\pi} \sin(z \cos \varphi) d\varphi = 0$$

we obtain

$$w(r,t) = \frac{1}{2bt} \int_0^{\infty} \rho f(\rho) J_0\left(\frac{r\rho}{2bt}\right) \sin\left(\frac{r^2+\rho^2}{4bt}\right) d\rho$$

for the displacement due to a symmetrical initial displacement $w = f(r)$— in agreement with the result (115) established by the method of Hankel transforms.

The forced vibrations of a thin plate can be treated similarly. If the plate is set in motion from rest in its equilibrium position, we may write the solution of the equation (146) in the form

$$W = 8bP(\xi,\eta) \int_{-\infty}^{t} \psi(\tau) \cos[\lambda(t-\tau)] d\tau$$

whence from the inversion theorem we have

$$w(x,y,t) = \frac{4b}{\pi} \int_{-\infty}^{t} \psi(\tau)d\tau \int_{-\infty}^{\infty} \int_{-\infty}^{\infty} P(\xi,\eta) \cos [\lambda(t - \tau)]e^{-i(\xi x + \eta y)} \, d\xi \, d\eta$$

The inner double integral can be expressed in terms of the function $p(x,y)$ by the method employed in the evaluation of the integral on the right-hand side of equation (148). In this way we obtain the solution

$$w(x,y,t) = \frac{2}{\pi} \int_{-\infty}^{t} \frac{\psi(\tau)d\tau}{t - \tau} \int_{-\infty}^{\infty} \int_{-\infty}^{\infty} p(\alpha,\beta) \sin \left[\frac{(x - \alpha)^2 + (y - \beta)^2}{4b(t - \tau)} \right] \\ \times \, d\alpha \, d\beta \quad (151)$$

As an example of the use of this formula we shall derive the Boussinesq result (125) for a concentrated force acting on the plate at the origin of coordinates. For a concentrated force of this type we may take

$$p(x,y) = \delta(x) \, \delta(y)$$

where $\delta(x)$ and $\delta(y)$ are Dirac delta functions. We then obtain

$$w = \frac{2}{\pi} \int_{-\infty}^{t} \sin \left[\frac{x^2 + y^2}{4b(t - \tau)} \right] \frac{\psi(\tau)}{t - \tau} \, d\tau$$

which may, by the substitutions $r^2 = x^2 + y^2$, $\xi = r^2/4b(t - \tau)$, be brought to the form (125).

20.5 Symmetrical vibrations of a thin plate of finite radius. Throughout the previous sections we have assumed the radius of the plate to be infinite. We now consider a possible approach to the corresponding problem of the determination of the vibrations of a circular plate of finite radius c, in the case where the vibrations are symmetrical. The method of integral transforms may again be applied, but we shall now employ the finite Hankel transform

$$\bar{w}_c = \int_0^c rw(r,t)J_0(\xi_i r)dr \quad (152)$$

where the quantity ξ_i is, as yet, unspecified. Integrating by parts, we obtain in the usual way

$$\int_0^c r \left(\frac{\partial^2 w}{\partial r^2} + \frac{1}{r} \frac{\partial w}{\partial r} \right) J_0(\xi_i r)dr = \left[r \frac{\partial w}{\partial r} J_0(\xi_i r) - \xi_i rwJ_0'(\xi_i r) \right]_0^c - \xi_i^2 \bar{w}_c$$

The expression in the brackets vanishes at the lower limit $r = 0$, and if we assume that $w = 0$ when $r = c$, it vanishes at the upper limit if ξ_i is chosen to be a root of the transcendental equation

$$J_0(\xi_i c) = 0 \quad (153)$$

Applying this result twice, we see that if the transverse displacement w satisfies the boundary conditions

$$w = 0, \qquad \frac{\partial^2 w}{\partial r^2} + \frac{1}{r}\frac{\partial w}{\partial r} = 0 \qquad \text{if } r = c \qquad (154)$$

then

$$\int_0^c rJ_0(\xi_i r)\left(\frac{\partial^2}{\partial r^2} + \frac{1}{r}\frac{\partial}{\partial r}\right)^2 w(r,t)dr = \xi_i^4 \bar{w}_c(\xi_i,t)$$

The analysis proceeds as before, and we have in place of equation (122) the equation

$$\frac{d^2\bar{w}_c}{dt^2} + \xi_i^4 \bar{w}_c = \frac{1}{2\rho h}\,\bar{Z}_c \qquad (155)$$

where $\bar{Z}_c$ is defined in a similar way to $\bar{w}_c$.

The boundary conditions (154) imply that the plate is held along the outer edge $r = c$ in such a way that the displacement of the plate is zero and also so that the mean curvature vanishes there. This latter condition seems at first sight to be of rather an artificial nature, but in the case of large plates, at least, it is approximately satisfied.

If a circular plate of radius c, held in such a fashion that equations (154) are satisfied, is set vibrating by being released from rest in the position $w = f(r)$, then, as before,

$$\bar{w}_c = \cos\,(bt\xi_i^2)\int_0^c uf(u)J_0(\xi_i u)du$$

and therefore, by equation (45), Chap. 3,

$$w(r,t) = \frac{2}{c^2}\sum_i \frac{\cos\,(bt\xi_i^2)}{[J_1(c\xi_i)]^2}\,J_0(\xi_i r)\int_0^c uf(u)J_0(\xi_i u)du$$

For example, if the plate is given the initial displacement

$$w = \epsilon\left(1 - \frac{r^2}{c^2}\right) \qquad 0 \le r \le c$$

where ϵ is small, then, since

$$\int_0^c uf(u)J_1(\xi_i u)du = 4\epsilon\,\frac{J_1(c\xi_i)}{c\xi_i^3}$$

we have, for the displacement of the plate at time t, the formula

$$w = \frac{8\epsilon}{c^3}\sum_i \frac{\cos\,(bt\xi_i^2)}{\xi_i^3}\frac{J_0(\xi_i r)}{J_1(\xi_i c)}$$

The summation with respect to i extends over all the positive roots of equation (153).

As an example of the forced vibrations produced in a circular plate by an external force we consider the dynamic bending of a plate by normal impact. If a force of magnitude $16\rho h b V$ uniformly distributed over a concentric circle of radius a acts on a thin plate of radius $c \geq a$ for a time T, then as before we find

$$\bar{w}_c = \frac{8VJ_1(a\xi_i)}{\pi a b \xi_i} \frac{1 - \cos(bt\xi_i^2)}{\xi_i^4}$$

if $0 \leq t \leq T$, with a corresponding formula for $t \geq T$. Then, inverting by the rule (45), Chap. 3, we obtain the series

$$w(r,t) = \frac{16VT}{\pi\alpha} \sum_i \frac{J_1(\gamma\eta_i)}{\gamma\eta_i} \frac{1 - \cos(\tau\alpha\eta_i^2)}{\eta_i^4} \frac{J_0(\eta_i\rho)}{[J_1(\eta_i)]^2} \qquad (156)$$

where $\gamma = a/c$, $\rho = r/c$, $\alpha = bT/c^2$, $\tau = t/T$ and the summation now extends over all the positive roots of the equation

$$J_0(\eta_i) = 0 \qquad (157)$$

In the case where the force is concentrated, $\gamma = 0$ and the factor $J_1(\gamma\eta_i)/\gamma\eta_i$ is replaced by $\frac{1}{2}$ to give

$$w = \frac{8VT}{\pi\alpha} \sum_i \left(\frac{1 - \cos\tau\alpha\eta_i^2}{\eta_i^4}\right) \frac{J_0(\eta_i\rho)}{[J_1(\eta_i)]^2} \qquad (158)$$

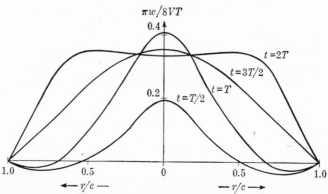

Fig. 17.   The dynamic bending of a circular plate by normal impact ($\alpha = 0.1$, $\gamma = 0$).

Because of the high power of η_i occurring in the denominators of the terms of these series, they are rapidly convergent (except when $\alpha\tau$ is very small) and can be easily computed. In the case $\alpha = 0.1$ a good approximation to the series is obtained by summing the first twenty terms—the first three significant figures of the result being exact. The results of such calculations for a few values of r and t are shown in Fig. 17.   It will be seen that for this value of T the agreement with the curves for a very large plate is reasonably close until $t = T$, after which time the waves reflected from the fixed boundary affect the form of the curves. It will also be noted that, whereas in the case of a plate of infinite radius the velocity of the center of the plate is zero for $t > T$, this is not so when the radius is finite.

The effect of varying the area of application of the impulsive force may readily be calculated from equation (156). The results for a typical case are shown in Fig. 18, where we have chosen $\alpha = 0.1$, $t = T$ and found

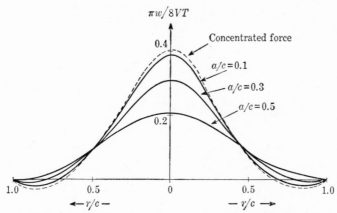

$\pi w/8VT$

0.4 — Concentrated force

$a/c = 0.1$

$a/c = 0.3$

$a/c = 0.5$

0.2

1.0　　　0.5　　　0　　　0.5　　　1.0

$\leftarrow r/c \rightarrow$　　　　$\leftarrow r/c \rightarrow$

Fig. 18. The effect of varying the area to which the impulsive force is applied ($\alpha = 0.1$, $t = T$).

the form of the plate for various values of a/c, the total force remaining constant. These curves show that, apart from a less intense displacement of the center, the general form of the plate during motion is not affected appreciably by distributing the external force over a circular area instead of concentrating it at the center of the plate.

21. Elastic Vibrations of Thick Cylinders and Spheres[1]

To illustrate the use of the Laplace inversion theorem in the solution of problems in the theory of vibrations, we shall now consider the vibrations produced in a thick elastic cylinder by the application of an internal pressure which varies with time. We consider a thick, isotropic, homogeneous cylinder of infinite length and of radii r_0 and r_1 deformed by an internal pressure $A(1 - \cos \omega t)$. The external surface is assumed to be free from external forces. The radial component u, at radius r, and time t are then determined by the differential equation

$$\frac{\partial^2 u}{\partial r^2} + \frac{1}{r}\frac{\partial u}{\partial r} - \frac{u}{r^2} = \frac{1}{a^2}\frac{\partial^2 u}{\partial t^2} \quad r_0 \leq r \leq r_1, t > 0 \quad (159)$$

where the quantity a is defined in terms of the density ρ of the cylinder

[1] C. J. Tranter, *Phil. Mag.*, **33**, 614 (1942).

and Lamé's elastic constants λ and μ by the equation

$$a^2 = \frac{\lambda + 2\mu}{\rho} \tag{160}$$

The radial component of stress is given by[1]

$$\sigma_r = (\lambda + 2\mu)\frac{\partial u}{\partial r} + \lambda\frac{u}{r} \tag{161}$$

so that the boundary conditions are

$$(\lambda + 2\mu)\frac{\partial u}{\partial r} + \lambda\frac{u}{r} = \begin{cases} -A(1 - \cos \omega t) & r = r_0,\, t > 0 \\ 0 & r = r_1,\, t > 0 \end{cases} \tag{162}$$

The initial conditions are that, at $t = 0$,

$$u = \frac{\partial u}{\partial t} = 0 \qquad r_0 \leq r \leq r_1 \tag{163}$$

Multiplying both sides of equation (159) by e^{-pt} and integrating with respect to t from 0 to ∞, we obtain the ordinary differential equation

$$\left(\frac{d^2}{dr^2} + \frac{1}{r}\frac{d}{dr} - \frac{1}{r^2} - \frac{p^2}{a^2}\right)\bar{u} = 0, \quad r_0 \leq r \leq r_1 \tag{164}$$

for the determination of the Laplace transform

$$\bar{u} = \int_0^\infty u(t)e^{-pt}\,dt \tag{165}$$

From equation (162) we see that the boundary conditions on the function $\bar{u}$ are

$$(\lambda + 2\mu)\frac{d\bar{u}}{dr} + \lambda\frac{\bar{u}}{r} = \begin{cases} -A\int_0^\infty (1 - \cos \omega t)e^{-pt}\,dt = \dfrac{-A\omega^2}{p(p^2 + \omega^2)} & r = r_0 \\[2mm] 0 \qquad r = r_1 \end{cases} \tag{166}$$

In the usual notation for Bessel functions of imaginary argument we may write the solution of equation (164) in the form

$$\bar{u} = CI_1\left(\frac{pr}{a}\right) + DK_1\left(\frac{pr}{a}\right) \tag{167}$$

where the constants C and D are determined from the equations (166). Making use of the recurrence relations

$$zI_1'(z) + I_1(z) = zI_0(z)$$
$$zK_1'(z) + K_1(z) = -zK_0(z)$$

and substituting in equation (166), we obtain for the determination of the constants C and D the equations

[1] Cf. Chap. 10.

$$C\left[I_1\left(\frac{pr_0}{a}\right) - \frac{\gamma pr_0}{a}I_0\left(\frac{pr_0}{a}\right)\right] + D\left[K_1\left(\frac{pr_0}{a}\right) + \frac{\gamma pr_0}{a}K_0\left(\frac{pr_0}{a}\right)\right]$$

$$= \frac{A\omega^2 r_0}{2\mu p(p^2 + \omega^2)}$$

$$C\left[I_1\left(\frac{pr_1}{a}\right) - \frac{\gamma pr_1}{a}I_0\left(\frac{pr_1}{a}\right)\right] + D\left[K_1\left(\frac{pr_1}{a}\right) + \frac{\gamma pr_1}{a}K_0\left(\frac{pr_1}{a}\right)\right] = 0$$

where

$$\gamma = \frac{\lambda + 2\mu}{2\mu} \tag{168}$$

Solving these equations and substituting in equation (167), we obtain for $\bar{u}$ the expression

$$\bar{u} = \frac{A\omega^2 r_0 F(p)}{2\mu(p^2 + \omega^2)pG(p)} \tag{169}$$

where $F(p)$ and $G(p)$ are the functions defined by the relations

$$F(p) = \left[K_1\left(\frac{pr_1}{a}\right) + \frac{\gamma pr_1}{a}K_0\left(\frac{pr_1}{a}\right)\right]I_1\left(\frac{pr}{a}\right) - \left[I_1\left(\frac{pr_1}{a}\right)\right.$$

$$\left. - \frac{\gamma pr_1}{a}I_0\left(\frac{pr_1}{a}\right)\right]K_1\left(\frac{pr}{a}\right) \tag{170}$$

$$G(p) = \left[I_1\left(\frac{pr_0}{a}\right) - \frac{\gamma pr_0}{a}I_0\left(\frac{pr_0}{a}\right)\right]\left[K_1\left(\frac{pr_1}{a}\right) + \frac{\gamma pr_1}{a}K_0\left(\frac{pr_1}{a}\right)\right]$$

$$- \left[K_1\left(\frac{pr_0}{a}\right) + \frac{\gamma pr_0}{a}K_0\left(\frac{pr_0}{a}\right)\right]\left[I_1\left(\frac{pr_1}{a}\right) - \frac{\gamma pr_1}{a}I_0\left(\frac{pr_1}{a}\right)\right] \tag{170a}$$

Applying the Laplace inversion theorem (Theorem 14) to the function (169), we obtain, for the displacement u,

$$\frac{2\mu u}{A\omega^2 r_0} = \frac{1}{2\pi i}\int_{c-i\infty}^{c+i\infty}\frac{e^{pt}F(p)dp}{p(p^2 + \omega^2)G(p)} \tag{171}$$

To evaluate the integral on the right-hand side of this equation, consider the integral taken round the closed contour consisting of a line at a distance c from the imaginary axis and the portion (lying to the left) of a circle whose center is the origin and whose radius is

$$R = (n + \tfrac{1}{2})\pi a/(r_1 - r_0)$$

—chosen so that the contour avoids all poles of the integrand (cf. Fig. 19). It can be shown that the limit of the integral around this circular arc tends to zero as n

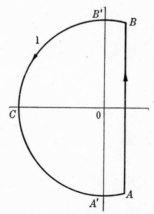

Fig. 19. The contour used in the evaluation of the integral (171).

tends to infinity so that Cauchy's theorem enables us to replace the line integral in equation (171) by the sum of the residues of the function

$$\frac{e^{pt}F(p)}{p(p^2 + \omega^2)G(p)}$$

lying to the left of the line $\mathsf{R}(p) = c$. The poles of this are at the points $p = 0, p = \pm i\omega$ and at the roots of the transcendental equation $G(p) = 0$, which have been shown by Tranter to be simple and purely imaginary; they will be written in the form $p = \pm i\alpha_s$. If $\omega \neq \alpha_s$ for any value of s, the sum of the residues of the function at $p = \pm i\omega$ is easily seen to be

$$-\frac{F(i\omega)\cos(\omega t)}{\omega^2 G(i\omega)} \tag{172}$$

and that at $p = 0$ is

$$\frac{F(0)}{\omega^2 G(0)} \tag{173}$$

The sum of the residues of the integrand at the remaining poles is

$$\sum_{s=1}^{\infty} \frac{1}{\omega^2 - \alpha_s^2}\left[\frac{e^{i\alpha_s t}F(i\alpha_s)}{(\alpha dG/d\alpha)_{\alpha=\alpha_s}} + \frac{e^{-i\alpha_s t}F(-i\alpha_s)}{(\alpha dG/d\alpha)_{\alpha=-\alpha_s}}\right] \tag{174}$$

After a little reduction we can show that

$$\left(\alpha\frac{dG}{d\alpha}\right)_{\alpha=\alpha_s} = \left(\alpha\frac{dG}{d\alpha}\right)_{\alpha=-\alpha_s}$$

$$= \xi\left(\frac{\gamma^2\alpha_s^2 r_0^2}{a^2} - 2\gamma + 1\right) - \frac{1}{\xi}\left(\frac{\gamma^2\alpha_s^2 r_1^2}{a^2} - 2\gamma + 1\right)$$

where

$$\xi = \frac{J_1(\alpha_s r_1/a) - (\gamma\alpha_s r_i/a)J_0(\alpha_s r_1/a)}{J_1(\alpha_s r_0/a) - (\gamma\alpha_s r_0/a)J_0(\alpha_s r_0/a)} = \frac{j(r_1)}{j(r_0)}, \text{ say}$$

and that

$$F(i\alpha_s) = F(-i\alpha_s) = -\frac{1}{2}\pi\left\{\left[Y_1\left(\frac{\alpha_s r_1}{a}\right) - \frac{\gamma\alpha_s r_1}{a}Y_0\left(\frac{\alpha_s r_1}{a}\right)\right]J_1\left(\frac{\alpha_s r}{a}\right)\right.$$

$$\left. - j(r_1)Y_1\left(\frac{\alpha_s r}{a}\right)\right\} \tag{175}$$

Substituting these results into equations (172) to (174), we obtain finally

$$\frac{2\mu u}{Ar_0} = \frac{r_0}{r}\left[\frac{r^2 + (2\gamma - 1)r_1^2}{(2\gamma - 1)(r_1^2 - r_0^2)}\right] - \frac{F(i\omega)}{G(i\omega)}\cos(\omega t)$$

$$+ 2\omega^2\sum_s^{\infty}\frac{F(i\alpha_s)(\omega^2 - \alpha_s^2)^{-1}j(r_0)j(r_1)\cos(\alpha_s t)}{(\gamma^2\alpha_s^2 r_0^2/a^2 - 2\gamma + 1)j(r_1) - (\gamma^2\alpha_s^2 r_1^2/a^2 - 2\gamma + 1)j(r_0)}$$

where γ is given by equation (168), F by equation (170), G by equation (170a) and the summation is taken over all the *positive* roots of the equation $G(i\alpha_s) = 0$.

The forced vibrations of a thick sphere may be treated in a similar fashion. With a similar notation we now have

$$\frac{\partial^2 u}{\partial r^2} + \frac{2}{r}\frac{\partial u}{\partial r} - \frac{2u}{r^2} = \frac{1}{a^2}\frac{\partial^2 u}{\partial t^2}, \quad r_0 \le r \le r_1, t > 0$$

with the boundary and initial conditions

$$(\lambda + 2\mu)\frac{\partial u}{\partial r} + 2\lambda\frac{u}{r} = \begin{cases} -A(1 - \cos \omega t), & r = r_0 \\ 0 & r = r_1 \end{cases}$$

$$u = \frac{\partial u}{\partial t} = 0, \quad t = 0, r_0 \le r \le r_1$$

Proceeding as before, we obtain the subsidiary equation

$$\frac{d^2\bar{u}}{dr^2} + \frac{2}{r}\frac{d\bar{u}}{dr} - \left(\frac{2}{r^2} + \frac{p^2}{a^2}\right)\bar{u} = 0, \quad r_0 < r < r_1$$

which has solution

$$\bar{u} = \frac{C[1 - (pr/a)]e^{pr/a} + D[1 + (pr/a)]e^{-pr/a}}{(pr/a)^2}$$

the constants C and D being determined from the conditions

$$(\lambda + 2\mu)\frac{d\bar{u}}{dr} + 2\lambda\frac{\bar{u}}{r} = \begin{cases} \dfrac{-A\omega^2}{p(p^2 + \omega^2)} & r = r_0 \\ 0 & r = r_1 \end{cases}$$

In this way we obtain the solution

$$\bar{u} = \frac{A\omega^2 r_0^3 F(p)}{4\mu r^2 p(p^2 + \omega^2)G(p)}$$

the functions $F(p)$ and $G(p)$ now being defined by the equations

$$F(p) = \left(1 - \frac{pr}{a}\right)\left(\frac{\gamma^2 p^2 r_1^2}{a^2} + \frac{pr_1}{a} + 1\right)e^{-p(r_1-r)/a}$$

$$- \left(1 + \frac{pr}{a}\right)\left(\frac{\gamma^2 p^2 r_1^2}{a^2} - \frac{pr_1}{a} + 1\right)e^{p(r_1-r)/a}$$

$$G(p) = \left(\frac{\gamma^2 p^2 r_0^2}{a^2} - \frac{pr_0}{a} + 1\right)\left(\frac{\gamma^2 p^2 r_1^2}{a^2} + \frac{pr_1}{a} + 1\right)e^{-p(r_1-r_0)/a}$$

$$- \left(\frac{\gamma^2 p^2 r_0^2}{a^2} + \frac{pr_0}{a} + 1\right)\left(\frac{\gamma^2 p^2 r_1^2}{a^2} - \frac{pr_1}{a} + 1\right)e^{p(r_1-r_0)/a}$$

in which

$$\gamma = \frac{\lambda + 2\mu}{4\mu}$$

and from which it follows that

$$\lim_{p \to 0} \frac{F(p)}{G(p)} = \frac{r^3 + (3\gamma - 1)r_1^3}{(3\gamma - 1)(r_1^3 - r_0^3)}$$

The inversion theorem then gives

$$\frac{4\mu r^2 u}{A\omega^2 r_0^3} = \frac{1}{2\pi i} \int_{c-i\infty}^{c+i\infty} \frac{F(p)e^{pt}\, dp}{p(p^2 + \omega^2)G(p)}$$

and we may evaluate the line integral in the same way as before.

CHAPTER 5

THE CONDUCTION OF HEAT IN SOLIDS

22. General Theory

22.1 Fundamental equations. It is known as a result of experience that if two parts of a solid body are at different temperatures heat flows through the material of the body itself from the region of higher temperature to that of lower temperature, by the process known as *conduction*. The fundamental experiment upon which the theory of this process is based is illustrated by Fig. 20. A very large plate bounded by two parallel planes at a distance h apart has its lower surface maintained at a constant temperature θ_0 and its upper surface maintained at a constant temperature θ_1 which is assumed to be lower than θ_0. Then heat will flow from the lower to the upper surface. If we consider a cylinder whose generators are perpendicular to the faces of the plate and whose cross section S is small in comparison with the surface areas of the bounding planes, then there will be no flow of heat across the surface of the cylinder, but only parallel to the generators. Supposing that a quantity of heat Q passes in this way through the cylinder in a time t, then we find that the results

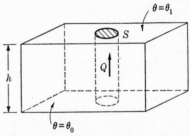

FIG. 20.   The basic experiment in the theory of thermal conductivity.

of the experiments may be interpreted by assuming that

$$Q = \frac{k(\theta_0 - \theta_1)St}{h} \tag{1}$$

where k is a constant, which we shall call the *thermal conductivity* of the material forming the plate.

The rate of flow per unit area between the faces of the plate is obtained by putting $S = 1$ in equation (1) and dividing by t,

$$\frac{Q}{t} = -\frac{k(\theta_1 - \theta_0)}{h} \tag{2}$$

Letting h tend to zero in this equation, we find that the rate of flow of heat per unit area across any plane is

$$q = -k \frac{\partial \theta}{\partial n} \tag{3}$$

where the operator $\partial/\partial n$ denotes differentiation along the normal. By means of this result we may establish the equation governing the conduction of heat in a solid.

Consider a rectangular parallelepiped whose vertices $A(x,y,z)$, $B(x,y + dy,z)$, $C(x,y + dy,z + dz)$, $D(x,y,z + dz)$, $A'(x + dx,y,z)$, $B'(x + dx,y + dy,z)$, $C'(x + dx,y + dy,z + dz)$, and $D'(x + dx,y,z + dz)$ all lie within the solid (cf. Fig. 21). Then it follows from equation (3) that the rate of flow of heat across the rectangular area $ABCD$ is

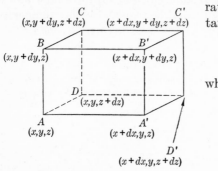

$$-k \, dx \, dy \left(\frac{\partial \theta}{\partial x}\right)_{x,y+\frac{1}{2}dy,z+\frac{1}{2}dz}$$

while that across the area $A'B'C'D'$ is

$$-k \, dy \, dz \left(\frac{\partial \theta}{\partial x}\right)_{x+dx,y+\frac{1}{2}dy,z+\frac{1}{2}dz}$$

$$= -k \, dy \, dz \left(\frac{\partial \theta}{\partial x}\right)_{x,y+\frac{1}{2}dy,z+\frac{1}{2}dz}$$

$$- dx \, dy \, dz \left(\frac{\partial}{\partial x} k \frac{\partial \theta}{\partial x}\right)_{x,y+\frac{1}{2}dy,z+\frac{1}{2}dz}$$

Fig. 21. Element of volume in a homogeneous solid.

by Taylor's theorem. The net flow of heat *into* the element of volume from these two planes is therefore

$$\left[\frac{\partial}{\partial x}\left(k \frac{\partial \theta}{\partial x}\right)\right] dx \, dy \, dz$$

The other faces of the element, taken in pairs, yield similar contributions so that, if the center of the cube is at temperature θ, heat flows into the element at a rate

$$\left[\frac{\partial}{\partial x}\left(k \frac{\partial \theta}{\partial x}\right) + \frac{\partial}{\partial y}\left(k \frac{\partial \theta}{\partial y}\right) + \frac{\partial}{\partial z}\left(k \frac{\partial \theta}{\partial z}\right)\right] dx \, dy \, dz \tag{4}$$

If, on the other hand, heat is *generated* in the element at a rate $Q(x,y,z)dx \, dy \, dz$, then, adding this to the expression (4), we see that the total rate of gain of heat by the element is

$$\left[Q(x,y,z) + \frac{\partial}{\partial x}\left(k \frac{\partial \theta}{\partial x}\right) + \frac{\partial}{\partial y}\left(k \frac{\partial \theta}{\partial y}\right) + \frac{\partial}{\partial z}\left(k \frac{\partial \theta}{\partial z}\right)\right] dx \, dy \, dz \tag{5}$$

Now if the density of the material is ρ, the mass of the element will be

$\rho \, dx \, dy \, dz$ so that, if c is the specific heat of the solid, the rate of gain of heat is given by the expression

$$\rho c \, \frac{\partial \theta}{\partial t} \, dx \, dy \, dz \tag{6}$$

Equating the expressions (5) and (6) and dividing throughout by $dx \, dy \, dz$, we obtain the partial differential equation

$$\rho c \, \frac{\partial \theta}{\partial t} = \frac{\partial}{\partial x} \left(k \, \frac{\partial \theta}{\partial x} \right) + \frac{\partial}{\partial y} \left(k \, \frac{\partial \theta}{\partial y} \right) + \frac{\partial}{\partial z} \left(k \, \frac{\partial \theta}{\partial z} \right) + Q(x,y,z) \tag{7}$$

governing the conduction of heat in a solid body.

If the conductivity k is a constant throughout the body and if we write

$$\kappa = \frac{k}{\rho c}, \qquad \Theta(x,y,z) = \frac{Q(x,y,z)}{\rho c} \tag{8}$$

equation (7) reduces to the simpler form

$$\frac{\partial \theta}{\partial t} = \kappa \, \nabla^2 \theta + \Theta(x,y,z,t) \tag{9}$$

∇^2 denoting the three-dimensional Laplacian operator.

22.2 Boundary conditions. The fundamental problem of the mathematical theory of the conduction of heat is the solution of equation (7)—or, in most cases, equation (9)—when it is known that the surfaces of the solid are treated in some prescribed way. The boundary conditions are usually of three main kinds[1]:

1. The temperature is prescribed along the surface.
2. The flux of heat across the surface is prescribed.
3. There is radiation from the surface into a medium of fixed temperature.

If we denote by P' any point on the surface under consideration, then in case 1 it is readily seen that

$$\theta(P',t) = F(P',t) \tag{10}$$

where $F(P',t)$ is a function of the position P' and of the time t. In case 2 it follows at once from equation (3) that the boundary condition can be expressed in the form

$$\frac{\partial \theta(P',t)}{\partial n} = F'(P',t) \tag{11}$$

where F' is a prescribed function of position and time.

[1] For the discussion of more complicated types of boundary conditions see H. S. Carslaw and J. C. Jaeger, "Conduction of Heat in Solids" (Oxford, New York, 1947), pp. 12–18.

To obtain the boundary condition in case 3, we make use of Newton's law of cooling in the form

$$k \frac{\partial \theta}{\partial n} + H(\theta - \theta_0) = 0$$

to obtain, for radiation into a medium at temperature θ_0,

$$\frac{\partial \theta}{\partial n} + h(\theta - \theta_0) = 0 \tag{12}$$

where $h = H/k > 0$.

If we introduce the differential operator λ defined by the equation

$$\lambda\{\theta\} = c_0\theta + c_1 \frac{\partial \theta}{\partial x} + c_2 \frac{\partial \theta}{\partial y} + c_3 \frac{\partial \theta}{\partial z} \tag{13}$$

where the coefficients of θ and its derivatives are functions of x, y, and z only, we may write all three of the conditions (10), (11), and (12) in the single form

$$\lambda[\theta(P',t)] = G(P',t) \tag{14}$$

where, it will be remembered, P' is a point on the boundary of the solid and $G(P',t)$ is a prescribed function of the time and of the coordinates of the point P'.

22.3 Resolution of boundary value problems in the theory of the conduction of heat.[1] If we assume that the function Θ occurring in the equation (9) is a linear function of the temperature of the form

$$\Theta(x,y,z,t) = C_0(x,y,z)\theta + F(x,y,z,t) \tag{15}$$

where C_0 is a function of x, y, and z only, then, introducing the differential operator

$$\Lambda\{\theta\} = \frac{1}{\rho c}\left[\frac{\partial}{\partial x}\left(k \frac{\partial \theta}{\partial x}\right) + \frac{\partial}{\partial y}\left(k \frac{\partial \theta}{\partial y}\right) + \frac{\partial}{\partial z}\left(k \frac{\partial \theta}{\partial z}\right) \right] + C_0\theta \tag{16}$$

and denoting by P a point in the interior of the solid, by P' a point on the boundary, it follows from equations (7) and (14) that the boundary value problem for the temperature $\theta(P,t)$ in the solid can be written in the form

$$\left. \begin{array}{ll} \dfrac{\partial}{\partial t}\,\theta(P,t) = \Lambda\{\theta\} + F(P,t) & t > 0 \\[2mm] \lambda[\theta(P',t)] = G(P',t) & t > 0 \\[2mm] \theta(P,0) = H(P) & \end{array} \right\} \tag{A}$$

The third of the equations (A) merely expresses the fact that at the instant $t = 0$ the distribution of temperature throughout the solid is known.

[1] R. C. F. Bartels and R. V. Churchill, *Bull. Am. Math. Soc.*, **48**, 276 (1942).

We shall now show how the theory of Laplace transforms may be used to resolve the complicated boundary value problem (A) into simpler problems. If we denote by $\bar{\theta}(P,s)$, $\bar{F}(P,s)$, and $\bar{G}(P',s)$ the Laplace transforms of the functions $\theta(P,t)$, $F(P,t)$, and $G(P',t)$, respectively (with regard to the variable t), then by the definition

$$\bar{\theta}(P,s) = \int_0^\infty \theta(P,t)e^{-st}\,dt \tag{17}$$

etc. Multiplying both sides of the equations (A) by e^{-st}, integrating with respect to t from 0 to ∞, and making use of the result

$$\int_0^\infty \frac{\partial \theta}{\partial t}\,e^{-st}\,dt = [\theta(P,t)e^{-st}]_0^\infty + s\int_0^\infty \theta(P,t)e^{-st}\,dt = -H(P) + s\bar{\theta}(P,s)$$

we see that the equations (A) are equivalent to the pair of relations

$$\left.\begin{array}{l} (s - \Lambda)[\bar{\theta}(P,s)] = H(P) + \bar{F}(P,s) \\ \lambda[\bar{\theta}(P',s)] = \bar{G}(P',s) \end{array}\right\} \tag{$\dot{A}'$}$$

between the Laplace transforms $\bar{\theta}, \bar{F}$, and $\bar{G}$.

Suppose now that the temperature function $\phi(P,t,t')$ depending on the *fixed* parameter t' is a solution of the boundary value problem (A) in the case in which the source function F and the surface temperature function G are functions of the space variables and of the parameter t', but not of the time t, so that we may write $F(P,t) = F(P,t')$, $G(P',t) = G(P',t')$ with Laplace transforms $\bar{F}(P,s) = s^{-1}F(P,t')$ and $G(P',s) = s^{-1}G(P',t')$. Then the function $\phi(P,t,t')$ satisfies the equations

$$\left.\begin{array}{l} \left(\dfrac{\partial}{\partial t} - \Lambda\right)\phi(P,t,t') = F(P,t') \\ \lambda[\phi(P',t,t')] = G(P',t') \\ \phi(P,0,t') = H(P) \end{array}\right\} \tag{B}$$

and if $\bar{\phi}(P,s,t')$ is its Laplace transform with respect to the variable t, then

$$(\Lambda - s)\bar{\phi}(P,s,t') + H(P) + s^{-1}F(P,t') = 0$$
$$\lambda[\bar{\phi}(P',s,t')] = s^{-1}G(P',t')$$

Multiplying both sides of these equations by $e^{-st'}$ and integrating with respect to t' from 0 to ∞, we find that

$$\left.\begin{array}{l} (s - \Lambda)\Phi(P,s) = s^{-1}H(P) + s^{-1}\bar{F}(P,s) \\ \lambda[\Phi(P',s)] = s^{-1}\bar{G}(P',s) \end{array}\right\} \tag{B'}$$

where

$$\Phi(P,s) = \int_0^\infty e^{-st'}\bar{\phi}(P,s,t')dt' = \int_0^\infty \int_0^\infty e^{-s(t+t')}\phi(P,t,t')dt\,dt'$$

is the iterated Laplace transform of the function $\phi(P,t,t')$ [cf. equation (118a), Chap. 1]. Multiplying each member of the pair (B') by s, we see immediately that the problems (A') and (B') are equivalent so that the function $s\Phi(P,s)$ is a solution of the boundary value problem (A'). If then we assume that the solution of this problem is unique, we must take

$$\bar{\theta}(P,s) = s\Phi(P,s) \tag{18}$$

Now, by equation (124), Chap. 1, it follows that $\Phi(P,s)$, which is the iterated Laplace transform of the function $\phi(P,t,t')$ is the Laplace transform of the generalized convolution

$$\int_0^t \phi(P,t-t',t')dt'$$

so that $s\Phi(P,s)$ is the Laplace transform of the function

$$\frac{1}{2\pi i}\int_{\gamma-i\infty}^{\gamma+i\infty} s\Phi(P,s)e^{st}\,ds = \frac{\partial}{\partial t}\int_0^t \phi(P,t-t',t')dt'$$

Multiplying both sides of equation (18) by e^{st} and integrating with respect to s along the contour $\mathsf{R}(s) = \gamma$ from $\gamma - i\infty$ to $\gamma + i\infty$, we find that

$$\theta(P,t) = \frac{\partial}{\partial t}\int_0^t \phi(P,t-t',t')dt' \tag{19}$$

This provides us with a proof of the following theorem:

Theorem 33 (Duhamel's Theorem).   *The solution $\theta(P,t)$ of the boundary value problem (A) with variable source and surface conditions is given in terms of the solution $\phi(P,t,t')$ of the boundary value problem (B) with constant source and surface conditions by the formula*

$$\theta(P,t) = \frac{\partial}{\partial t}\int_0^t \phi(P,t-t',t')dt'$$

This theorem, which is shown by the above analysis to hold for very general boundary and initial conditions, is of great value in the solution of boundary value problems in the conduction of heat, since it is often much easier to derive the solution in the case of constant source and boundary conditions (cf. Sec. 23.2, case 2).

It can further be shown that the complex boundary value problem (A) can be resolved into simpler problems. We may write the solution of the boundary value problem (B) in the form

$$\phi(P,t,t') = \phi_1(P,t') + \phi_2(P,t,t') + \chi(P,t,t') \tag{20}$$

where the functions ϕ_1, ϕ_2, and χ are solutions of the problems

$$\Lambda[\phi_1(P,t')] = 0, \qquad \lambda[\phi_1(P',t')] = G(P',t') \qquad (20a)$$

$$\left.\begin{array}{c}\left(\dfrac{\partial}{\partial t} - \Lambda\right)\phi_2(P,t,t') = 0, \qquad \lambda[\phi_2(P',t,t')] = 0 \\ \phi_2(P,0,t') = H(P) - \phi_1(P,t')\end{array}\right\} \qquad (20b)$$

and

$$\left(\frac{\partial}{\partial t} - \Lambda\right)\chi(P,t,t') = F(P,t'), \qquad \lambda[\chi(P',t,t')] = 0$$

$$\chi(P,0,t') = 0$$

In terms of the Laplace transform $\bar{\chi}(P,s,t')$ of the function $\chi(P,t,t')$ the third of these boundary value problems becomes

$$(s - \Lambda)\bar{\chi}(P,s,t') = s^{-1}F(P,t'), \qquad \lambda[\bar{\chi}(P',s,t')] = 0$$

Multiplying throughout by s, we see that $s\bar{\chi}(P,s,t')$ is the transform of a solution of the following problem:

$$\left.\begin{array}{c}\left(\dfrac{\partial}{\partial t} - \Lambda\right)\phi_3(P,t,t') = 0 \\ \lambda[\phi_3(P',t,t')] = 0, \qquad \phi_3(P,0,t') = F(P,t')\end{array}\right\} \qquad (20c)$$

Hence, proceeding as in the proof of Duhamel's theorem, we see that

$$\frac{\partial \chi}{\partial t} = \phi_3(P,t,t')$$

Integrating with respect to t and making use of the fact that $\chi(P,0,t')$ is zero, we find

$$\chi(P,t,t') = \int_0^t \phi_3(P,\tau,t')d\tau \qquad (21)$$

Hence if the functions ϕ_1, ϕ_2, and ϕ_3 are solutions of the boundary value problems (20a), (20b), and (20c), respectively, it follows that

$$\phi(P,t,t') = \phi_1(P,t') + \phi_2(P,t,t') + \int_0^t \phi_3(P,\tau,t')d\tau$$

and therefore, from equation (19), that the solution of the boundary value problem (A) is

$$\theta(P,t) = \frac{\partial}{\partial t}\int_0^t \left[\phi_1(P,t') + \phi_2(P,t-t',t') + \int_0^{t-t'} \phi_3(P,\tau,t')d\tau\right]dt'$$

which reduces to the expression

$$\theta(P,t) = \phi_1(P,t) + \frac{\partial}{\partial t}\int_0^t \phi_2(P,t-t',t')dt' + \int_0^t \phi_3(P,t-t',t')dt' \qquad (22)$$

The solution of the general boundary value problem (A) may therefore be obtained readily from the solutions of the three simpler boundary value problems $(20a)$, $(20b)$, and $(20c)$, of which the first is a steady-state problem and the other two are variable-state problems of the same type in which only the initial condition is inhomogeneous.

23. Conduction of Heat when There Are No Sources Present

In the remainder of this chapter we shall be concerned with the solution of the differential equation (9) for various forms of the function $\Theta(x,y,z,t)$, which expresses the rate at which heat is generated in the interior of the solid, and under various boundary and initial conditions. Since the application of the theory of Laplace transforms to the solution of problems of this type is already adequately covered in the literature,[1] we shall, in the main, confine our attention to applications of other types of transforms, noticeably the finite transforms discussed in Chap. 3. In many cases solutions which are derived by use of these finite transforms could also have been obtained by means of the Laplace transform, but a comparison of the two methods of solution will usually show that that based on the finite transform theory is quicker and easier to use.

We shall begin by considering conduction problems in media in which there are no sources of heat present; *i.e.*, we take the function $\Theta(x,y,z,t)$ occurring on the right-hand side of equation (9) to be identically zero.

23.1 Linear flow of heat in an infinite medium. If the flow of heat is linear so that the variation of θ with z and y may be neglected, and if we assume that no heat is generated in the medium, then the differential equation (9) reduces to the simple form

$$\frac{\partial \theta}{\partial t} = \kappa \frac{\partial^2 \theta}{\partial x^2} \tag{23}$$

In the first instance we shall consider the flow of heat in the infinite medium $-\infty < x < \infty$ when the initial distribution of temperature $\theta(x,0)$ is prescribed. We then have to solve the equation (23) subject to the initial condition

$$\theta = f(x) \qquad \text{when } t = 0 \tag{24}$$

$f(x)$ being a given function of x.

To solve this simple boundary value problem, we introduce the Fourier transform

$$\Theta(\xi,t) = \left(\frac{1}{2\pi}\right)^{\frac{1}{2}} \int_{-\infty}^{\infty} \theta(x,t) e^{i\xi x} \, dx \tag{25}$$

---

[1] See, for example, H. S. Carslaw and J. C. Jaeger, "Operational Methods in Applied Mathematics" (Oxford, New York, 1941), Chap. VI, and "Conduction of Heat in Solids" (Oxford, New York, 1947), Chaps. XI–XIV; R. V. Churchill, "Modern Operational Mathematics in Engineering" (McGraw-Hill, New York, 1944), Chap. VII.

of the temperature. Integrating both sides of equation (23) after it has been multiplied throughout by $e^{i\xi x}$, we obtain the ordinary differential equation

$$\frac{d\Theta}{dt} = -\kappa\xi^2\Theta$$

for the determination of the function Θ. It follows at once from equation (24) that, when $t = 0$,

$$\Theta = F(\xi) = \left(\frac{1}{2\pi}\right)^{\frac{1}{2}} \int_{-\infty}^{\infty} f(x)e^{i\xi x}\,dx$$

Thus we immediately have

$$\Theta = F(\xi)e^{-\kappa\xi^2 t}$$

and hence, by Theorem 10, that

$$\theta(x,t) = \left(\frac{1}{2\pi}\right)^{\frac{1}{2}} \int_{-\infty}^{\infty} F(\xi)e^{-\kappa\xi^2 t - i\xi x}\,d\xi \qquad (26)$$

Now the Fourier transform of the function $e^{-\kappa\xi^2 t}$ is

$$g(x) = \left(\frac{1}{2\pi}\right)^{\frac{1}{2}} \int_{-\infty}^{\infty} e^{-\kappa\xi^2 t - i\xi x}\,d\xi$$

which gives, as the result of a well-known integral,

$$g(x) = \frac{1}{\sqrt{2\kappa t}}\, e^{-x^2/4\kappa t}$$

By the Faltung theorem 12 the integral on the right-hand side of equation (26) has the value

$$\frac{1}{\sqrt{2\pi}} \int_{-\infty}^{\infty} f(u)g(x - u)\,du$$

Substituting for $g(x)$, we find

$$\theta(x,t) = \frac{1}{(4\pi\kappa t)^{\frac{1}{2}}} \int_{-\infty}^{\infty} f(u)e^{-(x-u)^2/4\kappa t}\,du$$

so that, changing the variable of integration to $\xi = (u - x)/2\sqrt{\kappa t}$, we obtain finally the solution

$$\theta(x,t) = \frac{1}{\sqrt{\pi}} \int_{-\infty}^{\infty} f(x + 2\sqrt{\kappa t}\,\xi)e^{-\xi^2}\,d\xi \qquad (26a)$$

23.2 Linear flow of heat in a semiinfinite medium. We next consider the linear flow of heat in the semiinfinite medium $0 \leq x < \infty$ under certain boundary conditions. The differential equation to be solved is again the equation (23), but, of course, in the present case x is restricted to take positive values only.

Case 1: In the first instance we shall suppose that the end $x = 0$ is kept at a constant temperature θ_0, say, and that initially the rod is at zero temperature throughout. We have then to solve equation (23) subject to the conditions (cf. Fig. 22)

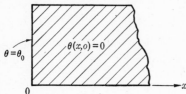

$$\theta = 0,\ t = 0,\ x > 0$$

Fig. 22. Boundary and initial conditions in case (1).   and

$$\theta = \theta_0,\ x = 0,\ t \geq 0 \qquad (27)$$

To solve this boundary value problem, let

$$\Theta_s(\xi,t) = \left(\frac{2}{\pi}\right)^{\frac{1}{2}} \int_0^\infty \theta(x,t)\ \sin\ (\xi x)dx \qquad (28)$$

be the Fourier sine transform of the temperature θ. Integrating by parts and assuming that $\theta(0,t) = \theta_0$, $\theta(\infty,t) = 0$, we see that

$$\int_0^\infty \frac{\partial^2\theta}{\partial x^2}\ \sin\ (\xi x)dx = \xi\theta_0 - \xi^2 \int_0^\infty \theta(x,t)\ \sin\ (\xi x)dx$$

Hence, multiplying both sides of equation (23) by $\sin\ (\xi x)$ and integrating with respect to x from 0 to ∞, we obtain the differential equation

$$\frac{d\Theta_s}{dt} + \kappa\xi^2\Theta_s = \sqrt{\frac{2}{\pi}}\ \kappa\xi\theta_0$$

Since $\theta = 0$ when $t = 0$, it follows by integration that $\Theta_s(\xi,0) = 0$ so that the solution of this last equation is

$$\Theta_s(\xi,t) = \sqrt{\frac{2}{\pi}} \left(\frac{1 - e^{-\kappa\xi^2 t}}{\xi}\right) \theta_0$$

Inverting the equation (28) by means of Theorem 9 and inserting this value for $\Theta_s(\xi,t)$, we obtain for the temperature at any instant in the interior of the medium

$$\theta(x,t) = \frac{2}{\pi}\ \theta_0 \int_0^\infty \frac{\sin\ (\xi x)}{\xi}\ (1 - e^{-\kappa\xi^2 t})d\xi$$

Making use of the integral

$$\int_0^\infty e^{-\xi^2} \frac{\sin\ (2\xi y)}{\xi}\ d\xi = \frac{1}{2}\ \pi\ \text{erf}\ (y) \qquad (29)$$

where

$$\text{erf }(y) = \frac{2}{\sqrt{\pi}} \int_0^y e^{-u^2}\, du$$

we obtain finally

$$\theta = \theta_0 - \frac{2}{\sqrt{\pi}}\, \theta_0 \int_0^{x/2(\kappa t)^{\frac{1}{2}}} e^{-u^2}\, du = \frac{2\theta_0}{\sqrt{\pi}} \int_{x/2(\kappa t)^{\frac{1}{2}}}^{\infty} e^{-u^2}\, du$$

The solution of this problem has also been derived by Jaeger,[1] using the theory of double Laplace transforms outlined in Sec. 7.1. It is instructive to give his derivation as an illustration of the use of these double transforms. We introduce the double Laplace transform of the temperature $\theta(x,t)$:

$$\Theta(p',p) = \int_0^{\infty} \int_0^{\infty} \theta(x,t) e^{-pt-p'x}\, dt\, dx \tag{30}$$

Then, in the notation of Sec. 7.1,

$$g_0(x) = \theta(x,0) = 0, \qquad h_0(t) = \theta(0,t) = \theta_0$$

and

$$h_1(t) = \left(\frac{\partial \theta}{\partial x}\right)_{x=0}$$

is unknown. By definition

$$\bar{h}_0(p) = \int_0^{\infty} h_0(t) e^{-pt}\, dt = \frac{\theta_0}{p}$$

so that we have from equations (113) and (116), Chap. 1,

$$\int_0^{\infty} \int_0^{\infty} e^{-pt-p'x} \frac{\partial \theta}{\partial t}\, dt\, dx = p\bar{\Theta}(p',p)$$

$$\int_0^{\infty} \int_0^{\infty} e^{-pt-p'x} \frac{\partial^2 \theta}{\partial x^2}\, dt\, dx = p'^2\bar{\Theta}(p',p) - p'\bar{h}_0(p) - \bar{h}_1(p)$$

Hence, if we multiply both sides of equation (23) by $\exp\,(-pt - p'x)$ and integrate over the positive quadrant of the xt plane, we obtain the algebraic equation

$$\left(p'^2 - \frac{p}{\kappa}\right) \bar{\Theta}(p',p) = \frac{p'}{p}\, \theta_0 + h_1(p)$$

for the double Laplace transform $\bar{\Theta}(p',p)$.

It follows from this equation that

$$\bar{\Theta}(p',p) = \frac{p'\theta_0 + p\bar{h}_1(p)}{p(p'^2 - p/\kappa)}$$

but it will be observed that in this equation $\bar{h}_1(p)$ is unknown as well as

[1] J. C. Jaeger, *Bull. Am. Math. Soc.*, **46**, 687 (1940).

$\bar{\Theta}(p',p)$. The function $\bar{h}_1(p)$ is determined by the condition that $\bar{\Theta}(p',p)$ is bounded in some half planes $\mathsf{R}(p') > \alpha'$, $\mathsf{R}(p) > \alpha$. We then have

$$\bar{h}_1(p) = -\frac{\theta_0}{\sqrt{\kappa p}}$$

so that

$$\bar{\Theta}(p',p) = \frac{\theta_0}{p[p' + \sqrt{(p/\kappa)}]}$$

and

$$
\begin{aligned}
\theta(x,t) &= -\frac{\theta_0}{4\pi^2} \int_{\gamma-i\infty}^{\gamma+i\infty} e^{pt}\frac{dp}{p} \int_{\gamma'-i\infty}^{\gamma'+i\infty} \frac{e^{p'x}\,dp'}{p' + (p/\kappa)^{\frac{1}{2}}} \\
&= \frac{\theta_0}{2\pi i} \int_{\gamma-i\infty}^{\gamma+i\infty} e^{pt-x(p/\kappa)^{\frac{1}{2}}}\frac{dp}{p} \\
&= \theta_0 - \frac{2\theta_0}{\sqrt{\pi}} \int_0^{x/2(\kappa t)^{\frac{1}{2}}} e^{-u^2}\,du
\end{aligned}
\tag{31}
$$

precisely as before.

Case 2: We shall now consider the case in which the initial temperature of the solid is zero and the face $x = 0$ is maintained at a temperature $\phi(t)$

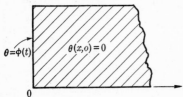

which varies with the time in a known way (cf. Fig. 23). The boundary conditions to be satisfied by the solution of equation (23) in this case are therefore

$$\theta = \phi(t),\ x = 0,\ t > 0;$$
$$\theta = 0,\ t = 0,\ x > 0 \tag{32}$$

FIG. 23. Boundary and initial conditions in case (2).

Now if t' is a fixed parameter, it follows from equation (31) that the solution of equation (23) which satisfies the boundary conditions

$$\theta = \phi(t'),\ x = 0,\ t > 0;\qquad \theta = 0,\ t = 0,\ x > 0 \tag{32a}$$

is

$$\theta = \frac{2}{\sqrt{\pi}}\,\phi(t') \int_{x/2(\kappa t)^{\frac{1}{2}}}^{\infty} e^{-u^2}\,du$$

It follows immediately from Theorem 33 that the solution of equation (23) which satisfies the conditions (32) is

$$
\begin{aligned}
\theta(x,t) &= \frac{\partial}{\partial t} \int_0^t \phi(t')dt' \int_{x/2(\kappa t-\kappa t')^{\frac{1}{2}}}^{\infty} e^{-u^2}\,du \\
&= \frac{x}{2\sqrt{\pi\kappa}} \int_0^t \phi(t')\frac{e^{-x^2/4\kappa(t-t')}}{(t-t')^{\frac{3}{2}}}\,dt'
\end{aligned}
$$

Changing the variable of integration from t' to η where

$$t' = t - \frac{x^2}{4\kappa\eta^2}$$

we see that the solution may be written in the form

$$\theta(x,t) = \frac{2}{\sqrt{\pi}} \int_{x/2(\kappa t)^{\frac{1}{2}}}^{\infty} \phi\left(t - \frac{x^2}{4\kappa\eta^2}\right) e^{-\eta^2}\, d\eta \qquad (33)$$

Case 3: As a final example of the conduction of heat in a semiinfinite medium $x \geq 0$, we shall consider the distribution of temperature in the medium when the end $x = 0$ is maintained at zero temperature and the initial distribution of temperature is known. We then have (cf. Fig. 24)

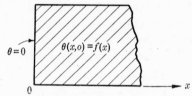

$$\theta = 0,\ x = 0,\ t > 0;$$
$$\theta = f(x),\ t = 0,\ x > 0$$

Defining the Fourier transform $\Theta_s(\xi,t)$ of the temperature θ by equation (28),

FIG. 24. Boundary and initial conditions in case (3).

multiplying both sides of equation (23) by sin (ξx), and making use of the result

$$\int_0^\infty \frac{\partial^2\theta}{\partial x^2} \sin\ (\xi x) dx = -\xi^2 \int_0^\infty \theta \sin\ (\xi x) dx$$

we see that $\Theta_s(\xi,t)$ is a solution of the ordinary differential equation

$$\frac{d\Theta_s}{dt} + \kappa\xi^2\Theta_s = 0 \qquad (34)$$

Now when $t = 0$, $\theta = f(x)$ so that

$$\Theta_s(\xi,0) = F_s(\xi) = \left(\frac{2}{\pi}\right)^{\frac{1}{2}} \int_0^\infty f(x) \sin\ (\xi x) dx$$

and the appropriate solution of equation (34) is

$$\Theta_s(\xi,t) = F_s(\xi)e^{-\kappa\xi^2 t}$$

By the Fourier inversion formula (36), Chap. 1, we then have

$$\theta(x,t) = \left(\frac{2}{\pi}\right)^{\frac{1}{2}} \int_0^\infty F_s(\xi)e^{-\kappa\xi^2 t} \sin\ (\xi x) d\xi$$

$$= \frac{2}{\pi} \int_0^\infty f(u)du \int_0^\infty \sin\ (\xi u) \sin\ (\xi x)e^{-\kappa\xi^2 t}\, d\xi$$

Now[1]

$$\int_0^\infty e^{-a^2x^2} \cos (2bx)dx = \frac{\sqrt{\pi}}{2a} e^{-b^2/a^2} \tag{35}$$

so that, since

$$\theta(x,t) = \frac{1}{\pi} \int_0^\infty f(u)du \int_0^\infty \{\cos [\xi(x - u)] - \cos [\xi(x + u)]\}e^{-\kappa t \xi^2} d\xi$$

we obtain finally

$$\theta(x,t) = \frac{1}{2\sqrt{\pi \kappa t}} \int_0^\infty f(u) [e^{-(x-u)^2/4\kappa t} - e^{-(x+u)^2/4\kappa t}]du \tag{36}$$

23.3 Conduction of heat in a solid bounded by two parallel planes. To illustrate the use of finite Fourier transforms in the solution of problems in the theory of the linear flow of heat, we shall determine the distribution of temperature in the solid $0 \le x \le a$ when the ends $x = 0$ and $x = a$ are kept at zero temperature and initially the distribution of temperature is $\theta(x,0) = f(x)$ (cf. Fig. 25). The boundary and initial conditions are therefore

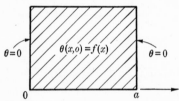

$$\theta = 0, x = 0,a, t > 0;$$
$$\theta = f(x), t = 0, 0 \le x \le a$$

FIG. 25. Boundary and initial conditions for the conduction of heat in a solid bounded by two parallel planes.

and the distribution of temperature is determined, as before, by equation (23). Multiplying both sides of equation (23) by $\sin (n\pi x/a)$ and integrating with respect to x from 0 to a, we find that the finite sine transform

$$\bar{\theta}_s(n,t) = \int_0^a \theta(x,t) \sin \left(\frac{n\pi x}{a}\right) dx$$

is a solution of the first-order ordinary differential equation

$$\frac{d\bar{\theta}_s}{dt} + \frac{\kappa n^2 \pi^2}{a^2} \bar{\theta}_s = 0$$

From the initial condition $\theta(x,0) = f(x)$ it follows that

$$\bar{\theta}_s(n,0) = \bar{f}_s(n) = \int_0^a f(x) \sin \left(\frac{n\pi x}{a}\right) dx$$

We have therefore

$$\bar{\theta}_s(n,t) = \bar{f}_s(n)e^{-\kappa n^2 \pi^2 t/a^2}$$

[1] T. M. MacRobert, "Functions of a Complex Variable," 2d ed. (Macmillan, London, 1933), p. 268.

so that by Theorem 27 we obtain the solution

$$\theta(x,t) = \frac{2}{a} \sum_{n=1}^{\infty} \bar{f}_s(n) e^{-\kappa n^2 \pi^2 t/a^2} \sin\left(\frac{n\pi x}{a}\right)$$

$$= \frac{2}{a} \sum_{n=1}^{\infty} e^{-\kappa n^2 \pi^2 t/a^2} \sin\left(\frac{n\pi x}{a}\right) \int_0^a f(u) \sin\left(\frac{n\pi u}{a}\right) du$$

23.4 Radiation at the surface of a semiinfinite solid.   In the previous examples we supposed that the temperatures of the surfaces of the solid were prescribed.   We shall now consider the more complicated case in which there is radiation from the surface into a medium of fixed temperature.   To fix our ideas, we shall consider the conduction of heat in the semiinfinite solid $x \geq 0$ when the initial temperature is $\theta(x,0) = f(x)$ and there is radiation from the surface $x = 0$ into a medium of temperature θ_0.   The temperature $\theta(x,t)$ then satisfies equations (9) and (12) and the above initial condition.   If we write

$$\phi(x,t) = \theta(x,t) - \theta_0 \tag{37}$$

we see that the function $\phi(x,t)$ satisfies the conditions

$$\frac{\partial \phi}{\partial t} = \kappa \frac{\partial^2 \phi}{\partial x^2} \tag{38}$$

$$\frac{\partial \phi}{\partial x} + h\phi = 0 \tag{39}$$

$$\phi(x,0) = f(x) - \theta_0 = g(x), \text{ say} \tag{40}$$

To solve the boundary value problem embodied in these equations, we make use of a modified form of Fourier's integral theorem.   Theorem 9, which states that, at a point of continuity of $f(x)$,

$$f(x) = \frac{2}{\pi} \int_0^{\infty} \int_0^{\infty} f(\xi) \sin(\xi\eta) \sin(\eta x) d\xi \, d\eta$$

may readily be generalized by means of the theory of Laplace transforms to give the theorem[1]

$$\phi(x) = \int_0^{\infty} K(\xi,x) d\xi \int_0^{\infty} \phi(\eta) K(\xi,\eta) d\eta \tag{41}$$

where the kernel $K(\xi,x)$ is defined by the equation

$$K(\xi,x) = \sqrt{\frac{2}{\pi}} \left[\frac{h \sin(\xi x) + \xi \cos(\xi x)}{(h^2 + \xi^2)^{\frac{1}{2}}} \right] \tag{42}$$

[1] For a proof of this theorem, see Churchill, *op. cit.*, pp. 206–210.

In the form of an inversion theorem this becomes: If

$$\Phi(\xi) = \int_0^\infty \phi(x)K(\xi,x)dx \tag{43}$$

then

$$\phi(x) = \int_0^\infty \Phi(\xi)K(\xi,x)d\xi \tag{44}$$

To solve our boundary value problem, we multiply both sides of equation (38) by $K(\xi,x)$, integrate with respect to x from 0 to ∞ and make use of the result

$$\int_0^\infty \frac{\partial^2 \phi}{\partial x^2} K(\xi,x)dx = \frac{\xi}{(h^2 + \xi^2)^{\frac{1}{2}}}\left(\frac{\partial \phi}{\partial x} + h\phi\right)_{x=0} - \xi^2\Phi(\xi) = -\xi^2\Phi(\xi)$$

to obtain the ordinary differential equation

$$\frac{d\Phi}{dt} + \kappa\xi^2\Phi = 0$$

Initially

$$\Phi(\xi,0) = G(\xi) = \int_0^\infty g(x)K(\xi,x)dx \tag{45}$$

so that

$$\Phi(\xi,t) = G(\xi)e^{-\kappa\xi^2 t}$$

Inverting this result by equation (44), we find that

$$\phi(x,t) = \int_0^\infty G(\xi)e^{-\kappa\xi^2 t}K(\xi,x)d\xi$$

so that

$$\theta(x,t) = \theta_0 + \int_0^\infty K(\xi,x)e^{-\kappa\xi^2 t}\,d\xi \int_0^\infty g(\eta)K(\xi,\eta)d\eta \tag{46}$$

23.5 Conduction of heat in an infinite cylinder. Next to the equation of linear flow the simplest case of the equation (9) which arises in the theory of conduction is that governing the conduction of heat in circular cylinders of great length. In cylindrical polar coordinates r,φ,z the partial differential equation (9) reduces in the case $\Theta = 0$ to the form

$$\frac{\partial\theta}{\partial t} = \kappa\left(\frac{\partial^2\theta}{\partial r^2} + \frac{1}{r}\frac{\partial\theta}{\partial r} + \frac{\partial^2\theta}{\partial z^2} + \frac{1}{r^2}\frac{\partial^2\theta}{\partial\varphi^2}\right) \tag{47}$$

If there is symmetry about the axis of the cylinder (the z axis), then the operator $\partial/\partial\varphi$ is identically zero, and if the cylinder is very long and the surface and initial conditions such that parallel sections of the cylinder normal to its axis have the same distribution of temperature, $\partial/\partial z$ is also identically zero. Equation (47) then becomes

$$\frac{\partial\theta}{\partial t} = \kappa\left(\frac{\partial^2\theta}{\partial r^2} + \frac{1}{r}\frac{\partial\theta}{\partial r}\right) \tag{48}$$

We shall now discuss the solution of this equation under differing surface and initial conditions.

Case 1: We shall begin by considering the distribution of temperature in the circular cylinder $0 \le r \le a$ when the surface $r = a$ is kept at a temperature $f(t)$ which varies with time. Our problem is then that of solving equation (48) subject to the conditions that $\theta = 0$ when $t = 0$ and $\theta = f(t)$ when $r = a(t > 0)$. From equation (61), Chap. 3, we find that under these circumstances

$$\int_0^a r\left(\frac{\partial^2\theta}{\partial r^2} + \frac{1}{r}\frac{\partial\theta}{\partial r}\right) J_0(\xi_i r)dr = a\xi_i J_1(\xi_i a)f(t) - \xi_i^2\bar\theta_a$$

if ξ_i is a root of the equation

$$J_0(\xi_i a) = 0 \tag{49}$$

and

$$\bar\theta_a = \int_0^a r\theta(r,t)J_0(\xi_i r)dr \tag{50}$$

Equation (48) is therefore equivalent to the equation

$$\frac{d\theta_a}{dt} + \kappa\xi_i^2\bar\theta_a = \kappa a\xi_i J_1(\xi_i a)f(t)$$

which, by virtue of the initial condition that $\bar\theta_a$ is zero when $t = 0$, has the solution

$$\theta_a = \kappa a\xi_i J_1(\xi_i a)\int_0^t f(\tau)e^{-\xi_i^2\kappa(t-\tau)}\,d\tau$$

Inverting this equation by means of Theorem 30, we obtain for the temperature at any instant

$$\theta(r,t) = \frac{2\kappa}{a}\sum_i \frac{\xi_i J_1(\xi_i r)}{J_1(\xi_i a)}\int_0^t f(\tau)e^{-\kappa\xi_i^2(t-\tau)}\,d\tau \tag{51}$$

the sum being taken over all the positive roots of equation (49). For instance, if the surface temperature is constant, *i.e.*, if $f(t) = \theta_0$, we have

$$\theta = \frac{2\theta_0}{a}\sum_i \frac{J_0(\xi_i r)}{\xi_i J_1(\xi_i a)}\left(1 - e^{-\kappa\xi_i^2 t}\right)$$

Now it follows immediately from equation (64), Chap. 3, and Theorem 30 that

$$\frac{2}{a}\sum_i \frac{J_0(\xi_i r)}{\xi_i J_1(\xi_i a)} = 1$$

so that we obtain for the temperature the expression

$$\theta = \theta_0 \left[1 - \frac{2}{a} \sum_i \frac{J_0(\xi_i r) e^{-\kappa \xi_i^2 t}}{\xi_i J_1(\xi_i a)} \right] \tag{52}$$

where the sum extends over all the positive roots of equation (49).

It will be observed that equation (51) can be derived from equation (52) by the application of Duhamel's theorem.

Case 2: In the next two cases we shall suppose that the initial distribution of temperature in the cylinder $0 \le r \le a$ is

$$\theta(r,0) = f(r) \qquad 0 \le r \le a \tag{53}$$

In the first case we shall assume further that the surface $r = a$ is maintained at zero temperature, so that

$$\theta(a,t) = 0 \qquad t > 0 \tag{54}$$

If we again define θ_a by equation (50) with ξ_i a root of equation (49), it follows from equation (61), Chap. 3, and from equation (54) that

$$\int_0^a r \left(\frac{\partial^2 \theta}{\partial r^2} + \frac{1}{r} \frac{\partial \theta}{\partial r} \right) J_0(\xi_i r) dr = - \xi_i^2 \bar{\theta}_a$$

Hence, multiplying both sides of equation (48) by $r J_0(\xi_i r)$ and integrating over the section of the cylinder, we obtain the ordinary differential equation

$$\frac{d \bar{\theta}_a}{dt} + \kappa \xi_i^2 \bar{\theta}_a = 0$$

which, because of (53), has the solution

$$\bar{\theta}_a = \bar{f}_a(\xi_i) e^{-\kappa \xi_i^2 t}$$

where

$$\bar{f}_a(\xi_i) = \int_0^a r f(r) J_0(\xi_i r) dr$$

It follows by a direct application of Theorem 30 that

$$\theta(r,t) = \frac{2}{a^2} \sum_i \frac{J_0(\xi_i r)}{[J_1(\xi_i a)]^2} e^{-\kappa \xi_i^2 t} \int_0^a u f(u) J_0(u \xi_i) du \tag{55}$$

where the sum is taken over all the positive roots of equation (49).

Case 3: We consider now the same problem except that, instead of the surface $r = a$ being maintained at zero temperature, there is radiation from it into a medium at zero temperature, *i.e.*, equation (54) is replaced by the condition

$$\frac{\partial \theta}{\partial r} + h \theta = 0 \qquad r = a, \, t > 0 \tag{56}$$

We again introduce a finite Hankel transform of the type (50), but now we take ξ_i to be a root of the equation

$$hJ_0(a\xi_i) = \xi_i J_1(a\xi_i) \tag{57}$$

Substituting from equation (56) into equation (69), Chap. 3, we see that, provided that ξ_i is a root of equation (57),

$$\int_0^a r\left(\frac{\partial^2 \theta}{\partial r^2} + \frac{1}{r}\frac{\partial \theta}{\partial r}\right) J_0(\xi_i r)dr = -\xi_i^2 \bar{\theta}_a$$

so that equations (48), (53), and (56) are equivalent to

$$\frac{d\bar{\theta}_a}{dt} + \kappa \xi_i^2 \bar{\theta}_a = 0$$

As before, we have

$$\theta_a(\xi_i,t) = e^{-\kappa \xi_i^2 t}\int_0^a uf(u)J_0(u\xi_i)du$$

whence by Theorem 30, we have

$$\theta(r,t) = \frac{2}{a^2}\sum_i \frac{\xi_i^2 e^{-\kappa \xi_i^2 t}J_0(\xi_i r)}{(h^2 + \xi_i^2)[J_0(\xi_i a)]^2}$$

$$\times \int_0^a uf(u)J_0(\xi_i u)du \tag{58}$$

where the sum is taken over all the positive roots of equation (57).[1]

Case 4: We shall conclude the discussion of the diffusion of heat in infinite circular cylinders by considering the flow of heat in the infinite cylinder bounded by the surfaces $r = a$, $r = b(a > b)$, when these surfaces are

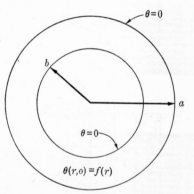

Fig. 26.   Boundary and initial conditions for the conduction of heat in an infinite hollow cylinder (case 4).

kept at zero temperature and the initial distribution of temperature in the cylinder is known (cf. Fig. 26). We again have equation (48), but now the boundary and initial conditions are

$$\theta = 0 \qquad \text{when } r = a \text{ or } r = b,\, t > 0 \tag{59}$$
$$\theta(r,0) = f(r) \qquad b \leq r \leq a \tag{60}$$

where $f(r)$ is a prescribed function of r.

[1] Numerical calculations based on equation (58) are greatly facilitated by the use of tables of the roots of equation (57) for various values of ha contained in Carslaw and Jaeger, *op. cit.*, p. 379.

Introducing the finite Hankel transform

$$\mathsf{H}[\theta(r)] = \theta_H(\xi_i)$$

defined by equation (51), Chap. 3, with $\mu = 0$ so that ξ_i is taken to be a root of the transcendental equation

$$J_0(\xi_i b)G_0(\xi_i a) - J_0(\xi_i a)G_0(\xi_i b) = 0 \tag{61}$$

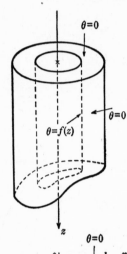

we may readily show that $\bar{\theta}_H$ satisfies

$$\frac{d\bar{\theta}_H}{dt} + \kappa\xi_i^2\bar{\theta}_H = 0$$

with the subsidiary condition $\bar{\theta}_H(\xi_i,0) = \bar{f}_H(\xi_i)$ so that

$$\bar{\theta}_H(\xi_i,t) = \bar{f}_H(\xi_i)e^{-\kappa\xi_i^2 t}$$

so that by the inversion theorem 32 we find immediately that

$$\theta = 2\sum_i \xi_i^2 \frac{J_0^2(\xi_i b)\bar{f}_H(\xi_i)e^{-\kappa\xi_i^2 t}}{J_0^2(a\xi_i) - J_0^2(b\xi_i)}$$
$$\times [J_0(r\xi_i)G_0(a\xi_i) - J_0(a\xi_i)G_0(r\xi_i)]$$

where $\bar{f}_H$ is defined to be

$$\bar{f}_H(\xi_i) = \int_b^a rf(r)[J_0(r\xi_i)G_0(a\xi_i)$$
$$- J_0(a\xi_i)G_0(r\xi_i)]dr$$

and the summation extends over all the positive roots of the transcendental equation (61).

23.6 Conduction of heat in a semiinfinite cylinder. To illustrate how we make use simultaneously of two different kinds of integral transform in the solution of a diffusion problem, we shall consider now the distribution of temperature in the semiinfinite cylinder bounded by the plane $z = 0$ and the cylindrical surfaces $r = a$, $r = b$ when the surfaces

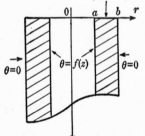

FIG. 27. Boundary and initial conditions for the conduction of heat in a semiinfinite hollow cylinder.

$z = 0$ and $r = a$ are maintained at zero temperature and the surface $r = b$ has a prescribed temperature distribution $f(z)$ (cf. Fig. 27).

It follows from equation (47) that the temperature θ must satisfy the partial differential equation

$$\frac{\partial^2\theta}{\partial r^2} + \frac{1}{r}\frac{\partial\theta}{\partial r} + \frac{\partial^2\theta}{\partial z^2} = \frac{1}{\kappa}\frac{\partial\theta}{\partial t} \tag{62}$$

with $b > r > a$, $z > 0$, $t > 0$, subject to the boundary and initial conditions

$$\theta = 0 \qquad a < r < b, t > 0, z = 0 \qquad (63)$$
$$\theta = 0 \qquad z > 0, t > 0, r = a \qquad (64)$$
$$\theta = f(z) \qquad z > 0, t > 0, r = b \qquad (65)$$
$$\theta = 0 \qquad a < r < b, z > 0, t = 0 \qquad (66)$$

the last equation arising from the additional assumption that initially the whole of the cylinder is at zero temperature. To solve equation (62), we write

$$\bar{\theta}_s(r,\xi,t) = \sqrt{\frac{2}{\pi}} \int_0^\infty \theta(r,z,t) \sin (\xi z)dz \qquad (67)$$

Then, since $\theta = 0$ when $z = 0$, we find

$$\sqrt{\frac{2}{\pi}} \int_0^\infty \frac{\partial^2\theta}{\partial z^2} \sin (\xi z)dz = -\xi^2\bar{\theta}_s \qquad (68)$$

so that, multiplying equation (62) by $(2/\pi)^{\frac{1}{2}} \sin (\xi z)$ and integrating over z, we obtain the partial differential equation

$$\frac{\partial^2\bar{\theta}_s}{\partial r^2} + \frac{1}{r}\frac{\partial\bar{\theta}_s}{\partial r} - \xi^2\bar{\theta}_s = \frac{1}{\kappa}\frac{\partial\bar{\theta}_s}{\partial t} \quad a < r < b; t > 0 \qquad (69)$$

for the function $\bar{\theta}_s(r,\xi,t)$. This function will also have to fulfill the conditions

$$\bar{\theta}_s = 0 \qquad\qquad r = a, t > 0 \qquad (70)$$
$$\bar{\theta}_s = \bar{f}_s(\xi) = \sqrt{\frac{2}{\pi}} \int_0^\infty f(z) \sin (\xi z)dz \quad r = b, t > 0 \qquad (71)$$
$$\bar{\theta}_s = 0 \qquad\qquad t = 0, a < r < b \qquad (72)$$

Equation (69) may be transformed to an ordinary differential equation by means of the finite Hankel transform employed in the last section. This we shall leave as an exercise to the reader and shall effect the reduction here by means of a Laplace transform. Writing

$$\Theta = \int_0^\infty e^{-pt}\bar{\theta}_s \, dt \qquad (73)$$

and making use of equation (72), we find that

$$\int_0^\infty \frac{\partial\bar{\theta}_s}{\partial t} e^{-pt} \, dt = p\Theta$$

Multiplying both sides of equation (69) by e^{-pt} and integrating with respect to t from 0 to ∞, we find that the function $\Theta(r,\xi,p)$ satisfies the ordinary differential equation

$$\frac{d^2\Theta}{dr^2} + \frac{1}{r}\frac{d\Theta}{dr} - \left(\xi^2 + \frac{p}{\kappa}\right)\Theta = 0 \qquad (74)$$

and, from equations (70) and (71), the boundary conditions

$$\Theta(a,\xi,p) = 0, \qquad \Theta(b,\xi,p) = p^{-1}\bar{f}_s(\xi) \tag{75}$$

If we define, in the usual notation for Bessel functions,

$$F(a,b,r,\mu) = \frac{I_0(\mu r)K_0(\mu a) - I_0(\mu a)K_0(\mu r)}{I_0(\mu b)K_0(\mu a) - I_0(\mu a)K_0(\mu b)} \tag{76}$$

then we may write the solution of (74) satisfying the conditions (75) in the form

$$\Theta(r,\xi,p) = p^{-1}\bar{f}_s(\xi)F\left[a,b,r,\left(\xi^2 + \frac{p}{\kappa}\right)^{\frac{1}{2}}\right] \tag{77}$$

To obtain θ_s from Θ, we make use of Theorem 14 to get

$$\bar{\theta}_s = \frac{\bar{f}_s}{2\pi i}\int_{\gamma-i\infty}^{\gamma+i\infty} F\left[a,b,r,\left(\xi^2 + \frac{p}{\kappa}\right)^{\frac{1}{2}}\right]e^{pt}\,dp \tag{78}$$

To evaluate this line integral, we transform it into a closed contour integral and make use of the methods of the calculus of residues. The integrand has poles at the point $p = 0$ and at the points $p = -\kappa(\xi^2 + \alpha_s^2)$ where $\pm\alpha_s$ are the roots of the transcendental equation (61) above.

The residue at $p = 0$ gives simply $\bar{f}_s F(a,b,r,\xi)$. To find the residue at the point $p = -\kappa(\xi^2 + \alpha_s^2)$, we require the result

$$\left\{ p\frac{d}{dp}\left[I_0(\mu b)K_0(\mu a) - I_0(\mu a)K_0(\mu b)\right]\right\}_{p=-\kappa(\xi^2+\alpha_s^2)}$$

$$= \left\{\frac{pb}{2\kappa\mu}\left[I_0'(\mu b)K_0(\mu a) - I_0(\mu a)K_0'(\mu b)\right]\right.$$

$$\left. + \frac{pa}{2\kappa\mu}\left[I_0(\mu b)K_0'(\mu a) - I_0'(\mu a)K_0(\mu b)\right]\right\}_{p=-\kappa(\xi^2+\alpha_s^2)} \tag{79}$$

where, for simplicity, we have written $\mu^2 = \xi^2 + p/\kappa$. Now when $p = -\kappa(\xi^2 + \alpha_s^2)$,

$$\frac{I_0(\mu b)}{I_0(\mu a)} = \frac{K_0(\mu b)}{K_0(\mu a)} = \frac{J_0(\alpha_s b)}{J_0(\alpha_s a)}$$

By the help of this result we may reduce the expression (79) to the neater form

$$\frac{\alpha_s^2 + \xi^2}{2\alpha_s^2}\frac{J_0^2(a\alpha_s) - J_0^2(b\alpha_s)}{J_0(a\alpha_s)J_0(b\alpha_s)}$$

Furthermore

$$[I_0(\mu r)K_0(\mu a) - I_0(\mu a)K_0(\mu r)]_{p=-\kappa(\xi^2+\alpha_s^2)}$$
$$= -\tfrac{1}{2}\pi[J_0(\alpha_s r)G_0(\alpha_s a) - J_0(\alpha_s a)G_0(\alpha_s r)]$$

so that we obtain for θ_s the expression

$$\bar{\theta}_s = \bar{f}_s \left\{ F(a,b,r,\xi) - \pi \sum_{s=1}^{\infty} e^{-\kappa(\xi^2+\alpha_s^2)t} \frac{\alpha_s^2 J_0(a\alpha_s)J_0(b\alpha_s)}{(\xi^2 + \alpha_s^2)[J_0^2(a\alpha_s) - J_0^2(b\alpha_s)]} \right.$$
$$\left. \times [J_0(\alpha_s r)G_0(\alpha_s a) - J_0(\alpha_s a)G_0(\alpha_s)] \right\}$$

Substituting this expression in Theorem 9, we find that, with the definition (71) of $\bar{f}_s$,

$$\theta(r,z,t) = \frac{2}{\pi} \int_0^{\infty} \int_0^{\infty} F(a,b,r,\xi)f(\eta) \sin(\xi z) \sin(\eta \xi)d\eta \, d\xi$$

$$- 2 \sum_s e^{-\kappa\alpha_s^2 t} \frac{\alpha_s^2 J_0(a\alpha_s)J_0(b\alpha_s)}{J_0^2(a\alpha_s) - J_0^2(b\alpha_s)} [J_0(\alpha_s r)G_0(\alpha_s a) - J_0(\alpha_s a)G_0(\alpha_s r)]$$

$$\times \int_0^{\infty} \int_0^{\infty} e^{-\kappa\xi^2 t}f(\eta) \sin(\xi z) \sin(\xi \eta) \frac{d\xi \, d\eta}{\xi^2 + \alpha_s^2} \quad (80)$$

where the sum is taken over all the positive roots of equation (61). The solution (80) was first derived in this way by Tranter[1]; the corresponding solution for the steady state ($t = \infty$) was obtained a little earlier by Lowan[2] by the classical method of separating the variables in the differential equation and representing $f(z)$ as a Fourier double integral.

A similar problem which can be tackled in precisely the same way is that of determining the distribution of temperature in a semiinfinite circular cylinder of radius a whose faces $z = 0$ and $r = a$ are kept at zero temperature and the flow of heat results from the initial distribution of temperature throughout the cylinder (cf. Fig. 28). We shall not employ the method of the last section, however, but shall make use of the simplest type of finite Hankel transform. The temperature $\theta(r,z,t)$ is again a solution of equation (62), but now the boundary and initial conditions are

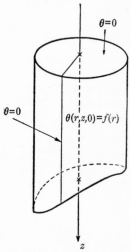

FIG. 28. Boundary and initial conditions for the conduction of heat in a semiinfinite solid cylinder.

$$\theta = 0, \quad z = 0 \quad 0 \le r \le a, t > 0 \quad (81)$$
$$\theta = 0, \quad r = a \quad z > 0, t > 0 \quad (82)$$
$$\theta(r,z,0) = f(r,z) \quad (83)$$

[1] C. J. Tranter, *Phil. Mag.*, **35**, 102 (1944).
[2] A. N. Lowan, *Phil. Mag.*, **34**, 502 (1943).

If we again employ the Fourier sine transform $\bar{\theta}_s(r,\xi,t)$ defined by equation (67), then making use of equation (81) we see that

$$\frac{\partial^2 \theta_s}{\partial r^2} + \frac{1}{r}\frac{\partial \bar{\theta}_s}{\partial r} - \xi^2 \bar{\theta}_s = \frac{1}{\kappa}\frac{\partial \theta_s}{\partial t} \qquad 0 \leq r \leq a \quad (84)$$

Now let

$$\Theta(\eta_i,\xi,t) = \int_0^a r\bar{\theta}_s(r,\xi,t)J_0(\eta_i r)dr \qquad (85)$$

where η_i is a root of the transcendental equation

$$J_0(\eta_i a) = 0 \qquad (86)$$

Making use of equation (82) and equation (62), Chap. 3, we find that $\Theta(\eta_i,\xi,t)$ satisfies the first-order equation

$$\frac{1}{\kappa}\frac{d\Theta}{dt} + (\xi^2 + \eta_i^2)\Theta = 0 \qquad t > 0 \quad (87)$$

When $t = 0$, the value of Θ is

$$F(\eta_i,\xi) = \sqrt{\frac{2}{\pi}}\int_0^\infty \sin(\xi z)dz \int_0^a rf(r,z)J_0(\eta_i r)dr \qquad (88)$$

so that the solution of equation (87) appropriate to our problem is

$$\Theta(\eta_i,\xi,t) = F(\eta_i,\xi)e^{-\kappa(\xi^2+\eta_i^2)t}$$

Inverting by means of equations (67) and (85) and Theorems 9 and 30 applied in succession, we obtain the solution of our boundary value problem in the form

$$\theta = \frac{2}{a^2}\sqrt{\frac{2}{\pi}}\sum_i \frac{J_0(\eta_i r)}{[J_1(\eta_i a)]^2}\int_0^\infty \Theta(\eta_i,\xi,t)\sin(\xi z)d\xi$$

so that

$$\theta = \frac{2}{a^2}\sqrt{\frac{2}{\pi}}\sum_i \frac{J_0(\eta_i r)}{J_1^2(\eta_i a)}e^{-\kappa\eta_i^2 t}\int_0^\infty F(\eta_i,\xi)e^{-\kappa\xi^2 t}\sin(\xi z)d\xi \qquad (89)$$

where the sum is taken over all the positive roots of the transcendental equation (86).

For instance, if

$$f(r,z) = f(r)g(z) \qquad (90)$$

then, by definition,

$$F(\eta_i,\xi) = \sqrt{\frac{2}{\pi}}\int_0^\infty g(u)\sin(\xi u)du \int_0^a vf(v)J_0(\eta_i v)dv$$

which we may write as

$$F(\eta_i,\xi) = \sqrt{\frac{2}{\pi}}\bar{f}_J(\eta_i)\int_0^\infty g(u)\sin(\xi u)du$$

Now, from equation (36), we have immediately that

$$\sqrt{\frac{2}{\pi}} \int_0^\infty F(\eta_i, \xi) e^{-\kappa t \xi^2} \sin(\xi z) d\xi$$

$$= \frac{\bar{f}_J(\eta_i)}{\sqrt{\pi \kappa t}} e^{-z^2/4\kappa t} \int_0^\infty g(u) \sinh\left(\frac{uz}{2\kappa t}\right) e^{-u^2/4\kappa t} du$$

so that, from equation (89), we obtain the solution

$$\theta = \frac{2e^{-z^2/4\kappa t}}{a^2 \sqrt{\pi \kappa t}} \sum_i \frac{J_0(\eta_i r) \bar{f}_J(\eta_i)}{J_1^2(\eta_i a)} e^{-\kappa \eta_i^2 t} \times \int_0^\infty g(u) \sinh\left(\frac{uz}{2\kappa t}\right) e^{-u^2/4\kappa t} du \qquad (91)$$

In particular, if $f(r,z)$ is a function of z alone, say

$$f(r,z) = g(z) \qquad (92)$$

then we may take $f(r) = 1$ in equation (90) and substitute

$$\bar{f}_J(\eta_i) = \frac{a}{\eta_i} J_1(a\eta_i)$$

in equation (91) to obtain

$$\theta = \frac{2e^{-z^2/4\kappa t}}{\sqrt{\pi \kappa t}} \sum_i \frac{J_0(\eta_i r) e^{-\kappa t \eta_i^2}}{a\eta_i J_1(a\eta_i)} \int_0^\infty g(u) \sinh\left(\frac{uz}{2\kappa t}\right) e^{-u^2/4\kappa t} du \qquad (93)$$

where the sum is taken over all the positive roots of equation (86).

24. Two- and Three-dimensional Boundary Value Problems

Throughout the whole of Sec. 23, with the exception of the last section (Sec. 23.6) the temperature θ in the interior of a solid body has been determined in terms of the time t and *one* spacelike variable (either x or r). The same methods of solution are available for more complicated boundary value problems involving two or more spacelike coordinates. In this section we shall illustrate how the procedures of the last section may be generalized to deal with these more complex situations by considering a few typical examples.

24.1 Flow of heat in a rectangle. We shall begin by considering the flow of heat in the rectangle $0 \leq x \leq a$, $0 \leq y \leq b$. If there are no sources of heat within the rectangle, equation (9) determining the flow of heat will assume the form

$$\kappa\left(\frac{\partial^2 \theta}{\partial x^2} + \frac{\partial^2 \theta}{\partial y^2}\right) = \frac{\partial \theta}{\partial t} \qquad (94)$$

The fundamental problem is the solution of this equation under certain boundary or initial conditions.   We shall now consider certain simple types of boundary value problem; the extension to more complicated cases is immediate and will not be undertaken here.

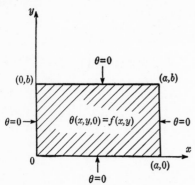

    Case 1: *Boundary at zero temperature and initial distribution of temperature prescribed.*   In the first instance we shall assume that the edges of the rectangle are kept at zero temperature and that the initial distribution of temperature

$$\theta(x,y,0) = f(x,y) \qquad (95)$$

Fig. 29.   Rectangle with its boundary at zero temperature and the initial distribution of temperature prescribed.

is known (cf. Fig. 29).   Our problem is then that of solving equation (94) subject to the initial condition (95) and the boundary conditions

$$\theta(0,y,t) = \theta(a,y,t) = \theta(x,0,t) = \theta(x,b,t) = 0 \qquad (96)$$

To solve this boundary value problem we introduce the double finite Fourier sine transforms

$$\Theta(m,n) = \int_0^a \int_0^b \theta(x,y) \sin\left(\frac{m\pi x}{a}\right) \sin\left(\frac{n\pi y}{b}\right) dx\,dy \qquad (97)$$

$$F(m,n) = \int_0^a \int_0^b f(x,y) \sin\left(\frac{m\pi x}{a}\right) \sin\left(\frac{n\pi y}{b}\right) dx\,dy \qquad (98)$$

Multiplying both sides of equation (94) by $\sin(m\pi x/a) \sin(n\pi y/b)$ and integrating with respect to x and y over the entire rectangle, we find that the transform Θ satisfies the first-order ordinary differential equation

$$\frac{d\Theta}{dt} + \kappa\pi^2\left(\frac{m^2}{a^2} + \frac{n^2}{b^2}\right)\Theta = 0 \qquad (99)$$

subject to the initial condition that $\Theta = F(m,n)$ when $t = 0$.   It follows at once that

$$\Theta(m,n,t) = F(m,n) \exp\left[-\kappa t\pi^2\left(\frac{m^2}{a^2} + \frac{n^2}{b^2}\right)\right]$$

and hence, by Theorem 29, that

$$(x,y,t) = \frac{4}{ab}\sum_{m=1}^{\infty}\sum_{n=1}^{\infty} F(m,n) \exp\left[-\kappa t\pi^2\left(\frac{m^2}{a^2} + \frac{n^2}{b^2}\right)\right]\sin\left(\frac{m\pi x}{a}\right)$$
$$\times \sin\left(\frac{n\pi y}{b}\right) \qquad (100)$$

Case 2: *Initial temperature zero throughout the solid and the temperature of the boundary prescribed.*   Next we consider the problem in which the surface temperature is prescribed.   For simplicity we shall assume that the edges $x = 0,a$ and $y = b$ are kept at zero temperature while the temperature along the edge $y = 0$ is made to vary according to the rule

$$\theta(x,0,t) = f(x)   \qquad 0 \leq x \leq a, \, t > 0$$
$$(101)$$

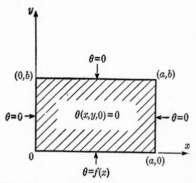

Fig. 30.   Rectangle with its boundary temperature prescribed and zero initial temperature.

(cf. Fig. 30).   If we assume further that the initial temperature in the solid is zero, then we have to solve equation (94) subject to equation (101) and the conditions

$$\theta(0,y,t) = \theta(a,y,t) = \theta(x,b,t) = \theta(x,y,0) = 0 \qquad (102)$$

Making use of the boundary conditions (101) and (102), we see that

$$\int_0^b \frac{\partial^2 \theta}{\partial y^2} \sin\left(\frac{n\pi y}{b}\right) dy = \frac{n\pi}{b} f(x) - \frac{n^2\pi^2}{b^2} \int_0^b \theta(x,y,t) \sin\left(\frac{n\pi y}{b}\right) dy$$

which gives immediately

$$\int_0^a dx \int_0^b \frac{\partial^2 \theta}{\partial y^2} \sin\left(\frac{m\pi x}{a}\right) \sin\left(\frac{n\pi y}{b}\right) dy = \frac{n\pi}{b} F_s(m) - \frac{n^2\pi^2}{b^2} \Theta(m,n)$$

where $\Theta(m,n,t)$ is defined by equation (97) and we have written

$$F_s(m) = \int_0^a f(u) \sin\left(\frac{m\pi u}{a}\right) du \qquad (103)$$

Hence, multiplying both sides of equation (94) by $\sin(m\pi x/a) \sin(n\pi y/b)$ and integrating over the rectangle, we see that Θ is that solution of the equation

$$\frac{d\Theta}{dt} + \kappa\mu_{mn}\Theta = \frac{\kappa n\pi}{b} F_s(m)$$

with

$$\mu_{mn} = \pi^2\left(\frac{m^2}{a^2} + \frac{n^2}{b^2}\right) \qquad (104)$$

which vanishes when $t = 0$.   In other words, if we suppose that $f(x)$ is independent of t, we have

$$\Theta(m,n,t) = \frac{n\pi}{b\mu_{mn}} F_s(m)(1 - e^{-\kappa\mu_{mn}t})$$

so that, by the inversion theorem 29,

$$\theta(x,y,t) = \frac{4\pi}{ab^2} \sum_{m=1}^{\infty} \sum_{n=1}^{\infty} \frac{n}{\mu_{mn}} F_s(m)(1 - e^{-\kappa\mu_{mn}t}) \sin\left(\frac{m\pi x}{a}\right) \sin\left(\frac{n\pi y}{b}\right) \quad (105)$$

To obtain the distribution of temperature in the steady state, we let $t \to \infty$ in equation (105) and find

$$\theta_\infty(x,y) = \frac{4}{\pi ab^2} \sum_{m=1}^{\infty} \sum_{n=1}^{\infty} \frac{nF_s(m)}{(m^2/a^2 + n^2/b^2)} \sin\left(\frac{m\pi x}{a}\right) \sin\left(\frac{n\pi y}{b}\right) \quad (106)$$

If we write

$$I_1 = \int_0^b \sinh\left[\frac{m\pi(b - y)}{a}\right] \sin\left(\frac{n\pi y}{b}\right) dy,$$

$$I_2 = \int_0^b \cosh\left[\frac{m\pi(b - y)}{a}\right] \cos\left(\frac{n\pi y}{b}\right) dy$$

then integrating by parts we obtain the relations

$$I_1 = \frac{b}{n\pi} \sinh\left(\frac{m\pi b}{a}\right) - \frac{bm}{an} I_2, \qquad I_2 = \frac{bm}{an} I_1$$

Eliminating I_2 between these two relations, we find that

$$I_1 = \frac{n}{\pi b(m^2/a^2 + n^2/b^2)} \sinh\left(\frac{m\pi b}{a}\right)$$

Making use of the finite Fourier sine inversion theorem 27, we may write this result in the form

$$\frac{2\pi}{b^2} \sum_{n=1}^{\infty} \frac{n \sin(n\pi y/b)}{(m^2/a^2) + (n^2/b^2)} = \frac{\sinh[m\pi(b - y)/a]}{\sinh(m\pi b/a)} \quad (107)$$

Substituting from equation (107) into equation (106), we obtain for the steady-state solution

$$\theta_\infty = \frac{2}{a} \sum_{m=1}^{\infty} \frac{\sinh[m\pi(b - y)/a]}{\sinh(m\pi b/a)} \sin\left(\frac{m\pi x}{a}\right) \int_0^a f(u) \sin\left(\frac{m\pi u}{a}\right) du \quad (108)$$

If, however, we are interested only in the steady solution, it is simpler to put the steady-state condition $\partial/\partial t = 0$ into the differential equation (94) at the beginning of the analysis. We then have to solve the harmonic equation

$$\frac{\partial^2 \theta}{\partial x^2} + \frac{\partial^2 \theta}{\partial y^2} = 0 \tag{109}$$

subject to the conditions (101) and (102)—with, of course, all reference to t omitted.

To solve equation (109), we introduce the finite Fourier sine transform

$$\bar{\theta}_s(m,y) = \int_0^a \theta(x,y) \sin\left(\frac{m\pi x}{a}\right) dx \tag{110}$$

Proceeding as before, we find that

$$\left(\frac{d^2}{dy^2} - \frac{m^2\pi^2}{a^2}\right) \bar{\theta}_s(m,y) = 0 \tag{111}$$

with $\bar{\theta}_s(m,b) = 0$, $\bar{\theta}_s(m,0) = F_s(m)$, the function $F_s(m)$ being defined by equation (103). The solution of equation (111) which satisfies these conditions is

$$\bar{\theta}_s(m,y) = F_s(m) \frac{\sinh [m\pi(b - y)/a]}{\sinh (m\pi b/a)}$$

so that by applying Theorem 27, and recalling the definition (103), we obtain the solution (108).

Case 3: Flow of heat when two edges of the rectangle are of infinite length. Roughly the same procedure is applicable to the case in which two parallel edges of the rectangle are infinitely long but instead of a double finite transform to solve equation (94) we employ the "mixed" transform

$$\Theta(\xi,n) = \int_0^\infty \sin (\xi x) dx$$
$$\times \int_0^b \theta(x,y) \sin\left(\frac{n\pi y}{b}\right) dy \tag{112}$$

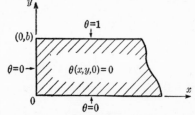

Fig. 31. Semiinfinite rectangle with constant boundary temperature and zero initial temperature.

Suppose, for example, that we wish to consider the flow of heat in the infinite strip $0 \leq y \leq b$, $x \geq 0$, when the initial temperature is zero and the surface temperature is given by the equations (cf. Fig. 31)

$$\theta = 0 \quad \text{when } x = 0 \text{ or when } y = 0 \tag{113}$$
$$\theta = 1 \quad \text{when } y = b \tag{114}$$

Integrating by parts and using the conditions (113) and (114), we see that

$$\int_0^b \frac{\partial^2 \theta}{\partial y^2} \sin\left(\frac{n\pi y}{b}\right) dy = (-1)^{n+1}\left(\frac{n\pi}{b}\right) - \frac{n^2\pi^2}{b^2} \int_0^b \theta \sin\frac{n\pi y}{b} \, dy$$

and since

$$\frac{2}{\pi} \int_0^\infty \frac{\sin(\xi x)d\xi}{\xi} = 1 \qquad x > 0$$

we may write formally[1]

$$\int_0^\infty \sin(\xi x)dx = \frac{1}{\xi} \tag{115}$$

so that

$$\int_0^\infty \int_0^b \frac{\partial^2 \theta}{\partial y^2} \sin(\xi x) \sin\left(\frac{n\pi y}{b}\right) dx \, dy = (-1)^{n+1}\frac{n\pi}{b\xi} - \frac{n^2\pi^2}{b^2}\theta$$

Multiplying both sides of equation (94) by $\sin(\xi x) \sin(n\pi y/b)$ and integrating over the whole strip, we see that the transform $\Theta(\xi,n)$ satisfies the equation

$$\frac{1}{\kappa}\frac{d\Theta}{dt} - \left(\xi^2 + \frac{n^2\pi^2}{b^2}\right)\Theta = \frac{n\pi}{b}(-1)^{n+1}\frac{1}{\xi}$$

Since the initial temperature is assumed to be zero the solution of this equation is readily seen to be

$$\Theta(\xi,n) = \frac{(-1)^{n+1}n\pi}{b\xi(\xi^2 + n^2\pi^2/b^2)}[1 - e^{-\kappa t(\xi^2 + n^2\pi^2/b^2)}] \tag{116}$$

By the successive applications of Theorems 9 and 27 we have

$$\theta(x,y,t) = \frac{4}{\pi b}\sum_{n=1}^\infty \sin\left(\frac{n\pi y}{b}\right)\int_0^\infty \Theta(\xi,n)\sin(\xi x)d\xi \tag{117}$$

From the integral

$$\int_0^\infty \frac{\sin(\xi x)d\xi}{\xi(\xi^2 + n^2\pi^2/b^2)} = \frac{b^2}{2\pi n^2}(1 - e^{-n\pi x/b})$$

it follows, on substituting from (116) into (117), that

$$\theta(x,y,t) = \frac{2}{\pi}\sum_{n=1}^\infty \frac{(-1)^{n+1}}{n}\sin\left(\frac{n\pi y}{b}\right) + \frac{2}{\pi}\sum_{n=1}^\infty e^{-n\pi x/b}\frac{(-1)^n}{n}\sin\left(\frac{n\pi y}{b}\right)$$

$$+ \frac{4}{b^2}\sum_{n=1}^\infty n(-1)^n \sin\left(\frac{n\pi y}{b}\right)\int_0^\infty \frac{e^{-\kappa t(\xi^2 + n^2\pi^2/b^2)}\sin(\xi x)}{\xi(\xi^2 + n^2\pi^2/b^2)}\, d\xi \tag{118}$$

---

[1] To be rigorous we should consider $\theta(x,b) = e^{-\epsilon x}$ and then let $\epsilon \to 0$ in the end. It is found that this gives the same result as the analysis based on the assumption (115).

By a direct application of Duhamel's theorem (Theorem 32) we can easily deduce from equation (118) the solution of the boundary value problem illustrated in Fig. 32.   The solution (118) may readily be established by the use of a double Laplace transform; for details of this method the reader is referred to the paper by J. C. Jaeger.[1]

24.2 Flow of heat in a rectangular parallelepiped.   The methods developed above for the solution of two-dimensional problems may be extended to three dimensions to cover cases in which heat diffuses through a rectangular parallelepiped. We shall consider only two very simple problems.

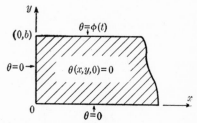

In the first we consider the flow of heat in the solid $0 \leq x \leq a, 0 \leq y \leq b, 0 \leq z \leq c$, arising from the initial distribution of temperature $\theta(x,y,z,0) = f(x,y,z)$, the faces of the parallelepiped being kept at zero temperature throughout the time.   Just

FIG.   32.   Semiinfinite   strip   with boundary temperature which varies with time in a prescribed fashion and zero initial temperature.

as in the two-dimensional case (Sec. 24.1, case 1), we see that, if we introduce the triple finite Fourier sine transforms

$$\Theta(m,n,q) = \int_0^a \int_0^b \int_0^c \theta(x,y,z,t) \sin\left(\frac{m\pi x}{a}\right) \sin\left(\frac{n\pi y}{b}\right) \sin\left(\frac{q\pi z}{c}\right) dx \, dy \, dz$$

$$(119)$$

$$F(m,n,q) = \int_0^a \int_0^b \int_0^c f(x,y,z) \sin\left(\frac{m\pi x}{a}\right) \sin\left(\frac{n\pi y}{b}\right) \sin\left(\frac{q\pi z}{c}\right) dx \, dy \, dz$$

$$(120)$$

then

$$\Theta(m,n,q,t) = F(m,n,q)e^{-\mu t}$$

where

$$\mu^2 = \pi^2 \kappa \left(\frac{m^2}{a^2} + \frac{n^2}{b^2} + \frac{q^2}{c^2}\right)$$

It follows then by applying the inversion theorem 29 in the form

$$\theta = \frac{8}{abc} \sum_{m=1}^{\infty} \sum_{n=1}^{\infty} \sum_{q=1}^{\infty} \Theta \sin\left(\frac{m\pi x}{a}\right) \sin\left(\frac{n\pi y}{b}\right) \sin\left(\frac{q\pi z}{c}\right)$$

that

$$\theta = \frac{8}{abc} \sum_m \sum_n \sum_q F(m,n,q)e^{-\mu t} \sin\left(\frac{m\pi x}{a}\right) \sin\left(\frac{n\pi y}{b}\right) \sin\left(\frac{q\pi z}{c}\right)$$

[1] *Op. cit.*, p. 690.

As a second illustration we consider the *steady* flow of heat in the same parallelepiped when the surface $x = a$ is kept at a constant temperature θ_0, the other faces being maintained at zero temperature. In this case equation (9) reduces to Laplace's equation

$$\frac{\partial^2\theta}{\partial x^2} + \frac{\partial^2\theta}{\partial y^2} + \frac{\partial^2\theta}{\partial z^2} = 0 \tag{121}$$

and we have to find the boundary conditions

$$\theta = 0 \quad \text{on the faces } y = 0,b \text{ or } z = 0,c \tag{122}$$
$$\theta = 0 \quad \text{on } x = 0, \qquad \theta = \theta_0 \text{ on } x = a \tag{123}$$

If we define double finite transforms of θ and θ_0 by the equations

$$\Theta = \int_0^b dy \int_0^c \theta(x,y,z) \sin\left(\frac{m\pi y}{b}\right) \sin\left(\frac{n\pi z}{c}\right) dz$$
$$\Theta_0 = \theta_0 \int_0^b dy \int_0^c \sin\left(\frac{m\pi y}{b}\right) \sin\left(\frac{n\pi z}{c}\right) dz$$

then, making use of the conditions (122), we can show in the usual way that equation (121) is equivalent to

$$\frac{d^2\Theta}{dx^2} = \mu^2\Theta$$

where $\mu^2 = \pi^2(m^2/b^2 + n^2/c^2)$. Similarly from equations (123) we have that $\Theta(0,m,n) = 0$ and $\Theta(a,m,n) = \theta_0$. Hence

$$\Theta = \Theta_0 \frac{\sinh(\mu x)}{\sinh(\mu a)} \tag{124}$$

Therefore, by the inversion theorem 29 for the case of double transforms, we have, from equation (124),

$$\theta(x,y,z) = \frac{4}{bc} \sum_{m=1}^{\infty} \sum_{n=1}^{\infty} \Theta_0 \frac{\sinh(\mu x)}{\sinh(\mu a)} \sin\left(\frac{m\pi y}{b}\right) \sin\left(\frac{n\pi z}{c}\right)$$

By direct integration we see that

$$\Theta_0(m,n) = \begin{cases} \dfrac{4bc\theta_0}{\pi^2 mn} & \text{if } m \text{ and } n \text{ are both } odd \\ 0 & \text{otherwise} \end{cases}$$

so that finally we obtain for the steady temperature at any point in the interior of the parallelepiped

$$\theta = \frac{16\theta_0}{\pi^2} \sum_{r=1}^{\infty} \sum_{s=1}^{\infty} \frac{1}{(2r+1)(2s+1)} \frac{\sinh (\mu x)}{\sinh (\mu a)} \sin \frac{(2r+1)\pi y}{b} \sin \frac{(2s+1)\pi z}{c}$$

(125)

with $\mu^2 = \pi^2[(2r+1)^2/b^2 + (2s+1)^2/c^2]$.

24.3 Flow of heat in a cylinder of finite height.   We shall conclude our
discussion of the conduction of heat
in media free from sources by considering the flow of heat through a cylinder of finite height.   We shall suppose for definiteness that the cylinder
has the equation

$$f(x,y) = 0 \qquad (126)$$

and that this surface is cut by the
plane $z = 0$ in the curve C (cf. Fig.
33).   The cylinder will be supposed
to be bounded by the surface whose
equation is (126) and by the parallel
planes $z = 0$, $z = h$ which cut its generators at right angles.   We shall consider steady flow only, so that the
temperature θ will satisfy equation
(121).   Further we shall take the

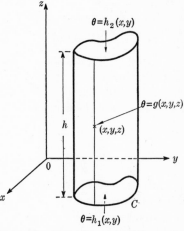

FIG. 33.   Boundary conditions for
the flow of heat in a cylinder of finite
height.

temperature as prescribed on the surfaces of the cylinder, that is,

$$g(x,y,z) \text{ on the curved surface} \qquad (127)$$

and

$$\theta = h_1(x,y) \text{ on } z = 0 \qquad \text{and} \qquad \theta = h_2(x,y) \text{ on } z = h \qquad (128)$$

To reduce this boundary value problem to one in two dimensions, we
introduce the finite Fourier sine transform

$$\bar{\theta}_s(x,y,n) = \int_0^h \theta(x,y,z) \sin\left(\frac{n\pi z}{h}\right) dz \qquad (129)$$

Integrating by parts in the usual way and making use of the boundary
conditions (128), we find that

$$\int_0^h \frac{\partial^2 \theta}{\partial z^2} \sin\left(\frac{n\pi z}{h}\right) dz = H(n) - n^2\bar{\theta}_s(n)$$

where $H(n) = n[h_1(x,y) - (-1)^n h_2(x,y)]$.   Multiplying both sides of
equation (121) by $\sin (n\pi z/h)$ and integrating along the length of the

cylinder, we see that $\theta_s(n)$ satisfies the differential equation

$$\nabla_1^2 \bar{\theta}_s - n^2 \bar{\theta}_s + H(n) = 0 \tag{130}$$

where ∇_1^2 denotes the two-dimensional Laplacian operator $\partial^2/\partial x^2 + \partial^2/\partial y^2$.
If, furthermore, we write

$$\bar{g}_s(x,y,n) = \int_0^h g(x,y,z) \sin\left(\frac{n\pi z}{h}\right) dz$$

it follows, from equation (127), that

$$\bar{\theta}_s(x,y,n) = \bar{g}_s(x,y,n) \text{ on the curve } C \tag{131}$$

The use of the finite transform (129) thus reduces the problem to one in two dimensions characterized by the equations (130) and (131). Once the solution of this problem has been found, the temperature $\theta(x,y,z)$ is found from the inversion theorem 27 to be

$$\theta(x,y,z) = \frac{2}{h} \sum_{n=1}^{\infty} \bar{\theta}_s(x,y,n) \sin\left(\frac{n\pi z}{h}\right) \tag{132}$$

It was observed by Tranter[1] that, whereas the three-dimensional problem originally proposed was not capable of solution by the relaxation methods developed by Southwell and his coworkers,[2] the reduced two-dimensional problem can be solved by the usual relaxation technique. The essentials of the relaxation method are the replacement of the partial differential equation (130) and the boundary conditions (131) by their finite difference approximations and the approximate solution of these at the nodal points of a regular (two-dimensional) network covering the area enclosed by the curve C, in the xy plane. Once two-dimensional maps of $\bar{\theta}_s$ have been constructed for integral values of n, the value of the temperature is given by the inversion formula (132).

Tranter illustrates the use of this method by calculating the steady temperature at the center of a cube of side π when all the faces are kept at zero temperature with the exception of the face $x = \pi$, which is maintained at a fixed temperature θ_0. In this case we have $h = \pi$, the functions $h_1(x,y)$ and $h_2(x,y)$ identically zero, and

$$g(x,y,z) = \begin{cases} \theta_0 & \text{when } x = \pi \\ 0 & \text{otherwise} \end{cases}$$

so that, when $x = \pi$,

$$\bar{g}_s(n) = \begin{cases} \dfrac{2\theta_0}{n} & \text{if } n \text{ is odd} \\ 0 & \text{if } n \text{ is even} \end{cases}$$

[1] C. J. Tranter, *Quart. Jour. Mech. Applied Math.*, **1**, 281 (1948).

[2] See, for example, R. V. Southwell, "Relaxation Methods in Theoretical Physics" (Oxford, New York, 1946).

Thus we require relaxation solutions to the problem

$$\nabla_1^2 \bar{\theta}_s(2r+1) - (2r+1)^2 \bar{\theta}_s(2r+1) = 0$$

$(r = 0,1,2, \ldots)$ with $\bar{\theta}_s(2r+1)$ zero on the lines $x = 0$, $y = 0$, and $y = \pi$ and equal to $2\theta_0/(2r+1)$ on the line $x = \pi$. Relaxation maps for this problem are given in the paper by Tranter cited above. For the center of the cube they give

$$\frac{\theta}{\theta_0} = \frac{2}{\pi}\left[0.267\sin\left(\frac{1}{2}\pi\right) + 0.005\sin\left(\frac{3}{2}\pi\right)\right] = 0.167$$

while the exact value given by equation (125) for this case is

$$\theta/\theta_0 = 0.1668$$

Even in this case, where an analytical solution exists, this combined use of relaxation methods and finite Fourier transforms gives numerical values with little, if any, more labor than numerical calculations from the analytical solution. For cylinders of irregular cross section or cases in which the surface temperatures are specified numerically, or both, the method outlined here could be extended with very little difficulty. For that reason it should provide a valuable tool for the solution of the types of problems which arise in engineering practice.

25. Diffusion of Heat in a Solid Medium Which Is Generating Heat

In the previous sections of this chapter we have assumed that there are no sources of heat within the solid in which we are interested. The more complicated case of solving the diffusion equation (9) for cases in which heat is generated in the interior of the medium arises frequently in physics and engineering. It occurs, for instance, when we consider the conduction of heat in a solid undergoing radioactive decay[1] or absorbing radiation.[2] Complications of a similar nature arise when there is generation or absorption of heat in the solid as a result of a chemical reaction; the hydration of cement is an example of a process of this kind. The particular case in which the rate of generation of heat is independent of the temperature arises in the theory of the ripening of apples and has been discussed by Awberry.[3]

In many cases of practical interest the rate of generation of heat may be taken as a linear function of the temperature. Explicit solutions of a very general kind have been given by Paterson[4] for this case with the additional assumption that the solid has constant thermal conductivity.

[1] A. N. Lowan, *Phys. Rev.*, **44**, 769 (1933).
[2] G. H. Brown, *Proc. Inst. Radio Engrs.*, **31**, 537 (1943).
[3] J. H. Awberry, *Phil. Mag.*, **4**, 629 (1927).
[4] S. Paterson, *Phil. Mag.*, **32**, 384 (1941).

No proofs are given by Paterson, but he indicates that the results may be obtained by the method of sources, an account of which is given in most textbooks on the conduction of heat.[1] We shall begin by showing how these solutions may be derived by the use of the theory of Fourier transforms.[2]

Equation (9) governs the variation with time of the temperature θ in a homogeneous isotropic solid within which heat is generated or absorbed. We assume that Θ is a known function of position and time and depends on the temperature in the manner

$$\Theta(x,y,z,t,\theta) = \phi(x,y,z,t) + \theta\psi(t) \tag{133}$$

where $\phi(x,y,z,t)$ is a function of the coordinates and the time but $\psi(t)$ is a function of the time only. If we now substitute from equation (133) into equation (9) and make the transformations

$$u = \theta \exp\left[-\int_0^t \psi(\tau)d\tau\right], \qquad \chi = \phi \exp\left[-\int_0^t \psi(\tau)d\tau\right] \tag{134}$$

we find that equation (9) assumes the equivalent form

$$\frac{\partial u}{\partial t} = \kappa \nabla^2 u + \chi(x,y,z,t) \tag{135}$$

We suppose further that the initial distribution of temperature is known, i.e., that

$$\theta(x,y,z,0) = \theta_0(x,y,z) \tag{136}$$

The initial condition on the function u is therefore

$$u(x,y,z,0) = \theta_0(x,y,z) \tag{137}$$

where the form of $\theta_0(x,y,z)$ is known.

25.1 Diffusion in an infinite solid. To solve equation (135) for an infinite solid subject to the initial condition (137), we reduce it to an ordinary differential equation by the introduction of the Fourier transform of the function $u(x,y,z,t)$ defined by the equation

$$U(\xi,\eta,\zeta,t) = \left(\frac{1}{2\pi}\right)^{\frac{3}{2}} \int_{-\infty}^{\infty} \int_{-\infty}^{\infty} \int_{-\infty}^{\infty} u(x,y,z,t)e^{i(\xi x+\eta y+\zeta z)}\, dx\, dy\, dz \tag{138}$$

Multiplying both sides of equation (135) by $\exp[i(\xi x + \eta y + \zeta z)]$ and integrating with respect to x, y, and z over the entire range of the variables, we find that

$$\frac{dU}{dt} + \kappa(\xi^2 + \eta^2 + \zeta^2)U = X(\xi,\eta,\zeta,t) \tag{139}$$

---

[1] See, for instance, Carslaw and Jaeger, *op. cit.*, Chap. X.
[2] Cf. I. N. Sneddon, *Proc. Glasgow Math. Assoc.* (in press).

where it is assumed that at infinity u vanishes and that $X(\xi,\eta,\zeta,t)$ is the Fourier transform of the function $\chi(x,y,z,t)$.

From equation (137) it follows that, at $t = 0$,

$$U = U_0(\xi,\eta,\zeta) = \left(\frac{1}{2\pi}\right)^{\frac{3}{2}} \int_{-\infty}^{\infty} \int_{-\infty}^{\infty} \int_{-\infty}^{\infty} \theta_0(x,y,z) e^{i(\xi x + \eta y + \zeta z)} \, dx \, dy \, dz$$

so that the solution of equation (139) is

$$U = U_0(\xi,\eta,\zeta) e^{-\kappa t(\xi^2+\eta^2+\zeta^2)} + \int_0^t X(\xi,\eta,\zeta,\tau) e^{-\kappa(t-\tau)(\xi^2+\eta^2+\zeta^2)} \, d\tau$$

Inverting this result by means of the inversion formula (111), Chap. 1, for multiple transforms, we have

$$u(x,y,z,t) = \left(\frac{1}{2\pi}\right)^{\frac{3}{2}} \int_{-\infty}^{\infty} \int_{-\infty}^{\infty} \int_{-\infty}^{\infty} U_0 e^{-\kappa t(\xi^2+\eta^2+\zeta^2) - i(\xi x + \eta y + \zeta z)} \, d\xi \, d\eta \, d\zeta$$

$$+ \left(\frac{1}{2\pi}\right)^{\frac{3}{2}} \int_{-\infty}^{\infty} \int_{-\infty}^{\infty} \int_{-\infty}^{\infty} \int_0^t X(\xi,\eta,\zeta,\tau) e^{-i\kappa(t-\tau)(\xi^2+\eta^2+\zeta^2) - i(\xi x + \eta y + \zeta z)} \, d\xi \, d\eta \, d\zeta \, d\tau$$

$$(140)$$

Now the function

$$G(\xi,\eta,\zeta) = e^{-\kappa t(\xi^2+\eta^2+\zeta^2)}$$

is readily seen, by direct integration, to be the Fourier transform of the function

$$g(x,y,z) = \left(\frac{1}{2\kappa t}\right)^{\frac{3}{2}} e^{-(x^2+y^2+z^2)/4\kappa t}$$

so that substituting this result in the Faltung theorem (112), Chap. 1, in the form

$$\int_{-\infty}^{\infty} \int_{-\infty}^{\infty} \int_{-\infty}^{\infty} U_0(\xi,\eta,\zeta) G(\xi,\eta,\zeta) e^{-i(\xi x + \eta y + \zeta z)} \, d\xi \, d\eta \, d\zeta$$

$$= \int_{-\infty}^{\infty} \int_{-\infty}^{\infty} \int_{-\infty}^{\infty} \theta_0(\alpha,\beta,\gamma) g(x - \alpha, y - \beta, z - \gamma) \, d\alpha \, d\beta \, d\gamma \quad (141)$$

we find that the first integral on the right-hand side of equation (140) has the value

$$\left(\frac{1}{4\pi\kappa t}\right)^{\frac{3}{2}} \int_{-\infty}^{\infty} \int_{-\infty}^{\infty} \int_{-\infty}^{\infty} \theta_0(\alpha,\beta,\gamma) \exp\left[-\frac{\Sigma(x-\alpha)^2}{4\kappa t}\right] d\alpha \, d\beta \, d\gamma$$

The second integral can be evaluated in an exactly similar way. Performing this integration and reverting to the original variables defined by equations (134), we have finally

$$\theta(x,y,z,t) = \left(\frac{1}{4\pi\kappa t}\right)^{\frac{3}{2}} \exp\left[\int_0^t \psi(\tau)d\tau\right] \int_{-\infty}^{\infty} \int_{-\infty}^{\infty} \int_{-\infty}^{\infty} \theta_0(\alpha,\beta,\gamma)$$

$$\times \exp\left[-\frac{\Sigma(x-\alpha)^2}{4\kappa t}\right] d\alpha\, d\beta\, d\gamma + \left(\frac{1}{4\pi\kappa}\right)^{\frac{3}{2}} \exp\left[\int_0^t \psi(\tau)d\tau\right] \int_0^t \frac{e^{-\int_0^\tau \psi\, d\tau}}{(t-\tau)^{\frac{3}{2}}}$$

$$\times d\tau \int_{-\infty}^{\infty} \int_{-\infty}^{\infty} \int_{-\infty}^{\infty} \exp\left[-\frac{\Sigma(x-\alpha)^2}{4\kappa(t-\tau)}\right] \phi(\alpha,\beta,\gamma,\tau)d\alpha\, d\beta\, d\gamma \quad (142)$$

If we take the functions ϕ and ψ to be identically zero, we obtain the solution corresponding to the case in which there is no generation of heat in the medium. Substituting $\phi = \psi = 0$,

$$(u,v,w) = (4\kappa t)^{\frac{1}{2}}(\alpha - x, \beta - y, \gamma - z)$$

in equation (142), we get Fourier's well-known solution[1]

$$\theta(x,y,z,t) = \left(\frac{1}{\pi}\right)^{\frac{3}{2}} \int_{-\infty}^{\infty} \int_{-\infty}^{\infty} \int_{-\infty}^{\infty}$$

$$\times \theta_0(x + 2u\sqrt{\kappa t}, y + 2v\sqrt{\kappa t}, z + 2w\sqrt{\kappa t})e^{-(u^2+v^2+w^2)}\, du\, dv\, dw \quad (143)$$

which is the three-dimensional analogue of the formula (26a) derived above. The general formula (142) was stated first by Paterson.

In the two-dimensional case the governing equation is

$$\frac{\partial\theta}{\partial t} = \kappa\left(\frac{\partial^2\theta}{\partial x^2} + \frac{\partial^2\theta}{\partial y^2}\right) + \phi(x,y,t) + \theta\psi(t)$$

By the use of two-dimensional Fourier transforms we can show similarly that the solution of this equation subject to the initial condition $\theta = \theta_0(x,y)$ is

$$\theta = \frac{\exp\left[\int_0^t \psi\, d\tau\right]}{4\pi\kappa t} \int_{-\infty}^{\infty} \int_{-\infty}^{\infty} \theta_0(\alpha,\beta) \exp\left[\frac{-(\alpha-x)^2 - (\beta-y)^2}{4\kappa t}\right] d\alpha\, d\beta$$

$$+ \frac{\exp\left[\int_0^t \psi\, d\tau\right]}{4\pi\kappa} \int_0^t \frac{e^{-\int_0^\tau \psi d\tau}}{t-\tau}\, d\tau \int_{-\infty}^{\infty} \int_{-\infty}^{\infty} \phi(\alpha,\beta,\tau) \exp$$

$$\times \left[\frac{-(x-\alpha)^2 - (y-\beta)^2}{4\kappa(t-\tau)}\right] d\alpha\, d\beta \quad (144)$$

The solution for the case in which there is symmetry about the z axis, so that the functions θ, θ_0, and ϕ are all functions of $\rho = (x^2 + y^2)^{\frac{1}{2}}$ and t only, can be deduced readily from the last equation. If the initial value of θ is $\theta_0(\rho)$, we obtain the expression for the temperature at a subsequent time t by substituting the values $x = \rho$, $y = 0$, $\alpha = \omega \cos\varphi$, $\beta = \omega \sin\varphi$,

[1] J. Fourier, "La Théorie analytique de la chaleur" (Paris, 1882), p. 372.

$\theta_0(\alpha,\beta) = \theta_0(\rho)$, $\phi(\alpha,\beta,\tau) = \phi(\rho,\tau)$ into equation (144). Making use of the result [cf. equation (24), Appendix A]

$$\int_0^{2\pi} e^{z \cos \varphi}\, d\varphi = 2\pi J_0(iz) = 2\pi I_0(z)$$

we then have

$$\theta(\rho,t) = \frac{\exp\left[\int_0^t \psi(\tau)d\tau - \dfrac{\rho^2}{4\kappa t}\right]}{4\pi\kappa t} \int_0^\infty \omega\theta_0(\omega)e^{-\omega^2/4\kappa t} I_0\left(\frac{\omega\rho}{2\kappa t}\right) d\omega$$

$$+ \frac{\exp\int_0^t \psi(\tau)d\tau}{4\pi\kappa} \int_0^t \frac{\exp\left[-\dfrac{\rho^2}{4\kappa(t-\tau)} - \displaystyle\int_0^\tau \psi(\lambda)d\lambda\right]}{t-\tau} d\tau$$

$$\times \int_0^\infty \omega\phi(\omega,\tau)e^{-\omega^2/4\kappa(t-\tau)} I_0\left[\frac{\omega\rho}{2\kappa(t-\tau)}\right] d\omega \quad (145)$$

It is of interest to note that this result can also be established directly from the equation of axially symmetrical flow,

$$\frac{\partial u}{\partial t} = \kappa\left(\frac{\partial^2 u}{\partial \rho^2} + \frac{1}{\rho}\frac{\partial u}{\partial \rho}\right) + \chi(\rho,t) \quad (146)$$

by means of the Hankel transform of zero order. If we denote by $\bar{u}(\xi,t)$ the Hankel transform of order zero of the function $u(\rho,t)$ so that

$$\bar{u}(\xi,t) = \int_0^\infty \rho u(\rho,t)J_0(\xi\rho)d\rho \quad (147)$$

then as a result of a pair of integrations by parts we have

$$\int_0^\infty \rho\left(\frac{\partial^2 u}{\partial \rho^2} + \frac{1}{\rho}\frac{\partial u}{\partial \rho}\right) J_0(\rho\xi)d\rho = -\xi^2\bar{u}(\xi,t) \quad (148)$$

Multiplying equation (146) throughout by $\rho J_0(\rho\xi)$ and integrating with respect to ρ over the range $(0, \infty)$, we find that $\bar{u}(\rho,t)$ is determined by the solution of the first-order linear differential equation

$$\frac{d\bar{u}}{dt} + \kappa\xi^2\bar{u} = \bar{\chi}(\xi,t) \quad (149)$$

where $\bar{\chi}(\xi,t)$ denotes the Hankel transform of the function $\chi(\rho,t)$. The solution of equation (149) is similar to that of equation (139), namely,

$$\bar{u}(\xi,t) = \bar{\theta}_0(\xi)e^{-\kappa t\xi^2} + \int_0^t \bar{\chi}(\xi,\tau)e^{-\kappa\xi^2(t-\tau)}\, d\tau \quad (150)$$

The expression for $u(\rho,t)$ is now found from this equation by the Hankel inversion theorem

$$u(\rho,t) = \int_0^\infty \xi\bar{u}(\xi,t)J_0(\xi\rho)d\xi \quad (151)$$

In this way we obtain two terms for $u(\rho,t)$ the first of which may be written, after the order of integrations has been interchanged, in the form

$$\int_0^\infty \eta\theta_0(\eta)d\eta \int_0^\infty \xi J_0(\xi\rho)J_0(\xi\eta)e^{-\kappa t\xi^2}\,d\xi$$

The inner integral may be evaluated by Weber's formula [cf. the derivation of equation (114), Chap. 4], which states that

$$\int_0^\infty \xi J_0(\xi\rho)J_0(\xi\eta)e^{-\kappa t\xi^2}\,d\xi = \frac{1}{2\kappa t}\exp\left(-\frac{\rho^2+\eta^2}{4\kappa t}\right)I_0\left(\frac{\rho\eta}{2\kappa t}\right)$$

to give

$$\frac{1}{2\kappa t}e^{-\rho^2/4\kappa t}\int_0^\infty \eta\theta_0(\eta)e^{-\eta^2/4\kappa t}I_0\left(\frac{\rho\eta}{2\kappa t}\right)d\eta$$

for the value of the first term.   In a similar fashion we find

$$\int_0^t \frac{\exp\left[-\rho^2/4\kappa(t-\tau)\right]}{2\kappa(t-\tau)}\,d\tau \int_0^\infty \eta\chi(\eta,\tau)e^{-\eta^2/4\kappa(t-\tau)}I_0\left[\frac{\rho\eta}{2\kappa(t-\tau)}\right]d\eta$$

for the second term.   Substituting for the original variables from equations (134), we establish the formula (145).

25.2 Conduction in a semiinfinite solid.   We now consider the conduction of heat in a medium which is bounded by the plane $x = 0$ but which is otherwise of unlimited extent.   The medium, which is taken to be isotropic and homogeneous, will be supposed to occupy the half space $x \geq 0$.   Since the range of variation of the variable x is now restricted to $(0,\infty)$, it is no longer possible to employ the exponential form of the Fourier transform.

Case 1: *No surface loss.*   Since we assume that there is zero flux of heat across the boundary, the problem here is to solve the partial differential equation (9) with Θ given by equation (133), subject to the initial condition (136) and the boundary condition $\partial\theta/\partial x = 0$ at $x = 0$.   This is then reduced to the solution of equation (135) with $u = \theta_0(x,y,z)$ when $t = 0$ and $\partial u/\partial x = 0$ on the surface $x = 0$.

To solve this boundary value problem, we first let

$$U(x,\eta,\zeta,t) = \frac{1}{2\pi}\int_{-\infty}^\infty \int_{-\infty}^\infty u(x,y,z,t)e^{i(\eta y+\zeta z)}\,dy\,dz \tag{152}$$

The problem then reduces to the solution of the partial differential equation

$$\frac{\partial U}{\partial t} = \kappa\left(\frac{\partial^2}{\partial x^2} - \eta^2 - \zeta^2\right)U + X(x,\eta,\zeta,t) \tag{153}$$

subject to the conditions

$$U = \Theta_0(x,\eta,\zeta), \ t = 0; \qquad \frac{\partial U}{\partial x} = 0, \ x = 0 \qquad (154)$$

If we now introduce the Fourier cosine transform defined by the relation

$$\bar{U}(\xi,\eta,\zeta,t) = \int_0^\infty U(x,\eta,\zeta,t) \cos (\xi x) dx$$

we find that, because of the boundary conditions,

$$\int_0^\infty \frac{\partial^2 U}{\partial x^2} \cos (\xi x) dx = -\xi^2 \bar{U}$$

We then obtain as before

$$\bar{U} = \bar{U}_0 e^{-\kappa t(\xi^2 + \eta^2 + \zeta^2)} + \int_0^t \bar{X}(\xi,\eta,\zeta,\tau) e^{-\kappa(t-\tau)(\xi^2+\eta^2+\zeta^2)} \, d\tau$$

so that

$$U(x,\eta,\zeta,t) = \frac{2}{\pi} e^{-\kappa t(\eta^2+\zeta^2)} \int_0^\infty \Theta_0(\alpha,\eta,\zeta,t) d\alpha \int_0^\infty e^{-\kappa t \xi^2} \cos (\alpha\xi) \cos (\xi x) d\xi$$

$$+ \frac{2}{\pi} \int_0^t e^{-\kappa(t-\tau)(\eta^2+\zeta^2)} \, d\tau \int_0^\infty X(\alpha,\eta,\zeta,\tau) d\alpha \int_0^\infty e^{-\kappa(t-\tau)\xi^2} \cos (\alpha\xi) \cos (\xi x) d\xi$$
$$(155)$$

Performing the ξ integrations by means of equation (35) and inverting the result by the rule (111), Chap. 1, we find on applying the corresponding Faltung theorem and returning to the original variables that

$$\theta(x,y,z,t) = \frac{\exp\left[\int_0^t \psi(\tau)d\tau\right]}{(4\pi\kappa)^{\frac{3}{2}}} \left\{ \int_0^t \frac{\exp\left[-\int_0^\tau \psi(\lambda)d\lambda\right]}{(t-\tau)^{\frac{3}{2}}} \, d\tau \int_0^\infty d\alpha \right.$$

$$\times \int_{-\infty}^\infty \int_{-\infty}^\infty d\beta \, d\gamma \, \phi(\alpha,\beta,\gamma,\tau) \exp\left[-\frac{\Sigma(x-\alpha)^2}{4\kappa(t-\tau)}\right] [1 + e^{-\alpha x/\kappa(t-\tau)}]$$

$$+ t^{-\frac{3}{2}} \int_0^\infty d\alpha \int_{-\infty}^\infty \int_{-\infty}^\infty d\beta \, d\gamma \, \theta_0(\alpha,\beta,\gamma) \exp\left[-\frac{\Sigma(x-\alpha)^2}{4\kappa t}\right] (1 + e^{-\alpha x/\kappa t}) \right\}$$
$$(156)$$

which is in agreement with Paterson's result.

If we substitute $\psi = \phi = 0$ in equation (156) and take for θ_0 the function $\delta(x-a)\delta(y)\delta(z)$, where, as before, the δ's denote Dirac delta functions, we obtain the elementary solution

$$\theta = \frac{e^{-(y^2+z^2)/4\kappa t}}{(4\pi\kappa t)^{\frac{3}{2}}} \left[e^{-(a-x)^2/4\kappa t} + e^{-(a+x)^2/4\kappa t} \right]$$

Case 2: Prescribed surface temperature. When the temperature is prescribed over the surface $x = 0$, the problem is that of solving equation (9) subject to the initial condition $\theta = \theta_0(x,y,z)$ when $t = 0$ and the boundary condition $\theta = \theta_1(y,z,t)$ when $x = 0$. The corresponding conditions on u are therefore that $u = \theta_0(x,y,z)$ when $t = 0$ and that

$$u = \theta_1(y,z,t) \exp\left[-\int_0^t \psi(\tau)d\tau \right] \equiv \theta_2(y,z,t)$$

when $x = 0$. Proceeding as in the case of no surface loss, we have to solve equation (153) subject now to the conditions

$$U = \Theta_0(x,\eta,\zeta), \; t = 0; \qquad U = \Theta_2(\eta,\zeta,t), \; x = 0$$

If we define the Fourier sine transform

$$\bar{U}(\xi,\eta,\zeta,t) = \int_0^\infty U(x,\eta,\zeta,t) \sin (\xi x)dx$$

and make use of the result

$$\int_0^\infty \frac{\partial^2 U}{\partial x^2} \sin (\xi x)dx = \xi\Theta_2(\eta,\zeta,t) - \xi^2\bar{U}(\xi,\eta,\zeta,t)$$

we find that equation (155) is replaced by

$$U(x,\eta,\zeta,t) = \frac{2}{\pi} e^{-\kappa t(\eta^2+\zeta^2)} \int_0^\infty \Theta_0(\alpha,\eta,\zeta,t)d\alpha \int_0^\infty e^{-\kappa t\xi^2} \sin (\alpha\xi) \sin (\xi x)d\xi$$

$$+ \frac{2}{\pi} \int_0^t \Theta_2(\eta,\zeta,\tau)e^{-\kappa(t-\tau)(\eta^2+\zeta^2)} d\tau \int_0^\infty \xi e^{-\kappa(t-\tau)\xi^2} \sin (\xi x)d\xi$$

$$+ \frac{2}{\pi} \int_0^t e^{-\kappa(t-\tau)(\eta^2+\zeta^2)} d\tau \int_0^\infty X(\alpha,\eta,\zeta,\tau)d\alpha \int_0^\infty e^{-\kappa(t-\tau)\xi^2} \cos (\alpha\xi) \cos (\xi x)d\xi$$

Using the result (35) and the equation

$$\frac{1}{\pi} \int_0^\infty \xi e^{-\kappa t\xi^2} \sin (\xi x)d\xi = \frac{x}{4\pi^{\frac{1}{2}}(\kappa t)^{\frac{3}{2}}} e^{-x^2/4\kappa t}$$

and then inverting by means of the inversion theorem for double Fourier transforms [equation (111), Chap. 1], we obtain finally the solution

$$\theta(x,y,z,t) = \frac{\exp\left[\int_0^t g(\tau)d\tau \right]}{(4\pi\kappa)^{\frac{3}{2}}}\left[t^{-\frac{3}{2}} \int_0^\infty d\alpha \int_{-\infty}^\infty \int_{-\infty}^\infty d\beta \, d\gamma \, \theta_0(\alpha,\beta,\gamma) \right.$$

$$\times \exp\left[-\frac{\Sigma(x-\alpha)^2}{4\kappa t} \right] (1-e^{-\alpha x/\kappa t}) + x \int_0^t \frac{\exp\left[-\int_0^\tau g(\lambda)d\lambda \right]}{(t-\tau)^{\frac{5}{2}}} d\tau \int_{-\infty}^\infty \int_{-\infty}^\infty$$

$$\times \theta_1(\beta,\gamma,\tau) \exp\left[-\frac{x^2 + (y-\beta)^2 + (z-\gamma)^2}{4\kappa(t-\tau)} \right] d\beta \, d\gamma$$

$$+ \int_0^t \frac{\exp\left[-\int_0^\tau g(\lambda)d\lambda \right]}{(t-\tau)^{\frac{3}{2}}} d\tau \int_{-\infty}^\infty \int_{-\infty}^\infty d\beta \, d\gamma \int_0^\infty d\alpha \, \phi(\alpha,\beta,\gamma,\tau)$$

$$\left. \times \exp\left[-\frac{\Sigma(x-\alpha)^2}{4\kappa(t-\tau)} \right] [1 - e^{-\alpha x/\kappa(t-\tau)}] \right] \quad (157)$$

25.3 Distribution of temperature produced by moving point sources.
As illustrations of the formulas derived above we shall now consider a
case of special interest, *viz.*, that in which the source of heat within the
solid is a point source of strength Q which is moving with velocity $v(t)$
along the line $x = a$, $z = 0$.   We then have

$$Q(x,y,z,t) = Q \, \delta(x - a) \, \delta(y - vt) \, \delta(z),$$

so that, in our notation,

$$\phi(x,y,z,t) = \frac{Q}{\rho c} \, \delta(x - a) \, \delta(y - vt) \, \delta(z), \qquad \psi(t) = 0 \qquad (158)$$

We shall further suppose that initially the temperature is zero so that

$$\theta_0(x,y,z) = 0 \qquad (159)$$

Substituting from equations (158) and (159) into equation (142) and
making use of the result (77), Chap. 1, we obtain the solution

$$\theta = \frac{Q}{8\rho c(\pi\kappa)^{\frac{3}{2}}} \int_0^t \exp\left[- \frac{(x - a)^2 + (y - vt)^2 + z^2}{4\kappa(t - \tau)} \right] \frac{d\tau}{(t - \tau)^{\frac{3}{2}}}$$

which may be put into the form

$$\theta = \frac{Q}{8\rho c(\pi\kappa)^{\frac{3}{2}}} \int_0^t \frac{e^{-R^2/4\kappa(t-\tau)}}{(t - \tau)^{\frac{3}{2}}} \, d\tau \qquad (160)$$

with

$$R^2 = (x - a)^2 + [y - \tau v(\tau)]^2 + z^2 \qquad (160a)$$

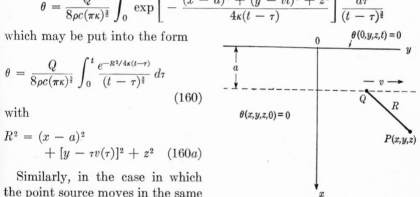

Similarly, in the case in which
the point source moves in the same
way in the interior of the semiinfinite isotropic solid $x \geq 0$, whose

FIG. 34.   Moving point source Q in a semiinfinite medium.

boundary is kept at zero temperature (cf. Fig. 34), and the initial temperature is zero, we obtain the solution

$$\theta = \frac{Q}{8\rho c(\pi\kappa)^{\frac{3}{2}}} \int_0^t \frac{d\tau}{(t - \tau)^{\frac{3}{2}}} [1 - e^{-ax/\kappa(t-\tau)}]e^{-R^2/4\kappa(t-\tau)} \qquad (161)$$

by substituting from equations (158) and (159) into equation (157) and
putting $\theta_1(x,y,z) = 0$.   If, instead of zero surface temperature, we have
the condition that there is no surface loss of heat, then it follows from
equation (156) with similar considerations that

$$\theta = \frac{Q}{8\rho c(\pi\kappa)^{\frac{3}{2}}} \int_0^t \frac{d\tau}{(t - \tau)^{\frac{3}{2}}} [1 + e^{-ax/\kappa(t-\tau)}]e^{-R^2/4\kappa(t-\tau)} \qquad (162)$$

where, as before, R is defined by equation (160a).

25.4 Diffusion in a finite region. Similar results may be obtained in the case in which the solid has finite dimensions. To illustrate the method, we shall merely consider the simplest type of problem of this kind. We shall restrict ourselves to linear flow of heat in the region $0 \leq x \leq a$, arising from a point source of strength Q situated at the point $x = b$. The surfaces $x = 0$ and $x = a$ are supposed to be maintained at zero temperature. If the initial temperature is zero throughout the medium, we then have to solve the partial differential equation

$$\frac{\partial \theta}{\partial t} = \kappa \frac{\partial^2 \theta}{\partial x^2} + \frac{Q}{\rho c} \delta(x - b) \qquad 0 < b < a \qquad (163)$$

subject to the conditions

$$\theta(x,0) = \theta(0,t) = \theta(a,t) = 0 \qquad (164)$$

To solve equation (163), multiply both sides of it by $\sin(n\pi x/a)$ and integrate from 0 to a with respect to x. Making use of equation (77), Chap. 1, and

$$\int_0^a \frac{\partial^2 \theta}{\partial x^2} \sin\left(\frac{n\pi x}{a}\right) dx = -\frac{n^2 \pi^2}{a^2} \bar{\theta}_s$$

where

$$\bar{\theta}_s(n,t) = \int_0^a \theta(x,t) \sin\left(\frac{n\pi x}{a}\right) dx \qquad (165)$$

we find that this transform satisfies the equation

$$\frac{d\bar{\theta}_s}{dt} + \frac{\kappa n^2 \pi^2}{a^2} \bar{\theta}_s = \frac{Q}{\rho c} \sin\left(\frac{n\pi b}{a}\right)$$

which, because of the initial condition, has solution

$$\bar{\theta}_s = \frac{Qa^2}{\rho c \kappa n^2 \pi^2} \sin\left(\frac{n\pi b}{a}\right)(1 - e^{-\kappa n^2 \pi^2 t/a^2})$$

which leads, by the inversion theorem 27, to the solution

$$\theta = \frac{2Qa}{\pi^2 k} \sum_{n=1}^{\infty} \frac{1}{n^2}(1 - e^{-\kappa n^2 \pi^2 t/a^2}) \sin\left(\frac{n\pi x}{a}\right) \sin\left(\frac{n\pi b}{a}\right)$$

25.5 Heat production in a cylinder. We shall consider finally the diffusion of heat in a cylinder of radius a when there are sources of heat within it which lead to an axially symmetrical temperature distribution. The fundamental differential equation is then of the form

$$\frac{\partial \theta}{\partial t} = \kappa \left(\frac{\partial^2 \theta}{\partial r^2} + \frac{1}{r} \frac{\partial \theta}{\partial r}\right) + \Theta(r,t) \qquad (166)$$

if we assume that the rate of generation of heat is independent of the temperature and that the cylinder is infinitely long, so the variation with z may be neglected. We shall, in addition, suppose that the surface $r = a$ is maintained at zero temperatute. Hence, if ξ_i is chosen to be a root of the equation

$$J_0(\xi_i a) = 0 \tag{167}$$

it follows from equation (62), Chap. 3, that

$$\int_0^a r\left(\frac{\partial^2 \theta}{\partial r^2} + \frac{1}{r}\frac{\partial \theta}{\partial r}\right) J_0(\xi_i r)dr = -\xi_i^2 \bar{\theta}_J$$

where

$$\bar{\theta}_J = \int_0^a r\theta(r,t)J_0(\xi_i r)dr$$

If, therefore, we multiply both sides of equation (166) by $rJ_0(\xi_i r)$ and integrate with respect to r from 0 to a, we find that $\bar{\theta}_J$ satisfies the equation

$$\frac{d\bar{\theta}_J}{dt} + \kappa\xi_i^2\bar{\theta}_J = \bar{\Theta}_J(\xi_i,t)$$

with the initial condition $\bar{\theta}_J(\xi_i,0) = 0$. We therefore have

$$\bar{\theta}_J = \int_0^t \bar{\Theta}_J(\xi_i,\tau)e^{-\kappa\xi_i^2(t-\tau)}\, d\tau$$

so that, by the inversion theorem 30,

$$\theta = \frac{2}{a^2}\sum_i \frac{J_0(r\xi_i)}{[J_1(a\xi_i)]^2}\int_0^t \bar{\Theta}_J(\xi_i,\tau)e^{-\kappa\xi_i^2(t-\tau)}\, d\tau$$

If, in particular, the rate of generation of heat may be written in the form

$$Q(r,t) = f(r)g(t)$$

where $f(r)$ is a function of r alone and $g(t)$ is a function of t alone, then

$$\Theta(r,t) = \frac{1}{\rho c}Q = \frac{\kappa}{k}f(r)g(t)$$

so that

$$\theta = \frac{2\kappa}{ka^2}\sum_i \frac{J_0(r\xi_i)}{[J_1(a\xi_i)]^2}\bar{f}_J(\xi_i)\int_0^t g(\tau)e^{-\kappa\xi_i^2(t-\tau)}\, d\tau \tag{168}$$

where $\bar{f}_J(\xi_i)$ is the finite Hankel transform of the function $f(r)$.

We shall consider two examples of the use of this formula:

Example 1. If the rate of generation of heat is independent of r, we may take $f(r)$ to be unity so that from equation (64), Chap. 3, we have

$$\bar{f}_J(\xi_i) = \frac{a}{\xi_i}J_1(a\xi_i)$$

whence it follows from equation (168) that

$$\theta = \frac{2\kappa}{k} \sum_i \frac{J_0(r\xi_i)}{a\xi_i J_1(a\xi_i)} \int_0^t g(\tau) e^{-\kappa \xi_i^2(t-\tau)} \, d\tau$$

For instance, if $g(t) = g_0$, a constant, we have

$$\theta = \frac{2g_0}{ka} \sum_i \frac{J_0(r\xi_i)}{\xi_i^3 J_1(a\xi_i)} (1 - e^{-\kappa t \xi_i^2}) \tag{169}$$

Now, from equation (65), Chap. 3, and Theorem 30, we see that, if the sum is taken over all the positive roots of equation (167),

$$\frac{2}{a} \sum_i \frac{J_0(r\xi_i)}{\xi_i^3 J_1(a\xi_i)} = \frac{1}{4}(a^2 - r^2) \qquad 0 \le r \le a$$

Substituting this result in equation (169), we have finally, for this case,

$$\theta = \frac{g_0(a^2 - r^2)}{4k} - \frac{2g_0}{ka} \sum_i \frac{J_0(r\xi_i) e^{-\kappa t \xi_i^2}}{\xi_i^3 J_1(a\xi_i)} \tag{170}$$

where the summation extends over all the positive roots of equation (167).

Similarly, if $g(t) = g_0 e^{-\beta t}$, where g_0 and β are constants, then, from equation (168),

$$\theta = \frac{2\kappa g_0}{ka} \sum_i \frac{J_0(r\xi_i)}{\xi_i J_1(a\xi_i)} \left[\frac{e^{-\beta t} - e^{-\xi_i^2 t}}{\kappa \xi_i^2 - \beta} \right]$$

But, from equation (68), Chap. 3, taken in conjunction with Theorem 30, we have

$$\frac{2}{a} \sum_i \frac{J_0(r\xi_i)}{\xi_i J_1(a\xi_i)} \left(\frac{\kappa \xi_i^2}{\beta} - 1 \right)^{-1} = \frac{J_0(r\sqrt{\beta/\kappa})}{J_0(a\sqrt{\beta/\kappa})} - 1$$

so that, in this case, we may write

$$\theta = \frac{\kappa g_0}{k\beta} \left[\frac{J_0(r\sqrt{\beta/\kappa})}{J_0(a\sqrt{\beta/\kappa})} - 1 \right] e^{-\beta t} - \frac{2\kappa g_0}{ka} \sum_i \frac{e^{-\kappa t \xi_i^2} J_0(r\xi_i)}{\xi_i(\kappa \xi_i^2 - \beta) J_1(a\xi_i)} \tag{171}$$

where, once again, the sum is taken over all the positive roots of equation (167).

It is readily verified by expanding the Bessel functions in ascending powers of β that equation (171) reduces to (170) as β tends to zero.

Example 2.　If the source of heat is along the axis of the cylinder (infinite line source), then, arguing as in Sec. 20.3, we see that we may take

$f(r) = \delta(r)/2\pi r$, where $\delta(r)$ denotes a Dirac delta function. In this instance $\bar{f}_J(\xi_i) = 1/2\pi$ so that, from equation (168), we obtain

$$\theta = \frac{\kappa}{\pi k a^2} \sum_i \frac{J_0(r\xi_i)}{[J_1(a\xi_i)]^2} \int_0^t g(\tau) e^{-\kappa(t-\tau)\xi_i^2} \, d\tau$$

the sum being taken over all the positive roots of equation (167).

The analysis for the case in which, instead of the surface temperature being kept constant, there is radiation into a medium at zero temperature may be set down in a precisely similar way, but with the use of the inversion theorem 31 instead of Theorem 30.

CHAPTER 6

THE SLOWING DOWN OF NEUTRONS IN MATTER

26. Fundamental Equations

26.1 Introduction. The motion of slow neutrons in matter is a process which is akin to the diffusion of heat, which we considered in the preceding chapter. The neutrons diffuse through the material as a result of collisions with the atoms forming it. The analogy with the diffusion of heat is more than superficial, for, as we shall see, it is possible to establish reliable results by making use of an approximate theory whose basic equation is of the type encountered in the theory of the conduction of heat in a solid containing sources.

It was early realized[1] that the discussion of the various methods of determining the position and width of nuclear resonance levels depended in the last resort on the investigation of the behavior of the neutrons, with which the experiments were performed, in the hydrogen-containing substances used to slow them down. The problem is also fundamental in the theory of nuclear chain reactions.[2] In a chain reaction of the kind which occurs in a nuclear pile, uranium nuclei undergo fission and as a result liberate neutrons. The velocity of the liberated neutrons is high but is soon reduced by their passage through the moderator, which is usually in the form of graphite, after which the neutrons diffuse through the material for a time before being finally absorbed. Most of the neutrons are absorbed by fissionable nuclei and consequently produce the neutrons of the next generation. In this way the chain reaction is built up. The discussion of the features of such a reactor obviously depends on a knowledge of the processes of slowing down and diffusion undergone by the neutrons in their passage through the moderator.

The discussion of the slowing down of neutrons is also relevant to the problem of determining the distribution of neutrons in the earth's atmosphere.[3] It is thought that the neutrons which are observed in the earth's

---

[1] For references, see H. A. Bethe, *Rev. Mod. Phys.*, **9**, 119–134 (1937).

[2] See, as an example, the article by F. L. Friedman entitled "Elementary Pile Theory" in "The Science and Engineering of Nuclear Power" (Addison-Wesley, Cambridge, Mass., 1947), pp. 111–186, and that by E. P. Wigner, *Jour. Applied Phys.*, **17**, 857 (1946).

[3] See, for instance, the article "On the Excitation of Neutrons by Cosmic Rays and Their Distribution in the Atmosphere," by S. Flugge in "Cosmic Radiation" (edited

atmosphere are not of cosmic origin but have been excited as secondaries in the course of the passage of some other cosmic ray particle through the upper atmosphere. An estimate of the distribution of neutrons in the atmosphere may then be obtained by assuming that a source of neutrons of definite (but unknown!) strength may be ascribed to the atmosphere and then applying the equations governing the motion of neutrons in matter.

Most of the recent work on the slowing down of neutrons in matter has been done by scientists working on the wartime atomic energy project. A great deal of theoretical work has been done in this direction by the Chicago group working under Professor E. P. Wigner, by the Los Alamos laboratory under Dr. R. E. Marshak, and by British and Canadian groups. Most of the work done under these circumstances remains unpublished, but various papers have appeared recently containing discussions of the more fundamental problems. The fullest of these are "Theory of the Slowing Down of Neutrons by Elastic Collision with Atomic Nuclei" by R. E. Marshak[1] and "Elementary Approximations in the Theory of Neutron Diffusion" by P. R. Wallace and J. LeCaine.[2] The discussion given in this chapter leans rather heavily on these two review articles.

26.2 Transport equation. We shall begin by establishing the equation governing the slowing down of neutrons, before introducing the approximations which lead to elementary solutions. We assume that the neutrons do *not* suffer *inelastic* collisions with the atoms of the material through which they are passing. In other words, we assume that there is no transfer of energy from the neutron to the atomic nucleus with which it collides. We are therefore restricted to neutron energies below the first excited level of the nucleus of the element forming the absorber. For light nuclei, such as carbon or oxygen, this energy limit is in the region of 4 to 6 Mev, but for heavier nuclei the lowest excited level is in the neighborhood of 100 kev. On the other hand we assume that the energy of the neutron is large compared with the energy of the chemical bond.

To simplify the complications which arise from the introduction of scattering processes, we assume further that the energy of the neutron is low enough for the deviations from s-wave scattering to be neglected. With this approximation the scattering is spherically symmetrical in the center of mass system (cf. Sec. 26.3).

---

by W. Heisenberg, translated by T. H. Johnson, Dover, New York, 1946), pp. 144–159.

[1] *Rev. Mod. Phys.*, **19**, 185 (1947).

[2] N. R. C. of Canada, Division of Atomic Energy, *Montreal Rept.* 12. See also P. R. Wallace, *Nucleonics*, **4**, 30 (1949).

Suppose that Ω is a unit vector coinciding with the direction of the velocity of the neutron when its energy is E. Instead of employing E as a variable we introduce the dimensionless energy parameter

$$u = \log\left(\frac{E_0}{E}\right) \tag{1}$$

where E_0 is some initial energy, and write $N(\mathbf{r},\Omega,u,t)d\mathbf{r}\,d\Omega\,du$ for the number of neutrons whose position vectors lie between $\mathbf{r}$ and $\mathbf{r} + d\mathbf{r}$, the direction of whose velocities lies between Ω and $\Omega + d\Omega$, and the magnitude of whose energy is between u and $u + du$, all measured at the time t. Then, precisely as in the theory of fluid motion (cf. Sec. 30.1), the time rate of change of the neutron distribution function moving with the neutron stream in the direction Ω is

$$\frac{\partial N}{\partial t} + \mathbf{v} \cdot \operatorname{grad}\,(N) \tag{2}$$

If we denote the scattering and the capture mean free paths by $L_s(u)$ and $L_c(u)$, respectively, then the total mean free path is $L(u)$, where

$$\frac{1}{L(u)} = \frac{1}{L_c(u)} + \frac{1}{L_s(u)}$$

and the number of neutrons removed from the beam by scattering and capture is

$$\frac{vN}{L} \tag{3}$$

Similarly, $v'N(\mathbf{r},\Omega',u',t)/L_s(u')$ is the number of collisions per second at the time t and the point r which befall neutrons whose velocity is determined by the parameters Ω' and u'. If now $f(\mu_0, u - u')$ is the relative probability of a neutron being left with velocity parameters (Ω,u) as a result of a collision before which its velocity was characterized by the pair (Ω',u') ($\mu_0 = \Omega \cdot \Omega'$ being the cosine of the angle through which the neutron is scattered), then the number of neutrons scattered into the beam will be

$$\int_0^u du' \int d\Omega' \frac{v'N(\mathbf{r},\Omega',u',t)}{L_s(u')} f(\mu_0, u - u') \tag{4}$$

We shall assume further that the function $f(\mu_0, u - u')$ is normalized to unity, *i.e.*, that

$$\int d\Omega \int du' f(\mu_0, u - u') = 1 \tag{5}$$

Finally we denote by

$$S(\mathbf{r},u,t) \tag{6}$$

the number of neutrons being produced per unit time and per unit volume at the time t and at the point whose position vector is $\mathbf{r}$.

From equations (2) to (6) we find from considerations of continuity that the function $N(\mathbf{r},\boldsymbol{\Omega},u,t)$ satisfies the time-dependent *transport equation*

$$\frac{\partial N(\mathbf{r},\boldsymbol{\Omega},u,t)}{\partial t} + \mathbf{v} \cdot \operatorname{grad} N(\mathbf{r},\boldsymbol{\Omega},u,t)$$

$$= \int_0^u du' \int d\boldsymbol{\Omega}' \frac{v' N(\mathbf{r},\boldsymbol{\Omega}',u',t)}{L_s(u')} f(\mu_0, u - u') + S(\mathbf{r},u,t) - \frac{vN(\mathbf{r},\boldsymbol{\Omega},u,t)}{L(u)} \quad (7)$$

If, in place of $N(\mathbf{r},\boldsymbol{\Omega},u,t)$, we introduce the function

$$\psi(\mathbf{r},\boldsymbol{\Omega},u,t) = \frac{v}{L(u)} N(\mathbf{r},\boldsymbol{\Omega},u,t) \tag{8}$$

and remember that $\mathbf{v} = v\boldsymbol{\Omega}$, we see that equation (7) assumes the equivalent form

$$L(u)\left(\frac{1}{v}\frac{\partial \psi}{\partial t} + \boldsymbol{\Omega} \cdot \operatorname{grad} \psi\right) + \psi(\mathbf{r},\boldsymbol{\Omega},u,t)$$

$$= \int_0^u du' \int d\boldsymbol{\Omega}' \, h(u')\psi(\mathbf{r},\boldsymbol{\Omega}',u',t)f(\mu_0, u - u') + S(\mathbf{r},u,t) \quad (9)$$

In the time-independent case S is a function of $\mathbf{r}$ and u only and ψ is a function of $\mathbf{r}$, $\boldsymbol{\Omega}$, and u. We obtain the basic equation in this instance by writing $\partial/\partial t \equiv 0$ in equation (9), that is,

$$L(u)\boldsymbol{\Omega} \cdot \operatorname{grad} \psi + \psi(\mathbf{r},\boldsymbol{\Omega},u,t)$$

$$= \int_0^u du' \int d\boldsymbol{\Omega}' \, h(u')\psi(\mathbf{r},\boldsymbol{\Omega},u)f(\mu_0, u - u') + S(\mathbf{r},u) \quad (10)$$

where, as in equation (9),

$$h(u) = \frac{L(u)}{L_s(u)} \tag{11}$$

From the definition (8) it is obvious that $\psi(\mathbf{r},\boldsymbol{\Omega},u,t)d\mathbf{r}\, d\boldsymbol{\Omega}\, du$ is the total number of collisions per unit time at time t and with $\mathbf{r}$ between $\mathbf{r}$ and $\mathbf{r} + d\mathbf{r}$, $\boldsymbol{\Omega}$ between $\boldsymbol{\Omega}$ and $\boldsymbol{\Omega} + d\boldsymbol{\Omega}$, and u between u and $u + du$.

The fundamental problem is that of solving the integrodifferential equation (9). Since a solution of this equation corresponding to an arbitrary distribution of sources (in u and t) is obtained by the superposition of solutions of the same equation with

$$S(\mathbf{r},u,t) = Q(\mathbf{r})\, \delta(u)\, \delta(t) \tag{12}$$

there is no loss in generality incurred by assuming that the source function S occurring in equation (9) is of the form (12).

26.3 Form of the scattering function. The solution of the integro-differential equation (9) depends on a knowledge of the scattering function $f(\mu_0, u - u')$ appearing under the integration sign on the right-hand side. We usually assume that the scattering is spherically symmetrical in the center of mass system. This assumption enables us to determine the form of the function $f(\mu_0, u - u')$ directly from the application of the laws of conservation of energy and momentum.

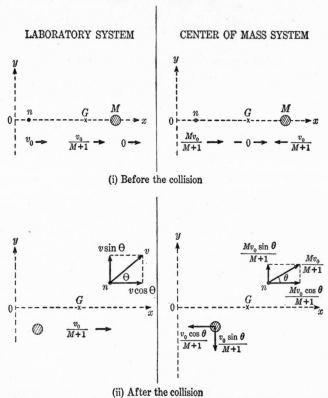

(i) Before the collision

(ii) After the collision

Fig. 35.   Relations between the laboratory and center of mass systems of coordinates.

Taking the mass of the neutron as the unit of mass, we suppose that the atoms of the absorber have mass M (*i.e.*, the mass number of the nucleus is M), and we assume that in the laboratory system the initial velocity of the neutron is v_0, that the final velocity after scattering by a single nucleus is v, and that the angle between the two is Θ (cf. Fig. 35). If the nucleus is originally at rest, then the velocity of the center of mass of the system is initially $v_0/(M + 1)$, so that, in the center of mass system the two particles have velocities $Mv_0/(M + 1)$ and $v_0/(M + 1)$ in the directions shown in Fig. 35. From the conservation of energy and momentum in the center of mass system we see that, after the collision, the components of velocity of the neutron are $\left(\dfrac{Mv_0}{M+1} \cos\theta, \dfrac{Mv_0}{M+1} \sin\theta \right)$ while those of the nucleus are $\left(\dfrac{-v_0}{M+1} \cos\theta, \dfrac{-v_0}{M+1} \sin\theta \right)$. Reverting to the laboratory system by adding the velocity $[v_0/(M+1),0]$ of the center of mass, we find that the velocity in the x direction of the neutron after the collision is

$$v \cos\Theta = \frac{Mv_0}{M+1} \cos\theta + \frac{v_0}{M+1} \tag{13}$$

Similarly, by considering the components of the neutron velocity in the y direction we obtain the equation

$$v \sin\Theta = \frac{Mv_0}{M+1} \sin\theta \tag{13a}$$

Squaring equations (13) and (13a) and adding, we find that

$$v^2 = \frac{M^2 v_0^2}{(M+1)^2} + \frac{2Mv_0^2}{(M+1)^2} \cos\theta + \frac{v_0^2}{(M+1)^2} \tag{14}$$

whence, from equation (1) and the relation $E/E_0 = v^2/v_0^2$, we derive the equation

$$\cos\theta = 1 - \frac{(M+1)^2}{2M}(1 - e^{-u}) \tag{15}$$

Substituting this result into equation (13) we see that the relation between the angle of scattering in the laboratory system and the energy parameter u is

$$\cos\Theta = \frac{M+1}{2} e^{-\frac{1}{2}u} - \frac{M-1}{2} e^{\frac{1}{2}u} \tag{16}$$

Now the maximum energy loss occurs when the neutron is scattered through an angle of 180° in the laboratory system; as is seen from equation (16), this corresponds to an energy loss u determined by the equation

$$[(M-1)e^{\frac{1}{2}u} - (M+1)](e^{\frac{1}{2}u} + 1) = 0$$

showing that the maximum possible logarithmic energy loss is

$$q_M = \log\left(\frac{M+1}{M-1}\right)^2 \tag{17}$$

Furthermore, it follows from equation (16) that scattering which changes the direction of the neutron velocity by an angle $\Theta = \cos^{-1}\mu_0$ in the laboratory system is possible only if

$$\mu_0 = \frac{M+1}{2} e^{-\frac{1}{2}u} - \frac{M-1}{2} e^{\frac{1}{2}u}$$

In other words, the function $f(\mu_0, u - u')$ is proportional to the Dirac delta function

$$\delta \left(\mu_0 - \frac{M+1}{2} e^{-\frac{1}{2}u} + \frac{M-1}{2} e^{\frac{1}{2}u} \right) \tag{18}$$

So far we have not made use of the assumption that in the center of mass system the scattering is spherically symmetrical. As is well known, this hypothesis is equivalent to assuming that the function $f(\mu_0, u)$ is proportional to $d(\cos \theta)/du$, so that from equation (15) it follows that f is proportional to

$$-\frac{(M+1)^2}{2M} e^{-u} \tag{19}$$

From the expressions (18) and (19) it follows that

$$f(\mu_0, u) = \begin{cases} Ce^{-u} \, \delta \left(\mu_0 - \frac{M+1}{2} e^{-\frac{1}{2}u} + \frac{M-1}{2} e^{\frac{1}{2}u} \right) & 0 \leq u \leq q_M \\ 0 & u > q_M \end{cases} \tag{20}$$

The constant C may be determined from the normalization condition (5). This gives

$$C = \frac{(M+1)^2}{8\pi M} \tag{21}$$

The scattering function is therefore determined by equations (20) and (21).

From this function we may readily determine by a simple integration the average logarithmic energy loss in one collision,

$$\xi = \int_0^{q_M} u \, du \int d\mathbf{\Omega}_0 \, f(\mu_0, u) = 1 - \frac{(M+1)^2}{4M} q_M e^{-q_M} \tag{22}$$

Similarly, the average value of the cosine of the angle of deflection (measured in the laboratory system) produced by one collision is

$$\langle \cos \Theta \rangle_{\mathrm{av}} = \int_0^{q_M} du \int d\mathbf{\Omega}_0 \, \mu_0 f(\mu_0, u) = \frac{2}{3M} \tag{23}$$

We shall find that these two quantities keep occurring in the subsequent analysis of the motion of neutrons in matter.

27. Age Theory

27.1 Basic equations of the age theory. We shall begin our discussion of the solutions of the transport equation by introducing certain assumptions which enable us to reduce this equation to one of a more familiar type.

For simplicity, we consider the time-independent equation (10) in the case in which there is no capture, so that $L(u) = L_s(u)$ and $h(u) = 1$. If, furthermore, we restrict ourselves to the one-dimensional case, we find that equation (10) reduces to the simple form

$$L(u)\mu \frac{\partial \psi}{\partial z} + \psi = \int_0^u du' \int d\Omega'\, \psi(z,u',\mu')f(\mu_0, u - u') + S(z,u) \quad (24)$$

where μ denotes the cosine of the angle which the neutron velocity makes with the z axis.

We now expand the functions ψ and f in spherical harmonics by means of the formulas

$$\psi = \frac{1}{4\pi} \sum_{n=1}^{\infty} (2n + 1)\psi_n(z,u)P_n(\mu) \quad (24a)$$

$$f = \frac{1}{4\pi} \sum_{n=1}^{\infty} (2n + 1)f_n(u)P_n(\mu) \quad (24b)$$

in which the coefficients ψ_n and f_n are defined by the relations

$$\psi_n = \int d\Omega\, P_n(\mu)\psi(z,\mu,u) \quad (25)$$
$$f_n = \int d\Omega\, P_n(\mu)f(\mu,u) \quad (25a)$$

In the age-theory approximation we assume that the distribution function $\psi(z,\mu,u)$ is almost isotropic so that we may neglect all but the first two terms of the expansions (24) and write

$$\psi(z,\mu,u) = \frac{1}{4\pi}[\psi_0(z,u) + 3\mu\psi_1(z,\mu)] \quad (26)$$

where

$$\psi_0(z,u) = \int \psi(z,\mu,u)d\Omega; \qquad \psi_1(z,u) = \int \mu\psi(z,\mu,u)d\Omega \quad (27)$$

If we take a similar number of terms in the expansion of the scattering function and substitute in equation (24), then integrating with respect to μ we obtain the relation

$$L(u)\frac{\partial \psi_1}{\partial z} + \psi_0(z,u) = \int_0^u du'\, \psi_0(z,u')f_0(u - u') + 4\pi S \quad (28)$$

If, on the other hand, we had multiplied both sides of the equation by μ and then integrated, we should have obtained the equation

$$\frac{1}{3}L(u)\frac{\partial \psi_0}{\partial z} + \psi_1(z,u) = \int_0^u du'\, \psi_1(z,u')f_1(u - u') \quad (29)$$

In both these equations it is understood that, as a result of equation (16), f_0 and f_1 are zero if $u - u' > q_M$, so that the integrals are taken over the interval q_M (except for $u < q_M$, which does affect the result since it will be assumed that $u \gg q_M$).

In the age-theory approximation we make the further assumption that the functions ψ_0 and ψ_1 occurring under the signs of integration in equations (28) and (29) vary slowly with u' so that we may write (assuming $\psi_1 \ll \psi_0$)

$$\left.\begin{aligned}
\psi_0(z,u') &= \psi_0(z,u) - (u - u')\frac{\partial\psi_0(z,u)}{\partial u} \\
\psi_1(z,u') &= \psi_1(z,u)
\end{aligned}\right\} \tag{30}$$

Substituting from these equations into equations (28) and (29) we find that

$$L(u)\frac{\partial\psi_1}{\partial z} + \psi_0 = \psi_0 \int_{u-q_M}^{u} f_0(u - u')du' + 4\pi S(z,u)$$
$$- \frac{\partial\psi_0}{\partial u}\int_{u-q_M}^{u}(u - u')f_0(u - u')du' \tag{31}$$

and

$$\frac{1}{3}L(u)\frac{\partial\psi_0}{\partial z} + \psi_1 = \psi_1 \int_{u-q_M}^{u} f_1(u - u')du' \tag{32}$$

But, from equations (5), (22), and (23), we have

$$\int_{u-q_M}^{u} f_0(u - u')du' = 1, \qquad \int_{u-q_M}^{u}(u - u')f_0(u - u')du' = \xi,$$
$$\int_{u-q_M}^{u} f_1(u - u')du' = \langle\cos\Theta\rangle_{av}$$

so that equations (31) and (32) reduce to the equivalent forms

$$L(u)\frac{\partial\psi_1}{\partial z} = -\xi\frac{\partial\psi_0}{\partial u} + 4\pi S(z,u) \tag{33}$$

$$\psi_1 = -\frac{L(u)}{3[1 - \langle\cos\Theta\rangle_{av}]}\frac{\partial\psi_0}{\partial z} \tag{34}$$

If, now, we introduce the "symbolic age" θ, defined by the equation

$$\theta = \frac{1}{3}\int_0^u \frac{L^2(u')du'}{\xi[1 - \langle\cos\Theta\rangle_{av}]} \tag{35}$$

we see that these equations are equivalent to the partial differential equation

$$\frac{\partial\chi(z,\theta)}{\partial\theta} = \frac{\partial^2\chi(z,\theta)}{\partial z^2} + T(z,\theta) \tag{36}$$

where T is related to the source function S by the equation

$$T(z,\theta) = 4\pi S(z,u)\frac{\partial u}{\partial\theta} \tag{37}$$

and $\chi(z,\theta) = \xi\psi_0(z,u)$ represents the number of neutrons per unit volume per unit time which reach the age θ; for that reason χ is called the *slowing-down density*.

Substituting from equation (34) into equation (26), we find that

$$\psi(z,\mu,u) = \frac{1}{4\pi\xi}\left\{\chi(z,\theta) - \mu\frac{L(u)}{[1 - \langle\cos\Theta_{\text{av}}\rangle]}\frac{\partial\chi}{\partial z}\right\} \tag{38}$$

from which it follows that

$$\int_0^1 \psi(z,\mu,u)\mu\,d\mu = \frac{1}{8\pi\xi}\left\{\chi(z,\mu) - \frac{2}{3}\frac{L(u)}{[1 - \langle\cos\Theta\rangle_{\text{av}}]}\frac{\partial\chi}{\partial z}\right\} \tag{39}$$

This represents the total neutron current incident upon the plane whose position is defined by the coordinate z, a fact of which we shall make use in the formulation of the boundary conditions to be satisfied in certain problems.

27.2 Solution for an infinite slowing-down medium. We shall begin our discussion of the solutions of the partial differential equation (36) by considering an infinite medium and a source function

$$T(z,\theta) = S\,\delta(z)\delta(\theta) \tag{40}$$

From the equation (36) and the properties of the Dirac delta function it follows that when $\theta = 0$ the slowing-down density is $S\,\delta(z)$, it being assumed that S is a constant. The boundary condition imposed on the slowing-down density is that it should tend to zero as $|z| \to \infty$.

The differential equation to be solved is

$$\frac{\partial\chi}{\partial\theta} = \frac{\partial^2\chi}{\partial z^2} + S\,\delta(z)\delta(\theta) \tag{41}$$

and the solution may be found by introducing the Fourier transform

$$\bar{\chi}(\xi,\theta) = \frac{1}{\sqrt{2\pi}}\int_{-\infty}^\infty e^{i\xi z}\chi(z,\theta)dz \tag{42}$$

of the slowing-down density. From the prescribed behavior of the slowing-down density at infinity, we have, as a result of an integration by parts, that

$$\frac{1}{\sqrt{2\pi}}\int_{-\infty}^\infty \frac{\partial^2\chi}{\partial z^2} e^{i\xi z}\,dz = -\xi^2\bar{\chi}(\xi,\theta)$$

so that equation (41) is equivalent to the ordinary differential equation

$$\frac{d\bar{\chi}}{d\theta} + \xi^2\bar{\chi} = \frac{1}{\sqrt{2\pi}}\delta(\theta)$$

which may be written in the form

$$\frac{d}{d\theta}\left(e^{\xi^2\theta}\bar{\chi}\right) = \frac{1}{\sqrt{2\pi}}\,\delta(\theta)e^{\xi^2\theta}$$

showing that its solution is

$$\bar{\chi} = \frac{1}{\sqrt{2\pi}}\,e^{-\xi^2\theta}$$

Inverting this result by means of Theorem 10, we find that

$$\chi = \frac{1}{2\pi}\int_{-\infty}^{\infty} e^{-\xi^2\theta - i\xi z}\,d\xi = \frac{1}{2\sqrt{\pi\theta}}\,e^{-z^2/4\theta} \tag{4}$$

We define a characteristic length Λ_s, called the *slowing-down length*,
the equation

$$\Lambda_s(u) = \left[\frac{\langle z^2(u)\rangle_{\mathrm{av}}}{2}\right]^{\frac{1}{2}} \tag{4}$$

where, as is usual,

$$\langle z^2(u)\rangle_{\mathrm{av}} = \frac{\displaystyle\int d\Omega \int_{-\infty}^{\infty} z^2\psi(z,\mu,u)du}{\displaystyle\int d\Omega \int_{-\infty}^{\infty} \psi(z,\mu,u)du}$$

For the solution (43) we have from this definition

$$\langle z^2(u)\rangle_{\mathrm{av}} = 4\theta\,\frac{\displaystyle\int_0^{\infty} u^2 e^{-u^2}\,du}{\displaystyle\int_0^{\infty} e^{-u^2}\,du} = 4\theta\,\frac{\Gamma(\frac{3}{2})}{\Gamma(\frac{1}{2})} = 2\theta$$

Inserting this result in equation (44), we see that for the solution (43)

$$\Lambda_s(u) = \theta^{\frac{1}{2}} \tag{45}$$

so that we can regard the variable θ as being the square of the characteristic length for slowing-down problem.

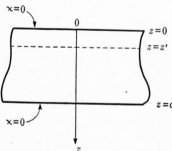

27.3 Slowing-down density in a slab of finite thickness and infinite extent. We consider now the problem in which the slowing-down medium is in the form of a thick slab (cf. Fig. 36) and the source function is of the form

$$T(z,\theta) = S\,\delta(z - z')\delta(\theta) \tag{46}$$

Fig. 36. Plane source of neutrons in a semiinfinite slowing-down medium.

With this form of source function and the fact that the plate is of infinite extent we are justified in using the linear diffusion equation (36). We assume further that the slowing-down density is zero on the faces $z = 0$

$z = a$ of the thick slab.   With this assumption we can readily show that

$$\int_0^a \sin\left(\frac{n\pi z}{a}\right) \frac{\partial^2 \chi}{\partial z^2}\, dz = -\frac{n^2 \pi^2}{a^2}\, \bar{\chi}(n,\theta) \tag{47}$$

where

$$\bar{\chi}(n,\theta) = \int_0^a \chi(z,\theta)\, \sin\left(\frac{n\pi z}{a}\right) dz \tag{48}$$

It follows at once, by multiplying throughout by $\sin (n\pi z/a)$ and integrating, that equation (36), with $T(z,\theta)$ given by (46), is equivalent to

$$\frac{d\bar{\chi}}{d\theta} + \frac{n^2 \pi^2}{a^2}\, \bar{\chi} = S \sin\left(\frac{n\pi z'}{a}\right) \delta(\theta)$$

Hence

$$\bar{\chi} = S \sin\left(\frac{n\pi z'}{a}\right) e^{-n^2 \pi^2 \theta / a^2}$$

so that from the definition (48) and the inversion theorem 27 we obtain the solution

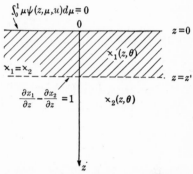

Fig. 37.   The boundary conditions in a semiinfinite slowing-down medium bounded by a vacuum and containing a plane source on $z = z'$.

$$\chi(z,\theta) = \frac{2S}{a} \sum_{n=1}^{\infty} \sin\left(\frac{n\pi z}{a}\right) \sin\left(\frac{n\pi z'}{a}\right) e^{-n^2 \pi^2 \theta / a^2} \tag{49}$$

It follows directly by integration of this result that, if $T(z,\theta)$ is of the form $S(z)\, \delta(\theta)$, then the corresponding solution is

$$\chi(z,\theta) = \frac{2}{a} \sum_{n=1}^{\infty} \sin\left(\frac{n\pi z}{a}\right) e^{-n^2 \pi^2 \theta / a^2} \int_0^a S(z') \sin\left(\frac{n\pi z'}{a}\right) dz' \tag{50}$$

27.4 Semiinfinite slowing-down medium bounded by a vacuum.   The boundary condition $\chi(z,\theta) = 0$ when $z = 0$ or a, which we used in the last section, is not strictly accurate.   In this section we shall solve the problem of a semiinfinite slowing-down medium with a source function of the form (46) and the correct boundary conditions.[1]   In this way we may hope to estimate the extent to which the boundary condition $\chi = 0$ at an outer boundary of a slowing-down medium is correct.

The age equation appropriate to this problem is (cf. Fig. 37)

$$\frac{\partial \chi(z,\theta)}{\partial \theta} = \frac{\partial^2 \chi(z,\theta)}{\partial z^2} + \delta(z - z')\, \delta(\theta) \tag{51}$$

[1] Marshak, *op. cit.*, pp. 216–218.

The boundary conditions are

1. The density of neutrons tends to zero as $z \to \infty$.

2. The total incoming current of neutrons across the plane $z = 0$ is zero.

From the second of these conditions and equation (39) it follows that, when $z = 0$, then, for all values of θ,

$$\chi(z,\theta) - \frac{2L(u)}{3(1 - \langle \cos \Theta \rangle_{av})} \frac{\partial \chi(z,\theta)}{\partial z} = 0 \tag{52}$$

Similarly the condition 1 may be written in the form

$$\chi(z,\theta) \to 0 \qquad \text{as } z \to \infty, \text{ for all } \theta \tag{53}$$

To solve equation (51) subject to these conditions, we introduce the Laplace transform

$$\phi(z,p) = \int_0^\infty \chi(z,\theta)e^{-p\theta}\, d\theta \tag{54}$$

of the function $\chi(z,\theta)$. Multiplying equation (51) by $e^{-p\theta}$ and integrating with respect to θ, we find that ϕ satisfies the differential equation

$$\frac{d^2\phi}{dz^2} - p\phi = -\delta(z - z') \tag{55}$$

If we denote the solution of this equation by

$$\phi(z,p) = \begin{cases} \phi_1(z,p) & 0 \le z \le z' \\ \phi_2(z,p) & z \ge z' \end{cases}$$

then we assume that

$$\phi_1(z,p) = \phi_2(z,p) \qquad \text{if } z = z' \tag{56}$$

and it follows from integrating equation (55) with respect to z over a small interval surrounding $z = z'$ that

$$\frac{\partial \phi_1(z,p)}{\partial z} - \frac{\partial \phi_2(z,p)}{\partial z} = 1 \tag{57}$$

With the assumption that $L(u)$ is constant, L_0 say, integration of equation (52) leads to the boundary condition

$$\phi_1(z,p) - \frac{2}{3} \bar{L}_0 \frac{\partial \phi_1(z,p)}{\partial z} = 0 \qquad \text{at } z = 0 \tag{58}$$

where we have written

$$\bar{L}_0 = \frac{L_0}{(1 - \langle \cos \Theta \rangle_{av})} \tag{58a}$$

From equation (55) we may write

$$\phi_1 = Ae^{-(z'-z)p^{\frac{1}{2}}} + Be^{(z'-z)p^{\frac{1}{2}}}, \qquad \phi_2 = Ce^{-(z-z')p^{\frac{1}{2}}}$$

Substituting these functions in equations (56), (57), and (58), we obtain
the equations

$$A + B - C = 0, \qquad p^{\frac{1}{2}}(A - B + C) = 1$$
$$Ae^{-2z'p^{\frac{1}{2}}}(1 - \tfrac{2}{3}\bar{L}_0 p^{\frac{1}{2}}) + B(1 + \tfrac{2}{3}\bar{L}_0 p^{\frac{1}{2}}) = 0$$

which may be solved to yield the solutions

$$\phi_1 = \tfrac{1}{2}p^{-\frac{1}{2}}e^{-(z'-z)p^{\frac{1}{2}}} - \tfrac{1}{2}p^{-\frac{1}{2}}e^{-(z+z')p^{\frac{1}{2}}} + \frac{4\bar{L}_0 p^{\frac{1}{2}}}{3p^{\frac{1}{2}}(1 + \tfrac{2}{3}\bar{L}_0 p^{\frac{1}{2}})} e^{-(z+z')p^{\frac{1}{2}}} \qquad (59)$$

$$\phi_2 = \frac{1}{2p^{\frac{1}{2}}}\left[1 - \left(\frac{1 - \tfrac{2}{3}\bar{L}_0 p^{\frac{1}{2}}}{1 + \tfrac{2}{3}\bar{L}_0 p^{\frac{1}{2}}}\right) e^{-2z'p^{\frac{1}{2}}} \right] e^{-(z-z')p^{\frac{1}{2}}} \qquad (59a)$$

The corresponding forms $\chi_1(z,\theta)$ and $\chi_2(z,\theta)$ are then obtained from the
Laplace inversion theorem

$$\chi_{1,2}(z,\theta) = \frac{1}{2\pi i} \int_{c-i\infty}^{c+i\infty} \phi_{1,2}(z,p)e^{p\theta}\, dp \qquad (60)$$

(Theorem 14).   The determination of the neutron density reduces in
this case to the evaluation of the two contour integrals

$$\frac{1}{2\pi i} \int_{c-i\infty}^{c+i\infty} \frac{e^{-\beta p^{\frac{1}{2}}+p\theta}}{p^{\frac{1}{2}}(1 + \alpha p^{\frac{1}{2}})}\, dp, \qquad \frac{1}{2\pi i} \int_{c-i\infty}^{c+i\infty} p^{-\frac{1}{2}}e^{-\beta p^{\frac{1}{2}}+p\theta}\, dp$$

Now we may write

$$\int_0^\infty e^{-pt}(\pi t)^{-\frac{1}{2}}e^{-a^2/4t}\, dt = \frac{e^{-ap^{\frac{1}{2}}}}{(\pi p)^{\frac{1}{2}}} \int_{-\infty}^\infty e^{-(u-ap^{\frac{1}{2}}/2u)^2}\, du$$

But it is readily proved[1] that, if b is real and positive,

$$\int_{-\infty}^\infty F\left[\left(u - \frac{b}{u}\right)^2\right] du = \int_{-\infty}^\infty F(u^2)du$$

so that, taking $F(u^2)$ to be e^{-u^2}, we have

$$\frac{1}{\pi^{\frac{1}{2}}} \int_{-\infty}^\infty e^{-(u-ap^{\frac{1}{2}}/2u)^2}\, du = 1$$

which yields the result

$$\int_0^\infty e^{-pt}(\pi t)^{-\frac{1}{2}}e^{-a^2/4t}\, dt = p^{-\frac{1}{2}}e^{-ap^{\frac{1}{2}}}$$

Inverting this equation by means of Theorem 14 and multiplying both
sides of the result by e^{-a}, we obtain the formula

$$\frac{1}{2\pi i} \int_{c-i\infty}^{c+i\infty} \frac{e^{-a(1+\alpha p^{\frac{1}{2}})+pt}}{p^{\frac{1}{2}}}\, dp = (\pi t)^{-\frac{1}{2}}e^{-a-a^2\alpha^2/4t}$$

---

[1] Cf. G. A. Gibson, "Advanced Calculus" (Macmillan, London, 1930), p. 500.

Integrating both sides of this equation with respect to a from a to ∞, we have

$$\frac{1}{2\pi i} \int_{c-i\infty}^{c+i\infty} \frac{e^{-a(1+\alpha p^{\frac{1}{2}})+pt}}{p^{\frac{1}{2}}(1+\alpha p^{\frac{1}{2}})}\, dp = (\pi t)^{-\frac{1}{2}} \int_a^\infty e^{-a^2\alpha^2/4t - a}\, da$$

Now we may put

$$\frac{a^2\alpha^2}{4t} + a = \frac{\alpha^2}{4t}\left(a + \frac{2t}{\alpha^2}\right)^2 - \frac{t}{\alpha^2}$$

so that

$$\frac{1}{2\pi i} \int_{c-i\infty}^{c+i\infty} \frac{e^{-a(1+\alpha p^{\frac{1}{2}})+pt}}{p^{\frac{1}{2}}(1+\alpha p^{\frac{1}{2}})}\, dp = \frac{2}{\alpha\pi^{\frac{1}{2}}} \int_{\frac{1}{2}a\alpha t^{-\frac{1}{2}} + t^{\frac{1}{2}}/\alpha}^{\infty} e^{-u^2}\, du\, e^{t/\alpha^2}$$

With the usual notation

$$\frac{2}{\sqrt{\pi}} \int_z^\infty e^{-u^2}\, du = 1 - \operatorname{erf}(z)$$

we may write this last result in the form

$$\frac{1}{2\pi i} \int_{c-i\infty}^{c+i\infty} \frac{e^{-\beta p^{\frac{1}{2}}+pt}}{p^{\frac{1}{2}}(1+\alpha p^{\frac{1}{2}})}\, dp = \frac{1}{\alpha} \exp\left(\frac{\beta}{\alpha} + \frac{t}{\alpha^2}\right)\left[1 - \operatorname{erf}\left(\frac{\beta}{2t^{\frac{1}{2}}} + \frac{t^{\frac{1}{2}}}{\alpha}\right)\right]$$

where we have put $\beta = a\alpha$.

Substituting from equation (59) into (60) and making use of these results, we find that, when $0 \leq z < z'$,

$$\chi(z,\theta) = \frac{1}{(4\pi\theta)^{\frac{1}{2}}} [e^{-(z-z')^2/4\theta} - e^{-(z+z')^2/4\theta}]$$
$$- \frac{3}{2\bar{L}_0} \exp\left[\frac{9\theta}{4\bar{L}_0^2} + \frac{3(z+z')}{2\bar{L}_0}\right]\left[1 - \operatorname{erf}\left(\frac{3\theta^{\frac{1}{2}}}{2\bar{L}_0} + \frac{z+z'}{2\theta^{\frac{1}{2}}}\right)\right] \quad (61)$$

It will be observed that the solution corresponding to the boundary condition $\chi(0,\theta) = 0$ is obtained by putting $\bar{L}_0 = 0$ in equation (61). In this case, therefore,

$$\chi(z,\theta) = \frac{1}{(4\pi\theta)^{\frac{1}{2}}} [e^{-(z-z')^2/4\theta} - e^{-(z+z')^2/4\theta}] \qquad (62)$$

so that the third term on the right-hand side of equation (61) represents the correction due to making use of the correct boundary conditions instead of the approximate ones we have been using so far.

In physical applications of calculations of this type it is of interest to determine the point at which the slowing-down density vanishes—the so-called *extrapolated end point*. If we denote this point by z_0, we have the condition $\chi(z_0,\theta) = 0$, with $\chi(z,\theta)$ given by equation (61). The numerical solution of this equation leads to the value $z_0 \simeq -0.70\bar{L}_0$.

27.5 Three-dimensional problems. It can readily be shown by methods similar to those employed in Sec. 27.2 that equation (36) may be generalized to three dimensions and a general source distribution to give

$$\frac{\partial \chi}{\partial \theta} = \nabla^2 \chi(\mathbf{r},\theta) + T(\mathbf{r},\theta) \tag{63}$$

where it is assumed that the form of the function $T(\mathbf{r},\theta)$ is prescribed by the known sources of neutrons in the material. In this section we shall consider the solution of this equation under certain boundary conditions.

Case 1: *Point source in an infinite medium.* We shall begin by considering the slowing-down density in an infinite medium when a point source is present. For simplicity we shall take the origin of coordinates at this point. Equation (63) then assumes the form

$$\frac{\partial \chi}{\partial \theta} = \frac{\partial^2 \chi}{\partial x^2} + \frac{\partial^2 \chi}{\partial y^2} + \frac{\partial^2 \chi}{\partial z^2} + \delta(x)\delta(y)\delta(z)S(\theta)$$

Multiplying both sides of this equation by $\exp[i(\xi x + \eta y + \zeta z)]$ and integrating throughout the entire space, we find that

$$\frac{d\bar{\chi}}{d\theta} = -\rho^2 \bar{\chi} + \left(\frac{1}{2\pi}\right)^{\frac{3}{2}} S(\theta) \tag{64}$$

where $\varrho = (\xi, \eta, \zeta)$ and $\bar{\chi}$ denotes the three-dimensional Fourier transform

$$\bar{\chi} = \left(\frac{1}{2\pi}\right)^{\frac{3}{2}} \int_{-\infty}^{\infty} \int_{-\infty}^{\infty} \int_{-\infty}^{\infty} \chi(\mathbf{r},\theta) e^{i(\varrho \cdot \mathbf{r})} \, dx \, dy \, dz$$

The solution of this equation is readily shown to be

$$\bar{\chi}(\varrho,\theta) = \left(\frac{1}{2\pi}\right)^{\frac{3}{2}} \int_0^\theta S(\theta') e^{-\rho^2(\theta-\theta')} \, d\theta'$$

so that inverting by the rule (111), Chap. 1, we find that

$$\chi(\mathbf{r},\theta) = \frac{1}{8\pi^3} \int_0^\theta S(\theta') d\theta' \int_{-\infty}^{\infty} \int_{-\infty}^{\infty} \int_{-\infty}^{\infty} e^{-\rho^2(\theta-\theta')-i(\varrho \cdot \mathbf{r})} \, d\xi \, d\eta \, d\zeta$$

Making use of the integral

$$\int_{-\infty}^{\infty} e^{-\xi^2 \theta - i\xi x} \, d\xi = \left(\frac{\pi}{\theta}\right)^{\frac{1}{2}} e^{-x^2/4\theta}$$

we see that the slowing-down density is

$$\chi(\mathbf{r},\theta) = \int_0^\theta \frac{S(\theta') e^{-r^2/4(\theta-\theta')} \, d\theta'}{[4\pi(\theta - \theta')]^{\frac{3}{2}}}$$

In the case $S(\theta) = \delta(\theta)$, this gives the solution

$$\chi(\mathbf{r},\theta) = \left(\frac{1}{4\pi\theta}\right)^{\frac{3}{2}} e^{-r^2/4\theta} \tag{65}$$

From equation (43) we see that, if $\chi(z,\theta)$ is the neutron density due to a plane source,

$$-\frac{1}{2\pi r}\left[\frac{d}{dz}\chi(z,\theta)\right]_{z=r} = \left(\frac{1}{4\pi\theta}\right)^{\frac{3}{2}} e^{-r^2/4\theta}$$

which is identical with the solution for a point source.

From the solution (65) we see that, in the case of a spherically symmetrical point source, the mean square distance, from the source, of neutrons of symbolic age θ is $\langle r^2\rangle_{\mathrm{av}} = 6\theta$, illustrating the relation $\langle r^2\rangle_{\mathrm{av}} = 3\langle z^2\rangle_{\mathrm{av}}$.

Case 2: Slowing-down density in an infinite pile. We shall now consider the variation of the slowing-down density in the infinite slab of material bounded by the planes $x = 0,a$; $y = 0,b$; $z = \pm\infty$ (cf. Fig. 38). We shall assume the approximate boundary condition that this density vanishes on the plane faces of the pile and shall suppose that $T(\mathbf{r},\theta)$ may be written in the form

$$T(\mathbf{r},\theta) = S(x,y,z)U(\theta) \tag{66}$$

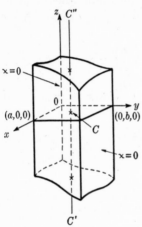

FIG. 38. The infinite pile $0 \le x \le a, 0 \le y \le b, -\infty \le z \le \infty$.

Substituting from equation (66) into equation (63), multiplying throughout by $e^{i\xi z}$ sin $(m\pi x/a)$ sin $(n\pi y/b)$, and integrating throughout the volume of the pile, we see that

$$\frac{d\bar{\chi}}{d\theta} + \left(\xi^2 + \frac{m^2\pi^2}{a^2} + \frac{n^2\pi^2}{b^2}\right)\bar{\chi} = \bar{S}(\xi,m,n)U(\theta) \tag{67}$$

where $\bar{\chi}(\xi,m,n)$ and $\bar{S}(\xi,m,n)$ denote the transforms

$$\bar{\chi}(\xi,m,n) = \frac{1}{\sqrt{2\pi}}\int_0^a dx \int_0^b dy \int_{-\infty}^\infty dz\,\chi(x,y,z)e^{i\xi z}\sin\left(\frac{m\pi x}{a}\right)\sin\left(\frac{n\pi y}{b}\right)$$

$$\bar{S}(\xi,m,n) = \frac{1}{\sqrt{2\pi}}\int_0^a dx \int_0^b dy \int_{-\infty}^\infty dz\,S(x,y,z)e^{i\xi z}\sin\left(\frac{m\pi x}{a}\right)\sin\left(\frac{n\pi y}{b}\right)$$

The solution of equation (67) is readily shown to be

$$\bar{\chi} = \bar{S}(\xi,m,n)\int^\theta U(\theta')\exp\left[-\left(\xi^2 + \frac{m^2\pi^2}{a^2} + \frac{n^2\pi^2}{b^2}\right)(\theta - \theta')\right]d\theta'$$

so that, making use of Theorems 9 and 28, we find that

$$\chi(x,y,z,\theta) = \frac{2}{ab} \sqrt{\frac{2}{\pi}} \sum_{n=1}^{\infty} \sum_{m=1}^{\infty} \sin\left(\frac{m\pi x}{a}\right) \sin\left(\frac{n\pi y}{b}\right)$$

$$\times \int_0^\theta U(\theta')d\theta' \int_{-\infty}^{\infty} e^{-i\xi z}\, d\xi\, \bar{S}(\xi,m,n) e^{-(\xi^2+m^2\pi^2/a^2+n^2\pi^2/b^2)(\theta-\theta')} \quad (68)$$

If the source is a point source at the point (x',y',z'), then we may take $S(x,y,z) = \delta(x - x')\delta(y - y')\delta(z - z')$, from which it follows that

$$\bar{S}(\xi,m,n) = (2\pi)^{-\frac{1}{2}}e^{i\xi z'} \sin\left(\frac{m\pi x'}{a}\right) \sin\left(\frac{n\pi y'}{b}\right)$$

The substitution of this expression in the general solution leads to the result

$$\chi(x,y,z,\theta) = \frac{2}{\sqrt{\pi}\, ab} \sum_{m=1}^{\infty} \sum_{n=1}^{\infty} \sin\left(\frac{m\pi x}{a}\right) \sin\left(\frac{m\pi x'}{a}\right) \sin\left(\frac{n\pi y}{b}\right) \sin\left(\frac{n\pi y'}{b}\right)$$

$$\times \int_0^\theta \frac{U(\theta')d\theta'}{(\theta - \theta')^{\frac{1}{2}}} \exp\left[-\left(\frac{m^2\pi^2}{a^2} + \frac{n^2\pi^2}{b^2}\right)(\theta - \theta') - \frac{(z - z')^2}{4(\theta - \theta')}\right]$$

In particular, if the point source is situated at the geometrical center C of the pile, we may take $x' = \frac{1}{2}a$, $y' = \frac{1}{2}b$, $z' = 0$, to obtain the solution

$$\chi(x,y,z,\theta) = \frac{2}{\sqrt{\pi}\, ab} \sum_{r=1}^{\infty} \sum_{s=1}^{\infty} \sin\left[\frac{(2r + 1)\pi x}{a}\right] \sin\left[\frac{(2s + 1)\pi y}{b}\right]$$

$$\times (-1)^{r+s} \int_0^\theta \frac{U(\theta')d\theta'}{(\theta - \theta')^{\frac{1}{2}}} \exp\left\{-\left[\frac{(2r + 1)^2\pi^2}{a^2} + \frac{(2s + 1)^2\pi^2}{b^2}\right](\theta - \theta') - \frac{z^2}{4(\theta - \theta')}\right\} \quad (69)$$

On the other hand, if the source of neutrons is a line source parallel to the axis $C'C''$ of the pile, we may write $S(x,y,z) = \delta(x - x')\delta(y - y')$, of which the required transform is

$$\bar{S}(\xi,m,n) = (2\pi)^{\frac{1}{2}}\delta(\xi) \sin\left(\frac{m\pi x'}{a}\right) \sin\left(\frac{n\pi y'}{b}\right)$$

Substituting this expression in equation (68) and performing the integration with respect to ξ, we obtain the solution

$$\chi(x,y,z,\theta) = \frac{4}{ab} \sum_{m=1}^{\infty} \sum_{n=1}^{\infty} \sin\left(\frac{m\pi x'}{a}\right) \sin\left(\frac{m\pi x}{a}\right) \sin\left(\frac{n\pi y}{b}\right) \sin\left(\frac{n\pi y'}{b}\right)$$

$$\times \int_0^\theta U(\theta')d\theta' \exp\left[-\left(\frac{m^2\pi^2}{a^2} + \frac{n^2\pi^2}{b^2}\right)(\theta - \theta')\right]$$

In the special case in which the line source coincides with the axis of the pile this formula reduces to the simpler form

$$\chi(x,y,z,\theta) = \frac{4}{ab} \sum_{r=1}^{\infty} \sum_{s=1}^{\infty} (-1)^{r+s} \sin\left[\frac{(2r+1)\pi x}{a}\right] \sin\left[\frac{(2s+1)\pi y}{b}\right]$$

$$\times \int_0^\theta U(\theta')d\theta' \exp\left\{-\left[\frac{(2r+1)^2\pi^2}{a^2} + \frac{(2s+1)^2\pi^2}{b^2}\right](\theta-\theta')\right\}$$

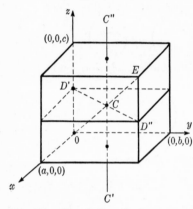

Fig. 39. The finite pile $0 \le x \le a$, $0 \le y \le b$, $0 \le z \le c$.

We could have established this result by taking the two-dimensional form of equation (63) and choosing $T(\mathbf{r},\theta)$ to be $\delta(x - x')\delta(y - y')U(\theta)$.

Case 3: Case of a finite pile. We consider now the solution of equation (63) in the case where

$$T(\mathbf{r},\theta) = S(x,y,z)\delta(\theta) \qquad (70)$$

and the absorbing material is in the form of the rectangular parallelepiped $0 \le x \le a, 0 \le y \le b, 0 \le z \le c$ (cf. Fig. 39). As in the previous cases in this section we assume that the boundary condition is that the slowing-down density vanishes on the faces of the pile. We therefore have to solve the equation

$$\frac{\partial \chi}{\partial \theta} = \nabla^2\chi + S(x,y,z)\delta(\theta) \qquad (71)$$

subject to the boundary conditions

$$\chi = 0 \qquad \text{on } x = 0,a;\ y = 0,b;\ z = 0,c \qquad (72)$$

If we introduce the Fourier triple finite sine transform,

$$\bar{\chi}(m,n,q) = \int_0^a dx \int_0^b dy \int_0^c dz\, \chi(x,y,z,\theta) \sin\left(\frac{m\pi x}{a}\right) \sin\left(\frac{n\pi y}{b}\right) \sin\left(\frac{q\pi z}{c}\right)$$

$$(73)$$

then, because of the conditions (72), we see that equation (71) is equivalent to

$$\frac{d\bar{\chi}}{d\theta} + \mu_{mnq}^2\bar{\chi} = \bar{S}(m,n,q)\delta(\theta)$$

with $\mu_{mnq}^2 = \pi^2(m^2/a^2 + n^2/b^2 + q^2/c^2)$, and in which $\bar{S}(m,n,q)$ is the transform of $S(x,y,z)$. The solution of this ordinary differential equation is

$$\bar{\chi}(m,n,q,\theta) = \bar{S}(m,n,q,\theta)e^{-\mu^2_{mnq}\theta}$$

so that, inverting the result by means of Theorem 29, we obtain the expression

$$\chi(x,y,z,\theta) = \frac{8}{abc} \sum_{m=1}^{\infty} \sum_{n=1}^{\infty} \sum_{q=1}^{\infty} \bar{S}e^{-\mu^2_{mnq}\theta} \sin\left(\frac{m\pi x}{a}\right) \sin\left(\frac{n\pi y}{b}\right)$$

$$\times \sin\left(\frac{q\pi z}{c}\right) \quad (74)$$

for the slowing-down density.

We shall now consider the form of this solution for two simple examples of source function $S(x,y,z)$.

Example 1. If the source of neutrons is a plane source in the plane $z = z'$, then $S(x,y,z) = S_0(x,y)\delta(z - z')$ and $\bar{S}(m,n,q)$ reduces to $\bar{S}_0(m,n)$ $\sin(q\pi z'/c)$, where

$$\bar{S}_0(m,n) = \int_0^a \int_0^b S_0(x,y) \sin\left(\frac{m\pi x}{a}\right) \sin\left(\frac{n\pi y}{b}\right) dx\, dy$$

Example 2. On the other hand, if the source of neutrons is a point source at the point (x',y',z') within the pile, then

$$S(x,y,z) = S_0\delta(x - x')\delta(y - y')\delta(z - z')$$

so that

$$\bar{S}(m,n,q) = S_0 \sin\left(\frac{m\pi x'}{a}\right) \sin\left(\frac{n\pi y'}{b}\right) \sin\left(\frac{q\pi z'}{c}\right)$$

Substituting this expression in equation (74), we obtain for the slowing-down density

$$\chi(x,y,z,\theta) = \frac{8S_0}{abc} \sum_{m=1}^{\infty} \sum_{n=1}^{\infty} \sum_{q=1}^{\infty} e^{-\mu^2_{mnq}\theta} \sin\left(\frac{m\pi x'}{a}\right) \sin\left(\frac{m\pi x}{a}\right)$$

$$\times \sin\left(\frac{n\pi y'}{b}\right) \sin\left(\frac{n\pi y}{b}\right) \sin\left(\frac{q\pi z'}{c}\right) \sin\left(\frac{q\pi z}{c}\right)$$

In particular, if the source is at the center C of the pile,

$$\chi(x,y,z,\theta) = \frac{8S_0}{abc} \sum_{r=0}^{\infty} \sum_{s=0}^{\infty} \sum_{t=0}^{\infty} (-1)^{r+s+t} \sin\left[\frac{(2r + 1)\pi x}{a}\right]$$

$$\times \sin\left[\frac{(2s + 1)\pi y}{b}\right] \sin\left[\frac{(2t + 1)\pi z}{c}\right] \exp\left\{-\pi^2\theta\left[\frac{(2r + 1)^2}{a^2} + \frac{(2s + 1)^2}{b^2}\right.\right.$$

$$\left.\left. + \frac{(2t + 1)^2}{c^2}\right]\right\} \quad (75)$$

Let us now consider, in more detail, the form of the solution (75) in the case of a pile of cubical form, the half length of each side of which is $(\langle r^2 \rangle_{\rm av})^{\frac{1}{2}}$ for an infinite medium. Then, by the results of Sec. 27.5 we have $a = b = c = 2(6\theta)^{\frac{1}{2}}$.

Along the axis $C'C''$ of the pile, $x = (6\theta)^{\frac{1}{2}}$, $y = (6\theta)^{\frac{1}{2}}$, $z = \rho\theta^{\frac{1}{2}}$, where ρ is a dimensionless parameter. The slowing-down density is seen from equation (75) to be $S_0\phi_1/\theta^{\frac{3}{2}}$, where

$$\phi_1(\rho) = \frac{1}{6\sqrt{6}} \sum_{r=0}^{\infty} \sum_{s=0}^{\infty} \sum_{t=0}^{\infty} (-1)^t E \sin\left(\frac{2t+1}{2\sqrt{6}} \pi\rho\right) \qquad (75a)$$

and

$$E = \exp\left\{-\frac{\pi^2}{24}[(2r+1)^2 + (2s+1)^2 + (2t+1)^2]\right\}$$

Similarly, along a diagonal of the cross-section plane through the source $(D'CD'')$ we may take $x = \rho(\theta/2)^{\frac{1}{2}}$, $y = \rho(\theta/2)^{\frac{1}{2}}$, $z = \frac{1}{2}c$, so that the slowing-down density is given by equation (75) in the form $S_0\phi_2/\theta^{\frac{3}{2}}$, where

$$\phi_2(\rho) = \frac{1}{6\sqrt{6}} \sum_{r=0}^{\infty} \sum_{s=0}^{\infty} \sum_{t=0}^{\infty} (-1)^{r+s} E \sin\left[\frac{(2r+1)\pi\rho}{4\sqrt{3}}\right] \sin\left[\frac{(2s+1)\pi\rho}{4\sqrt{3}}\right]$$
$$(75b)$$

Finally, since along the diagonal OCE of the cube we may write

$$x = y = z = \rho(\theta/3)^{\frac{1}{2}}$$

we see, from equation (75), that the slowing-down density is $S_0\phi_3/\theta^{\frac{3}{2}}$, where ϕ_3 is given by the equation

$$\phi_3(\rho) = \frac{1}{6\sqrt{6}} \sum_{r=0}^{\infty} \sum_{s=0}^{\infty} \sum_{t=0}^{\infty} (-1)^{r+s+t} E \sin\left[\frac{(2r+1)\pi\rho}{6\sqrt{2}}\right]$$
$$\times \sin\left[\frac{(2s+1)\pi\rho}{6\sqrt{2}}\right] \sin\left[\frac{(2t+1)\pi\rho}{6\sqrt{2}}\right] \qquad (75c)$$

The variation of the functions ϕ_1, ϕ_2, and ϕ_3 with the dimensionless variable ρ is shown in Fig. 40.[1]

27.6 Problems with spherical symmetry. In this section we shall consider two problems in which the slowing-down density and the source function T are functions of $r = (x^2 + y^2 + z^2)^{\frac{1}{2}}$ alone. In this instance equation (63) assumes the form

$$\frac{\partial\chi}{\partial\theta} = \frac{1}{r^2} \frac{\partial}{\partial r}\left(r^2 \frac{\partial\chi}{\partial r}\right) + S(r)\delta(\theta)$$

---

[1] The numerical data on which Figs. 40 to 43 are based are taken from the report by Wallace and LeCaine, *op. cit.*

which may be written as

$$\frac{\partial(r\chi)}{\partial\theta} = \frac{\partial^2}{\partial r^2}(r\chi) + rS(r)\delta(\theta) \tag{76}$$

If we suppose that the medium is bounded by the spherical surface $r = a$

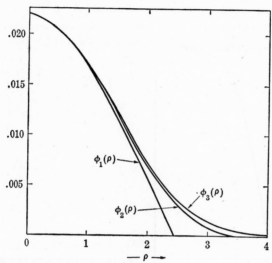

FIG. 40.   Variation of the slowing-down density along the lines $C'CC''$, $D'CD''$, OCE of the finite pile.

and that the slowing-down density vanishes there, we may solve the equation (76) by introducing the finite Fourier sine transform

$$\bar{\phi}_s(n) = \int_0^a r\chi(r) \sin\left(\frac{n\pi r}{a}\right) dr \tag{77}$$

If, similarly, we define $\bar{T}_s(n)$ to be

$$\int_0^a rS(r) \sin\left(\frac{n\pi r}{a}\right) dr$$

it follows, at once, by making use of the condition that $r\chi(r)$ vanishes when $r = a$ that equation (76) is equivalent to

$$\frac{d\bar{\phi}_s}{d\theta} + \frac{n^2\pi^2}{a^2}\bar{\phi}_s = \bar{T}_s(n)\delta(\theta)$$

The solution of this equation is readily seen to be

$$\bar{\phi}_s(n) = \bar{T}_s(n)e^{-n^2\pi^2\theta/a^2}$$

so that, inverting equation (77) by Theorem 27, we find for the slowing-down density

$$\chi(r,\theta) = \frac{2}{ar} \sum_{n=1}^{\infty} \sin\left(\frac{n\pi r}{a}\right) e^{-n^2\pi^2\theta/a^2} \int_0^a \rho S(\rho) \sin\left(\frac{n\pi\rho}{a}\right) d\rho \qquad (78)$$

Case 1: *Point source at the center of a sphere.* If the source function $S(r)$ is that appropriate to a point source at the center of the sphere, then

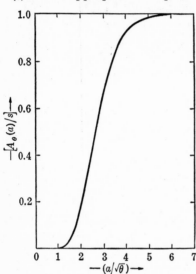

$$S(\rho) = S\delta(\rho)/4\pi\rho^2, \text{ so that}$$

$$\int_0^a \rho S(\rho) \sin\left(\frac{n\pi\rho}{a}\right) d\rho = \frac{nS}{4a}$$

and it follows from equation (78) that

$$\chi(r,\theta) = \frac{S}{2a^2 r} \sum_{n=1}^{\infty} n \sin$$

$$\times \left(\frac{n\pi r}{a}\right) e^{-n^2\pi^2\theta/a^2}$$

As a result we see that the total number of neutrons, in the sphere, passing symbolic age θ per unit time is

$$A_\theta(a) = \int_0^a 4\pi r^2 \, dr \, \chi(r,\theta) = 2S$$

$$\times \sum_{n=1}^{\infty} (-1)^{n+1} e^{-n^2\pi^2\theta/a^2} \qquad (79)$$

FIG. 41.   The variation with the radius of the total number of neutrons in a sphere passing symbolic age θ per unit time.

The variation of this function $A_\theta(a)$ with the radius a of the sphere is shown in Fig. 41.

Case 2: *Concentric spherical shell source.* If the source of neutrons is a spherical shell source, we may take $S(\rho) = S\,\delta(\rho - b)/4\pi b^2$, where the shell has radius b lying between 0 and a. For this function,

$$\bar{T}_s(n) = \frac{S}{4\pi b} \sin\left(\frac{n\pi b}{a}\right)$$

so that it follows from equation (78) that

$$\chi(r,\theta) = \frac{S}{2\pi abr} \sum_{n=1}^{\infty} \sin\left(\frac{n\pi b}{a}\right) \sin\left(\frac{n\pi r}{a}\right) e^{-n^2\pi^2\theta/a^2} \qquad (80)$$

Case 3: Infinite medium with spherical cavity: point source at the center of the cavity. Since, in this case, the actual source is not in the medium, we must first determine the effective sources over the surface of the cavity. If we assume the radius of the cavity to be a, then, as a first approximation, these are obviously given by

$$\frac{S\ \delta(r-a)}{4\pi a^2}$$

if $S\ \delta(r)$ is the source at the center of the sphere. The boundary conditions are that χ should tend to zero as $r \to \infty$ and that $\partial\chi/\partial r = 0$ when $r = a$. The differential equation to be solved is

$$\frac{\partial(r\chi)}{\partial\theta} = \frac{\partial^2(r\chi)}{\partial r^2} + \frac{S}{4\pi a}\,\delta(r-a)\delta(\theta)$$

since $r\,\delta(r-a) = a\,\delta(r-a)$. If we let $f = r\chi$, $x = r - a$, then

$$\left.\begin{array}{ll} f \to 0 & \text{as } x \to \infty \\[2mm] \dfrac{\partial f}{\partial x} - \dfrac{f}{a} = 0 & \text{if } x = 0 \end{array}\right\} \tag{81}$$

where f satisfies the equation

$$\frac{\partial f}{\partial\theta} = \frac{\partial^2 f}{\partial x^2} + \frac{S}{4\pi a}\,\delta(x)\delta(\theta) \tag{81a}$$

To solve the partial differential equation (81a) subject to the boundary conditions (81), we make use of the inversion theorem introduced in Sec. 23.4, equations (43) and (44). Define a function $\bar{f}(\alpha,\theta)$ by the equation

$$\bar{f}(\alpha,\theta) = \int_0^\infty f(x,\theta)K(\alpha,x)dx$$

where

$$K(\alpha,x) = \sqrt{\frac{2}{\pi}}\,\frac{\alpha\cos(\alpha x) + a^{-1}\sin(\alpha x)}{(\alpha^2 + a^{-2})^{\frac{1}{2}}}$$

Then, as a result of equation (81), it follows by integrating by parts that the transform $\bar{f}$ satisfies the differential equation

$$\frac{d\bar{f}}{d\theta} + \alpha^2\bar{f} = \frac{S\ \delta(\theta)}{4\pi a}\int_0^\infty K(\alpha,x)\delta(x)dx$$

$$= \frac{S\ \delta(\theta)}{4\pi a}\sqrt{\frac{2}{\pi}}\,\frac{\alpha}{(\alpha^2 + a^{-2})^{\frac{1}{2}}}$$

which has solution

$$\bar{f} = \frac{S}{4\pi a}\sqrt{\frac{2}{\pi}}\,\frac{\alpha e^{-\alpha^2\theta}}{(\alpha^2 + a^{-2})^{\frac{1}{2}}}$$

Now, by equation (44), Chap. 5, we have

$$f(x,\theta) = \int_0^\infty \bar{f}(\alpha,\theta)K(\alpha,x)d\alpha$$

so that

$$f(x,\theta) = \frac{S}{2\pi^2 a} \int_0^\infty \left[\frac{\alpha^2 \cos (\alpha x) + \alpha a^{-1} \sin (\alpha x)}{\alpha^2 + a^{-2}} \right] e^{-\alpha^2 \theta}\, d\alpha$$

which may be written in the form

$$f(x,\theta) = \frac{S}{2\pi^2 a} \left[\int_0^\infty e^{-\alpha^2 \theta} \cos (\alpha x)d\alpha \right.$$
$$\left. + a^{-2} \int_0^\infty \frac{(a\alpha) \sin (\alpha x) - \cos (\alpha x)}{\alpha^2 + a^{-2}}\, e^{-\alpha^2 \theta}\, d\alpha \right] \quad (82)$$

If we write

$$f(x) = \frac{1}{\sqrt{2\theta}}\, e^{-x^2/4\theta}, \qquad g(x) = \frac{1}{b}\sqrt{\frac{\pi}{2}}\, e^{-bx}$$

then their cosine transforms are

$$F_c(p) = e^{-\theta p^2}, \qquad G_c(p) = (b^2 + p^2)^{-1}$$

so that, by equation (43), Chap. 1,

$$\int_0^\infty \frac{e^{-\theta p^2} \cos (px)}{b^2 + p^2}\, dp = \frac{1}{4b}\sqrt{\frac{\pi}{\theta}} \int_0^\infty [e^{-b\eta-(\eta-x)^2/4\theta} + e^{-b\eta-(\eta+x)^2/4\theta}]d\eta$$

Now

$$b\eta + \frac{(\eta \pm x)^2}{4\theta} = \left(\frac{\eta}{2\sqrt{\theta}} + b\sqrt{\theta} \pm \frac{x}{2\sqrt{\theta}} \right)^2 - \left(b\sqrt{\theta} \pm \frac{x}{2\sqrt{\theta}} \right)^2 + \frac{x^2}{4\theta}$$

so that making use of the result

$$\int_0^\infty e^{-(\alpha\eta+\beta)^2}\, d\eta = \frac{1}{\alpha} \int_\beta^\infty e^{-u^2}\, du = \frac{\sqrt{\pi}}{2\alpha} (1 - \operatorname{erf} \beta)$$

we find that

$$\int_0^\infty \frac{e^{-\theta p^2} \cos (px)dp}{b^2 + p^2}$$
$$= \frac{\pi}{4b}\, e^{-x^2/4\theta} \left\{ \exp\left(b\sqrt{\theta} - \frac{x}{2\sqrt{\theta}} \right)^2 \left[1 - \operatorname{erf}\left(b\sqrt{\theta} - \frac{x}{2\sqrt{\theta}} \right) \right] \right.$$
$$\left. + \exp\left(b\sqrt{\theta} + \frac{x}{2\sqrt{\theta}} \right)^2 \left[1 - \operatorname{erf}\left(b\sqrt{\theta} + \frac{x}{2\sqrt{\theta}} \right) \right] \right\}$$

Similarly by considering the pairs $f(x) = (2\theta)^{-\frac{1}{2}}e^{-x^2/4\theta}$, $F_c(p) = e^{-\theta p^2}$,

$g(x) = (\pi/2)^{\frac{1}{2}}e^{-bx}$, $G_s(p) = p(b^2 + p^2)^{-1}$ in equation (44), Chap. 1, we obtain the result

$$\int_0^\infty \frac{pe^{-\theta p^2}\sin{(px)}}{p^2 + b^2}\,dp$$

$$= \frac{\pi}{4}\,e^{-x^2/4\theta}\left\{\exp\left(b\,\sqrt{\theta} - \frac{x}{2\,\sqrt{\theta}}\right)^2\left[1 - \operatorname{erf}\left(b\,\sqrt{\theta} - \frac{x}{2\,\sqrt{\theta}}\right)\right]\right.$$

$$\left. - \exp\left(b\,\sqrt{\theta} + \frac{x}{2\,\sqrt{\theta}}\right)^2\left[1 - \operatorname{erf}\left(b\,\sqrt{\theta} + \frac{x}{2\,\sqrt{\theta}}\right)\right]\right\}$$

Substituting these results and the integral

$$\int_0^\infty e^{-\alpha^2\theta}\cos{(\alpha x)}d\alpha = \frac{1}{2}\sqrt{\frac{\pi}{\theta}}\,e^{-x^2/4\theta}$$

in equation (82), we have

$$f(x,\theta) = \frac{Se^{-x^2/4\theta}}{2\pi^2 a}\left\{\frac{1}{2}\sqrt{\frac{\pi}{\theta}} - \frac{\pi}{2a}\exp\left(\frac{x}{2\,\sqrt{\theta}} + \frac{\sqrt{\theta}}{a}\right)^2\right.$$

$$\left. \times\left[1 - \operatorname{erf}\left(\frac{x}{2\,\sqrt{\theta}} + \frac{\sqrt{\theta}}{a}\right)\right]\right\}$$

Reverting to the original variables r and χ, we obtain the solution

$$\chi(r,\theta) = \frac{Se^{-(r-a)^2/4\theta}}{4ar(\pi^3\theta)^{\frac{1}{2}}}\left\{1 - \frac{\sqrt{\pi\theta}}{a}\exp\left(\frac{r-a}{2\,\sqrt{\theta}} + \frac{\sqrt{\theta}}{a}\right)^2\right.$$

$$\left. \times\left[1 - \operatorname{erf}\left(\frac{r-a}{2\,\sqrt{\theta}} + \frac{\sqrt{\theta}}{a}\right)\right]\right\} \quad (83)$$

The asymptotic behavior of the slowing-down density at great distances from the surface of the cavity may be obtained from equation (83) by means of the asymptotic expansion

$$\operatorname{erf}{(x)} \simeq 1 - \frac{e^{-x^2}}{x\,\sqrt{\pi}}$$

for the error function. If $r - a \gg 2\theta^{\frac{1}{2}}$, this gives

$$\chi(r,\theta) \simeq \frac{Se^{-(r-a)^2/4\theta}}{(4\pi\theta)^{\frac{3}{2}}}\,\frac{1}{1 + \dfrac{(r-a)a}{2\theta}}$$

The variation of the slowing-down density with r and with the radius of the cavity is shown in Fig. 42, in which is plotted the dimensionless quantity $\chi\theta^{\frac{1}{2}}/S$ as a function of $(r - a)/\theta^{\frac{1}{2}}$ for the values 0, 0.25, 1, 2, and

4 of the ratio $a/\theta^{\frac{1}{2}}$. When the radius of the cavity is zero ($a\theta^{-\frac{1}{2}} = 0$), the curve is Gaussian in shape. For the remaining values of a the curves have a nonzero slope at the surface of the cavity and behave like

$$\frac{\text{Const.}}{r - a} \exp\left[-\frac{(r - a)^2}{4\theta} \right]$$

for large values of r.

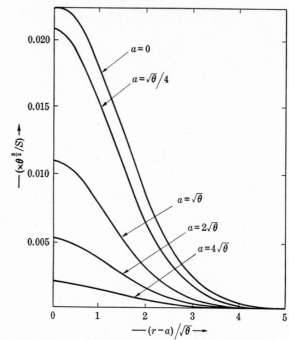

Fig. 42. The variation of the slowing-down density in the vicinity of a spherical cavity with a point source at its center.

The number of neutrons with radius vector between r and $r + dr$ is proportional to $r^2\chi(r,\theta)$. Figure 43 shows the variation of this function for the values of $a\theta^{-\frac{1}{2}}$ cited above. It will be observed that each of these curves has a maximum which is nearer to the boundary of the cavity the larger the radius of the cavity is. In the case of zero radius the maximum is given by $r = 2\theta^{\frac{1}{2}}$.

27.7 Two different slowing-down media.[1] In the problems considered in the above sections we have applied the age theory to problems involving one homogeneous slowing-down medium. In this section we shall con-

[1] Cf. Marshak, *op. cit.*, pp. 218–221, and R. Bellman, R. E. Marshak, and G. M. Wing, *Phil. Mag.*, **40**, 297 (1949).

sider the case of two media separated by a plane interface in order to exhibit the boundary conditions which obtain at the interface between two different slowing-down media, and also to illustrate the simultaneous

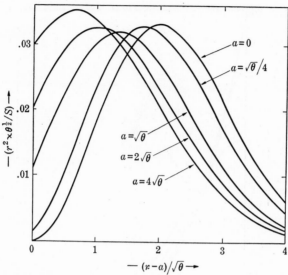

FIG. 43.   The variation of $r^2\chi$ in the neighborhood of a spherical cavity containing a point source at its center.

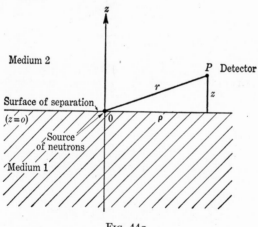

FIG. 44a.

use of Laplace and Hankel transforms in problems of neutron aging in which there is axial symmetry. The problem we shall consider is that of determining the slowing-down density everywhere in the media when there is a point source of fast monoenergetic neutrons situated at the interface between two semiinfinite media which possess different slowing-down properties (cf. Fig. 44a).   If we denote the two media by the suffixes 1 and 2 and the slowing-down densities in them by χ_1 and χ_2, then, taking the interface to be the plane $z = 0$ and the point source to

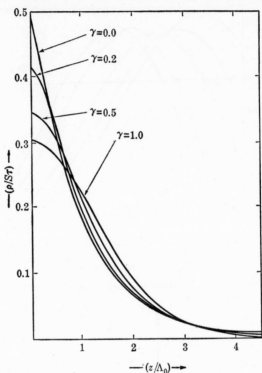

Fig. 44.   The density of thermal neutrons in an infinite solid when there is a source of strength S at $z = 0$.

be the origin of coordinates, we see that the equations governing the slowing-down density at every point are

$$\frac{\partial \chi_1}{\partial \theta_1} = \nabla^2 \chi_1 + \delta(x)\,\delta(y)\,\delta(z)\,\delta(\theta_1) \tag{84}$$

and

$$\frac{\partial \chi_2}{\partial \theta_2} = \nabla^2 \chi_2 + \delta(x)\,\delta(y)\,\delta(z)\,\delta(\theta_2) \tag{85}$$

where θ_1 and θ_2 are defined by the equations

$$\theta_{1,2} = \int_0^u \frac{L_{1,2}^2(u')\,du'}{3\xi_{1,2}(1 - \langle \cos \Theta_{1,2} \rangle_{\text{av}})} \tag{86}$$

To determine the conditions on the interface, we make use of the rela tion $\chi = \xi v N_0 / L$ between the neutron density N_0 and the slowing-down density χ to obtain the condition

$$\frac{L_1(u)\chi_1}{\xi_1} = \frac{L_2(u)\chi_2}{\xi_2} \qquad \text{on } z = 0 \qquad (87)$$

We now assume that the mean free paths $L_1(u)$ and $L_2(u)$ vary arbitrarily but in such a way that their ratio remains constant. With this assumption we introduce two constants D and Δ which are defined by the equations

$$D = \frac{L_2^2(u)}{L_1^2(u)} \frac{\xi_1(1 - \langle\cos\Theta_1\rangle_{\text{av}})}{\xi_2(1 - \langle\cos\Theta_2\rangle_{\text{av}})}$$

$$\Delta = \frac{\xi_1(1 - \langle\cos\Theta_2\rangle_{\text{av}})}{\xi_2(1 - \langle\cos\Theta_1\rangle_{\text{av}})}$$

From equation (86) we then have $\theta_2 = D\theta_1$ so that, using the relation $\delta(\theta_1) = \delta(\theta_2/D) = D\,\delta(\theta_2)$, we see that equation (84) may be written in the form

$$D \frac{\partial\chi_1}{\partial\theta_2} = \nabla^2\chi_1 + D\,\delta(x)\delta(y)\delta(z)\delta(\theta_2) \qquad (88)$$

We now transform equations (85) and (88) to cylindrical polar coordinates ρ and z. Writing $\delta(x)\delta(y)\delta(z) = \delta(\rho)\delta(z)/2\pi\rho$, we see that they reduce to the forms

$$D \frac{\partial\chi_1}{\partial\theta_2} = \frac{1}{\rho}\frac{\partial}{\partial\rho}\left(\rho\frac{\partial\chi_1}{\partial\rho}\right) + \frac{\partial^2\chi_1}{\partial z^2} + \frac{D\,\delta(\rho)\delta(z)\delta(\theta_2)}{2\pi\rho}$$

$$\frac{\partial\chi_2}{\partial\theta_2} = \frac{1}{\rho}\frac{\partial}{\partial\rho}\left(\rho\frac{\partial\chi_2}{\partial\rho}\right) + \frac{\partial^2\chi_2}{\partial z^2} + \frac{\delta(\rho)\delta(z)\delta(\theta_2)}{2\pi\rho}$$

We now introduce the Laplace transforms

$$\phi_{1,2}(p) = \int_0^\infty \chi_{1,2}e^{-p\theta_2}\,d\theta_2$$

and write these equations in the equivalent forms

$$\left.\begin{array}{l} \dfrac{1}{\rho}\dfrac{\partial}{\partial\rho}\left(\rho\dfrac{\partial\phi_1}{\partial\rho}\right) + \dfrac{\partial^2\phi_1}{\partial z^2} = Dp\phi_1 - D\dfrac{\delta(\rho)\delta(z)}{2\pi\rho} \\[2mm] \dfrac{1}{\rho}\dfrac{\partial}{\partial\rho}\left(\rho\dfrac{\partial\phi_2}{\partial\rho}\right) + \dfrac{\partial^2\phi_2}{\partial z^2} = p\phi_2 - \dfrac{\delta(\rho)\delta(z)}{2\pi\rho} \end{array}\right\} \qquad (89)$$

From equation (87) we get the condition

$$\phi_1 = (D\Delta)^{\frac{1}{2}}\phi_2 \qquad \text{on } z = 0 \qquad (90)$$

and, integrating equation (88), we find that the boundary condition on $\partial\phi/\partial z$ is

$$\frac{\partial\phi_1}{\partial z} = D\frac{\partial\phi_2}{\partial z} + D\frac{\delta(\rho)}{2\pi\rho} \qquad \text{on } z = 0 \qquad (91)$$

Our problem is thus reduced to the solution of the pair of equations (89) subject to the conditions (90) and (91) and the further conditions that $\chi_2 \to 0$ as $z \to \infty$ and $\chi_1 \to 0$ as $z \to -\infty$. To solve this boundary value problem we make use of the Hankel transforms of order zero of the functions ϕ_1 and ϕ_2, defined by the equations

$$\bar{\phi}_{1,2}(\xi) = \int_0^\infty \rho J_0(\xi\rho)\phi_{1,2}(\rho)d\rho$$

Multiplying both sides of equations (89) by $\rho J_0(\xi\rho)$ and integrating with respect to ρ from 0 to ∞, we obtain the pair of ordinary differential equations

$$\frac{d^2\bar{\phi}_1}{dz^2} = (Dp + \xi^2)\bar{\phi}_1 - \frac{D}{2\pi}\delta(z), \qquad \frac{d^2\bar{\phi}_2}{dz^2} = (p + \xi^2)\bar{\phi}_2 - \frac{\delta(z)}{2\pi} \quad (92)$$

Similarly, equations (90) and (91) are transformed to

$$\bar{\phi}_1 = (D\Delta)^{\frac{1}{2}}\bar{\phi}_2, \qquad \frac{d\bar{\phi}_1}{dz} = D\frac{d\bar{\phi}_2}{dz} + \frac{D}{2\pi}, \quad \text{on } z = 0 \quad (93)$$

We may take the solutions of these equations to be

$$\bar{\phi}_1 = Ae^{(\xi^2+pD)^{\frac{1}{2}}z}, \qquad \bar{\phi}_2 = Be^{-(\xi^2+p)^{\frac{1}{2}}z}$$

where, as a consequence of the relations (93), A and B satisfy the equations

$$A = (D\Delta)^{\frac{1}{2}}B, \qquad (\xi^2 + pD)^{\frac{1}{2}}A + D(\xi^2 + p)^{\frac{1}{2}}B = \frac{D}{2\pi}$$

so that they are given by the expressions

$$A = \frac{D\Delta^{\frac{1}{2}}}{2\pi} \frac{1}{\{[\Delta(\xi^2 + pD)]^{\frac{1}{2}} + [D(\xi^2 + p)]^{\frac{1}{2}}\}}, \qquad B = (D\Delta)^{-\frac{1}{2}}A$$

Making use of the Laplace and Hankel inversion theorems (Theorems 1 and 19) in succession, we see that χ_1 and χ_2 are related to the functions $\bar{\phi}_1$ and $\bar{\phi}_2$, which we have just determined, by the equations

$$\chi_{1,2} = \frac{1}{2\pi i} \int_{c-i\infty}^{c+i\infty} e^{p\theta_2}\,dp \int_0^\infty \xi J_0(\xi\rho)d\xi\,\bar{\phi}_{1,2}(p,\xi)$$

Therefore, the expressions for the slowing-down density are

$$\chi_1 = \frac{D\Delta^{\frac{1}{2}}}{4\pi^2 i} \int_{c-i\infty}^{c+i\infty} e^{p\theta_2}\,dp \int_0^\infty \frac{\xi J_0(\xi\rho)e^{(\xi^2+pD)^{\frac{1}{2}}z}\,d\xi}{[\Delta(\xi^2 + pD)]^{\frac{1}{2}} + [D(\xi^2 + p)]^{\frac{1}{2}}} \quad (94$$

and

$$\chi_2 = \frac{D^{\frac{1}{2}}}{4\pi^2 i} \int_{c-i\infty}^{c+i\infty} e^{p\theta_2}\,dp \int_0^\infty \frac{\xi J_0(\xi\rho)e^{-(\xi^2+p)^{\frac{1}{2}}z}\,d\xi}{[\Delta(\xi^2 + pD)]^{\frac{1}{2}} + [D(\xi^2 + p)]^{\frac{1}{2}}} \quad (95$$

The evaluation of the double integrals (94) and (95) may be carried out for arbitrary values of $D, \Delta, \rho,$ and z. To illustrate the method, we shall consider only the limiting case in which $\Delta = 1$ and $z = 0$. We then have

$$\chi_2(\rho,0,\theta_2) = \frac{1}{(1 - 1/D)4\pi^2 i} \int_{c-i\infty}^{c+i\infty} e^{p\theta_2}\,dp \int_0^\infty \frac{J_0(\xi\rho)d\xi}{\xi}\left[(\xi^2 + p)^{\frac{1}{2}} - \left(\frac{\xi^2}{D} + p\right)^{\frac{1}{2}} \right]$$

Making use of the integrals

$$\frac{1}{2\pi i}\int_{c-i\infty}^{c+i\infty} e^{p\theta_2}\,dp \left[(\xi^2 + p)^{\frac{1}{2}} - \left(\frac{\xi^2}{D} + p\right)^{\frac{1}{2}} \right] = \frac{1}{2(\pi\theta_2^3)^{\frac{1}{2}}}(e^{-\xi^2\theta_2/D} - e^{-\xi^2\theta_2})$$

and

$$\int_0^\infty \xi e^{-\theta_2\xi^2}J_0(\xi\rho)d\xi = \frac{1}{2\theta_2}e^{-\rho^2/4\theta_2}$$

we find after a little manipulation that

$$\chi_2(\rho,0,\theta_2) = \frac{1}{(4\pi\theta_2)^{\frac{3}{2}}(1 - 1/D)}\left[Ei\left(-\frac{\rho^2 D}{4\theta_2}\right) - Ei\left(-\frac{\rho^2}{4\theta_2}\right) \right] \quad (96)$$

where $Ei(x)$ is the exponential integral function

$$-Ei(-x) = \int_x^\infty e^{-t}\frac{dt}{t} \qquad 0 < x < \infty$$

Making use of Taylor's theorem, we see that when D is approximately equal to unity,

$$Ei\left(-\frac{\rho^2 D}{4\theta_2}\right) = Ei\left(-\frac{\rho^2}{4\theta_2}\right) + (D - 1)e^{-\rho^2/4\theta_2}$$

so that in the limit, as $D \to 1$, the solution (96) reduces to the expression for the slowing-down density corresponding to a point source in a homogeneous medium [equation (65)], namely

$$\chi_2(\rho,0,\theta_2) = \frac{1}{(4\pi\theta_2)^{\frac{3}{2}}}e^{-\rho^2/4\theta_2} \quad (96a)$$

Equation (96) gives the expression for the slowing-down density in the less dense of the two media for which the ratio of the densities is $(D)^{\frac{1}{2}}$. For small values of ρ the function (96) is greater than (96a) as is to be expected since the denser medium 1 enhances the slow neutron density in the less dense medium 2, through more efficient aging. On the other hand, for larger values of ρ the function (96) is less than (96a) for a given value of the symbolic age θ_2, showing that the greater aging in medium 1 carries a greater percentage of neutrons beyond the symbolic age θ_2 as compared with the situation when only the medium 2 is present.

27.8 Effects of capture and of time variation. The problems we have just been considering were solved on the basis of absence of capture and time variations. We shall now consider briefly the modifications we must make to our basic age equations if we wish to include the effects of time dependence and capture. If we return to equation (9) and make precisely the same assumptions as we made in establishing equation (36), with the exception of stationarity and no capture, we arrive at the equations

$$\frac{L(u)}{v}\frac{\partial \psi_0}{\partial t} + L(u)\frac{\partial \psi_1}{\partial z} + [1 - h(u)]\psi_0 = -\xi \frac{\partial \psi_0}{\partial u} + \delta(z)\delta(u)\delta(t) \quad (97)$$

and

$$\frac{1}{3}L_t(u)\frac{\partial \psi_0}{\partial z} + \psi_1 = 0 \quad (98)$$

where $L_t(u) = L(u)/(1 - \langle \cos \Theta \rangle_{av})$ and $L(u)$ is the mean free path for scattering. Equations (97) and (98) are the forms resulting from assuming that the capture is weak and that only the time variation of ψ_0 need be considered; ψ_1 is taken to be constant throughout the time. Introducing the symbolic age and the slowing-down density as before, we may combine equations (97) and (98) into the single partial differential equation

$$\frac{\partial \chi(z,\theta,t)}{\partial \theta} + \frac{3}{vL_t(u)}\frac{\partial \chi}{\partial t} + \frac{3[1 - h(u)]\chi}{L(u)L_t(u)} = \frac{\partial^2 \chi}{\partial z^2} + \delta(z)\delta(\theta)\delta(t) \quad (99)$$

If we now make the transformation

$$\chi(z,\theta,t) = \chi(z,\theta)F_1(h)F_2(t) \quad (100)$$

we find that $\chi(z,\theta)$ satisfies equation (36) with $T(z,\theta)$ of the simple form $\delta(z)\delta(\theta)$ provided that the functions $F_1(h)$ and $F_2(t)$ are chosen to be of the form

$$F_1(h) = \exp\left\{ -\int_0^u [1 - h(u')]\frac{du'}{\xi} \right\} \quad (101)$$

and

$$F_2(t) = \delta\left[t - \int_0^u \frac{L(u')du'}{v\xi} \right] \quad (102)$$

Within the limits of the age theory the effects of capture and time dependence may therefore be included simply by multiplying the appropriate solution of equation (36) by the factors F_1 and F_2 defined by equations (101) and (102). A similar result holds in the three-dimensional case.

28. Diffusion of Thermal Neutrons with Sources Given by the Age Theory

28.1 Diffusion of thermal neutrons.   When the neutrons reach a certain velocity, they cease to lose energy and we may describe their motion by means of classical diffusion theory.   If we denote by $\rho(\mathbf{r},t)$ the density of the neutrons and by $\mathbf{j}(\mathbf{r},t)$ the neutron current,[1] we have the continuity equation

$$\frac{\partial \rho}{\partial t} + \operatorname{div} \mathbf{j} + \frac{\rho}{\tau} = q(\mathbf{r}) \tag{103}$$

where $q(\mathbf{r})$ is the number of neutrons produced per unit volume and per unit time at the point $\mathbf{r}$ and $\tau = L_c/v$ is the mean lifetime of thermal neutrons.   The basic assumption of classical diffusion theory is that

$$\mathbf{j} = -D \operatorname{grad} \rho \tag{104}$$

where D is a constant which, on the basis of the exact transport equation, is given in terms of the velocity v and the mean free path L by the expression

$$D = \frac{L(u)v}{3[1 - h(u)\langle \cos \Theta \rangle_{\text{av}}]} = \frac{1}{3} L_t v, \text{ say} \tag{105}$$

Substituting from equation (104) into equation (103), we obtain the diffusion equation

$$\nabla^2 \rho - \frac{\rho}{\Lambda^2} = \frac{\tau}{\Lambda^2} \frac{\partial \rho}{\partial t} - \frac{\tau}{\Lambda^2} q(\mathbf{r}) \tag{106}$$

in which

$$\Lambda = (D\tau)^{\frac{1}{2}} = \left(\frac{L_c L_t}{3}\right)^{\frac{1}{2}} \tag{106a}$$

is known as the *diffusion length*.   In the steady state (ρ independent of the time) we have, therefore,

$$\nabla^2 \rho - \frac{\rho}{\Lambda^2} = -\frac{\tau q}{\Lambda^2} \tag{107}$$

In first approximation in the diffusion theory, we take as our boundary condition the vanishing of the neutron density at a free surface.   It follows from equation (52) that the true value (which we shall denote by ρ_t) of the density at a boundary is of the form

$$\rho_t = \frac{\sqrt{3}}{v(1 + \epsilon)} j_0 \tag{108}$$

where j_0 is the surface current as determined from equation (104) and ϵ is, in general, a small quantity.

[1] The neutron current is defined to be such that the flux of neutrons across a unit surface normal to the direction $\mathbf{n}$ is $(\mathbf{n} \cdot \mathbf{j})$.

Before proceeding to the discussion of the use of these equations in conjunction with the equations of the age theory we shall outline briefly the method of their solution in a particular case. We shall consider only the case of laminar symmetry when equation (107) reduces to

$$\frac{d^2\rho}{dz^2} - \frac{\rho}{\Lambda^2} = -\frac{\tau}{\Lambda^2}\, q(z) \tag{109}$$

If the medium is infinite, we solve this equation by introducing the pair of Fourier transforms

$$(R,Q) = \frac{1}{\sqrt{2\pi}} \int_{-\infty}^{\infty} (\rho,q)e^{i\xi z}\, dz$$

when equation (109) will assume the equivalent form

$$R(\xi) = \frac{\tau}{\Lambda^2} \frac{Q(\xi)}{\xi^2 + 1/\Lambda^2} \tag{110}$$

Thus, inverting by means of Theorem 10, we find that

$$\rho(z) = \frac{(\tau/\Lambda^2)}{\sqrt{2\pi}} \int_{-\infty}^{\infty} \frac{Q(\xi)e^{-i\xi z}}{(\xi^2 + 1/\Lambda^2)}\, d\xi$$

This integral may be evaluated in terms of the function $q(z)$ by means of the Faltung theorem 12. In this way we obtain the solution

$$\rho(z) = \frac{\tau}{2\Lambda} \int_{-\infty}^{\infty} q(u)e^{-|z-u|/\Lambda}\, du \tag{111}$$

Similarly, if the medium is semiinfinite ($z \geq 0$) and we assume that $\rho = 0$ when $z = 0$ and that both ρ and $d\rho/dz$ tend to zero as $z \to \infty$, then, if we write

$$(R_s,Q_s) = \sqrt{\frac{2}{\pi}} \int_0^{\infty} (\rho,q)\, \sin{(\xi z)}dz$$

it follows that we again obtain equation (110) but with (R,Q) replaced by (R_s,Q_s). Hence we have the solution

$$\begin{aligned}
\rho &= \frac{\tau}{\Lambda^2} \sqrt{\frac{2}{\pi}} \int_0^{\infty} \frac{Q(\xi)\, \sin{(\xi z)}}{\xi^2 + 1/\Lambda^2}\, d\xi \\
&= \frac{\tau}{2\Lambda} \int_0^{\infty} q(u)(e^{-|z-u|/\Lambda} - e^{-|z+u|/\Lambda})du
\end{aligned}$$

From this expression we obtain for the surface current

$$j_0 = -D\left(\frac{\partial\rho}{\partial z}\right)_{z=0} = \int_0^{\infty} e^{-u/\Lambda}q(u)du$$

so that, on the surface $z = 0$,

$$\rho_t(0) = \frac{\sqrt{3}}{v(1 + \epsilon)} \int_0^\infty e^{-u/\Lambda} q(u) du$$

From equation (111) it follows that the same distribution of sources[1] in an infinite medium leads to a value

$$\rho_i(0) = \frac{\tau}{2\Lambda} \int_0^\infty e^{-u/\Lambda} q(u) du$$

Therefore we have

$$\frac{\rho_i(0)}{\rho_t(0)} = \frac{v\tau(1 + \epsilon)}{2\sqrt{3}\Lambda} = \frac{1 + \epsilon}{2} \left(\frac{L_c}{L_t}\right)^{\frac{1}{2}} \tag{112}$$

Now, if β is the coefficient of diffuse reflection, or *albedo*, that is, the probability that a neutron which passes from $z > 0$ to $z < 0$ is reflected back again, and if the density at $z = 0$ in the semiinfinite medium is $\rho_t(0)$, the density in the infinite medium will be

$$\rho_i(0) = \rho_t(0)(1 + \beta + \beta^2 \cdots) = \frac{\rho_t(0)}{1 - \beta}$$

Eliminating $\rho_i(0)/\rho_t(0)$ from this equation by means of equation (112) and solving for β, we obtain the relation

$$\beta = 1 - \frac{2}{1 + \epsilon} \left(\frac{L_t}{L_c}\right)^{\frac{1}{2}}$$

For scattering which is isotropic in the laboratory system we may take $\epsilon = 0$ and $L_c/L_t \simeq L_c/L = N$, the average number of collisions a neutron experiences before capture. In this case we find that

$$\beta = 1 - \frac{2}{\sqrt{N}}$$

in agreement with a conjecture of Fermi's.[2]

28.2 Neutron density due to a source of fast neutrons. We shall now make use of the age theory to determine the sources of thermal neutrons which we must employ in the diffusion theory. In Sec. 27 the quantity $\chi(\mathbf{r}, \theta)$ denoted the number of neutrons reaching a given energy per unit time. If we denote by θ_0 the symbolic age of thermal neutrons, $\chi(\mathbf{r}, \theta_0)$ will be the number of neutrons becoming thermal per unit volume and per unit time, *i.e.*, the function $q(\mathbf{r})$ of equation (107). Our procedure is then to determine the appropriate solutions of the equation

[1] That is, $q(z) = q(z)$ $(z \geq 0)$; $q(z) = 0$ $(z < 0)$.
[2] E. Fermi, *Ricerca sci.*, **7**, 13 (1936).

$$\nabla^2 \rho - \frac{\rho}{\Lambda^2} = -\frac{\tau}{\Lambda^2} \chi(\mathbf{r},\theta_0) \tag{113}$$

in which $\chi(\mathbf{r},\theta_0)$ is derived from the solution of the age equation

$$\frac{\partial \chi}{\partial \theta} = \nabla^2 \chi + S(\mathbf{r})\delta(\theta) \tag{114}$$

To solve these equations, we multiply both sides throughout by $e^{i\boldsymbol{\xi}\cdot\mathbf{r}}$ and integrate throughout all space $[\boldsymbol{\xi} = (\xi,\eta,\zeta)]$. If we write

$$(\bar{\rho},\bar{\chi},\bar{S}) = \left(\frac{1}{2\pi}\right)^{\frac{3}{2}} \int_{-\infty}^{\infty} \int_{-\infty}^{\infty} \int_{-\infty}^{\infty} (\rho,\chi,S)e^{i\boldsymbol{\xi}\cdot\mathbf{r}} \, dx \, dy \, dz$$

for the Fourier transforms of the functions ρ,χ, and S, then we find that

$$\left(\xi^2 + \frac{1}{\Lambda^2}\right)\bar{\rho} = \frac{\tau}{\Lambda^2} \bar{\chi}(\boldsymbol{\xi},\theta_0) \tag{113a}$$

where $\bar{\chi}(\boldsymbol{\xi},\theta_0)$ is determined from the equation

$$\frac{d\bar{\chi}}{d\theta} = -\xi^2\bar{\chi} + \bar{S}(\boldsymbol{\xi})\delta(\theta) \tag{114a}$$

Solving this equation and inserting the particular value $\theta = \theta_0$, we obtain

$$\bar{\chi}(\boldsymbol{\xi},\theta_0) = \bar{S}(\boldsymbol{\xi})e^{-\xi^2\theta_0}$$

and, hence, from equation (113a), it follows that

$$\bar{\rho} = \frac{\tau}{\Lambda^2} \frac{\bar{S}(\boldsymbol{\xi})e^{-\xi^2\theta_0}}{\xi^2 + 1/\Lambda^2}$$

By the inversion theorem for multiple Fourier transforms—equation (111). Chap. 1—we obtain for the density of thermal neutrons

$$\rho = \left(\frac{1}{2\pi}\right)^{\frac{3}{2}} \frac{\tau}{\Lambda^2} \int_{-\infty}^{\infty} \int_{-\infty}^{\infty} \int_{-\infty}^{\infty} \frac{\bar{S}(\boldsymbol{\xi})e^{-\xi^2\theta_0 - i(\boldsymbol{\xi}\cdot\mathbf{r})}}{\xi^2 + 1/\Lambda^2} \, d\xi \, d\eta \, d\zeta \tag{115}$$

As an example of the use of equation (115) we shall consider the density of thermal neutrons in an infinite medium due to the uniform plane source $S(\mathbf{r}) = S \, \delta(z)$ of fast neutrons. The Fourier transform of this function is readily seen to be $\bar{S}(\boldsymbol{\xi}) = S(2\pi)^{\frac{1}{2}}\delta(\xi)\delta(\eta)$, so that, substituting in equation (115) and performing the ξ and η integrations, we obtain the expression

$$\rho = \frac{S\tau}{2\pi\Lambda^2} \int_{-\infty}^{\infty} \frac{e^{-\zeta^2\theta_0 - i\zeta z}}{\zeta^2 + 1/\Lambda^2} \, d\zeta$$

for the density of thermal neutrons in the medium.   This integral has
already been evaluated in Sec. 27.6, case (3); it leads to the solution

$$\rho = \frac{\tau S}{4\Lambda} e^{\theta_0/\Lambda^2} \left\{ e^{-z/\Lambda} \left[1 - \mathrm{erf}\left(\frac{\sqrt{\theta_0}}{\Lambda} - \frac{z}{2\sqrt{\theta_0}} \right) \right] \right.$$
$$\left. + e^{z/\Lambda} \left[1 - \mathrm{erf}\left(\frac{\sqrt{\theta_0}}{\Lambda} + \frac{z}{2\sqrt{\theta_0}} \right) \right] \right\} \quad (116)$$

Now, by definition,

$$\langle z^2 \rangle_{\mathrm{av}} = \frac{\displaystyle\int_{-\infty}^{\infty} z^2 \rho \, dz}{\displaystyle\int_{-\infty}^{\infty} \rho \, dz} = \left(\frac{\partial^2 \bar{\rho}/\partial \zeta^2}{\bar{\rho}} \right)_{\zeta=0} \quad (117)$$

which with the present value of $\bar{\rho}$ gives

$$\langle z^2 \rangle_{\mathrm{av}} = 2(\theta_0 + \Lambda^2) \quad (118)$$

so that the characteristic length for problems in the diffusion of thermal
neutrons resulting from known sources of fast neutrons is the *migration
length* defined by

$$\Lambda_0 = (\tfrac{1}{2}\langle z^2 \rangle_{\mathrm{av}})^{\frac{1}{2}} = \Lambda(1 + \gamma^2)^{\frac{1}{2}}$$

where $\gamma = \sqrt{\theta_0}/\Lambda$.   The migration length is therefore the root of the
sum of the squares of the characteristic lengths for the slowing-down and
thermal-diffusion problems.

The variation of the function (116) with z/Λ_0 and γ has been calculated
by Wallace and LeCaine.   Their results are shown graphically in Fig.
44(*i*).   The case $\gamma = 0$ corresponds, of course, to the case of pure thermal
diffusion.

28.3 Multiplication of neutrons in a medium containing sources.   In

the preceding sections we have made no assumptions as to the nature of
the processes resulting from the capture of a neutron by a nucleus of the
slowing-down material.   The process which is of most interest in the
theory of nuclear reactors is that in which the capture of the neutron is
followed by the emission of new fast neutrons.   We shall now discuss the
modifications which this imposes on our equations, assuming, for simplicity, that *each* capture results in the emission of k fast neutrons.

In the diffusion theory for thermal neutrons $1/\tau$ denotes the probability
of capture per unit time so that, as a consequence of capture, $\rho k/\tau$ new
fast neutrons will be produced per unit time in unit volume.   Because
of this new effective source we must modify equation (114) to read

$$\frac{\partial \chi}{\partial \theta} = \nabla^2 \chi + \left[S(\mathbf{r}) + \frac{k\rho}{\tau} \right] \delta(\theta) \quad (119)$$

As an example of the use of this equation we consider the density of thermal neutrons arising from a distribution of sources of fast neutrons in an infinite medium in which neutron multiplication is possible. Proceeding as in Sec. 28.2, we see that equation (119) is equivalent to

$$\frac{d\bar{\chi}}{d\theta} = -\xi^2\bar{\chi} + \left[\bar{S}(\xi) + \frac{k\bar{\rho}}{\tau} \right] \delta(\theta)$$

which has solution

$$\bar{\chi}(\xi,\theta_0) = \left[\bar{S}(\xi) + \frac{k\bar{\rho}}{\tau} \right] e^{-\theta_0\xi^2}$$

Equation (113a) remains unaltered so that, inserting this expression for $\bar{\chi}(\xi,\theta_0)$, we have

$$\bar{\rho} = \frac{\tau\bar{S}}{(1 + \Lambda^2\xi^2)e^{\theta_0\xi^2} - k} \tag{120}$$

Inverting this result with the help of equation (111), Chap. 1, we obtain for the density of thermal neutrons

$$\rho = \left(\frac{1}{2\pi}\right)^{\frac{3}{2}} \int_{-\infty}^{\infty} \int_{-\infty}^{\infty} \int_{-\infty}^{\infty} \frac{\tau\bar{S}(\xi)e^{-i\xi\cdot r}\,d\xi\,d\eta\,d\zeta}{(1 + \Lambda^2\xi^2)e^{\theta_0\xi^2} - k}$$

In the case of a plane source $S\,\delta(z)$ we find for the density in an infinite medium

$$\rho = \frac{S\tau}{2\pi} \int_{-\infty}^{\infty} \frac{e^{-i\zeta z}}{(1 + \zeta^2\Lambda^2)e^{\theta_0\zeta^2} - k}\,d\zeta$$

For this solution the characteristic length is the *multiplication length*

$$c = \left(\frac{1}{2}\langle z^2\rangle_{\text{av}}\right)^{\frac{1}{2}} = \left(\frac{1}{\bar{\rho}}\frac{\partial^2\bar{\rho}}{\partial\zeta^2}\right)_{\zeta=0} = \sqrt{\frac{\theta_0 + \Lambda^2}{1 - k}}$$

Integrating round a contour consisting of the real axis and an infinite semicircle with center at the origin, we find that

$$\rho = \frac{1}{2}S\tau \sum_{n=-\infty}^{\infty} \frac{\exp\left(\alpha_n^2\theta_0 - \alpha_n|z|\right)}{\alpha_n[\Lambda^2 + (1 - \alpha_n^2\Lambda^2)\theta_0]}$$

where the sum is taken over the roots of the transcendental equation

$$(1 - \alpha^2\Lambda_0)e^{-\alpha^2\theta_0} = k$$

In the particular case $\theta_0 = 0$ the roots of this equation are $\alpha = \pm 1/$ so that the expression for the density of thermal neutrons is

$$\rho = \frac{1}{2}S\tau \frac{e^{-|z|/c}}{c(1 - k)}$$

As a second example we shall consider the density of thermal neutrons in the slab $0 \leq z \leq a$, when there is a plane source $S(z)$ in its interior. Taking the vanishing of the neutron density on the surfaces $z = 0$, a as our boundary conditions and introducing the finite sine transforms

$$(\bar{\rho}, \bar{\chi}) = \int_0^a (\rho, \chi) \sin\left(\frac{n\pi z}{a}\right) dz$$

we have, by analogy with equation (120), the relation

$$\bar{\rho}(n) = \frac{\tau \bar{S}(n)}{(1 + n^2\pi^2\Lambda^2/a^2)e^{n^2\pi^2\theta_0/a^2} - k}$$

so that, by Theorem 27, we obtain the solution

$$\rho = \frac{2\tau}{a} \sum_{n=1}^{\infty} \frac{\bar{S}(n) \sin (n\pi z/a)}{(1 + n^2\pi^2\Lambda^2/a^2)e^{n^2\pi^2\theta_0/a^2} - k} \tag{121}$$

By means of this solution we may deduce the minimum thickness of a slab in which a divergent chain reaction will occur in the presence of sources for a given value of the multiplication factor $k(> 1)$. This gives what is known as the *critical dimensions* of the slab for a prescribed value of k. Mathematically the critical value a_c of a is that value which makes the first term of the series (121) infinite for all values of z (except, perhaps, $z = 0, a$). It follows immediately that a_c is a root of the equation

$$k = \left(1 + \frac{\pi^2\Lambda^2}{a^2}\right) e^{\pi^2\theta_0/a^2} \tag{122}$$

in which the value of k is prescribed. Expanding in powers of a_c^{-2} and reversing the series, we may show that

$$a_c = \frac{\pi\Lambda_0}{\sqrt{k-1}} [1 + \eta(\gamma, k - 1)] \tag{123}$$

where $\gamma^2 = \theta_0/\Lambda^2$ and $\eta(\gamma, k - 1)$ denotes the power series

$$\eta(\gamma, k - 1) = \frac{\gamma^2(2 + \gamma^2)(k - 1)}{4(1 + \gamma^2)^2} - \frac{\gamma^4(36 + 28\gamma^2 + 7\gamma^4)(k - 1)^2}{96(1 + \gamma^2)^4} + \cdots \tag{124}$$

In the neighborhood of the critical value the density of the thermal neutrons will be given by the first term of the series (121); that is,

$$\rho \simeq \frac{2\bar{S}(1)}{a} \frac{\sin (\pi z/a)}{(1 + \pi^2\Lambda^2/a^2)e^{\pi^2\theta_0/a^2} - k} \tag{125}$$

28.4 Neutron multiplication in a medium without sources. Finally, in this section, we shall determine, for a simple system, the conditions under which a distribution of neutrons is just self-sustaining without sources. We shall consider the case of a sphere of finite radius a and take as our boundary conditions the vanishing of the functions $r\rho$ and $r\chi$ when $r = 0,a$. In the case of spherical symmetry, equations (113) and (114) assume the forms

$$\frac{\partial^2(r\rho)}{\partial r^2} - \frac{r\rho}{\Lambda^2} = -\frac{\tau}{\Lambda^2}(r\chi) \tag{126}$$

and

$$\frac{\partial(r\chi)}{\partial\theta} = \frac{\partial^2(r\chi)}{\partial r^2} + \frac{(r\rho)k}{\tau}\delta(\theta) \tag{127}$$

From the nature of the boundary conditions it seems most convenient to make use of the finite sine transforms

$$(R,X) = \int_0^a r(\rho,\chi)\sin\left(\frac{n\pi r}{a}\right)dr$$

If we multiply both sides of the equations (126) and (127) by $\sin(n\pi r/a)$ and integrate throughout the sphere, we find that these transforms satisfy the relations

$$\left(\frac{n^2\pi^2}{a^2} + \frac{1}{\Lambda^2}\right)R(n) = \frac{\tau}{\Lambda^2}X(n,\theta_0)$$

$$\frac{dX}{d\theta} = -\frac{n^2\pi^2}{a^2}X + \frac{Rk}{\tau}\delta(\theta)$$

Integrating this last equation we have

$$X = \frac{Rk}{\tau}e^{-n^2\pi^2\theta/a^2}$$

from which it follows that

$$R(n)\left[\left(1 + \frac{n^2\pi^2\Lambda^2}{a^2}\right)e^{n^2\pi^2\theta_0/a^2} - k\right] = 0$$

Thus $R(n)$ must be zero except possibly for one value of n, which, or physical grounds, must be the lowest value $n = 1$, that is, $R(n) = ($ $(n = 2,3,4, \ldots)$, and the critical value of the radius is a_c where

$$\left(1 + \frac{\pi^2\Lambda^2}{a_c^2}\right)e^{\pi^2\theta_0/a_c^2} = k$$

The critical value of the radius of the sphere is therefore given by equa tions (123) and (124). When $a = a_c$, the value of the constant $R(1)$ i arbitrary and $r\rho_c$ is $(2/a)R(1) \sin (\pi r/a)$, so that we may write

$$\rho_c = A \frac{\sin (\pi r/a_c)}{r}, \qquad \chi_c = \frac{Ak}{\tau} e^{-\pi^2\theta_0/a_c^2} \left[\frac{\sin (\pi r/a_c)}{r} \right]$$

in which the constant A is arbitrary. The total number of thermal neutrons in the sphere is

$$N = \int_0^a 4\pi r^2\rho_c \, dr = 4Aa_c^2$$

so that we may write the solution in the form

$$\rho_c = \frac{N}{4a_c^3} \frac{\sin (\pi r/a_c)}{(r/a_c)}$$

The variation of $r^2\rho_c$ with r, as calculated from this equation, is shown in Fig. 45.

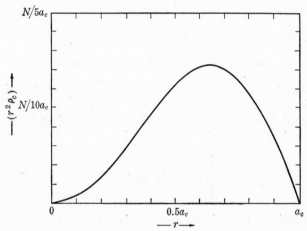

FIG. 45.   The variation of $r^2\rho_c$ in a sphere of critical radius a_c containing no sources. The total number of thermal neutrons in the sphere is N.

29. Exact Solutions of the Transport Equation

In Secs. 27 and 28 we considered the distribution of neutrons in a slowing-down medium under the age theory. However, the age theory is valid only if the average number of slowing-down collisions is large and if the fractional rate of change of mean free path per collision interval is small. If the mean free path changes rapidly or the number of collisions is small, the age theory is a poor approximation and we must return to the consideration of the transport equation (7). In this section we shall consider some exact solutions of this equation.

29.1 Energy distribution of slowed-down neutrons. In the firs
instance we shall suppose that we are interested only in the energy dis
tribution of the slowed-down neutrons and *not* in their spatial distribution
If we are not concerned with the spatial distribution of neutrons, we ma
integrate equation (9) throughout all space. Then

$$\Psi_0(u,t) = \int d\mathbf{r} \int \chi(\mathbf{r},\mathbf{\Omega},u,t)d\mathbf{\Omega} \qquad (128$$

which represents the number of collisions a neutron experiences per uni
time per unit logarithmic energy interval, satisfies the integrodifferentia
equation

$$\frac{L(u)}{v}\frac{\partial \Psi_0}{\partial t} + \Psi_0(u,t) - Q\,\delta(u)\delta(t) = \int_0^u \Psi_0(u',t)h(u')f_0(u-u')du' \qquad (129$$

in the case in which the function S is given by equation (12). In equa
tion (129)

$$Q = \int Q(\mathbf{r})d\mathbf{r}d\mathbf{\Omega}$$

is the total source strength and

$$f_0(u-u') = \int f(\mu_0,u-u')d\mathbf{\Omega}_0 \qquad (130$$

is the relative probability that a neutron will be scattered into the
logarithmic energy interval $(u,u+du)$ from the logarithmic energy
interval $(u',u'+du')$. If we write $d\mathbf{\Omega}_0 = 2\pi\,d\mu_0$ and make use of equa
tions (20) and (21), we find

$$f_0(u) = \begin{cases} (M+1)^2\dfrac{e^{-u}}{4M} & u \leq q_M \\ 0 & u > q_M \end{cases} \qquad (131$$

Case 1: *Stationary case in the absence of capture.* As the simplest cas
of equation (129) we shall consider the case in which there is no captur
and the distribution of neutrons arises from a monoenergetic source con
tinuously emitting neutrons of energy E_0 (stationary case). In th
stationary case $\partial/\partial t \equiv 0$, and if there is no capture, $h(u') \equiv 1$ so tha
equation (129) reduces to the simple form

$$\Psi_0(u) = \int_0^u \Psi_0(u')f_0(u-u')du' + \delta(u) \qquad (132$$

Now, by the Faltung theorem for Laplace transforms [equation (69)
Chap. 1], we may write

$$\frac{1}{2\pi i}\int_{\gamma-i\infty}^{\gamma+i\infty} \Phi_0(p)F_0(p)e^{pu}\,dp = \int_0^u \Psi_0(u')f_0(u-u')du'$$

where

$$\Phi_0(p) = \int_0^\infty \Psi_0(u)e^{-pu}\, du, \qquad F_0(p) = \int_0^\infty f_0(u)e^{-pu}\, du \qquad (133)$$

are the Laplace transforms of $\Psi_0(u)$ and $f_0(u)$.   Hence, using the inversion theorem 14, we may write

$$\int_0^\infty e^{-pu}\, du \int_0^u \Psi_0(u')f_0(u - u')du' = \Phi_0(p)F_0(p) \qquad (134)$$

Hence, multiplying both sides of equation (132) by e^{-pu} and integrating with respect to u from 0 to ∞, we find that

$$\Phi_0(p) = \Phi_0(p)F_0(p) + 1$$

where $F_0(p)$ and $\Phi_0(p)$ are defined by the equations (133).   Solving this equation for $\Phi_0(p)$, we obtain

$$\Phi_0(p) = 1 + \frac{F_0(p)}{1 - F_0(p)}$$

Using the inversion theorem and the result (85), Chap. 1, we see that

$$\Psi_0(u) = \delta(u) + \frac{1}{2\pi i} \int_{\gamma - i\infty}^{\gamma + i\infty} \frac{F_0(p)}{1 - F_0(p)}\, e^{pu}\, dp$$

Now, for the scattering function (131), we have

$$F_0(p) = \int_0^{q_M} \alpha e^{-(1+p)u}\, du = \frac{\alpha}{1 + p}[1 - e^{-(1+p)q_M}]$$

where $\alpha = (M + 1)^2/4M$.   Hence

$$\frac{F_0(p)}{1 - F_0(p)} = \frac{1 - e^{-(1+p)q_M}}{\dfrac{p + 1}{\alpha} - [1 - e^{-(1+p)q_M}]} = \frac{F_1(p)}{F_2(p)}, \text{ say}$$

The poles of the integrand are therefore given by the roots of the equation

$$F_2(p) \equiv \frac{p + 1}{\alpha} - 1 + e^{-(1+p)q_M} = 0 \qquad (135)$$

We therefore have

$$\Psi_0(u) = \delta(u) + \sum_{p_i} \frac{F_1(p_i)}{F_2'(p_i)}\, e^{p_i u} \qquad (136)$$

where the sum is taken over all the roots of equation (135); that is,

$$\Psi_0(u) = \delta(u) + \sum_{p_i} \frac{(p_i + 1)e^{p_i u}}{1 + q_M(p_i - \alpha + 1)} \qquad (137)$$

It is found that $R(p_i) < 0$,† except in the one case $p_0 = 0$. Separating off the contribution from p_0, we find that

$$\Psi_0(u) = \delta(u) + \frac{1}{1 + q_M(1 - \alpha)} + \sum_{p_i} \frac{(p_i + 1)e^{p_i u}}{1 + q_M(p_i - \alpha + 1)}$$

As $u \to \infty$,

$$\Psi_0(u) \to \Psi_{As}(u) = \frac{1}{1 + q_M(1 - \alpha)}$$

so that if $u \neq 0$ we may write

$$\frac{\Psi_0(u) - \Psi_{As}(u)}{\Psi_{As}(u)} = \sum_{p_i} \frac{1 + q_M(1 - \alpha)}{1 + q_M(p_i - \alpha + 1)} (p_i + 1)e^{p_i u} \qquad (138)$$

It follows at once from the values of the roots given by Marshak that when $M \gg 2$, the ratio $[\Psi_0(u) - \Psi_{As}(u)]/\Psi_{As}(u)$ is of order $Me^{-0.52Mu}$.

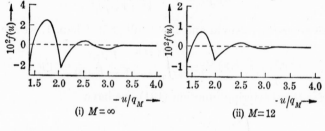

(i) $M = \infty$ (ii) $M = 12$

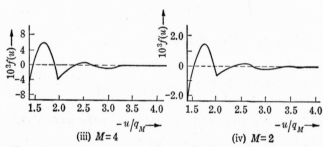

(iii) $M = 4$ (iv) $M = 2$

Fig. 46. The variation with u/q_M of $f(u) = [\Psi_0(u) - \Psi_{As}(u)]/\Psi_{As}(u)$ in the four cases $M = 2, 4, 12$, and ∞. (*After Placzek.*)

The above derivation of formula (138) is due to Adler.[1] More recently, Placzek[2] has solved the problem by an alternative method and calculated

† R. E. Marshak, *Montreal Rept.* 18, where it is further shown that the next pair of roots is

$$p_{1,2} = -1.55 \pm 3.37i \qquad M = 2$$
$$p_{1,2} = -0.52M \pm 1.87i \qquad M \gg 2$$

[1] F. T. Adler, *Phys. Rev.*, **60**, 279 (1941).
[2] G. Placzek, *Phys. Rev.*, **69**, 423 (1946).

the variation of the ratio

$$f(u) = \frac{\Psi_0(u) - \Psi_{As}(u)}{\Psi_{As}(u)}$$

with u/q_M in the cases $M = 2, 4, 12$, and ∞. The results of these calculations are shown graphically in Fig. 46.

Case 2: Time-dependent distribution in the absence of capture. We shall now consider a simple case of the time-dependent form of equation (129). In the absence of capture and for a monoenergetic source of neutrons of energy E_0 emitted at time $t = 0$, the fundamental equation becomes

$$\frac{L(u)}{v} \frac{\partial \Psi_0}{\partial t} + \Psi_0(u,t) = \int_0^u \Psi_0(u',t) f_0(u - u') du' + Q\, \delta(u)\delta(t)$$

We shall distinguish between two physical cases.

$M = 1$ *(hydrogen): Variable mean free path.* If we introduce the Laplace transform

$$\Phi_0(u,s) = \int_0^\infty \Psi_0(u,t) e^{-st}\, dt$$

the transport equation assumes the equivalent form

$$\left[1 + \frac{sL(u)}{v}\right] \Phi_0(u,s) = \int_0^u \Phi_0(u',s) e^{-(u-u')}\, du' + Q\, \delta(u) \qquad (139)$$

Making the substitution

$$\Phi_0(u,s) = \frac{Q\, \delta(u)}{1 + \dfrac{sL(0)}{v(0)}} + \chi(u,s)$$

and using the result

$$\frac{f(u)}{f(0)} \delta(u) \equiv \delta(u)$$

we find that

$$\left[1 + \frac{sL(u)}{v(u)}\right] \chi(u,s) = \int_0^u \chi(u',s) e^{-(u-u')}\, du' + \frac{Qe^{-u}}{1 + sL_0/v_0}$$

with $L_0 \equiv L(0)$. Differentiating both sides of this equation with respect to u, we obtain the equation

$$\frac{d}{du}\left\{ \left[1 + \frac{sL(u)}{v(u)}\right] \chi(u,s) \right\}$$

$$= \chi(u,s) - \int_0^u \chi(u',s) e^{-(u-u')}\, du' - \frac{Qe^{-u}}{1 + sL_0/v_0}$$

$$= -\frac{s}{s + v(u)/L(u)} \left\{ \left[1 + \frac{sL(u)}{v(u)}\right] \chi(u,s) \right\}$$

The solution of this equation subject to

$$\chi(0,s) = \frac{Q}{(1 + sL_0/v_0)^2}$$

is

$$\chi(u,s) = \frac{Q}{(1 + sL_0/v_0)[1 + sL(u)/v(u)]} \exp\left[-s \int_0^u \frac{du'}{s + v(u')/L(u')}\right]$$

Hence by the Laplace inversion theorem 14 we obtain the result[1]

$$\Psi_0(u,t) = \frac{1}{2\pi i} \int_{\gamma-i\infty}^{\gamma+i\infty} \left[\frac{Q\,\delta(u)}{1 + sL_0/v_0} + \chi(u,s)\right] e^{st}\,ds$$

$$= Q\frac{v_0}{L_0} e^{-v_0 t/L_0}\,\delta(u) + \frac{Q}{2\pi i} \int_{\gamma-i\infty}^{\gamma+i\infty} \frac{\exp s\left[t - \int_0^u \dfrac{du'}{s + v(u')/L(u')}\right]}{[1 + s + L(u)/v(u)](1 + sL_0/v_0)} \qquad (140)$$

where the contour of integration is chosen to the right of all the poles of the integrand.

If the scattering mean free path is assumed to vary directly as the velocity, so that the scattering cross section obeys a $1/v$ law, we may write $L(u)/v(u) = L_0/v_0$, in which case equation (140) reduces to

$$\Psi_0(u,t) = \frac{Qv}{L} e^{-vt/L}\,\delta(u) + \frac{Qe^{-u}}{2\pi i} \int_{\gamma-i\infty}^{\gamma+i\infty} \frac{\exp\left(st + \dfrac{u}{1 + sL/v}\right)}{(1 + sL/v)^2}\,ds$$

which may be transformed to

$$\Psi_0(u,t) = \frac{Qv}{L} e^{-vt/L}\,\delta(u) + Qe^{-u-vt/L}\left(\frac{v}{L}\right)\frac{1}{2\pi i} \int_{\gamma'-i\infty}^{\gamma'+i\infty} \exp\left(\frac{\sigma vt}{L} + \frac{u}{\sigma}\right)\frac{d\sigma}{\sigma^2}$$

Now, by equation (116), Chap. 4, we have

$$\int_0^\infty t^{\frac{1}{2}\nu} I_\nu(2\alpha t^{\frac{1}{2}}) e^{-pt}\,dt = \alpha^\nu p^{-\nu-1} e^{\alpha^2/p}$$

where, as usual, $I_\nu(z)$ denotes the νth-order Bessel function of the first kind with imaginary argument. By the Laplace inversion theorem 14 we therefore have

$$\frac{1}{2\pi i} \int_{\gamma'-i\infty}^{\gamma'+i\infty} \exp\left(pt + \frac{\alpha^2}{p}\right)\frac{dp}{p^{\nu+1}} = \left(\frac{t}{\alpha^2}\right)^{\frac{1}{2}\nu} I_\nu(2\alpha t^{\frac{1}{2}})$$

so that, finally

$$\Psi_0(u,t) = \frac{Qv}{L} e^{-vt/L}\,\delta(u) + Q\left(\frac{v}{L}\right)\left(\frac{vt}{uL}\right)^{\frac{1}{2}} I_1\left[2\left(\frac{vut}{L}\right)^{\frac{1}{2}}\right] e^{-u-vt/L}$$

[1] Cf. L. S. Ornstein and G. E. Uhlenbeck, *Physica*, **4**, 478 (1937).

Heavy element: Constant mean free path. We shall consider now the case in which the element forming the absorber is heavy but is such that the mean free path of neutrons may be assumed to be constant. In this instance equation (139) is replaced by

$$\left(1 + \frac{sL_0}{v}\right)\Phi_0(u,s) = \frac{(M+1)^2}{4M}\int_{u-q_M}^{u}\Phi_0(u',s)e^{-(u-u')}\,du' + \delta(u) \quad (141)$$

If we assume further that $u > q_M$, we may neglect $\delta(u)$ on the right-hand side. Introducing a new independent variable $w = sL_0/v$ and remembering that

$$u - u' = \log\left(\frac{E'}{E}\right) = 2\log\left(\frac{v'}{v}\right) = 2\log\left(\frac{w}{w'}\right)$$

we see that equation (141) may be written in the form

$$\phi(w,s) = \frac{2}{w^2(1-r^2)}\int_{rw}^{w}\frac{w'\phi(w',s)}{1+w'}\,dw' \quad (142)$$

where

$$\phi(w,s) = (1+w)\Phi_0(u,s) \quad (143)$$

and

$$r = \frac{M-1}{M+1} \quad (144)$$

In the case of hydrogen, $r = 0$, so that equation (142) becomes simply

$$\phi(w,s) = \frac{2}{w^2}\int_0^w\frac{w'\phi(w',s)}{1+w'}\,dw' \quad (145)$$

As a trial solution of this equation, let

$$\phi(w,s) = \frac{a(s)}{(1+w)^n}$$

Then substituting in equation (145) we see that n must be chosen so that

$$(1+w)^n - \left[\frac{n(n-1)}{2}w^2 + nw + 1\right] = 0$$

from which it follows immediately that $n = 2$ and hence that

$$\phi(w,s) = \frac{a(s)}{(1+w)^2} \quad (146)$$

when $M = 1$.

When $M = 1$, we obtain a solution of equation (142) by taking it to be represented by the Maclaurin series

$$\phi(w,s) = \sum_{n=0}^{\infty} a_n(s)w^n \tag{147}$$

Since

$$\int_{rw}^{w} \frac{w'^{n+1}}{1 + w'} dw' = (-1)^n \sum_{j=n}^{\infty} \frac{(-1)^j}{j+2} w^{j+2}(1 - r^{j+2})$$

we find on substituting from equation (147) into (142) that

$$\sum_{n=0}^{\infty} a_n w^n = \sum_{n=0}^{\infty} (-1)^n a_n \sum_{j=n}^{\infty} (-1)^j \lambda_j w^j$$

where

$$\lambda_j = \frac{2(1 - r^{j+2})}{(j+2)(1 - r^2)} \tag{148}$$

Equating powers of w^p in this equation, we find that the a's satisfy the relation

$$a_p = (-1)^p \lambda_p \sum_{n=0}^{p} (-1)^n a_n$$

From this relation we see that a_0 may be chosen arbitrarily and that, in general,

$$a_j = (-1)^j \frac{\lambda_j}{\prod_{i=1}^{j} (1 - \lambda_i)} a_0 \qquad j \geq 1 \tag{149}$$

From equations (143) and (147) and Theorem 14 we see that

$$\Psi_0(u,t) = \sum_{n=0}^{\infty} \left[\frac{1}{2\pi i} \int_{\gamma-i\infty}^{\gamma+i\infty} a_n(s) \frac{w^n}{1+w} e^{st} ds \right] \tag{150}$$

The evaluation of the contour integral on the right-hand side of equation (150) is exceedingly difficult; therefore we resort to an approximate method. If we define $\langle t^n \rangle_{\mathrm{av}}$ by the relation

$$\langle t^n \rangle_{\mathrm{av}} = \frac{\displaystyle\int_0^{\infty} t^n \Psi_0(u,t)dt}{\displaystyle\int_0^{\infty} \Psi_0(u,t)dt}$$

it follows at once that, if $\Psi_0(u,t)$ is normalized to unity,

$$\langle t^n \rangle_{\mathrm{av}} = (-1)^n \frac{\partial^n}{\partial s^n} \left[\sum_{j=0}^{\infty} \frac{a_j(s)w^j}{1+w} \right]_{s=0}$$

ᴏr, what is the same thing,

$$\langle x^n \rangle_{av} = (-1)^n \left[\frac{\partial^n}{\partial w^n} \sum_{j=0}^{\infty} \frac{a_j(s)w^j}{1+w} \right]_{w=0}$$

ᴡhere $x = vt/L_0$. Taking $a_0(s)$ to be unity and $a_j(s)$ $(j > 0)$ to be given ᴄy equation (149), Placzek[1] has calculated that

$$\langle x^n \rangle_{av} = n! \prod_{j=1}^{n} (1 - \lambda_j)^{-1} \tag{151}$$

Now from equation (148)

$$\log \prod_{j=1}^{n} (1 - \lambda_j)^{-1} \sim \sum_{j=1}^{n} \log \left[1 - \frac{2}{(j+2)(1-r^2)} \right]^{-1}$$

$$\sim \frac{2}{1-r^2} \sum_{j=1}^{n} \frac{1}{j+2} \sim \frac{2}{1-r^2} \log_e n$$

Thus we have the approximate expression

$$\langle x^n \rangle_{av} \sim (n!) n^{2/(1-r^2)} \tag{152}$$

In principle the expression (151) for the moments $\langle x^n \rangle_{av}$ defines a generating function $F(x)$ which is closely related to $\Psi_0(u,t)$. The exact determination of this function is difficult, but it follows from equation (152) that, for large values of x,

$$F(x) \sim e^{-x} x^{2/(1-r^2)}$$

so that, as a first approximation to the generating function $F(x)$, we may take

$$F_1(x) = A e^{-(x+b/x)} x^{2/(1-r^2)}$$

where A is a constant chosen so that $F_1(x)$ is normalized to unity and b is determined by minimizing $F_1(x)$ at the point $x = \langle x \rangle_{av}$. We find that, to a close approximation,

$$\int_0^{\infty} x^n F_1(x) dx = [1 + a(n+1)] \langle x^n \rangle_{av}$$

where $\langle x^n \rangle_{av}$ is given by (152) and a is a constant. A closer approximation to $F(x)$ is therefore given by $F_2(x)$, where

$$\int_0^{\infty} x^n F_1(x) dx = [1 + a(n+1)] \int_0^{\infty} x^n F_2(x) dx = \int_0^{\infty} x^n [F_2(x) - axF_2'(x)] dx$$

[1] G. Placzek, *Manhattan Project Rept.* **A-25**.

Thus $F_2(x)$ is determined by the differential equation

$$ax \frac{dF_2}{dx} - F_2(x) + F_1(x) = 0$$

that is, by

$$F_2(x) = \frac{1}{a} x^{1/a} \int_x^\infty \frac{F_1(u)}{u^{1+1/a}} \, du$$

The variation of the function $\log F_2(x)$ with x in the three cases $M = 2$, 9, and 15 is shown in Fig. 47, which is based on the numerical values of the constants a and b given by Marshak.[1]

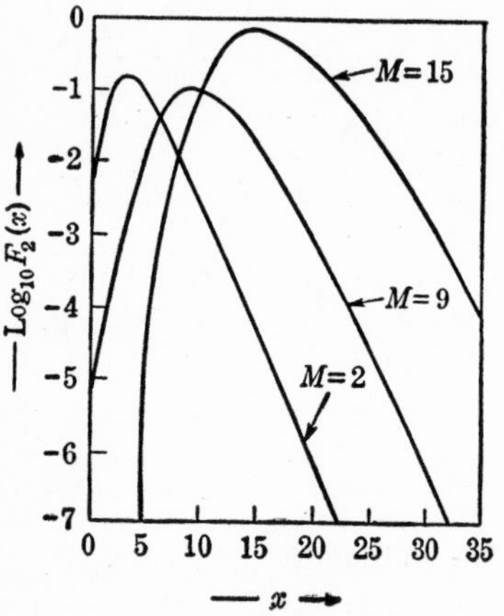

FIG. 47. The variation with x of $F_2(x)$ in the cases $M = 2$, 9, and 15

29.2 Spatial distribution of slowed-down neutrons: calculation of the second spatial moment. In the preceding section we considered typical problems of the determination of the energy distribution of neutrons slowed down as a result of their elastic collisions with atomic nuclei. For many purposes we require a knowledge of the spatial distribution of the neutrons in addition to the energy distribution. In Secs. 27 and 28 we saw how the approximate nature of these distributions could in certain circumstances be determined by means of the age theory and the theory of diffusion. In this section we shall consider the problem more exactly. In many cases the calculation of the complete spatial distribution is laborious, but that of the second spatial moment $\langle z^2 \rangle_{av}$ is relatively simple. Next to the actual neutron density a knowledge of the second spatial moment is of greatest interest and in some cases, such as the design of a slow neutron pile, is sufficient.

Taking $S(z,u) = \delta(z)\delta(u)/4\pi$ in equation (24), we see that it becomes

$$L(u)\mu \frac{\partial \psi}{\partial z} + \psi(z,\mu,u) = \int_0^u du' \int \psi(z,\mu',u')f(\mu_0, u - u')d\Omega'$$

$$+ \frac{1}{4\pi} \delta(z)\delta(u) \quad (153)$$

so that, introducing the Fourier transform

$$\phi(\xi,\mu,u) = \frac{1}{\sqrt{2\pi}} \int_{-\infty}^\infty e^{i\xi z}\psi(z,\mu,u)dz \quad (154)$$

[1] R. E. Marshak, *Rev. Mod. Phys.*, **19**, 197 (1947), Table I.

we find that

$$[1 - \xi\mu L(u)]\phi(\xi,\mu,u) = \int_0^u du' \int \phi(\xi,\mu',u')f(\mu_0,u - u')d\Omega' \\ + 2^{-\frac{5}{2}}\pi^{-\frac{3}{2}}\,\delta(u) \quad (155)$$

If we expand $f(\mu,u)$ in spherical harmonics according to equations (24b) and (25a) and similarly write

$$\phi(\xi,\mu,u) = \frac{1}{4\pi}\sum_{n=0}^{\infty}(2n + 1)\phi_n(\xi,u)P_n(\mu) \quad (156)$$

where

$$\phi_n(\xi,u) = \int\phi(\xi,\mu,u)P_n(\mu)d\Omega \quad (156a)$$

we obtain, by equating coefficients of the powers of μ in (155), the infinite set of integral equations

$$\phi_0(\xi,u) - i\xi L(u)\phi_1(\xi,u) = \int_0^u du'\,\phi_0(\xi,u')f_0(u - u') + (2\pi)^{-\frac{1}{2}}\,\delta(u) \quad (157)$$

$$\phi_n(\xi,u) - \frac{i\xi L(u)}{2n + 1}\,[n\phi_{n-1}(\xi,u) + (n + 1)\phi_{n+1}(\xi,u)] \\ = \int_0^u \phi_n(\xi,u')f_n(u - u')du' \quad n \geq 1 \quad (157a)$$

To find the slowing-down length $\Lambda_s(u)$ defined by equation (44), we need to evaluate

$$\langle z^2\rangle_{\mathrm{av}} = \frac{\displaystyle\int_{-\infty}^{\infty}dz\int z^2\psi(z,\mu,u)d\mu}{\displaystyle\int_{-\infty}^{\infty}dz\int\psi(z,\mu,u)d\mu} = -\left[\frac{\dfrac{\partial^2\phi_0(\xi,u)}{\partial\xi^2}}{\phi_0(\xi,u)}\right]_{\xi=0} \quad (158)$$

It follows from the system of equations (157) and (157a) that $\phi_0(0,u)$ and $\phi_0''(0,u)$ may be determined from (157) and the equation of the set (157a) obtained by putting $n = 1$ and omitting ϕ_2. Equation (157a) is then replaced by

$$\phi_1(\xi,u) - \frac{i\xi L(u)}{3}\,\phi_0(\xi,u) = \int_0^u \phi_1(\xi,u')f_1(u - u')du' \quad (157b)$$

Multiplying both sides of the equations (157) and (157b) by $e^{-\eta u}$, integrating with respect to u from 0 to ∞, and writing

$$\Phi_{0,1}(\xi,\eta) = \int_0^{\infty}\phi_{0,1}(\xi,u)e^{-\eta u}\,du, \qquad \Lambda_{0,1}(\xi,\eta) = \int_0^{\infty}\phi_{0,1}(\xi,u)L(u)e^{-\eta u}\,du$$

$$\gamma_{0,1}(\eta) = 1 - g_{0,1}(\eta) = 1 - \int_0^{\infty}f_{0,1}(u)e^{-\eta u}\,du$$

we find, on making use of the Faltung theorem—equation (69), Chap. 1—that

$$\gamma_0(\eta)\Phi_0(\xi,\eta) - i\xi\Lambda_1(\xi,\eta) = (2\pi)^{-\frac{1}{2}}$$
$$\gamma_1(\eta)\Phi_1(\xi,\eta) - \tfrac{1}{3}i\xi\Lambda_0(\xi,\eta) = 0$$

Substituting the Maclaurin expansions

$$\Phi_{0,1}(\xi,\eta) = \sum_{n=0}^{\infty} \frac{\xi^n}{n!} \Phi_{0,1}^{(n)}(0,\eta)$$

$$\Lambda_{0,1}(\xi,\eta) = \sum_{n=0}^{\infty} \frac{\xi^n}{n!} \Lambda_{0,1}^{(n)}(0,\eta)$$

in these equations and equating powers of ξ, we find the relations

$$\Phi_0(0,\eta) = \frac{1}{\sqrt{2\pi}\,\gamma_0(\eta)}, \qquad \Phi_1'(0,\eta) = \frac{i}{3\gamma_1(\eta)}\Lambda_0(0,\eta)$$

$$\Phi_0''(0,\eta) = \frac{2i}{\gamma_0(\eta)}\Lambda_1'(0,\eta)$$

If we suppose now that $1/\gamma_{0,1}(\eta)$ are the Laplace transforms of two functions $\bar{\gamma}_{0,1}(u)$, then using the notation

$$\mathsf{L}_u^{-1}\left[\frac{1}{\gamma_{0,1}(\eta)}\right] = \bar{\gamma}_{0,1}(u)$$

it follows from the first of these equations that

$$\mathsf{L}_u^{-1}[\Phi_0(0,\eta)] = (2\pi)^{-\frac{1}{2}}\bar{\gamma}_0(u)$$

From the second of these equations we find, by the Faltung theorem, that

$$\mathsf{L}_u^{-1}[\Phi_0'(0,\eta)] = \frac{i}{3}\int_0^u du'\,\bar{\gamma}_1(u - u')L(u')\mathsf{L}_{u'}^{-1}[\Phi_0(0,\eta)]$$
$$= \frac{i}{3}\int_0^u \bar{\gamma}_1(u - u')L(u')(2\pi)^{-\frac{1}{2}}\bar{\gamma}_0(u')du'$$

and similarly, from the third,

$$\mathsf{L}_u^{-1}[\Phi_0''(0,\eta)] = -\frac{2}{3(2\pi)^{\frac{1}{2}}}\int_0^u \bar{\gamma}_0(u - u')L(u')du'$$
$$\times \int_0^{u'} \bar{\gamma}_1(u' - u'')L(u'')\bar{\gamma}_0(u'')du''$$

Now from equations (44) and (158) and the definition of the $\Phi^{(n)}$'s,

$$\Lambda_s^2(u) = -\frac{1}{2}\left\{\frac{L_u^{-1}[\Phi''(0,\eta)]}{L_u^{-1}[\Phi(0,\eta)]}\right\}$$

so that finally we obtain

$$\Lambda_s^2(u) = \frac{1}{3\bar{\gamma}_0(u)}\int_0^u \bar{\gamma}_0(u-u')L(u')du'\int_0^{u'}\bar{\gamma}_1(u'-u'')L(u'')\bar{\gamma}_0(u'')du'' \quad (159)$$

—a result due to Marshak and Schwinger. The derivation given here is due to Marshak.

As an illustration of the use of this formula we shall consider the case of hydrogen, for which

$$f(\mu,u) = \frac{1}{2\pi}e^{-u}\delta(\mu - e^{-\frac{1}{2}u}) \qquad 0 < u < \infty$$

so that, by equation (25a),

$$f_n = e^{-u}\int_{-1}^1 P_n(\mu)\delta(\mu - e^{-\frac{1}{2}u})d\mu = e^{-u}P_n(e^{-\frac{1}{2}u})$$

and, in particular, $f_0 = e^{-u}$, $f_1 = e^{-3u/2}$. It follows by direct integration that

$$\frac{1}{\gamma_0(\eta)} = 1 + \frac{1}{\eta}, \qquad \frac{1}{\gamma_1(\eta)} = 1 + \frac{1}{\eta + \frac{1}{2}}$$

and therefore that

$$\bar{\gamma}_0(u) = \delta(u) + 1, \qquad \bar{\gamma}_1(u) = \delta(u) + e^{-\frac{1}{2}u} \quad (160)$$

Substituting from equations (160) into equation (159), we obtain in the case of hydrogen

$$\Lambda_s^2(u) = \frac{1}{3}\left[L^2(0) + L^2(u) + L(0)L(u)e^{-\frac{1}{2}u} + L(u)\int_0^u L(u')e^{-\frac{1}{2}(u-u')}\,du'\right.$$
$$\left. + \int_0^u L^2(u')du' + L(0)\int_0^u L(u')e^{-\frac{1}{2}u'}\,du'\right.$$
$$\left. + \int_0^u L(u')du'\int_0^{u'} L(u'')e^{-\frac{1}{2}(u'-u'')}\,du''\right] \quad (161)$$

Alternative derivations of equation (161) have been given by Fermi[1] and by Ornstein and G. E. Uhlenbeck.[2]

For the extension of these calculations to heavy elements and mixtures and to the determination of higher spatial moments the reader is referred to R. E. Marshak's review article cited above.

[1] Fermi, *op. cit.*
[2] Ornstein and Uhlenbeck, *op. cit.*

29.3 Milne problem for a half space with isotropic scattering. In conclusion we shall consider the problem of determining the stationary neutron distribution in a semiinfinite medium ($z > 0$) bounded by the plane $z = 0$ when there are no sources in the medium and no neutrons cross the plane $z = 0$ from without. It will be assumed, however, that a current density of magnitude j and in the $-z$ direction exists in the medium.[1] For simplicity we shall assume that the medium is noncapturing and that collisions between the neutrons and the nuclei of the medium take place without change in the neutron velocity. If we denote by $f(\mathbf{v}, \mathbf{v}' - \mathbf{v})d\mathbf{v}$ the probability per unit time that a particle suffer a collision removing it from the "point" $(\mathbf{r}, \mathbf{v}')$ into the interval $d\mathbf{v}$ at $(\mathbf{r}, \mathbf{v})$, then, in the absence of capture, the transport equation governing the variation of $w(\mathbf{r}, \mathbf{v}, t)$, the probability that at time t a neutron has position vector $\mathbf{r}$ and velocity $\mathbf{v}$, is

$$\frac{\partial w}{\partial t} + \mathbf{v} \cdot \operatorname{grad} (w) + \Gamma w = \int w(\mathbf{r}, \mathbf{v}', t) f(\mathbf{v}, \mathbf{v}' - \mathbf{v}) d\mathbf{v}' \qquad (162)$$

where Γ is the total probability per unit time of scattering. Since the particle is assumed to lose no energy in scattering, the velocity is uniquely determined by the cosine μ of the angle the direction of motion makes with the positive z direction. Denoting by $\psi(z, \mu)d\mu$ the number of neutrons per unit volume whose μ value lies between μ and $\mu + d\mu$, and by v_0 the velocity of the neutrons, we find therefore that in the stationary case

$$v_0 \mu \frac{\partial \psi}{\partial z} + \Gamma \psi = \int_{-1}^{1} \psi(z, \mu') f(\mu, \mu' - \mu) d\mu' \qquad (163)$$

To simplify the problem still further, we shall suppose that the scattering is isotropic in the laboratory system of coordinates so that we may assume

$$f(\mu, \mu' - \mu) = \tfrac{1}{2}\Gamma \qquad (164)$$

Substituting from equation (164) into equation (163) and choosing the neutron velocity to be the unit of velocity and the scattering mean free path as unit of length, we see that equation (163) is equivalent to the simple transport equation

$$\mu \frac{\partial \psi}{\partial z} + \psi = \frac{1}{2} \psi_0 \qquad (165)$$

where

$$\psi_0(z) = \int_{-1}^{1} \psi(z, \mu) d\mu \qquad (166)$$

denotes the neutron density.

[1] Cf. G. Placzek and W. Seidel, *Phys. Rev.*, **72**, 550 (1947). A similar problem is considered by O. Halpern, R. Lueneburg, and O. Clark, *Phys. Rev.*, **53**, 173 (1938).

Since no neutrons enter the medium from without, the boundary condition of our problem is

$$\psi(0,\mu) = 0 \qquad\qquad \mu > 0 \qquad (167)$$

This problem is identical with that of determining the law of darkening at the sun's surface—the "Milne problem" of astrophysical literature.[1]

Integrating equation (165) with respect to μ from -1 to 1, we obtain the relation $\partial j/\partial z = 0$, where

$$j = - \int_{-1}^{1} \mu\psi(z,\mu)d\mu$$

is the neutron current density. It follows at once that j is a constant which, if we normalize $\psi(z,\mu)$ for unit current density, may be taken to be unity.

Similarly, multiplying both sides of equation (165) by μ and then integrating, we find that $\partial K/\partial z = 1$, where

$$K(z) = \int_{-1}^{1} \mu^2\psi(z,\mu)d\mu$$

Thus

$$K(z) = z + z_0$$

where z_0 is a constant which, by virtue of equation (167), is given by

$$z_0 = K(0) = \int_{-1}^{0} \psi(0,\mu)\mu^2\,d\mu \qquad (168)$$

The transformation

$$\psi(z,\mu) = \chi(z,\mu)e^{-z/\mu}$$

substituted in equation (165) yields the results

$$\psi(z,\mu) = \begin{cases} \dfrac{1}{2\mu}\displaystyle\int_0^z \psi_0(z')e^{(z'-z)/\mu}\,dz' & \mu > 0 \\[2ex] -\dfrac{1}{2\mu}\displaystyle\int_z^{\infty} \psi_0(z')e^{(z'-z)/\mu}\,dz' & \mu < 0 \end{cases} \qquad (169)$$

Integrating both sides of these equations with respect to μ from -1 to 1, we find that $\psi_0(z)$ satisfies the integral equation

$$\psi_0(z) = \frac{1}{2}\int_0^{\infty} \psi_0(z')E(|z - z'|)dz' \qquad (165a)$$

in which the kernel $E(x)$ is defined by the relation

$$E(x) = -Ei(-x) = \int_x^{\infty} \frac{e^{-u}}{u}\,du$$

[1] See, for instance, E. A. Milne, "Handbuch der Astrophysik" (Verlag Julius Springer, Berlin, 1930), Bd. III/I, p. 141.

Equation (165a) is known as *Milne's integral equation.* The solution of this equation is discussed in the article by Milne cited above and in the book by Hopf.[1] In the solution of the problem considered here we shall regard equation (165) as our fundamental equation rather than (165a). If we write

$$\phi(s,\mu) = \int_0^\infty \psi(z,\mu)e^{-sz}\,dz, \qquad \mathsf{R}(s) > 0 \qquad (170)$$

$$\phi_0(s) = \int_{-1}^1 \phi(s,\mu)d\mu = \int_0^\infty \psi_0(z)e^{-sz}\,dz, \qquad \mathsf{R}(s) > 0 \quad (170a)$$

we find, by multiplying both sides by e^{-sz} and integrating with respect to z from 0 to ∞, that equation (165) is equivalent to the relation

$$\phi(s,\mu) = \frac{\frac{1}{2}\phi_0(s) + \mu\psi(0,\mu)}{1 + s\mu} \qquad (171)$$

Integrating over the complete range of μ and making use of the integral

$$\frac{1}{2}\int_{-1}^1 \frac{d\mu}{1 + s\mu} = \frac{1}{s}\tanh^{-1}(s) \qquad (172)$$

we see that

$$\phi_0(s) = \frac{\int_{-1}^0 \mu\psi(0,\mu)d\mu/(1 + s\mu)}{1 - (1/s)\tanh^{-1} s} \qquad (173)$$

Now putting $z = 0$ in the second of equations (169) and remembering the definition of $\phi_0(s)$, we see that

$$\mu\psi(0,\mu) = -\frac{1}{2}\phi_0\left(-\frac{1}{\mu}\right) \qquad (174)$$

Substituting from equation (174) into equation (173), we find that we may write this latter equation in the form

$$\phi_0(s)\left(1 - \frac{1}{s}\tanh^{-1} s\right) = g(s) \qquad (175)$$

where

$$g(s) = \int_{-1}^0 \frac{\mu\psi(0,\mu)d\mu}{1 + s\mu} = -\frac{1}{2}\int_{-1}^0 \frac{\phi_0(-1/\mu)}{1 + s\mu}\,d\mu \qquad (176)$$

We solve the integral equation (175) by what is known as the *Wiener-Hopf method.*[2] This method consists essentially in determining the

[1] E. Hopf, "Mathematical Problems of Radiative Equilibrium," *Cambridge Tracts* 31 (Cambridge, London, 1934).

[2] N. Wiener and E. Hopf, *Berlin. Ber. Math. Phys. Klasse,* **1931,** 696. See also R. E. A. C. Paley and N. Wiener, "Fourier Transforms in the Complex Domain" (American Mathematical Society Colloquium Publications, Vol. 19, New York, 1934), Chap. IV, and Hopf, *op. cit.*

domains in the complex s plane in which the functions occurring in the equation are analytic. We then form a certain function containing $\phi_0(s)$ and the function $s^{-1} \tanh^{-1}(s)$ which has the property that it is bounded and analytic throughout the entire s plane. According to Liouville's theorem in the theory of functions of a complex variable, such a function must be simply a constant. It is then possible to determine the unknown function $\phi_0(s)$ in terms of the function $s^{-1} \tanh^{-1}(s)$.

From the definition (170a) it follows immediately that $\phi_0(s)$ is analytic in the half plane $\mathsf{R}(s) > 0$. Similarly, from its expression as a definite integral—equation (172)—it is obvious that the function $s^{-1} \tanh^{-1}(s)$ is analytic in the strip $-1 < \mathsf{R}(s) < 1$. From these results and the definition (176) it follows that $g(s)$ is analytic throughout the half space $\mathsf{R}(s) < 1$.

In order to obtain a solution of equation (175), we must rewrite it so that its left-hand side is analytic in a certain half plane and its right-hand side is analytic in a second half plane overlapping the first, both half planes covering the entire s plane. If we achieve this result, we may then regard each side of the equation as the analytical continuation of the other. The function, so extended by analytical continuation, will be analytic over the entire s plane; thus, if it can further be shown to be bounded, it will, by the application of Liouville's theorem, be a constant.

To write equation (175) in the desired form, we must first express the function $1 - s^{-1} \tanh^{-1}(s)$ as the quotient of two functions each of which is analytic in a half plane. It is readily shown that this function has a double zero at the origin and no other zero in the strip $-1 < \mathsf{R}(s) < 1$. Hence if we form the function

$$\tau(s) = \frac{1}{s^2}(s^2 - 1)\left[1 - \frac{1}{s}\tanh^{-1}(s)\right] \tag{177}$$

we see that it has no zeros in the strip $-1 < \mathsf{R}(s) < 1$ and tends to unity as $|s| \to \infty$ in the strip. To obtain the required decomposition of $\tau(s)$, we consider the function $\log \tau(s)$ which is single-valued in the strip $-1 < \mathsf{R}(s) < 1$ provided that we take $\log 1 = 0$. Since $\log \tau(s) \to 0$ as $|s| \to \infty$ in the strip, it can, by Cauchy's integral theorem, be represented by the formula

$$\log \tau(s) = \log \tau_+(s) - \log \tau_-(s) \tag{178}$$

where

$$\tau_-(s) = \exp\left[\frac{1}{2\pi i}\int_{-\beta-i\infty}^{-\beta+i\infty} \frac{du}{u-s} \log \tau(u)du\right] \tag{179}$$

$$\tau_+(s) = \exp\left[\frac{1}{2\pi i}\int_{\beta-i\infty}^{\beta+i\infty} \frac{du}{u-s} \log \tau(u)du\right] \tag{180}$$

with $0 < \beta < 1$ and $-\beta < \mathsf{R}(s) < \beta$. From equation (178) and the definitions (179) and (180), it follows that we may write

$$\tau(s) = \frac{\tau_+(s)}{\tau_-(s)} \tag{181}$$

where $\tau_-(s)$ is regular and different from zero in the half plane $\mathsf{R}(s) > -\beta$, while $\tau_+(s)$ is regular and different from zero in the half plane $\mathsf{R}(s) < \beta$. Substituting this value for $\tau(s)$ into equation (177) and eliminating the function $1 - s^{-1} \tanh^{-1}(s)$ between this equation and (175), we see that the latter equation may be written in the form

$$\frac{s^2 \phi_0(s)}{(s+1)\tau_-(s)} = \frac{(s-1)g(s)}{\tau_+(s)} \tag{182}$$

The left-hand side of this equation is regular in the positive half plane $\mathsf{R}(s) > 0$, and the right-hand side is regular in the half plane $\mathsf{R}(s) < \beta$, where, it will be recalled, $0 < \beta < 1$. Since the two half planes overlap, each side of equation (182) represents the analytic continuation of the other, so that either side is regular in the whole finite s plane. It is readily shown[1] that each side is bounded at infinity. Hence by Liouville's theorem we have that

$$\phi_0(s) = C \frac{s+1}{s^2} \tau_-(s) \tag{183}$$

where C is a constant, whose value we have still to determine. Expanding the right-hand side of equation (183) in a Laurent series, we find

$$\phi_0(s) = \frac{C\tau_-(0)}{s^2} + \frac{C[\tau_-(0) + \tau_-'(0)]}{s} + \cdots$$

If, however, we expand equation (173) in a Laurent series and make use of the fact that

$$\int_{-1}^{1} \mu\psi(z,\mu)d\mu = -1$$

and that z_0 is defined by equation (168), we find

$$\phi_0(s) = \frac{3}{s^2} + \frac{3z_0}{s} + \cdots$$

Comparing the two series, it follows immediately that

$$C = \frac{3}{\tau_-(0)}, \qquad z_0 = 1 + \frac{\tau_-'(0)}{\tau_-(0)} \tag{184}$$

---

[1] For details see Placzek and Seidel, *op. cit.*, pp. 553, 555.

Now, from equation (179), we have

$$\frac{1}{\tau_-(0)} = \exp\left[-\frac{1}{2\pi i}\int_{-\beta-i\infty}^{-\beta+i\infty}\frac{\log\tau(u)}{u}\,du\right]$$

We deform the path of integration into the two segments $(-i\infty, -i\rho)$ and $(i\rho, i\infty)$ of the imaginary axis and the semicircle of center the origin and radius ρ (cf. Fig. 48). The total contribution from the segments is zero, and in the limit $\rho \to 0$ the contribution from the semicircle is

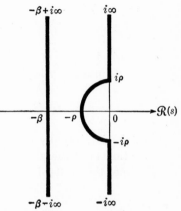

$$\frac{1}{\tau_-(0)} = \exp\left[\frac{1}{2}\log\tau(0)\right] = \sqrt{\tau(0)}$$

From the definition (177) we have $\tau(0) = \frac{1}{3}$ so that $C = \sqrt{3}$ and we obtain from equation (183)

$$\phi_0(s) = \frac{\sqrt{3}\,(1+s)\tau_-(s)}{s^2} \quad (185)$$

Similarly we may evaluate

$$\frac{\tau'_-(0)}{\tau_-(0)} = \frac{1}{2\pi i}\int_{-i\infty}^{i\infty}\frac{\tau'(u)du}{u\tau(u)}$$

FIG. 48. The path of integration for the evaluation of $1/\tau_-(0)$.

Inserting the explicit form for $\tau(u)$ and changing the variable of integration from s to t where $s = it$, we find from this equation and the second of equations (184) that

$$z_0 = \frac{1}{\pi}\int_0^\infty\left\{\frac{3}{t^2} - \frac{1}{(1+t^2)[1-(1/t)\tan^{-1}t]}\right\}dt \quad (186)$$

Computing this integral numerically, Wallace and Carlson showed that $z_0 = 0.71044609$.

The angular distribution of the neutrons emerging from the plane boundary is given by equations (174) and (183) in the form

$$\psi(0,\mu) = \frac{1}{2}\sqrt{3}\,(1-\mu)\tau_-\left(-\frac{1}{\mu}\right) \qquad \mu < 0 \quad (187)$$

Deforming the contour of integration in the definition (179) to that shown on the right of Fig. 48 and then letting ρ tend to 0, we find that

$$\log\tau_-(s) = \frac{s}{\pi i}\int_{i0}^{i\infty}\frac{\log\tau(u)}{u^2-s^2}\,du = -\frac{s}{\pi}\int_0^\infty\frac{\log\tau(it)}{t^2+s^2}\,dt$$

so that substituting for $\tau(it)$ from (177) we find

$$\log [\tau_-(s)] = -\frac{s}{\pi} \int_0^\infty \log \left[\frac{t^2+1}{t^2} \left(1 - \frac{\tan^{-1} t}{t} \right) \right] \frac{dt}{t^2+s^2}$$

Making the transformation $t = \tan (x)$ in this integral and substituting $s = -1/\mu$, we find, from equation (187), that

$$\psi(0,\mu) = \frac{1}{2} \sqrt{3} \, (1 - \mu) \exp \left\{ -\frac{\mu}{\pi} \int_0^{\frac{1}{2}\pi} \frac{\log [\sin^2 x/(1 - x \cot x)]}{\cos^2 x + \mu^2 \sin^2 x} \, dx \right\}$$
(188)

The numerical values of this expression have been given by Placzek.[1]
The neutron density is given, by Theorem 14, in the form

$$\psi_0(z) = \frac{1}{2\pi i} \int_{\gamma-i\infty}^{\gamma+i\infty} \phi_0(s)e^{sz} \, ds$$

where $\phi_0(s)$ is given by equation (185). The numerical evaluation of this function near the plane surface has been carried out by Mark,[2] to whose paper the reader is referred for details.

[1] G. Placzek, *Phys. Rev.*, **72**, 556 (1947).
[2] C. Mark, *Phys. Rev.*, **72**, 558 (1947).

CHAPTER 7

HYDRODYNAMIC PROBLEMS

30. Hydrodynamic Equations

We shall consider in this chapter the application of the theory of integral transforms to the solution of boundary value problems in hydrodynamics. The field of hydrodynamics is so vast that we can consider only a few representative problems which illustrate the methods of solution involved. Before discussing the solution of special problems we shall briefly outline the general theory underlying the establishment of the equations of motion of a fluid.

30.1 Equation of continuity.

In the first instance we consider the mathematical expression of the principle of continuity. If we consider any closed surface in the fluid, fixed in space, then, in the absence of sources or sinks in the interior of the surface, the rate of increase of mass within the surface is equal to the rate at which mass flows into the volume enclosed by the surface. If ρ denotes the density of the fluid, then the mass enclosed by the surface is $\int_V \rho \, d\tau$, where V is the volume enclosed by the surface S. Now if $\mathbf{v}$ denotes the velocity of a particle of the fluid, its component in the direction $\mathbf{n}$ will be $(\mathbf{v} \cdot \mathbf{n})$ so that the rate at which mass flows *out* of the volume V is $\int_S (\mathbf{v} \cdot \mathbf{n})\rho \, dS$, which, by Gauss' theorem, may be written as the volume integral $\int_V \operatorname{div}(\rho\mathbf{v}) d\tau$. The amount of fluid which flows per unit time *into* the volume will be this integral multiplied by -1, so that we have the equation

$$\frac{\partial}{\partial t} \int_V \rho \, d\tau = -\int_V \operatorname{div}(\rho\mathbf{v}) d\tau$$

The volume V is arbitrary so that the continuity condition is simply

$$\frac{\partial \rho}{\partial t} + \operatorname{div}(\rho\mathbf{v}) = 0 \tag{1}$$

Now, if θ is any physical quantity associated with the fluid, $\partial\theta/\partial t$ is the rate of change of θ measured at the fixed point $\mathbf{r} = (x,y,z)$ and may be called the *local rate of change* of θ. In calculating the total rate of change of θ we must, however, include the rate of change arising from the fact that θ is being convected by the fluid. A particle which is at the point $\mathbf{r}$ at time t is at the point $\mathbf{r} + \mathbf{v}\,\Delta t$ at time $t + \Delta t$ so that the total change in θ is $\theta(\mathbf{r} + \mathbf{v}\,\Delta t, t + \Delta t) - \theta(\mathbf{r},t)$. If we denote this change by

$$\frac{D\theta}{Dt}\,\Delta t$$

we then find, from Taylor's theorem for a function of two variables, that

$$\frac{D\theta}{Dt} = \frac{\partial\theta}{\partial t} + \mathbf{v}\cdot\operatorname{grad}\theta \tag{2}$$

The equation of continuity (1) may thus be written in the form

$$\frac{\partial\rho}{\partial t} + \rho\operatorname{div}(\mathbf{v}) + \mathbf{v}\cdot\operatorname{grad}\rho = 0$$

that is,

$$\frac{1}{\rho}\frac{D\rho}{Dt} + \operatorname{div}\mathbf{v} = 0 \tag{3}$$

30.2 Equations of motion of a nonviscous fluid. In a fluid at rest or in a nonviscous fluid in motion the pressure over an element of area is wholly normal and independent of the orientation of the area. We may denote it therefore by a scalar function of position $p(\mathbf{r})$. To establish the equations of motion of a nonviscous fluid, we consider the rate of change of momentum of a small rectangular parallelepiped centered at the point (x,y,z) and having sides of length dx, dy, and dz. The rate of change of momentum of this element is

$$\rho\frac{D}{Dt}(\mathbf{v}\cdot dx\,dy\,dz)$$

The net result of the pressures acting on the yz faces of the element is

$$\left(p - \frac{1}{2}\frac{\partial p}{\partial x}\,dx\right)dy\,dz - \left(p + \frac{1}{2}\frac{\partial p}{\partial x}\,dx\right)dy\,dz = -\frac{\partial p}{\partial x}\,dx\,dy\,dz$$

so that the total force arising from the differences in fluid pressure is $-(\operatorname{grad} p)dx\,dy\,dz$. On the other hand, the external force $\mathbf{F}$, per unit mass of the fluid, gives a contribution $\rho\mathbf{F}\cdot dx\,dy\,dz$, so that, by Newton's second law of motion, we obtain the equation of motion of the fluid in the form

$$\frac{D\mathbf{v}}{Dt} = \mathbf{F} - \frac{1}{\rho}\operatorname{grad} p \tag{4}$$

As a special case of equation (2) we have

$$\frac{D\mathbf{v}}{Dt} = \frac{\partial \mathbf{v}}{\partial t} + \frac{1}{2}\operatorname{grad}(\mathbf{v}^2) - 2\mathbf{v} \times \boldsymbol{\omega} \tag{5}$$

where

$$\boldsymbol{\omega} = \tfrac{1}{2}\operatorname{curl}\mathbf{v} \tag{6}$$

the *vorticity* of the fluid at the point (x,y,z), is the angular velocity with which an element at that point would rotate if it were suddenly solidified. If we assume further that the external forces are derivable from a potential Ω so that

$$\mathbf{F} = -\operatorname{grad}\Omega \tag{7}$$

it follows from equations (4), (5), and (7) that the equations of motion of a nonviscous fluid may be written in the vector form

$$\frac{\partial \mathbf{v}}{\partial t} - 2\mathbf{v} \times \boldsymbol{\omega} + \operatorname{grad}\left(\Omega + \frac{1}{2}\mathbf{v}^2 + \int\frac{dp}{\rho}\right) = 0 \tag{8}$$

30.3 Irrotational motion of a perfect fluid. In the case in which the motion of the fluid is irrotational the equations of motion assume a particularly simple form. The motion of a fluid is said to be irrotational if the vorticity $\boldsymbol{\omega}$ is zero at every point of the fluid. In other words, curl $\mathbf{v} = 0$ everywhere so that we may express the velocity vector $\mathbf{v}$ in terms of a scalar quantity ϕ by means of the equation

$$\mathbf{v} = -\operatorname{grad}\phi \tag{9}$$

A perfect fluid is one which is nonviscous and which has *constant* density ρ. For such a fluid the equation of continuity (1) becomes simply

$$\operatorname{div}\mathbf{v} = 0 \tag{10}$$

or, by virtue of equation (9),

$$\nabla^2\phi = 0 \tag{11}$$

showing that the velocity potential ϕ is a harmonic function.

30.4 Equations of motion of a viscous fluid. In a viscous fluid in motion the pressure on a small area is no longer normal to that area so that at any point the principal stresses differ from their mean value $-p$ by a function of the rates of distortion. In formulating this relation we introduce a constant μ which is called the *coefficient of viscosity* of the fluid and we find that,[1] in the case where the fluid is incompressible (that is, ρ constant) equation (8) is replaced by the equation

$$\frac{\partial \mathbf{v}}{\partial t} - 2\mathbf{v} \times \boldsymbol{\omega} + \operatorname{grad}\left(\Omega + \frac{1}{2}\mathbf{v}^2 + \frac{p}{\rho}\right) + 2\nu\operatorname{curl}\boldsymbol{\omega} = 0 \tag{12}$$

[1] Cf. S. Goldstein (ed.), "Recent Developments in Fluid Dynamics" (Oxford, New York, 1938), p. 97.

where $\nu = \mu/\rho$ is called the *kinematical viscosity*. Since the density is constant, the equation of continuity is of the simple form (10), and since we may, in general, write

$$\nabla^2 \mathbf{v} = \text{grad (div } \mathbf{v}) - 2 \text{ curl } \omega$$

it follows that, in this case, (12) may be written in the equivalent form

$$\frac{\partial \mathbf{v}}{\partial t} - 2\mathbf{v} \times \omega + \text{grad}\left(\Omega + \frac{1}{2} \mathbf{v}^2 + \frac{p}{\rho} \right) - \nu\nabla^2\mathbf{v} = 0 \qquad (13)$$

The two-dimensional form of this equation is of some interest. In this case the vectors $\mathbf{v}$ and ω assume the simple forms $(u,v,0)$ and $(0,0,\zeta)$, respectively, so that we may write equation (13) in the forms

$$\frac{\partial u}{\partial t} - 2v\zeta + \frac{\partial \Omega'}{\partial x} - \nu \nabla^2 u = 0 \qquad (13a)$$

$$\frac{\partial v}{\partial t} + 2u\zeta + \frac{\partial \Omega'}{\partial y} - \nu \nabla^2 v = 0 \qquad (13b)$$

Eliminating the quantity $\Omega' = \Omega + \frac{1}{2}(u^2 + v^2) + p/\rho$ from these equations, we obtain the single equation

$$\frac{\partial \zeta}{\partial t} + u \frac{\partial \zeta}{\partial x} + v \frac{\partial \zeta}{\partial y} = \nu \nabla_1^2 \zeta \qquad (14)$$

Also, if we write

$$u = -\frac{\partial \psi}{\partial y}, \qquad v = \frac{\partial \psi}{\partial x} \qquad (15)$$

it follows from the definition of the vorticity that $\zeta = \nabla_1^2 \psi$ and also that the continuity equation (10) is satisfied. Substituting from equations (15) into equation (14) we find that

$$\frac{\partial}{\partial t} \nabla_1^2 \psi + \left(\frac{\partial \psi}{\partial y} \frac{\partial}{\partial x} - \frac{\partial \psi}{\partial x} \frac{\partial}{\partial y} \right) \nabla_1^2 \psi = \nu \nabla_1^4 \psi \qquad (16)$$

In the steady state $\partial/\partial t = 0$, so that if the velocity of the fluid be very small and the viscosity large all the terms on the left-hand side of equation (16) arising from the inertia of the fluid and not its viscosity may be neglected in first approximation, so reducing equation (16) to the biharmonic equation

$$\nabla_1^4 \psi = 0 \qquad (17)$$

31. Irrotational Flow of a Perfect Fluid

We shall begin our discussion of typical boundary value problems in hydrodynamics by considering the irrotational flow of a perfect fluid under certain circumstances.

31.1 Two-dimensional flow. In the first instance we shall consider the irrotational two-dimensional flow of a perfect fluid filling the half space $y \geq 0$. It follows from equations (9) and (11) that, in terms of a velocity potential ϕ, we have

$$u = -\frac{\partial \phi}{\partial x}, \qquad v = -\frac{\partial \phi}{\partial y} \tag{18}$$

where the scalar velocity potential ϕ satisfies the two-dimensional form of Laplace's equation

$$\nabla_1^2 \phi \equiv \frac{\partial^2 \phi}{\partial x^2} + \frac{\partial^2 \phi}{\partial y^2} = 0 \tag{19}$$

We shall suppose that fluid is introduced to the half space through the strip $|x| \leq a$ of the plane $y = 0$. First we shall assume that the fluid is introduced normally with prescribed velocity so that, along $y = 0$, we have the boundary condition

$$\frac{\partial \phi}{\partial y} = \left\{ \begin{array}{ll} -f(x) & 0 < |x| < a \\ 0 & |x| > a \end{array} \right\} \tag{20}$$

where $f(x)$ is a prescribed function of position. We further make the assumption that at a great distance from the plane $y = 0$ the fluid is at rest, that is,

$$(u,v) \to 0 \qquad \text{as } y \to \infty \tag{20a}$$

If, now, we introduce the Fourier transforms

$$\Phi(\xi,y) = \frac{1}{\sqrt{2\pi}} \int_{-\infty}^{\infty} e^{i\xi x} \phi(x,y)\,dx, \qquad F(\xi) = \frac{1}{\sqrt{2\pi}} \int_{-\infty}^{\infty} e^{i\xi x} f(x)\,dx$$

we find that equations (19) and (20) are equivalent to the ordinary differential equation

$$\frac{d^2\Phi}{dy^2} - \xi^2 \Phi = 0$$

taken with the boundary condition $d\Phi(\xi,0)/dy = -F(\xi)$. The solution of this problem subject to the condition (20a) is obviously

$$\Phi = \frac{F(\xi)}{|\xi|} e^{-|\xi|y}$$

whence, by the inversion theorem 10,

$$\phi = \frac{1}{\sqrt{2\pi}} \int_{-\infty}^{\infty} \frac{F(\xi)}{|\xi|} e^{i\xi x - |\xi| y}\,d\xi \tag{21}$$

In particular, if

$$f(x) = \begin{cases} U, & 0 < |x| < a \\ 0, & |x| > a \end{cases}$$

we have

$$F(\xi) = \frac{U}{\sqrt{2\pi}} \frac{\sin(\xi a)}{\xi}$$

so that

$$\phi = \frac{U}{2\pi} \int_{-\infty}^{\infty} \frac{\sin(\xi a)}{\xi} \frac{e^{i\xi x}}{|\xi|} e^{-|\xi|y} d\xi$$

and the component of the fluid velocity in the y direction is given by

$$v = -\frac{\partial \phi}{\partial y} = \frac{U}{2\pi} \int_{-\infty}^{\infty} \frac{\sin(\xi a)}{\xi} e^{-|\xi|y + i\xi x} d\xi$$

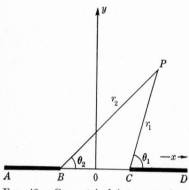

FIG. 49. Geometrical interpretation of r_1, r_2, θ_1, and θ_2. C is the point $(a,0)$ and $B(-a,0)$.

Making use of the result

$$\int_0^{\infty} \frac{\sin(\alpha\xi)}{\xi} e^{-\xi y} d\xi = \frac{\pi}{2} - \tan^{-1}\frac{y}{\alpha}$$

we find that

$$v = \frac{U}{2\pi} (\theta_1 - \theta_2)$$

where $\tan \theta_1 = y/(x - a)$ and

$$\tan \theta_2 = y/(x + a)$$

(cf. Fig. 49).

In a similar fashion we find for the component of the fluid velocity in the x direction

$$u = -\frac{\partial \phi}{\partial x} = -\frac{iU}{2\pi} \int_{-\infty}^{\infty} \frac{\sin(\xi a)}{|\xi|} e^{i\xi x - |\xi|y} d\xi = \frac{U}{2\pi} \log \frac{r_2}{r_1}$$

where $r_2^2 = (x + a)^2 + y^2$ and $r_1^2 = (x - a)^2 + y^2$.

If we introduce a complex potential $w = \phi + i\psi$, we have

$$\frac{dw}{dz} = \frac{\partial \phi}{\partial x} - i\frac{\partial \phi}{\partial y} = -u + iv \tag{22}$$

so that, inserting the above values for the components of velocity, we obtain the expression

$$\frac{dw}{dz} = \frac{U}{2\pi} \left[\log \frac{r_1}{r_2} + i(\theta_1 - \theta_2) \right] = \frac{U}{2\pi} \log \frac{z - a}{z + a}$$

Integrating this expression with respect to z, we obtain for the complex potential

$$w = \frac{U}{2\pi} [2a + (z - a) \log (z - a) - (z + a) \log (z + a)] \quad (23)$$

31.2 Steady flow of a perfect fluid through a slit. We shall next consider the problem of determining the two-dimensional steady flow of a perfect fluid through a slit in a plane rigid boundary. With the center of the slit as origin (cf. Fig. 49), and with the y axis perpendicular to the plane of the thin screen, we have to solve the differential equation (19) subject to the boundary conditions

$$\phi = \text{const.}, \ |x| \leq a; \qquad v = -\frac{\partial \phi}{\partial y} = 0, \ |x| > a$$

when $y = 0$.

If along $y = 0$ we have

$$v = \begin{cases} (a^2 - x^2)^{-\frac{1}{2}}, & 0 < |x| < a \\ 0, & |x| > a \end{cases}$$

then by the analysis of Sec. 31.1 we find that the velocity potential is given by equation (21) with

$$F(\xi) = \frac{1}{\sqrt{2\pi}} \int_{-a}^{a} \frac{e^{-i\xi x}}{(a^2 - x^2)^{\frac{1}{2}}} \, dx = \sqrt{\frac{2}{\pi}} \int_{0}^{a} \frac{\cos (\xi x) dx}{(a^2 - x^2)^{\frac{1}{2}}} = \sqrt{\frac{\pi}{2}} J_0(a\xi)$$

Hence we have for the velocity potential

$$\phi = \frac{1}{2} \int_{-\infty}^{\infty} \frac{J_0(a\xi)}{|\xi|} e^{i\xi x - |\xi| y} \, d\xi$$

so that from equations (18) we have for the components of the velocity vector

$$v = -\frac{\partial \phi}{\partial y} = \int_{0}^{\infty} e^{-\xi y} J_0(a\xi) \cos (\xi x) d\xi \quad (24)$$

$$u = -\frac{\partial \phi}{\partial x} = \int_{0}^{\infty} e^{-\xi y} J_0(a\xi) \sin (\xi x) d\xi \quad (25)$$

Also, when $y = 0$,

$$\frac{\partial \phi}{\partial x} = -\int_{0}^{\infty} \sin (\xi x) J_0(a\xi) d\xi = 0 \qquad \text{if } |x| < a$$

verifying that ϕ is a constant on the segment $y = 0$, $|x| < a$.

Substituting from equations (24) and (25) into equation (22), we find that the complex potential of the flow is given by the solution of the equation

$$\frac{dw}{dz} = i \int_0^\infty e^{i\xi z} J_0(a\xi) d\xi = (z^2 - a^2)^{-\frac{1}{2}}$$

Integrating this equation, we obtain the standard solution[1]

$$z = a \cosh(w)$$

31.3 Flow of a jet of perfect fluid through a circular aperture in a plane rigid screen. The solution to the problem of determining the steady flow of a perfect fluid through a circular aperture in a plane rigid wall is given on page 138 of Lamb's treatise. We shall now show how this three-dimensional analogue of the problem considered in Sec. 31.2 may be generalized by the use of the theory of dual integral equations developed in Sec. 12.

With the center of the aperture as origin and with the z axis perpendicular to the plane of the thin rigid screen we may describe any point in the fluid by means of cylindrical polar coordinates r and z. The solution of the steady flow problem requires the determination of a velocity potential function $\phi(r,z)$ satisfying Laplace's equation (11) in these coordinates,

$$\frac{\partial^2 \phi}{\partial r^2} + \frac{1}{r}\frac{\partial \phi}{\partial r} + \frac{\partial^2 \phi}{\partial z^2} = 0 \tag{26}$$

together with the boundary conditions

$$\phi = g(r) \qquad\qquad r < a \tag{27}$$

$$\frac{\partial \phi}{\partial z} = 0 \qquad\qquad r > a \tag{28}$$

over the plane $z = 0$. The function $g(r)$ occurring in equation (27) is prescribed. In the special case considered by Lamb it is a constant.

Multiplying both sides of equation (26) by $rJ_0(\xi r)$ and integrating with respect to r from 0 to ∞, we find that this equation is equivalent to the second-order ordinary differential equation

$$\frac{d^2 \bar{\phi}}{dz^2} - \xi^2 \bar{\phi} = 0 \tag{29}$$

for the determination of the Hankel transform

$$\bar{\phi}(\xi,z) = \int_0^\infty r\phi(r,z)J_0(\xi r)dr \tag{30}$$

of the velocity potential. If we are interested in flow into the half space $z \geq 0$, then, since the velocity potential must tend to zero as $z \to \infty$, we

[1] H. Lamb, "Hydrodynamics," 6th ed. (Cambridge, London, 1932), p. 73.

must take a solution of equation (29) of the form

$$\bar{\phi} = A(\xi)e^{-\xi z} \tag{31}$$

where $A(\xi)$ is to be determined by the conditions (27) and (28). Differentiating equation (31) with respect to z, we have

$$\int_0^\infty r\frac{\partial\phi}{\partial z}J_0(\xi r)dr = -\xi A(\xi)e^{-\xi z}$$

and inverting these equations by means of the Hankel inversion theorem 19, we obtain the expressions

$$\phi = \int_0^\infty \xi A(\xi)e^{-\xi z}J_0(\xi r)d\xi, \qquad \frac{\partial\phi}{\partial z} = -\int_0^\infty \xi^2 A(\xi)e^{-\xi z}J_0(\xi r)d\xi$$

If we substitute from these equations into equations (27) and (28) and write $\rho = r/a$, $F(u) = uA(u/a)$, $G(\rho) = a^2g(r)$, we obtain the dual integral equations

$$\left.\begin{array}{ll} \displaystyle\int_0^\infty F(u)J_0(\rho u)du = G(\rho) & 0 < \rho < 1 \\[3mm] \displaystyle\int_0^\infty uF(u)J_0(\rho u)du = 0 & \rho > 1 \end{array}\right\} \tag{32}$$

for the determination of the function $F(u)$, from which we derive the value of $A(\xi)$ by the equation

$$A(\xi) = \frac{F(a\xi)}{a\xi}$$

The dual integral equations (32) are of the type considered in Sec. 12. It follows immediately from equation (47), Chap. 2, that the solution of these equations is

$$F(u) = \frac{2}{\pi}\cos u\int_0^1 \frac{yG(y)dy}{(1-y^2)^{\frac{1}{2}}} + \frac{2}{\pi}\int_0^1 \frac{y\,dy}{(1-y^2)^{\frac{1}{2}}}\int_0^1 G(yu)xu\,\sin\,(xu)du \tag{33}$$

In the particular case in which the function $G(\rho)$ is a constant, C, say, we find that

$$F(u) = \frac{2C}{\pi}\left(\frac{\sin u}{u}\right) \tag{34}$$

Thus $g(r)$ is a constant γ where $C = a^2\gamma$ and

$$A(\xi) = \frac{2\gamma}{\pi}\frac{\sin\,(\xi a)}{\xi^2}$$

so that, finally,

$$\phi = \frac{2\gamma}{\pi} \int_0^\infty \frac{\sin (\xi a)}{\xi} e^{-\xi z} J_0(\xi r) d\xi \tag{35}$$

which is the solution derived otherwise by Lamb.

We can perform a similar analysis in the case in which $\partial\phi/\partial z$ is prescribed all along the plane $z = 0$. If $\partial\phi/\partial z = -F(r)$ (which is assumed to be zero when r exceeds a), and if we denote its Hankel transform of zero order by

$$\bar{F}(\xi) = \int_0^a rF(r)J_0(\xi r)dr$$

then it is readily shown that

$$\bar{\phi} = -\frac{\bar{F}(\xi)}{\xi}$$

and so, by Theorem 19, that

$$\phi = -\int_0^\infty \bar{F}(\xi)e^{-\xi z}J_0(\xi r)d\xi$$

If the aperture is very small, we may take

$$F(r) = \frac{S}{2\pi r} \delta(r)$$

of which the Hankel transform is $\bar{F}(\xi) = S/2\pi$, giving

$$\phi(r,z) = -\frac{S}{2\pi} \int_0^\infty e^{-\xi z}J_0(\xi r)d\xi = -\frac{S}{2\pi(r^2 + z^2)^{\frac{1}{2}}}$$

Similarly, if we take $F(r) = (a^2 - r^2)^{-\frac{1}{2}}$, we arrive at the solution (35).

32. Surface Waves

32.1 Fundamental equations. Another subject of interest in hydrodynamics is that of the propagation of waves in a perfect fluid. We shall now consider this problem under certain specific assumptions. We shall confine ourselves primarily to the consideration of fluid motion in two dimensions. The elevation of the free surface will then have the appearance of a series of parallel ridges running normal to the xy plane.

If the motion is generated originally from rest by the action of ordinary forces or impulses, it will be irrotational throughout all time and we may describe the motion in terms of a velocity potential ϕ satisfying the two-dimensional form of equation (11),

$$\frac{\partial^2\phi}{\partial x^2} + \frac{\partial^2\phi}{\partial y^2} = 0 \tag{36}$$

From the definition (9) of the potential it follows at once that, at any fixed boundary, the function ϕ must satisfy the condition

$$\frac{\partial \phi}{\partial n} = 0 \tag{37}$$

where $\partial/\partial n$ denotes differentiation along the direction of the normal to the boundary. Also, substituting from equation (9) into equation (8), we find in the irrotational case that

$$\mathrm{grad}\left(\Omega + \frac{1}{2}\, \mathbf{v}^2 + \frac{p}{\rho} - \frac{\partial \phi}{\partial t} \right) = 0$$

If we take the y axis to be vertical and the x axis horizontal, we may write $\Omega = gy$ and the integrated form of the above equation becomes, on neglect of the term $\frac{1}{2}\mathbf{v}^2$, which is small if the oscillations are small,

$$\frac{p}{\rho} = \frac{\partial \phi}{\partial t} - gy + F(t) \tag{38}$$

where $F(t)$ is an arbitrary function of t. If we absorb this function in $\partial\phi/\partial t$, we see that the elevation η of the surface at time t above its equilibrium position is given by the expression

$$\eta = \frac{1}{g}\left(\frac{\partial \phi}{\partial t} \right)_{y=\eta} - \frac{p_0(x,t)}{g\rho} \tag{39}$$

where $p_0(x,t)$ denotes the pressure at the surface.

If the surface is free from external pressure, we may put $p_0(x,t) = 0$ and write $(\partial\phi/\partial t)_{y=0}$ as a first approximation to $(\partial\phi/\partial t)_{y=\eta}$ to obtain the relation

$$\eta = \frac{1}{g}\left(\frac{\partial \phi}{\partial t} \right)_{y=0} \tag{40}$$

Also, by the definition of the velocity we have

$$\frac{\partial \eta}{\partial t} = v_0 = -\left(\frac{\partial \phi}{\partial y} \right)_{y=0} \tag{41}$$

Eliminating η between equations (40) and (41), we obtain the condition

$$\frac{\partial^2 \phi}{\partial t^2} + g\frac{\partial \phi}{\partial y} = 0 \tag{42}$$

valid when $y = 0$.

If, on the other hand, an impulsive pressure is applied to the surface of the fluid, equation (39) becomes

$$\left(\frac{\partial \phi}{\partial t}\right)_{y=0} = \frac{1}{\rho}\, p_0(x,t)$$

that is, when $y = 0$,

$$\phi = \frac{P_0(x)}{\rho} \tag{43}$$

where $P_0(x) = \int p_0(x,t)dt$ is the impulsive pressure.

32.2 Surface waves generated by an impulsive pressure.   In the first boundary value problem of this type which we shall consider we suppose that the fluid is of infinite depth, $y \leq 0$, and that waves are generated by the action of an impulsive pressure on the surface $y = 0$ of the fluid.   To determine the wave system so produced we have, therefore, to solve equations (36) and (42) subject to the boundary condition (43) together with the initial condition that $\eta = 0$ when $t = 0$.

If we introduce the Fourier transform

$$\Phi(\xi,y,t) = \frac{1}{\sqrt{2\pi}} \int_{-\infty}^{\infty} \phi(x,y,t)e^{i\xi x}\, dx$$

then equation (36) is equivalent to

$$\frac{d^2\Phi}{dy^2} - \xi^2\Phi = 0$$

of which the solution which tends to zero as $y \to -\infty$ is

$$\Phi(\xi,y,t) = A(\xi,t)e^{|\xi|y} \tag{44}$$

Multiplying both sides of equation (42) by $(2\pi)^{-\frac{1}{2}}e^{i\xi x}$ and integrating over the entire range of variation of x, we find that

$$\frac{d^2A}{dt^2} + g|\xi|A(\xi,t) = 0$$

whence it follows that

$$A(\xi,t) = \alpha(\xi)e^{i(g|\xi|)^{\frac{1}{2}}t} + \beta(\xi)e^{-i(g|\xi|)^{\frac{1}{2}}t} \tag{45}$$

where $\alpha(\xi)$ and $\beta(\xi)$ are constants of integration.   Along $y = 0$ we have

$$\frac{d\Phi}{dt} = i(g|\xi|)^{\frac{1}{2}}[\alpha(\xi)e^{i(g|\xi|)^{\frac{1}{2}}t} - \beta(\xi)e^{-i(g|\xi|)^{\frac{1}{2}}t}]$$

so that if η is zero initially we must take $\alpha(\xi) = \beta(\xi)$.   Using this condition with that on ϕ, which may be written in the form $\Phi(\xi,0,0) = \bar{P}_0(\xi)/\rho$, we find that

$$\Phi = \frac{P_0(\xi)}{\rho} \cos\, (g|\xi|)^{\frac{1}{2}}te^{|\xi|y}$$

which by the application of the inversion theorem 10 leads to the result

$$\phi(x,y,t) = \frac{1}{\rho}\sqrt{\frac{1}{2\pi}} \int_{-\infty}^{\infty} \bar{P}_0(\xi) \cos (g|\xi|)^{\frac{1}{2}}te^{|\xi|y-i\xi x}\,d\xi$$

$$= \frac{1}{\pi\rho} \int_0^{\infty} d\xi \int_{-\infty}^{\infty} P_0(\alpha) \cos [(g|\xi|)^{\frac{1}{2}}t] \cos [(x-\alpha)]e^{\xi y}\,d\alpha \quad (46)$$

In particular, if $\bar{P}_0(\xi)$ is an *even* function of ξ, the first of these two equations may be put into the form

$$\phi(x,y,t) = \frac{1}{\rho\sqrt{2\pi}} \left[\int_0^{\infty} e^{\xi y}\bar{P}_0(\xi) \cos (\xi x - g^{\frac{1}{2}}\xi^{\frac{1}{2}}t)d\xi \right.$$

$$\left. + \int_0^{\infty} e^{\xi y}\bar{P}_0(\xi) \cos (\xi x + g^{\frac{1}{2}}\xi^{\frac{1}{2}}t)d\xi \right] \quad (47)$$

The evaluation of definite integrals of this type is, in general, troublesome and can often be achieved only by the use of numerical or approximate methods. We shall return to this problem in the next section. For the moment we shall confine our attention to the evaluation of these integrals in a special case—that in which the waves are generated by the application of an impulsive pressure to a single point, the origin, say. In this case we may take $P_0(x) = P\delta(x)$, where P is a constant, so that $\bar{P}_0(\xi) = (2\pi)^{-\frac{1}{2}}P$. When $y = 0$, it follows from equation (47) that

$$\phi(x,0,t) = \frac{P}{2\pi\rho} \int_0^{\infty} [\cos (\xi x - g^{\frac{1}{2}}\xi^{\frac{1}{2}}t) + \cos (\xi x + g^{\frac{1}{2}}\xi^{\frac{1}{2}}t)]d\xi \quad (48)$$

Substituting η^2 for $g\xi$ in these integrals, we find that

$$\phi(x,0,t) = -\frac{P}{\pi\rho g}\frac{dJ}{dt} \quad (49)$$

where J denotes the integral

$$J = \int_0^{\infty} \left[\sin \left(\frac{\eta^2 x}{g} + \eta t\right) - \sin \left(\frac{\eta^2 x}{g} - \eta t\right) \right]d\eta \quad (50)$$

Making the substitutions

$$\zeta = \frac{x^{\frac{1}{2}}}{g^{\frac{1}{2}}}\left(\eta \mp \frac{gt}{2x}\right), \qquad \omega = \left(\frac{gt^2}{4x}\right)^{\frac{1}{2}}$$

we find that

$$J = -\frac{2g^{\frac{1}{2}}}{x^{\frac{1}{2}}} \int_0^{\omega} \sin (\omega^2 - \zeta^2)d\zeta \quad (51)$$

from which it follows immediately that

$$\frac{dJ}{dt} = -\left(\frac{g}{x}\right)^{\frac{3}{2}} t \int_0^\omega \cos(\omega^{\iota} - \zeta^2)d\zeta \qquad (52)$$

Substituting from equation (52) into equation (49), we obtain for the velocity potential

$$\phi(x,0,t) = \frac{P}{\pi\rho} \frac{g^{\frac{1}{2}}t}{x^{\frac{3}{2}}} \int_0^\omega \cos(\omega^2 - \zeta^2)d\zeta \qquad (53)$$

With the usual notation for Fresnel's integrals,[1]

$$C(u) = \int_0^u \cos\left(\frac{1}{2}\pi x^2\right) dx, \qquad S(u) = \int_0^u \sin\left(\frac{1}{2}\pi x^2\right) dx \qquad (54)$$

we may write the solution (52) in the form

$$\phi(x,0,t) = \frac{Pu}{\rho x}\left[\cos\left(\frac{1}{2}\pi u^2\right) C(u) + \sin\left(\frac{1}{2}\pi u^2\right) S(u)\right] \qquad (55)$$

where

$$u^2 = \frac{gt^2}{2\pi x} \qquad (56)$$

The value of the velocity potential along $y = 0$ can therefore be determined readily from the calculated values of the Fresnel integrals $C(u)$ and $S(u)$. The variation of these functions with u is shown in Fig. 50(i) and (ii). A simple geometrical interpretation of this result is, however, possible. Equation (55) shows that we may consider the velocity potential ϕ to be the real part of the expression

$$\frac{Pu}{\rho x} e^{-\frac{1}{2}\pi i u^2}[C(u) + iS(u)]$$

If we now plot the curve whose freedom equations are

$$x = C(u), \qquad y = S(u)$$

we get the well-known Cornu spiral (cf. Fig. 51) so that, if P is the point on the spiral corresponding to the value u, we may write

$$C(u) + iS(u) = re^{i\theta}$$

where r denotes the distance OP of P from the origin and θ is the angle xOP, as shown in Fig. 51. With this notation ϕ is the real part of the expression

$$\frac{Pur}{\rho x} e^{-i(\frac{1}{2}\pi u^2 - \theta)}$$

[1] E. Jahnke and F. Emde, "Funktionentafeln mit Formeln und Kurven" (B. G. Teubner, Leipzig, 1933), p. 108.

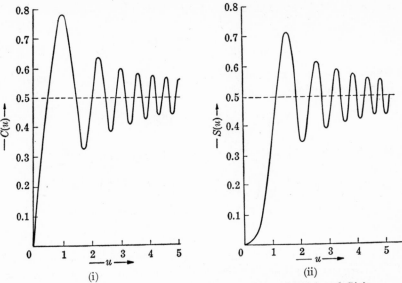

FIG. 50.   The variation with u of Fresnel's integrals $C(u)$ and $S(u)$.

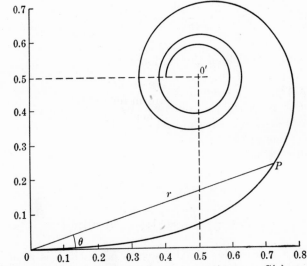

FIG. 51.   The Cornu spiral with freedom equations $x = C(u)$, $y = S(u)$.

from which it follows at once that

$$\phi = \frac{Pur}{\rho x} \cos\left(\frac{1}{2}\pi u^2 - \theta\right)$$

Now, since $C(\infty) = S(\infty) = \frac{1}{2}$, we see that for large values of u the point P approaches the limit point $O'(\frac{1}{2}, \frac{1}{2})$ of the spiral and $r = OO' = 1/\sqrt{2}$,

$\theta = \pi/4$ so that for large values of gt^2/x we have the asymptotic expression

$$\phi(x,0,t) \sim \frac{P}{2\rho}\left(\frac{gt^2}{\pi x^3}\right)^{\frac{1}{2}}\cos\left(\frac{gt^2}{4x} - \frac{\pi}{4}\right) \tag{57}$$

for the velocity potential on $y = 0$.

Using the relations (40) and (56), we obtain

$$\eta = (2\pi gx)^{-\frac{1}{2}}\frac{\partial\phi}{\partial u}$$

so that from the solution (55) we obtain the equation

$$\eta = \frac{P}{\rho(2\pi gx^3)^{\frac{1}{2}}}\left\{C(u)\left[\cos\left(\frac{1}{2}\pi u^2\right) - \pi u^2\sin\left(\frac{1}{2}\pi u^2\right)\right]\right.$$
$$\left. + S(u)\left[\sin\left(\frac{1}{2}\pi u^2\right) + \pi u^2\cos\left(\frac{1}{2}\pi u^2\right)\right] + 1\right\} \tag{58}$$

for the elevation of the free surface. For large values of u we may take $C(u) = S(u) = \frac{1}{2}$ and neglect terms of order u and 1 in comparison with those of order u^2. Equation (58) then reduces to

$$\eta \sim \frac{Pg^{\frac{1}{2}}t^2}{4\pi^{\frac{1}{2}}\rho x^{\frac{5}{2}}}\cos\left(\frac{gt^2}{4x} + \frac{\pi}{4}\right) \tag{59}$$

for large values of gt^2/x.

32.3 Kelvin's principle of the stationary phase. We shall now return to the consideration of the evaluation of integrals of the kind occurring in equation (47) with a complicated form for the function $\bar{P}_0(\xi)$. In the preceding section we saw that even when $\bar{P}_0(\xi)$ was unity the evaluation of these integrals even in the simplest case $y = 0$ was a fairly complicated process. For general values of y and more involved forms of $\bar{P}_0(\xi)$ recourse must be had to an approximate method due to Kelvin[1] and known generally as the *principle of the stationary phase*.

To begin with we confine our attention to the integral

$$I_1 = \frac{1}{2\pi}\int_0^\infty \cos\{u[x - tf(u)]\}\,du \tag{60}$$

where $f(u)$ is a real single-valued function of u which is positive for all positive values of u. In the case of the integrals occurring in equation (48), $f(u) = (g/u)^{\frac{1}{2}}$. Kelvin *asserted* that an approximate value of the integral I_1 valid for large values of x and t can be obtained by considering

---

[1] Lord Kelvin, *Phil. Mag.*, [5] **23**, 252 (1887); *Proc. Roy. Soc. (London)*, **A42**, 80 (1887). See also T. H. Havelock, "The Propagation of Disturbances in Dispersive Media," *Cambridge Tract* 17 (Cambridge, London, 1914), Chap. III.

only the contributions from small ranges of integration in the neighborhood of points at which the phase

$$u[x - tf(u)] \tag{61}$$

is stationary. Since the integral represents the superposition of the effects of an infinite number of trains of simple waves of equal amplitude and all possible wavelengths, we consider the effect of the remainder of the range of integration to vanish as a result of interference.

Suppose, for simplicity, that the function (61) has a simple turning value at the point $u = \lambda$ and nowhere else; then according to Kelvin's conjecture the approximate value of I_1 is

$$I_1^{(0)} = \frac{1}{2\pi} \int_{\lambda-\epsilon}^{\lambda+\epsilon} \cos \{u[x - tf(u)]\} du \tag{62}$$

where ϵ is a small positive quantity and λ satisfies the equation

$$t[f(\lambda) + \lambda f'(\lambda)] = x \tag{63}$$

Changing the variable of integration from u to $\zeta = u - \lambda$ and making use of Taylor's theorem and equation (63) in the form

$$(\zeta + \lambda)[x - tf(\zeta + \lambda)] = \lambda^2 tf'(\lambda) + \mu^2 \zeta^2$$

where

$$\mu^2 = -\tfrac{1}{2}t[\lambda f''(\lambda) + 2f'(\lambda)] > 0$$

we find that $I_1^{(0)}$ is the real part of the integral

$$I = \frac{1}{\pi} e^{i\lambda^2 tf'(\lambda)} \int_0^{\epsilon} e^{i\mu^2 \zeta^2} d\zeta$$

which reduces by the substitution $\mu^2 \zeta^2 = v$ to the form

$$\frac{1}{2\pi\mu} e^{i\lambda^2 tf'(\lambda)} \int_0^{\mu^2 \epsilon^2} e^{iv} v^{-\frac{1}{2}} dv$$

Now as $t \to \infty$, $\mu \to \infty$ and ϵ, though it is small, is fixed so that $\mu\epsilon \to \infty$ and we have approximately

$$I = \frac{1}{2\pi\mu} e^{i\lambda^2 tf'(\lambda)} e^{\frac{1}{4}\pi i} \Gamma\left(\frac{1}{2}\right)$$

Taking the real part of this expression and substituting for μ, we see that, when x and t are large, I_1 is given approximately by

$$I_1^{(0)} = \frac{\cos[\lambda^2 tf'(\lambda) + \tfrac{1}{4}\pi]}{\{-2\pi t[2f'(\lambda) + \lambda f''(\lambda)]\}^{\frac{1}{2}}} \tag{64}$$

where λ is the root of equation (63). If we introduce the group velocity[1] U, defined by the relation

$$U(\xi) = \frac{d}{d\xi}[\xi f(\xi)]$$

then it is obvious that we may write equation (64) in the equivalent form

$$I_1^{(0)} = \frac{\cos\{[x - tf(\lambda)]\lambda + \tfrac{1}{4}\pi\}}{[-2\pi t U'(\lambda)]^{\frac{1}{2}}} \tag{64a}$$

where, by equation (63), λ is a root of the equation

$$U(\lambda) = \frac{x}{t} \tag{63a}$$

The formula (64a) breaks down if $U'(\lambda)$ is zero; in this case we must consider the terms in ζ^3. Using the expansion

$$u[x - tf(u)] = \lambda[x - tf(\lambda)] + \tfrac{1}{6}tU''(\lambda)\zeta^3$$

we find that

$$I_1^{(0)} = \frac{1}{2\pi}\left[\frac{6}{-tU''(\lambda)}\right]^{\frac{1}{3}}\int_{-\infty}^{\infty}\cos\{[x - f(\lambda)t] + v^3\}dv$$

$$= \frac{1}{2\pi}\left[\frac{6}{-tU''(\lambda)}\right]^{\frac{1}{3}}\frac{2}{3}\sin\left(\frac{\pi}{3}\right)\Gamma\left(\frac{1}{3}\right)\cos\{\lambda[x - f(\lambda)t]\} \tag{64b}$$

provided that λ has neither of the values 0 or ∞; in both of these cases we obtain the desired result by dividing the right-hand side of equation (64b) by 2.

It will be observed that in deriving the expression (64) for the integral (60) we assumed that:

1. The total value of the integral arises from a small range of integration in the immediate vicinity of the point $u = \lambda$.

2. In the integration over this small range it is possible to neglect all powers of $(u - \lambda)$ higher than the second.

It should also be noted that the method as developed by Kelvin does not yield an estimate of the error $I_1 - I_1^{(0)}$. By making use of a generalization of Dirichlet's integral, due to Bromwich, Watson[2] has shown that it is possible to establish the validity of the principle of the stationary phase for a wide class of integrals involving rapidly oscillating functions. More recently, the method has been investigated rigorously by van der Corput,[3] mainly with a view to applications in the analytical theory of

[1] C. A. Coulson, "Waves, A Mathematical Account of the Common Types of Wave Motion" (Oliver & Boyd, Edinburgh and London, 1941), p. 133.

[2] G. N. Watson, *Proc. Cambridge Phil. Soc.*, **19**, 49 (1918).

[3] J. van der Corput, *Compositio Math.*, **1**, 14 (1935); **3**, 328 (1936).

numbers.   The results of these investigations confirm that *the major part of the integral of a rapidly oscillating trigonometrical function arises from that part of the region of integration near which the phase of the oscillating function is stationary.*

If, for example, we apply the result (64) to the first of the integrals occurring in equation (48), we have $f(u) = (g/u)^{\frac{1}{2}}$ so that equation (63) reduces to $\lambda = gt^2/4x^2$ and the formula (64) gives

$$\frac{1}{2\pi} \int_0^\infty \cos\left[ux - g^{\frac{1}{2}}u^{\frac{1}{2}}t\right]du = \frac{1}{2}\left(\frac{gt^2}{\pi x^3}\right)^{\frac{1}{2}} \cos\left(\frac{gt^2}{4x} - \frac{\pi}{4}\right)$$

Now in the expression (48) there are symmetrical groups of waves moving in the two directions from the origin.   If x and t are both positive, the chief contribution comes from the first of the two integrals and we find

$$\phi \sim \frac{P}{2\rho}\left(\frac{gt^2}{\pi x^3}\right)^{\frac{1}{2}} \cos\left(\frac{gt^2}{4x} - \frac{\pi}{4}\right)$$

in agreement with equation (57).

If the function $F(u)$ is appreciably constant in a small neighborhood of the point $u = \lambda$ defined by (63), it follows by arguments similar to those outlined above that the integral

$$I_2 = \frac{1}{2\pi} \int_0^\infty F(u) \cos\{u[x - tf(u)]\}du \qquad (65)$$

has the approximate value

$$I_2^{(0)} = \frac{F(\lambda) \cos\left[\lambda^2 tf'(\lambda) + \frac{1}{4}\pi\right]}{\sqrt{-2\pi t[2f'(\lambda) + \lambda f''(\lambda)]}} \qquad (66)$$

for large values of x and t.

Applying this result to equation (47), we see that for large values of x and t, both positive, we have approximately

$$\phi \sim \frac{1}{\rho}\left(\frac{gt^2}{2x^3}\right)^{\frac{1}{2}} e^{gt^2y/4x^2}\bar{P}_0\left(\frac{gt^2}{4x^2}\right) \cos\left(\frac{gt^2}{4x} - \frac{\pi}{4}\right)$$

32.4 Surface waves due to an initial displacement.   If we consider again the semiinfinite fluid $y \leq 0$ but suppose that the wave motion is produced by an initial displacement of the surface, then, by equations (40) and (43), our boundary conditions become

$$\frac{\partial \phi}{\partial t} = gf(x) \qquad\qquad \phi = 0 \qquad (67)$$

when $y = 0$ and $t = 0$.

Just as in Sec. 32.2, the Fourier transform Φ of the velocity potential is determined by equations (44) and (45) but, because of (67), the constants $\alpha(\xi)$ and $\beta(\xi)$ are now obtained from the equations

$$\alpha(\xi) + \beta(\xi) = 0$$
$$i(|\xi|)^{\frac{1}{2}}[\alpha(\xi) - \beta(\xi)] = g^{\frac{1}{2}}F(\xi)$$

in which $F(\xi)$ denotes the Fourier transform of the function $f(x)$. Hence

$$\Phi = \left(\frac{g}{|\xi|}\right)^{\frac{1}{2}} F(\xi) \sin [(g|\xi|)^{\frac{1}{2}}t] e^{|\xi|y}$$

so that, by Theorem 10, we find, for the velocity potential,

$$\phi = \frac{g}{\sqrt{2\pi}} \int_{-\infty}^{\infty} F(\xi) \frac{\sin [(g|\xi|)^{\frac{1}{2}}t]}{(g|\xi|)^{\frac{1}{2}}} e^{|\xi|y - i\xi x} \, d\xi$$

or, in the particular case in which $F(\xi)$ is an even function of ξ

$$\phi = \frac{g}{\sqrt{2\pi}} \int_0^{\infty} \frac{F(\xi)e^{\xi y}}{(g\xi)^{\frac{1}{2}}} [\sin (\xi x + g^{\frac{1}{2}}\xi^{\frac{1}{2}}t) - \sin (\xi x - g^{\frac{1}{2}}\xi^{\frac{1}{2}}t)]d\xi \quad (68)$$

With this value of the velocity potential we find from equation (40) that the elevation of the free surface at any subsequent time t is

$$\eta = \frac{1}{\sqrt{2\pi}} \int_0^{\infty} F(\xi)[\cos (\xi x + g^{\frac{1}{2}}\xi^{\frac{1}{2}}t) + \cos (\xi x - g^{\frac{1}{2}}\xi^{\frac{1}{2}}t)]d\xi \quad (69)$$

Using Kelvin's approximation (66) with $\lambda = gt^2/4x^2$, we see that for large values of x and t, both positive, the elevation of the free surface is given by the equation

$$\eta \sim \left(\frac{gt^2}{2x^3}\right)^{\frac{1}{2}} F\left(\frac{gt^2}{4x^2}\right) \cos\left(\frac{gt^2}{4x} - \frac{\pi}{4}\right) \quad (70)$$

For example, if the initial displacement is

$$f(x) = \frac{\epsilon a^2}{a^2 + x^2}$$

it follows that

$$F(\xi) = \left(\frac{\pi}{2}\right)^{\frac{1}{2}} a\epsilon e^{-a\xi}$$

so that, for large values of x and t,

$$\eta \sim \epsilon \left(\frac{a}{2x}\right) \left(\frac{\pi gt^2}{x}\right)^{\frac{1}{2}} e^{-agt^2/4x^2} \quad (71)$$

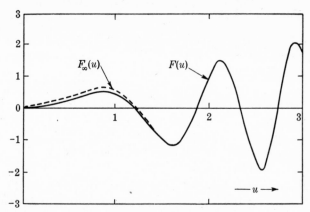

FIG. 52.   The variation with u of the function $F(u)$ defined by (74a).   The dotted curve shows the asymptotic form

$$F_\infty(u) = \frac{u}{\sqrt{2}} \cos\left[\frac{\pi}{2}\left(u^2 - \frac{1}{2}\right)\right]$$

If, however, the initial displacement is confined to the immediate vicinity of the origin, so that $f(x)$ vanishes for all but infinitesimal values of x, we may take $f(x) = \epsilon\ \delta(x)$, where ϵ is the area between the y axis and the initial displacement.   For this form of $f(x)$ we have $F(\xi) = (2\pi)^{-\frac{1}{2}}\epsilon$, leading to the asymptotic expression

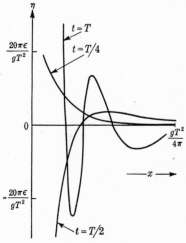

$$\eta \sim \epsilon\left(\frac{gt^2}{4\pi x^3}\right)^{\frac{1}{2}} \cos\left(\frac{gt^2}{4x} - \frac{\pi}{4}\right) \quad (72)$$

valid for large values of x and t.

In this case the integral (69) can be evaluated exactly.   It follows from an inspection of equations (48), (55), and (69) that we may write the expression for the elevation of the free surface in the dimensionless form

$$\frac{\eta}{(\epsilon/\frac{1}{2}gT^2)} = \left(\frac{\frac{1}{2}gT^2}{x}\right)F(u) \quad (73)$$

FIG. 53.   The form of the free surface at three times after the application of a displacement confined to the immediate vicinity of the origin.

where T denotes a unit of time and u and $F(u)$ are defined by the relations

$$F(u) = u[\cos\left(\tfrac{1}{2}\pi u^2\right)C(u) + \sin\left(\tfrac{1}{2}\pi u^2\right)S(u)] \quad (74)$$

$$u = \frac{1}{\sqrt{\pi}}\left(\frac{t}{T}\right)\left(\frac{\frac{1}{2}gT^2}{x}\right)^{\frac{1}{2}} \quad (74a)$$

With this notation it follows that, as $u \to \infty$,

$$\frac{\eta}{(\epsilon/\frac{1}{2}gT^2)} \sim \left(\frac{\frac{1}{2}gT^2}{x}\right) \frac{u}{\sqrt{2}} \cos\left(\frac{\pi u^2}{2} - \frac{\pi}{4}\right)$$

in agreement with equation (72).

The variation of $F(u)$ and of its asymptotic expansion

$$F_\infty(u) = \frac{u}{\sqrt{2}} \cos\left[\frac{1}{2}\left(u^2 - \frac{1}{2}\right)\pi\right]$$

with u is shown in Fig. 52. The form of these curves gives some idea of the accuracy of the Kelvin approximation. By means of Fig. 52 it is possible to draw out the form of the surface elevation at any time. The results of some calculations of this kind are shown in Fig. 53.

32.5 Waves on fluid of finite depth. In the problems on surface waves which we have considered in the previous sections it has been assumed that the fluid filled the entire half space $y \leq 0$. Now, we shall suppose the depth of the fluid to be finite, h, say, so that the range of variation of y is $-h \leq y \leq 0$. The wave motion is again determined from the solutions of equations (36) and (42), but the condition that $\phi \to 0$ as $y \to -\infty$ is replaced by the boundary condition

$$\frac{\partial\phi}{\partial y} = 0 \qquad\qquad y = -h \qquad (75)$$

which comes directly from equation (37). Instead of equation (44) we therefore have the solution

$$\Phi(\xi,y,t) = A(\xi,t) \cosh\left[|\xi|(y + h)\right]$$

for the Fourier transform Φ of the velocity potential ϕ of the wave motion. Multiplying both sides of equation (42) by $(2\pi)^{-\frac{1}{2}}e^{i\xi x}$ and integrating with respect to x from $-\infty$ to ∞, we find that $A(\xi,t)$ satisfies the equation

$$\frac{d^2A}{dt^2} + \sigma^2 A = 0$$

where

$$\sigma^2 = g|\xi|v \tanh\left(|\xi|h\right) \qquad (76)$$

whence it follows that, in terms of two arbitrary constants $\alpha(\xi)$ and $\beta(\xi)$,

$$\Phi = [\alpha(\xi)e^{i\sigma t} + \beta(\xi)e^{-i\sigma t}] \cosh\left[|\xi|(y + h)\right] \qquad (77)$$

If the motion is due to a prescribed initial displacement of the free surface, the conditions determining $\alpha(\xi)$ and $\beta(\xi)$ are equations (67), which may be written in the equivalent form

$$\frac{1}{g}\frac{d\Phi}{dt} = F(\xi) \qquad\qquad \Phi = 0 \qquad\qquad (78)$$

when $y = 0$ and $t = 0$. Substituting from (77) into (78), we obtain the pair of simultaneous equations

$$\alpha(\xi) + \beta(\xi) = 0$$

$$\frac{i\sigma}{g}[\alpha(\xi) - \beta(\xi)] \cosh(|\xi|h) = F(\xi)$$

which lead to the solution

$$\Phi = \frac{g}{\sigma} F(\xi) \sin(\sigma t) \frac{\cosh[|\xi|(y + h)]}{\cosh(|\xi|h)}$$

Inverting this result by means of Theorem 10, we find that

$$\phi = \frac{g}{\sqrt{2\pi}} \int_{-\infty}^{\infty} \frac{\sin(\sigma t)}{\sigma} F(\xi) e^{-i\xi x} \frac{\cosh[|\xi|(y + h)]}{\cosh(|\xi|h)} d\xi$$

which reduces in the case in which $F(\xi)$ is an even function of ξ to

$$\phi = \frac{g}{\sqrt{2\pi}} \int_{0}^{\infty} \frac{F(\xi)}{\sigma} \frac{\cosh[\xi(y + h)]}{\cosh(\xi h)} [\sin(\xi x + \sigma t) - \sin(\xi x - \sigma t)]d\xi \quad (79)$$

with σ^2 given by equation (76).

From equations (79) and (40) we obtain for the elevation of the free surface

$$\eta = \frac{1}{\sqrt{2\pi}} \int_{0}^{\infty} F(\xi)[\cos(\xi x - \sigma t) + \cos(\xi x + \sigma t)]d\xi \qquad (80)$$

In this case the function $f(u)$ of equation (60) is given by

$$f(u) = \left(\frac{g}{u}\right)^{\frac{1}{2}} \tanh^{\frac{1}{2}}(uh)$$

so that the group velocity occurring in (64a) has the form

$$U(u) = \frac{1}{2}\left[\frac{g}{u}\tanh(hu)\right]^{\frac{1}{2}}\left[1 + \frac{2uh}{\sinh(2uh)}\right]$$

and in particular $U(0) = (gh)^{\frac{1}{2}}$. Equation (63a) has, in general, one positive real root, and we can obtain an approximate expression for the integrals occurring in (80) by a straightforward application of the formula

(64a). This latter formula breaks down, however, in the case in which $x/t = (gh)^{\frac{1}{2}}$, which leads to a value $\lambda = 0$, for then $U'(\lambda) = U'(0) = 0$. Recourse is then had to (64b), which yields[1]

$$\eta \sim \frac{1}{3\sqrt{2\pi}}\, \Gamma\left(\frac{1}{3}\right)\left[\frac{-tU''(0)}{6}\right]^{-\frac{1}{3}} F(0)\, \sin\left(\frac{\pi}{3}\right)$$

If $f(x) = \epsilon\, \delta(x)$, so that $F(0) = (2\pi)^{-\frac{1}{2}}\epsilon$, we see that, for $x = (gh)^{\frac{1}{2}}t$,

$$\eta \sim \frac{\epsilon}{6\pi}\, \Gamma\left(\frac{1}{3}\right)\left(\frac{xh^2}{6}\right)^{-\frac{1}{3}} \sin\left(\frac{\pi}{3}\right)$$

since $U''(0) = -(gh^5)^{\frac{1}{2}}$.

If the motion arises from an initial impulsive pressure, then we must have (in the notation of Sec. 32.2)

$$\Phi = \frac{P_0(\xi)}{\xi}, \qquad \frac{d\Phi}{dt} = 0$$

when $y = 0$, $t = 0$, yielding

$$\Phi = \frac{P_0(\xi)}{\rho}\, \frac{\cos(\sigma t)}{\sinh(|\xi|h)}\, \cosh\left[|\xi|(y+h)\right]$$

from which it follows by Theorem 10 that the velocity potential is given by

$$\phi = \frac{1}{\rho\sqrt{2\pi}}\int_{-\infty}^{\infty} \frac{\cos(\sigma t)}{\sinh(|\xi|h)}\, \bar{P}_0(\xi)\, \cosh\left[|\xi|(y+h)\right]e^{-i\xi x}\, d\xi$$

In the case in which $\bar{P}_0(\xi)$ is an even function of ξ, this reduces to

$$\phi = \frac{1}{\rho\sqrt{2\pi}}\int_{0}^{\infty} \frac{\cosh(\xi y + \xi h)}{\sinh(\xi h)}\, \bar{P}_0(\xi)[\cos(\xi x - \sigma t) + \cos(\xi x + \sigma t)]d\xi$$

with σ given by equation (76). This integral may now be evaluated by methods similar to those employed above.

32.6 Wave propagation in two dimensions. Finally we shall consider the case of the propagation of surface waves in two horizontal directions we shall take to be the directions x and y. This removes the restriction, introduced in Sec. 32.1, that the elevation of the free surface will have the appearance of a series of parallel ridges. If we draw the z axis vertically upward so that the fluid is in the half space $z \leq 0$, the previous equations of motion (36) and (42) are replaced by

$$\frac{\partial^2\phi}{\partial x^2} + \frac{\partial^2\phi}{\partial y^2} + \frac{\partial^2\phi}{\partial z^2} = 0 \tag{81}$$

---

[1] It should be noted that since $\lambda = 0$ the factor $\frac{1}{2}$ has to be applied to the right-hand side of equation (64b).

and

$$\frac{\partial^2 \phi}{\partial t^2} + g \frac{\partial \phi}{\partial z} = 0 \qquad z = 0 \qquad (82)$$

with

$$\zeta = \frac{1}{g}\left(\frac{\partial \phi}{\partial t}\right)_{z=0} \qquad (83)$$

for the elevation of the free surface.

In the case of symmetry about the z axis we may describe the motion in terms of two cylindrical coordinates $r = (x^2 + y^2)^{\frac{1}{2}}$ and z. Equation (81) then assumes the familiar form

$$\frac{\partial^2 \phi}{\partial r^2} + \frac{1}{r}\frac{\partial \phi}{\partial r} + \frac{\partial^2 \phi}{\partial z^2} = 0 \qquad (84)$$

To solve this equation we introduce the zero-order Hankel transform

$$\bar{\phi}(\xi,z,t) = \int_0^\infty r\phi(r,z,t)J_0(\xi r)dr \qquad (85)$$

of the velocity potential ϕ. Multiplying both sides of (84) by $rJ_0(\xi r)$ and integrating with respect to r from 0 to ∞, we find that $\bar{\phi}$ satisfies

$$\frac{d^2\bar{\phi}}{dz^2} - \xi^2\bar{\phi} = 0$$

of which the solution, suitable to the discussion of cases in which $\phi \to 0$ as $z \to -\infty$, is

$$\bar{\phi} = A(\xi,t)e^{\xi z}$$

Multiplying (82) throughout by $rJ_0(\xi r)$, integrating over r, substituting from the last equation, and putting $z = 0$, we find

$$\frac{d^2 A}{dt^2} + g\xi A = 0$$

If the initial conditions are

$$\zeta = f(r), \qquad \phi = 0 \qquad \text{when } t = 0, z = 0$$

then by equation (83) we have

$$\frac{dA}{dt} = g\bar{f}(\xi) \qquad A = 0, t = 0$$

where $\bar{f}(\xi)$ is the zero-order Hankel transform of the function $f(r)$. Hence

$$A = \left(\frac{g}{\xi}\right)^{\frac{1}{2}} \bar{f}(\xi) \sin{[(g\xi)^{\frac{1}{2}}t]}$$

so that, by the Hankel inversion theorem 19, we obtain for the velocity potential

$$\phi = \int_0^\infty (g\xi)^{\frac{1}{2}}\bar{f}(\xi) \sin\left[(g\xi)^{\frac{1}{2}}t\right]J_0(\xi r)e^{\xi z}\,d\xi \tag{86}$$

Equation (83) then gives the expression

$$\zeta = \int_0^\infty \xi\bar{f}(\xi)J_0(\xi r) \cos\left[(g\xi)^{\frac{1}{2}}t\right]d\xi \tag{87}$$

for the elevation of the free surface.

For large values of α we have the asymptotic expression

$$J_0(\alpha) \sim \left(\frac{2}{\pi\alpha}\right)^{\frac{1}{2}} \sin\left(\alpha + \frac{1}{4}\pi\right)$$

so that, for large values of r, equation (86) yields the asymptotic formula

$$\phi \sim \left(\frac{g}{2\pi r}\right)^{\frac{1}{2}} \int_0^\infty \bar{f}(\xi)e^{\xi z} \left\{\cos\left[(g\xi)^{\frac{1}{2}}t - \xi r - \frac{1}{4}\pi\right]\right.$$
$$\left. - \cos\left[(g\xi)^{\frac{1}{2}}t + \xi r + \frac{1}{4}\pi\right]\right\}\,d\xi$$

Since $r > 0$, the main contribution in the case $t > 0$ comes from the first term so that

$$\phi \sim \left(\frac{g}{2\pi r}\right)^{\frac{1}{2}} \int_0^\infty \bar{f}(\xi)e^{\xi z} \cos\left[(g\xi)^{\frac{1}{2}}t - \xi r - \frac{1}{4}\pi\right]d\xi$$

Evaluating this integral by means of the approximate formula (66), we obtain the asymptotic expression

$$\phi \sim \left(\frac{gt}{2^{\frac{1}{2}}r^2}\right)\bar{f}\left(\frac{gt^2}{4r^2}\right) e^{gt^2z/4r^2} \sin\left(\frac{gt^2}{4r}\right) \tag{88}$$

Similarly, from equation (87), we have, approximately, for large values of r and t,

$$\zeta \sim \frac{gt^2}{2^{\frac{3}{2}}r^3}\bar{f}\left(\frac{gt^2}{4r^2}\right) \cos\left(\frac{gt^2}{4r}\right) \tag{89}$$

In particular, if the initial elevation of the free surface is concentrated in the neighborhood of the origin, we may write $f(r) = (2\pi r)^{-1}\epsilon\,\delta(r)$, where ϵ is the total volume of the fluid displaced, so that $\bar{f}(\xi) = \epsilon/2\pi$ and equation (86) gives

$$\phi_{r=0} = \frac{\epsilon}{2\pi} \int_0^\infty (g\xi)^{\frac{1}{2}} \sin\left[(g\xi)^{\frac{1}{2}}t\right]e^{\xi z}\,d\xi$$

Expanding $(g\xi)^{\frac{1}{2}} \sin (g\xi)^{\frac{1}{2}} t$ in ascending powers of ξ; we have

$$\phi_{r=0} = \frac{\epsilon g t}{2\pi} \sum_{s=0}^{\infty} \frac{(-1)^s}{(2s+1)!} (gt^2)^s \int_0^{\infty} e^{-\xi(-z)} \xi^{s+1} \, d\xi$$

$$= \frac{\epsilon g t}{2\pi} \sum_{s=0}^{\infty} \frac{(-gt^2)^s}{(2s+1)!} \frac{(s+1)!}{(-z)^{s+2}}$$

This expression gives the value of the velocity potential ϕ at points on the vertical axis of symmetry. By a well-known property of harmonic functions[1] we may write down its value at other points merely by replacing $(-z)^{-s-2}$ by $P_{s+1}(\mu)/R^{s+2}$, where $R^2 = x^2 + y^2 + z^2$ and $\mu = z/R$. $P_n(\mu)$ denotes the Legendre polynomial of order n. Hence at a general point

$$\phi = \frac{\epsilon g t}{2\pi} \sum_{s=0}^{\infty} \frac{(-1)^s (gt^2)^s (s+1)!}{R^{s+2}(2s+1)!} P_{s+1}(\mu)$$

From equation (83) with the results

$$P_{2s+1}(0) = 0, \qquad P_{2s}(0) = (-1)^s \frac{1 \cdot 3 \cdot 5 \cdots (2s-1)}{2 \cdot 4 \cdots 2s}$$

and the fact that $R = r$ when $z = 0$, we find that the elevation of the free surface is given by the equation

$$\zeta = \frac{\epsilon}{2\pi r^2} \left[\frac{1^2}{2!} \left(\frac{gt^2}{r} \right) - \frac{1^2 \cdot 3^2}{6!} \left(\frac{gt^2}{r} \right)^3 + \frac{1^2 \cdot 3^2 \cdot 5^2}{10!} \left(\frac{gt^2}{r} \right)^5 - \cdots \right]$$

33. Slow Motion of a Viscous Fluid

We shall now turn to the discussion of problems in which the viscous nature of the fluid plays an important role. The complete equations of motion of an incompressible viscous fluid [equations (13)] are too difficult to solve exactly in any particular problem because they are nonlinear. In the case of very slow motions the equations reduce, in first approximation, to linear equations since the terms $\mathbf{v} \times \boldsymbol{\omega}$ and $\mathbf{v}^2$ will be of the second order. In the subsequent pages we shall discuss certain boundary value problems which may be treated under this approximation and then, in Sec. 36, consider how far the methods of Fourier analysis may be applied to the nonlinear case.

[1] L. A. Pipes, "Applied Mathematics for Engineers and Physicists" (McGraw-Hill, New York, 1946), p. 416.

33.1 Motion under gravity of a viscous fluid contained between two parallel planes.

As a first example we shall consider the motion of a viscous fluid down an inclined plane with the assumption that the velocity of the fluid at the free surface is known (cf. Fig. 54). For slow motions equations (13) reduce to the form

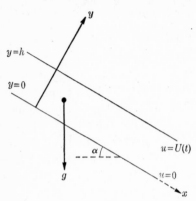

$$\frac{\partial \mathbf{v}}{\partial t} - \mathbf{F} + \frac{1}{\rho} \operatorname{grad} (p) = \nu \, \nabla^2 \mathbf{v} \quad (90)$$

If we consider a viscous fluid of density ρ filling the space between parallel plane boundaries $y = 0$, $y = h$ and moving under gravity, then we may take

$$\mathbf{F} = g(\sin \alpha, - \cos \alpha, 0) \quad (91)$$

FIG. 54. Flow under gravity of a viscous fluid confined between two parallel planes.

Since the motion may be assumed to be the same in all planes parallel to the plane xOy, the vector $\mathbf{v}$ will be of the form $(u,0,0)$ where u is a function of x,y, and t. With this form of velocity vector and the assumption that the fluid is incompressible the equation of continuity becomes simply

$$\frac{\partial u}{\partial x} = 0$$

showing that u is a function only of y and t. Under these circumstances equation (90) becomes

$$\frac{\partial u}{\partial t} = g \sin \alpha - \frac{1}{\rho} \frac{\partial p}{\partial x} + \nu \frac{\partial^2 u}{\partial y^2}$$

$$0 = g \cos \alpha + \frac{1}{\rho} \frac{\partial p}{\partial y}$$

It follows from the first of these equations that $g \sin \alpha - (1/\rho)(\partial p/\partial x)$ is a function of y alone, and hence from the second equation we have

$$p = g\rho(x \sin \alpha - y \cos \alpha) + x\rho X$$

where X is constant. The first of the equations of motion then gives

$$\frac{\partial u}{\partial t} = -X + \nu \frac{\partial^2 u}{\partial y^2} \quad (92)$$

If we introduce the finite Fourier sine transform

$$\bar{u}_s(n,t) = \int_0^h u(y,t) \sin \left(\frac{n\pi y}{h} \right) dy$$

then, integrating by parts and making use of the boundary conditions $u = U(t)$ on $y = h$ and $u = 0$ on $y = 0$, we find that

$$\int_0^h \frac{\partial^2 u}{\partial y^2} \sin\left(\frac{n\pi y}{h}\right) dy = (-1)^{n+1} \frac{n\pi}{h} U(t) - \frac{n^2\pi^2}{h^2} \bar{u}_s(n,t)$$

so that equation (92) is equivalent to

$$\frac{d\bar{u}_s}{dt} + \frac{n^2\pi^2}{h^2} \bar{u}_s = (-1)^{n+1} \frac{n\pi}{h} U(t) - X \tag{93}$$

which has solution

$$\bar{u}_s = -\frac{1}{n^2} \frac{Xh^2}{\pi^2} + (-1)^{n+1} \frac{\pi n}{h} \int_{t_0}^t U(\tau) e^{-n^2\pi^2(t-\tau)/h^2} d\tau$$

where t_0 is an arbitrary time defined by the initial conditions. Inverting this result by means of Theorem 27 and making use of the series

$$\frac{2}{h} \sum_{n=1}^{\infty} \frac{1}{n^2} \sin\left(\frac{n\pi y}{h}\right) = \frac{y(h-y)}{2h^2}$$

we find that

$$u(y,t) = -\frac{Xy(h-y)}{2} + 2\pi \sum_{n=1}^{\infty} (-1)^{n+1} n \sin\left(\frac{n\pi y}{h}\right) \int_{t_0}^t$$
$$\times U(\tau) e^{-n^2\pi^2(t-\tau)/h^2} d\tau$$

If the flow is steady, so that $U(t)$ is a constant, equation (93) reduces to

$$\bar{u}_s = (-1)^{n+1} \frac{hU}{n\pi} - \frac{Xh^2}{n^2\pi^2}$$

Using Theorem 27 and the series

$$\frac{2}{\pi} \sum_{n=1}^{\infty} \frac{(-1)^{n+1}}{n} \sin\frac{n\pi y}{h} = \frac{y}{h}$$

we find that

$$u(y,t) = \frac{Uy}{h} - \frac{1}{2} y(h-y)X$$

33.2 Flow of viscous fluid through a slit. As a further example of the application of the theory of integral transforms to problems of the slow motion of viscous fluids we shall examine the case of a fluid bounded by two semiinfinite plane boundaries, the boundaries being coplanar and having their straight edges parallel at a finite distance apart. We shall consider the motion to be due to a jet of fluid of finite width $BC = 2a$, say (cf. Fig. 49).

We shall assume that the fluid is bounded by the plane $y = 0$ and that, through a strip $|x| \leq a$ of this plane, fluid is introduced. In terms of a stream function ψ the component velocities u and v of the fluid are given by equations (15), where ψ is a solution of equation (16) or, in the slow motion approximation, of equation (17). It is this latter case which we shall consider first.

If, in the first instance, we assume that fluid is introduced normally with a prescribed velocity, we have the boundary conditions

$$\frac{\partial \psi}{\partial y} = 0, \qquad \frac{\partial \psi}{\partial x} = f(x) \qquad y = 0 \tag{94}$$

where $f(x)$ is a prescribed function of x which is identically zero when $|x| \geq a$.

To solve the biharmonic equation (17) subject to the boundary conditions (94), we introduce the Fourier transform

$$\Psi(\xi, y) = \frac{1}{\sqrt{2\pi}} \int_{-\infty}^{\infty} \psi(x, y) e^{i\xi x} \, dx \tag{95}$$

of the stream function. Then, multiplying both sides of equation (17) by $e^{i\xi x}$ and integrating over x, we find, as a result of an integration by parts, that

$$\left(\frac{d^2}{dy^2} - \xi^2 \right)^2 \Psi(\xi, y) = 0 \tag{96}$$

If we are interested only in solutions which tend to zero at great distances from the slit, then, in the region $y \geq 0$, this ordinary differential equation has the general solution

$$\Psi(\xi, y) = (A + B|\xi|y)e^{-|\xi|y}$$

To satisfy the first of equations (94), we must take $d\Psi/dy = 0$, when $y = 0$, so that $A = B$. Furthermore from the second equation of the pair (94) we have

$$-i\xi\Psi = F(\xi)$$

where $F(\xi)$ is the Fourier transform of $f(x)$ which, since $f(x)$ vanishes outside of the strip $|x| \leq a$, may be written as

$$F(\xi) = \frac{1}{\sqrt{2\pi}} \int_{-a}^{a} f(x) e^{i\xi x} \, dx$$

Thus for the solution of equation (96) we obtain

$$\Psi(\xi,y) = \frac{i}{\xi}[1 + |\xi|y]e^{-|\xi|y}F(\xi)$$

whence, by the Fourier transform theorem 10, we find

$$\psi(x,y) = \frac{1}{\sqrt{2\pi}} \int_{-\infty}^{\infty} H(\xi)F(\xi)e^{-i\xi x}\,d\xi \tag{97}$$

where

$$H(\xi) = \frac{i}{\xi}[1 + |\xi|y]e^{-|\xi|y}$$

By means of the Faltung theorem for Fourier transforms (Theorem 12) we may write equation (97) in the form

$$\psi(x,y) = \frac{1}{\sqrt{2\pi}} \int_{-\infty}^{\infty} f(u)h(x-u)du \tag{98}$$

with

$$h(x) = \frac{1}{\sqrt{2\pi}} \int_{-\infty}^{\infty} H(\xi)e^{-i\xi x}\,d\xi$$

$$= \sqrt{\frac{2}{\pi}}\left[\tan^{-1}\left(\frac{x}{y}\right) + \frac{xy}{x^2 + y^2}\right] \tag{99}$$

Substituting from equation (99) into equation (98), we obtain finally for the solution of this boundary value problem

$$\psi(x,y) = \frac{1}{\pi} \int_{-\infty}^{\infty} f(u)\left[\tan^{-1}\left(\frac{x-u}{y}\right) + \frac{y(x-u)}{(x-u)^2 + y^2}\right]du \tag{100}$$

Similarly, if we replace the conditions (94) by the boundary conditions

$$\frac{\partial\psi}{\partial y} = g(x), \qquad \frac{\partial\psi}{\partial x} = 0 \qquad \text{on } y = 0 \tag{101}$$

we find that

$$\Psi(\xi,y) = G(\xi)ye^{-|\xi|y}$$

where $G(\xi)$ is the Fourier transform of the function $g(x)$. Thus, by use of the inversion and Faltung theorems, we obtain the solution

$$\psi(x,y) = \frac{y^2}{\pi} \int_{-\infty}^{\infty} \frac{g(u)du}{(x-u)^2 + y^2} \tag{102}$$

Adding the solutions (100) and (102), we see that the function

$$\psi(x,y) = \frac{1}{\pi} \int_{-\infty}^{\infty} f(u)\left[\tan^{-1}\left(\frac{x-u}{y}\right) + \frac{y(x-u)}{(x-u)^2 + y^2}\right]du$$

$$+ \frac{y^2}{\pi} \int_{-\infty}^{\infty} \frac{g(u)du}{(x-u)^2 + y^2} \tag{103}$$

is that solution of the biharmonic equation (17) which satisfies the boundary conditions

$$\frac{\partial \psi}{\partial x} = f(x), \qquad \frac{\partial \psi}{\partial y} = g(x) \qquad \text{on } y = 0 \qquad (104)$$

As a special case of the conditions (104) we may take

$$\frac{\partial \psi}{\partial x} = V\pi, \qquad \frac{\partial \psi}{\partial y} = \kappa V\pi \qquad \text{on } y = 0$$

In this instance the solution (103) reduces to

$$\psi(x,y) = Vy \int_{(x-a)/y}^{(x+a)/y} \left[\tan^{-1}(v) + \frac{v}{1 + v^2} + \kappa \frac{1}{1 + v^2} \right] dv$$

$$= Vy \left[(v + \kappa) \tan^{-1}(v) \right]_{v=(x-a)/y}^{v=(x+a)/y}$$

If we write

$$\tan^{-1}\left(\frac{x + a}{y}\right) = \frac{1}{2}\pi - \tan^{-1}\left(\frac{y}{x + a}\right) = \frac{1}{2}\pi - \theta_2$$

$$\tan^{-1}\left(\frac{x - a}{y}\right) = \frac{1}{2}\pi - \tan^{-1}\left(\frac{y}{x - a}\right) = \frac{1}{2}\pi - \theta_1$$

where θ_1 and θ_2 are the angles shown in Fig. 49, then

$$\psi(x,y) = V[(x + \kappa y - a)\theta_1 - (x + \kappa y + a)\theta_2 + \pi a] \qquad (105)$$

The solution (105) was first obtained by Dean,[1] using a different method of attack. This solution corresponds physically to the case in which the fluid is introduced through the strip BC at a constant velocity which is inclined at an angle $\tan^{-1} \kappa$ to the normal to the wall AD.

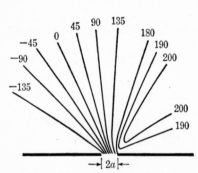

The streamlines, $\psi = $ const., of the motion represented by the solution (105) are shown in Fig. 55 for the case in which κ is unity. Along each of these curves the value of ψ/Va, reckoned in degrees, is constant and has the value shown.

Fig. 55. The streamlines of the flow of a fluid through the strip BC at a constant velocity inclined at 45° to the wall.

The solution we have obtained in this way is, of course, only a first approximation, since we have completely neglected the term

[1] W. R. Dean, *Phil. Mag.* (vii) **21**, 727 (1936).

$$\left(\frac{\partial \psi}{\partial y}\frac{\partial}{\partial x} - \frac{\partial \psi}{\partial x}\frac{\partial}{\partial y}\right)\nabla_1^2\psi$$

occurring on the left-hand side of equation (16). If we denote this first approximation by ψ_1, then we see that it satisfies the conditions

$$\nabla_1^4\psi_1 = 0 \qquad\qquad y \geq 0$$

$$\frac{\partial \psi_1}{\partial x} = f(x), \qquad \frac{\partial \psi_1}{\partial y} = g(x) \qquad\qquad y = 0$$

It follows immediately that a more exact solution to the problem posed by equations (16) and (104) will be $\psi = \psi_1 + \psi_2$, where the function ψ_2 satisfies the equations

$$\frac{\partial \psi_2}{\partial x} = \frac{\partial \psi_2}{\partial y} = 0 \qquad\qquad y = 0 \qquad (106)$$

and

$$\nabla_1^4\psi_2 = f(x,y) \qquad\qquad y \geq 0 \qquad (107)$$

with

$$f(x,y) = \frac{1}{\nu}\left(\frac{\partial \psi_1}{\partial y}\frac{\partial}{\partial x} - \frac{\partial \psi_1}{\partial x}\frac{\partial}{\partial y}\right)\nabla_1^2\psi_1 \qquad (108)$$

To solve the partial differential equation (107) subject to the conditions (106), we introduce the double Fourier transform

$$\Psi_2(\xi,\eta) = \frac{1}{\pi}\int_{-\infty}^{\infty} dx \int_0^{\infty} dy\, \psi_2(x,y)e^{i\xi x}\cos(\eta y) \qquad (109)$$

Multiplying both sides by $e^{i\xi x}\cos(\eta y)$ and integrating over the entire upper half plane, we see that equation (107) is equivalent to the relation

$$(\xi^2 + \eta^2)^2\Psi_2(\xi,\eta) = F(\xi,\eta)$$

where $F(\xi,\eta)$ is defined in terms of $f(x,y)$ by an equation of the type (109). Inverting this equation by means of Theorems 8 and 10, we obtain for ψ_2 the expression

$$\psi_2(x,y) = \frac{1}{\pi}\int_{-\infty}^{\infty} d\xi \int_0^{\infty} d\eta\, \frac{F(\xi,\eta)}{(\xi^2 + \eta^2)^2}e^{-i\xi x}\cos(\eta y)$$

Making use of the Faltung theorem 12, we may show that this solution is equivalent to

$$\psi_2(x,y) = \frac{1}{8\pi}\int_{-\infty}^{\infty} d\alpha \int_0^{\infty} d\beta\left[\frac{1}{2}(R'^2 - R^2) - R^2\log\left(\frac{R'}{R}\right)\right]f(\alpha,\beta) \qquad (110)$$

where $R^2 = (x - \alpha)^2 + (y - \beta)^2$, $R'^2 = (x - \alpha)^2 + (y + \beta)^2$.

In this way we have a procedure for obtaining a better approximation. The evaluation of the integral (110) is, however, often very difficult. For instance, even in the simplest case in which the solution is given by equation (105) with $\kappa = 0$, it is readily shown that

$$f(x,y) = \frac{V}{\nu}\left[-2\left(\frac{\theta_1 \cos 2\theta_1}{r_1^2} + \frac{\theta_2 \cos 2\theta_2}{r_2^2}\right) + 2\left(\frac{\theta_1 \cos 2\theta_2}{r_2^2} + \frac{\theta_2 \cos 2\theta_1}{r_1^2}\right) \right.$$
$$\left. + \left(\frac{1}{r_1^2} - \frac{1}{r_2^2}\right)\sin 2(\theta_1 - \theta_2) \right]$$

so that it is better to make use of a more tentative method, such as that devised by Dean,[1] to obtain the second approximation. Equation (110) is, however, useful in determining the nature of the flow at infinity.

33.3 Diffusion of vorticity. In the two-dimensional case in which either the motion is very slow or ζ is a function of ψ we may write equation (14) in the form

$$\frac{\partial \zeta}{\partial t} = \nu \nabla_1^2 \zeta \tag{111}$$

which is the equation for the two-dimensional flow of heat (cf. Chap. 5). If the fluid fills the whole space and if, when $t = 0$,

$$\zeta = \zeta_0(x,y) \tag{112}$$

then we may solve equation (111) by multiplying both sides by $(1/2\pi)e^{i(\omega_1 x + \omega_2 y)}$ and integrating throughout the whole xy plane. In this way we obtain the equation

$$\frac{dZ}{dt} = -\nu(\omega_1^2 + \omega_2^2)Z(\omega_1,\omega_2,t) \tag{113}$$

for the rate of change of the Fourier transform

$$Z(\omega_1,\omega_2,t) = \frac{1}{2\pi}\int_{-\infty}^{\infty}\int_{-\infty}^{\infty} \zeta(x,y,t)e^{i(\omega_1 x + \omega_2 y)}\, dx\, dy$$

of the vorticity $\zeta(x,y,t)$. The solution of equation (113) satisfying the initial condition (112) is

$$Z = Z_0 e^{-\nu(\omega_1^2 + \omega_2^2)t}$$

where Z_0 is the Fourier transform of the function $\zeta_0(x,y)$. Hence, making use of the inversion theorem for double Fourier transforms [$n = 2$ in equation (111), Chap. 1], we have

$$\zeta(x,y,t) = \frac{1}{2\pi}\int_{-\infty}^{\infty}\int_{-\infty}^{\infty} Z_0(\omega_1,\omega_2)e^{-\nu(\omega_1^2+\omega_2^2)t - i(\omega_1 x + \omega_2 y)}\, d\omega_1\, d\omega_2$$

[1] *Ibid.*

In the special case in which we may write $\zeta_0(x,y) = f(x)g(y)$ this solution reduces to the form

$$\zeta(x,y,t) = \frac{1}{2\pi} \int_{-\infty}^{\infty} F(\omega_1)e^{-\nu\omega_1^2 t - i\omega_1 x}\, d\omega_1 \int_{-\infty}^{\infty} G(\omega_2)e^{-\nu\omega_2^2 t - i\omega_2 y}\, d\omega_2$$

in which F and G are the usual (one-dimensional) transforms of the functions $f(x)$ and $g(y)$. For example, if initially there is a vortex sheet in the plane $x = 0$, we may write $\zeta_0 = U\, \delta(x)$ so that, taking $f(x) = U\, \delta(x)$ and $g(y) = 1$, we readily calculate that $F(\omega_1) = (2\pi)^{-\frac{1}{2}}U$ and

$$G(\omega_2) = (2\pi)^{\frac{1}{2}}\, \delta(\omega_2),$$

giving

$$\zeta = \frac{1}{2\pi} \int_{-\infty}^{\infty} e^{-\nu\omega_1^2 t - i\omega_1 x}\, d\omega_1 = \frac{U}{2\sqrt{\pi\nu t}}\, e^{-x^2/4\nu t}$$

From the relation $\partial u/\partial x = 2\zeta$, we find that

$$u(x,t) = \frac{2U}{\sqrt{\pi}} \int_0^{x/2(\nu t)^{\frac{1}{2}}} e^{-\nu^2}\, dv$$

If, on the other hand, there was initially a vortex filament of strength κ along the z-axis, then $\zeta_0 = \frac{1}{2}\kappa\, \delta(x)\, \delta(y)$ and so $Z_0 = \kappa/4\pi$, whence

$$\zeta = \frac{\kappa}{8\pi^2} \int_{-\infty}^{\infty} e^{-\nu\omega_1^2 t - i\omega_1 x}\, d\omega_1 \int_{-\infty}^{\infty} e^{-\nu\omega_2^2 t - i\omega_2 y}\, d\omega_2$$

The integrations are elementary and give

$$\zeta = \frac{\kappa}{8\pi\nu t}\, e^{-(x^2+y^2)/4\nu t}$$

In the case of axial symmetry about the z axis, equation (111) may be written as

$$\frac{\partial \zeta}{\partial t} = \nu\left(\frac{\partial^2 \zeta}{\partial r^2} + \frac{1}{r}\frac{\partial \zeta}{\partial r}\right)$$

Multiplying both sides of this equation by $rJ_0(\omega r)$ and integrating with respect to r from 0 to ∞, we find that the transform

$$\bar{\zeta}(\omega,t) = \int_0^{\infty} rJ_0(\omega r)\zeta(r,t)dr$$

satisfies the first-order equation

$$\frac{d\bar{\zeta}}{dt} = -\nu\omega^2\bar{\zeta}$$

Subject to the initial condition $\zeta = f(r)$, this equation has the solution

$$\bar{\zeta} = \bar{f}(\omega)e^{-\nu\omega^2 t}$$

so that, by the application of the Hankel inversion theorem 19, we find

$$\zeta = \int_0^\infty \omega J_0(\omega r) e^{-\nu\omega^2 t} \bar{f}(\omega) d\omega$$

For the case of a line filament we have $f(r) = \kappa \, \delta(r)/4\pi r$, so that $\bar{f}(\omega) = \kappa/4\pi$ and

$$\zeta = \frac{\kappa}{4\pi} \int_0^\infty \omega J_0(\omega r) e^{-\nu\omega^2 t} \, d\omega$$

Making use of equation (16), Appendix A, with $\nu = 0$, we get the same result as we did by employing the theory of two-dimensional Fourier transforms.

34. Motion of a Viscous Fluid Contained between Two Infinite Coaxal Cylinders

34.1 Introduction. As an example of the use of finite Hankel transforms in the discussion of boundary value problems in the theory of the motion of viscous fluids we consider the motion of such a fluid contained between two infinite coaxal cylinders. We regard the cylinders as being of infinite length and, as is usually done in problems of this type, assume that the velocities involved are sufficiently small for their squares to be neglected.

If we take the z axis along the common axis of the cylinders and the x and y axes normal to it, then, denoting the components of the velocity in the x and y directions by u and v, respectively, and neglecting terms involving the squares of the components of velocity, we may write the basic equations (13) in the form

$$\frac{\partial p}{\partial x} = \mu \left(\frac{\partial^2 u}{\partial x^2} + \frac{\partial^2 u}{\partial y^2} \right) - \rho \frac{\partial u}{\partial t}$$

$$\frac{\partial p}{\partial y} = \mu \left(\frac{\partial^2 v}{\partial x^2} + \frac{\partial^2 v}{\partial y^2} \right) - \rho \frac{\partial v}{\partial t}$$

where p is the pressure at the point (x,y) in the fluid and μ and ρ denote, respectively, the coefficient of viscosity and density of the fluid. For rotational motion we may write

$$u = -V \sin \theta, \qquad v = V \cos \theta$$

so that, making use of the relations

$$\frac{\partial}{\partial x} = \cos \theta \frac{\partial}{\partial r} - \frac{\sin \theta}{r} \frac{\partial}{\partial \theta}, \qquad \frac{\partial}{\partial y} = \sin \theta \frac{\partial}{\partial r} + \frac{\cos \theta}{r} \frac{\partial}{\partial \theta}$$

we may put the equations of motion in the form

$$\frac{\partial p}{\partial r} - \frac{1}{r}\frac{\partial p}{\partial \theta}\tan\theta = -\tan\theta\left[\mu\left(\frac{\partial^2 V}{\partial r^2} + \frac{1}{r}\frac{\partial V}{\partial r} - \frac{V}{r^2}\right) - \rho\frac{\partial V}{\partial t}\right]$$

$$\frac{\partial p}{\partial r} + \frac{1}{r}\frac{\partial p}{\partial \theta}\cot\theta = \cot\theta\left[\mu\left(\frac{\partial^2 V}{\partial r^2} + \frac{1}{r}\frac{\partial V}{\partial r} - \frac{V}{r^2}\right) - \rho\frac{\partial V}{\partial t}\right]$$

Further, if the motion is symmetrical about the z axis,

$$\frac{\partial p}{\partial \theta} = 0 \tag{114}$$

from which it follows immediately that the above equations are equivalent to the pair

$$\frac{\partial p}{\partial r} = 0 \tag{115}$$

and

$$\frac{\partial^2 V}{\partial r^2} + \frac{1}{r}\frac{\partial V}{\partial r} - \frac{V}{r^2} = \frac{1}{\nu}\frac{\partial V}{\partial t} \quad a \leq r \leq b, t > 0 \tag{116}$$

where ν denotes the kinematic viscosity μ/ρ. The inequalities in equation (116) merely express the fact that we are interested only in the region bounded by cylinders of radii a and b and in positive values of the time. It is an immediate consequence of equations (114) and (115) that, with the assumptions we have made, the pressure p is a constant throughout the fluid. This is hardly surprising when we remember that the squares of the velocities have been neglected. The fundamental equation (116) may be derived directly as follows: Consider an annular element of fluid of radius r and thickness Δr, and let ω be the angular velocity of the fluid. Then the frictional force per unit area on a cylindrical shell of radius r is $2\pi r r\mu(\partial\omega/\partial r)$ per unit length, and the equation of motion of the annular element is

$$2\pi r^3\rho\,\Delta r\,\frac{\partial\omega}{\partial t} = \frac{\partial}{\partial r}\left(2\pi r^3\mu\,\frac{\partial\omega}{\partial r}\right)\Delta r$$

or

$$\frac{\partial^2\omega}{\partial r^2} + \frac{3}{r}\frac{\partial\omega}{\partial r} = \frac{1}{\nu}\frac{\partial\omega}{\partial t}$$

On putting $\omega = V/r$ we immediately obtain equation (116).

34.2 Motion when the outer cylinder rotates at a constant speed.
Suppose viscous fluid is contained between two infinite coaxal cylinders of radii a and b and that the fluid is set in motion by the outer cylinder $r = b$ starting to rotate with uniform angular velocity Ω at the instant $t = 0$, the inner cylinder being kept at rest. Then $V = \Omega b$ when $r = b$,

and $V = 0$ when $r = a$. Multiplying the left-hand side of equation (116) by the function

$$r[J_1(\xi_i r)G_1(\xi_i a) - G_1(\xi_i r)J_1(\xi_i a)]$$

where ξ_i is a positive root of the equation

$$J_1(\xi_i b)G_1(\xi_i a) - G_1(\xi_i b)J_1(\xi_i a) = 0 \tag{117}$$

then, using equation (73), Chap. 3, we find that

$$\int_a^b r[J_1(\xi_i r)G_1(\xi_i a) - J_1(\xi_i a)G_1(\xi_i r)]\left(\frac{\partial^2 V}{\partial r^2} + \frac{1}{r}\frac{\partial V}{\partial r} - \frac{V}{r^2}\right)dr$$
$$= -\xi_i^2 \bar{V}_H + V(a) - V(b)\frac{J_1(\xi_i a)}{J_1(\xi_i b)} \tag{118}$$

where $\bar{V}_H$ denotes the finite Hankel transform

$$\bar{V}_H = \int_a^b r[J_1(\xi_i r)G_1(\xi_i a) - J_1(\xi_i a)G_1(\xi_i r)]V(r)dr \tag{119}$$

of the velocity $V(r)$. Substituting the boundary conditions $V(a) = 0$' $V(b) = \Omega b$, we see that the right-hand side of equation (118) becomes simply

$$-\xi_i^2 \bar{V}_H - \Omega b \frac{J_1(\xi_i a)}{J_1(\xi_i b)}$$

Thus we obtain the first-order ordinary linear equation

$$\frac{1}{\nu}\frac{dV_H}{dt} + \xi_i^2 \bar{V}_H + \Omega b \frac{J_1(\xi_i a)}{J_1(\xi_i b)} = 0 \tag{120}$$

for the determination of the finite Hankel transform $\bar{V}_H$.

Since the outer cylinder starts from rest when $t = 0$, we have the initial condition $\bar{V}_H = 0$ when $t = 0$, so that the appropriate solution of equation (120) is

$$\bar{V}_H = -\frac{\Omega b}{\xi_i^2}\frac{J_1(\xi_i a)}{J_1(\xi_i b)}(1 - e^{-\nu \xi_i^2 t}) \tag{121}$$

Substituting this value for $\bar{V}_H$ into the inversion formula (53), Chap. 3, for the finite Hankel transform employed here we have

$$V(r) = -2\Omega b \sum_i \frac{J_1(\xi_i a)J_1(\xi_i b)}{J_1^2(\xi_i a) - J_1^2(\xi_i b)}(1 - e^{-\nu \xi_i^2 t})[J_1(\xi_i r)G_1(\xi_i a)$$
$$- G_1(\xi_i r)J_1(\xi_i a)]$$

where the sum is taken over all the positive roots of equation (117).

Now from equations (53) and (77), Chap. 3, it follows at once that

$$\frac{\Omega b^2}{r}\left(\frac{r^2 - a^2}{b^2 - a^2}\right) = -2\Omega b \sum_i \frac{J_1(\xi_i a)J_1(\xi_i b)}{J_1^2(\xi_i a) - J_1^2(\xi_i b)} [J_1(\xi_i r)G_1(\xi_i a)$$
$$- J_1(\xi_i a)G_1(\xi_i r)] \quad (122)$$

so that we may write the solution finally in the form

$$V(r) = \frac{\Omega b^2}{r}\left(\frac{r^2 - a^2}{b^2 - a^2}\right) + 2\Omega b \sum_i \frac{J_1(\xi_i a)J_1(\xi_i b)}{J_1^2(\xi_i a) - J_1^2(\xi_i b)} e^{-\nu \xi_i^2 t}$$
$$\times [J_1(\xi_i r)G_1(\xi_i a) - G_1(\xi_i r)J_1(\xi_i a)]$$

where the sum is taken over the positive roots of equation (117).

34.3 Oscillations of a cylinder in a viscous fluid contained in a fixed coaxal cylinder. A problem which arises in a certain experimental method of determining the coefficient of viscosity of molten slags may be stated as follows: Viscous fluid is contained in a fixed cylinder, and a second cylinder, coaxal with the first, is suspended in the fluid. The problem is to determine the couple exerted on the inner cylinder when it is constrained to execute a prescribed damped oscillation. If we denote the velocity of the fluid by $V(r)$ as before, then, in this case, $V(b) = 0$ and $V(a) = a\omega_0(t)$. Substituting these values in the right-hand side of equation (118), we see that, in this instance, the Hankel transform $\bar{V}_H$ defined by equation (119) satisfies the ordinary equation

$$\frac{1}{\nu}\frac{d\bar{V}_H}{dt} + \xi_i^2 \bar{V}_H = a\omega_0(t)$$

in which it is assumed that the function $\omega_0(t)$ is known. Since $V(r) = 0$ when $t = 0$, it follows that $\bar{V}_H = 0$ initially and the requisite solution is

$$\bar{V}_H = \nu a \int_0^t e^{-\xi_i^2 \nu(t-\tau)}\omega_0(\tau)d\tau \quad (123)$$

Integrating the expression on the right by means of the rule for integration by parts, we have

$$\bar{V}_H = \frac{a\omega_0(t)}{\xi_i^2} - \frac{a}{\xi_i^2}\int_0^t e^{-\nu\xi_i^2(t-\tau)}\omega_0'(\tau)d\tau \quad (124)$$

when we take account of the fact that $\omega_0(t) = 0$, when $t = 0$. Substituting from equation (124) into the inversion formula (53), Chap. 3, we obtain the expression

$$V(r) = \sum_i \left\{ \frac{2a\omega_0(t)J_1^2(\xi_i b)}{J_1^2(\xi_i a) - J_1^2(\xi_i b)} [J_1(\xi_i r)G_1(\xi_i a) - G_1(\xi_i r)J_1(\xi_i a)] \right.$$
$$\left. - \frac{2aJ_1^2(\xi_i b)}{J_1^2(\xi_i a) - J_1^2(\xi_i b)} [J_1(\xi_i r)G_1(\xi_i a) - G_1(\xi_i r)J_1(\xi_i a)] \int_0^t e^{-\nu\xi_i^2(t-\tau)}\omega_0'(\tau)d\tau \right\}$$

the summation extending over all the positive roots of equation (117). The relation

$$\frac{a^2(b^2 - r^2)}{r(b^2 - a^2)} = \sum_i \frac{2aJ_1^2(\xi_i b)}{J_1^2(\xi_i a) - J_1^2(\xi_i b)} [J_1(\xi_i r)G_1(\xi_i a) - G_1(\xi_i r)J_1(\xi_i a)]$$

may be established by a method similar to that used in establishing equation (122) so that the expression for the velocity $V(r)$ becomes

$$V(r) = \frac{a^2(b^2 - r^2)}{r(b^2 - a^2)} \omega_0(t) - 2a \sum_i \frac{J_1^2(\xi_i b)}{J_1^2(\xi_i a) - J_1^2(\xi_i b)}$$

$$\times [J_1(\xi_i r)G_1(\xi_i a) - J_1(\xi_i a)G_1(\xi_i r)] \int_0^t e^{-\nu \xi_i^2 (t-\tau)} \omega_0'(\tau) d\tau$$

the summation being taken, as before, over the positive roots of equation (117). The solution in this form is due to D. Martin.[1] It follows immediately that if $\omega_0(t)$ is a constant, Ω_0, say, then the angular velocity $\omega = V/r$ of the fluid is given by the simple formula

$$\omega(r) = \frac{a^2(b^2 - r^2)}{r^2(b^2 - a^2)} \Omega_0$$

Now the couple on the inner cylinder is of magnitude

$$M = 2\pi\mu a^3 \left(\frac{d\omega}{dr}\right)_{r=a} \tag{125}$$

The simplest way to calculate the value of the quantity $d\omega/dr$ on the cylinder $r = a$ is to make use of the expression (123) for $\bar{V}_H$. Inverting this expression by means of the formula (53), Chap. 3, and then dividing by r, we obtain the expression

$$\omega(r) = \frac{2a\nu}{r} \sum_i \frac{\xi_i^2 J_1^2(\xi_i b)}{J_1^2(\xi_i a) - J_1^2(\xi_i b)} [J_1(\xi_i r)G_1(\xi_i a) - G_1(\xi_i r)J_1(\xi_i a)]$$

$$\times \int_0^t \omega_0(\tau) e^{-\nu \xi_i^2 (t-\tau)} d\tau$$

for the angular velocity of the fluid. Differentiating with respect to r, putting $r = a$, and making use of the relation[2]

$$J_1'(\xi_i a)G_1(\xi_i a) - G_1'(\xi_i a)J_1(\xi_i a) = \frac{1}{\xi_i a}$$

---

[1] D. Martin, "Some Problems of Fluid Motion with Special Reference to the Flow of Compressible Fluids" (Ph.D. thesis, University of Glasgow, 1948), p. 79.

[2] T. M. MacRobert, "Spherical Harmonics" (Methuen, London, 1934), p. 284.

we find that

$$\left(\frac{d\omega}{dr}\right)_{r=a} = \frac{2\nu}{a} \sum_i \frac{\xi_i^2 J_1^2(\xi_i b)}{J_1^2(\xi_i a) - J_1^2(\xi_i b)} \int_0^t \omega_0(\tau) e^{-\nu \xi_i^2(t-\tau)} \, d\tau$$

from which it follows that

$$M = 4\pi\mu\nu a^2 \sum_i \frac{\xi_i^2 J_1^2(\xi_i b)}{J_1^2(\xi_i a) - J_1^2(\xi_i b)} \int_0^t \omega_0(\tau) e^{-\nu \xi_i^2(t-\tau)} \, d\tau$$

For example, if the angular velocity of the inner cylinder is prescribed to be

$$\omega_0(t) = \Omega_0 e^{-\kappa t} \sin (pt)$$

then the integrations are elementary and the couple M may be calculated from the formula

$$M = 2\pi\Omega_0 \mu a^3 \sum_i \{P_i e^{-\nu \xi_i^2 t} - e^{-\kappa t}[Q_i \sin (pt) + P_i \cos (pt)]\} \quad (126)$$

where, for brevity, we have written

$$P_i = \frac{2p\nu}{a} \frac{\xi_i^2 J_1^2(\xi_i b)}{[(\kappa - \nu \xi_i^2)^2 + p^2][J_1^2(\xi_i a) - J_1^2(\xi_i b)]}, \qquad Q_i = \frac{\kappa - \nu \xi_i^2}{p} P_i$$

and the summations are taken over the positive roots of equation (117). Equation (126) provides the solution of the problem.

35. Motion of a Viscous Fluid under a Surface Load

35.1 Introduction. In the discussion of the plastic recoil of the earth after the disappearance of the Pleistocene ice sheets a boundary value problem in the theory of viscous fluids arises[1] which can be solved by means of the theory of Hankel transforms. The curvature of the earth is neglected, and as a model we treat the motion of a semiinfinite, incompressible, viscous fluid under the action of a radially symmetrical pressure applied to the free surface. Since, in the case of the earth, we are dealing with extremely small accelerations and very high viscosity, we may neglect the inertial terms in the equations of motion in comparison with those arising from viscous forces.

Neglecting the terms arising from the acceleration, the equations of motion (13) of a fluid in a gravitational field may be written in the vector form

$$\mu \nabla^2 \mathbf{v} = \text{grad } p - (0,0,\rho g) \quad (127)$$

[1] N. A. Haskell, *Physics*, **6**, 265 (1935).

provided that the positive z axis is taken as pointing downward. The velocity $\mathbf{v}$ at the point (x,y,z) in the fluid must also satisfy the equation of continuity (10). Transforming to cylindrical coordinates (r,z,φ) and assuming cylindrical symmetry, we see that the equations (127) become

$$\frac{1}{r}\frac{\partial}{\partial r}\left(r\frac{\partial v_r}{\partial r}\right) - \frac{v_r}{r^2} + \frac{\partial^2 v_r}{\partial z^2} = \frac{1}{\mu}\frac{\partial \bar{p}}{\partial r} \tag{128}$$

$$\frac{1}{r}\frac{\partial}{\partial r}\left(r\frac{\partial v_z}{\partial r}\right) + \frac{\partial^2 v_z}{\partial z^2} = \frac{1}{\mu}\frac{\partial \bar{p}}{\partial z} \tag{128a}$$

where we have written $\bar{p} = p - g\rho z$. Similarly the equation of continuity (10) transforms to

$$\frac{1}{r}\frac{\partial}{\partial r}(rv_r) + \frac{\partial v_z}{\partial z} = 0 \tag{129}$$

The components of stress associated with the z direction are

$$\sigma_z = -p + 2\mu\frac{\partial v_z}{\partial z} \tag{130}$$

and

$$\tau_{rz} = \mu\left(\frac{\partial v_r}{\partial z} + \frac{\partial v_z}{\partial r}\right) \tag{131}$$

The boundary conditions are that, on the free surface, the shearing stress τ_{rz} is zero and that the normal component of stress σ_z is equal to the applied pressure. In addition, it is assumed that at infinity the stresses and the components of velocity are zero. If we suppose that the equation of the free surface is $z = \zeta(r,t)$ and that the equation of the undisturbed free surface is $z = 0$, then we take ζ to be small in comparison with the other distances which enter into the problem, such as, for instance, the radius of the circle to which the load is applied. Just as in the case of surface waves (Sec. 32.1), we may take, at least in first approximation, the free surface to be $z = 0$. Thus we replace the value of $\partial v_z/\partial z$ at $z = \zeta$ by its value at $z = 0$, and similarly with the other quantities except $g\rho z = g\rho\zeta(r,t)$. If we denote the applied pressure by $\sigma(r,t)$, we have $\sigma_z = -\sigma(r,t)$ when $z = \zeta(r,t)$, or, by means of equation (130) with the "surface wave approximation,"

$$\bar{p} + g\rho\zeta(r,t) - 2\mu\frac{\partial v_z}{\partial z} = \sigma(r,t) \qquad \text{on } z = 0 \tag{132}$$

The relation between ζ and v_z is that, at the free surface, the rate of change of ζ is equal to v_z; hence we have

$$\frac{\partial \zeta}{\partial t} = (v_z)_{z=0} \tag{133}$$

Finally, the condition that the shearing stress on the free surface is zero becomes, in this approximation,

$$(\tau_{rz})_{z=0} = 0 \tag{134}$$

35.2 General solution for arbitrary impressed circular load. To solve the equations of motion, we multiply equation (128) by $rJ_1(\xi r)$ and integrate with respect to r from 0 to ∞ to obtain

$$\int_0^\infty r\left(\frac{\partial^2 v_r}{\partial r^2} + \frac{1}{r}\frac{\partial v_r}{\partial r} - \frac{v_r}{r^2}\right)J_1(\xi r)dr + \frac{\partial^2}{\partial z^2}\int_0^\infty rv_r J_1(\xi r)dr$$

$$= \frac{1}{\mu}\int_0^\infty r\frac{\partial \bar{p}}{\partial r}J_1(\xi r)dr$$

It follows from equation (32), Chap. 2, that

$$\int_0^\infty r\left(\frac{\partial^2 v_r}{\partial r^2} + \frac{1}{r}\frac{\partial v_r}{\partial r} - \frac{v_r}{r^2}\right)J_1(\xi r)dr = -\xi^2\int_0^\infty rv_r J_1(\xi r)dr$$

and from (33), Chap. 2, that

$$\int_0^\infty r\frac{\partial \bar{p}}{\partial r}J_1(\xi r)dr = -\xi\int_0^\infty r\bar{p}J_0(\xi r)dr$$

so that, if we write

$$R = \int_0^\infty rv_r J_1(\xi r)dr, \qquad P = \int_0^\infty r\bar{p}J_0(\xi r)dr \tag{135}$$

we see that equation (128) is equivalent to

$$\left(\frac{d^2}{dz^2} - \xi^2\right)R = -\frac{\xi}{\mu}P \tag{136}$$

Similarly, multiplying equation (128a) by $rJ_0(\xi r)$ and integrating with respect to r over its complete range, we find that

$$\left(\frac{d^2}{dz^2} - \xi^2\right)Z = \frac{1}{\mu}\frac{dP}{dz} \tag{137}$$

where Z denotes the zero-order Hankel transform of v_z,

$$Z = \int_0^\infty rv_z J_0(\xi r)dr \tag{138}$$

If we now multiply the equation of continuity (129) by $rJ_0(\xi r)$ and integrate, we obtain the relation

$$\int_0^\infty \frac{\partial}{\partial r}\left(r\frac{\partial v_r}{\partial r}\right)J_0(\xi r)dr + \frac{dZ}{dz} = 0$$

Integrating by parts and making use of the relation

$$\frac{\partial}{\partial r} J_0(\xi r) = -\xi J_1(\xi r)$$

we obtain

$$\xi R + \frac{dZ}{dz} = 0 \tag{139}$$

Eliminating the functions P and R from the three equations (136), (137), and (139), we find that Z satisfies the fourth-order differential equation

$$\left(\frac{d^2}{dz^2} - \xi^2\right)^2 Z = 0$$

The solution of this equation, which tends to zero as $z \to \infty$, is

$$Z = (A + B\xi z)e^{-\xi z} \tag{140}$$

where A and B are arbitrary functions of the parameter ξ. Substituting this value of Z into equation (139), we obtain

$$R = (A - B + B\xi z)e^{-\xi z} \tag{141}$$

Multiplying both sides of equation (131) by $rJ_1(\xi r)$ and integrating over r, we find, as a result of integrating by parts, that

$$\frac{1}{\mu} \int_0^\infty r\tau_{rz} J_1(\xi r) dr = \frac{dR}{dz} - \xi Z = -2\xi(A - B + B\xi z)e^{-\xi z} \tag{142}$$

Putting $z = 0$ in this equation and making use of the boundary condition (134), we find that $A = B = \alpha(\xi)/\xi$, say, from which it follows that

$$Z = \frac{\alpha(\xi)}{\xi}(1 + \xi z)e^{-\xi z}, \qquad R = z\alpha(\xi)e^{-\xi z} \tag{143}$$

Equation (136) then yields

$$P = 2\mu\alpha(\xi)e^{-\xi z} \tag{144}$$

Now, by the Hankel inversion theorem 19, we have

$$v_z = \int_0^\infty \xi Z J_0(\xi r) d\xi$$

and, similarly, we may express v_r and $\bar{p}$ in terms of R and P. Equations (143) and (144) interpreted in this way then give the expressions

$$\left. \begin{array}{l} v_r = z \int_0^\infty \xi\alpha(\xi)e^{-\xi z}J_1(\xi r)d\xi \\[2mm] v_z = \int_0^\infty (1 + \xi z)\alpha(\xi)e^{-\xi z}J_0(\xi r)d\xi \\[2mm] \bar{p} = 2\mu \int_0^\infty \alpha(\xi)e^{-\xi z}J_0(\xi r)d\xi \end{array} \right\} \tag{145}$$

Substituting from these equations into equation (132), we obtain

$$2\mu \int_0^\infty \xi\alpha(\xi)J_0(\xi r)d\xi + g\rho\zeta = \sigma(r,t)$$

which, on differentiation with respect to the time, leads to

$$2\mu \int_0^\infty \xi\frac{\partial\alpha}{\partial t}J_0(\xi r)d\xi + g\rho\frac{\partial\zeta}{\partial t} = \frac{\partial\sigma}{\partial t}$$

Equation (133) leads, in a similar way, to the relation

$$\frac{\partial\zeta}{\partial t} = \int_0^\infty \alpha(\xi)J_0(\xi r)d\xi$$

which, when substituted in the last equation, yields

$$\int_0^\infty \xi\left(2\mu\frac{\partial\alpha}{\partial t} + \frac{g\rho\alpha}{\xi}\right)J_0(\xi r)d\xi = \frac{\partial\sigma}{\partial t}$$

Inverting this equation by means of the Hankel inversion theorem 19, we obtain the first-order differential equation

$$2\mu\frac{\partial\alpha}{\partial t} + \frac{g\rho}{\xi}\alpha = S(\xi,t)$$

in which

$$S(\xi,t) = \int_0^\infty r\frac{\partial\sigma(r,t)}{\partial t}J_0(\xi r)dr \tag{146}$$

Noticing that $\exp(g\rho t/2\mu\xi)$ is an integrating factor, we may integrate this equation to obtain

$$\alpha(\xi) = K(\xi)e^{-g\rho t/2\mu\xi} + \frac{1}{2\mu}\int_0^t e^{g\rho(\tau-t)/2\mu\xi}S(\xi,\tau)d\tau \tag{147}$$

where the function $K(\xi)$ is determined from the initial conditions. Denoting $\sigma(r,0)$ by σ_0 and integrating by parts, we have

$$\int_0^t \frac{\partial\sigma}{\partial t}e^{g\rho t/2\mu\xi}dt = \sigma e^{g\rho t/2\mu\xi} - \sigma_0 - \frac{g\rho}{2\mu\xi}\int_0^t e^{g\rho t/2\mu\xi}dt$$

giving finally

$$\alpha(\xi) = K(\xi)e^{-g\rho t/2\mu\xi} + \frac{1}{2\mu}\int_0^\infty r\sigma J_0(\xi r)dr - \frac{1}{2\mu}e^{-g t\rho/2\mu\xi}\int_0^\infty r\sigma_0 J_0(\xi r)dr$$

$$- \frac{g\rho}{4\mu^2\xi}e^{-g\rho t/2\mu\xi}\int_0^t\int_0^\infty \sigma e^{g\rho t/2\mu\xi}J_0(\xi r)r\,dr\,dt \tag{148}$$

This equation with the formulas (145) is the formal solution of the problem.

35.3 Subsidence of a cylindrical body. If we suppose that the fluid is initially at rest and that at $t = 0$ a uniform circular load distributed over a circle of radius a is applied to the surface, then, when $t \leq 0$, $\sigma(r,t) = 0$ and, when $t > 0$,

$$\sigma(r,t) = \begin{cases} \sigma & 0 \leq r \leq a \\ 0 & r > a \end{cases}$$

Thus $\sigma_0 = 0$, and $K(\xi) = 0$ so that, making use of

$$\int_0^a rJ_0(\xi r)dr = \frac{a}{\xi} J_1(a\xi)$$

we obtain the solution

$$\alpha(\xi) = \frac{a\sigma}{2\mu\xi} e^{-\rho g t/2\mu\xi} J_1(a\xi)$$

Substituting this expression into the equations (145), we find

$$v_r = \frac{a\sigma z}{2\mu} \int_0^\infty e^{-\rho g t/2\mu\xi - \xi z} J_1(\xi a) J_1(\xi r) d\xi$$

$$v_z = \frac{a\sigma}{2\mu} \int_0^\infty e^{-\rho g t/2\mu\xi - \xi z}(1 + \xi z) J_1(\xi a) J_0(\xi r) \frac{d\xi}{\xi}$$

$$p = g\rho z + a\sigma \int_0^\infty e^{-g\rho t/2\mu\xi - \xi z} J_1(\xi a) J_0(\xi r) d\xi$$

To obtain the expression for the displacement of the free surface we make use of equation (133) in the form

$$\frac{\partial \zeta}{\partial t} = (v_z)_{z=0} = \frac{a\sigma}{2\mu} \int_0^\infty e^{-\rho g t/2\mu\xi} J_1(\xi a) J_0(\xi r) \frac{d\xi}{\xi} \qquad (149)$$

and find that

$$\zeta = \int_0^t (v_z)_{z=0} \, dt = \frac{a\sigma}{g\mu} \int_0^\infty (1 - e^{-\rho g t/2\mu\xi}) J_1(\xi a) J_0(\xi r) d\xi$$

As $t \to \infty$, we note that

$$\zeta \to \frac{a\sigma}{g\mu} \int_0^\infty J_1(\xi a) J_0(\xi r) d\xi = \begin{cases} 0 & r > a \\ \dfrac{\sigma}{g\mu} & 0 < r < a \end{cases}$$

showing that the system approaches asymptotically the configuration of hydrostatic equilibrium, as we should expect it to.

It does not appear to be possible to obtain simple closed forms for the integrals occurring in the expressions for the components of velocity and pressure, but they may readily be put into a dimensionless form suitable for numerical or mechanical integration by means of the substitutions $u = \xi a$, $\lambda = r/a$, $w = z/a$, $\tau = \rho g a t/2\mu$, which lead to the results

$$\frac{2\mu v_r}{a\sigma} = w \int_0^\infty e^{-\tau/u - wu} J_1(u) J_1(\lambda u) du$$

$$\frac{2\mu v_z}{a\sigma} = \int_0^\infty e^{-\tau/u - wu} (1 + wu) J_1(u) J_0(\lambda u) du$$

$$\frac{p}{\sigma} = \frac{g\rho z}{\sigma} + \int_0^\infty e^{-\tau/u - wu} J_1(u) J_0(\lambda u) du$$

$$\frac{g\rho\zeta}{\sigma} = \int_0^\infty (1 - e^{-\tau/u}) J_1(u) J_0(\lambda u) du$$

As a special case of the solution for a constant circular load we shall consider the case in which the pressure σ applied to the surface is zero all over the surface. Taking $\sigma(r,t) = 0 (t > 0)$, it follows from the definition of the function $S(\xi,t)$—equation (146)—that this latter function is zero for $t > 0$ and hence, from equation (147), that

$$\alpha(\xi) = K(\xi) e^{-\rho g t/2\mu\xi} \tag{150}$$

The arbitrary function $K(\xi)$ is as yet unspecified. Its value can, however, be determined either from the initial velocity at the surface or from the initial configuration of the surface. If $v_z = f(r)$ when $z = 0$ and $t = 0$, it follows from equation (150) and the second equation of the set (145) that

$$f(r) = \int_0^\infty K(\xi) J_0(\xi r) d\xi$$

Inverting this equation by the Hankel inversion theorem 19, we derive the relation

$$K(\xi) = \xi \int_0^\infty r f(r) J_0(\xi r) dr \tag{151}$$

for the determination of the function $K(\xi)$ when the initial velocity is known.

On the other hand, when the initial displacement is known we make use of equation (149) in the form

$$\zeta(r,t) = \zeta(r,0) + \int_0^t v_z(r,0,t) dt$$

$$= \zeta(r,0) + \frac{2\mu}{g\rho} \int_0^\infty K(\xi)(1 - e^{-\rho g t/2\mu\xi}) J_0(\xi r) \xi \, d\xi$$

Letting $t \to \infty$ and remembering that $\zeta(r,t)$ will tend to zero, we find that

$$\zeta(r,0) = -\frac{2\mu}{g\rho} \int_0^\infty \xi K(\xi) J_0(\xi r) d\xi \tag{152}$$

which, on inversion by Theorem 19, yields the formula

$$K(\xi) = -\frac{g\rho}{2\mu} \int_0^\infty r\zeta(r,0)J_0(\xi r)dr$$

for the determination of $K(\xi)$ from the initial configuration of the surface.

In geophysical applications the function $f(r)$ may usually be represented with sufficient accuracy by the exponential function

$$f(r) = -\beta e^{-b^2 r^2} \tag{153}$$

Substituting from equation (153) into equation (151), we obtain the equation

$$K(\xi) = -\beta\xi \int_0^\infty re^{-b^2 r^2} J_0(\xi r)dr$$

Putting $\nu = 0$, $\mu = 2$ in Hankel's formula (15), Appendix A, we have

$$K(\xi) = -\frac{\beta\xi}{2b^2} e^{-\xi^2/4b^2}$$

Inserting this value for $K(\xi)$ into equation (152), we find that the surface displacement is given by

$$\zeta(r,0) = \frac{\mu\beta}{g\rho b^2} \int_0^\infty \xi^2 e^{-\xi^2/4b^2} J_0(\xi r)d\xi$$

Again using equation (15), Appendix A, but this time with $\nu = 0$, $\mu = 3$, we find that

$$\zeta(r,0) = 2\sqrt{\pi}\left(\frac{b\mu\beta}{g\rho}\right) {}_1F_1\left(\frac{3}{2};1;-r^2 b^2\right)$$

where, as usual, ${}_1F_1$ denotes a confluent hypergeometric function.[1] When $r = 0$, this hypergeometric function reduces to unity so that

$$\zeta(0,0) = 2\sqrt{\pi}\left(\frac{b\mu\beta}{g\rho}\right) \tag{154}$$

From this it follows that

$$\frac{\zeta(r,0)}{\zeta(0,0)} = {}_1F_1\left(\frac{3}{2};1;-r^2 b^2\right)$$

so that, inserting the definition of the hypergeometric function,

$$\frac{\zeta(r,0)}{\zeta(0,0)} = \frac{2}{\sqrt{\pi}} \sum_{n=0}^\infty (-1)^n \frac{\Gamma(n+\frac{3}{2})}{(n!)^2} r^{2n}b^{2n} \tag{155}$$

---

[1] For definition see equation (14), Appendix A.

The series on the right-hand side of this equation may be evaluated easily. A sequence of values calculated by Haskell is given in Table 1

TABLE 1

rb	0.0	0.2	0.4	0.6	0.8	1.0	1.5	2.0	2.5
$\dfrac{\zeta(r,0)}{\zeta(0,0)}$	1.000	0.922	0.780	0.562	0.328	0.155	−0.076	−0.068	−0.023

and the variation with rb represented graphically in Fig. 56.

An expression for the kinematic viscosity $\nu = \mu/\rho$ is readily derived from equation (154),

$$\nu = \frac{g\zeta(0,0)}{2\sqrt{\pi}\, b\beta}$$

If we express β in meters per hundred years, b in kilometers, and $\zeta(0,0)$ in meters, then ν is given, in cgs units, by

$$\nu = \frac{\zeta(0,0)}{b\beta}\, 8.73 \times 10^{16}$$

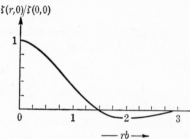

Fig. 56. Variation with rb of $\zeta(r,0)/\zeta(0,0)$.

Applying this formula to the plastic recoil of the earth after the disappearance of the Pleistocene ice sheets, Haskell found that the geological data led to a value of the order of 3.10^{21} cgs units for the kinematic viscosity.

35.4 Load in the form of an infinitely long strip.[1] We shall now treat the simpler problem of determining the distribution of velocities for the case of an instantaneously applied load of constant thickness having parallel sides and whose length is sufficiently greater than the width to be regarded as effectively infinite. In this instance we refer the equations of motion to a rectangular coordinate system having the plane $z = 0$ in the undisturbed surface of the fluid, the positive z axis directed downward and the y axis parallel to the length of the load, whose width is taken to be $2L$. Both v_y and the operator $\partial/\partial y$ are zero in these circumstances, and we obtain, from the equations of motion,

$$\frac{\partial^2 v_x}{\partial x^2} + \frac{\partial^2 v_x}{\partial z^2} = \frac{1}{\mu}\frac{\partial \bar{p}}{\partial x} \tag{156}$$

$$\frac{\partial^2 v_z}{\partial x^2} + \frac{\partial^2 v_z}{\partial z^2} = \frac{1}{\mu}\frac{\partial \bar{p}}{\partial z} \tag{157}$$

[1] N. A. Haskell, *Physics*, **7**, 56 (1936).

with $\bar{p} = p - g\rho z$, as before. The equation of continuity (10) then becomes

$$\frac{\partial v_x}{\partial x} + \frac{\partial v_z}{\partial z} = 0 \qquad (158)$$

If we let the equation of the free surface be of the form $z = \zeta(x,t)$ and let the pressure exerted by the load be $\sigma(x,t)$, the boundary conditions assume the forms

$$\bar{p} + g\rho\zeta(x,t) - 2\mu\frac{\partial v_z}{\partial z} = \sigma(x,t) \quad \text{when } z = 0 \quad (159)$$

and

$$\frac{\tau_{xz}}{\mu} = \frac{\partial v_x}{\partial z} + \frac{\partial v_z}{\partial x} = 0 \qquad \text{when } z = 0 \qquad (160)$$

in exact analogy with the axially symmetrical case. In the applications we shall consider we have $\sigma(x,t) = 0$ $(t \leq 0)$ and, for $t > 0$,

$$\sigma(x,t) = \begin{cases} \sigma & |x| < L \\ 0 & |x| > L \end{cases}$$

where σ is a constant.

Multiplying both sides of equation (156) by $\sin(\xi x)$ and integrating with respect to x from 0 to ∞, we obtain the equation

$$\left(\frac{d^2}{dz^2} - \xi^2\right) X_s = -\frac{\xi}{\mu} P_c \qquad (161)$$

where X_s and P_c denote the Fourier transforms

$$X_s = \int_0^\infty v_x \sin(\xi x)dx, \qquad P_c = \int_0^\infty \bar{p} \cos(\xi x)dx$$

Similarly, introducing the Fourier cosine transform

$$Z_c = \int_0^\infty v_z \cos(\xi x)dx$$

of the velocity v_z, we see that equation (157) is equivalent to

$$\left(\frac{d^2}{dz^2} - \xi^2\right) Z_c = \frac{1}{\mu}\frac{dP_c}{dz} \qquad (162)$$

and that the equation of continuity (157) may be written as

$$\xi X_s + \frac{dZ_c}{dz} = 0 \qquad (163)$$

Eliminating the functions P_c and X_s from equations (161), (162), and (163), we find that Z_c satisfies the equation

$$\left(\frac{d^2}{dz^2} - \xi^2\right)^2 Z_c = 0$$

so that, if we are seeking a solution which tends to zero as $z \to \infty$, we must take

$$Z_c = (A + B\xi z)e^{-\xi z}$$

If we multiply both sides of equation (160) by $\sin(\xi x)$, we see that one boundary condition is equivalent to

$$\frac{dX_s}{dz} - \xi Z_c = 0 \qquad\qquad z = 0$$

Eliminating X_s between this equation and (163), we obtain the condition

$$\frac{d^2 Z_c}{dz^2} + \xi^2 Z_c = 0 \qquad\qquad \text{on } z = 0$$

which shows that $A = B$, giving

$$Z_c = A(1 + \xi z)e^{-\xi z}, \qquad X_s = A\xi z e^{-\xi z} \qquad P_c = 2\mu A \xi e^{-\xi z}$$

Inverting these equations by means of the Fourier cosine and sine formulas, we obtain

$$\left.\begin{aligned}
v_x &= \frac{2z}{\pi} \int_0^\infty \xi A(\xi) e^{-\xi z} \sin(\xi x) d\xi \\
v_y &= \frac{2}{\pi} \int_0^\infty (1 + \xi z) A(\xi) e^{-\xi z} \cos(\xi x) d\xi \\
\bar{p} &= \frac{4\mu}{\pi} \int_0^\infty \xi A(\xi) e^{-\xi z} \cos(\xi x) d\xi
\end{aligned}\right\} \qquad (164)$$

Now

$$\frac{\partial\zeta}{\partial t} = (v_z)_{z=0} = \frac{2}{\pi} \int_0^\infty A(\xi) \cos(\xi x) d\xi$$

so that it follows from equation (159) that

$$\frac{4\mu}{\pi} \int_0^\infty \xi \frac{\partial A}{\partial t} e^{-\xi z} \cos(\xi x) d\xi + \frac{2g\rho}{\pi} \int_0^\infty A(\xi) \cos(\xi x) d\xi = \frac{\partial\sigma}{\partial t}$$

which, on inversion, gives

$$2\mu\xi \frac{\partial A}{\partial t} + g\rho A = S(\xi,t)$$

where

$$S(\xi,t) = \int_0^\infty \frac{\partial\sigma(x,t)}{\partial t} \cos(\xi x) dx$$

This equation has solution

$$A(\xi) = K(\xi)e^{-g\rho t/2\mu\xi} + \frac{1}{2\mu\xi} e^{-g\rho t/2\mu\xi} \int_0^t S(\xi,\tau)e^{g\rho t/2\mu\xi} \, d\tau$$

where $K(\xi)$ depends on the initial conditions. Now

$$\int_0^t S(\xi,\tau)e^{g\rho t/2\mu\xi} \, d\tau = \int_0^\infty \cos{(\xi x)}dx \int_0^t \frac{\partial\sigma}{\partial\tau} e^{g\mu\tau/2\mu\xi} \, d\tau$$

$$= \int_0^L \sigma \cos{(\xi x)}dx = \sigma \frac{\sin{(\xi L)}}{\xi}$$

for the choice of σ we have made, so that, if $K(\xi)$ is taken to be zero as a result of the initial conditions, we have

$$A(\xi) = \frac{\sigma \sin{(\xi L)}}{2\mu\xi^2} e^{-g t \rho/2\mu\xi}$$

Substituting this value for $A(\xi)$ into the formulas (164), we obtain the expressions

$$v_x = \frac{\sigma z}{\pi\mu} \int_0^\infty \frac{\sin{(\xi L)}}{\xi} \sin{(\xi x)}e^{-\rho g t/2\mu\xi} \, e^{-\xi z}d\xi$$

$$v_z = \frac{\sigma}{\pi\mu} \int_0^\infty \frac{\sin{(\xi L)}}{\xi^2} (1 + \xi z) \cos{(\xi x)}e^{-\xi z - g\rho t/2\mu\xi} \, d\xi$$

$$\bar{p} = \frac{\sigma}{\pi} \int_0^\infty \frac{\sin{(\xi L)}}{\xi} \cos{(\xi x)}e^{-\xi z - g\rho t/2\mu\xi} \, d\xi$$

When $z = 0$,

$$v_z = \frac{\sigma}{\pi\mu} \int_0^\infty \frac{\sin{(\xi L)}}{\xi^2} \cos{(\xi x)}e^{-g\rho t/2\mu\xi} \, d\xi$$

and so

$$\zeta = \int_0^t (v_z)_{z=0} \, dt = \frac{2\sigma}{\pi\rho g} \int_0^\infty (1 - e^{-g\rho t/2\mu\xi}) \frac{\sin{(\xi L)}}{\xi} \cos{(\xi x)}d\xi$$

In dimensionless form these expressions become

$$v_x' = \frac{2\mu v_x}{\sigma L} = \frac{2w}{\pi} \int_0^\infty e^{-\tau/\eta - w\eta} \sin{(\eta)} \sin{(u\eta)}d\eta$$

$$v_z' = \frac{2\mu v_z}{\sigma L} = \frac{2}{\pi} \int_0^\infty e^{-\tau/\eta - w\eta} \sin{(\eta)} \cos{(u\eta)} \frac{(1 + w\eta)d\eta}{\eta^2}$$

$$p' = \frac{\bar{p}}{\sigma} = \frac{2}{\pi} \int_0^\infty e^{-\tau/\eta - w\eta} \frac{\sin{(\eta)}}{\eta} \cos{(u\eta)}d\eta$$

$$\zeta' = \frac{g\rho\zeta}{\sigma} = \frac{2}{\pi} \int_0^\infty (1 - e^{-\tau/\eta}) \frac{\sin{(\eta)}}{\eta} \cos{(u\eta)}d\eta$$

(165)

where $u = x/L$, $w = z/L$, and $\tau = g\rho L t/2u$.

The components of the displacement are given by

$$u_x = \int_0^t v_x \, dt = \frac{\sigma}{g\rho} \int_0^\tau v_x' \, d\tau, \qquad u_z = \int_0^t v_z \, dt = \frac{\sigma}{g\rho} \int_0^\tau v_z' \, d\tau$$

so that, with $\xi = g\rho\mathbf{u}/\sigma$, we have

$$\left. \begin{aligned}
\xi_x &= \frac{2w}{\pi} \int_0^\infty (1 - e^{-\tau/\eta}) e^{-w\eta} \sin(\eta) \sin(u\eta) d\eta \\
\xi_z &= \frac{2}{\pi} \int_0^\infty (1 - e^{-\tau/\eta}) e^{-w\eta} \frac{\sin(\eta)}{\eta} (1 + w\eta) \cos(u\eta) d\eta
\end{aligned} \right\} \tag{166}$$

The integrals occurring in these expressions can be evaluated in terms of Bessel functions of the second kind with complex argument by means of the result

$$\int_0^\infty \exp\left(-\frac{\tau}{\eta} - \eta w - i\gamma\eta\right) \frac{d\eta}{\eta^{n+1}} = 2^{n+1} \left(\frac{w + i\gamma}{4\tau}\right)^{\frac{1}{2}n} K_n[4\tau \sqrt{(w + i\gamma)}]$$

Thus if we let

$$N_n^{(+)} = 2^{n+1} \left(\frac{w + iu + i}{4\tau}\right)^{\frac{1}{2}n} K_n[4\tau \sqrt{(w + iu + i)}]$$

$$N_n^{(-)} = 2^{n+1} \left(\frac{w + iu - i}{4\tau}\right)^{\frac{1}{2}n} K_n[4\tau \sqrt{(w + iu - i)}]$$

it is readily shown that

$$v_x' = \frac{w}{\pi} \mathsf{R}[N_0^{(-)} - N_0^{(+)}]$$

$$v_z' = \frac{1}{\pi} \mathsf{I}[N_1^{(-)} - N_1^{(+)}] + \frac{w}{\pi} \mathsf{I}[N_0^{(-)} - N_0^{(+)}]$$

$$p' = \frac{1}{\pi} \mathsf{I}[N_0^{(-)} - N_0^{(+)}]$$

where R denotes "the real part of" and I "the imaginary part of."

As $t \to \infty$,

$$\xi_x \to \xi_x^\infty = \frac{2w}{\pi} \int_0^\infty e^{-\eta w} \sin(\eta) \sin(u\eta) d\eta$$

which may be integrated by ordinary means to give

$$\xi_x^\infty = \frac{4}{\pi} \frac{uw^2}{[w^2 + (u - 1)^2][w^2 + (u + 1)^2]}$$

Similarly, as $t \to \infty$,

$$\xi_z \to \xi_z^\infty = \frac{1}{\pi} \tan^{-1}\left(\frac{2w}{w^2 + u^2 - 1}\right)$$

The displacements then come out to be

$$\xi_x = \xi_x^\infty - \frac{w}{\pi} \, \mathrm{R}[N_{-1}^{(-)} - N_{-1}^{(+)}]$$

$$\xi_z = \xi_z^\infty - \frac{1}{\pi} \, \mathrm{I}[N_0^{(-)} - N_0^{(+)}] - \frac{w}{\pi} \, \mathrm{I}[N_{-1}^{(-)} - N_{-1}^{(+)}]$$

From the last two equations of the set (165) we obtain the relation

$$\frac{g\rho}{\sigma} \, \zeta(x,t) = \frac{g\rho}{\sigma} \, \zeta^\infty - \left(\frac{\bar{p}}{\sigma}\right)_{w=0}$$

where

$$\frac{g\rho}{\sigma} \, \zeta^\infty = \frac{2}{\pi} \int_0^\infty \frac{\sin(\eta)}{\eta} \cos(u\eta) d\eta = \begin{cases} 1 & \text{if } |u| < 1 \\ 0 & \text{if } |u| > 1 \end{cases}$$

This equation giving the configuration of the surface at any time may

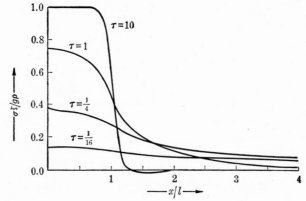

Fɪɢ. 57. The form of the displacement $\zeta(x,t)$ at various times.

readily be simplified by expressing the functions in terms of the Hankel function $H_0^{(1)}(i^{\frac{1}{2}}x)$, where x is real, for which tables are available.[1]

$$\left(\frac{\bar{p}}{\sigma}\right)_{w=0} = \frac{2}{\pi} \, \mathrm{I} \{K_0[4\tau i^{\frac{1}{2}}(1 + u)^{\frac{1}{2}}] - K_0[4\tau i^{\frac{1}{2}}(u - 1)^{\frac{1}{2}}]\}$$

Introducing the quantities

$$x_2 = 4\tau(1 + u)^{\frac{1}{2}}, \qquad x_1 = \begin{cases} 4\tau(u - 1)^{\frac{1}{2}}, & u > 1 \\ 4\tau(1 - u)^{\frac{1}{2}}, & u < 1 \end{cases}$$

and making use of the relation

$$\frac{2}{\pi} K_0(z) = i H_0^{(1)}(iz)$$

[1] Jahnke and Emde, *op. cit.*, pp. 302–305.

we find finally that

$$\zeta(x,t) = \begin{cases} \dfrac{g\rho}{\sigma} \, \mathrm{R}[H_0^{(1)}(x_1 i^{\frac{1}{2}}) - H^{(1)}(x_2 i^{\frac{1}{2}})] & u > 1 \\[3mm] \dfrac{g\rho}{\sigma} \, \{1 - \mathrm{R}[H_0^{(1)}(x_1 i^{\frac{1}{2}}) + H_0^{(1)}(x_2 i^{\frac{1}{2}})]\} & 0 < u < 1 \end{cases}$$

This function may readily be computed from the set of tables cited above.[1] Some idea of the variation of the surface displacement $\zeta(x,t)$ with x and t may be derived from Fig. 57.

36. Harmonic Analysis of Nonlinear Viscous Flow

In Secs. 33 to 35 we have discussed problems in viscous fluid flow by assuming that the motion was so slow that the terms of the second order in the velocity could be neglected. Thus, in the discussion of the diffusion of vorticity (Sec. 33.3) we made use of the approximate equation (111) instead of the exact equation (14) for the variation of the vorticity. In this section we shall consider this latter equation. Because of its nonlinearity this equation does not lend itself readily to the application of methods based on the theory of integral transforms, but some progress has recently been made in this direction by Kampé de Fériet.[2] It is possible to set up relations between the double Fourier transforms of the various physical quantities entering into the problem and then, with the help of these relations, to form an integrodifferential equation governing the behavior of the double transform of the vorticity. The study of this equation is very difficult but would seem to be the rational starting point for the rigorous discussion of the behavior of the transform of the vorticity and the related spectral function. Though the solution of particular boundary value problems by this method will be exceedingly complicated, it should be possible to investigate in this way the validity of several of the working hypotheses which have been made in the past, such as the assumption that the big eddies have a tendency to degenerate into smaller ones.

We shall first of all write down some important properties of double Fourier transforms of which we shall make use. If $f(x,y)$ is a *real* function of the variables x and y, then its double Fourier transform

$$F(\omega_1, \omega_2) = \frac{1}{2\pi} \int_{-\infty}^{\infty} \int_{-\infty}^{\infty} f(x,y) e^{i(\omega_1 x + \omega_2 y)} \, dx \, dy$$

---

[1] A series of computations of this kind is included in N. A. Haskell, *Physics*, **7**, 61 (1936).

[2] J. Kampé de Fériet, *Quart. Applied Math.*, **6**, 1 (1948).

has complex conjugate

$$F^*(\omega_1,\omega_2) = \frac{1}{2\pi} \int_{-\infty}^{\infty} \int_{-\infty}^{\infty} f(x,y)e^{-i(\omega_1 x+\omega_2 y)}\, dx\, dy$$

Then, by a method similar to that employed in establishing the Faltung theorem (112), Chap. 1, we may readily show that

$$\int_{-\infty}^{\infty} \int_{-\infty}^{\infty} f(x,y)g(x,y)e^{i(\theta_1 x+\theta_2 y)}\, dx\, dy$$

$$= \int_{-\infty}^{\infty} \int_{-\infty}^{\infty} F(\omega_1,\omega_2)G^*(\omega_1 - \theta_1, \omega_2 - \theta_2)d\omega_1\, d\omega_2 \quad (167)$$

where $f(x,y)$ and $g(x,y)$ are real functions of x and y. In particular, we shall make use of the special case $g = f$,

$$\int_{-\infty}^{\infty} \int_{-\infty}^{\infty} f^2(x,y)dx\, dy = \int_{-\infty}^{\infty} \int_{-\infty}^{\infty} |F(\omega_1,\omega_2)|^2\, d\omega_1\, d\omega_2 \quad (168)$$

If we introduce the double Fourier transform $\Psi(\omega_1,\omega_2,t)$ of the stream function $\psi(x,y,t)$ through the equation

$$\Psi(\omega_1,\omega_2,t) = \frac{1}{2\pi} \int_{-\infty}^{\infty} \int_{-\infty}^{\infty} \psi(x,y,t)e^{i(\omega_1 x+\omega_2 y)}\, dx\, dy$$

then it follows from equations (15) that the Fourier transforms $U(\omega_1,\omega_2,t)$ and $V(\omega_1,\omega_2,t)$ of the velocity components $u(x,y,t)$ and $v(x,y,t)$ satisfy the relations

$$U(\omega_1,\omega_2,t) = i\omega_2\Psi(\omega_1,\omega_2,t), \qquad V(\omega_1,\omega_2,t) = -i\omega_1\Psi(\omega_1,\omega_2,t)$$

Similarly, by multiplying both sides of the equation

$$\zeta = -\tfrac{1}{2}\nabla_1^2\psi$$

by $e^{i(\omega_1 x+\omega_2 y)}$ and integrating over the whole xy plane, we obtain the equation

$$Z = \tfrac{1}{2}(\omega_1^2 + \omega_2^2)\Psi$$

for the double transform $Z(\omega_1,\omega_2,t)$ of the vorticity $\zeta(x,y,t)$.

From these relations it follows immediately that

$$\left.\begin{aligned}
\Psi(\omega_1,\omega_2,t) &= \frac{2}{\omega_1^2 + \omega_2^2}\, Z(\omega_1,\omega_2,t) \\
U(\omega_1,\omega_2,t) &= \frac{2i\omega_2}{\omega_1^2 + \omega_2^2}\, Z(\omega_1,\omega_2,t) \\
V(\omega_1,\omega_2,t) &= -\frac{2i\omega_1}{\omega_1^2 + \omega_2^2}\, Z(\omega_1,\omega_2,t)
\end{aligned}\right\} \quad (169)$$

Now, from equation (168), we have that

$$E = \frac{1}{2} \int_{-\infty}^{\infty} \int_{-\infty}^{\infty} (u^2 + v^2)dx\, dy = \frac{1}{2} \int_{-\infty}^{\infty} \int_{-\infty}^{\infty} (UU^* + VV^*)d\omega_1\, d\omega_2 \tag{170}$$

so, substituting for U and V and their complex conjugates from the last two of the equations (169), we obtain the expression

$$E = \int_{-\infty}^{\infty} \int_{-\infty}^{\infty} \frac{2ZZ^*}{\omega_1^2 + \omega_2^2}\, d\omega_1\, d\omega_2 \tag{170a}$$

This integral E has a simple physical interpretation—it represents the kinetic energy of the fluid flow. If we form the *spectral decomposition* of this function, we write

$$E = \int_{-\infty}^{\infty} \int_{-\infty}^{\infty} \gamma(\omega_1, \omega_2, t)d\omega_1\, d\omega_2 \tag{171}$$

where the function $\gamma(\omega_1, \omega_2, t)$ is called the *spectral function*. A simple expression for this spectral function is obtained by identifying equations (170a) and (171). We find that

$$\gamma(\omega_1, \omega_2, t) = \frac{2}{\omega_1^2 + \omega_2^2} |Z(\omega_1, \omega_2, t)|^2 \tag{172}$$

These equations show that the harmonic analysis of the flow of a viscous fluid can be based on the study of the Fourier transform $Z(\omega_1, \omega_2, t)$ of the vorticity, but even in the rather special case we are considering here, in which the fluid fills the entire space, we have no simple method of determining the form of the function $Z(\omega_1, \omega_2, t)$. We shall now set up the nonlinear integrodifferential equation upon whose solutions the determination of $Z(\omega_1, \omega_2, t)$ rests. From equation (167) we have

$$\int_{-\infty}^{\infty} \int_{-\infty}^{\infty} u(x,y) \frac{\partial \zeta}{\partial x} e^{i(\omega_1 x + \omega_2 y)}\, dx\, dy$$
$$= \int_{-\infty}^{\infty} \int_{-\infty}^{\infty} - iU(\theta_1, \theta_2)(\theta_1 - \omega_1)Z^*(\theta_1 - \omega_1, \theta_2 - \omega_2)d\theta_1\, d\theta_2$$

Now the Fourier transform $U(\theta_1, \theta_2)$ is, by equations (169), of the form

$$\frac{2i\theta_2}{\theta_1^2 + \theta_2^2} Z(\theta_1, \theta_2, t)$$

so that

$$\int_{-\infty}^{\infty} \int_{-\infty}^{\infty} u \frac{\partial \zeta}{\partial x} e^{i(\omega_1 x + \omega_2 y)}\, dx\, dy = 2 \int_{-\infty}^{\infty} \int_{-\infty}^{\infty} \frac{\theta_2(\theta_1 - \omega_1)}{\theta_1^2 + \theta_2^2}$$
$$Z(\theta_1, \theta_2)Z^*(\theta_1 - \omega_1, \theta_2 - \omega_2)d\theta_1\, d\theta_2$$

Similarly it may be shown that

$$\int_{-\infty}^{\infty}\int_{-\infty}^{\infty} v(x,y)\,\frac{\partial \zeta}{\partial y}\,e^{i(\omega_1 x + \omega_2 y)}\,dx\,dy$$

$$= -2\int_{-\infty}^{\infty}\int_{-\infty}^{\infty}\frac{\theta_1(\theta_2 - \omega_2)}{\theta_1^2 + \theta_2^2}\,Z(\theta_1,\theta_2)Z^*(\theta_1 - \omega_1, \theta_2 - \omega_2)d\theta_1\,d\theta_2$$

Hence it follows that equation (14) is equivalent to

$$\frac{\partial Z(\omega_1,\omega_2,t)}{\partial t} + \nu(\omega_1^2 + \omega_2^2)Z(\omega_1,\omega_2,t)$$

$$= 2\int_{-\infty}^{\infty}\int_{-\infty}^{\infty}\frac{\theta_2\omega_1 - \theta_1\omega_2}{\theta_1^2 + \theta_2^2}\,Z(\theta_1,\theta_2,t)Z^*(\theta_1 - \omega_1, \theta_2 - \omega_2,t)d\theta_1\,d\theta_2 \quad (173)$$

It will be observed that, in the case in which $\theta_2\omega_1 - \theta_1\omega_2 = 0$, this equation reduces to the approximate equation (113) which we used previously to obtain the solution of special problems. This suggests that in a case in which the term on the right-hand side of equation (173) would appear to be small we may obtain approximate solutions of the equation by writing $Z = Z_0 + Z_1$, where Z_0 is the appropriate solution of the corresponding initial value problem on the equation (113). If we then insert this form in equation (173) and retain only terms in Z_0 on the right, we obtain the equation

$$\frac{\partial Z_1(\omega_1,\omega_2,t)}{\partial t} + \nu(\omega_1^2 + \omega_2^2)Z_1(\omega_1,\omega_2,t)$$

$$= 2\int_{-\infty}^{\infty}\int_{-\infty}^{\infty}\frac{\theta_2\omega_1 - \theta_1\omega_2}{\theta_1^2 + \theta_2^2}\,Z_0(\theta_1,\theta_2,t)Z_0^*(\theta_1 - \omega_1, \theta_2 - \omega_2,t)d\theta_1\,d\theta_2$$

for the determination of the small quantity Z_1. This equation being linear in Z_1 may be solved readily under the initial condition $Z_1 = 0$ to give the first approximation to Z_1. The process may then be repeated, retaining terms of the next highest order of small quantities on the right. In this way we may build up the solution in cases in which the nonlinear terms represent a small perturbation of the linear flow described by equation (111). In the general case in which the nonlinear term is appreciable there does not appear to be any general method of attack.

In the above analysis we have assumed that the viscous fluid fills the whole of the xy plane. If it is bounded by a curve C which encloses a domain D of finite area S, then we may employ finite Fourier transforms of the type

$$F(\omega_1,\omega_2) = \frac{1}{2\pi}\int\int_D f(x,y)e^{-i(\omega_1 x + \omega_2 y)}\,dx\,dy$$

to obtain some general inequalities governing the behavior of certain physical quantities. It is obvious that

$$|F(\omega_1,\omega_2)| \leq \frac{1}{2\pi} \int\int_D |f(x,y)| dx\, dy$$

so that, by Schwarz's inequality, we have

$$|F(\omega_1,\omega_2)|^2 \leq \frac{S}{4\pi^2} \left[\int\int_D f^2(x,y) dx\, dy \right]$$

since $S = \int\int_D dx\, dy$. Extracting the square root, we obtain

$$F(\omega_1,\omega_2) \leq \frac{S^{\frac{1}{2}}}{2\pi} \left[\int\int_D f^2(x,y) dx\, dy \right]^{\frac{1}{2}}$$

In particular, if U denotes the finite transform of $u(x,y)$, then

$$|U| \leq \frac{S^{\frac{1}{2}}}{2\pi} \left(\int\int_D u^2\, dx\, dy \right)^{\frac{1}{2}} \leq \frac{(2SE)^{\frac{1}{2}}}{2\pi} \tag{174}$$

where E is the total energy of the fluid, defined by the analogue of equation (170). Similarly

$$|V| \leq \frac{(2SE)^{\frac{1}{2}}}{2\pi} \tag{175}$$

Now from equations (169) it follows that

$$2iZ(\omega_1,\omega_2) = \omega_2 U - \omega_1 V$$

and hence

$$|Z(\omega_1,\omega_2)| \leq \tfrac{1}{2}(|\omega_2||U| + |\omega_1||V|) \tag{176}$$

Substituting from equations (174) and (175) into equation (176), we find that

$$|Z(\omega_1,\omega_2)| \leq \frac{(2SE)^{\frac{1}{2}}}{4\pi}(|\omega_1| + |\omega_2|)$$

Equation (172) then gives an upper bound for $\gamma(\omega_1,\omega_2,t)$,

$$\gamma(\omega_1,\omega_2) \leq \frac{SE}{4\pi^2} \frac{(|\omega_1| + |\omega_2|)^2}{\omega_1^2 + \omega_2^2}$$

from which it follows immediately that

$$\gamma(\omega_1,\omega_2) \leq \frac{SE}{2\pi^2}$$

Indeed it can be proved that[1]

$$\gamma(\omega_1, \omega_2) \leq \frac{SE_0}{2\pi^2} e^{-8\nu t/K_D^{\frac{1}{2}}}$$

where K_D is a positive quantity depending on the nature of D and, E_0 is the value of E at time $t = 0$.

[1] J. Kampé de Fériet, *Compt. rend.*, **223**, 1096 (1946).

CHAPTER 8

APPLICATIONS TO ATOMIC AND NUCLEAR PHYSICS

Since the fundamental equations of quantum theory, which are designed to deal with problems arising in atomic and nuclear systems, are of comparatively recent origin, the theory of integral transforms has not been applied extensively to their solution. This is also due, in part, to the fact that quantum theoretical problems frequently are *eigenvalue* problems; *i.e.*, interest is focused not on the determination of the behavior of a function in a prescribed region of space but on finding the values of a certain parameter, occurring in the appropriate differential equation, which will lead to solutions of a specified nature.

There are, however, several problems which are of interest in atomic physics and which are based on the differential equations of classical physics. We shall begin this chapter by considering a few problems of this type (Secs. 37 to 40). In these sections no use is made of quantum mechanics though in Sec. 40 it is necessary to make use of the *results* of certain wave-mechanical calculations to obtain explicit expressions for some of the functions whose nature cannot be discussed by purely classical methods. In the remaining three sections use is made of nonrelativistic quantum theory. Although an attempt has been made to make these sections self-contained, they will probably prove difficult to a reader unacquainted with wave mechanics. Such a reader may omit these sections, if he so desires, since none of the results derived therein is quoted in the remaining two chapters of the book.

37. Theory of Radioactive Transformations

The general theory of radioactive transformations, based on the assumption that radioactive atoms are unstable and disintegrate according to the laws of chance, was first put forward by Rutherford and Soddy.[1] A parent substance decays into a daughter substance which may be either stable or radioactive. If we denote the number of atoms of the parent substance at time t by $N_1(t)$, then the law of radioactive transformation states that the number of atoms $(-\Delta N_1)$ which decay to the daughter substance during the time interval $(t, t + \Delta t)$ is proportional to both Δt

---

[1] E. Rutherford and F. Soddy, *Phil. Mag.*, **4**, 370 (1902). See also J. D. Stranathan, "The Particles of Modern Physics" (Blakiston, Philadelphia, 1942), Chap. 8.

and $N_1(t)$. That is, we have

$$-\Delta N_1(t) \,=\, \lambda_1 N_1(t)\Delta t \tag{1}$$

where λ_1 is a constant called the *disintegration constant* of the parent substance. If the daughter substance is itself radioactive, then, similarly,

$$-\Delta N_2(t) \,=\, -\lambda_1 N_1 \,\Delta t \,+\, \lambda_2 N_2 \,\Delta t \tag{2}$$

where $N_2(t)$ is the number of atoms of the daughter substance present at time t. The radioactive series continues in this way, the $(r-1)$th product decaying into the rth according to the rule

$$-\Delta N_{r+1} \,=\, -\lambda_r N_r \,\Delta t \,+\, \lambda_{r+1} N_{r+1} \,\Delta t \tag{3}$$

If, finally, the nth product is stable, it will increase according to the rule

$$\Delta N_{n+1} \,=\, \lambda_n N_n \,\Delta t \tag{4}$$

Equations (1) to (4) are equivalent to the $n+1$ first-order equations

$$\left.\begin{array}{c} \dfrac{dN_1}{dt} \,=\, -\lambda_1 N_1 \\[2mm] \dfrac{dN_{r+1}}{dt} \,=\, \lambda_r N_r - \lambda_{r+1} N_{r+1} \qquad 1 \le r \le n-1 \\[2mm] \dfrac{dN_{n+1}}{dt} \,=\, \lambda_n N_n \end{array}\right\} \tag{5}$$

These equations may be solved by the use of Laplace transforms.[1] If we write

$$\bar{N}_r(p) \,=\, \int_0^\infty N_r(t)e^{-pt}\,dt$$

then, integrating by parts,

$$\int_0^\infty \frac{dN_r}{dt}\,e^{-pt}\,dt \,=\, -N_r(0) \,+\, p\bar{N}_r(p) \tag{6}$$

Assuming that initially only the parent substance is present, we have the initial conditions

$$N_1(0) \,=\, N_0, \qquad N_r(0) \,=\, 0 \qquad\qquad r \neq 1 \tag{7}$$

Multiplying both sides of each of the equations (5) by e^{-pt}, integrating with respect to t from 0 to ∞, and making use of the equations (6) and

---

[1] Cf. H. Jeffreys, "Operational Methods in Mathematical Physics," *Cambridge Tract* 32 (Cambridge, London, 1927), p. 36, and W. F. Sedgwick, *Proc. Cambridge Phil. Soc.*, **38**, 280 (1942).

(7), we have the relations

$$(\lambda_1 + p)\bar{N}_1 = N_0; \qquad (\lambda_{r+1} + p)\bar{N}_{r+1} = \lambda_r\bar{N}_r \qquad 1 \leq r \leq n - 1 \left.\begin{matrix} \\ \\ \end{matrix}\right\} \quad (8)$$
$$p\bar{N}_{n+1} = \lambda_n\bar{N}_n$$

The solution of these algebraic equations is readily seen to be

$$\bar{N}_{r+1} = \frac{N_0}{\lambda_{r+1}} \prod_{i=1}^{r+1} \left(1 + \frac{p}{\lambda_i}\right)^{-1} \qquad 1 \leq r \leq n - 1 \left.\begin{matrix} \\ \\ \\ \\ \\ \end{matrix}\right\} \quad (9)$$
$$\bar{N}_1 = N_0(\lambda_1 + p)^{-1}, \qquad \bar{N}_{n+1} = \frac{N_0}{p} \prod_{i=1}^{n} \left(1 + \frac{p}{\lambda_i}\right)^{-1}$$

Inverting these results by means of the Laplace inversion theorem 14, we have

$$N_1 = \frac{1}{2\pi i} \int_{c-i\infty}^{c+i\infty} \frac{N_0 e^{pt}}{p + \lambda_1} dp$$

$$N_{r+1} = \frac{1}{2\pi i} \int_{c-i\infty}^{c+i\infty} \frac{N_0}{\lambda_{r+1}} e^{pt} \prod_{i=1}^{r+1} \left(1 + \frac{p}{\lambda_i}\right)^{-1} dp \qquad 1 \leq r \leq n - 1 \quad (10)$$

$$N_{n+1} = \frac{1}{2\pi i} \int_{c-i\infty}^{c+i\infty} \frac{N_0}{p} e^{pt} \prod_{i=1}^{n} \left(1 + \frac{p}{\lambda_i}\right)^{-1} dp$$

These integrals may be evaluated by expressing the rational function part of the integrand in partial fractions and making use of the results

$$\frac{1}{2\pi i} \int_{c-i\infty}^{c+i\infty} \frac{e^{pt}}{p + \lambda_r} dp = e^{-\lambda_r t}, \qquad \frac{1}{2\pi i} \int_{c-i\infty}^{c+i\infty} \frac{e^{pt}}{p(p + \lambda_r)} dp = \frac{1 - e^{-\lambda_r t}}{\lambda_r} \quad (11)$$

We shall now examine certain special cases.

Case 1: n = 1. In this instance the first daughter substance is stable. We then have from the set of relations (9),

$$\bar{N}_1 = \frac{N_0}{p + \lambda_1}, \qquad \bar{N}_2 = \frac{\lambda_1 N_0}{p(p + \lambda_1)}$$

so that by Theorem 14 and the formulas (11) we find that

$$N_1 = N_0 e^{-\lambda_1 t}, \qquad N_2 = N_0(1 - e^{-\lambda_1 t})$$

The variation of N_1 and N_2 with time is shown in Fig. 58. It will be observed that, as we should expect, the sum of N_1 and N_2 is the number of atoms of the parent substance present initially.

Case 2: $n = 2$. In this case equations (9) reduce to the simple forms

$$\bar{N}_1 = \frac{N_0}{p + \lambda_1}, \qquad \bar{N}_2 = \frac{\lambda_1}{\lambda_1 - \lambda_2}\left(\frac{1}{p + \lambda_2} - \frac{1}{p + \lambda_1}\right)N_0, \qquad \bar{N}_3 = \frac{\lambda_2}{p}\,\bar{N}_2$$

so that, inverting by means of Theorem 14 and making use of the integra-

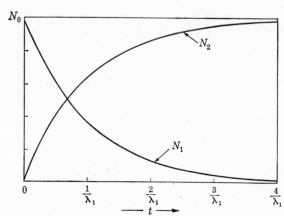

Fig. 58.   Decay of a radioactive nucleus to a stable daughter nucleus.

tions (11), we find that at time t the numbers of atoms of the various substances present are

$$N_1 = N_0 e^{-\lambda_1 t} \tag{12}$$

$$N_2 = \frac{N_0 \lambda_1}{\lambda_2 - \lambda_1}\left(e^{-\lambda_1 t} - e^{-\lambda_2 t}\right) \tag{13}$$

$$N_3 = N_0\left(1 - \frac{\lambda_2}{\lambda_2 - \lambda_1}e^{-\lambda_1 t} + \frac{\lambda_1}{\lambda_2 - \lambda_1}e^{-\lambda_2 t}\right) \tag{14}$$

The variation of these numbers with time is shown in Fig. 59, from which (or from the above equations) it is obvious that here also the total number of atoms present at any instant is equal to the number of atoms of the parent substance from which the process is begun.

When $t \simeq 0$, it follows from equations (13) and (14) that

$$\frac{N_2}{N_0} \simeq \lambda_1 t, \qquad \frac{N_3}{N_0} \simeq \frac{\lambda_2}{2\lambda_1}\,(\lambda_1 t)^2$$

On the other hand, if λ_2 is very much greater than λ_1, we find that for large values of t ($\gg 1/\lambda_1$)

$$N_2 \simeq \frac{\lambda_1}{\lambda_2}\,N_0 e^{-\lambda_1 t}, \qquad N_3 = N_0(1 - e^{-\lambda_1 t})$$

so that we get approximately the same state of affairs as in the case in which $n = 1$. If, however, $\lambda_2 \ll \lambda_1$, then

$$N_2 \simeq N_0 e^{-\lambda_2 t}, \qquad N_3 \simeq N_0(1 - e^{-\lambda_2 t})$$

so that the parent substance decays so rapidly that the substance N_2 is built up very soon, but because of the low decay constant it is then transformed to N_3 by the kind of process discussed in case 1.

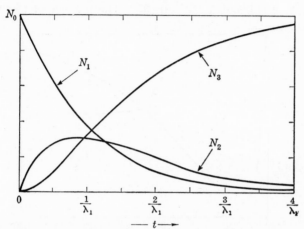

Fig. 59.   Growth of the decay products in the case $n = 2$.

Case 3: $n = 3$.   Similar results can be derived in the case in which $n = 3$.   It follows at once from equations (9) that $\bar{N}_1$ and $\bar{N}_2$ have the same values as in case 2 and that

$$\bar{N}_3 = \lambda_1 \lambda_2 N_0 \left[\frac{1}{(\lambda_2 - \lambda_1)(\lambda_3 - \lambda_1)(p + \lambda_1)} + \frac{1}{(\lambda_1 - \lambda_2)(\lambda_3 - \lambda_2)(p + \lambda_2)} \right.$$
$$\left. + \frac{1}{(\lambda_1 - \lambda_3)(\lambda_2 - \lambda_3)(p + \lambda_3)} \right]$$

$$\bar{N}_4 = \frac{\lambda_3 \bar{N}_3}{p}$$

Inverting these expressions by the usual process, we find that N_1 and N_2 are given by equations (12) and (13) but that now

$$N_3 = \lambda_1 \lambda_2 N_0 \left[\frac{e^{-\lambda_1 t}}{(\lambda_2 - \lambda_1)(\lambda_3 - \lambda_1)} + \frac{e^{-\lambda_2 t}}{(\lambda_1 - \lambda_2)(\lambda_3 - \lambda_2)} \right.$$
$$\left. + \frac{e^{-\lambda_3 t}}{(\lambda_1 - \lambda_3)(\lambda_2 - \lambda_3)} \right] \quad (15)$$

and

$$N_4 = N_0 \left[\frac{\lambda_2\lambda_3(1 - e^{-\lambda_1 t})}{(\lambda_2 - \lambda_1)(\lambda_3 - \lambda_1)} + \frac{\lambda_3\lambda_1(1 - e^{-\lambda_2 t})}{(\lambda_1 - \lambda_2)(\lambda_3 - \lambda_2)} \right. $$
$$\left. + \frac{\lambda_1\lambda_2(1 - e^{-\lambda_3 t})}{(\lambda_1 - \lambda_3)(\lambda_2 - \lambda_3)} \right] \quad (16)$$

In the case of the transformation of RaA to RaD we have the experimental values $\lambda_1 = 3.79 \times 10^{-3}$, $\lambda_2 = 4.31 \times 10^{-4}$, $\lambda_3 = 5.86 \times 10^{-4}$, so that $\lambda_2/\lambda_1 = 0.114$ and $\lambda_3/\lambda_1 = 0.155$. The number of atoms of RaA

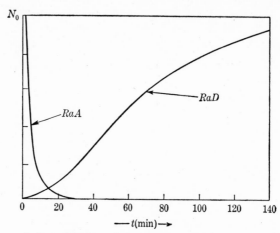

FIG. 60. The variation with time of the amounts of RaA and RaD present during the transformation of RaA to RaD, through RaB and RaC.

at time t is given by inserting these numerical values in equation (12), while that of RaD is given by inserting them in (16). The variation with time of the amounts of RaA and RaD, calculated in this way, is shown in Fig. 60.

38. Van der Waals Attraction between Spherical Particles

The problem of computing the energy of interaction between two spheres under a general law of force is one which arises frequently in modern physics, as, for instance, in the discussion of the cohesive force between solid surfaces and the surface energy of solids.[1] We shall now show how the theory of Laplace transforms may be used to obtain an expression for this energy on the assumption that $v(r)$, the mutual potential energy of two unit masses situated at a distance r apart, is a function of r alone. The method of calculation, which is due to Bouwkamp,[2] is

[1] See, *e.g.*, R. S. Bradley, *Phil. Mag.*, **13**, 853 (1932).
[2] C. J. Bouwkamp, *Physica*, **13**, 501 (1947).

not restricted to spherical particles. For instance, the interaction energy of the two disklike particles lying in the same plane, as discussed by Dube and Dasgupta,[1] can be calculated along similar lines.

When the law of force between two point masses is Newton's law, it is well known that the mutual energy between two spheres is the same as that obtained by imagining the total masses of the spheres to be concentrated at their centers. The general question which arises immediately is whether there exists a law of interaction, other than Newton's, such that two homogeneous spheres shall attract each other as if certain reduced masses were located at the centers. More precisely, we wish to determine whether it is possible to choose $v(r)$ such that the mutual energy of the two spheres is given by $\phi(a,b)v(c)$, where $\phi(a,b)$ is a function of a and b, the radii of the spheres, and c is the distance between their centers.

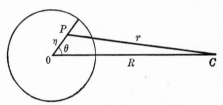

FIG. 61. The coordinates η and θ.

We begin by considering the energy of interaction of a unit point mass and a sphere of radius a. Let R denote the distance between the point mass and the center of the sphere, and introduce spherical coordinates η,θ at the center of the sphere, the polar axis pointing toward the unit mass (cf. Fig. 61). Then the mutual energy between the point mass and the sphere is

$$w = \int_0^a d\eta \int_0^\pi 2\pi\eta^2 \sin\ (\theta)d\theta\ \rho(\eta)v(r) \tag{17}$$

where $\rho(\eta)$ is the density of the sphere and

$$r^2 = \eta^2 - 2\eta R \cos \theta + R^2 \tag{18}$$

If we let

$$V(r) = \int_{r_0}^r rv(r)dr \tag{19}$$

where r_0 is arbitrary, then

$$\frac{\partial V}{\partial \theta} = rv(r) \frac{\partial r}{\partial \theta} = Rv(r)\eta \sin \theta$$

so that the energy of interaction between the unit point mass and the sphere is

$$w = \frac{2\pi}{R} \int_0^a \eta\rho(\eta)d\eta \int_0^\pi Rv(r)\eta \sin \theta\, d\theta$$

$$= \frac{2\pi}{R} \int_0^a \eta\rho(\eta)d\eta[V(R + \eta) - V(R - \eta)] \tag{20}$$

[1] G. P. Dube and H. K. Dasgupta, *Indian Jour. Phys.*, **13**, 411 (1939).

Suppose now that

$$V(R + \eta) - V(R - \eta) = V'(R)f(\eta) \qquad (21)$$

where $f(\eta)$ is a function of η alone and $V'(R) = dV/dr$. Then, since

$$\frac{1}{R} [V(R + \eta) - V(R - \eta)] = \frac{1}{R} V'(R)f(\eta) = v(R)f(\eta)$$

the expression for the energy reduces to

$$w = m(a)v(R) \qquad (22)$$

where

$$m(a) = 2\pi \int_0^a \eta f(\eta)\rho(\eta)d\eta \qquad (23)$$

In other words, if the law of interaction is such that the function $V(r)$ satisfies equation (21), the interaction between the point mass and the sphere is as if the mass $m(a)$, defined by equation (23), were located at the center of the sphere. It can readily be shown[1] that $V(r) = e^{-\lambda r}$, in which λ is zero or a constant (real or complex) is the only form of $V(r)$ which satisfies equation (21). Now if $V(r) = e^{-\lambda r}$, it follows that

$$V(R + \eta) - V(R - \eta) = -2e^{-\lambda R} \sinh (\lambda \eta)$$

so that, since $V'(R) = -\lambda e^{-\lambda R}$, equation (21) is satisfied with

$$f(\eta) = \frac{2}{\lambda} \sinh (\lambda \eta)$$

If the density of the sphere is constant, then

$$m(a) = \rho \int_0^a \frac{4\pi}{\lambda} \eta \sinh (\lambda \eta)d\eta = \left(\frac{2\pi a}{\lambda}\right)^{\frac{3}{2}} \rho I_{\frac{3}{2}}(\lambda a) \qquad (24)$$

where

$$I_{\frac{3}{2}}(z) = \left(\frac{2}{\pi z}\right)^{\frac{1}{2}} \left[\cosh (z) - \frac{\sinh (z)}{z} \right] \qquad (25)$$

Since equation (22) gives the energy of interaction of a point of unit mass and a sphere of radius a, it follows that the energy of interaction between two spheres of radii a and b is

$$w = m(a)m(b)v(R) \qquad (26)$$

where R is the distance between the centers of the spheres. Taking ρ to be constant and putting $V(r) = e^{-\lambda r}$, that is,

$$v(r) = \frac{1}{r} e^{-\lambda r} \qquad (27)$$

[1] I. N. Sneddon and C. K. Thornhill, *Proc. Cambridge Phil. Soc.*, **45**, 318 (1949).

we see from equations (24) and (26) that the interaction energy is

$$w = \frac{8\pi^3(ab)^{\frac{3}{2}}\rho^2}{\lambda^3} I_{\frac{3}{2}}(\lambda a)I_{\frac{3}{2}}(\lambda b)\frac{e^{-\lambda R}}{R}$$

Suppose, now, that the law of attraction is $v(R)$; then, writing

$$g(\lambda) = \frac{1}{2\pi i}\int_{c-i\infty}^{c+i\infty} Rv(R)e^{\lambda R}\,dR \tag{28}$$

we have, by the Laplace inversion theorem 14,

$$v(R) = \int_0^\infty g(\lambda)\frac{e^{-\lambda R}}{R}\,d\lambda \tag{29}$$

The energy of interaction between two spheres is then

$$w = \frac{8\pi^3(ab)^{\frac{3}{2}}}{R}\rho^2\int_0^\infty g(\lambda)I_{\frac{3}{2}}(\lambda a)I_{\frac{3}{2}}(\lambda b)e^{-\lambda R}\lambda^{-3}\,d\lambda \tag{30}$$

For instance, if $v(R) = R^{-n}(n > 1)$, then, since

$$\int_0^\infty \lambda^{n-2}e^{-\lambda R}\,d\lambda = \Gamma(n-1)R^{-n+1}$$

we have $g(\lambda) = \lambda^{n-2}/\Gamma(n-1)$, so that, if $w_n(a,b,R)$ denotes the energy of interaction of two spheres of radii a and b at a distance R apart, when the law of force is $v(r) = r^{-n}(n > 1)$, we have

$$Rw_n(a,b,R) = \frac{8\pi^3(ab)^{\frac{3}{2}}\rho^2}{\Gamma(n-1)}\int_0^\infty e^{-\lambda R}I_{\frac{3}{2}}(\lambda a)I_{\frac{3}{2}}(\lambda b)\lambda^{n-5}\,d\lambda$$

The integrand of the integral on the right of this equation is an elementary function, and all the integrals involved are easily evaluated with the aid of Euler's integral for the gamma function. Evaluating this integral, and arranging the result in a form which shows the symmetry between a and b, we obtain

$$\frac{(n-2)(n-3)(n-4)(n-5)Rw_n(a,b,R)}{4\pi^2\rho^2}$$

$$= ab[(R+a+b)^{5-n} + (R-a-b)^{5-n} + (R-a+b)^{5-n}$$
$$+ (R+a-b)^{5-n}]$$

$$- \frac{R}{n-6}[(R+a+b)^{6-n} + (R-a-b)^{6-n} + (R-a+b)^{6-n}$$
$$+ (R+a-b)^{6-n}]$$

$$+ \frac{1}{n-7}[(R+a+b)^{7-n} + (R-a-b)^{7-n} + (R-a+b)^{7-n}$$
$$+ (R+a-b)^{7-n}]$$

Some difficulty is encountered in the evaluation of the function $w_n(a,b,R)$ when n is one of the integers 2,3,4,5,6, and 7.   In these cases a limiting process has to be applied, leading to logarithmic terms.   The most important case in physical applications (*e.g.*, in the theory of van der Waals' forces) is that for which $n = 6$.   In this case it is easily shown that

$$w_6(a,b,R) = \frac{\pi^2\rho^2}{6} \left\{ \frac{4ab(R^2 - a^2 - b^2)}{[R^2 - (a - b)^2][R^2 - (a + b)^2]} + \log_e \frac{R^2 - (a + b)^2}{R^2 - (a - b)^2} \right\}$$

in agreement with Hamaker's result.[1]

It is further of interest to note that the function $w_n(a,b,R)$ for $n > 2$ can be found by a simple differentiation once it is known for $1 \leq n \leq 2$. For it can easily be shown that

$$w_{n+1}(a,b,R) = \frac{1}{n - 1} \frac{1}{R} \frac{\partial}{\partial R} [Rw_n(a,b,R)]   n > 1$$

39. Interaction of Radiation with an Electron

We shall now consider the interaction between an electron and radiation in certain circumstances, on the basis of classical electrodynamics.

39.1 Retarded potentials.   In the classical theory of the electromagnetic field the electric and magnetic field strengths **E** and **H** may be expressed in terms of a vector potential **A** and a scalar potential ϕ by means of the relations

$$\mathbf{H} = \operatorname{curl} \mathbf{A}, \qquad \mathbf{E} = -\frac{1}{c}\frac{\partial \mathbf{A}}{\partial t} - \operatorname{grad}(\phi) \tag{31}$$

where, as a consequence of Maxwell's equations, **A** and ϕ satisfy the inhomogeneous wave equations

$$\nabla^2\mathbf{A} - \frac{1}{c^2}\frac{\partial^2}{\partial t^2}\mathbf{A} + \frac{4\pi}{c}\mathbf{i} = 0 \tag{32}$$

$$\nabla^2\phi - \frac{1}{c^2}\frac{\partial^2\phi}{\partial t^2} + 4\pi\rho = 0 \tag{33}$$

where **i** and ρ denote the current and charge density, respectively.   The solutions **A** and ϕ of these equations are related by the Lorentz condition

$$\operatorname{div} \mathbf{A} + \frac{1}{c}\frac{\partial \phi}{\partial t} = 0 \tag{34}$$

so that, once the solution of (32) has been found, the value of ϕ may be obtained by integrating equation (34) with respect to the time.

[1] H. C. Hamaker, *Physica*, **4**, 1058 (1937).

To solve equation (32), we introduce the four-dimensional Fourier transforms

$$\bar{A}(\xi,\eta,\zeta,\omega) = \frac{1}{4\pi^2} \int_{-\infty}^{\infty} \int_{-\infty}^{\infty} \int_{-\infty}^{\infty} \int_{-\infty}^{\infty} A(x,y,z,t)e^{i(\xi x+\eta y+\zeta z+\omega t)} \, dx \, dy \, dz \, dt$$

$$\bar{i}(\xi,\eta,\zeta,\omega) = \frac{1}{4\pi^2} \int_{-\infty}^{\infty} \int_{-\infty}^{\infty} \int_{-\infty}^{\infty} \int_{-\infty}^{\infty} i(x,y,z,t)e^{i(\xi x+\eta y+\zeta z+\omega t)} \, dx \, dy \, dz \, dt$$

Then, multiplying both sides of equation (32) by $e^{i(\xi x+\eta y+\zeta z+\omega t)}$ and integrating throughout all space and over all times, we obtain the relation

$$\left[\frac{\omega^2}{c^2} - (\xi^2 + \eta^2 + \zeta^2)\right] \bar{A} + \frac{4\pi}{c} \bar{i} = 0$$

so that

$$\bar{A} = \frac{4\pi c}{c^2(\xi^2 + \eta^2 + \zeta^2) - \omega^2} \bar{i}$$

and as a result of the inversion theorem stated in equation (111), Chap. 1, we have

$$\bar{A} = \frac{c}{\pi} \int_{-\infty}^{\infty} \int_{-\infty}^{\infty} \int_{-\infty}^{\infty} \int_{-\infty}^{\infty} \frac{\bar{i}(\xi,\eta,\zeta,\omega)e^{-i(\xi \cdot r+\omega t)}}{c^2(\xi^2 + \eta^2 + \zeta^2) - \omega^2} \, d\xi \, d\eta \, d\zeta \, d\omega$$

Now we may write

$$\bar{i}(\xi,\eta,\zeta,\omega) = \left(\frac{1}{2\pi}\right)^{\frac{3}{2}} \int_{-\infty}^{\infty} \int_{-\infty}^{\infty} \int_{-\infty}^{\infty} I(x,y,z,\omega)e^{i(\xi \cdot r)} \, dx \, dy \, dz$$

with

$$I(x,y,z,\omega) = \left(\frac{1}{2\pi}\right)^{\frac{1}{2}} \int_{-\infty}^{\infty} i(x,y,z,t)e^{i\omega t} \, dt$$

and by the Faltung theorem (112), Chap. 1, and the result

$$\left(\frac{1}{2\pi}\right)^{\frac{3}{2}} \int_{-\infty}^{\infty} \int_{-\infty}^{\infty} \int_{-\infty}^{\infty} \frac{e^{-i(\xi \cdot r)}}{\xi^2 + \eta^2 + \zeta^2 - \gamma^2} \, d\xi \, d\eta \, d\zeta = \left(\frac{\pi}{2}\right)^{\frac{1}{2}} \frac{e^{i\gamma r}}{r}$$

with $r^2 = x^2 + y^2 + z^2$, we have

$$\int_{-\infty}^{\infty} \int_{-\infty}^{\infty} \int_{-\infty}^{\infty} \frac{\bar{i}(\xi,\eta,\zeta,\omega)e^{-i(\xi \cdot r)}}{\xi^2 + \eta^2 + \zeta^2 - \omega^2/c^2} \, d\xi \, d\eta \, d\zeta$$

$$= \left(\frac{\pi}{2}\right)^{\frac{1}{2}} \int_{-\infty}^{\infty} \int_{-\infty}^{\infty} \int_{-\infty}^{\infty} \frac{e^{i\omega|r-r'|/c}}{|r - r'|} I(x',y',z',\omega)dx' \, dy' \, dz'$$

Thus

$$A = \frac{1}{c} \int_{-\infty}^{\infty} \int_{-\infty}^{\infty} \int_{-\infty}^{\infty} \frac{dx' \, dy' \, dz'}{|r - r'|} \left(\frac{1}{2\pi}\right)^{\frac{1}{2}} \int_{-\infty}^{\infty} I(x',y',z',\omega)e^{i\omega\left(t-\frac{|r-r'|}{c}\right)} \, d\omega$$

Since

$$\left(\frac{1}{2\pi}\right)^{\frac{1}{2}} \int_{-\infty}^{\infty} \mathbf{I}(x',y',z',\omega)e^{-i\omega t}\, d\omega = \mathbf{i}(x',y',z',t)$$

it follows that

$$\left(\frac{1}{2\pi}\right)^{\frac{1}{2}} \int_{-\infty}^{\infty} \mathbf{I}(x',y',z',\omega)e^{-i\omega\left(t-\frac{|\mathbf{r}-\mathbf{r}'|}{c}\right)}\, d\omega = \mathbf{i}\left(x',y',z',t-\frac{|\mathbf{r}-\mathbf{r}'|}{c}\right)$$

and hence that

$$\mathbf{A}(x,y,z,t) = \frac{1}{c}\int_{-\infty}^{\infty}\int_{-\infty}^{\infty}\int_{-\infty}^{\infty} \frac{\mathbf{i}\left(x',y',z',t-\dfrac{|\mathbf{r}-\mathbf{r}'|}{c}\right)}{|\mathbf{r}-\mathbf{r}'|}\, dx'\, dy'\, dz' \quad (35)$$

On account of its physical interpretation this solution is known as a *retarded potential*. By a precisely similar argument we may show that

$$\phi = \int_{-\infty}^{\infty}\int_{-\infty}^{\infty}\int_{-\infty}^{\infty} \frac{\rho\left(x',y',z',t-\dfrac{|\mathbf{r}-\mathbf{r}'|}{c}\right)}{|\mathbf{r}-\mathbf{r}'|}\, dx'\, dy'\, dz' \quad (36)$$

It should be noted that in deriving these formulas we assumed that both $\mathbf{A}$ and ϕ tended to zero as $r \to \infty$ and $|t| \to \infty$.

39.2 Radiation from a moving electron. If at time t an electron is at the point (x_0,y_0,z_0), we may take $\mathbf{i}(x',y',z',t) = e\, \delta(\mathbf{r}' - \mathbf{r}_0)\mathbf{v}(t)$, where $\delta(\mathbf{r})$ denotes the product $\delta(x)\, \delta(y)\, \delta(z)$. Substituting this expression in equation (35), we obtain the solution

$$\mathbf{A}(\mathbf{r},t) = \frac{e}{c}\int_{-\infty}^{\infty}\int_{-\infty}^{\infty}\int_{-\infty}^{\infty} \frac{\delta(\mathbf{r}' - \mathbf{r}_0)\mathbf{v}\left(t-\dfrac{|\mathbf{r}-\mathbf{r}'|}{c}\right)}{|\mathbf{r}-\mathbf{r}'|}\, dx'\, dy'\, dz' \quad (37)$$

with $\mathbf{v} = d\mathbf{r}_0/dt'$, where $t' = t - |\mathbf{r} - \mathbf{r}'|/c$. Thus

$$\frac{\partial x_0}{\partial x'} = \frac{\partial x_0}{\partial t'}\frac{\partial t'}{\partial x'} = -\frac{(x'-x)v_x}{c|\mathbf{r}-\mathbf{r}'|}, \qquad \frac{\partial y_0}{\partial x'} = \frac{\partial y_0}{\partial t'}\frac{\partial t'}{\partial x'} = -\frac{(x'-x)v_y}{c|\mathbf{r}-\mathbf{r}'|}$$

so that if we change the variables of integration from (x',y',z') to (λ,μ,ν), where

$$\boldsymbol{\lambda} = \mathbf{r}' - \mathbf{r}_0 \quad (38)$$

we have

$$\frac{\partial\lambda}{\partial x'} = 1 + \frac{(x'-x)v_x(t')}{c|\mathbf{r}-\mathbf{r}'|}, \qquad \frac{\partial\lambda}{\partial y'} = \frac{(y'-y)v_x(t')}{c|\mathbf{r}-\mathbf{r}'|}, \text{ etc.}$$

so that

$$\frac{\partial(\lambda,\mu,\nu)}{\partial(x',y',z')} = 1 + \frac{(\mathbf{r}'-\mathbf{r})\cdot\mathbf{v}(t')}{c|\mathbf{r}-\mathbf{r}'|}$$

from which it follows that

$$\frac{dx'\,dy'\,dz'}{|\mathbf{r} - \mathbf{r}'|} = \frac{d\lambda\,d\mu\,d\nu}{|\mathbf{r} - \mathbf{r}'| + (1/c)(\mathbf{r}' - \mathbf{r})\cdot\mathbf{v}} \tag{39}$$

Substituting from equations (38) and (39) into equation (37) and performing the integrations which are immediate, because of the result (76), Chap. 1, we find that

$$\mathbf{A}(\mathbf{r},t) = \frac{e\mathbf{v}\left(t - \dfrac{|\mathbf{r} - \mathbf{r}_0|}{c}\right)}{c|\mathbf{r} - \mathbf{r}_0| + (\mathbf{r}_0 - \mathbf{r})\cdot\mathbf{v}\left(t - \dfrac{|\mathbf{r} - \mathbf{r}_0|}{c}\right)}$$

which, by the substitutions $\mathbf{R} = \mathbf{r}_0 - \mathbf{r}$, $t' = t - R/c$, may be put in the neater form

$$\mathbf{A}(\mathbf{r},t) = \frac{e\mathbf{v}(t')}{cR + \mathbf{R}\cdot\mathbf{v}(t')} \tag{40}$$

The scalar potential ϕ may be obtained similarly from equation (30) by the substitution $\rho(\mathbf{r},t) = e\,\delta(\mathbf{r} - \mathbf{r}_0)$. We find

$$\phi(\mathbf{r},t) = \frac{ec}{cR + \mathbf{R}\cdot\mathbf{v}(t')} \tag{41}$$

These expressions for the vector and scalar potentials of a moving charge were first obtained by Lienard and Wiechert.[1] The method of proof given here is due to D. L. Pursey.

In the nonrelativistic range of velocities ($v \ll c$) we may write equation (40) in the form

$$\mathbf{A}(\mathbf{r},t) = \frac{e}{cR}\,\mathbf{v}(t')$$

so that it follows from equation (31) that for large values of R we may write

$$\mathbf{H} = -\frac{e}{c^2 R^2}\,(\mathbf{R} \times \dot{\mathbf{v}}) \tag{42}$$

Similarly it can be shown that

$$\mathbf{E} = \frac{1}{R}\,(\mathbf{R} \times \mathbf{H}) \tag{43}$$

Forming the expression for the Poynting vector $c(\mathbf{E} \times \mathbf{H})/4\pi$ and integrating over a sphere of large radius R, we find that the energy radiated per unit time by an accelerated particle moving with small velocity $\mathbf{v}$ is

[1] W. Heitler, "The Quantum Theory of Radiation," 2d ed. (Oxford, New York, 1944), p. 20.

$2e^2\dot{\mathbf{v}}^2/3c^3$. To take account of this energy loss, we have to introduce a self-force $\mathbf{F}_s$, which is such that the work performed by it in a given time interval $t_1 < t < t_2$, in which the state of motion at t_2 is the same as it was at t_1, is equal to the energy loss. That is, we have

$$\int_{t_1}^{t_2} (\mathbf{F}_s \cdot \mathbf{v})dt = -\frac{2e^2}{3c^3} \int_{t_1}^{t_2} \dot{\mathbf{v}}^2 \, dt$$

Integration by parts on the right of this equation leads to the expression

$$\mathbf{F}_s = \frac{2e^2}{3c^3} \ddot{\mathbf{v}} \tag{44}$$

If $\mathbf{F}$ is the external force acting on a particle, the equation of the nonrelativistic motion of the particle then becomes

$$m\dot{\mathbf{v}} = \mathbf{F} + \frac{2e^2}{3c^3} \ddot{\mathbf{v}} \tag{45}$$

39.3 Scattering of inhomogeneous light by bound electrons. By means of the theory developed above we may give an account of the motion which an external electromagnetic field, say a light wave, imposes on a particle such as an electron. In this section we shall consider the scattering of inhomogeneous light with field strength $E(t)$ by a bound electron. As a model of the bound electron we consider an oscillator such that if the electron performs only the free vibration, but no forced vibration due to the light wave, its motion will be periodic with frequency ω_0. Under these circumstances the force $\mathbf{F}$ of equation (45) may be taken to be

$$\mathbf{F} = -m\omega_0^2\mathbf{x} + e\mathbf{E}(t) + \frac{e}{c} (\mathbf{v} \times \mathbf{H}) \tag{46}$$

where $\dot{\mathbf{x}} = \mathbf{v}$. By making use of the equation of motion (45) we are committed to the consideration of nonrelativistic motions only. Since, then, $v \ll c$, we may neglect the magnetic force $e(\mathbf{v} \times \mathbf{H})/c$ in comparison with the electric force $e\mathbf{E}$. With this approximation, we find, on inserting for $\mathbf{F}$ from equation (46), that (45) yields the equation of motion

$$\ddot{\mathbf{x}} - \frac{2e^2}{3mc^3} \dddot{\mathbf{x}} + \omega_0^2\mathbf{x} = \frac{e}{m} \mathbf{E}(t) \tag{47}$$

To solve this equation, we write

$$\xi(\omega) = \frac{1}{\sqrt{2\pi}} \int_{-\infty}^{\infty} x(t)e^{i\omega t} \, dt, \qquad \epsilon(\omega) = \frac{1}{\sqrt{2\pi}} \int_{-\infty}^{\infty} E(t)e^{i\omega t} \, dt$$

and multiply both sides of equation (47) by $e^{i\omega t}$ to obtain, on integrating with respect to t over all times,

$$\left[(\omega_0^2 - \omega^2) + \frac{2e^2}{3mc^3} i\omega^3 \right] \xi(\omega) = \frac{e}{m} \varepsilon(\omega)$$

Writing $\gamma = 2e^2\omega_0/3mc^3$ and solving this equation for $\xi(\omega)$, we find

$$\xi(\omega) = \frac{e}{m} \frac{\epsilon(\omega)}{(\omega_0^2 - \omega^2) + i\gamma\omega^3/\omega_0} \tag{48}$$

and consequently that

$$|\xi(\omega)|^2 = \frac{e^2}{m^2} \frac{|\epsilon(\omega)|^2}{(\omega_0^2 - \omega^2)^2 + \gamma^2\omega^6/\omega_0^2} \tag{49}$$

Since the energy radiated per unit time by an accelerated particle moving with velocity $\mathbf{v}$ is $2e^2\dot{\mathbf{v}}^2/3c^3$, the total energy radiated by the electron is

$$R = \frac{2e^2}{3c^3} \int_{-\infty}^{\infty} \dot{\mathbf{v}}^2 \, dt \tag{50}$$

Now $\dot{\mathbf{v}} = \partial^2\mathbf{x}/\partial t^2$ so that $-\omega^2\xi(\omega)$ is the Fourier transform of $\dot{\mathbf{v}}$. Making use of this result and the theorem (50), Chap. 1, in the form

$$\int_{-\infty}^{\infty} f^2(t)dt = \int_{-\infty}^{\infty} |F(\omega)|^2 \, d\omega \tag{51}$$

where $F(\omega)$ is the Fourier transform of $f(t)$, we find that

$$R = \frac{2e^2}{3c^3} \int_{-\infty}^{\infty} \omega^4 |\xi(\omega)|^2 \, d\omega$$

Substituting for $|\xi(\omega)|^2$ from equation (49) we find, for the total energy radiated by the electron, the expression

$$R = \frac{2e^4}{3m^2c^3} \int_{-\infty}^{\infty} \frac{\omega^4 |\varepsilon(\omega)|^2}{(\omega_0^2 - \omega^2)^2 + \gamma^2\omega^6/\omega_0^2} \, d\omega \tag{52}$$

or, in terms of the classical electronic radius $r_0 = e^2/mc^2$,

$$R = \frac{4}{3} r_0^2 c \int_0^{\infty} \frac{\omega^4 |\varepsilon(\omega)|^2}{(\omega_0^2 - \omega^2)^2 + \gamma^2\omega^6/\omega_0^2} \, d\omega \tag{53}$$

If we introduce a spectral distribution function $R(\omega)$ defined by the relation

$$R = \int_0^{\infty} R(\omega)d\omega$$

we find that

$$R = \frac{4}{3} r_0^2 c \omega^4 \frac{|\boldsymbol{\varepsilon}(\omega)|^2}{(\omega_0^2 - \omega^2)^2 + \gamma^2 \omega^6 / \omega_0^2} \tag{54}$$

so that the spectral function of the emitted radiation is determined readily in terms of the square of the modulus of the Fourier transform of the electric field strength $E(t)$.

On the other hand, the total work done by the light wave is

$$W = \int_{-\infty}^{\infty} e\dot{\mathbf{x}} \cdot \mathbf{E}\, dt$$

Using equation (50), Chap. 1, in the form

$$\int_{-\infty}^{\infty} F(t)G(t)dt = \int_{-\infty}^{\infty} f(\omega)g^*(\omega)d\omega$$

and the fact that the Fourier transform of x is $-i\omega\boldsymbol{\xi}(\omega)$, we have

$$W = \frac{e^2}{m} \int_{-\infty}^{\infty} \frac{-i\omega|\boldsymbol{\varepsilon}(\omega)|^2\, d\omega}{(\omega_0^2 - \omega^2) - i\gamma\omega^3/\omega_0} = \frac{2\gamma e^2}{m\omega_0} \int_{0}^{\infty} \frac{\omega^4|\boldsymbol{\varepsilon}(\omega)|^2\, d\omega}{(\omega_0^2 - \omega^2)^2 + \gamma^2\omega^6/\omega_0^2}$$

Substituting the value of γ, we see that $R = W$.

In the case of monochromatic radiation we may take $E = E_0 e^{i\nu t}$ so that, by equation (86), Chap. 1, $\boldsymbol{\varepsilon}(\omega) = \mathbf{E}_0(2\pi)^{\frac{1}{2}}\delta(\nu + \omega)$, and it follows from equation (48) that

$$\boldsymbol{\xi}(\omega) = \frac{(2\pi)^{\frac{1}{2}}e\mathbf{E}_0\,\delta(\nu + \omega)}{m[(\omega^2 - \omega_0^2) + i\gamma\omega^3/\omega_0]}$$

From the inversion theorem 10 and the result (77), Chap. 1, we then have

$$\mathbf{x}(t) = \frac{e\mathbf{E}_0 e^{i\nu t}}{m[(\nu^2 - \omega_0^2) + i\gamma\nu^3/\omega_0]}$$

for which

$$|\dot{\mathbf{v}}(t)|^2 = \frac{e^2\mathbf{E}_0^2\nu^4}{m^2[(\nu^2 - \omega_0^2)^2 + \gamma^2\nu^6/\omega_0^2]}$$

It follows that the energy radiated per unit time by the electron $(2e^2\dot{\mathbf{v}}^2/3c^3)$ is

$$R = \frac{2}{3} r_0^2 c E_0^2 \frac{\nu^4}{(\nu^2 - \omega_0^2)^2 + \gamma^2\nu^6/\omega_0^2}$$

But the energy crossing unit area per unit time in the incident beam is $S = cE_0^2/4\pi$ so that the area σ which takes enough energy at this rate S to supply energy R in the form of radiation is the *cross section*

$$\sigma = \frac{R}{S} = \frac{8\pi}{3} r_0^2 f(\nu)$$

where $f(\nu)$ denotes the function

$$f(\nu) = \frac{\nu^4}{(\nu^2 - \omega_0^2)^2 + \gamma^2 \nu^6 / \omega_0^2}$$

39.4 Breadth of spectral lines. As in the last section we take a linear harmonic oscillator as a simple model for a source of light whose frequency is ω_0. The reaction force (44) has the effect of damping the amplitude of such an oscillator. The equation of motion is simply

$$\ddot{x} - \frac{\gamma}{\omega_0} \dddot{x} + \omega_0^2 x = 0$$

Since the reaction force is small, we may write in first approximation $\ddot{x} = -\omega_0^2 x$. Differentiating both sides of this equation with respect to

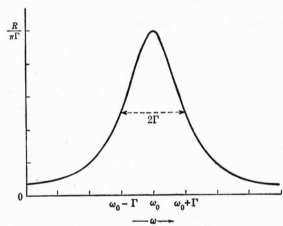

FIG. 62   The shape of a spectral line.

t, we have approximately $\dddot{x} = -\omega_0^2 \dot{x}$, which gives for the equation of motion

$$\ddot{x} + 2\Gamma\dot{x} + \omega_0^2 x = 0$$

where we have written $\Gamma = \frac{1}{2}\gamma\omega_0$. If $x = 0$ when $t < 0$ and $x = x_0$ at $t = 0$, we have approximately (since $\Gamma^2 \ll \omega_0^2$),

$$x = x_0 e^{-\Gamma t - i\omega_0 t} \qquad t > 0$$

from which it follows that

$$\dot{v} = \begin{cases} 0 & t < 0 \\ \dot{v}_0 e^{-\Gamma t - i\omega_0 t} & t \geq 0 \end{cases}$$

where $\dot{v}_0$ is a constant. Now the Fourier transform of $\dot{v}$ is

$$V(\omega) = \frac{\dot{v}_0}{\sqrt{2\pi}} \int_0^\infty e^{-\Gamma t + i(\omega - \omega_0)t} \, dt = \frac{\dot{v}_0}{\sqrt{2\pi}\, [\Gamma + i(\omega_0 - \omega)]}$$

so that the total energy radiated by the electron is

$$R = \frac{2e^2}{3c^3} \int_{-\infty}^{\infty} \dot{\mathbf{v}}^2 \, dt = \frac{2e^2}{3c^3} \int_{-\infty}^{\infty} |V(\omega)|^2 \, d\omega = \frac{e^2 \dot{\mathbf{v}}_0^2}{3\Gamma c^3}$$

Introducing the spectral distribution function $R(\omega)$ defined by

$$R = \int_{-\infty}^{\infty} R(\omega) d\omega$$

we find that

$$R(\omega) = \frac{R\Gamma/\pi}{(\omega_0^2 - \omega^2)^2 + \Gamma^2}$$

Since $R(\omega_0 \pm \Gamma) = \frac{1}{2}R(\omega_0)$, the quantity 2Γ is called the *breadth at half maximum* (cf. Fig. 62).

39.5 D functions of quantum electrodynamics. We shall not attempt to outline here the quantum theory of the interaction of an electron with a radiation field. There are, however, two results of a purely mathematical nature which are of importance in this theory and which we shall derive here. In the theory of quantum electrodynamics[1] a function $D_0(x,y,z,t)$ is introduced in the discussion of the circumstances in which measurements of the electromagnetic field strengths at different points in space-time influence each other. We shall now determine this function, taking it to be that solution of the wave equation

$$\nabla^2 D_0 = \frac{1}{c^2} \frac{\partial^2 D_0}{\partial t^2} \tag{55}$$

which satisfies the initial conditions

$$D_0(x,y,z,0) = 0, \qquad \frac{\partial D_0(x,y,z,0)}{\partial t} = \delta(x)\, \delta(y)\, \delta(z) \tag{56}$$

If we define by the equation

$$\bar{D}_0(\xi,\eta,\zeta,t) = \left(\frac{1}{2\pi}\right)^{\frac{3}{2}} \int_{-\infty}^{\infty} \int_{-\infty}^{\infty} \int_{-\infty}^{\infty} D_0(x,y,z,t) e^{i(\xi x + \eta y + \zeta z)} \, dx \, dy \, dz \tag{57}$$

the three-dimensional Fourier transform $\bar{D}_0(\xi,\eta,\zeta,t)$ of the function $D_0(x,y,z,t)$, it follows from these equations that $\bar{D}_0$ satisfies the differential equation

$$\frac{d_0^2 \bar{D}}{dt^2} + c^2(\xi^2 + \eta^2 + \zeta^2)\bar{D}_0 = 0$$

[1] P. Jordan and W. Pauli, Z. Physik, **47**, 151 (1928); L. I. Schiff, "Quantum Mechanics" (McGraw-Hill, New York, 1949), p. 371; G. Wentzel, "Quantum Theory of Fields" (Interscience Publishers, New York, 1949), p. 115.

and the initial conditions

$$\bar{D}_0(\xi,\eta,\zeta,0) = 0, \qquad \frac{d}{dt}\,\bar{D}_0(\xi,\eta,\zeta,0) = (2\pi)^{-\frac{3}{2}} \tag{58}$$

If we write $\rho^2 = \xi^2 + \eta^2 + \zeta^2$, it follows that

$$\bar{D}_0 = \left(\frac{1}{2\pi}\right)^{\frac{3}{2}} \frac{\sin(c\rho t)}{c\rho}$$

and hence, by theorem (111), Chap. 1, that

$$D_0 = \left(\frac{1}{2\pi}\right)^3 \int_{-\infty}^{\infty} \int_{-\infty}^{\infty} \int_{-\infty}^{\infty} \frac{\sin(c\rho t)}{c\rho}\, e^{-i(\xi x + \eta y + \zeta z)}\, d\xi\, d\eta\, d\zeta$$

Writing $\xi x + \eta y + \zeta z = \rho r \cos(\theta)$, $d\xi\, d\eta\, d\zeta = 2\pi\rho^2 \sin(\theta)d\rho\, d\theta$, we see that

$$D_0 = \frac{1}{2\pi^2 c} \int_0^{\infty} \rho \sin(c\rho t)d\rho \int_0^{\pi} e^{-i\rho r \cos\theta} \sin\theta\, d\theta$$

Now the θ integration is elementary and gives

$$D_0 = \frac{1}{8\pi^2 cr} \int_{-\infty}^{\infty} [e^{-i\rho(r-ct)} - e^{-i\rho(r+ct)}]d\rho$$

Using equation (86), Chap. 1, we have finally

$$D_0(\mathbf{r},t) = \frac{1}{4\pi cr} [\delta(r - ct) - \delta(r + ct)]$$

A similar function $D(\mathbf{r},t)$ arises in the quantized field theory representing the motion of a number of noninteracting free electrons in the Dirac theory.[1] This function satisfies exactly the same initial conditions as the function $D_0(\mathbf{r},t)$—equations (56)—but instead of (55) it satisfies the Klein-Gordon equation

$$(\nabla^2 - \kappa^2)D = \frac{1}{c^2} \frac{\partial^2 D}{\partial t^2} \tag{59}$$

It follows at once that the three-dimensional Fourier transform $\bar{D}(\xi,t)$, defined by an equation similar to (57), satisfies the initial conditions (58) and the ordinary differential equation

$$\frac{d^2 D}{dt^2} + c^2(\rho^2 + \kappa^2)\bar{D} = 0 \tag{60}$$

[1] P. A. M. Dirac, *Proc. Cambridge Phil. Soc.*, **30**, 150 (1934); W. Pauli, *Rev. Mod. Phys.*, **13**, 203 (1941); Schiff, *op. cit.*, Sec. 47, p. 348.

so that it is of the form

$$\bar{D} = \left(\frac{1}{2\pi}\right)^{\frac{3}{2}} \frac{\sin\left[c(\rho^2 + \kappa^2)^{\frac{1}{2}}t\right]}{c(\rho^2 + \kappa^2)^{\frac{1}{2}}}$$

Inverting this equation by means of theorem (111), Chap. 1, we have

$$D(\mathbf{r},t) = \left(\frac{1}{2\pi}\right)^3 \int_{-\infty}^{\infty} \int_{-\infty}^{\infty} \int_{-\infty}^{\infty} \frac{\sin\left[c(\rho^2 + \kappa^2)^{\frac{1}{2}}t\right]}{c(\rho^2 + \kappa^2)^{\frac{1}{2}}} e^{-i(\xi x + \eta y + \zeta z)} \, d\xi \, d\eta \, d\zeta$$

Proceeding as in the evaluation of the integral expression for D_0, we find that

$$D(\mathbf{r},t) = -\frac{1}{4\pi^2 cr} \frac{\partial}{\partial r} \int_{-\infty}^{\infty} \frac{\sin\left[c(\rho^2 + \kappa^2)^{\frac{1}{2}}t\right] \cos\left(\rho r\right)}{(\rho^2 + \kappa^2)^{\frac{1}{2}}} \, d\rho$$

To evaluate the integral

$$I = 2 \int_{-\infty}^{\infty} \frac{\sin\left[c(\rho^2 + \kappa^2)^{\frac{1}{2}}t\right] \cos\left(\rho r\right)}{(\rho^2 + \kappa^2)^{\frac{1}{2}}} \, d\rho$$

we make the substitutions $\rho = \kappa \sinh(\chi)$ to obtain the expression

$$I = \int_{-\infty}^{\infty} \{\sin\left[\kappa(ct \cosh \chi + r \sinh \chi)\right] + \sin\left[\kappa(ct \cosh \chi - r \sinh \chi)\right]\} d\chi$$

If $ct > r > 0$, we may write

$$ct \cosh(\chi) \pm r \sinh(\chi) = (c^2 t^2 - r^2)^{\frac{1}{2}} \cosh(\chi \pm \alpha)$$

with $\tanh \alpha = r/ct$, while if $r > ct > -r$, we have

$$ct \cosh(\chi) \pm r \sinh(\chi) = \pm (r^2 - c^2 t^2)^{\frac{1}{2}} \cosh(\chi \pm \beta)$$

with $\tanh \beta = ct/r$, so that, using the result[1]

$$\pi J_0(\zeta) = \int_{-\infty}^{\infty} \sin\left[\zeta \cosh(\chi + \alpha)\right] d\chi$$

we find that

$$D(\mathbf{r},t) = -\frac{1}{4\pi cr} \frac{\partial}{\partial r} F(r,t) \tag{60a}$$

where the function $F(r,t)$ is defined by the equations

$$F(r,t) = \begin{cases} J_0[\kappa(c^2 t^2 - r^2)^{\frac{1}{2}}] & ct > r \\ 0 & -r < ct < r \\ -J_0[\kappa(c^2 t^2 - r^2)^{\frac{1}{2}}] & ct < -r \end{cases}$$

With the usual convention, r is always regarded as being positive so that we may represent the variation of $F(r,t)$ with r and t by a diagram of the type of Fig. 63.

[1] E. T. Whittaker and G. N. Watson, "A Course of Modern Analysis," 4th ed., (Cambridge, London, 1935), p. 382.

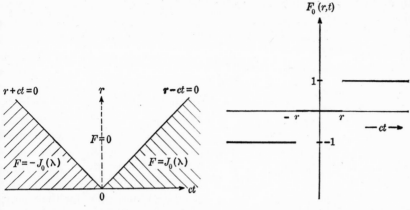

FIG. 63. The variation of $F(r,t)$ over the half plane $r > 0$, $-\infty < ct < \infty$. λ denotes the quantity $\kappa(c^2t^2 - r^2)^{\frac{1}{2}}$.

FIG. 64. The variation with ct of the function $F_0(r,t)$.

We should naturally expect that as κ tends to zero the function $D(\mathbf{r},t)$ tends in form to the function $D_0(\mathbf{r},t)$. To determine the value of $D(\mathbf{r},t)$ when $\kappa = 0$, we first note that equation (60a) may be written in the form

$$D(\mathbf{r},t) = \frac{1}{4\pi c(ct)} \frac{\partial}{\partial(ct)} [F(r,t)]$$

Now, in the case $\kappa = 0$, we have

$$F_0(r,t) = \begin{cases} 1 & ct > r \\ 0 & -r < ct < r \\ -1 & ct < -r \end{cases}$$

(cf. Fig. 64), so that, making use of the fact that the derivative of an increasing step function is a positive delta function—equation (84), Chap. 1—we find that

$$\lim_{\kappa \to 0} D(\mathbf{r},t) = \frac{1}{4\pi c(ct)} [\delta(r - ct) + \delta(r + ct)] \equiv \frac{1}{4\pi cr} [\delta(r - ct) - \delta(r + ct)]$$

showing that as κ tends to zero $D(\mathbf{r},t)$ tends to $D_0(\mathbf{r},t)$.

40. Cascade Theory of Cosmic Ray Showers

40.1 Introduction. It is well known that charged particles, in their passage through matter, lose energy by collisions and by radiation.[1] The energy lost in a collision is transferred from the charged particle to

---

[1] Cf. B. Rossi and K. Greisen, *Rev. Mod. Phys.*, **13**, 240 (1941), and L. Janossy, "Cosmic Rays" (Oxford, New York, 1948), Chap. III.

an atom of the medium through which it is passing and results in the ejection from the atom of a low-energy electron or in raising it to an excited level.   In both cases the energy of the liberated electron or photon is so small that the particles can no longer be thought of as still belonging to the cosmic radiation.   On the other hand, the energy lost by radiation is spent in the production of photons of high energy.   These high-energy quanta will, in turn, produce high-energy electrons by Compton collisions or will lead to the creation of pairs of positive and negative electrons.   As a result of both these processes high-energy electrons are produced, and they, for their part, will radiate more photons of an energy sufficiently high to create positron-electron pairs or to eject high-energy Compton electrons. In this way is created a cascade shower at every new step of which the number of particles increases. Figure 65 is a schematic representation of such a shower; it is assumed in this diagram that the shower is initiated by an electron, but it could equally well have been initiated by a high-energy quantum. Showers of this type form the principal part (the soft component) of the cosmic radiation from a height of about 7 km upward.

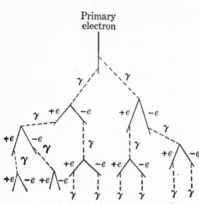

Fig. 65.   Schematic representation of the creation of a cascade shower in matter by a high-energy electron.

The theory of cosmic ray showers of this kind was instituted independently by Carlson and Oppenheimer[1] and by Bhabha and Heitler[2] and developed by various authors.[3]   In the subsequent sections we shall outline the theory in the form established by Landau and Rümer and by Rossi and Greisen.

[1] J. F. Carlson and J. R. Oppenheimer, *Phys. Rev.*, **51**, 220 (1937).

[2] H. J. Bhabha and W. Heitler, *Proc. Roy. Soc. (London)*, **A159**, 432 (1937).

[3] W. H. Furry, *Phys. Rev.*, **52**, 569 (1937); L. Landau and G. Rümer, *Proc. Roy. Soc. (London)*, **A166**, 213 (1938); H. Snyder, *Phys. Rev.*, **53**, 960 (1938); R. Serber, *Phys. Rev.*, **54**, 317 (1938); D. Iwaneko and A. Sokolow, *Phys. Rev.*, **53**, 910 (1938); H. Euler, *Z. Physik.*, **110**, 450 (1938); W. Heisenberg and H. Euler, Ergeb. exakt. Naturw., **17**, 1 (1938); N. Arley, *Proc. Roy. Soc. (London)*, **A168**, 519 (1938); I. Tamm and S. Belenky, *Jour. Phys. U.S.S.R.*, **1**, 177 (1939); L. W. Nordheim and M. H. Hebb, *Phys. Rev.*, **56**, 494 (1939); A. Nordsieck, W. E. Lamb, and G. E. Uhlenbeck, *Physica*, **7**, 344 (1940); Rossi and Greisen, *loc. cit.*; H. J. Bhabha and K. Chakrabarty, *Proc. Roy. Soc. (London)*, **A181**, 267 (1943); L. Janossy, *Comm. Dublin Inst. Adv. Studies*, **A**, No. 4 (1947); I. Tamm and S. Belenky, *Phys. Rev.*, **70**, 660 (1946).

40.2 Fundamental equations. In the first instance the calculations are simplified by the assumption that all the particles and photons in the shower are emitted in the forward direction, *i.e.*, in the direction of the primary particle. Since the change in path length due to scattering is generally negligible, it is usual to treat the lateral spread of showers as a second-order process.[1] If the primary particle of the shower is an electron of energy E_0, we denote by $\pi(E_0,E,x)dE$ the average number of electrons (of either charge) at a distance x from the boundary of the layer at which the primary electron is incident, and with energy between E and $E + dE$. Similarly $\gamma(E_0,W,x)dW$ is the number of photons with energy between W and $W + dW$ at the distance x. On the other hand, when the primary particle is a photon of energy W_0, these quantities will be denoted by $\pi(W_0,E,x)dE$ and $\gamma(W_0,W,x)dW$, respectively.

In the energy range in which we are interested the energy losses due to the Compton effect and to collisions is small in comparison with those due to radiation and the creation of pairs. If we neglect losses due to collisions and the Compton process, then in a given thickness dx the number of electrons with energy between E and $E + dE$ is changed as a result of the following effects:

1. A number π_1 is produced as a result of pair creation by photons.

2. A number π_2 of electrons whose energy was originally greater than $E + dE$ lose energy by radiation and now enter the energy interval $(E,E + dE)$.

3. A number π_3 of electrons originally in the range $(E,E + dE)$ lose sufficient energy, as a result of radiation, to leave the interval.

In a like manner, in the thickness dx the number of photons with energy between W and $W + dW$ changes because:

4. A number γ_1 is produced by the radiation of photons by electrons whose energy E is greater than W.

5. A number γ_2 is absorbed in the process of pair production. We then have the fundamental equations

$$\frac{\partial \pi(E,x)}{\partial x} dx\, dE = \pi_1 + \pi_2 - \pi_3 \tag{61}$$

$$\frac{\partial \gamma(W,x)}{\partial x} dx\, dW = \gamma_1 - \gamma_2 \tag{62}$$

If we denote by $\Psi_0(W,E)dE$ the probability per unit length of path of the production of an electron with energy between E and $E + dE$ by a photon of energy W, it follows that

$$\pi_1 = 2\, dE\, dx \int_E^\infty \gamma(W,x)\Psi_0(W,E)dW$$

[1] See, for example, H. A. Bethe, *Phys. Rev.*, **59**, 684 (1941).

the factor 2 arising from the fact that there are always two particles created. In a similar way we see that

$$\pi_3 = dE \, dx \int_0^E \Phi_0(E,W) \pi(E,x) dW$$

where $\Phi_0(E,W)dW$ is the probability of the radiation of a photon with energy in the range $(W, W + dW)$ by an electron of energy E. Furthermore

$$\pi_2 = dE \, dx \int_E^\infty \Phi_0(E',E' - E) \pi(E',x) dE'$$

In a precisely similar fashion it can be shown that

$$\gamma_1 = dW \, dx \int_E^\infty \pi(E,x) \Phi_0(E,W) dE$$

and that

$$\gamma_2 = dW \, dx \, \sigma_0 \gamma(W,x)$$

where σ_0 is the total probability per unit length for pair production. It is found that for sufficiently high energies we may write

$$\Psi_0(W,E) = \frac{1}{W} \psi_0\left(\frac{E}{W}\right), \qquad \Phi_0(E,W) = \frac{1}{E} \phi_0\left(\frac{W}{E}\right) \tag{63}$$

—equations which are valid when the screening of the atomic electrons is complete for the collision process. Substituting from equations (63) into the expressions for π_1, π_2, π_3, γ_1, and γ_2, we obtain from equations (61) and (62) the diffusion equations

$$\frac{\partial \pi(E,x)}{\partial x} = 2 \int_E^\infty \gamma(W,x) \psi_0\left(\frac{E}{W}\right) \frac{dW}{W} + \int_E^\infty \pi(E',x) \phi_0\left(\frac{E' - E}{E'}\right) \frac{dE'}{E'}$$
$$- \pi(E,x) \int_0^E \phi_0\left(\frac{W}{E}\right) \frac{dW}{E}$$

$$\frac{\partial \gamma(W,x)}{\partial x} = \int_W^\infty \pi(E,x) \phi_0\left(\frac{W}{E}\right) \frac{dE}{E} - \sigma_0 \gamma(W,x)$$

which may readily be transformed to

$$\frac{\partial \pi(E,x)}{\partial x} = 2 \int_0^1 \gamma\left(\frac{E}{u}, x\right) \psi_0(u) \frac{du}{u}$$
$$- \int_0^1 \left[\pi(E,x) - \frac{1}{1 - v} \pi\left(\frac{E}{1 - v}, x\right)\right] \phi_0(v) dv \tag{64}$$

and

$$\frac{\partial \gamma(W,x)}{\partial x} = \int_0^1 \pi\left(\frac{W}{v}, x\right) \phi_0(v) \frac{dv}{v} - \sigma_0 \gamma(W,x) \tag{65}$$

40.3 Landau-Rümer solution.[1] To solve the shower equations, we introduce the Mellin transforms

$$\bar{\pi}(s,x) = \int_0^\infty \pi(E,x)E^s\,dE, \qquad \bar{\gamma}(s,x) = \int_0^\infty \gamma(W,x)W^s\,dW \quad (66)$$

Multiplying both sides of equation (64) by E^s and integrating with respect to E from 0 to ∞, we obtain the relation

$$\frac{d\bar{\pi}(s,x)}{dx} = 2\int_0^\infty E^s\,dE \int_0^1 \gamma\left(\frac{E}{u},x\right)\psi_0(u)\frac{du}{u}$$

$$- \int_0^\infty E^s\,dE \int_0^1 \left[\pi(E,x) - \frac{1}{1-v}\pi\left(\frac{E}{1-v},x\right)\right]\phi_0(v)dv$$

Now

$$2\int_0^\infty E^s\,dE \int_0^1 \gamma\left(\frac{E}{u},x\right)\psi_0(u)\frac{du}{u} = 2\int_0^1 \psi_0(u)\frac{du}{u}\int_0^\infty E^s\gamma\left(\frac{E}{u},x\right)dE$$

$$= \bar{\gamma}(s,x)B(s)$$

where

$$B(s) = 2\int_0^1 u^s\psi_0(u)du \qquad (67)$$

The second double integral may be written in the form

$$-\int_0^\infty E^s\,dE\,\pi(E,x)\int_0^1 \phi_0(v)dv + \int_0^\infty \left(\frac{E}{1-v}\right)^s\pi\left(\frac{E}{1-v},x\right)\frac{dE}{1-v}$$

$$\times \int_0^1 (1-v)^s\phi_0(v)dv = -\bar{\pi}(s,x)A(s)$$

where

$$A(s) = \int_0^1 [1 - (1-v)^s]\phi_0(v)dv \qquad (68)$$

In this way we see that equation (64) is equivalent to

$$\frac{d\bar{\pi}(s,x)}{dx} = -A(s)\bar{\pi}(s,x) + B(s)\bar{\gamma}(s,x) \qquad (69)$$

Similarly, by multiplying both sides of equation (65) by W^s and integrating with respect to W from 0 to ∞, we find equation (65) is equivalent to

$$\frac{d\bar{\gamma}(s,x)}{dx} = C(s)\bar{\pi}(s,x) - \sigma_0\bar{\gamma}(s,x) \qquad (70)$$

the function $C(s)$ being defined by the relation

$$C(s) = \int_0^1 v^s\phi_0(v)dv \qquad (71)$$

[1] Landau and Rümer, *loc. cit.*

The solution of the pair of simultaneous ordinary differential equations (69) and (70) is effected by the introduction of the Laplace transforms

$$\bar{\Pi}(s,p) = \int_0^\infty \bar{\pi}(s,x)e^{-px}\,dx, \qquad \bar{\Gamma}(s,p) = \int_0^\infty \bar{\gamma}(s,x)e^{-px}\,dx \qquad (72)$$

Then if $\bar{\pi}(s,x) = \bar{\pi}_0(s)$, when $x = 0$ we have

$$\int_0^\infty \frac{d\bar{\pi}(s,x)}{dx}\,e^{-px}\,dx = -\bar{\pi}_0(s) + p\bar{\Pi}(s,p)$$

and, similarly,

$$\int_0^\infty \frac{d\bar{\gamma}(s,x)}{dx}\,e^{-px}\,dx = -\bar{\gamma}_0(s) + p\bar{\Gamma}(s,p)$$

so that equations (69) and (70) are equivalent to the pair of simultaneous algebraic equations

$$p\bar{\Pi}(s,p) - \bar{\pi}_0(s) = -A(s)\bar{\Pi}(s,p) + B(s)\bar{\Gamma}(s,p)$$
$$p\bar{\Gamma}(s,p) - \bar{\gamma}_0(s) = C(s)\bar{\Pi}(s,p) - \sigma_0\bar{\Gamma}(s,p)$$

which have the solution

$$\bar{\Pi}(s,p) = \frac{B(s)\bar{\gamma}_0(s) + (p + \sigma_0)\bar{\pi}_0(s)}{[p + A(s)](p + \sigma_0) - B(s)C(s)} \qquad (73)$$

$$\bar{\Gamma}(s,p) = \frac{C(s)\bar{\pi}_0(s) + [p + A(s)]\bar{\gamma}_0(s)}{[p + A(s)](p + \sigma_0) - B(s)C(s)} \qquad (74)$$

If we now define two new functions $p_1(s)$ and $p_2(s)$ by the equations

$$p_1(s) = -\tfrac{1}{2}[A(s) + \sigma_0] + \tfrac{1}{2}[(A - \sigma_0)^2 - BC]^{\frac{1}{2}}$$
$$p_2(s) = -\tfrac{1}{2}[A(s) + \sigma_0] - \tfrac{1}{2}[(A - \sigma_0)^2 - BC]^{\frac{1}{2}}$$

we may write these equations in the alternative forms

$$\bar{\Pi}(s,p) = \frac{1}{p_1(s) - p_2(s)}\left\{ \frac{B(s)\bar{\gamma}_0(s) + [\sigma_0 + p_1(s)]\bar{\pi}_0(s)}{p - p_1(s)} \right.$$
$$\left. - \frac{B(s)\bar{\gamma}_0(s) + [\sigma_0 + p_2(s)]\bar{\pi}_0(s)}{p - p_2(s)} \right\} \qquad (75)$$

$$\bar{\Gamma}(s,p) = \frac{1}{p_1(s) - p_2(s)}\left\{ \frac{C(s)\bar{\pi}_0(s) + [A(s) + p_1(s)]\bar{\gamma}_0(s)}{p - p_1(s)} \right.$$
$$\left. - \frac{C(s)\bar{\pi}_0(s) + [A(s) + p_2(s)]\bar{\gamma}_0(s)}{p - p_2(s)} \right\} \qquad (76)$$

Making use of the Laplace inversion theorem 14 and the elementary result

$$e^{bx} = \frac{1}{2\pi i}\int_{c-i\infty}^{c+i\infty} \frac{e^{px}}{p - b}\,dp$$

we find that

$$\bar{\pi}(s,x) = \frac{1}{p_1(s) - p_2(s)} \left(\{B(s)\bar{\gamma}_0(s) + [\sigma_0 + p_1(s)]\bar{\pi}_0(s)\}e^{p_1(s)x} \right.$$
$$\left. - \{\dot{B}(s)\bar{\gamma}_0(s) + [\sigma_0 + p_2(s)]\bar{\pi}_0(s)\}e^{p_2(s)x} \right) \quad (77)$$

from which result we may obtain the expression for $\pi(E,x)$ by means of the Mellin inversion theorem 15, namely,

$$\pi(E,x) = \frac{1}{2\pi i} \int_{c-i\infty}^{c+i\infty} \bar{\pi}(s,x)E^{-s-1}\,ds$$

Likewise we find that

$$\bar{\gamma}(s,x) = \frac{1}{p_1(s) - p_2(s)} \left(\{C(s)\bar{\pi}_0(s) + [A(s) + p_1(s)]\bar{\gamma}_0(s)\}e^{p_1(s)x} \right.$$
$$\left. - \{C(s)\bar{\pi}_0(s) + [A(s) + p_2(s)]\bar{\gamma}_0(s)\}e^{p_2(s)x} \right) \quad (78)$$

from which the expression for the differential photon spectrum may be obtained formally by the use of the Mellin inversion theorem.

40.4 Calculation of the differential spectra. Two cases are of special interest—that in which the shower is initiated by a single primary electron of energy E_0 and that in which it is due to a single primary photon of energy W_0.

Case 1: Shower initiated by a single primary electron. In this case we may write as our boundary conditions

$$\pi(E,0) = \delta(E - E_0), \qquad \gamma(W,0) = 0$$

from which it follows at once that

$$\bar{\pi}_0(s) = E_0^s, \qquad \bar{\gamma}_0(s) = 0 \quad (79)$$

Substituting from equation (79) into equations (73) and (74), we have the expressions

$$\bar{\Pi}(s,p) = \frac{(\sigma_0 + p)E_0^s}{[p - p_1(s)][p - p_2(s)]} \quad (80)$$

$$\bar{\Gamma}(s,p) = \frac{C(s)E_0^s}{[p - p_1(s)][p - p_2(s)]} \quad (81)$$

so that by the Laplace inversion theorem 14 or, what is the same thing, from equations (77) and (78), we find that

$$\bar{\pi}(s,x) = \frac{E_0^s}{p_1(s) - p_2(s)} \{[\sigma_0 + p_1(s)]e^{xp_1(s)} - [\sigma_0 + p_2(s)]e^{xp_2(s)}\}$$

and that

$$\bar{\gamma}(s,x) = \frac{C(s)E_0^s}{p_1(s) - p_2(s)} [e^{xp_1(s)} - e^{xp_2(s)}]$$

Inverting the former of these equations by means of the Mellin inversion theorem 15, we find for the differential electron spectrum

$$\pi(E_0,E,x) = \frac{1}{2\pi i E} \int_{c-i\infty}^{c+i\infty} \left[\frac{\sigma_0 + p_1(s)}{p_1(s) - p_2(s)} e^{xp_1(s)} - \frac{\sigma_0 + p_2(s)}{p_1(s) - p_2(s)} e^{xp_2(s)} \right] \times \left(\frac{E_0}{E} \right)^s ds$$

Writing $y = \log (E_0/E)$, $H_1(s) = [\sigma_0 + p_1(s)]/[p_1(s) - p_2(s)]$, and

$$H_2(s) = [\sigma_0 + p_2(s)]/[p_1(s) - p_2(s)]$$

we see that this last equation may be written in the simplified form

$$\pi(E_0,E,x)dE = -\frac{dy}{2\pi i} \int_{c-i\infty}^{c+i\infty} H_1(s)e^{ys+xp_1} ds - \frac{dy}{2\pi i} \int_{c-i\infty}^{c+i\infty} H_2(s)e^{ys+xp_2} ds \tag{82}$$

Similarly it is readily shown that

$$\gamma(E_0,W,x) = \frac{1}{2\pi i W} \int_{c-i\infty}^{c+i\infty} \frac{C(s)}{p_1(s) - p_2(s)} (e^{xp_1} - e^{xp_2}) \left(\frac{E_0}{W} \right)^s ds$$

which may be put in the form

$$\gamma(E_0,W,x)dW = -\frac{dy}{2\pi i} \int_{c-i\infty}^{c+i\infty} L(s)[e^{ys+xp_1-\frac{1}{2}\log (s)} - e^{ys+xp_2-\frac{1}{2}\log (s)}]ds \tag{83}$$

with $y = \log (E_0/W)$, $L(s) = s^{\frac{1}{2}}C(s)/[p_1(s) - p_2(s)]$.

Case 2: Shower initiated by a single primary photon. Here $\pi(E,0) = 0$, $\gamma(W,0) = \delta(W - W_0)$, so that

$$\bar{\pi}_0(s) = 0, \qquad \bar{\gamma}_0(s) = W_0^s \tag{84}$$

Substituting from equation (84) into equations (73) and (74), we obtain the equations

$$\bar{\Pi}(s,p) = \frac{B(s)W_0^s}{[p - p_1(s)][p - p_2(s)]}$$

$$\bar{\Gamma}(s,p) = \frac{[p + A(s)]W_0^s}{[p - p_1(s)][p - p_2(s)]}$$

which yield the expressions

$$\pi(W_0,E,x) = \frac{1}{2\pi i E} \int_{c-i\infty}^{c+i\infty} \frac{B(s)}{p_1(s) - p_2(s)} [e^{xp_1(s)} - e^{xp_2(s)}] \left(\frac{W_0}{E} \right)^s ds$$

$$\gamma(W_0,W,x)$$
$$= \frac{1}{2\pi i W} \int_{c-i\infty}^{c+i\infty} \left[\frac{A(s) + p_1(s)}{p_1(s) - p_2(s)} e^{xp_1(s)} - \frac{A(s) + p_2(s)}{p_1(s) - p_2(s)} e^{xp_2(s)} \right] \left(\frac{W_0}{W} \right)^s ds$$

These equations are readily seen to be equivalent to the relations

$$\pi(W_0,E,x)dE = \frac{-dy}{2\pi i} \int_{c-i\infty}^{c+i\infty} M(s)[e^{ys+xp_1+\frac{1}{2}\log(s)} - e^{ys+xp_2+\frac{1}{2}\log(s)}]ds \quad (85)$$

with

$$y = \log \frac{W_0}{E}, \qquad M(s) = -\frac{[\sigma_0 + p_1(s)][\sigma_0 + p_2(s)]}{s^{\frac{1}{2}}C(s)[p_1(s) - p_2(s)]}$$

and

$$\gamma(W_0,W,x)dW = \frac{-dy}{2\pi i} \int_{c-i\infty}^{c+i\infty} [H_2(s)e^{ys+xp_1} + H_1(s)e^{ys+xp_2}]ds \quad (86)$$

with $y = \log(W_0/W)$ and $H_1(s)$ and $H_2(s)$ as in equation (82).

To evaluate the integrals involved in these expressions for the differential spectra, we need first to evaluate the functions $A(s)$, $B(s)$, and $C(s)$ on which depend the functions which appear in the integrands. It is known from the quantum theory of radiation that the function $\phi_0(v)$ is given by an expression of the form[1]

$$\phi_0(v) = \frac{1 + (1 - v)^2 - (1 - v)(\frac{2}{3} - 2b)}{v}$$

where $b^{-1} = 18 \log(183Z^{-\frac{1}{3}})$, Z being the charge of the nuclei of the atoms forming the shower-producing medium. The value of b is 0.012 for air and 0.015 for lead, and hence it does not vary appreciably throughout the periodic table. Good agreement with experiment is obtained by taking b to be 0.0135 for *all* elements. It follows at once from equations (68) and (71) that the functions $A(s)$ and $C(s)$ then assume the forms

$$A(s) = 1.36 \frac{d}{ds}[\log(s+1)!] - \frac{1}{(s+1)(s+2)} - 0.0750$$

$$C(s) = \frac{1}{s+2} + \frac{1.36}{s(s+1)}$$

Similarly the function $\psi_0(u)$ is found to have the form

$$\psi_0(u) = u^2 + (1 - u)^2 + (\tfrac{2}{3} - 2b)u(1 - u)$$

so that equation (67) gives

$$B(s) = 2\left[\frac{1}{s+1} - \frac{1.36}{(s+2)(s+3)}\right]$$

and the relation $\sigma_0 = \int_0^1 \psi_0(u)du$ leads to the value $\frac{7}{9} - (b/3)$ for the constant σ_0.

[1] Rossi & Greisen, *op. cit.*, p. 255.

From these expressions we may readily calculate the functions $p_1(s)$ and $p_2(s)$. The variation of these functions and of $p_1'(s)$ and $p_1''(s)$ with positive real values of s is shown in Fig. 66. Once the functions $p_1(s)$ and $p_2(s)$ have been calculated, it is a simple matter to determine the values of the functions $H_1(s)$, $H_2(s)$, $L(s)$, and $M(s)$ occurring in the expressions (82), (83), (85), and (86) for the differential spectra. Figure 67 shows the results of such a calculation for the range of values of s chosen for Fig. 66.

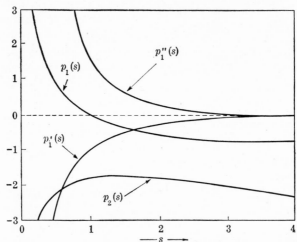

FIG. 66. The variation of $p_1(s)$, $p_1'(s)$, $p_1''(s)$ for positive real values of s.

From an inspection of equations (82), (83), (85), and (86) and the curves of Fig. 67 we see that all the integrals occurring in the expressions for the differential spectra are of the form

$$\frac{1}{2\pi i}\int_{c-i\infty}^{c+i\infty} \chi(s) \exp\left[ys + p(s)x - n \log (s)\right]ds$$

where $\chi(s)$ is a *slowly varying* function of the variable s. An integral of this type can be evaluated by the saddle-point method (cf. Appendix B). The exponential term has a saddle point at the point s_0 for which

$$y + p'(s_0)x - \frac{n}{s_0} = 0$$

and the approximate value of the integral is

$$\frac{1}{(2\pi)^{\frac{1}{2}}} \frac{\chi(s_0)}{[p''(s_0)x + n/s_0^2]^{\frac{1}{2}}} \exp\left[ys_0 + p(s_0)x - n \log (s_0)\right]$$

$$= \frac{1}{\sqrt{2\pi}}\left(\frac{E_0}{E}\right)^{s_0} \frac{\chi(s_0)e^{xp(s_0)}}{s_0^n[xp''(s_0) + n/s_0^2]^{\frac{1}{2}}}$$

Furthermore $p_2 < 0$, and $|p_2| > |p_1|$ so that unless x is very small we may neglect the terms in p_2 in comparison with those in p_1.

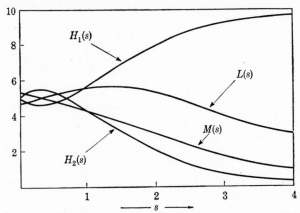

FIG. 67.   The variation of $H_1(s)$, $H_2(s)$, $L(s)$, and $M(s)$ for real values of s.

Hence from equations (82) and (83) we have, on dropping the subscript 0 from s_0, the expressions

$$\pi(E_0,E,x)dE = \frac{H_1(s)e^{xp_1(s)}}{[2\pi x p_1''(s)]^{\frac{1}{2}}}\left(\frac{E_0}{E}\right)^s \frac{dE}{E}, \quad x = -\frac{\log (E_0/E)}{p_1'(s)} \quad (82a)$$

and

$$\gamma(E_0,W,x)dW = \frac{L(s)e^{xp_1(s)}}{[2\pi x s p_1''(s) + \pi/s]^{\frac{1}{2}}}\left(\frac{E_0}{E}\right)^s \frac{dW}{W}$$

$$x = -\frac{\log (E_0/E) - \frac{1}{2}s}{p_1'(s)} \quad (83a)$$

for the differential spectra in the case in which the shower is initiated by a single primary electron of energy E_0.

When the primary particle is a photon of energy W_0, the differential spectra are found to be

$$\left. \begin{aligned} \pi(W_0,E,x)dE &= \frac{s^{\frac{1}{2}}M(s)e^{xp_1(s)}}{[2\pi p_1''(s)x - \pi/s^2]^{\frac{1}{2}}}\left(\frac{W_0}{E}\right)^s \frac{dE}{E} \\ x &= -\frac{1}{p_1'(s)}\left[\log\left(\frac{W_0}{E}\right) + \frac{1}{2}s\right] \end{aligned} \right\} \quad (85a)$$

with

and

$$\left. \begin{aligned} \gamma(W_0,W,x)dW &= \frac{H_2(s)e^{xp_1(s)}}{[2\pi p_1''(s)x]^{\frac{1}{2}}}\left(\frac{W_0}{W}\right)^s \frac{dW}{W} \\ x &= -\frac{\log (W_0/W)}{p_1'(s)} \end{aligned} \right\} \quad (86a)$$

with

It follows from these formulas that the differential spectra may easily be calculated from tables of the functions $p_1(s), p_1'(s), p_1''(s), H_1(s), H_2(s), L(s),$

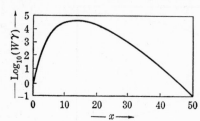

FIG. 68. The differential photon spectrum $\gamma(E_0, W, t)$ for a shower initiated by an electron of energy E_0 for

$$W = 10^{-6} E_0.$$

and $M(S)$ (cf. Figs. 66 and 67). Tables of these functions are given in the paper by Rossi and Greisen cited above. A typical curve calculated in this way is shown in Fig. 68. This curve shows the variation of $\log_{10} [W\gamma(E_0, W, x)]$ with x, calculated from equation (82a), for the case in which $W = E_0 \times 10^{-6}$.

40.5 Calculation of the integral spectra. An important physical quantity is the number of electrons at the thickness x which possess an energy larger than E. It is obvious from the definition of the differential spectrum $\pi(E,x)$ that this integral spectrum is given by the formula

$$\Pi(E,x) = \int_E^\infty \pi(E',x)dE'$$

When it is necessary to indicate the nature of the primary particle of the shower, we write $\Pi(E_0,E,x)$ or $\Pi(W_0,E,x)$, whichever is appropriate. There are similar definitions for the integral photon spectra $\gamma(E_0,W,x)$ and $\gamma(W_0,W,x)$.

We shall illustrate the method of calculating these integral spectra by considering the value of $\Pi(E_0,E,x)$. The calculation of the others proceeds along similar lines and is left to the reader. From equation (82) we find, on making use of the result

$$\int_E^\infty dE' \frac{1}{2\pi i} \int_{c-i\infty}^{c+i\infty} \frac{dy}{dE'} e^{y's} ds = \frac{1}{2\pi i} \int_{c-i\infty}^{c+i\infty} e^{ys - \log(s)} ds$$

that

$$\Pi(E_0,E,x) = \frac{1}{2\pi i} \int_{c-i\infty}^{c+i\infty} [H_1(s)e^{ys+xp_1 - \log(s)} + H_2(s)e^{ys+xp_2 - \log(s)}]ds$$

Evaluating this integral by the saddle-point method, we find that, when $E \ll E_0$,

$$\Pi(E_0,E,x) = \frac{H_1(s)e^{xp_1(s)}}{s[2\pi x p_1''(s) + \pi/s]^{\frac{1}{2}}} \left(\frac{E_0}{E}\right)^s$$

with

$$x = -\frac{1}{p_1'(s)} \left[\log\left(\frac{E_0}{E}\right) - \frac{1}{s}\right]$$

The variation of $\Pi(E_0,E,x)$ with the distance x, for three values of the ratio E/E_0, is shown in Fig. 69.

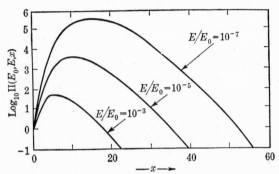

FIG. 69. The average number $\Pi(E_0,E,x)$ of electrons at depth x with energy greater than E produced by a primary electron of energy E_0.

40.6 Average behavior of showers. In the preceding sections we saw that it was necessary to use the saddle-point method to obtain approximate expressions for the contour integrals involved in the expressions for the differential and integral spectra. We shall now show how it is possible, by making use of the theory of Laplace transforms, to derive information about the *average* behavior of showers which is not based on the use of the saddle-point method.

The differential electron track length $z_\pi(E)dE$ is defined to be the total distance traveled by all shower electrons while their energy lies between E and $E + dE$, so that

$$z_\pi(E) = \int_0^\infty \pi(E,x)dx \qquad (87)$$

Similarly the differential photon track length $z_\gamma(W)dW$ is defined by the equation

$$z_\gamma(W) = \int_0^\infty \gamma(W,x)dx \qquad (88)$$

The position $\bar{x}(E)$ of the center of mass of shower electrons of energy E is defined by the relation

$$\bar{x}(E) = \frac{\int_0^\infty x\pi(E,x)dx}{\int_0^\infty \pi(E,x)dx} = \frac{1}{z_\pi(E)} \int_0^\infty x\pi(E,x)dx \qquad (89)$$

and the longitudinal spread $\tau_\pi(E)$ of shower electrons of energy E is given by the equation

$$\tau_\pi^2(E) = \frac{\int_0^\infty [x - \bar{x}_\pi(E)]^2 \pi(E,x)dx}{\int_0^\infty \pi(E,x)dx}$$

$$= \frac{1}{z_\pi(E)} \int_0^\infty x^2 \pi(E,x)dx - \bar{x}_\pi^2(E) \tag{90}$$

Similar expressions give the position $\bar{x}_\gamma(W)$ of the center of mass of photons of energy W and the longitudinal spread $\tau_\gamma(W)$ of such photons.

It follows from these equations that if we introduce the Laplace transform

$$P(E,p) = \int_0^\infty \pi(E,x)e^{-px} dx$$

then

$$z_\pi(E) = P(E,0) \tag{91}$$

$$\bar{x}_\pi(E) = \left(-\frac{1}{P}\frac{\partial P}{\partial p}\right)_{p=0} \tag{92}$$

$$\tau_\pi^2(E) = \left(\frac{1}{P}\frac{\partial^2 P}{\partial p^2}\right)_{p=0} - \bar{x}_\pi^2(E) \tag{93}$$

Similarly we may write

$$z_\gamma(W) = G(W,0) \text{ etc.} \tag{94}$$

where

$$G(W,p) = \int_0^\infty \gamma(W,x)e^{-px} dx \tag{95}$$

is the Laplace transform of the function $\gamma(W,x)$.

From equations (66) and (72) it follows at once from the Mellin inversion theorem 15 that

$$P(E,p) = \frac{1}{2\pi i} \int_{c-i\infty}^{c+i\infty} \bar{\Pi}(s,p)E^{-s-1} ds$$

and

$$G(W,p) = \frac{1}{2\pi i} \int_{c-i\infty}^{c+i\infty} \bar{\Gamma}(s,p)W^{-s-1} ds$$

In particular when the shower is initiated by a single electron of energy E_0 it follows from equation (80) that

$$P(E,p) = \frac{1}{2\pi i E} \int_{c-i\infty}^{c+i\infty} \frac{(\sigma_0 + p)}{[p - p_1(s)][p - p_2(s)]} \left(\frac{E_0}{E}\right)^s ds \tag{96}$$

and

$$G(W,p) = \frac{1}{2\pi i W} \int_{c-i\infty}^{c+i\infty} \frac{C(s)ds}{[p - p_1(s)][p - p_2(s)]} \left(\frac{E_0}{W}\right)^s \tag{97}$$

We shall now consider the case in which $E \ll E_0$. For $p > -\sigma_0$ the pole lying on the real axis and defined by the equation

$$p_1(s) = p \tag{98}$$

is the only pole on the positive half plane of s, but because of the behavior of the logarithmic derivative of the factorial function which enters into the definition of $A(s)$ there is an infinite number of poles in the negative half plane. As $s \rightarrow -\infty$, the integrand tends to zero since $E \ll E_0$ so that, deforming the contour to the left, we may replace the integral by the sum of the residues at all the poles. Each pole contributes a term of order $(E_0/E)^s$ so that if $E \ll E_0$ the dominant term comes from the pole on the positive real axis. Hence we may write for equation (96)

$$P(E,p) = -\frac{1}{E}\left(\frac{E_0}{E}\right)^s \frac{\sigma_0 + p_1(s)}{[p_1(s) - p_2(s)]p_1'(s)} \qquad E \ll E_0 \tag{99}$$

where s is the positive root of equation (98). Likewise

$$G(W,p) = -\frac{1}{W}\left(\frac{E_0}{W}\right)^s \frac{C(s)}{[p_1(s) - p_2(s)]p_1'(s)} \qquad W \ll E_0 \tag{100}$$

Now when p is zero, it follows from Fig. 66 that $s = 1$ is the positive real root of equation (98) so that

$$P(E,0) = -\frac{\sigma_0}{p_2(1)p_1'(1)} \frac{E_0}{E^2}$$

From curves of the kind shown in Fig. 66 it is found that $p_2(1) = -1.7868$, $p_1'(1) = -0.9908$, so that, taking the radiation length to be the unit of length, we have

$$z_\pi(E_0,E) = 0.437 \frac{E_0}{E^2}$$

Similarly we find that

$$z_\gamma(E_0,W) = \frac{C(1)}{p_2(1)p_1'(1)} \frac{E_0}{W_2} = 0.572 \frac{E_0}{W^2}$$

since $C(1) = 1.0135$.

Expressions of a like nature can be derived for the center of mass of the particles and their longitudinal spread. The derivation of these results is left to the reader; the final expressions are given on page 282 of the review article by Rossi and Greisen cited above.

The modifications to the theory rendered necessary by taking into account the energy losses due to ionization and the lateral spread of the showers may be included by an analysis similar to that given above, in which it is assumed that these effects are negligible. The details of these calculations are given in the article by Rossi and Greisen.

41. Distribution of Momentum in Atomic and Molecular Systems

41.1 Momentum distribution function. The spatial distribution of electrons in an atom has been fully studied in recent years both experimentally and theoretically. Experiments on X-ray scattering have confirmed the electron density curves computed theoretically. Although it was early realized by Dirac and Jordan[1] that the velocity distribution was equally fundamental, it is only in recent years, largely owing to the efforts of Coulson and Duncanson, that theoretical expressions have been obtained for the momentum distribution of the electrons in atoms of different atomic number. This enables density curves to be drawn for the momentum p from which may be calculated the shapes of the modified Compton lines scattered from these atoms.

When a homogeneous beam of X rays falls on an atom in which all the electrons are at rest, the Compton line should have a single modified frequency. If, however, the electrons are in motion, there is a Doppler effect which causes the modified line to become a band whose profile determines the velocity distribution.[2] The shape of the Compton profile depends on the incident wavelength λ_i and the angle of scattering θ. The peak of the modified line is given by

$$\lambda_c = \lambda_i + \frac{2h}{mc} \sin^2 \left(\frac{\theta}{2}\right)$$

where h is Planck's constant, m the mass of the electron, and c the velocity of light. Then the intensity of the Compton band at a displacement L from λ_c is given by

$$J(q) = \frac{1}{2} \int_q^\infty \frac{I(p)dp}{p} \tag{101}$$

where

$$q = \frac{cL}{2[\lambda_c^2 + \lambda_i^2 - 2\lambda_c\lambda_i \cos (\theta)]^{\frac{1}{2}}}$$

and $I(p)dp$ is the probability that p, the momentum of an electron in the atom, has magnitude between p and $p + dp$. This simple photon theory of DuMond has been shown by Schaidt and Burkhardt[3] to give effectively the same results as the complete quantum theory due to Wentzel.[4] The problem of determining the profile of the modified Compton line therefore reduces to that of finding the momentum density function $I(p)$.

[1] P. Jordan, *Z. Physik*, **40**, 809 (1927).
[2] J. W. M. DuMond, *Rev. Mod. Phys.*, **5**, 1 (1933).
[3] K. Schaidt, *Ann. Physik*, **21**, 89 (1934); G. Burkhardt, *Ann. Physik*, **26**, 567 (1936).
[4] G. Wentzel, *Z. Physik*, **43**, 1, 779 (1927); **58**, 348 (1929).

It is well known[1] that, for a system containing one electron, the probability that the electron is to be found in the volume element $dx\,dy\,dz$ situated at the point (x,y,z) is $|\psi(x,y,z)|^2\,dx\,dy\,dz$ where $\psi(x,y,z)$ is the appropriate solution of the Schrödinger equation

$$\nabla^2\psi + \frac{8\pi^2 m}{h^2}(W - V)\psi = 0$$

In this equation W is the total energy of the electron and $V(x,y,z)$ the potential of the field in which it moves. The frequent repetition of the constant $8\pi^2 m/h^2$ in this equation is avoided by the use of *atomic units* first introduced by D. R. Hartree.[2] If we take the electronic charge e, the electronic mass m, and the length $r_0 = h^2/4\pi^2 m e^2$ as the units of charge, mass, and length, then the Schrödinger equation becomes simply

$$\nabla^2\psi + 2(W - V)\psi = 0 \tag{102}$$

and the units of energy and velocity are now e^2/r_0 and $2\pi e^2/h = c/137$, respectively.

In order to compute the function $I(p)$ of equation (101) for a one-electron system, we must first construct a momentum wave function $\chi(\mathbf{p})$ with the property that $|\chi(\mathbf{p})|^2\,dp_x\,dp_y\,dp_z$ is the probability of finding the electron with its momentum in the band $(p_x,p_y,p_z) \leq \mathbf{p} \leq (p_x + dp_x, p_y + dp_y, p_z + dp_z)$. It turns out, on the basis of the Dirac transformation theory,[3] that, in atomic units, $\chi(\mathbf{p})$ is merely the three-dimensional Fourier transform of the wave function $\psi(\mathbf{r})$,

$$\chi(\mathbf{p}) = \left(\frac{1}{2\pi}\right)^3 \int_{-\infty}^{\infty}\int_{-\infty}^{\infty}\int_{-\infty}^{\infty} \psi(\mathbf{r})e^{-i(\mathbf{p}\cdot\mathbf{r})}\,dx\,dy\,dz \tag{103}$$

so that the study of the momentum distribution function is based on that of the Fourier transforms of the spatial wave functions. For, from the definitions of $\chi(\mathbf{p})$ and $I(p)$, we have

$$I(p) = \int |\chi(\mathbf{p})|^2 p^2\,d\omega \tag{104}$$

where $d\omega$ is the element of solid angle for p.

It follows from the Faltung theorem (112), Chap. 1, that

$$\int_{-\infty}^{\infty}\int_{-\infty}^{\infty}\int_{-\infty}^{\infty} |\psi(\mathbf{r})|^2\,dx\,dy\,dz = \int_{-\infty}^{\infty}\int_{-\infty}^{\infty}\int_{-\infty}^{\infty} |\chi(\mathbf{p})|^2\,dp_x\,dp_y\,dp_z$$

[1] N. F. Mott and I. N. Sneddon, "Wave Mechanics and Its Applications" (Oxford, New York, 1948), Chap. I. Hereafter in this chapter this work will be referred to as "Wave Mechanics."

[2] D. R. Hartree, *Proc. Cambridge Phil. Soc.*, **24**, 89 (1928). Cf. "Wave Mechanics," p. 127.

[3] P. A. M. Dirac, "The Principles of Quantum Mechanics," 3d ed. (Oxford, New York, 1947), p. 103, or "Wave Mechanics," p. 34.

so that, if, as is usual, $\psi(\mathbf{r})$ is normalized to unity, *i.e.*, if

$$\int_{-\infty}^{\infty} \int_{-\infty}^{\infty} \int_{-\infty}^{\infty} |\psi(\mathbf{r})|^2 \, dx \, dy \, dz = 1$$

then $\chi(\mathbf{p})$ is automatically normalized to unity. In other words,

$$\int_0^{\infty} I(p)dp = 1$$

as we should expect, on the probability interpretation.

Further, in the Schrödinger theory, the momentum p is represented by the operator $-i$ grad so that with the probability interpretation of ψ the mean value of p_x is

$$\bar{p}_x = -\int_{-\infty}^{\infty} \int_{-\infty}^{\infty} \int_{-\infty}^{\infty} \psi^* \left(i \frac{\partial}{\partial x} \right) \psi \, dx \, dy \, dz$$

Now $\psi(\mathbf{r})$ is the Fourier transform of $\chi(\mathbf{p})$ so that $-i \, \partial\psi/\partial x$ is the Fourier transform of $p_x \chi(\mathbf{p})$. Using these results in the Faltung theorem (112), Chap. 1, we find that

$$\bar{p}_x = \int_{-\infty}^{\infty} \int_{-\infty}^{\infty} \int_{-\infty}^{\infty} p_x \chi(\mathbf{p}) \chi^*(\mathbf{p}) dp_x \, dp_y \, dp_z$$

as we should require if $\chi(\mathbf{p})$ is to have the desired interpretation. Similarly the mean momentum is given by

$$\bar{p} = \int_0^{\infty} p I(p) dp \tag{105}$$

In the more complicated case of an atomic or molecular system with n electrons we number the electrons $1, 2, \ldots, n$ and use $\mathbf{r}_1, \mathbf{r}_2, \ldots, \mathbf{r}_n$ for their spatial coordinates and $\mathbf{p}_1, \mathbf{p}_2, \ldots, \mathbf{p}_n$ for their momentum coordinates. Then the momentum wave function $(\mathbf{p}_1, \mathbf{p}_2, \ldots, \mathbf{p}_n)$ is obtained from the spatial wave function $\Psi(\mathbf{r}_1, \mathbf{r}_2, \ldots, \mathbf{r}_n)$ by means of the $3n$-dimensional Fourier transform

$$\chi(\mathbf{p}_1, \mathbf{p}_2, \ldots, \mathbf{p}_n)$$
$$= \left(\frac{1}{\sqrt{2\pi}} \int_{-\infty}^{\infty} \right)^{3n} e^{-i(\mathbf{p}_1 \cdot \mathbf{r}_1 \cdots \mathbf{p}_n \cdot \mathbf{r}_n)} \Psi(\mathbf{r}_1, \mathbf{r}_2, \ldots, \mathbf{r}_n) d\mathbf{r}_1 \, d\mathbf{r}_2 \cdots d\mathbf{r}_n \tag{106}$$

In this instance the wave function Ψ is a solution of the equation

$$(\nabla_1^2 + \nabla_2^2 \cdots + \nabla_n^2)\Psi + 2(W - V)\Psi = 0 \tag{107}$$

in which

$$\nabla_s^2 = \frac{\partial^2}{\partial x_s^2} + \frac{\partial^2}{\partial y_s^2} + \frac{\partial^2}{\partial z_s^2}$$

By multiplying both sides of equation (107) by $\exp[-i(\mathbf{p}_1 \cdot \mathbf{r}_1 + \cdots + \mathbf{p}_n \cdot \mathbf{r}_n)]$ and integrating through the space of the coordinates of the electrons, we obtain an integral equation for the determination of the momentum wave function $\chi(\mathbf{p}_1, \mathbf{p}_2, \ldots, \mathbf{p}_n)$, of which we might hope to obtain solutions. We shall consider this problem later (Sec. 42) in relation to problems in nuclear physics. In the present section we shall assume that the spatial wave function $\Psi(r_1, r_2, \ldots, r_n)$ is known. The determination of the momentum wave function reduces then to the calculation of the Fourier transform of the function Ψ.

41.2 Electron momenta in hydrogenlike atoms. With the system of units we have chosen the potential of the single electron in a hydrogenlike atom of nuclear charge Z is

$$V(x,y,z) = -\frac{Z}{r} \qquad r^2 = x^2 + y^2 + z^2$$

Examples of atoms of this type are hydrogen, ionized helium, and doubly ionized lithium, in which $Z = 1, 2, 3$, respectively. It is readily verified by direct substitution in equation (102) that

$$\psi(\mathbf{r}) = \left(\frac{Z^3}{\pi}\right)^{\frac{1}{2}} e^{-Zr} \tag{108}$$

is a solution of the corresponding Schrödinger equation provided that $W = -\frac{1}{2}Z^2$. The constant on the right of equation (108) is chosen so that $\psi(\mathbf{r})$ is normalized to unity. Using the integral

$$\int_{-\infty}^{\infty} \int_{-\infty}^{\infty} \int_{-\infty}^{\infty} e^{-\alpha r + i(\mathbf{p} \cdot \mathbf{r})} \, d\mathbf{r} = \frac{8\pi}{(p^2 + \alpha^2)^{\frac{1}{2}}} \tag{109}$$

we see that the momentum wave function corresponding to the spatial wave function (108) is

$$\chi(\mathbf{p}) = \frac{(8Z^5)^{\frac{1}{2}}}{\pi(p^2 + Z^2)^2} \tag{110}$$

so that

$$I(p) = 4\pi p^2 |\chi(\mathbf{p})|^2 = \frac{32p^2 Z^2}{\pi(p^2 + Z^2)^4} \tag{111}$$

It follows immediately from equation (101) that the intensity of the Compton band is given by

$$J(q) = \frac{32Z^5}{\pi} \int_q^{\infty} \frac{p \, dp}{(p^2 + Z^2)^4} = \frac{8Z^5}{3\pi} \frac{1}{(q^2 + Z^2)^3} \tag{112}$$

and from equation (105) that the mean momentum is

$$\bar{p} = \frac{32Z^5}{\pi}\left[\int_0^\infty \frac{p\,dp}{(p^2+Z^2)^3} - Z^2 \int_0^\infty \frac{p\,dp}{(p^2+Z^2)^4}\right] = \frac{8Z}{3\pi} \quad (113)$$

where, it will be recalled, the unit is $mc/137$. In the nomenclature of spectroscopy the function (108) is the $1s$ wave function of a hydrogenlike atom; thus equation (113) states that in a $1s$ orbit the mean momentum of the electron is $8Zmc/401\pi$.

The evaluation of the momentum wave function in the general case has been carried out by Podolsky and Pauling.[1] The calculation is cumbersome but will be repeated in outline here since it illustrates the method of evaluating the types of triple integrals encountered in work of this kind. If we write

$$\mathbf{p} = p(\sin\Theta\cos\Phi, \sin\Theta\sin\Phi, \cos\Theta),$$
$$\mathbf{r} = r(\sin\theta\cos\phi, \sin\theta\sin\phi, \cos\phi)$$

we may put equation (103) in the form

$$\chi(p,\Theta,\Phi) = \left(\frac{1}{2\pi}\right)^{\frac{3}{2}} \int_0^\infty r^2\,dr \int_0^\pi \sin\theta\,d\theta \int_0^{2\pi} \psi(r,\theta,\phi)e^{-i\mu}\,d\phi \quad (114)$$

where

$$\mu = pr[\sin\theta\sin\Theta\cos(\Phi-\phi) + \cos\theta\cos\Theta]$$

Now, for a hydrogenlike atom, it may be shown that the wave function

$\psi(r,\theta,\phi)$ is of the form $\sum_{lmn} c_{lmn}\psi_{nlm}$, where[2]

$$\psi_{nlm}(r,\theta,\phi) = Ce^{\pm im\phi}P_l^m(\cos\theta)e^{-\gamma r}r^l L_{l+n}^{2l+1}(2\gamma r) \quad (115)$$

In this expression $\gamma = Z/n$, $P_l^m(\cos\theta)$ is Ferrar's associated Legendre function of degree l and order m, $L_{l+n}^{2l+1}(2\gamma r)$ is an associated Laguerre function, and C is the normalizing constant

$$C = \frac{1}{\sqrt{2\pi}}\left[\frac{(2l+1)(l-m)!}{2(l+m)!}\right]^{\frac{1}{2}} \frac{(2\gamma)^{l+1}}{(n+l)!}\left[\frac{\gamma(n-l-1)!}{n(n+l)!}\right]^{\frac{1}{2}}$$

If we substitute from equation (115) into equation (114) and write

$$I_1 = \int_0^{2\pi} e^{\pm im\phi + ib\cos(\Phi-\phi)}\,d\phi, \qquad I_2 = \int_0^\pi e^{ic\cos\theta}\,I_1 P_l^m(\cos\theta)\sin\theta\,d\theta$$

[1] B. Podolsky and L. Pauling, *Phys. Rev.*, **34**, 109 (1929).

[2] L. Pauling and E. B. Wilson, "Introduction to Quantum Mechanics—with Applications to Chemistry" (McGraw-Hill, New York, 1935), p. 132.

with $b = -rp \sin\theta \sin\Theta$ and $c = -rp$, we find that

$$\chi(p,\Theta,\Phi) = \frac{C}{(2\pi)^{\frac{3}{2}}} \int_0^\infty I_2 e^{-\gamma r} r^{l+2} L_{n+l}^{2l+1}(2\gamma r)dr \tag{116}$$

Now it is well known that

$$I_1 = e^{\pm im\Phi} \int_0^{2\pi} e^{\pm im\omega + ib\cos\omega} \, d\omega = 2\pi(i)^{\pm m} e^{\pm im\Phi} J_m(b)$$

Using the relation $J_{-m}(b) = i^{2m} J_m(b)$, we find that

$$I_1 = 2\pi i^m J_m(b) e^{\pm im\Phi}$$

Furthermore, from the result[1]

$$\int_0^\pi e^{ic\cos\theta\cos\Theta} J_m(c\sin\theta\sin\Theta) P_l^m(\cos\theta)\sin\theta \, d\theta$$
$$= \left(\frac{2\pi}{c}\right)^{\frac{1}{2}} i^{l-m} P_l^m(\cos\theta) J_{l+\frac{1}{2}}(c)$$

it follows that

$$I_2 = -2\pi(-i)^l e^{\pm im\Phi} P_l^m(\cos\Theta) \left(\frac{2}{pr}\right)^{\frac{1}{2}} J_{l+\frac{1}{2}}(pr)$$

Substituting this expression for I_2 into equation (116), we find that

$$\chi_{nlm}(p,\Theta,\Phi) = -\frac{(-i)^l C}{p^{\frac{1}{2}}} e^{\pm im\Phi} P_l^m(\cos\Theta) \int_0^\infty e^{-\gamma r} r^{l+\frac{3}{2}} J_{l+\frac{1}{2}}(pr) L_{n+l}^{2l+1}(2\gamma r)dr$$

This integral may be expressed in terms of the Gegenbauer function C_k defined by the relation[2]

$$(1 - 2ut + u^2)^{-\nu} = \sum_{k=0}^\infty C_k(t)u^k$$

We find after some manipulation that

$$\chi_{nlm}(p,\Theta,\Phi)$$
$$= C e^{\pm im\Phi} P_l^m(\cos\Theta)\left[-\frac{(-1)^l \pi 2^{l+4} l!}{(2\pi\gamma)^{\frac{3}{2}}}\right] \frac{\zeta^l}{(\zeta^2+1)^{l+2}} C_{n-l-1}^{l+1}\left(\frac{\zeta^2-1}{\zeta^2+1}\right)$$

in which $\zeta = pn/Z = p/p_n$, p_n being the momentum of the electron in a circular Bohr orbit characterized by the total quantum number n and the nuclear charge Z.

[1] G. N. Watson, "The Theory of Bessel Functions" (Cambridge, London, 1922), p. 379.

[2] For explicit expressions for the functions C_k see Whittaker and Watson, *op. cit.*, p. 329.

From equation (104) it follows that the corresponding mean radial distribution function is

$$I_{n,l}(p) = p^2 \int_0^\pi \int_0^{2\pi} |\chi_{nlm}(p,\Theta,\Phi)|^2 \sin\Theta \, d\Theta \, d\Phi$$

which reduces to

$$I_{n,l}(p) = \frac{1}{2\pi Z} \frac{2^{4l+6} n^2 (l!)^2 (n-l-1)!}{(n+l)!} \frac{\zeta^{2l+2}}{(\zeta^2+1)^{2l+4}} \left[C_{n-l-1}^{l+1}\left(\frac{\zeta^2-1}{\zeta^2+1}\right) \right]^2 \tag{116a}$$

For the 1s state, $l = 0$, $n = 1$, so that using the fact that $C_0^1 = 1$ we find

$$I_{1,0}(p) = \frac{32Z^5}{\pi} \frac{p^2}{(p^2+Z^2)^4} \tag{117}$$

in agreement with equation (112). Similarly putting $l = 1$, $n = 2$, and $C_0^2 = 1$, we find for a 2p state

$$I_{2,1}(p) = \frac{512Z^5}{3\pi} \frac{p^4}{(p^2+Z^2)^6} \tag{118}$$

In the case of a 2s state, $l = 0$, $n = 2$, $C_1^1(t) = 2t$, so that

$$I_{2,0}(p) = \frac{32Z^5 p^2 (p^2 - Z^2)}{(p^2+Z^2)^5} \tag{119}$$

41.3 Distribution of momenta in atoms.[1] In the case of atoms with more than one electron we have to make use of the formula (106) for the determination of the momentum wave function $\chi(\mathbf{p}_1,\mathbf{p}_2, \ldots ,\mathbf{p}_n)$. It has been shown by Slater[2] that the spatial wave function $\Psi(\mathbf{r}_1,\mathbf{r}_2, \ldots , \mathbf{r}_n)$ may be written as a sum of determinants of the type

$$\begin{vmatrix} \psi_1(\mathbf{r}_1)\phi_1(\mathbf{\sigma}_1) & \psi_1(\mathbf{r}_2)\phi_1(\mathbf{\sigma}_2) & \cdots & \psi_1(\mathbf{r}_n)\phi_1(\mathbf{\sigma}_n) \\ \psi_2(\mathbf{r}_1)\phi_2(\mathbf{\sigma}_1) & \psi_2(\mathbf{r}_2)\phi_2(\mathbf{\sigma}_2) & \cdots & \psi_2(\mathbf{r}_n)\phi_2(\mathbf{\sigma}_n) \\ \cdot & \cdot & & \cdot \\ \cdot & \cdot & & \cdot \\ \cdot & \cdot & & \cdot \\ \psi_n(\mathbf{r}_1)\phi_n(\mathbf{\sigma}_1) & \psi_n(\mathbf{r}_2)\phi_n(\mathbf{\sigma}_2) & \cdots & \psi_n(\mathbf{r}_n)\phi_n(\mathbf{\sigma}_n) \end{vmatrix} \tag{120}$$

in which the ϕ's denote spin wave functions. On expansion of this determinant we see that $\Psi(\mathbf{r}_1,\mathbf{r}_2, \ldots ,\mathbf{r}_n)$ may be regarded as the sum of a large number of distinct terms each of which is the product of n atomic orbitals, that is,

[1] C. A. Coulson and W. E. Duncanson, *Proc. Phys. Soc.* (*London*), **57**, 190 (1945); **60**, 175 (1948).

[2] J. C. Slater, *Phys. Rev.*, **34**, 1293 (1929), or "Wave Mechanics," p. 130.

$$\Psi(\mathbf{r}_1, \mathbf{r}_2, \ldots, \mathbf{r}_n) = \sum_s A_s \psi_{a_s}(\mathbf{r}_1) \psi_{b_s}(\mathbf{r}_2) \cdots \psi_{c_s}(\mathbf{r}_n) \tag{121}$$

Since the coordinates of each electron appear once and only once in each of these terms, the integration (106) for any term of the series (121) is immediate and gives

$$\chi(\mathbf{p}_1, \mathbf{p}_2, \ldots, \mathbf{p}_n) = \sum_s A_s \chi_{a_s}(\mathbf{p}_1) \chi_{b_s}(\mathbf{p}_2) \cdots \chi_{c_s}(\mathbf{p}_n) \tag{122}$$

where

$$\chi_m(p_q) = \frac{1}{\sqrt{2\pi}} \int_{-\infty}^{\infty} \chi_m(r_q) e^{-i(\mathbf{p}_q \cdot \mathbf{r}_q)} \, dx_q \, dy_q \, dz_q \tag{123}$$

The result of the integration is therefore simply that obtained by replacing each spatial wave function $\chi_m(\mathbf{r}_q)$ by the corresponding momentum wave function $\chi_m(\mathbf{p}_q)$ defined by equation (121). It follows at once that, if the spatial wave function of the n electron system is the sum of Slater determinants of the type (120), the corresponding momentum wave function is precisely the same sum of determinants of the type

$$\begin{vmatrix} \chi_1(\mathbf{p}_1)\phi_1(\delta_1) & \chi_1(\mathbf{p}_2)\phi_1(\delta_2) & \cdots & \chi_1(\mathbf{p}_n)\phi_1(\delta_n) \\ \chi_2(\mathbf{p}_1)\phi_2(\delta_1) & \chi_2(\mathbf{p}_2)\phi_2(\delta_2) & \cdots & \chi_2(\mathbf{p}_n)\phi_2(\delta_n) \\ \cdot & \cdot & & \cdot \\ \cdot & \cdot & & \cdot \\ \cdot & \cdot & & \cdot \\ \chi_n(\mathbf{p}_1)\phi_n(\delta_1) & \chi_n(\mathbf{p}_2)\phi_n(\delta_2) & \cdots & \chi_n(\mathbf{p}_n)\phi_n(\delta_n) \end{vmatrix}$$

Once the momentum wave function $\chi(\mathbf{p}_1, \mathbf{p}_2, \ldots, \mathbf{p}_n)$ is known the calculation of the generalized mean distribution function $I(p_1, p_2, \ldots, p_n)$ is effected by means of an integration completely analogous to that of equation (104). The simplest method of giving graphical expression to the function $I(p_1, p_2, \ldots, p_n)$ is to integrate it over all values of $p_2, p_3, \ldots, p_n$ to obtain a function

$$I(p_1) = \int_0^{\infty} dp_2 \cdots \int_0^{\infty} dp_n \, I(p_1, p_2, \ldots, p_n) \tag{124}$$

which may be called the mean radial momentum density for the electron 1. From the fact that it is physically impossible to distinguish between two electrons (or, what is the same thing, from the character of the determinantal wave functions used) it follows that

$$I(p_1) = I(p_2) = I(p_3) = \cdots = I(p_n) = I(p), \text{ say}$$

The function $I(p)$, which is normalized to unity, may be regarded therefore as giving a measure of the distribution of momentum in the atom, in just the same way as the spatial distribution is measured by the density function $\rho(r)$.

The calculation of $I(p)$ is particularly simple if all the original atomic orbitals $\psi_m(\mathbf{r})$ are orthogonal and normalized to unity, *i.e.*, if

$$\int \psi_m(\mathbf{r})\psi_{m'}^*(\mathbf{r})d\mathbf{r} = \delta_{mm'} = \begin{cases} 1 & \text{if } m = m' \\ 0 & \text{if } m \neq m' \end{cases}$$

for then, by the Faltung theorem (112), Chap. 1, it follows at once that

$$\int \psi_m(\mathbf{p})\psi_{m'}^*(\mathbf{p})d\mathbf{p} = \delta_{mm'} \tag{125}$$

Now from equation (122) we have

$$\chi\chi^* = \sum_s \sum_t A_s A_t^* \chi_{a_s}(\mathbf{p}_1)\chi_{a_t}^*(\mathbf{p}_1) \cdots \chi_{c_s}(\mathbf{p}_n)\chi_{c_t}^*(\mathbf{p}_n)$$

so that from equation (124) it follows that if the integrations are over the whole momentum space $0 \leq p_i \leq \infty$ $(i = 2,3, \ldots ,n)$, then

$$\int dp_2 \cdots \int dp_n\, \chi\chi^* = \sum_{s,t} A_s A_t^* \chi_{a_s}(p_1)\chi_{a_t}^*(p_1)\delta_{b_s b_t} \cdots \delta_{c_s c_t}$$

Hence by the definition of $I(p)$ it follows that we may write

$$I(p) = \sum_s \sum_t A_s A_t^* I_{a_s a_t}(p)\delta_{b_s b_t} \cdots \delta_{c_s c_t} \tag{126}$$

where

$$I_{a_s a_t}(p) = \int p^2 \chi_{a_s}(p)\chi_{a_t}^*(p)d\omega_p$$

The shape of the Compton profile is then obtained by substituting from equation (126) into equation (101).

Ground State of the Helium Atom. Next to the hydrogenlike atoms considered in Sec. 41.2 the simplest atom is helium. Accurate wave functions have been determined for helium, but, in order to illustrate the procedure outlined above, we shall make use of one-particle wave functions to construct a wave function of the Slater type. In the ground state of the helium atom the spin wave function is antisymmetric so that to preserve the antisymmetry of the wave function as a whole (*i.e.*, in order to obey the Pauli exclusion principle) the spatial part must be symmetric. Since the configuration in the ground state is $(1s)^2\, {}^1S$ we may, therefore, write

$$\Psi(\mathbf{r}_1,\mathbf{r}_2) = \psi_{1s}(\mathbf{r}_1)\psi_{1s}(\mathbf{r}_2) \tag{127}$$

The connection of this wave function with the Slater determinant arises from the fact that in this instance the determinant (120) is of the form

$$\frac{1}{\sqrt{2}} \begin{vmatrix} \psi_{1s}(\mathbf{r}_1)\phi_\alpha(\mathfrak{d}_1) & \psi_{1s}(\mathbf{r}_2)\phi_\alpha(\mathfrak{d}_2) \\ \psi_{1s}(\mathbf{r}_1)\phi_\beta(\mathfrak{d}_1) & \psi_{1s}(\mathbf{r}_2)\phi_\beta(\mathfrak{d}_2) \end{vmatrix} \tag{128}$$

which reduces to $\psi_{1s}(\mathbf{r}_1)\psi_{1s}(\mathbf{r}_2)S(\mathfrak{d}_1,\mathfrak{d}_2)$, where

$$S(\mathfrak{d}_1,\mathfrak{d}_2) = \frac{1}{\sqrt{2}}\left[\phi_\alpha(\mathfrak{d}_1)\phi_\beta(\mathfrak{d}_2) - \phi_\alpha(\mathfrak{d}_2)\phi_\beta(\mathfrak{d}_1)\right]$$

Since in the end we integrate over the spin variables, it follows, from the fact that the spin wave $S(\mathfrak{d}_1,\mathfrak{d}_2)$ is normalized to unity, that we may make use of the wave function (127) instead of the Slater determinant (128).

Multiplying both sides of equation (127) by $e^{-i(\mathbf{p}_1 \cdot \mathbf{r}_1 + \mathbf{p}_2 \cdot \mathbf{r}_2)}$ and integrating with respect to r_1 and r_2, we find that the momentum wave function is given by

$$\chi(\mathbf{p}_1,\mathbf{p}_2) = \chi_{1s}(\mathbf{p}_1)\chi_{1s}(\mathbf{p}_2) \tag{127a}$$

It follows at once from equations (127a), (122), and (126) that in this instance $I(p) = I_{1s}(p)$, where

$$I_{1s}(p) = p^2\int|\chi_{1s}(\mathbf{p})|^2\,d\omega_p$$

and $\chi_{1s}(\mathbf{p})$ is the Fourier transform of the assumed function $\chi_{1s}(\mathbf{r})$.

For an electron in the ground state of the helium atom we may take, in first approximation

$$\psi_{1s}(\mathbf{r}) = \left(\frac{\alpha^3}{\pi}\right)^{\frac{1}{2}} e^{-\alpha r}$$

with $\alpha = 1.7$, so that making use of the integral (109) we find that

$$\chi_{1s}(\mathbf{p}) = \frac{2^{\frac{3}{2}}\alpha^{\frac{5}{2}}}{\pi^2(p^2 + \alpha^2)^2}$$

so that

$$I_{1s}(p) = 4\pi p^2|\chi_{1s}(\mathbf{p})|^2 = \frac{32\alpha^5 p^2}{(p^2 + \alpha^2)^4} \tag{127b}$$

By comparison with equations (111) and (113) we see that the mean momentum in the ground state of the helium atom is $\bar{p} = 8\alpha/3\pi$, which is equivalent to a velocity in the region of $c/100$.

Putting $\alpha = 1.70$ in equation (127b), we obtain the value of $I(p)$ for the ground state of helium. The variation of this $I(p)$ with p is shown in Fig. 70 together with the curves for the ground states of hydrogen and ionized helium, obtained by putting $Z = 1,2$ respectively in equation (111).

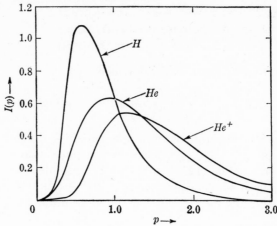

FIG. 70. The mean radial distribution function $I(p)$ for hydrogen, helium, and ionized helium.

From equations (127*b*) and (101) it follows that the intensity of the Compton band is given by

$$J(q) = \frac{8\alpha^5}{3\pi(q^2 + \alpha^2)^3} \tag{129}$$

In Fig. 71 are shown the normalized $J(q)$ curves for helium and hydrogen [$\alpha = 1.70$ and 1.00, respectively, in equation (129)]. Since the corrections to be made for binding and relativistic effects are small, the profile is very nearly symmetrical and, for that reason, only half of each profile is shown.

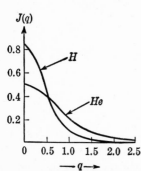

FIG. 71. The shape of the Compton profiles for hydrogen and helium.

As there are only two electrons in the helium atom, it is possible to refine the spatial wave function considerably by explicit inclusion of the distance between the two electrons. Using wave functions of this kind, Hicks[1] has calculated the more accurate form of the momentum wave function of the two electrons in the ground state of the helium atom.

Ground State of Atoms from Lithium to Neon.[2] The most suitable wave functions for the series of atoms from Li to Ne are those derived by Duncanson and Coulson.[3]

[1] B. Hicks, *Phys. Rev.*, **52**, 436 (1936).

[2] W. E. Duncanson and C. A. Coulson, *Proc. Phys. Soc.* (*London*), **57**, 190 (1945).

[3] W. E. Duncanson and C. A. Coulson, *Proc. Roy. Soc. Edinburgh*, **62A**, 37 (1944).

They are formed by suitable linear combinations of determinants whose elements are the separate orbitals

$$\psi_{1s}(\mathbf{r}) = \left(\frac{\alpha^3}{\pi}\right)^{\frac{1}{2}} e^{-\alpha r}, \qquad \psi_{2s}(\mathbf{r}) = \left(\frac{\mu^5}{3\pi N}\right)^{\frac{1}{2}} \left(re^{-\mu r} - \frac{3A}{\mu} e^{-\beta r}\right)$$

$$\psi_{2p_0}(\mathbf{r}) = \left(\frac{\gamma^5}{\pi}\right)^{\frac{1}{2}} re^{-\gamma r} \cos\theta, \qquad \psi_{2p_\pm}(\mathbf{r}) = \left(\frac{\gamma^5}{\pi}\right)^{\frac{1}{2}} re^{-\gamma r \pm i\phi} \sin\theta$$

In these expressions the constant A is determined by the condition that $\psi_{1s}(\mathbf{r})$ is orthogonal to $\psi_{2s}(\mathbf{r})$. N is a normalizing constant, and the values of the parameters are given for each separate atom.[1]

If all the $1s, 2s$, and $2p$ orbitals are mutually orthogonal, it follows from equation (126) that $I(p)$ reduces to the sum of a suitable number of functions $I_{1s}(p), I_{2s}(p), I_{2p}(p)$. From the definition of $J(q)$ it follows, in turn, that it will be the same sum of separate functions $J_{1s}(q), J_{2s}(q), J_{2p}(q)$ related to the I's by equations of the type (101). By integrations of the type (109) it is readily shown that

$$I_{1s}(p) = \frac{32\alpha^5 p^2}{(p^2 + \alpha^2)^4}, \qquad I_{2s}(p) = \frac{32\mu^5 p^2}{3\pi N}\left[\frac{3\mu^2 - p^2}{(p^2 + \mu^2)^3} - \frac{3A}{\mu(p^2 + \beta^2)^2}\right]^2$$

$$I_{2p}(p) = \frac{512\gamma^7 p^4}{3\pi(p^2 + \gamma^2)^6}$$

From the definition (101) it follows as a result of elementary integrations that

$$J_{1s}(q) = \frac{8\alpha^5}{3\pi(q^2 + \alpha^2)^3}$$

$$J_{2s}(q) = \frac{16\mu^5}{3\pi N}\left\{\frac{5q^4 - 20q^2\mu^2 + 23\mu^4}{30(q^2 + \mu^2)^5} + \frac{3\beta^2 A^2}{2\mu^2(q^2 + \beta^2)^3}\right.$$
$$- \frac{3\beta A}{\mu(\mu^2 - \beta^2)^4}\left[2(5\mu^2 + \beta^2)\log\frac{q^2 + \beta^2}{q^2 + \mu^2} + \frac{2\mu^2(\mu^2 - \beta^2)^2}{(q^2 + \mu^2)^2}\right.$$
$$\left.\left. + (\mu^2 - \beta^2)\left(\frac{3\mu^2 + \beta^2}{q^2 + \beta^2} + \frac{7\mu^2 + \beta^2}{q^2 + \mu^2}\right)\right]\right\}$$

$$J_{2p}(q) = \frac{32\gamma^7(5q^2 + \gamma^2)}{15\pi(q^2 + \gamma^2)^5}$$

The problem of determining the shape of the Compton profile thus reduces to the determination of the coefficients A_s which occur in the spatial wave function (121). By this method Duncanson and Coulson have computed the function $I(p)$ for the ground state of the atoms from Li to Ne. The results of their calculations are shown in Fig. 72.

---

[1] See, for instance, "Wave Mechanics," p. 144, in which the constants α, β, γ are referred to as $a\mu, b\mu, c\mu$, respectively.

Ground State of Atoms from Neon to Potassium.[1] For atoms with atomic number, Z, between 11 and 20 the atomic orbitals making up the Slater determinants may be taken to be

$$\psi_{nlm}(r) = Cr^{n-1}e^{-cr}P_l^m(\cos\theta)e^{\pm im\phi} \tag{130}$$

where C is a normalizing factor, n is the effective quantum number, and c is a constant whose value for any particular atom may be calculated

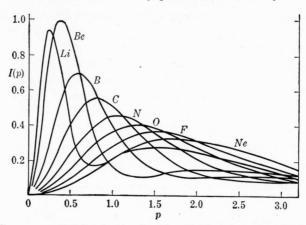

Fɪɢ. 72.   The mean radial distribution function $I(p)$ for atoms from lithium to neon.

by means of simple rules due to Slater.[2] By means of an integration similar to that involved in the derivation of equation (116) it can readily be shown that the mean radial distribution function (normalized to unity) is

$$I(p) = \frac{2}{\pi}\frac{(2c)^{2n^*+1}}{\Gamma(2n^*+1)}\,p^2[R_l(p)]^2 \tag{131}$$

where

$$R_l(p) = \int_0^\infty r^{n^*+1}e^{-cr}\left(\frac{\pi}{2pr}\right)^{\frac{1}{2}}J_{l+\frac{1}{2}}(pr)dr$$

For the first three rows of the periodic table n^* is an integer, and equation (131) leads to the algebraic functions

$$I_{1s}(p) = \frac{32c^5p^2}{(p^2+c^2)^4}, \qquad I_{2s}(p) = \frac{32c^5p^2(p^2-3c^2)^2}{3\pi(p^2+c^2)^6}$$

$$I_{2p}(p) = \frac{512c^7p^2}{3\pi(p^2+c^2)^6}, \qquad I_{3s}(p) = \frac{1{,}024c^9p^2(p^2-c^2)^2}{5\pi(p^2+c^2)^8}$$

$$I_{3p}(p) = \frac{1{,}024c^7p^4(5c^2-p^2)^2}{45\pi(p^2+c^2)^8}, \qquad I_{3d}(p) = \frac{4{,}096c^9p^6}{5\pi(p^2+c^2)^8}$$

[1] W. E. Duncanson and C. A. Coulson, *Proc. Phys. Soc. (London),* **60,** 175 (1948).
[2] J. C. Slater, *Phys. Rev.,* **36,** 57 (1930).

If n^* is not an integer, it is readily shown from (131) that

$$pR_0(p) = S(n^*)$$
$$p^2R_1(p) = S(n^* - 1) - pC(n^*)$$
$$p^3R_2(p) = 3S(n^* - 2) - 3pC(n^* - 1) - p^2S(n^*)$$
$$p^4R_3(p) = 15S(n^* - 3) - 15pC(n^* - 2) - 6p^2(n^* - 1) + p^3C(n^*)$$

where

$$C(n) = \int_0^\infty r^n e^{-cr} \cos (pr)dr = \Gamma(n + 1) \cos [(n + 1)\alpha](\cos \alpha)^{n+1}$$
$$S(n) = \int_0^\infty r^n e^{-cr} \sin (pr)dr = \Gamma(n + 1) \sin [(n + 1)\alpha](\cos \alpha)^{n+1}$$

with $\alpha = \tan^{-1} (p/c)$.

The corresponding mean momenta are readily shown to be

$$\bar{p}_{1s} = \frac{8c}{3\pi}, \ \bar{p}_{2s} = \frac{8c}{5\pi}, \ \bar{p}_{3s} = \frac{128c}{105\pi}, \ \bar{p}_{2p} = \frac{128c}{45\pi}, \ \bar{p}_{3p} = \frac{9,472c}{4,725\pi}$$

By means of these formulas Duncanson and Coulson have calculated the function $I(p)$ and the mean momentum $\bar{p}$ for the elements from Ne to K.

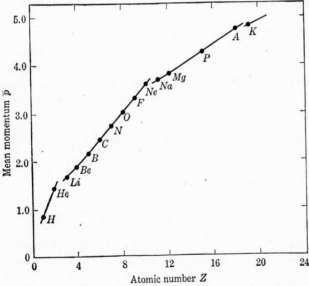

Fig. 73. The variation with Z of the mean momentum $\bar{p}$ for atoms between hydrogen and potassium.

The variation with the atomic number Z of $\bar{p}$ for these elements and those discussed under Ground State of Atoms from Lithium to Neon is shown in Fig. 73. The variation of $\bar{p}$ is almost linear for each shell, but the gradient of each successive shell is less than that of the preceding one. Further, there is a small change in $\bar{p}$ in going from a rare gas to an alkali metal atom. This is just what we should expect when we recall that, in atomic units, the total electronic energy E is related to $\bar{p}$ in some such way as $\bar{p} \simeq (2E/Z)^{\frac{1}{2}}$. Along each row of the periodic table there is a steady increase in E/Z, but, because of the small binding of the valence electron in the alkali atom, there is only a small change in E at the beginning of a new shell.

41.4 Momentum distribution in molecular systems.[1]   Since our knowledge of precise molecular wave functions is small, we have to make use of one of two alternative approximations which we shall now consider in turn.

Molecular Orbital Method.   In this method we may write (neglecting the spin terms)

$$\Psi(\mathbf{r_1},\mathbf{r_2}, \ldots ,\mathbf{r}_n) = \psi_1(\mathbf{r}_1)\psi_2(\mathbf{r}_2) \cdots \psi_n(\mathbf{r}_n) \tag{132}$$

For an inner shell electron ψ is a suitably chosen atomic orbital, but for a bonding electron ψ is a polynuclear orbital. By the Pauli principle only two of the ψ's can be the same, and they must then correspond to opposite spins.

In the case of inner shell electrons the integration is just the same as in the calculation of the momentum wave function in an atom and may be obtained by the method outlined above. We need therefore only investigate the molecular orbital for an electron forming part of a bond between two nuclei A and B. If these nuclei are identical, giving rise to a homopolar bond (for example, H_2), we write

$$\psi(\mathbf{r}) = \frac{\psi_a(\mathbf{r}) + \psi_b(\mathbf{r})}{[2(1 + S_{ab})]^{\frac{1}{2}}} \tag{133}$$

where ψ_a,ψ_b are atomic orbitals round A and B, respectively, and S_{ab} is the overlap integral

$$S_{ab} = \int \psi_a(\mathbf{r})\psi_b(\mathbf{r})d\mathbf{r} \tag{133a}$$

If ψ_a and ψ_b are similar except for the different origins of coordinates, then, denoting the position vectors of A and B by $\mathbf{r}_a$ and $\mathbf{r}_b$, we have

$$\psi(\mathbf{r}) = \frac{\psi_a(\mathbf{r} - \mathbf{r}_a) + \psi_a(\mathbf{r} - \mathbf{r}_b)}{[2(1 + S_{ab})]^{\frac{1}{2}}}$$

Using the result

$$\int e^{-i(\mathbf{p}\cdot\mathbf{r})}\psi_a(\mathbf{r} - \mathbf{r}_a)d\mathbf{r} = e^{-i\mathbf{p}\cdot\mathbf{r}_a} \int e^{-i\mathbf{p}\cdot\mathbf{r}'}\psi_a(\mathbf{r}')d\mathbf{r}' = e^{-i\mathbf{p}\cdot\mathbf{r}_a}\chi_a(\mathbf{p}) \tag{134}$$

[1] C. A. Coulson, *Proc. Cambridge Phil. Soc.*, **37**, 55 (1941).

we see that

$$\chi(\mathbf{p}) = \frac{e^{-i\mathbf{p}\cdot\mathbf{r}_a} + e^{-i\mathbf{p}\cdot\mathbf{r}_b}}{[2(1 + S_{ab})]^{\frac{1}{2}}} \chi_a(\mathbf{p})$$

The density function then comes out to be

$$\chi(\mathbf{p})\chi^*(\mathbf{p}) = \frac{1 + \cos \mathbf{p}\cdot(\mathbf{r}_a - \mathbf{r}_b)}{1 + S_{ab}} \chi_a(p)\chi_a^*(p)$$

which is the same as it would be if the valence electrons were confined each to its own particular nucleus, except for the occurrence of the diffraction factor

$$\frac{1 + \cos (\mathbf{p}\cdot\mathbf{R})}{1 + S_{ab}} = \frac{1 + \cos (pR \cos \vartheta)}{1 + S_{ab}}$$

where $\mathbf{R} = \mathbf{r}_a - \mathbf{r}_b$ and ϑ is the angle between the directions $\mathbf{p}$ and $\mathbf{R}$. From equation (104) we have for the corresponding value of $I(p)$

$$I(p) = \frac{p^2}{1 + S_{ab}} \int \int |\chi_a(\mathbf{p})|^2 [1 + \cos (pR \cos \vartheta)] \sin \vartheta \, d\vartheta \, d\varphi$$

As an example of the use of this method we shall consider the simplest possible molecule—the hydrogen molecular ion H_2. For the single electron in this molecule we may write $\psi_a(r) = (\alpha^3/\pi)^{\frac{1}{2}}e^{-\alpha r}$, so that

$$I(p) = \frac{32\alpha^5 p^2}{\pi(1 + S)(p^2 + \alpha^2)^4}\left[1 + \frac{\sin (pR)}{pR}\right] \tag{135}$$

and

$$\bar{p} = \frac{4\alpha}{\pi(1 + S)} + \frac{32\alpha^5}{\pi(1 + S)R}\int_0^\infty \frac{p^2 \sin (pR)}{(p^2 + \alpha^2)^4} \, dp$$

In atomic units $R = 2.0$, $c = 1.228$, $S = 0.445$, and the integral

$$\int_0^\infty \frac{p^2 \sin (pR)}{(p^2 + \alpha^2)^4} \, dp$$

may readily be put in the form of a rapidly convergent series,[1] so that we find that numerically $\bar{p} = 0.907$, whereas in the case of the simple hydrogen atom $\bar{p} = 8/3\pi = 0.849$. The mean momentum is thus greater for the molecular ion than for the atom.

Similar results hold when the nuclei A and B are not identical but give a heteropolar bond (for example, HCl), but now we replace (133) by

$$\psi(\mathbf{r}) = \frac{\psi_a(\mathbf{r}) + \lambda\psi_b(\mathbf{r})}{(1 + 2\lambda S_{ab} + \lambda^2)^{\frac{1}{2}}}$$

[1] E. T. Copson, *Proc. Cambridge Phil. Soc.*, **37**, 102 (1941).

whence

$$\chi(p) = \frac{e^{-i\mathbf{p}\cdot\mathbf{r}_a}\chi_a(p) + \lambda e^{-i\mathbf{p}\cdot\mathbf{r}_b}\chi_b(p)}{(1 + 2\lambda S_{ab} + \lambda^2)^{\frac{1}{2}}}$$

Multiplying this function by its complex conjugate, we find for the momentum density function the expression

$$|\chi(\mathbf{p})|^2 = \frac{|\chi_a(\mathbf{p})|^2 + 2\lambda|\chi_a(\mathbf{p})||\chi_b(\mathbf{p})|\cos(\mathbf{p}\cdot\mathbf{R} + \phi) + \lambda^2|\chi_b(\mathbf{p})|^2}{1 + 2\lambda S_{ab} + \lambda^2}$$

with $\phi = \arg[\chi_a(\mathbf{p})/\chi_b(\mathbf{p})]$, from which may be derived the quantities which are of physical interest.

Electron-pair Method.   In the second of the two approximate methods we group the electrons in pairs having opposite spins.   Pairing together the electrons 1 and 2, 3 and 4, . . . , $n - 1$ and n, then[1] apart from the spin factor, we may write

$$\Psi(\mathbf{r}_1,\mathbf{r}_2, \ldots ,\mathbf{r}_n) = \psi_{1,2}(\mathbf{r}_1,\mathbf{r}_2) \cdots \psi_{n-1,n}(\mathbf{r}_{n-1},\mathbf{r}_n) \tag{136}$$

If the electrons 1 and 2 belong to inner shells, then

$$\psi_{1,2}(\mathbf{r}_1,\mathbf{r}_2) = \psi(\mathbf{r}_1)\psi(\mathbf{r}_2) \tag{137}$$

where $\psi(\mathbf{r})$ is an atomic orbital, but if they are outer valence electrons paired into bonds of the Heitler-London type between the nuclei A and B, we must write[2]

$$\psi_{1,2}(\mathbf{r}_1,\mathbf{r}_2) = \frac{\psi_a(\mathbf{r}_1)\psi_b(\mathbf{r}_2) + \psi_a(\mathbf{r}_2)\psi_b(\mathbf{r}_1)}{[2(1 + S_{ab}^2)]^{\frac{1}{2}}} \tag{138}$$

ψ_a and ψ_b being atomic orbitals round the nuclei A and B and S_{ab} the overlap integral (133a).   In this approximation, exchange between electrons which are not paired is neglected, but this effect, though important, is not so important as the exchange between electrons of the same bond.

From equation (134) it follows that the momentum wave function corresponding to (138) is

$$\chi_{1,2} = \frac{e^{-i(\mathbf{p}_1\cdot\mathbf{r}_a+\mathbf{p}_2\cdot\mathbf{r}_b)}\chi_a(\mathbf{p}_1)\chi_b(\mathbf{p}_2) + e^{-i(\mathbf{p}_1\cdot\mathbf{r}_b+\mathbf{p}_2\cdot\mathbf{r}_a)}\chi_a(\mathbf{p}_2)\chi_b(\mathbf{p}_1)}{[2(1 + S_{ab}^2)]^{\frac{1}{2}}}$$

so that the momentum density is

$$|\chi_{1,2}(\mathbf{p}_1,\mathbf{p}_2)|^2 = \frac{1}{2(1 + S_{ab}^2)} \{|\chi_a(\mathbf{p}_1)|^2|\chi_b(\mathbf{p}_2)|^2$$
$$+ |\chi_a(\mathbf{p}_2)|^2|\chi_b(\mathbf{p}_1)|^2 2|\chi_a(\mathbf{p}_1)\chi_b(\mathbf{p}_1)\chi_a(\mathbf{p}_2)\chi_b(\mathbf{p}_2)| \cos[(\mathbf{p}_1 - \mathbf{p}_2)\cdot\mathbf{R} + \phi]\}$$

[1] Here it is assumed that, as in the case of all simple molecules, n is an even number. If n is odd, we have to multiply the expression (136) by the molecular orbital of the extra electron.

[2] "Wave Mechanics," p. 176.

where $\phi = \arg [\chi_a(\mathbf{p}_1)/\chi_b(\mathbf{p}_1)] - \arg [\chi_a(\mathbf{p}_2)/\chi_b(\mathbf{p}_2)]$. If the two nuclei are identical, this expression reduces to

$$|\chi_{1,2}(\mathbf{p}_1,\mathbf{p}_2)|^2 = \frac{1 + \cos [\mathbf{R} \cdot (\mathbf{p}_1 - \mathbf{p}_2)]}{1 + S_{ab}^2} |\chi_a(\mathbf{p}_1)|^2 |\chi_a(\mathbf{p}_2)|^2 \qquad (139)$$

The diffraction factor

$$\frac{1 + \cos \mathbf{R} \cdot (\mathbf{p}_1 - \mathbf{p}_2)}{1 + S_{ab}^2}$$

which multiplies the atomic function $|\chi_a(\mathbf{p}_1)|^2 |\chi_a(\mathbf{p}_2)|^2$, is similar to, but not identical with, that found in the molecular orbital case.

For example, for the hydrogen molecule we may make use of the Wang wave function $\psi_a(\mathbf{r}) = (\alpha^3/\pi)^{\frac{1}{2}} e^{-\alpha r}$, with $\alpha = 1.1166$. It follows at once from equation (139) and the results of Sec. 41.3, Ground State of Atoms from Lithium to Neon, that

$$|\chi(\mathbf{p}_1,\mathbf{p}_2)|^2 = \frac{64\alpha^{10}}{\pi^4(1 + S^2)} \frac{1 + \cos [(\mathbf{p}_1 - \mathbf{p}_2) \cdot (\mathbf{r}_a - \mathbf{r}_b)]}{(p_1^2 + \alpha^2)^4 (p_2^2 + \alpha^2)^4} \qquad (140)$$

Both the methods outlined above have been applied to the determination of the distribution of momentum in more complex molecules by Coulson and Duncanson in a series of papers[1] to which the reader is referred for details.

42. Binding Energies of the Lightest Nuclei

Calculations in the theory of nuclear forces differ from the usual quantum-mechanical calculations in that the precise form of $V(\mathbf{r}_1,\mathbf{r}_2)$, the interaction potential between two fundamental nuclear particles, is unknown. The values of the binding energies of the nuclei are known as a result of experiment for certain states of nuclei. The theoretical problem is that of determining from these values information about the nature of $V(\mathbf{r}_1,\mathbf{r}_2)$. The fact that nuclear forces are of short range renders invalid the kind of approximation which is used extensively in atomic physics. In this section we shall show how the theory of Fourier integrals may be employed to overcome this latter difficulty.

In Sec. 41.1 we noted that by multiplying both sides of equation (107) by $(2\pi)^{-3n/2} e^{-i(\mathbf{p}_1 \cdot \mathbf{r}_1 + \cdots + \mathbf{p}_n \cdot \mathbf{r}_n)}$ and integrating from $-\infty$ to ∞ over all $3n$ of the variables $x_1, y_1, z_1, \ldots, x_n, y_n, z_n$ we should obtain an integral equation for the determination of the momentum wave function $\chi(\mathbf{p}_1, \mathbf{p}_2, \ldots, \mathbf{p}_n)$. The solution of this integral equation would enable us to determine the spatial wave function $\Psi(\mathbf{r}_1, \mathbf{r}_2, \ldots, \mathbf{r}_n)$ by a series of

---

[1] Coulson, *op. cit.*, pp. 55, 74; W. E. Duncanson, *Proc. Cambridge Phil. Soc.*, **37**, 397 (1941); C. A. Coulson and W. E. Duncanson, *ibid.*, **37**, 67, 406 (1941), **38**, 100 (1942).

integrations.   This method of transforming the eigenvalue problem to momentum space has been used by Svartholm[1] to investigate eigenvalue problems in the theory of nuclear forces.   In addition Svartholm developed a special method of calculation (Sec. 42.3) which is particularly suited to the calculation of binding energies when the forces are of short range.

42.1 One-body problem in momentum space.   Before considering the many-body problems which are of interest in nuclear theory we shall outline the method for the case of one-body problems.   If we take as our unit of mass the mass of the nuclear particle concerned, then the Schrödinger equation may be written in the form (102).   Multiplying both sides of this equation by $e^{-i(\mathbf{p \cdot r})}$ and integrating throughout all space, we find, on assuming that $\psi \to 0$ as $r \to \infty$, that

$$\int_{-\infty}^{\infty} \int_{-\infty}^{\infty} \int_{-\infty}^{\infty} \nabla^2 \psi(\mathbf{r}) e^{-i\mathbf{p \cdot r}} \, d\mathbf{r} = -\mathbf{p}^2 \chi(\mathbf{p}) = -(\xi^2 + \eta^2 + \zeta^2)\chi(\mathbf{p})$$

where $\mathbf{p} = (\xi, \eta, \zeta)$ and $\chi(\mathbf{p})$ is defined by equation (103).

If $v(\xi, \eta, \zeta)$ is the Fourier transform of the potential $V(x, y, z)$, then, by the Faltung theorem (112), Chap. 1, we have

$$\int_{-\infty}^{\infty} \int_{-\infty}^{\infty} \int_{-\infty}^{\infty} V(\mathbf{r})\psi(\mathbf{r}) e^{-i\mathbf{p \cdot r}} \, d\mathbf{r} = \int_{-\infty}^{\infty} \int_{-\infty}^{\infty} \int_{-\infty}^{\infty} v(\mathbf{p} - \mathbf{p'})\chi(\mathbf{p'})d\mathbf{p'}$$

Hence the Schrödinger equation (102) is equivalent to

$$\left(\frac{1}{2}\mathbf{p}^2 - W\right)\chi(\mathbf{p}) + \left(\frac{1}{2\pi}\right)^{\frac{3}{2}} \int_{-\infty}^{\infty} \int_{-\infty}^{\infty} \int_{-\infty}^{\infty} v(\mathbf{p} - \mathbf{p'})\chi(\mathbf{p'})d\mathbf{p'} = 0 \quad (141)$$

Since we are interested in the calculation of binding energies, we may assume that W is negative and write

$$\phi(\mathbf{p}) = (\mathbf{p}^2 - 2W)^{\frac{1}{2}}\chi(\mathbf{p}), \qquad K(\mathbf{p},\mathbf{p'}) = \frac{-v(p - p')}{\pi[2\pi(p^2 - 2W)(p'^2 - 2W)]^{\frac{1}{2}}}$$

to transform equation (141) to the linear homogeneous form

$$\phi(\mathbf{p}) = \int_{-\infty}^{\infty} \int_{-\infty}^{\infty} \int_{-\infty}^{\infty} K(\mathbf{p},\mathbf{p'})\phi(\mathbf{p'})d\mathbf{p'} \quad (142)$$

in which the kernel corresponds to the nuclear interaction.

It will be observed that in the case of one-dimensional problems equation (141) reduces simply to

$$\left[\left(\frac{1}{2}p^2 - W\right)\right]\chi(p) + \frac{1}{\sqrt{2\pi}} \int_{-\infty}^{\infty} v(\mathbf{p} - \mathbf{p'})\chi(\mathbf{p'})d\mathbf{p'} = 0 \quad (143)$$

---

[1] N. Svartholm, "The Binding Energies of the Lightest Atomic Nuclei" (thesis, Lund, 1945); see also *Arkiv. Mat. Astron. Fysik*, **35A**, Nos. 7 and 8 (1947).

In Sec. 42.3 we shall consider approximate methods of solution of equations of this type.   It is possible, in certain simple cases, to obtain exact solutions of equation (143), and we shall consider one such case[1] before proceeding to the consideration of approximate methods.   Suppose

$$V(x) = V_0 e^{-a|x|}$$

Then its Fourier transform is

$$v(p) = \left(\frac{2}{\pi}\right)^{\frac{1}{2}} \frac{V_0 a}{a^2 + p^2}$$

so that we may write equation (143) in the form

$$(p^2 + p_0^2)\chi(p) = \frac{\lambda}{\pi} \int_{-\infty}^{\infty} \frac{a^3 \chi(p')dp'}{a^2 + (p - p')^2} \tag{144}$$

where $p_0^2 = -2W$, $\lambda = -2V_0/a^2$.

As a solution of the integral equation (144) we assume a power series of the form

$$\chi(p) = \sum_{m=0}^{\infty} \frac{\alpha_m p}{p^2 + (am + p_0)^2} \tag{145}$$

Substituting from (145) into (144) and making use of the integral

$$\frac{a^3}{\pi} \int_{-\infty}^{\infty} \frac{p'\,dp'}{[a^2 + (\mathbf{p} - \mathbf{p'})^2]^2(\mathbf{p'}^2 + \nu^2)} = \frac{a^2 p}{p^2 + (a + \nu)^2}$$

we obtain the relation

$$\sum_{m=0}^{\infty} p\alpha_m \left[1 - \frac{am(am + 2p_0)}{p^2 + (am + p_0)^2} \right] = \lambda a^2 \sum_{m=1}^{\infty} \alpha_{m-1} \frac{p}{p^2 + (am + p_0)^2}$$

Each side of this equation represents exactly the same function if the coefficients α_m satisfy the relations

$$m\alpha_m \left(\frac{m + 2p_0}{a}\right) + \lambda\alpha_{m-1} = 0, \qquad \sum_{m=0}^{\infty} \alpha_m = 0$$

Solving the former of these equations for α_m in terms of α_0, which is assumed to be nonzero, and substituting in the second equation, we obtain the relation

$$\alpha_0 \left[1 + \sum_{m=1}^{\infty} \frac{(-\lambda)^m}{m!} \frac{1}{(1 + 2p_0/a)(2 + 2p_0/a) \cdots (m + 2p_0/a)} \right] = 0$$

[1] L. H. Thomas, *Phys. Rev.*, **51**, 202 (1937).

From the definition of the nth-order Bessel function of the first kind, $J_n(z)$, we see that this equation may be put in the form

$$\lambda^{-p_0/a} J_{2p_0/a}(2\lambda^{\frac{1}{2}}) = 0 \tag{146}$$

In atomic problems of this kind it is assumed that V_0 and a are prescribed and that it is our object to find the possible values of the energy W of the system. Knowing the values of λ and a in equation (146), we can determine p_0, and hence W, from tables of the zeros of Bessel functions. The wave function $\chi(p)$ is then found, apart from the normalizing constant α_0, from equation (145). In nuclear theory, on the other hand, the law of force is not known accurately, and it is more usual to assume that W is known and that we wish to determine a relation between V_0 and a. As an example of this latter type of problem, let us assume that $W = 0$. Equation (146) then reduces to the simpler form

$$J_0(2\lambda^{\frac{1}{2}}) = 0$$

From tables of the zeros of Bessel functions we find $\lambda = 1.44580$, leading to the relation

$$V_0 = -0.72290a^2$$

between the constants V_0 and a.

42.2 Reduction of a two-body problem to a one-body problem. It is well known[1] that, if the potential energy of two particles whose position vectors are $\mathbf{r}_1$ and $\mathbf{r}_2$ is of the form $V(\mathbf{r}_1 - \mathbf{r}_2)$, then the problem of solving the Schrödinger equation for two particles can be reduced to that of solving an equivalent one-body problem. We shall now show how this reduction may be effected when the eigenvalue problem is formulated in momentum space.

If V is of the form $V(\mathbf{r}_1 - \mathbf{r}_2)$ and if the particles are of the same mass (chosen to be the unit of mass), then, by analogy with equation (107), the Schrödinger equation for the system may be written in the form

$$[V(\mathbf{r}_1 - \mathbf{r}_2) - \tfrac{1}{2}(\nabla_1^2 + \nabla_2^2)]\psi(\mathbf{r}_1,\mathbf{r}_2) = W\psi(\mathbf{r}_1,\mathbf{r}_2)$$

If we now introduce the Fourier transform

$$\chi(\mathbf{p}_1,\mathbf{p}_2) = \left(\frac{1}{\sqrt{2\pi}}\int_{-\infty}^{\infty}\right)^6 \psi(\mathbf{r}_1,\mathbf{r}_2)e^{-i(\mathbf{p}_1\cdot\mathbf{r}_1+\mathbf{p}_2\cdot\mathbf{r}_2)}\, d\mathbf{r}_1\, d\mathbf{r}_2$$

we see that this equation is equivalent to

$$[\tfrac{1}{2}(p_1^2 + p_2^2) - W]\chi(\mathbf{p}_1,\mathbf{p}_2) + I(\mathbf{p}_1,\mathbf{p}_2) = 0 \tag{147}$$

[1] "Wave Mechanics," p. 102.

where

$$I(\mathbf{p}_1, \mathbf{p}_2) = \left(\frac{1}{\sqrt{2\pi}} \int_{-\infty}^{\infty}\right)^6 V(\mathbf{r}_1 - \mathbf{r}_2)e^{-i(\mathbf{p}_1 \cdot \mathbf{r}_1 + \mathbf{p}_2 \cdot \mathbf{r}_2)}\, d\mathbf{r}_1\, d\mathbf{r}_2$$

Now the Fourier transform of $V(\mathbf{r}_1 - \mathbf{r}_2)$ is

$$I(\mathbf{p}_1, \mathbf{p}_2) = \left(\frac{1}{\sqrt{2\pi}} \int_{-\infty}^{\infty}\right)^6 V(\mathbf{r}_1 - \mathbf{r}_2)e^{-i(\mathbf{p}_1 \cdot \mathbf{r}_1 + \mathbf{p}_2 \cdot \mathbf{r}_2)}\, d\mathbf{r}_1\, d\mathbf{r}_2$$

Let $\mathbf{r} = \mathbf{r}_1 - \mathbf{r}_2$, $\mathbf{R} = \frac{1}{2}(\mathbf{r}_1 + \mathbf{r}_2)$; then

$$
\begin{aligned}
&v(\mathbf{p}_1, \mathbf{p}_2) \\
&= \left(\frac{1}{2\pi}\right)^{\frac{3}{2}} \int_{-\infty}^{\infty} \int_{-\infty}^{\infty} \int_{-\infty}^{\infty} e^{-i(\mathbf{p}_1 + \mathbf{p}_2) \cdot \mathbf{R}}\, d\mathbf{R} \left(\frac{1}{2\pi}\right)^{\frac{3}{2}} \int_{-\infty}^{\infty} \int_{-\infty}^{\infty} \int_{-\infty}^{\infty} e^{-\frac{1}{2}i(\mathbf{p}_1 - \mathbf{p}_2) \cdot \mathbf{r}} \\
&\qquad\qquad\qquad \times V(\mathbf{r})d\mathbf{r} = (2\pi)^{\frac{3}{2}}\, \delta(\mathbf{p}_1 + \mathbf{p}_2)\, v[\tfrac{1}{2}(\mathbf{p}_1 - \mathbf{p}_2)]
\end{aligned}
$$

where

$$v(\mathbf{p}) = \left(\frac{1}{2\pi}\right)^{\frac{3}{2}} \int_{-\infty}^{\infty} \int_{-\infty}^{\infty} \int_{-\infty}^{\infty} V(\mathbf{r})e^{-i\mathbf{p}\cdot\mathbf{r}}\, d\mathbf{r}$$

Thus

$$v(\mathbf{p}_1 - \mathbf{p}_1', \mathbf{p}_2 - \mathbf{p}_2') = (2\pi)^{\frac{3}{2}}\, \delta(\mathbf{p}_1 + \mathbf{p}_2 - \mathbf{p}_1' - \mathbf{p}_2')\, v[\tfrac{1}{2}(\mathbf{p}_1 - \mathbf{p}_2 - \mathbf{p}_1' + \mathbf{p}_2')]$$

Now, by the Faltung theorem (112), Chap. 1,

$$
\begin{aligned}
I(\mathbf{p}_1, \mathbf{p}_2) &= \left(\frac{1}{\sqrt{2\pi}} \int_{-\infty}^{\infty}\right)^6 \chi(\mathbf{p}_1', \mathbf{p}_2')v(\mathbf{p}_1 - \mathbf{p}_1', \mathbf{p}_2 - \mathbf{p}_2')d\mathbf{p}_1'\, d\mathbf{p}_2' \\
&= \left(\frac{1}{2\pi}\right)^{\frac{3}{2}}\left(\int_{-\infty}^{\infty}\right)^6 \delta(\mathbf{p}_1 + \mathbf{p}_2 - \mathbf{p}_1' - \mathbf{p}_2')\, v\left[\frac{1}{2}(\mathbf{p}_1 - \mathbf{p}_2 - \mathbf{p}_1' + \mathbf{p}_2')\right] \\
&\qquad\qquad\qquad\qquad\qquad\qquad \times \chi(\mathbf{p}_1', \mathbf{p}_2')\, d\mathbf{p}_1'\, d\mathbf{p}_2'
\end{aligned}
$$

Performing the integration over $\mathbf{p}_2'$, we find that

$$I(\mathbf{p}_1, \mathbf{p}_2) = \left(\frac{1}{2\pi}\right)^{\frac{3}{2}} \int_{-\infty}^{\infty} \int_{-\infty}^{\infty} \int_{-\infty}^{\infty} v(\mathbf{p}_1 - \mathbf{p}_1')\chi(\mathbf{p}_1', \mathbf{p}_1 + \mathbf{p}_2 - \mathbf{p}_1')d\mathbf{p}_1'$$

so that the Schrödinger equation (147) is equivalent to

$$\left[\frac{1}{2}(\mathbf{p}_1^2 + \mathbf{p}_2^2) - W\right]\chi(\mathbf{p}_1, \mathbf{p}_2) + \left(\frac{1}{2\pi}\right)^{\frac{3}{2}} \int_{-\infty}^{\infty} \int_{-\infty}^{\infty} \int_{-\infty}^{\infty} \chi(\mathbf{p}_1', \mathbf{p}_1 + \mathbf{p}_2 - \mathbf{p}_1')$$
$$\times v(\mathbf{p}_1 - \mathbf{p}_1')d\mathbf{p}_1' = 0$$

If we now let $\chi(\mathbf{p}_1, \mathbf{p}_2) = \delta(\mathbf{p}_1 + \mathbf{p}_2)\, \chi(\mathbf{p}_1)$, then, using the relations $(p_1^2 + p_2^2)\, \delta(\mathbf{p}_1 + \mathbf{p}_2) = 2p_1^2\, \delta(\mathbf{p}_1 + \mathbf{p}_2)$ and

$$\chi(\mathbf{p}_1', \mathbf{p}_1 + \mathbf{p}_2 - \mathbf{p}_1') = \delta(\mathbf{p}_1 + \mathbf{p}_2)\, \chi(\mathbf{p}_1')$$

we find that

$$(p_1^2 - W)\chi(\mathbf{p}_1) + \left(\frac{1}{2\pi}\right)^{\frac{3}{2}} \int_{-\infty}^{\infty} \int_{-\infty}^{\infty} \int_{-\infty}^{\infty} v(\mathbf{p}_1 - \mathbf{p}_1')\chi(\mathbf{p}_1')d\mathbf{p}_1' = 0 \quad (148)$$

The solutions of this integral equation are quite different in the two cases $W > 0$ and $W < 0$. In the latter case, but not in the former, the equation (148) may be symmetrized to the form (142) by dropping the subscript 1 and making the substitutions

$$\phi(p) = (\mathbf{p}^2 - W)^{\frac{1}{2}}\chi(\mathbf{p}), \qquad K(\mathbf{p},\mathbf{p}') = \frac{-v(\mathbf{p} - \mathbf{p}')}{(2\pi)^{\frac{3}{2}}[(\mathbf{p}^2 - W)(\mathbf{p}'^2 - W)]^{\frac{1}{2}}}$$

42.3 Variation-iteration method of Svartholm. Integral equations of the type (148) are not readily solved for the forms of function $v(\mathbf{p}_1 - \mathbf{p}_1')$ which occur in nuclear physics. Exact solutions are in fact known in only very few cases so that recourse must be had to approximate methods. To this end Svartholm has devised an approximate method of solution based on two well-known methods of the theory of integral equations, *viz.*, the Gauss-Hilbert variational principle and the method of iterated functions due to Kellogg.

It is easily seen that integral equations of the type (148) for problems in which the potential V depends linearly on a parameter λ can be written in the form

$$T(p)\chi(p) = \lambda \int S(p,p')\chi(p')dp' \tag{149}$$

where p denotes the three-dimensional momentum space and $T(p)$ is a positive function. The kernel $S(p,p') = S^*(p',p)$ is assumed to be *positive definite*, that is,

$$X_f \equiv \iint f^*(p)S(p,p')f(p')dp\,dp' \geq 0 \tag{150}$$

for all functions $f(p)$. Similarly, since $T(p)$ is a positive function

$$T_f \equiv \int f^*(p)T(p)f(p)dp \geq 0 \tag{151}$$

Starting from an arbitrary function $\chi_0(p)$, we may construct a set of functions $\chi_1, \chi_2, \ldots$ by means of the formula

$$\chi_{r+1}(p) = \frac{1}{T(p)} \int S(p,p')\chi_r(p')dp' \tag{152}$$

and from these functions we may calculate the two sets of integrals

$$T_r = \int \chi_r^*(p)T(p)\chi_r(p)dp, \qquad X_r = \iint \chi_r^*(p)S(p,p')\chi_r(p')dp\,dp' \tag{153}$$

with $r = 0,1,2, \ldots$, it being assumed that the initial choice of $\chi_0(p)$ is such that these integrals exist.

If we let $f(p) = \alpha\chi_r(p) + \beta\chi_{r+1}(p)$ in equations (150) and (151) and assume that α and β are real, we find

$$\alpha^2 T_r + 2\alpha\beta X_r + \beta^2 T_{r+1} \geq 0, \qquad \alpha^2 X_r + 2\alpha\beta T_{r+1} + \beta^2 X_{r+1} \geq 0$$

These results are valid for all values of α and β. Putting $\beta = 0$, we obtain the conditions $T_r \geq 0$, $X_r \geq 0$. Furthermore the condition that these quadratic forms should be positive definite is that $T_r T_{r+1} \geq X_r^2$ and $X_r X_{r+1} \geq T_{r+1}^2$. Introducing the ratios

$$\lambda_r = \frac{T_r}{X_r}, \qquad \lambda_{r+\frac{1}{2}} = \frac{X_r}{T_{r+1}} \tag{154}$$

we may write the above inequalities in the form

$$\lambda_r \geq \lambda_{r+\frac{1}{2}} \geq \lambda_{r+1} \tag{155}$$

Now the variational principle states that the lowest eigenvalue λ is a lower bound of the ratio $\lambda_f = T_f/X_f$ for arbitrary functions f. Especially with $f(p) = \chi_r(p)$ we have $\lambda_r \geq \lambda$. Hence the numbers λ_0, $\lambda_{\frac{1}{2}}$, λ_1, . . . form a monotonic decreasing sequence no member of which is less than the lowest eigenvalue λ. It can further be proved[1] that the limit $\bar{\lambda}$ of this sequence is an eigenvalue of (149) and is equal to the lowest eigenvalue λ in the case in which $\chi_0(p)$ satisfies the condition

$$\int \chi_0^*(p) T(p) \chi(p) dp \neq 0$$

where $\chi(p)$ is the exact eigenfunction corresponding to the lowest eigenvalue λ. Under these circumstances the sequence of functions $\chi_r(p) T_r^{-\frac{1}{2}}$ converges uniformly to $\chi(p)$.

We assume usually that the initial function $\chi_0(p)$ is a simple analytical function of the variables p, containing a parameter, b, say. This enables us to calculate λ_0 as a function of b. We then choose b to be such that λ_0 is a minimum with respect to it, *i.e.*, such that

$$\frac{\partial \lambda_0}{\partial b} = 0 \tag{156}$$

This value of b is retained in the ensuing calculations of $\lambda_{\frac{1}{2}}$, λ_1, ... The calculation of λ_0 in this way is equivalent to the ordinary variational method of atomic theory. The improvements effected by the calculation of $\lambda_{\frac{1}{2}}$, λ_1, . . . are substantial, especially in the case of the short-range potentials of nuclear theory, for which the variational method yields bad results.

To illustrate the use of the variation-iteration method,[2] we shall consider the problem solved exactly in Sec. 42.1. To solve equation (144), we take

$$\chi_0(p) = \frac{p}{(p^2 + b^2)(p^2 + p_0^2)}$$

[1] O. D. Kellogg, *Math. Ann.*, **86**, 14 (1922); L. Collatz, *Math. Z.*, **46**, 692 (1940); Thomas, *op. cit.*, **51**, 202 (1937).

[2] Hereafter referred to simply as the V-I method.

Calculating the integrals T_0 and X_0 with this form of $\chi_0(p)$, we find

$$\lambda_0(b) = \frac{T_0}{X_0} = \frac{(a + b + p_0)(a + 2b)(a + 2p_0)}{4a^2b}$$

The condition (156) then leads to the relation $b^2 = \frac{1}{2}a(a + p_0)$ so that

$$\lambda_0 = \frac{1}{4}\left(1 + \frac{2p_0}{a}\right)\left[1 + 2^{\frac{1}{2}}\left(1 + \frac{p_0}{a}\right)^{\frac{1}{2}}\right]^2 \tag{157}$$

We now construct the function $\chi_1(p)$ and determine the ratios $\lambda_{\frac{1}{2}}$ and λ_1. To take a numerical example, we shall suppose $p_0 = 0$. Then equation (157) becomes $\lambda_0 = (a + b)(a + 2b)/4ab$, and it is readily shown that

$$\lambda_{\frac{1}{2}} = \frac{4(a + b)^2(2a + b)}{(a + 2b)(5a^2 + 5ab + b^2)}$$

and

$$\lambda_1 = \frac{3(3a + b)(3a + 2b)(5a^2 + 5ab + b^2)}{2(a + b)(2a + b)(23a^2 + 13ab + 2b^2)}$$

Putting $b = 2^{-\frac{1}{2}}a$ in order that equation (156) may be satisfied, we find $\lambda_0 = 1.457$, $\lambda_{\frac{1}{2}} = 1.4466$, $\lambda_1 = 1.44587$, showing that the monotonic decreasing sequence (λ_n) is converging rapidly to the limit $\lambda = 1.44580$ obtained from the exact solution. It will be observed that, in this instance, λ_0 is out by less than 1 per cent and λ_1 by less than one-hundredth of 1 per cent.

42.4 Ground state of the deuteron. The determination of the energy levels of the deuteron, which consists of two elementary nuclear particles ("nucleons"), is a problem of fundamental importance in theoretical nuclear physics. By the very simplicity of its structure, the deuteron is destined to play, in nuclear physics, a role similar to that assumed by the hydrogen atom in atomic physics. The experimental discovery of an electric quadrupole moment of the deuteron suggests that a not inconsiderable contribution is made to the binding energy by an angle-dependent interaction, of the dipole-dipole type, but as a preparatory study it seems adequate to consider only central forces. We shall consider two short-range potentials—the error-function potential and the Yukawa potential.

Error-function Potential. If the range of the nuclear forces is a, we may take as the potential $V(r) = -V_0 e^{r^2/a^2}$ so that

$$v(p) = -V_0(a^2/2)^{\frac{3}{2}}e^{-\frac{1}{4}a^2p^2}$$

and equation (148) takes the form

$$(\mathbf{p}^2 + \mathbf{p}_0^2)\chi(\mathbf{p}) + \frac{\lambda a}{(4\pi)^{\frac{3}{2}}}\int_{-\infty}^{\infty}\int_{-\infty}^{\infty}\int_{-\infty}^{\infty}e^{-\frac{1}{4}a^2(\mathbf{p}-\mathbf{p}')^2}\chi(\mathbf{p}')d\mathbf{p}' = 0$$

where $p_0^2 = -W > 0$ and $\lambda = V_0a^2$.

As the initial function in the Svartholm V-I method we take

$$\chi_0(\mathbf{p}) = e^{-\frac{1}{2}b^2\mathbf{p}^2}$$

From their definition, T and X are given by

$$T_0 = \int_{-\infty}^{\infty} \int_{-\infty}^{\infty} \int_{-\infty}^{\infty} (\mathbf{p}_0^2 + \mathbf{p}^2)e^{-\frac{1}{2}b^2\mathbf{p}^2}\, d\mathbf{p} = (2\pi)^{\frac{3}{2}}\left(\frac{p_0}{b^3} + \frac{3}{b^5}\right)$$

$$X_0 = \frac{a}{(4\pi)^{\frac{3}{2}}}\left(\int_{-\infty}^{\infty}\right)^6 e^{-\frac{1}{4}(\mathbf{p}-\mathbf{p}')^2 a^2 - \frac{1}{4}b^2(\mathbf{p}^2+\mathbf{p}'^2)}\, d\mathbf{p}\, d\mathbf{p}' = \frac{(4\pi)^{\frac{3}{2}}a}{b^3(2a^2+b^2)^{\frac{3}{2}}} \quad (158)$$

so that

$$\lambda_0 = \frac{T_0}{X_0} = \frac{1}{a}\left(p_0^2 + \frac{3}{b^2}\right)\left(a^2 + \frac{1}{2}b^2\right)^{\frac{3}{2}}$$

Using the condition (156), we see that b^2 should be chosen to be the positive root of the equation

$$b^4p_0^2 + b^2 - 4a^2 = 0$$

If we write $k = 2a^2/b^2$, we see that the relation between λ_0 and p_0 may be expressed by the freedom equations

$$a^2p_0^2 = k^2 - \tfrac{1}{2}k, \qquad \lambda_0 = k^{-\frac{3}{2}}(k+1)^{\frac{3}{2}} \quad (159)$$

For the calculation of $\lambda_{\frac{1}{2}}$ we must first determine the iterated function $\chi_1(\mathbf{p})$. It is

$$\chi_1(\mathbf{p}) = \frac{a}{(4\pi)^{\frac{3}{2}}(\mathbf{p}^2 + \mathbf{p}_0^2)}\int_{-\infty}^{\infty}\int_{-\infty}^{\infty}\int_{-\infty}^{\infty} e^{-\frac{1}{4}a^2(\mathbf{p}-\mathbf{p}')^2}\chi_0(\mathbf{p}')\, d\mathbf{p}'$$

$$= \frac{a}{(\mathbf{p}^2 + \mathbf{p}_0^2)(a^2+b^2)^{\frac{3}{2}}}\exp\left[\frac{-a^2b^2\mathbf{p}^2}{4(a^2+b^2)}\right]$$

It follows from the definition that

$$T_1 = \frac{a^2}{(a^2+b^2)^3}\int_{-\infty}^{\infty}\int_{-\infty}^{\infty}\int_{-\infty}^{\infty} \frac{1}{\mathbf{p}^2 + \mathbf{p}_0^2}\exp\left[-\frac{1}{2}\left(\frac{x}{p_0}\mathbf{p}\right)^2\right]d\mathbf{p}$$

where

$$x = \frac{abp_0}{a^2 + b^2} \quad (160)$$

To evaluate this integral, we write

$$\frac{1}{\mathbf{p}^2 + \mathbf{p}_0^2} = \int_0^{\infty} e^{-(\mathbf{p}^2 + \mathbf{p}_0^2)u}\, du$$

and interchange the order of integrations to obtain

$$T_1 = \frac{a^2}{(a^2 + b^2)^3} \int_0^\infty e^{-p_0{}^2 u}\, du \int_{-\infty}^\infty \int_{-\infty}^\infty \int_{-\infty}^\infty e^{-p^2 u - \frac{1}{2}x^2 p^2/p_0{}^2}\, d\mathbf{p}$$

$$= \frac{a^2 \pi^{\frac{3}{2}}}{(a^2 + b^2)^3} \int_0^\infty e^{-p_0{}^2 u} \left(u + \frac{x^2}{2p_0{}^2} \right)^{-\frac{3}{2}} du$$

If we introduce a function $F(x)$ defined by the equation

$$F(x) = e^{\frac{1}{2}x^2} \int_0^\infty e^{-\frac{1}{2}u^2}\, du \tag{161}$$

it follows immediately that

$$T_1 = \frac{(2\pi)^{\frac{3}{2}} p_0 a^2}{(a^2 + b^2)^3} \left[\frac{1}{x} - F(x) \right] \tag{162}$$

From the expressions (158) and (162) and the definition of $\lambda_{\frac{1}{2}}$ we find

$$\lambda_{\frac{1}{2}} = \frac{X_0}{T_1} = \frac{(a^2 + b^2)^3}{ab^3 p_0 (a^2 + \frac{1}{2}b^2)^{\frac{3}{2}}} \left[\frac{1}{x} - F(x) \right]^{-1} \tag{163}$$

a relation which may be expressed in the parametric form

$$a^2 p_0{}^2 = k^2 - \frac{1}{2}k, \qquad \lambda = \frac{(k+2)^3}{2k^{\frac{1}{2}}(k+1)^{\frac{3}{2}}(2k-1)^{\frac{1}{2}}} \left[\frac{1}{x} - F(x) \right]^{-1} \tag{164}$$

with $x^2 = k(2k - 1)/(k + 2)$.

The variation with a of λ_0 and $\lambda_{\frac{1}{2}}$ as given by equations (159) and (164) is shown in Fig. 74, the value of p_0 being chosen to correspond to a bind-ing energy of 2.18 Mev, which is the experimental value for the deuteron.[1]

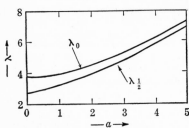

FIG. 74.   The variation with the range a (in 10^{-13} cm) of the approximations λ_0 and $\lambda_{\frac{1}{2}}$ to the force constant λ for the deuteron.

In a similar way we may calculate the integral X_1 and hence the ratio $\lambda_1 = T_1/X_1$. For details of the cal-culation the reader is referred to Svartholm's thesis, where it is shown that the difference $\lambda_{\frac{1}{2}} - \lambda_1$ is very small compared with $\lambda_0 - \lambda_1$. For values of a between 0 and 4×10^{-13} cm it turns out that $\lambda_{\frac{1}{2}} - \lambda_1$ is approx-imately 0.2 per cent of the value of $\lambda_{\frac{1}{2}}$.

Yukawa Potential. We shall now consider the Yukawa potential $V(r) = -V_0 e^{-\kappa r}/\kappa r$, which arises in the meson theory of nuclear forces

---

[1] This is the value given by F. E. Myers and L. C. van Atta, *Phys. Rev.*, **61**, 19 (1942). For a comparison of this with other experimental values see H. A. Bethe, "Elementary Nuclear Theory" (Wiley, New York, 1947), p. 29.

and has been applied to the two-body problem by many authors.[1] This potential differs from the error-function potential, considered under Error-function Potential, in that it has a singularity at the origin.

The Fourier transform of this potential is

$$v(\mathbf{p}) = -\frac{V_0}{(2\pi)^{\frac{3}{2}}} \int_{-\infty}^{\infty} \int_{-\infty}^{\infty} \int_{-\infty}^{\infty} e^{-\kappa r - i(\mathbf{p}\cdot\mathbf{r})} \frac{dr}{\kappa r} = -\frac{V_0}{\kappa}\left(\frac{2}{\pi}\right)^{\frac{1}{2}} \frac{1}{\kappa^2 + \mathbf{p}^2}$$

If we substitute this value of $v(p)$ in equation (148) and put $p_0^2 = -W$, $\lambda = V_0/\kappa^2$, we see that it reduces to

$$(\mathbf{p}^2 + \mathbf{p}_0^2)\chi(\mathbf{p}) = \frac{\kappa\lambda}{2\pi^2} \int_{-\infty}^{\infty} \int_{-\infty}^{\infty} \int_{-\infty}^{\infty} \frac{\chi(\mathbf{p}')d\mathbf{p}'}{\kappa^2 + (\mathbf{p} - \mathbf{p}')^2} \tag{165}$$

As a first approximation we take

$$\chi_0(\mathbf{p}) = \frac{\beta}{\pi(\beta^2 + p^2)^2} \tag{166}$$

and, substituting this expression into the definitions of T_0 and X_0, we find, on evaluating the integrals by means of the calculus of residues, that

$$T_0 = \frac{p_0^2 + \beta^2}{8\beta^3}, \qquad X_0 = \frac{\kappa}{2(2\beta + \kappa)^2}$$

from which it follows that

$$\lambda_0 = \frac{(p_0^2 + \beta^2)(2\beta + \kappa)^2}{4\kappa\beta^3} \tag{167}$$

Minimizing λ_0 with respect to the parameter β, we find that β is determined by the equation

$$p_0^2 = \beta^2 \frac{2\beta - \kappa}{2\beta + 3\kappa} \tag{168}$$

The iterated function is readily shown to be

$$\chi_1(\mathbf{p}) = \frac{\kappa}{2\pi(p^2 + p_0^2)[p^2 + (\beta + \kappa)^2]}$$

by means of which the values of T_1, X_1 and hence those of $\lambda_{\frac{1}{2}}$ and λ_1 can be computed. $\chi_2(p)$ and T_2 can also be calculated, though the results are somewhat complicated. The integrations are given in Svartholm's thesis. The results of Svartholm's numerical calculations are shown in Table 2; these values show that for short-range forces (small values of p_0/κ) the iteration process improves the variational value λ_0 but that for long-range forces the variational value derived from equation (156) is a

[1] See, for instance, H. Frohlich, K. Huang, and I. N. Sneddon, *Proc. Roy. Soc. (London)*, **A191**, 61 (1947).

TABLE 2*

p_0/κ	0.0	0.25	0.5	1.0	1.5	2.0
λ_0	2.00	2.31	2.81	3.80	4.85	5.87
$\lambda_{\frac{1}{2}}$	1.6799	2.2335	2.7695	3.8168	4.8470	5.8684

* The values of $\lambda_{\frac{1}{2}}$ are in agreement with those computed by L. Hulthen, *Arkiv Mat. Astron. Fysik*, **28A**, No. 5 (1942), using a very accurate variational method.

very good approximation which is only slightly improved by using the iteration process.

Using the function

$$\chi_0(p) = \frac{1}{(p^2 + a^2)(p^2 + b^2)}$$

instead of the initial function (166), McWeeny[1] has shown that the corresponding variational value λ_0 is easily computed and is more accurate than the corresponding value derived by Svartholm. For instance, in the case $p_0/\kappa = 0.25$ the numerical value of λ_0 comes out to be 2.2333, which is in very good agreement with Hulthen's accurate value.

42.5 n-body problem in momentum space. We shall now generalize the results of the preceding sections to the case in which the nuclear system consists of n nucleons. In this way we are able to reduce the problem of determining the binding energies of nuclei to that of finding the eigenvalues of a certain integral equation. To this equation we may then apply the Svartholm V-I procedure.

The state of a system of n nuclear particles will be supposed to be governed by the Schrödinger equation (107), which is an equation in the $3n$ independent variables $x_1, y_1, z_1, \ldots, x_n, y_n, z_n$. It is usual, at least in first approximation, to assume that the potential function of such a system can be written in the form

$$V(\mathbf{r}_1, \ldots, \mathbf{r}_n) = \sum_{i<j} V_{ij}(\mathbf{r}_i - \mathbf{r}_j)$$

To find the $3n$-dimensional Fourier transform of such a function, we note that the Fourier transform of one of its constituent terms is

$$v_{ij}(\mathbf{p}_1, \ldots, \mathbf{p}_n) = \left(\frac{1}{\sqrt{2\pi}} \int_{-\infty}^{\infty}\right)^6 V_{ij}(\mathbf{r}_i - \mathbf{r}_j)e^{-i(\mathbf{p}_i \cdot \mathbf{r}_i + \mathbf{p}_j \cdot \mathbf{r}_j)} \, d\mathbf{r}_i \, d\mathbf{r}_j$$

$$\times \prod_{k \neq i,j} \left(\frac{1}{\sqrt{2\pi}} \int_{-\infty}^{\infty}\right) e^{-i(\mathbf{p}_k \cdot \mathbf{r}_k)} \, dr_k$$

The integrals occurring to the right of the product sign are simple Dirac delta functions, and the first factor is evaluated in the same way as

[1] R. McWeeny, *Proc. Cambridge Phil. Soc.*, **45**, 315 (1949).

$v(\mathbf{p}_1, \mathbf{p}_2)$ at the beginning of Sec. 42.2. In this way we obtain, for the $3n$-dimensional Fourier transform of the potential function $V(\mathbf{r}_1, \ldots, \mathbf{r}_n)$,

$$v(\mathbf{p}_1, \ldots, \mathbf{p}_n) = (2\pi)^{(3n-3)/2}\, \delta(\mathbf{p}_1)\delta(\mathbf{p}_2) \cdots \delta(\mathbf{p}_n)$$
$$\times \sum_{i<j} \frac{\delta(\mathbf{p}_i + \mathbf{p}_j)}{\delta(\mathbf{p}_i)\delta(\mathbf{p}_j)}\, v_{ij}\left(\frac{1}{2}\,\mathbf{p}_i - \frac{1}{2}\,\mathbf{p}_j\right) \quad (169)$$

where

$$v_{ij}(\mathbf{p}) = \left(\frac{1}{2\pi}\right)^{\frac{3}{2}} \int_{-\infty}^{\infty} \int_{-\infty}^{\infty} \int_{-\infty}^{\infty} v_{ij}(\mathbf{r})e^{-i\mathbf{p}\cdot\mathbf{r}}\, d\mathbf{r}$$

If, now, we multiply equation (107) by $e^{-i(\mathbf{p}_1\cdot\mathbf{r}_1 + \cdots + \mathbf{p}_n\cdot\mathbf{r}_n)}$ and integrate from $-\infty$ to ∞ over all $3n$ variables $x_1, \ldots, z_n$, we obtain the integral equation

$$[\tfrac{1}{2}(\mathbf{p}_1^2 + \mathbf{p}_2^2 + \cdots + \mathbf{p}_n^2) - W]\chi(\mathbf{p}_1, \mathbf{p}_2, \ldots, \mathbf{p}_n)$$
$$+ \left(\frac{1}{\sqrt{2\pi}} \int_{-\infty}^{\infty}\right)^{3n} \Psi(\mathbf{r}_1, \ldots, \mathbf{r}_n) V(\mathbf{r}_1, \ldots, \mathbf{r}_n)e^{-i(\mathbf{p}_1\cdot\mathbf{r}_1 + \cdots + \mathbf{p}_n\cdot\mathbf{r}_n)}$$
$$\times\, d\mathbf{r}_1 \cdots d\mathbf{r}_n = 0$$

governing the Fourier transform of the nuclear wave function. Making use of the Faltung theorem (112), Chap. 1, we see that the integral occurring in this equation may be written in the form

$$\left(\frac{1}{\sqrt{2\pi}} \int_{-\infty}^{\infty}\right)^{3n} \chi(\mathbf{p}_1', \mathbf{p}_2', \ldots, \mathbf{p}_n')v(\mathbf{p}_1 - \mathbf{p}_1', \ldots, \mathbf{p}_n - \mathbf{p}_n')d\mathbf{p}_1' \cdots d\mathbf{p}_n'$$

Substituting the value (169) for $v(\mathbf{p}_1, \ldots, \mathbf{p}_n)$ and performing the trivial integrations involving the δ functions, we find that the Schrödinger equation (107) is equivalent to the integral equation

$$\left(\frac{1}{2}\sum_{i=1}^{n} p_i^2 - W\right)\chi(\mathbf{p}_1, \mathbf{p}_2, \ldots, \mathbf{p}_n)$$

$$+ \left(\frac{1}{2\pi}\right)^{\frac{3}{2}} \sum_{i<j}^{n} \int_{-\infty}^{\infty} \int_{-\infty}^{\infty} \int_{-\infty}^{\infty} v_{ij}(\mathbf{p}_i - \mathbf{p}_i')$$
$$\times \chi(\mathbf{p}_1, \ldots, \mathbf{p}_i', \ldots, \mathbf{p}_j - \mathbf{p}_i' + \mathbf{p}_i \cdots \mathbf{p}_n)d\mathbf{p}_i' = 0 \quad (170)$$

If we now write

$$\chi(\mathbf{p}_1, \ldots, \mathbf{p}_n) = \delta(\mathbf{p}_1 + \mathbf{p}_2 + \cdots + \mathbf{p}_n)\chi(\mathbf{p}_1, \mathbf{p}_2, \ldots, \mathbf{p}_{n-1})$$

and make use of the identity

$$\left(\frac{1}{2}\sum_{i=1}^{n}\mathbf{p}_i^2\right)\delta(\mathbf{p}_1 + \mathbf{p}_2 + \cdots + \mathbf{p}_n)$$

$$= \left[\sum_{i=1}^{n-1}\mathbf{p}_i^2 + \sum_{i<j}^{n-1}(\mathbf{p}_i \cdot \mathbf{p}_j)\right]\delta(\mathbf{p}_1 + \cdots + \mathbf{p}_n)$$

we see that equation (170) may be written in the form

$$T(p_1, \ldots, p_{n-1})\chi(p_1, \ldots, p_{n-1})$$

$$+ \sum_{i<j}^{n-1}\int_{-\infty}^{\infty}\int_{-\infty}^{\infty}\int_{-\infty}^{\infty}v_{ij}(\mathbf{p}_i - \mathbf{p}_i')$$

$$\times \chi(\mathbf{p}_1, \ldots, \mathbf{p}_i', \ldots, \mathbf{p}_i + \mathbf{p}_j - \mathbf{p}_i', \ldots, \mathbf{p}_{n-1})d\mathbf{p}_i'$$

$$+ \sum_{i=1}^{n-1}\int_{-\infty}^{\infty}\int_{-\infty}^{\infty}\int_{-\infty}^{\infty}v_{in}(\mathbf{p}_i - \mathbf{p}_i')$$

$$\times \chi(\mathbf{p}_1, \ldots, \mathbf{p}_i', \ldots, \mathbf{p}_j, \ldots, \mathbf{p}_{n-1})d\mathbf{p}_i' = 0 \qquad (171)$$

where

$$T(p_1, \ldots, p_{n-1}) = (2\pi)^{\frac{3}{2}}\left[p_0^2 + \sum_{i=1}^{n-1}\mathbf{p}_i^2 + \sum_{i<j}^{n-1}(\mathbf{p}_i \cdot \mathbf{p}_j)\right] \qquad (172)$$

and $p_0^2 = -W$.

The method outlined in Sec. 42.3 for the calculation of the force constant in terms of the energy W of the ground state of the nucleus can be taken over step by step to the more complicated case (171). An initial function $\chi_0(p_1, \ldots, p_{n-1})$ is introduced in all terms containing integrals, while the iterated function has the coefficient $T(p)$ defined by equation (172). The definitions of T_j and X_j are the same as before—equation (153)—except that dp now means integration over all $3(n-1)$ of the momentum coordinates $(p_1, \ldots, p_{n-1})$.

The fact that in nuclear theory the forces depend on the spin coordinates $\mathfrak{d}_i$ of the nucleons does not affect the V-I scheme appreciably. Since in the n-body problem the spin-dependent part of the wave function cannot be separated off, we obtain in general a system of partial integral equations. Integration with respect to the momentum coordinates must then be accompanied by summation over the spin coordinates. Apart from this the method of calculation is the same as before.

The V-I method has been applied, in this way, by Svartholm to derive information about the ground state of the lightest atomic nuclei—H_3, He_3, He_4. For the details of these calculations the reader is referred to the papers by Svartholm cited above. The problem of calculating exactly the energy levels of a heavy nucleus is a much more formidable one. In the absence of exact theoretical predictions of the position of the energy levels, an estimate of the average spacing of the enormous number of levels possessed by a highly excited nucleus is obviously of great value. Such an estimate has been derived by Sneddon and Touschek[1] by applying the theory of Laplace transforms to Bethe's model of the nucleus, which assumes that, at high energies, the interaction of the nucleons is so weak that the nucleus can be treated as a gas.

42.6 Dirac's one-body problem in momentum representation. In Secs. 41 and 42 we have considered the solution of problems in quantum mechanics based on the nonrelativistic Schrödinger equation (102). If, however, we wish to fulfill the requirements of the special theory of relativity, we must take as our electron wave equations the Dirac equations[2]

$$\left(\frac{i}{c} \frac{\partial}{\partial t} - \frac{V}{c} - i\boldsymbol{\alpha} \cdot \text{grad} + \alpha_4 c \right) \Psi = 0$$

(in atomic units), where the quantities $(\alpha_1, \alpha_2, \alpha_3) = \boldsymbol{\alpha}$ and α_4 satisfy the relations $\alpha_\lambda \alpha_\mu + \alpha_\mu \alpha_\lambda = 2\delta_{\lambda\mu} (\lambda,\mu = 1,2,3,4)$. If we put $\Psi = \psi e^{-iWt}$, we have the equation

$$\left(\frac{W + \alpha_4 c^2 - V}{c} - i\boldsymbol{\alpha} \cdot \text{grad} \right) \psi = 0$$

The α's may be represented by 4×4 matrices; therefore ψ may be written as a column matrix

$$\psi = \begin{pmatrix} \psi_1 \\ \psi_2 \\ \psi_3 \\ \psi_4 \end{pmatrix} \equiv \{\psi_1, \psi_2, \psi_3, \psi_4\}$$

If we introduce the transforms

$$\chi_j(\xi,\eta,\zeta) = \left(\frac{1}{2\pi} \right)^{\frac{3}{2}} \int_{-\infty}^{\infty} \int_{-\infty}^{\infty} \int_{-\infty}^{\infty} \psi_j(\mathbf{r}) e^{-i\mathbf{p}\cdot\mathbf{r}} \, d\mathbf{r}$$

with $\mathbf{p} = (\xi,\eta,\zeta)$ and write χ for the column matrix $(\chi_1, \chi_2, \chi_3, \chi_4)$, it follows that χ satisfies the equations

$$[W + \alpha_4 c^2 + c(\boldsymbol{\alpha} \cdot \mathbf{p})]\chi = \left(\frac{1}{2\pi} \right)^{\frac{3}{2}} \int_{-\infty}^{\infty} \int_{-\infty}^{\infty} \int_{-\infty}^{\infty} v(\mathbf{p} - \mathbf{p}')\chi(\mathbf{p}')d\mathbf{p}' \quad (173)$$

where $v(\mathbf{p})$ is the Fourier transform of the potential $V(\mathbf{r})$.

This is a system of four linear integral equations for the determination of the four functions χ_j, for if we make use of the matrix expressions for

[1] I. N. Sneddon and B. F. Touschek, *Proc. Cambridge Phil. Soc.*, **44**, 391 (1948).
[2] "Wave Mechanics," p. 296.

the α's,† we find that equation (173) when written out in components has the form

$$
\begin{aligned}
(W + c^2)\chi_1 + c(p_1 - ip_2)\chi_4 + cp_3\chi_3 &= I_1(p) \\
(W + c^2)\chi_2 + c(p_1 + ip_2)\chi_3 + cp_3\chi_4 &= I_2(p) \\
(W - c^2)\chi_3 + c(p_1 - ip_2)\chi_2 + cp_3\chi_1 &= I_3(p) \\
(W - c^2)\chi_4 + c(p_1 + ip_2)\chi_1 + cp_3\chi_2 &= I_4(p)
\end{aligned}
\right\}
\quad (174)
$$

where

$$
I_j(p) = \left(\frac{1}{2\pi}\right)^{\frac{3}{2}} \int_{-\infty}^{\infty} \int_{-\infty}^{\infty} \int_{-\infty}^{\infty} v(\mathbf{p} - \mathbf{p}')\chi_j(\mathbf{p}')d\mathbf{p}' \quad (175)
$$

From Sec. 42.4, *Yukawa Potential*, we see that in the case of a hydrogen-like atom, for which $V(r) = -Z/r$, we have

$$
I_j(p) = -\frac{Z}{2\pi^2} \int_{-\infty}^{\infty} \int_{-\infty}^{\infty} \int_{-\infty}^{\infty} \frac{\chi_j(\mathbf{p}')d\mathbf{p}'}{(\mathbf{p} - \mathbf{p}')^2} \quad (176)
$$

The solution of the equations (174) for this case has been given by Rubinowicz.[1]   The method he employs is not one belonging to the theory of integral equations, but that of determining directly the Fourier transforms of the known spatial wave functions ψ_1, ψ_2, ψ_3, and ψ_4. For details of the integrations, which are similar to those of Sec. 41.2, the reader should consult Rubinowicz's paper.

This solution of Rubinowicz appears to be the only exact solution of the equations (174) so far derived, but it is possible to set up a V-I method, of the type discussed above, for the derivation of approximate solutions.

† See "Wave Mechanics," p. 299.
[1] A. Rubinowicz, *Phys. Rev.*, **73**, 1330 (1948).

CHAPTER 9

TWO-DIMENSIONAL STRESS SYSTEMS

43. Equations of Motion

43.1 Introduction. The problem of determining the state of stress in an elastic body under the action of given forces has been attacked, by reason of its many varied applications to engineering and physical problems, by most of the great applied mathematicians since the time of Euler. It was soon found that the problem was one of great difficulty, more so than is encountered, say, in the solution of boundary value problems in the mathematical theory of electricity or hydrodynamics, where the existence of a potential function greatly simplifies the analysis. The great general theorems which exist in these subjects arise from the fact that the differential equations of equilibrium and the boundary conditions can be expressed simply in terms of this function in the regions of space in which we are interested. No such general propositions exist in the mathematical theory of elasticity. Consequently the solutions of all but a few of the three-dimensional problems of elasticity have proved to be unattainable, at least in simple form. Problems of this type may, however, be simplified by reducing them to problems in two dimensions. The two-dimensional problems then solved can, of course, be subjected to experimental verification only in an imperfect fashion, but their solution provides us with a sufficiently good picture of the distribution of stress set up in the corresponding three-dimensional case to be of use in the design of structures. In this chapter we shall consider how the solution of certain of these two-dimensional problems may be obtained by the use of the theory of Fourier transforms.

43.2 Plane strain. It is found as a result of experiment that, when a very long cylinder of isotropic elastic material is strained as a result of the action of surface tractions or of body forces, acting normal to the axis of the cylinder, normal sections of the cylinder remain plane and the body retains its cylindrical form. Any distortion possessing these characteristics is termed a *plane strain*. Mathematically, we may describe a plane strain as one in which one of the Cartesian components of the displacement vector may be taken to be zero (with a suitable choice of axes). If we take the generators of the cylinder to be parallel to the z axis, then $u_z \equiv 0$ where $\mathbf{u} = (u_x, u_y, u_z)$ denotes the displacement at the point (x,y,z).

In plane strain for which $u_z \equiv 0$ we need consider only a section normal to the z axis. Figure 75 represents such a section of a body in equilibrium. The effect of body or surface forces will be to produce internal forces between the various parts of the body. If we consider the body to be divided into two parts by a plane, parallel to the z axis, which cuts

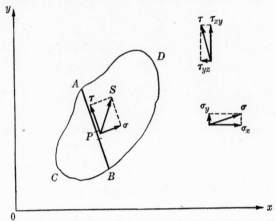

FIG. 75. Specification of stress in a two-dimensional medium.

the section in a line AB, then the part ACB will be in equilibrium under the action of the external forces and the internal forces distributed over AB. The magnitudes of these internal forces may be defined by their intensity (*i.e.*, the ratio of the force to the area over which it acts), and this intensity is called the *average stress*.

Suppose that the force acting on a small area ΔA situated at a point P of the dividing plane is $\Delta \mathbf{F}$; then the magnitude of the stress at the point P is

$$\lim_{A \to 0} \frac{\Delta \mathbf{F}}{\Delta A}$$

In general this resultant $\mathbf{S}$ is *not* normal to the area ΔA, and for that reason we resolve it into two components: σ normal to ΔA and τ in ΔA. These components may, in turn, be resolved along the x and y directions, as shown in Fig. 75. The components of σ are σ_x, σ_y, respectively, and we adopt the convention that the stress σ is taken to be positive when a tension is produced and negative when a compression occurs. The components of τ are similarly τ_{yx} and τ_{xy} though it is readily shown[1] that $\tau_{xy} = \tau_{yx}$. The components σ_x and σ_y are called the *normal components of stress*, and τ_{xy} is called the *shearing stress* at the point (x,y) of the section.

[1] S. Timoshenko, "Theory of Elasticity" (McGraw-Hill, New York, 1934), p. 5

The differential equations satisfied by the components of stress in a medium in which a force of components (X,Y) per unit mass acts may be obtained by considering the motion of a small rectangular element with sides of length dx, dy, and unity in the x,y, and z directions, respectively. A cross section of such a parallelepiped is shown in Fig. 76; the vertex A has coordinates (x,y) and $B(x + dx, y + dy)$. We assume that the

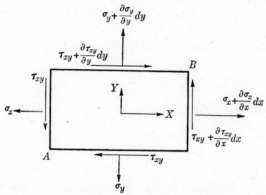

FIG. 76.   Forces acting on an element of an elastic body.

lengths dx, dy are small enough for the force on any of the sides of the element to be the product of the length of the side and the stress at its mid-point. Equating the total force in the x direction to the rate of change of momentum, in the x direction, of the element, we obtain the equation of motion

$$\rho \frac{\partial^2 u}{\partial t^2} = \rho X \, dx \, dy + \left(\sigma_x + \frac{\partial \sigma_x}{\partial x} dx\right) dy + \left(\tau_{xy} + \frac{\partial \tau_{xy}}{\partial y} dy\right) dx$$
$$- \sigma_x \, dy - \tau_{xy} \, dx$$

where now we have written $\mathbf{u} = (u,v,0)$ for the displacement vector. From this equation and the similar one expressing the rate of change of momentum of the element in the y direction we thus obtain the equations of motion for a two-dimensional elastic medium,

$$\frac{\partial \sigma_x}{\partial x} + \frac{\partial \tau_{xy}}{\partial y} + \rho X = \rho \frac{\partial^2 u}{\partial t^2}, \qquad \frac{\partial \tau_{xy}}{\partial x} + \frac{\partial \sigma_y}{\partial y} + \rho Y = \rho \frac{\partial^2 v}{\partial t^2} \qquad (1)$$

Most of the problems we shall consider will be equilibrium problems. The equilibrium equations

$$\frac{\partial \sigma_x}{\partial x} + \frac{\partial \tau_{xy}}{\partial y} + \rho X = 0, \qquad \frac{\partial \tau_{xy}}{\partial x} + \frac{\partial \sigma_y}{\partial y} + \rho Y = 0 \qquad (2)$$

are then obtained by taking the operator $\partial^2/\partial t^2$, which occurs in the equations of motion (1), to be identically zero.

43.3 The Airy stress function. To determine the equilibrium distribution of stress in a two-dimensional elastic medium we have to solve the differential equations (2), subject to the appropriate boundary conditions but these equations are not sufficient for the determination of the stresses. In order to obtain the complete solution, we have to take into account the condition for the compatibility of the distribution of stress with the existence of a displacement vector with continuous components $(u,v,0)$. In this case the components of strain are given by the equations

$$\epsilon_x = \frac{\partial u}{\partial x}, \qquad \epsilon_y = \frac{\partial v}{\partial y}, \qquad \gamma_{xy} = \frac{\partial u}{\partial y} + \frac{\partial v}{\partial x}$$

from which we may derive by differentiation the relation

$$\frac{\partial^2 \epsilon_x}{\partial y^2} + \frac{\partial^2 \epsilon_y}{\partial x^2} = \frac{\partial^2 \gamma_{xy}}{\partial x\, \partial y} \tag{3}$$

If we denote the Poisson ratio of the material by σ, its Young's modulus by E, the relations between stress and strain give, for the component of strain in the z direction,

$$E\epsilon_z = \sigma_z - \sigma(\sigma_x + \sigma_y)$$

But in the case of plane strain $\epsilon_z = 0$, so that the normal component of stress in the z direction is, in the case of plane strain,

$$\sigma_z = \sigma(\sigma_x + \sigma_y) \tag{4}$$

Now, from the other stress-strain relations we obtain the equations

$$\left.\begin{aligned} E\epsilon_x &= \sigma_x - \sigma(\sigma_y + \sigma_z) = (1 - \sigma^2)\sigma_x - \sigma(1 + \sigma)\sigma_y \\ E\epsilon_y &= \sigma_y - \sigma(\sigma_x + \sigma_z) = (1 - \sigma^2)\sigma_y - \sigma(1 + \sigma)\sigma_x \\ E\gamma_{xy} &= 2(1 + \sigma)\tau_{xy} \end{aligned}\right\} \tag{5}$$

Substituting from equations (5) into equation (3), we have finally

$$\frac{\partial^2}{\partial y^2}\left[\sigma_x - \sigma(\sigma_x + \sigma_y)\right] + \frac{\partial^2}{\partial x^2}\left[\sigma_y - \sigma(\sigma_x + \sigma_y)\right] = 2\frac{\partial^2 \tau_{xy}}{\partial x\, \partial y} \tag{6}$$

In practical examples the body force is usually derived from a potential function $V(x,y)$ such that

$$X = -\frac{\partial V}{\partial x}, \qquad Y = -\frac{\partial V}{\partial y}$$

and the equations of equilibrium (2) become

$$\frac{\partial \sigma_x}{\partial x} + \frac{\partial \tau_{xy}}{\partial y} - \frac{\partial V}{\partial x} = 0, \qquad \frac{\partial \tau_{xy}}{\partial x} + \frac{\partial \sigma_y}{\partial y} - \frac{\partial V}{\partial y} = 0$$

To solve these equations we let

$$\tau_{xy} = - \frac{\partial^2 \chi}{\partial x \, \partial y}$$

n which case they reduce to

$$\frac{\partial}{\partial x} \left(\sigma_x - \frac{\partial^2 \chi}{\partial y^2} - V \right) = 0, \qquad \frac{\partial}{\partial y} \left(\sigma_y - \frac{\partial^2 \chi}{\partial x^2} - V \right) = 0$$

It follows immediately that the equations of equilibrium are satisfied by ₋he expressions

$$\sigma_x = \frac{\partial^2 \chi}{\partial y^2} + V, \qquad \sigma_y = \frac{\partial^2 \chi}{\partial x^2} + V, \qquad \tau_{xy} = - \frac{\partial^2 \chi}{\partial x \, \partial y} \qquad (7)$$

₊nd that the compatibility relation (6) is satisfied if the function χ is a ₅olution of the partial differential equation

$$\nabla_1^4 \chi + \frac{1 - 2\sigma}{1 - \sigma} \nabla_1^2 V = 0 \qquad (8)$$

ᵥhere ∇_1^2 denotes the two-dimensional Laplacian operator $\partial^2/\partial x^2 + \partial^2/\partial y^2$. [n the absence of body forces we may take V to be zero; the function χ ₊hen satisfies the two-dimensional biharmonic equation

$$\nabla_1^4 \chi = 0 \qquad (9)$$

The function χ was first introduced by Airy[1] and is known as the *Airy stress function*.

It might have been supposed that Airy's introduction of a single stress ᶠunction would have led to the development of a two-dimensional theory ₒf elasticity based on the theory of functions of a complex variable. That this has not been found to be true is due, in no small measure, to the greater difficulties which attend the solution of the two-dimensional ᵇiharmonic equation as compared with those of Laplace's equation in ₊wo dimensions. The second-order equation has certain simple properties, analogues of which do not appear to exist in the case of the fourth-order equation. Recently, however, a theory of plane strain based on the theory of functions of a complex variable, but not formulated in terms of an Airy stress function, has been developed by Green, Stevenson, and Milne-Thomson.[2] In the hands of Green and Stevenson this method

[1] G. Airy, Brit. Assoc. Advancement Sci. Rept., 1862, p. 82.

[2] A. E. Green, *Proc. Cambridge Phil. Soc.*, **41**, 224 (1945), and the papers referred to therein; A. C. Stevenson, *Phil. Mag.*, **34**, 766 (1943); L. M. Milne-Thomson, *Jour. London Math. Soc.*, **17**, 115 (1942).

has been successfully applied to the solution of many special problems in two-dimensional elasticity, but it is difficult to see how this method could be extended easily to cover the three-dimensional case. The solution of some special problems will be obtained below by use of the theory of integral transforms; this method has the advantage that it lends itself naturally to extension to three-dimensional problems—as we shall see in Chap. 10.

43.4 Plane stress. Suppose that, instead of a very long cylinder, we consider a very short cylinder—*i.e.*, a flat plate. If the z axis is chosen to be normal to the plate, or, what is the same thing, parallel to the generators of the cylinder, and if the prescribed body forces and surface tractions have directions normal to Oz, the faces of the plate being free from stress, we may write the boundary conditions in the form

$$\sigma_z = \tau_{zx} = \tau_{zy} = 0 \qquad\qquad z = \pm h$$

When the plate is very thin, it is evident that σ_z, τ_{zx}, and τ_{zy} will be small everywhere. It is therefore assumed that these equations hold at all points in the interior of the plate. We then have what is called a state of *plane stress*. The equations of plane stress can be formulated and solved in precisely the same way as those for plane strain, the solutions of one set being derivable from those of the other merely by a change of constants; hence we shall confine our attention to plane strain in the sequel.

44. Infinite Elastic Solid with Body Forces

In the first instance we shall suppose that the elastic solid is of infinite extent and that it is deformed by the action of known body forces $X(x,y)$ and $Y(x,y)$. We shall further suppose that, as $|x|$ or $|y| \to \infty$, all the components of the displacement and of the stress tensor tend to zero. To solve the equations of equilibrium (2) and the compatibility equation we introduce the two-dimensional Fourier transforms

$$(\bar{\sigma}_x, \bar{\sigma}_y, \bar{\tau}_{xy}, \bar{X}, \bar{Y}) = \frac{1}{2\pi} \int_{-\infty}^{\infty} \int_{-\infty}^{\infty} (\sigma_x, \sigma_y, \tau_{xy}, X, Y) e^{i(\xi x + \eta y)} \, dx \, dy$$

Multiplying both sides of the equations (2) by $e^{i(\xi x + \eta y)}$ and integrating over the entire xy plane, we find on integrating by parts that the equations (2) are equivalent to the relations

$$\xi\bar{\sigma}_x + \eta\bar{\tau}_{xy} + i\rho\bar{X} = 0, \qquad \xi\bar{\tau}_{xy} + \eta\bar{\sigma}_y + i\rho\bar{Y} = 0$$

Similarly, equation (6) can be shown to be equivalent to

$$\bar{\sigma}_x[(1 - \sigma)\eta^2 - \sigma\xi^2] + \bar{\sigma}_y[(1 - \sigma)\xi^2 - \sigma\eta^2] = 2\xi\eta\bar{\tau}_{xy}$$

In these three equations we may assume that $\bar{X}$ and $\bar{Y}$ are known, *i.e.*, that the distribution of body forces is known. We may then solve these equations to obtain the expressions

$$\bar{\sigma}_x + \bar{\sigma}_y = -\rho\frac{1}{1-\sigma}\cdot\frac{i\xi\bar{X} + i\eta\bar{Y}}{(\xi^2 + \eta^2)} \tag{10}$$

$$\bar{\sigma}_x - \bar{\sigma}_y = -\rho\frac{1-2\sigma}{1-\sigma}\cdot\frac{\xi^2 - \eta^2}{(\xi^2 + \eta^2)^2}(i\xi\bar{X} + i\eta\bar{Y}) - 4\rho\frac{\xi\eta(i\eta\bar{X} - i\xi\bar{Y})}{(\xi^2 + \eta^2)^2} \tag{11}$$

$$\bar{\tau}_{xy} = -\rho\frac{\xi^2 - \eta^2}{(\xi^2 + \eta^2)^2}(i\xi\bar{X} - i\eta\bar{Y}) - \frac{1-2\sigma}{1-\sigma}\rho\frac{\xi\eta(i\eta\bar{X} + i\xi\bar{Y})}{(\xi^2 + \eta^2)^2} \tag{12}$$

Inverting equation (10) by means of the formula (111), Chap. 1, we see that

$$\sigma_x + \sigma_y = -\frac{\rho}{2\pi(1-\sigma)}\int_{-\infty}^{\infty}\int_{-\infty}^{\infty}\frac{(i\xi\bar{X} + i\eta\bar{Y})e^{-i(\xi x + \eta y)}}{(\xi^2 + \eta^2)}\,d\xi\,d\eta$$

Now

$$\int_{-\infty}^{\infty}\int_{-\infty}^{\infty}\frac{i\xi}{\xi^2 + \eta^2}e^{-i(\xi x + \eta y)}\,d\xi\,d\eta = 4\int_0^{\infty}\xi\sin(\xi x)d\xi\int_0^{\infty}\frac{\cos(\eta y)d\eta}{\eta^2 + \xi^2}$$

The integrations are elementary and show that $i\xi/(\xi^2 + \eta^2)$ is the Fourier transform of the function $x/(x^2 + y^2)$. Hence by the Faltung theorem (112), Chap. 1, we have

$$\int_{-\infty}^{\infty}\int_{-\infty}^{\infty}\frac{i\xi\bar{X}(\xi,\eta)}{\xi^2 + \eta^2}e^{-i(\xi x + \eta y)}\,d\xi\,d\eta = \int_{-\infty}^{\infty}\int_{-\infty}^{\infty}\frac{(x - \alpha)X(\alpha,\beta)d\alpha\,d\beta}{(x - \alpha)^2 + (y - \beta)^2}$$

Similarly it may be shown that

$$\int_{-\infty}^{\infty}\int_{-\infty}^{\infty}\frac{i\eta\bar{Y}(\xi,\eta)}{\xi^2 + \eta^2}e^{-i(\xi x + \eta y)}\,d\xi\,d\eta = \int_{-\infty}^{\infty}\int_{-\infty}^{\infty}\frac{(y - \beta)Y(\alpha,\beta)d\alpha\,d\beta}{(x - \alpha)^2 + (y - \beta)^2}$$

so that

$$\sigma_x + \sigma_y = -\frac{\rho}{2\pi(1-\sigma)}\int_{-\infty}^{\infty}\int_{-\infty}^{\infty}\frac{(x - \alpha)X(\alpha,\beta) + (y - \beta)Y(\alpha,\beta)}{(x - \alpha)^2 + (y - \beta)^2}\,d\alpha\,d\beta \tag{13}$$

By a similar process we can show that

$$\sigma_x - \sigma_y = -\frac{1-2\sigma}{\pi(1-\sigma)}\rho\int_{-\infty}^{\infty}\int_{-\infty}^{\infty}\frac{(x - \alpha)(y - \beta)}{[(x - \alpha)^2 + (y - \beta)^2]^2}$$
$$\times[(y - \beta)X(\alpha,\beta) - (x - \alpha)Y(\alpha,\beta)]d\alpha\,d\beta$$
$$-\frac{\rho}{\pi}\int_{-\infty}^{\infty}\int_{-\infty}^{\infty}\frac{[(x - \alpha)^2 - (y - \beta)^2]}{[(x - \alpha)^2 + (y - \beta)^2]^2}[(x - \alpha)X(\alpha,\beta) + (y - \beta)Y(\alpha,\beta)]$$
$$\times d\alpha\,d\beta \tag{14}$$

and that

$$\tau_{xy} = -\frac{(1-2)\rho}{4\pi(1-\sigma)} \int_{-\infty}^{\infty} \int_{-\infty}^{\infty} \frac{[(y-\alpha)^2 - (x-\beta)^2]}{[(x-\alpha)^2 + (y-\beta)^2]^2} [(y-\beta)X(\alpha,\beta)$$
$$- (x-\alpha)Y(\alpha,\beta)]d\alpha\, d\beta$$
$$-\frac{\rho}{\pi} \int_{-\infty}^{\infty} \int_{-\infty}^{\infty} \frac{(x-\alpha)(y-\beta)}{[(x-\alpha)^2 + (y-\beta)^2]^2} [(x-\alpha)X(\alpha,\beta)$$
$$+ (y-\beta)Y(\alpha,\beta)]d\alpha\, d\beta \quad (15)$$

A special case of some interest is that in which a point force of magnitude F acts at the origin of coordinates in the negative direction of x. We may then take $X(\alpha,\beta) = k\,\delta(\alpha)\delta(\beta)$, $Y(\alpha,\beta) = 0$, where the constant k is found from the condition

$$\iint X(\alpha,\beta)\rho\, d\alpha\, d\beta = -F$$

to be $-F/\rho$. We then have, from equations (13), (14), and (15), the expressions for the components of stress.

$$\sigma_x = \frac{Fx}{4\pi(1-\sigma)r^2}\left[(1-2\sigma) + \frac{2x^2}{r^2}\right]$$
$$\sigma_y = \frac{Fx}{4\pi(1-\sigma)r^2}\left[(1+2\sigma) - \frac{2x^2}{r^2}\right] \Bigg\} \quad (16)$$
$$\tau_{xy} = \frac{Fy}{4\pi(1-\sigma)r^2}\left[(1-2\sigma) + \frac{2x^2}{r^2}\right]$$

expressions for the components of stress. The fourth component of stress σ_z is obtained readily from equation (4).

45. Application of Pressure to the Surfaces of a Two-dimensional Elastic Solid

We shall now consider the equilibrium of a solid body when it is deformed by the application of pressure to its bounding surfaces, the body forces being assumed to be zero throughout the solid.

45.1 Solution of the two-dimensional biharmonic equation.
In the absence of body forces the solution of the equations of equilibrium of a two-dimensional elastic body reduces, as we have seen, to the solution of the two-dimensional biharmonic equation (9). Now, it follows from Theorem 13 that

$$\int_{-\infty}^{\infty} \nabla_1^2 f e^{i\xi y}\, dy = \left(\frac{d^2}{dx^2} - \xi^2\right) \int_{-\infty}^{\infty} f e^{i\xi y}\, dy \quad (17)$$

Repeating the operation, we obtain the result

$$\int_{-\infty}^{\infty} \nabla_1^4 f e^{i\xi y}\, dy = \left(\frac{d^2}{dx^2} - \xi^2\right)^2 \int_{-\infty}^{\infty} f e^{i\xi y}\, dy \tag{18}$$

Thus, if we denote by G the integral

$$\int_{-\infty}^{\infty} \chi e^{i\xi y}\, dy$$

it follows from equation (18) that if χ is a solution of (9) then G is a solution of the equation

$$\left(\frac{d^2}{dx^2} - \xi^2\right)^2 G = 0 \tag{19}$$

whose general solution may be written in the form

$$G = (A + Bx)e^{-|\xi|x} + (C + Dx)e^{+|\xi|x} \tag{20}$$

where the constants A,B,C,D, which are, in general, functions of ξ, are determined from the boundary conditions imposed in the particular problem under consideration. By Fourier's inversion theorem 10 we obtain immediately

$$\chi(x,y) = \frac{1}{2\pi} \int_{-\infty}^{\infty} G(x,\xi)e^{-i\xi y}\, d\xi \tag{21}$$

by which the Airy stress function χ may be derived from equation (20) by a simple integration.

To determine the arbitrary constants A,B,C, and D, we require to obtain expressions for the components of the stress tensor in terms of the function $G(x,\xi)$ and its derivatives with respect to x. In the first of the equations (7) we put $V = 0$, multiply throughout by $e^{i\xi y}$, and integrate with respect to y over the range $(-\infty, \infty)$ to obtain

$$\int_{-\infty}^{\infty} \sigma_x e^{i\xi y}\, dy = \int_{-\infty}^{\infty} \frac{\partial^2 \chi}{\partial y^2} e^{i\xi y}\, dy = -\xi^2 G \tag{22}$$

as a result of an integration by parts. Similarly the second and third equations of the set (7) give

$$\int_{-\infty}^{\infty} \sigma_y e^{i\xi y}\, dy = \frac{d^2 G}{dx^2} \tag{23}$$

and

$$\int_{-\infty}^{\infty} \tau_{xy} e^{i\xi y}\, dy = i\xi \frac{dG}{dx} \tag{24}$$

Inverting these equations by means of the Fourier inversion theorem 10, we obtain the expressions

$$\sigma_x = -\frac{1}{2\pi} \int_{-\infty}^{\infty} \xi^2 G e^{-i\xi y}\, d\xi \tag{25}$$

$$\sigma_y = \frac{1}{2\pi} \int_{-\infty}^{\infty} \frac{d^2G}{dx^2}\, e^{-i\xi y}\, d\xi \tag{26}$$

$$\tau_{xy} = \frac{1}{2\pi} \int_{-\infty}^{\infty} i\xi \frac{dG}{dx}\, e^{-i\xi y}\, d\xi \tag{27}$$

To determine the corresponding expressions for the components of the displacement vector, we write the second of the equations (5) in the form

$$\frac{E}{1+\sigma} \frac{\partial v}{\partial y} = \sigma_y - \sigma(\sigma_x + \sigma_y)$$

and then multiply by $e^{i\xi y}$ to obtain, on integrating over y,

$$-\frac{i\xi E}{1+\sigma} \int_{-\infty}^{\infty} v e^{i\xi y}\, dy = (1-\sigma)\frac{d^2G}{dx^2} + \sigma \xi^2 G$$

whence we obtain the expression

$$v = \frac{1+\sigma}{2\pi E} \int_{-\infty}^{\infty} \left[(1-\sigma)\frac{d^2G}{dx^2} + \sigma \xi^2 G \right] i e^{-i\xi y} \frac{d\xi}{\xi} \tag{28}$$

In a similar fashion the equation

$$\frac{E}{2(1+\sigma)} \left(\frac{\partial v}{\partial x} + \frac{\partial u}{\partial y} \right) = \tau_{xy}$$

leads to the expression

$$u = \frac{1+\sigma}{2\pi E} \int_{-\infty}^{\infty} \left[(1-\sigma)\frac{d^3G}{dx^3} + (2+\sigma)\xi^2 \frac{dG}{dx} \right] e^{-i\xi y} \frac{d\xi}{\xi^2} \tag{29}$$

45.2 Semiinfinite elastic medium. We shall begin by considering the distribution of stress in a semiinfinite elastic solid due to the application of an external pressure to its surface.   It will be assumed that the elastic medium is bounded by a plane of infinite extent, which we shall take to be $x = 0$.   The x axis is taken normal to this plane to point *into* the medium.   The medium is otherwise unbounded.

We shall suppose that this domain is compressed by a surface pressure p, which varies along the surface.   Then the boundary conditions are

$$\sigma_x = -p(y), \qquad \tau_{xy} = 0 \qquad \text{on } x = 0$$

it being assumed that p is a function of y. In the case of a semiinfinite medium, the solution we derive must be such that the stress components σ_x, σ_y, and τ_{xy} all tend to zero as x tends to infinity.   Inserting this last condition in equation (20), we find $C = D = 0$. Substituting the conditions at the boundary in equations (22) and (24), we have

$$-\xi^2 A = -\int_{-\infty}^{\infty} p(y)e^{i\xi y}\,dy = -\bar{p}(\xi), \qquad 0 = B - |\xi|A \qquad (30)$$

whence we deduce $A = \bar{p}(\xi)/\xi^2$, $B = \bar{p}(\xi)/|\xi|$ so that

$$G = \frac{\bar{p}(\xi)}{\xi^2}(1 + |\xi|x)e^{-|\xi|x} \qquad (31)$$

Substituting this expression in equations (25) to (27), we obtain for the components of stress

$$\sigma_x = -\frac{1}{2\pi}\int_{-\infty}^{\infty} \bar{p}(\xi)e^{-|\xi|x-i\xi y}(1 + |\xi|x)d\xi \qquad (32)$$

$$\sigma_y = -\frac{1}{2\pi}\int_{-\infty}^{\infty} \bar{p}(\xi)e^{-|\xi|x-i\xi y}(1 - |\xi|x)d\xi \qquad (32a)$$

$$\tau_{xy} = -\frac{i}{2\pi}\int_{-\infty}^{\infty} x\xi\bar{p}(\xi)e^{-|\xi|x-i\xi y}\,d\xi \qquad (32b)$$

From equation (4) it follows that

$$\sigma_z = -\frac{\sigma}{\pi}\int_{-\infty}^{\infty} \bar{p}(\xi)e^{-|\xi|x-i\xi y}\,d\xi$$

The corresponding components of the displacement vector are then, from equations (28) and (29), found to be

$$u = \frac{1+\sigma}{2\pi E}\int_{-\infty}^{\infty} |\xi|\bar{p}(\xi)e^{-|\xi|x-i\xi y}[2(1-\sigma) + |\xi|x]d\xi \qquad (33)$$

and

$$v = -\frac{1+\sigma}{2\pi E}\int_{-\infty}^{\infty} |\xi|\bar{p}(\xi)e^{-|\xi|x-i\xi y}[(1-2\sigma) - |\xi|x]d\xi \qquad (33a)$$

Two particular cases are in general use. When $\bar{p}(\xi)$ is an *even* function of ξ, these equations reduce to

$$\sigma_x = -\frac{2}{\pi}\int_0^{\infty} \bar{p}(\xi)(1 + \xi x)e^{-\xi x}\cos(\xi y)d\xi \qquad (34)$$

$$\sigma_y = -\frac{2}{\pi}\int_0^{\infty} \bar{p}(\xi)(1 - \xi x)e^{-\xi x}\cos(\xi y)d\xi \qquad (34a)$$

$$\tau_{xy} = -\frac{2x}{\pi}\int_0^{\infty} \xi\bar{p}(\xi)e^{-\xi x}\sin(\xi y)d\xi \qquad (34b)$$

$$u = \frac{2(1+\sigma)}{\pi E}\int_0^{\infty} \bar{p}(\xi)e^{-\xi x}[2(1-\sigma) + \xi x]\frac{\cos(\xi y)}{\xi}\,d\xi \qquad (35)$$

$$v = -\frac{2(1+\sigma)}{\pi E}\int_0^{\infty} \bar{p}(\xi)e^{-\xi x}(1 - 2\sigma - \xi x)\frac{\sin(\xi y)}{\xi}\,d\xi \qquad (35a)$$

where, now,

$$\bar{p}(\xi) = \int_0^\infty p(y) \cos(\xi y) dy \tag{36}$$

On the other hand, if $\bar{p}(\xi)$ is an *odd* function of ξ, we find that the components of stress become

$$\sigma_x = -\frac{2}{\pi} \int_0^\infty \bar{p}(\xi)(1 + \xi x)e^{-\xi x} \sin(\xi y) d\xi \tag{37}$$

$$\sigma_y = -\frac{2}{\pi} \int_0^\infty \bar{p}(\xi)(1 - \xi x)e^{-\xi x} \sin(\xi y) d\xi \tag{37a}$$

$$\tau_{xy} = \frac{2x}{\pi} \int_0^\infty \xi\bar{p}(\xi)e^{-\xi x} \cos(\xi y) d\xi \tag{37b}$$

where, in this case,

$$\bar{p}(\xi) = \int_0^\infty p(y) \sin(\xi y) dy \tag{38}$$

and the components of displacement are

$$u = \frac{2(1 + \sigma)}{\pi E} \int_0^\infty \bar{p}(\xi)[2(1 - \sigma) + \xi x]e^{-\xi x} \frac{\sin(\xi y)}{\xi} d\xi \tag{39}$$

$$v = \frac{2(1 + \sigma)}{\pi E} \int_0^\infty \bar{p}(\xi)[(1 - 2\sigma) - \xi x]e^{-\xi x} \frac{\cos(\xi y)}{\xi} d\xi \tag{39a}$$

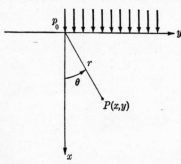

FIG. 77. Semiinfinite band of pressure applied to a semiinfinite solid.

Example 1. As an example of the use of the formulas (32), (32a), and (32b) let us consider the case in which $p(y) = p_0 S_+(y)$, where p_0 is a constant and $S_+(y)$ denotes the function

$$S_+(y) = \begin{cases} 1 & y > 0 \\ 0 & y < 0 \end{cases} \tag{40}$$

Let us consider the Heisenberg delta function[1]

$$\delta_+(x) = \frac{1}{2} \delta(x) - \frac{1}{2\pi i x} \tag{41}$$

Then

$$\int_{-\infty}^\infty \delta_+(\xi)e^{-i\xi y} d\xi = \frac{1}{2} + \frac{1}{\pi} \int_0^\infty \frac{\sin(\xi y)}{\xi} d\xi = \begin{cases} 1 & \text{if } y > 0 \\ 0 & \text{if } y < 0 \end{cases}$$

Now the function on the right is merely $S_+(y)$ so that, inverting this equation by means of Theorem 10, we have

[1] Cf. W. Pauli, "Meson Theory of Nuclear Forces" (Interscience Publishers, New York, 1946), p. 47.

$$\int_{-\infty}^{\infty} S_+(y)e^{i\xi y}\, dy = 2\pi\, \delta_+(\xi)$$

Hence, in this case, $\bar{p}(\xi) = 2\pi p_0\, \delta_+(\xi)$. From the equation (32a) we therefore have

$$\sigma_x = -p_0 \int_{-\infty}^{\infty} \delta_+(\xi)e^{-|\xi|x - i\xi y}(1 + \xi x)d\xi = -\frac{1}{2}\, p_0$$

$$-\frac{p_0}{\pi} \int_0^{\infty} (1 + \xi x)e^{-\xi x} \sin\,(\xi y)\, \frac{d\xi}{\xi}$$

$$= -p_0\left[1 - \frac{1}{\pi} \tan^{-1}\left(\frac{x}{y}\right) + \frac{xy}{\pi(x^2 + y^2)}\right]$$

If we write $x = r\cos\theta$, $y = r\sin\theta$, we have

$$\sigma_x = -p_0\left[\frac{1}{2} + \frac{\theta}{\pi} + \frac{1}{2\pi} \sin\,(2\theta)\right]$$

The two remaining independent components of stress are similarly found to be

$$\sigma_y = -p_0\left[\frac{1}{2} + \frac{\theta}{\pi} - \frac{1}{2\pi} \sin\,(2\theta)\right], \qquad \tau_{xy} = \frac{p_0}{\pi} \cos^2\theta$$

Example 2. As an example of the use of the formulas (34), (34a), and (34b) we shall consider the stress set up in a semiinfinite elastic solid when a uniform pressure p_0 acts over a segment $-a \le y \le a$ of the y axis. In this case the stresses are given by equations (34), (34a), and (34b) with

$$\bar{p}(\xi) = p_0 \int_0^a \cos\,(\xi y)dy = p_0\, \frac{\sin\,(\xi a)}{\xi} \tag{42}$$

Substituting this value for $\bar{p}(\xi)$ into equations (34), (34a), and (34b), we have, for the components of stress,

$$\left.\begin{aligned}
\sigma_x &= -\frac{2p_0}{\pi} \int_0^{\infty} \frac{1 + \xi x}{\xi} e^{-\xi x} \sin\,(\xi a)\cos\,(\xi y)d\xi \\
\sigma_y &= -\frac{2p_0}{\pi} \int_0^{\infty} \frac{1 - \xi x}{\xi} e^{-\xi x} \sin\,(\xi a)\cos\,(\xi y)d\xi \\
\tau_{xy} &= -\frac{2p_0 x}{\pi} \int_0^{\infty} e^{-\xi x} \sin\,(\xi a)\sin\,(\xi y)d\xi
\end{aligned}\right\} \tag{43}$$

Writing $x + iy = re^{i\theta}$, $x + i(y - a) = r_1 e^{i\theta_1}$, $x + i(y + a) = r_2 e^{i\theta_2}$ in the notation of Fig. 78, we see that the expressions for the components of stress may be put into the forms

$$\sigma_x = -\frac{p_0}{2\pi} \left[2(\theta_1 - \theta_2) - \sin(2\theta_1) + \sin(2\theta_2) \right]$$

$$\sigma_y = -\frac{p_0}{2\pi} \left[2(\theta_1 - \theta_2) + \sin(2\theta_1) - \sin(2\theta_2) \right] \Bigg\} \quad (44)$$

$$\tau_{xy} = \frac{p_0}{2\pi} \left[\cos(2\theta_2) - \cos(2\theta_1) \right]$$

These formulas were obtained otherwise by Okobu.[1] It follows at once that the maximum shearing stress

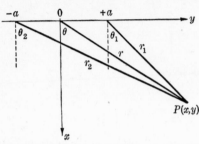

$$\tau = \left[\left(\tfrac{1}{2}\sigma_x - \tfrac{1}{2}\sigma_y \right)^2 + \tau_{xy}^2 \right]^{\frac{1}{2}}$$

at any point is given by

$$\tau = \frac{p_0}{\pi} \left| \sin(\theta_1 - \theta_2) \right| \quad (45)$$

Fig. 78. The coordinates r_1, r_2, θ_1, and θ_2.

so that the loci of points at which the maximum shearing stress has a given value are members of the family

$$\left| \sin(\theta_1 - \theta_2) \right| = k$$

where k is a parameter. This family of curves is easily seen to be a system of coaxal circles passing through the points $(0, -a)$ and $(0, a)$ as shown in Fig. 79. Because of an important optical property which they possess,[2] the loci of points at which the maximum shearing stress has a given value are known as *isochromatic lines*. They are often drawn to illustrate the distribution of stress in an elastic system.

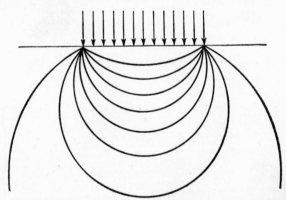

Fig. 79. Isochromatic lines produced by a finite band of uniform pressure.

[1] S. Okobu, *Science Repts. Tôhoku Imp. Univ.*, **25**, 114 (1937).

[2] E. G. Coker and L. N. G. Filon, "Photoelasticity" (Cambridge, London, 1934), p. 248.

In a similar fashion we define the *isoclinic lines* to be the loci of points at which the directions of mean principal stress are parallel to fixed directions. In the present example it is readily proved that the isoclinic lines form a family of hyperbolas.

If a point force of magnitude P acts at the origin of coordinates on the boundary, then we may put $p_0 = P/2a$ in (42) and obtain

$$\bar{p}(\xi) = \lim_{a \to 0} \frac{P}{2a} \frac{\sin (\xi a)}{\xi} = \frac{1}{2} P$$

so that from equations (34), (34a), and (34b) we obtain, for the components of stress, the expressions

$$\sigma_x = -\frac{P}{\pi} \int^{\infty} (1 + \xi x)e^{-\xi x} \cos (\xi y)d\xi = -\frac{2Px^3}{\pi(x^2 + y^2)^2} \qquad (46)$$

$$\tau_{xy} = -\frac{Px}{\pi} \int_0^{\infty} \xi e^{-\xi x} \sin (\xi y)d\xi = -\frac{2Px^2y}{\pi(x^2 + y^2)^2} \qquad (46a)$$

$$\sigma_y = -\frac{P}{\pi} \int_0^{\infty} (1 - \xi x)e^{-\xi x} \cos (\xi y)d\xi = -\frac{2Pxy^2}{\pi(x^2 + y^2)^2} \qquad (46b)$$

Also, the maximum shearing stress is

$$\tau = \frac{Py}{\pi(x^2 + y^2)} = \frac{P \cos \theta}{\pi r}$$

so that the isochromatic lines are $r = k \cos \theta$—a family of circles passing through the point of application of the force and tangential to the boundary.

It follows from equation (46), by a simple integration, that the normal component of stress due to a pressure $p(y)$ distributed over the surface is

$$\sigma_x = -\frac{2x^3}{\pi} \int_{-\infty}^{\infty} \frac{p(\eta)d\eta}{[x^2 + (y - \eta)^2]^2} \qquad (47)$$

—a result which could equally easily have been obtained by applying the Faltung theorem 12 to the formula (32). In the case in which $p(y)$ is an *even* function of y equation (47) may be written in the form

$$\sigma_x = -\frac{2x^3}{\pi} \int_0^{\infty} \left\{ \frac{p(\eta)}{[x^2 + (y - \eta)^2]^2} + \frac{p(\eta)}{[x^2 + (y + \eta)^2]^2} \right\} d\eta \qquad (48)$$

Similarly equations (46a) and (46b) lead to the formulas

$$\tau_{xy} = -\frac{2x^2}{\pi} \int_0^{\infty} p(\eta) \left\{ \frac{y - \eta}{[x^2 + (y - \eta)^2]^2} + \frac{y + \eta}{[x^2 + (y + \eta)^2]^2} \right\} d\eta \qquad (49)$$

and

$$\sigma_y = -\frac{2x}{\pi} \int_0^\infty p(\eta) \left\{ \frac{(y - \eta)^2}{[x^2 + (y - \eta)^2]^2} + \frac{(y + \eta)^2}{[x^2 + (y + \eta)^2]^2} \right\} d\eta \quad (50)$$

The verification that the substitution

$$p(\eta) = p_0, \ 0 \leq |\eta| \leq a, \qquad p(\eta) = 0, \ |\eta| > a$$

in these formulas leads to the expressions (46), (46a), and (46b) is left to the reader.

45.3 Constant deflection along the loaded part of the boundary. As a further example of the use of equations (34), (34a), and (34b) consider the distribution of stress in a semiinfinite medium when the prescribed pressure $p(y)$ on the free surface is defined by the relations

$$p(y) = \begin{cases} \dfrac{P}{\pi} (a^2 - y^2)^{-\frac{1}{2}} & 0 \leq |y| \leq a \\ 0 & |y| > a \end{cases}$$

For such a pressure the total force acting on the boundary is

$$\int_{-\infty}^{\infty} p(y) dy = \frac{P}{\pi} \int_{-a}^{a} (a^2 - y^2)^{-\frac{1}{2}} dy = P$$

Also the function $\bar{p}(\xi)$ defined by equation (36) becomes in this case

$$\bar{p}(\xi) = \frac{P}{\pi} \int_0^a \frac{\cos (\xi y) dy}{(a^2 - y^2)^{\frac{1}{2}}}$$

Now, from equation (20), Appendix A, we know that

$$\int_0^\infty \cos (\xi y) J_0(\xi a) d\xi = \begin{cases} (a^2 - y^2)^{\frac{1}{2}} & 0 < y < a \\ 0 & y > a \end{cases}$$

so that, inverting this result by the Fourier cosine rule, we obtain

$$\frac{2}{\pi} \int_0^a \frac{\cos (\xi y) dy}{(a^2 - y^2)^{\frac{1}{2}}} = J_0(\xi a)$$

which yields the formula $\bar{p}(\xi) = \frac{1}{2} P J_0(\xi a)$. It follows immediately from equations (34), (34a), and (34b) that the components of stress are given by the equations

$$\sigma_x + \sigma_y = -\frac{2P}{\pi} \int_0^\infty J_0(\xi a) e^{-\xi x} \cos (\xi y) d\xi$$

$$\sigma_y - \sigma_x + 2i\tau_{xy} = \frac{2Px}{\pi} \int_0^\infty \xi J_0(\xi a) e^{-\xi z} d\xi$$

where $z = x + iy$. The integral on the right has been evaluated in equation (20), Appendix A, so that we obtain

$$\sigma_y - \sigma_x + 2i\tau_{xy} = \frac{2Px}{\pi} \frac{z}{(z + ia)^{\frac{3}{2}}(z - ia)^{\frac{3}{2}}}$$

Writing $z = re^{i\theta}$, $z - ia = r_1 e^{i\theta_1}$, $z + ia = r_2 e^{i\theta_2}$ (cf. Fig. 78), we have

$$\frac{1}{2}(\sigma_y - \sigma_x) + i\tau_{xy} = \frac{Pxr}{(r_1 r_2)^{\frac{3}{2}}} \exp\left[i\theta - \frac{3}{2}(\theta_1 + \theta_2)i\right]$$

from which it is at once obvious that the maximum shearing stress τ is given by the equation

$$\tau = \frac{Pr^2 \cos \theta}{\pi (r_1 r_2)^{\frac{3}{2}}}$$

Similarly, by the use of equation (20), Appendix A, we can evaluate the integral for $\sigma_x + \sigma_y$. We find

$$\sigma_x + \sigma_y = -\frac{2P}{\pi} \mathsf{R} \int_0^\infty e^{-\xi z} J_0(\xi a) d\xi = -\frac{2P}{\pi} \mathsf{R}(a^2 + z^2)^{-\frac{1}{2}}$$

$$= -\frac{2P}{\pi} \frac{\cos\left[\frac{1}{2}(\theta_1 + \theta_2)\right]}{(r_1 r_2)^{\frac{1}{2}}}$$

The expression for $\sigma_y - \sigma_x$ can be obtained by equating real parts of both sides of the equation for $\sigma_y - \sigma_x + 2i\tau_{xy}$. In this way we obtain the expressions

$$\sigma_x = -\frac{P}{\pi(r_1 r_2)^{\frac{1}{2}}} \left\{\cos\left[\frac{1}{2}(\theta_1 + \theta_2)\right] + \frac{r^2}{r_1 r_2} \cos \theta \cos\left[\theta - \frac{3}{2}(\theta_1 + \theta_2)\right]\right\}$$

$$\sigma_y = -\frac{P}{\pi(r_1 r_2)^{\frac{1}{2}}} \left\{\cos\left[\frac{1}{2}(\theta_1 + \theta_2)\right] - \frac{r^2}{r_1 r_2} \cos \theta \cos\left[\theta - \frac{3}{2}(\theta_1 + \theta_2)\right]\right\}$$

$$\tau_{xy} = \frac{Pr^2 \cos \theta}{\pi(r_1 r_2)^{\frac{3}{2}}} \sin\left[\theta - \frac{3}{2}(\theta_1 + \theta_2)\right]$$

for the components of stress.

It follows from equation (35) that, for this applied pressure, the component of displacement in the x direction satisfies the relation

$$\left(\frac{\partial u}{\partial y}\right)_{y=0} = -\frac{2P}{\pi E}(1 - \sigma^2) \int_0^\infty J_0(\xi a) \sin(\xi y) d\xi$$

so that

$$\left(\frac{\partial u}{\partial y}\right)_{y=0} = \begin{cases} 0 & |y| < a \\ -\dfrac{2P(1 - \sigma^2)}{\pi E(y^2 - a^2)^{\frac{1}{2}}} & |y| > a \end{cases}$$

showing that u is constant along the strip $|y| < a$ of the boundary $x = 0$, as shown previously by Sadowsky.[1]

45.4 Infinite strip of finite thickness symmetrically loaded. We shall now briefly indicate how the analysis of the preceding section may be extended to the case where the elastic medium is bounded by the two parallel planes $x = \pm b$ to form a thick elastic plate of infinite radius. The plate will be considered to be deformed by the application of normal pressures to infinitely long strips of these plane surfaces. If the edges of the strips are straight and parallel, we have a state of plane strain as before. The boundary conditions then assume the forms

(i) $$\sigma_x = -p_1(y), \qquad \tau_{xy} = 0 \qquad \text{on } x = b$$
(ii) $$\sigma_x = -p_2(y), \qquad \tau_{xy} = 0 \qquad \text{on } x = -b$$

To preserve the equilibrium of the plate as a whole, we must either have

$$\int_{-\infty}^{\infty} p_1(y)dy = \int_{-\infty}^{\infty} p_2(y)dy$$

or ensure that the plate is held "at infinity."

If both the functions $p_1(y)$ and $p_2(y)$ are *even* functions, then equations (25), (26), and (27) take the forms

$$\sigma_x = -\frac{2}{\pi} \int_0^\infty \xi^2 G \cos (\xi y)d\xi \tag{51}$$

$$\tau_{xy} = \frac{2}{\pi} \int_0^\infty \xi \frac{dG}{dx} \sin (\xi y)d\xi \tag{52}$$

and

$$\sigma_y = \frac{2}{\pi} \int_0^\infty \frac{d^2G}{dx^2} \cos (\xi y)d\xi \tag{53}$$

where G may be taken to be a solution of equation (19) of the form

$$G = (A + B\xi x) \cosh (\xi x) + (C + D\xi x) \sinh (\xi x) \tag{54}$$

Inserting this function and the boundary conditions (i) and (ii) into equations (51) and (52), we obtain four equations for the four unknowns A, B, C, D, in terms of the Fourier cosine transforms

$$\bar{p}_1(\xi) = \int_0^\infty p_1(y) \cos (\xi y)dy, \qquad \bar{p}_2 = \int_0^\infty p_2(y) \cos (\xi y)dy$$

of the applied surface pressures. Solving these simultaneous equations for A, B, C, and D and substituting these values into equation (54), we obtain an expression for the function $G(x,\xi)$ which when substituted into the equations (51), (52), and (53) gives for the components of stress

[1] M. Sadowsky, *Z. angew. Math. u. Mech.*, **8**, 107 (1928).

$$\sigma_y - \sigma_x = \frac{2}{\pi b} \{(1 - \eta)[I_1(1 + \eta) + J_1(1 + \eta)] + (1 + \eta)[I_1(1 - \eta) $$
$$+ J_1(1 - \eta)]\} \quad (55)$$

$$\sigma_y + \sigma_x = -\frac{2}{\pi b}[I_2(1 + \eta) + J_2(1 + \eta) + I_2(1 - \eta) + J_2(1 - \eta)] \quad (56)$$

$$\tau_{xy} = \frac{2}{\pi b} \{(1 - \eta)[I_3(1 + \eta) + J_3(1 + \eta)]$$
$$- (1 + \eta)[I_3(1 - \eta) + J_3(1 - \eta)]\} \quad (57)$$

where $\eta = x/b$, $\xi = y/b$ and the integrals I_i and J_i are defined by the formulas

$$\begin{matrix} I_1(\lambda) \\ J_1(\lambda) \end{matrix} = \int_0^\infty \left[\bar{p}_1\left(\frac{u}{b}\right) \pm \bar{p}_2\left(\frac{u}{b}\right)\right] \frac{u \cosh(\lambda u) \cos(\xi u) du}{\sinh(2u) \pm 2u} \quad (58)$$

$$\begin{matrix} I_2(\lambda) \\ J_2(\lambda) \end{matrix} = \int_0^\infty \left[\bar{p}_1\left(\frac{u}{b}\right) \pm \bar{p}_2\left(\frac{u}{b}\right)\right] \frac{\sinh(\lambda u) \cos(\xi u) du}{\sinh(2u) \pm 2u} \quad (59)$$

$$\begin{matrix} I_3(\lambda) \\ J_3(\lambda) \end{matrix} = \int_0^\infty \left[\bar{p}_1\left(\frac{u}{b}\right) \pm \bar{p}_2\left(\frac{u}{b}\right)\right] \frac{u \sinh(\lambda u) \sin(\xi u) du}{\sinh(2u) \pm 2u} \quad (60)$$

It is easily verified from these expressions that, when $\eta = 1$, $\tau_{xy} = 0$, $\sigma_x = -p_1(y)$ and that, when $\eta = -1$, $\tau_{xy} = 0$, $\sigma_x = -p_2(y)$.

The problem of determining the distribution of stress in the interior of the strip is thus reduced to the evaluation of the infinite integrals defined by the equations (58), (59), and (60). This can be effected only after the functions $\bar{p}_1$ and $\bar{p}_2$ have been determined. Even then the evaluation of the integrals is troublesome. In any practical case it would be best to determine their values by a series of numerical integrations, though approximate methods of evaluating them have been devised.[1]

We shall now give the integral expressions for the components of stress for the case in which both boundaries of the strip are subjected to a force distributed over the regions $-a \le y \le a$ with uniform pressure p (see Fig. 80). In this case the boundary conditions are that, on $x = \pm b$, $\tau_{xy} = 0$ and σ_x is equal to $-p$ if $-a \le y \le a$ but is zero otherwise. We then have

$$\bar{p}_1(\xi) = \bar{p}_2(\xi) = p\frac{\sin(\xi a)}{\xi}$$

so that

$$\sigma_x = -\frac{4p}{\pi}\int_0^\infty \left[\frac{(\sinh \zeta + \zeta \cosh \zeta) \cosh(\zeta \eta) - \zeta \eta \sinh \zeta \sinh(\zeta \eta)}{2\zeta + \sinh(2\zeta)}\right]$$
$$\times \frac{\sin(\alpha \zeta)}{\zeta} \cos(\zeta \xi) d\zeta \quad (61)$$

[1] Cf. L. N. G. Filon, *Phil. Trans.*, **A201**, 63 (1903); I. N. Sneddon, *Proc. Cambridge Phil. Soc.*, **42**, 260 (1945) and Sec. 53.4 below.

$$\tau_{xy} = -\frac{4p}{\pi} \int_0^\infty \left[\frac{\zeta\eta \sinh \zeta \cosh (\zeta\eta) - \zeta \cosh \zeta \sinh (\zeta\eta)}{2\zeta + \sinh (2\zeta)} \right] \frac{\sin (\alpha\zeta)}{\zeta}$$
$$\sin (\zeta\xi)d\zeta \quad (62)$$

$$\sigma_y = -\frac{4p}{\pi} \int_0^\infty \left[\frac{(\sinh \zeta - \zeta \cosh \zeta) \cosh (\zeta\eta) + \zeta\eta \sinh \zeta \sinh (\zeta\eta)}{\sinh (2\zeta) + 2\zeta} \right]$$
$$\times \frac{\sin (\alpha\zeta)}{\zeta} \cos (\zeta\xi)d\zeta \quad (63)$$

where $\alpha = a/b$, $\eta = x/b$, and $\xi = y/b$. These results have been derived otherwise by Filon,[1] who also considered in some detail the problem of the approximate evaluation of the integrals.

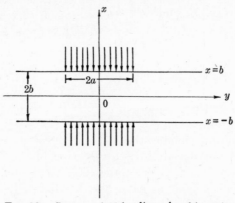

FIG. 80.   Symmetrical loading of a thin strip.

45.5 Asymmetrical distribution of external force. In the problems considered in the preceding section the occurrence of symmetry about the y axis enabled us to make use of the formulas (51) to (53). In problems where no such symmetry exists it is necessary to make use of the more general results (25) to (27). To illustrate the use of these formulas we shall consider the problem of determining the distribution of stress in an infinite strip of width $2d$, loaded symmetrically as shown in Fig. 81. If we suppose that the two loads P are distributed with uniform pressure p over two segments of length a, then the boundary conditions are

(i) On $x = d$, $\tau_{xy} = 0$ for all values of y, and σ_x is equal to $-p$ within the band $b < y < a + b$ but is otherwise zero.

(ii) On $x = -d$, $\tau_{xy} = 0$ for all values of y, $\sigma_x = -p$ within the band $-b - a < y < -b$ and is zero outside it.

Taking

$$G = (A + Bx)e^{-\xi x} + (C + Dx)e^{\xi x} \quad (64)$$

[1] Filon, *loc. cit.*

and making use of the boundary conditions (i) and (ii) in equations (22) and (24), we obtain four equations for the constants A,B,C,D, whose solution may be written in the form

$$A = \frac{2p}{\xi^3} \{\sin [(a + b)\xi] - \sin (b\xi)\} \frac{\sinh (\xi d) + \xi d \cosh (\xi d)}{2\xi d + \sinh (2\xi d)}$$

$$B = - \frac{2p}{i\xi^2} \{\cos [(a + b)\xi] - \cos (b\xi)\} \frac{\cosh (\xi d)}{2\xi d + \sinh (2\xi d)}$$

$$C = \frac{2p}{i\xi^3} \{\cos [(a + b)\xi] - \cos (b\xi)\} \frac{\xi d \sinh (\xi d) + \cosh (\xi d)}{2\xi d + \sinh (2\xi d)}$$

$$D = - \frac{2p}{\xi^2} \{\sin [(a + b)\xi] - \sin (b\xi)\} \frac{\sinh (\xi d)}{2\xi d + \sinh (2\xi d)}$$

Substituting these expressions into equation (64) and putting the resulting expression for $G(x,\xi)$ into equations (25) to (27), we obtain integral

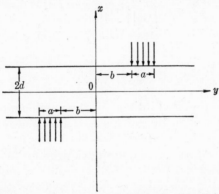

FIG. 81.   Asymmetrical loading of a thin strip.

expressions for the components of stress within the strip.   Once again, the values of these integrals are best found numerically.

46. Distribution of Stress Due to a Force in the Interior of a Semiinfinite Elastic Medium

46.1 Introduction.   A boundary value problem which arises frequently in applied mechanics, for example in soil mechanics and the theory of armor penetration, is that of determining the distribution of stress in a semiinfinite elastic solid due to the action of a force applied to the interior of the medium.   In this section we give an analysis of the case in which the force acts in a direction normal to that of the boundary of the solid. The analysis is similar when the line of action is not normal to the boundary, and therefore it will not be given in detail here.   The equations of plane strain parallel to the xy plane are again employed.   Physically, this is equivalent to assuming that the applied force is acting along an infinite line parallel to the z axis.

In the first instance the external force is assumed to be concentrated, *i.e.*, applied to a single point in the xy plane. Expressions for the components of stress in this case have been given by Melan;[1] they are derived by a different method in Secs. 46.2 and 46.4. The advantage of this method over Melan's is that the corresponding expressions for the components of the displacement vector can be deduced readily. Subsequent to the publication of this analysis[2] a third solution was given by Green,[3] using a complex variable method. It is very difficult to see how this result could be extended to three dimensions by Green's method, whereas the extension of the method given here is obvious and is carried out in Sec. 53.7.

46.2 Fundamental solution for a point force. If a force of magnitude F acts at the origin of coordinates in the negative direction of x, then the stress produced in an infinite elastic medium is determined from the equations (16) and the corresponding displacements are readily shown to be

$$u = \frac{(1+\sigma)F}{4\pi(1-\sigma)E}\left[(3-4\sigma)\log(r) + \frac{y^2}{r^2}\right], \qquad v = -\frac{(1+\sigma)Fxy}{4\pi(1-\sigma)Er^2} \quad (65)$$

Consider now the equilibrium of the semiinfinite elastic medium $x \geq 0$ when a force of magnitude F acts at the point $(h,0)$ in the negative x direction. The components of stress must satisfy the differential equations (2) and must have the same singularities at the point $(h,0)$ as the components defined by equations (16) have at the origin. Furthermore, if we assume that the boundary $x = 0$ is free from stress, we must have

$$\sigma_x = \tau_{xy} = 0 \qquad\qquad \text{on } x = 0 \qquad (66)$$

Combining the solutions (16) and (7) with $V = 0$ (since there are no body forces), we may write for the stress components

$$\sigma_x = \frac{F}{4\pi(1-\sigma)}\left[(1-2\sigma)\left(\frac{x-h}{\rho^2} - \frac{x+h}{\rho_2^2}\right) + \frac{2(x-h)^3}{\rho_1^4} - \frac{2(x+h)^3}{\rho_2^4}\right]$$
$$+ \frac{\partial^2\chi}{\partial y^2} \quad (67)$$

$$\tau_{xy} = \frac{Fy}{4\pi(1-\sigma)}\left[(1-2\sigma)\left(\frac{1}{\rho_1^2} - \frac{1}{\rho_2^2}\right) + \frac{2(x-h)^2}{\rho_1^4} - \frac{2(x+h)^2}{\rho_2^4}\right]$$
$$- \frac{\partial^2\chi}{\partial x\,\partial y} \quad (68)$$

[1] E. Melan, *Z. angew. Math. u. Mech.*, **12**, 343 (1932).
[2] I. N. Sneddon, *Proc. Cambridge Phil. Soc.*, **40**, 229 (1944).
[3] Green, *loc. cit.*

$$\sigma_y = \frac{F}{4\pi(1 - \sigma)}\left[(1 + 2\sigma)\left(\frac{(x - h)}{\rho_1^2} - \frac{(x + h)}{\rho_2^2}\right) - \frac{2(x - h)^3}{\rho_1^4}\right.$$
$$\left. + \frac{2(x + h)^3}{\rho_2^4}\right] + \frac{\partial^2\chi}{\partial x^2} \quad (69)$$

where $\rho_1^2 = (x - h)^2 + y^2$ and $\rho_2^2 = (x + h)^2 + y^2$. Then, since the stress components given by these equations satisfy the equations of equilibrium and have the correct singularities at the point $(h,0)$, the problem will be solved if we can determine a biharmonic function χ of the two variables x and y satisfying the boundary conditions

$$\frac{\partial^2\chi}{\partial x\,\partial y} = 0, \qquad \frac{\partial^2\chi}{\partial y^2} = -p(y) = \frac{Fh}{2\pi(1 - \sigma)}\left[\frac{1 - 2\sigma}{h^2 + y^2} + \frac{2h^2}{(h^2 + y^2)^2}\right] \quad (70)$$

when $x = 0$, and of such a nature as to ensure that all the components of stress tend to zero as x tends to infinity. This problem has already been discussed in Sec. 45.2. The components of stress and displacement can be calculated from equations (34) to (35a) if we make the substitution

$$\bar{p}(\xi) = \int_0^\infty p(y) \cos (\xi y) dy = -\frac{1}{2}F\left[1 + \frac{h\xi}{2(1 - \sigma)}\right]e^{-h\xi} \quad (71)$$

46.3 Conditions on the bounding surface. In problems of this kind most interest is usually attached to the variation of stress along the free surface $x = 0$, and in the two-dimensional case we have the additional advantage that there is only one nonvanishing component of stress there. Before proceeding to the analysis of the distribution of stress in the interior of the medium we shall therefore consider the surface stress. It is of interest to note that the result can be written down without further calculation. This arises from the fact that, when $x = 0$,

$$\frac{\partial^2\chi}{\partial x^2} = \frac{\partial^2\chi}{\partial y^2} = -\frac{2}{\pi}\int_0^\infty \bar{p}(\xi) \cos (\xi y) d\xi = -p(y)$$

as is immediately obvious from equations (7), (34), and (34a). Thus from equations (69) and (70) we find that the surface stress due to a point force of magnitude F acting at $(h,0)$ in the negative x direction is given by the equation

$$(\sigma_y)_0 = \frac{Fh}{2\pi(1 - \sigma)}\left[\frac{1 - 2\sigma}{h^2 + y^2} - \frac{y^2}{(h^2 + y^2)^2}\right] - p(y)$$

the other components of stress being zero. Inserting the value (70) for $p(y)$, we have finally

$$(\sigma_y)_0 = \frac{2Fh}{\pi}\frac{h^2 - \dfrac{\sigma}{1 - \sigma}y^2}{(h^2 + y^2)^2} \quad (72)$$

showing that $(\sigma_y)_0$ is initially positive, decreases steadily through zero at the point $y = h[(1 - \sigma)/\sigma]^{\frac{1}{2}}$, and reaches the minimum value $-\sigma F/h(1 - \sigma)$ when $y = h[(2 - \sigma)/\sigma]^{\frac{1}{2}}$.

We shall now consider the surface stress produced by a force which is distributed over the length of the strip $x = h$, $-a \leq y \leq a$, and acting in the direction of the negative x axis. The stress $(\sigma_y)_0$ at the point $(0,y)$ due to the action of the elementary force $f(u)du$ acting at the point (h,u) can be deduced immediately from equation (72) by replacing F by $f(u)du$ and y by $(y - u)$. Integrating the result over u from $-a$ to a, we then obtain

$$(\sigma_y)_0 = \frac{2h}{\pi} \int_{-a}^{a} \frac{h^2 - \dfrac{\sigma}{1 - \sigma}(y - u)^2}{[h^2 + (y - u)^2]^2} f(u)du \tag{73}$$

for the surface stress due to the distributed force whose resultant in the negative x direction is

$$F = \int_{-a}^{a} f(u)du$$

If the force is *uniformly* distributed over the length of the strip, we may write $f(u) = F/2a$; the integrations are then immediate and yield

$$(\sigma_y)_0 = \frac{Fh}{\pi(1 - \sigma)} \left[\frac{1 - 2\sigma}{2ah} \tan^{-1}\left(\frac{2ah}{h^2 - a^2 + y^2} \right) + \frac{a^2 + h^2 - y^2}{(a^2 + h^2 + y^2)^2 - 4a^2y^2} \right] \tag{74}$$

for the surface stress due to a uniformly distributed force. It may readily be verified that, as $a \to 0$, equation (74) reduces to equation (72)

46.4 Determination of the stress within the medium. Returning now to the problem of determining the components of stress in the interior of the medium, we have from equations (34b) and (71) that

$$\frac{\partial^2 \chi}{\partial x\, \partial y} = -\frac{Fx}{\pi} \int_0^\infty \left[1 + \frac{\xi h}{2(1 - \sigma)} \right] e^{-\xi(h+x)} \sin(\xi y)d\xi$$

$$= -\frac{Fxy}{\pi(1 - \sigma)} \left[\frac{2(1 - \sigma)x + (1 - 2\sigma)h}{\rho_2^4} + \frac{4h(x + h)^2}{\rho_2^6} \right]$$

and that

$$\frac{\partial^2 \chi}{\partial y^2} - \frac{\partial^2 \chi}{\partial x^2} = \frac{2Fx}{\pi(1 - \sigma)} \int_0^\infty \xi \left[(1 - \sigma) + \frac{1}{2}\xi h \right] e^{-\xi(h+x)} \cos(\xi y)d\xi$$

$$= \frac{2Fx}{\pi(1 - \sigma)} \left\{ (1 - \sigma)\left[\frac{2(h + x)^2}{\rho_2^4} - \frac{1}{\rho_2^2} \right] + h(h + x) \times \left[\frac{4(h + x)^2}{\rho_2^6} - \frac{3}{\rho_2^4} \right] \right\}$$

Substituting from these equations into equations (67) to (69), we obtain the expressions

$$\tau_{xy} = \frac{Fy}{4\pi(1-\sigma)}\left[(1-2\sigma)\left(\frac{1}{\rho_1^2} - \frac{1}{\rho_2^2}\right) + \frac{2(x-h)^2}{\rho_1^4}\right.$$
$$\left. + \frac{2(3-4\sigma)x^2 - 8\sigma hx - 2h^2}{\rho_2^4} + \frac{16hx(h+x)^2}{\rho_2^6}\right] \quad (75)$$

and

$$\sigma_x - \sigma_y = \frac{F}{\pi(1-\sigma)}\left\{\frac{(x-h)^3}{\rho_1^4} - \frac{\sigma(x-h)}{\rho_1^2} + \frac{\sigma h - (2-3\sigma)x}{\rho_1^2}\right.$$
$$\left. + \frac{8hx(h+x)^3}{\rho_2^6} + \frac{(x+h)[(3-4\sigma)x^2 + 4(1+\sigma)hx - h^2]}{\rho_2^4}\right\} \quad (76)$$

By means of these expressions the maximum shearing stress across any plane through the point (x,y) can be calculated from the formula

$$\tau = [(\tfrac{1}{2}\sigma_x - \tfrac{1}{2}\sigma_y)^2 + \tau_{xy}^2]^{\frac{1}{2}} \quad (77)$$

If the values of the stress components σ_x and σ_y are desired, use can be made of the result

$$\frac{\partial^2\chi}{\partial x} + \frac{\partial^2\chi}{\partial y^2} = \frac{4}{\pi}\int_0^\infty \bar{p}(\xi)e^{-\xi x}\cos(\xi y)d\xi$$
$$= \frac{F}{\pi(1-\sigma)}\left[\frac{2(1-\sigma)x + (1-2\sigma)h}{\rho_2^2} + \frac{2h(h+x)^2}{\rho_2^4}\right]$$

to yield

$$\sigma_x + \sigma_y = \frac{F}{2\pi(1-\sigma)}\left[\frac{x-h}{\rho_1^2} + \frac{(3-4\sigma)x + (1-4\sigma)h}{\rho_2^2} + \frac{4h(h+x)^2}{\rho_2^4}\right] \quad (78)$$

In a similar fashion we have for the components of the displacement vector at the point (x,y)

$$u = -\frac{(1+\sigma)F}{\pi E}\left\{2(1-\sigma)\log(\rho_2^{-1}) - \frac{3-4\sigma}{4(1-\sigma)}\log\left(\frac{\rho_1}{\rho_2}\right)\right.$$
$$\left. + \frac{y^2}{4(1-\sigma)}\left(\frac{1}{\rho_1^2} - \frac{1}{\rho_2^2}\right) + \frac{(h+x)^2}{\rho_2^2} + \frac{hx}{2(1-\sigma)}\left[\frac{2(h+x)^2}{\rho_2^4} - \frac{1}{\rho_2^2}\right]\right\}$$

and

$$v = \frac{(1+\sigma)F}{\pi E}\left\{(1-2\sigma)\tan^{-1}\left(\frac{y}{h+x}\right) + \left[\frac{(1-2\sigma)h}{2(1-\sigma)} - x\right]\frac{y}{\rho_2^2}\right.$$
$$\left. - \frac{hxy(h+x)}{(1-\sigma)\rho_2^4} - \frac{y}{4(1-\sigma)}\left[\frac{x-h}{\rho_1^2} - \frac{x+h}{\rho_2^2}\right]\right\}$$

46.5 Stress due to a force distributed over a strip. The components of stress at a point (x,y) in the interior of a semiinfinite elastic medium due to the action of a force of magnitude F distributed uniformly over the strip $x = h$, $-a \leq y \leq a$, and in the direction of the negative x direction can readily be calculated. The shearing stress τ_{xy} due to the elementary force $(F/2a)du$ acting at the point (h,u) can be written down from equation (75). Integrating with respect to u over the range $(-a,a)$, we find that the shearing stress produced by the distributed force is given by the integral

$$\frac{4\pi(1 - \sigma)\tau_{xy}}{F} = \int_{-a}^{a} \left\{ (1 - 2\sigma) \left[\frac{1}{(x - h)^2 + (y - u)^2} \right. \right.$$
$$\left. - \frac{1}{(x + h)^2 + (y - u)^2} \right] + \frac{2(3 - 4\sigma)x^2 - 8\sigma hx - 2h^2}{[(x + h)^2 + (y - u)^2]^2}$$
$$\left. + \frac{2(x - h)^2}{[(x - h)^2 + (y - u)^2]^2} + \frac{16hx(h + x)^2}{[(x + h)^2 + (y - u)^2]^3} \right\} (y - u)du$$

The integrals involved in this expression can be readily expressed in terms

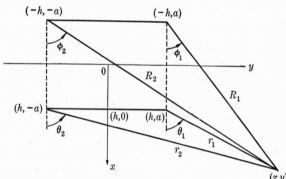

Fig. 82.   The coordinates R_1, R_2, r_1, r_2, θ_1, θ_2, ϕ_1, and ϕ_2.

of elementary functions. If we adopt the notation

$$r_1^2 = (x - h)^2 + (y - a)^2, \qquad r_2^2 = (x - h)^2 + (y + a)^2$$
$$R_1^2 = (x + h)^2 + (y - a)^2, \qquad R_2^2 = (x + h)^2 + (y + a)^2$$

(cf. Fig. 82), we then have, in the case of a distributed force,

$$\tau_{xy} = \frac{F}{8\pi a(1 - \sigma)} \left\{ (1 - 2\sigma) \log\left(\frac{r_2 R_1}{r_1 R_2}\right) + (x - h)^2 \left(\frac{1}{r_1^2} - \frac{1}{r_2^2}\right) \right.$$
$$\left. + 4hx(h + x)^2 \left(\frac{1}{R_1^4} - \frac{1}{R_2^4}\right) + [(3 - 4\sigma)x^2 - 4\sigma hx - h^2] \left(\frac{1}{R_1^2} - \frac{1}{R_2^2}\right) \right\}$$
$$(79)$$

Similarly, if we write $\tan\theta_1 = (y - a)/(x - h)$, $\tan\theta_2 = (y + a)/(x - h)$, $\tan\phi_1 = (y - a)/(x + h)$, $\tan\phi_2 = (y + a)/(x + h)$, we find from equation (78)

$$\sigma_x + \sigma_y = \frac{F}{4\pi a(1 - \sigma)}\left[\theta_2 - \theta_1 + (3 - 4\sigma)(\phi_2 - \phi_1)\right.$$

$$\left. + \frac{h}{h + x}\left(\sin 2\phi_2 - \sin 2\phi_1\right)\right] \quad (80)$$

and from equation (76)

$$\sigma_x - \sigma_y = \frac{F}{4\pi a(1 - \sigma)}\left[(1 - 2\sigma)(\theta_2 - \theta_1 - \phi_2 + \phi_1)\right.$$

$$+ \frac{1}{2}(\sin 2\theta_2 - \sin 2\theta_1) + \frac{(3 - 4\sigma)x^2 + 4(1 - \sigma)hx - h^2}{2(h + x)^2}$$

$$\left. \times (\sin 2\phi_2 - \sin 2\phi_1) + \frac{hx}{2(h + x)^2}(\sin 4\phi_2 - \sin 4\phi_1)\right] \quad (81)$$

As a check on these results we may determine the stress produced in a semiinfinite elastic medium by a uniform surface pressure—a problem which has been considered above (Sec. 45.2, Example 2). Putting $h = 0$, and noting that $\phi_1 = \theta_1$, $\phi_2 = \theta_2$, $R_1 = r_1$, $R_2 = r_2$ in equations (79) to (81), we find that they reduce to equations (44) apart from the difference in sign caused by the fact that the external force system of this section is equivalent, in the limiting case, to an applied tension instead of an applied pressure.

The maximum shearing stress τ can easily be calculated from equations (77), (79), and (81). This was done for various values of y/a and x/a in the special case of an incompressible solid ($\sigma = \frac{1}{2}$) and $h = a$. Tables of this and the other components are given in the

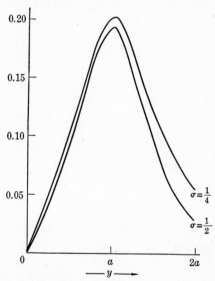

FIG. 83. The variation with σ and y of τ_{xy} in the plane $x = \frac{1}{2}a$.

original paper[1] to which the reader is referred for details.

By calculating, in the incompressible case, the value of τ_{xy} in the planes

[1] I. N. Sneddon, *Proc. Cambridge Phil. Soc.*, **40**, 229 (1944).

$x = a$, $\frac{1}{2}a$, $\frac{1}{4}a$, we see that by far the greatest values of τ_{xy} occur in the plane $x = \frac{1}{2}a$; therefore we shall estimate the effect of incompressibility by confining our attention to the variation of τ_{xy} in this plane. The results for $\sigma = \frac{1}{2}$ and $\sigma = \frac{1}{4}$ are shown in Fig. 83. It is obvious from this diagram that there is no significant difference between the shearing stress in a compressible medium and that in an incompressible one—a fact of which we make use to simplify greatly the analysis in the three-dimensional case. This is borne out by calculations of the stress components in other planes; hence we may conclude that the assumption that the medium is incompressible does not affect the physics of the problem in any significant manner.

47. Distribution of Stress in the Neighborhood of a Griffith Crack

47.1 Introduction. A theory of rupture of nonductile materials such as glass has been put forward by Griffith on the assumption of the existence of a large number of cracks in the interior of the solid body.[1] The fundamental concept of the Griffith theory is that the bounding surfaces of a solid possess a surface tension, just as those of a liquid do, and that, when a crack spreads, the decrease in the strain energy is balanced by an increase in the potential energy due to this surface tension. The calculation of the effect of the presence of a crack on the energy of an elastic body is based on Inglis's solution[2] of the two-dimensional equations of elastic equilibrium in the space bounded by two concentric ellipses, the crack then being taken to be an ellipse of zero minor axis. Denoting the surface tension of the material forming the solid body by T, the Young's modulus by E, and the width of the crack by $2c$, Griffith showed that in the case of plane strain the crack will spread when the stress P applied normally to the direction of the crack exceeds the critical value

$$P_c = \left[\frac{2ET}{\pi c(1 - \sigma^2)} \right]^{\frac{1}{2}} \tag{82}$$

Because of the nature of the coordinate system employed by Griffith the expressions he derives for the components of stress in the neighborhood of a crack do not lend themselves easily to computation. An alternative method of determining the distribution of stress in the vicinity of a Griffith crack is to suppose that the body is deformed by the opening of a crack under the action of a uniform hydrostatic pressure acting over

---

[1] A. A. Griffith, *Phil. Trans.*, **A221**, 180 (1921); *Proc. Intern. Congr. Applied Mech. (Delft)*, 1924, p. 55.

[2] C. E. Inglis, *Engineering*, **95**, 415 (1913); *Trans. Inst. Naval Arch.*, **55**, 219 (1913).

its surface.[1]   In the case of a uniform pressure the calculations may be based on a solution of the elastic equations given by Westergaard.[2]   The advantage of this form of analysis is not only that it is simpler than Inglis's but that Cartesian coordinates are employed throughout, thus facilitating the interpretation of the numerical results.   This method, however, suffers from the disadvantage that the Westergaard stress function refers only to the case in which the Griffith crack is opened under the action of a *uniform* pressure.   The stress function corresponding to a variable internal pressure can, however, be constructed by making use of the theory of Fourier transforms and dual integral equations.[3]   It is this method which we shall consider here.   It consists essentially in considering the corresponding boundary value problem for a semiinfinite medium. This method has the added advantage that it can readily be extended to the three-dimensional problem of determining the stress in the neighborhood of a "penny-shaped" crack—except that there we employ a Hankel transform in place of the Fourier cosine transform used here (see Sec. 54).

47.2 Derivation of the dual integral equations.   We consider the distribution of stress in the interior of an infinite two-dimensional elastic medium when a very thin internal crack $-c \leq y \leq c$, $x = 0$, is opened under the action of a pressure which may be considered to vary in magnitude along the length of the crack.   The stress in such a medium may be described by the three stress components σ_x, σ_y, τ_{xy} satisfying the partial differential equations (2).   Denoting the displacement vector by $(u,v,0)$, then we see that the boundary conditions to be satisfied are that u,v and all the components of stress must vanish as $x^2 + y^2$ tends to infinity and that

$$\tau_{xy} = 0, \qquad \sigma_x = -p_0(y) \qquad \text{on } x = 0, \; -c \leq y \leq c \quad (83)$$

It is obvious from the symmetry about the y axis that the problem of determining the distribution of stress in the neighborhood of the crack is equivalent to that of determining the stress in the semiinfinite solid $x \geq 0$ when the boundary $x = 0$ is subjected to the following conditions:

(i) $$\tau_{xy} = 0 \qquad \text{for all values of } y$$
(ii) $$\sigma_x = -p_0(y), \; |y| \leq c; \qquad u = 0, \; |y| \geq c$$

From the symmetry about the x axis we may take as solutions of the elastic equations the expressions (34), (34a), and (34b).   These expressions satisfy the equations of equilibrium and the boundary condition (i) above.   The function $\bar{p}(\xi)$ occurring in these expressions is then

[1] I. N. Sneddon, *Proc. Roy. Soc. (London)*, **A187**, 229 (1946).
[2] H. M. Westergaard, *Jour. Applied Mech.*, **6**, A49 (1939).
[3] I. N. Sneddon and H. A. Elliott, *Quart. Applied Math.*, **4**, 262 (1946).

determined from the pair of conditions (ii). When $x = 0$, it follows from equation (34) that

$$\sigma_x = -\frac{2}{\pi} \int_0^\infty \bar{p}(\xi) \cos(\xi y) d\xi \tag{84}$$

and from equation (35) that

$$u = \frac{4(1 - \sigma^2)}{\pi E} \int_0^\infty \bar{p}(\xi) \frac{\cos(\xi y)}{\xi} d\xi \tag{85}$$

From (ii) we see therefore that the equations determining $\bar{p}(\xi)$ are the dual integral equations

$$\frac{2}{\pi} \int_0^\infty \bar{p}(\xi) \cos(\xi y) d\xi = p_0(y) \qquad 0 \leq y \leq c$$

$$\int_0^\infty \bar{p}(\xi) \frac{\cos(\xi y)}{\xi} d\xi = 0 \qquad y \geq c$$

If, now, we make the substitutions

$$\xi = \frac{\rho}{c}, \qquad g(\eta) = c\left(\frac{\pi}{2\eta}\right)^{\frac{1}{2}} p_0(\eta c)$$

$$\left. y = \eta c, \qquad \bar{p}\left(\frac{\rho}{c}\right) = \rho^{\frac{1}{2}} F(\rho), \qquad \cos(\rho\eta) = \left(\frac{\pi\rho\eta}{2}\right)^{\frac{1}{2}} J_{-\frac{1}{2}}(\rho\eta) \right\} \tag{86}$$

we find that the equations may be written in the form

$$\left. \int_0^\infty \rho F(\rho) J_{-\frac{1}{2}}(\rho\eta) d\rho = g(\eta) \qquad 0 \leq \eta \leq 1 \\ \int_0^\infty F(\rho) J_{-\frac{1}{2}}(\rho\eta) d\rho = 0 \qquad \eta > 1 \right\} \tag{87}$$

From this pair of dual integral equations we may determine the function $F(\rho)$. Once $F(\rho)$ has been found, $\bar{p}(\xi)$ can be written down and the components of stress calculated by means of equations (34), (34a), and (34b).

47.3 Solution of the dual integral equations. The dual integral equations (87) are a special case of the pair of equations considered by Busbridge (Sec. 12). The solution may be obtained by substituting $\alpha = 1$, $\nu = -\frac{1}{2}$ in the general solution (47) given there. In this way we obtain

$$F(\rho) = \left(\frac{2\rho}{\pi}\right)^{\frac{1}{2}} \left[J_0(\rho) \int_0^1 y^{\frac{1}{2}}(1 - y^2)^{\frac{1}{2}} g(y) dy \right.$$
$$\left. + \rho \int_0^1 u^{\frac{1}{2}}(1 - u^2)^{\frac{1}{2}} du \int_0^1 g(yu) y^{\frac{1}{2}} J_1(\rho y) dy \right] \tag{88}$$

Thus if the applied pressure $p_0(y)$ is given by a Maclaurin series of the form

$$p_0(y) = p_0 \sum_{n=0}^{\infty} a_n \left(\frac{y}{c}\right)^n \tag{89}$$

convergent for $-c \leq y \leq c$, then the corresponding expression for $\bar{p}(\xi)$ is, with the aid of equations (88) and (86), readily found to be

$$\bar{p}(\xi) = \frac{1}{4} p_0 c^2 \pi^{\frac{1}{2}} \xi \sum_{n=0}^{\infty} \frac{2\Gamma(\frac{1}{2}n + \frac{1}{2})}{\Gamma(\frac{1}{2}n + 2)} a_n \left[J_0(c\xi) + c\xi \int_0^1 y^{n+2} J_1(c\xi y) dy \right] \tag{90}$$

Substituting from equation (90) into equation (85), we find that $w(y)$, the value of u when $x = 0$, is given by the equation

$$w(y) = \frac{2(1 - \sigma^2)}{\pi^{\frac{1}{2}} E} p_0 c^2 \sum_{n=0}^{\infty} \frac{\Gamma(\frac{1}{2}n + \frac{1}{2})}{\Gamma(\frac{1}{2}n + 2)} a_n \left[\int_0^{\infty} J_0(c\xi) \cos(\xi y) d\xi \right.$$

$$\left. + c \int_0^1 y^{n+2} dy \int_0^{\infty} \xi J_1(c\xi y) \cos(\xi y) d\xi \right]$$

Making use of the results[1]

$$\int_0^{\infty} J_0(c\xi) \cos(\xi y) d\xi = \begin{cases} (c^2 - y^2)^{-\frac{1}{2}} & 0 \leq y < c \\ 0 & y > c \end{cases}$$

$$\int_0^{\infty} \xi J_1(c\xi) \cos(\xi y) d\xi = \begin{cases} c(c^2 - y^2)^{-\frac{3}{2}} & 0 \leq y < c \\ 0 & y > c \end{cases}$$

we verify that $w(y) = 0$ when $y > c$ and find that the normal component of displacement along the crack is given by

$$w(y) = \frac{2(1 - \sigma^2)}{\pi^{\frac{1}{2}} E} p_0 c \sum_{n=0}^{\infty} \frac{\Gamma(\frac{1}{2}n + \frac{1}{2})}{\Gamma(\frac{1}{2}n + 2)} a_n \left[\frac{c}{(c^2 - y^2)^{\frac{1}{2}}} \right.$$

$$\left. + \left(\frac{y}{c}\right)^{n+1} \int_1^{c/y} \frac{u^{n+3} du}{(u^2 - 1)^{\frac{3}{2}}} \right] \tag{91}$$

For the case of a uniform pressure p_0, we take $a_0 = 1$, $a_n = 0$ $(n \geq 1)$, in which case equation (91) reduces to

$$w = \frac{2(1 - \sigma^2) p_0}{E} (c^2 - y^2)^{\frac{1}{2}} \tag{92}$$

[1] G. N. Watson, "The Theory of Bessel Functions" (Cambridge, London, 1922), p. 401.

If we write

$$b = \frac{2(1 - \sigma^2)p_0 c}{E} \qquad (92a)$$

equation (92) assumes the form $y^2/c^2 + w^2/b^2 = 1$, which shows that the effect of the uniform pressure is to widen the crevice into an elliptical crack.

47.4 Distribution of pressure producing a crack of prescribed shape. It is also of interest to determine what distribution of pressure will produce a crack of prescribed shape. In this instance we assume that the value of the normal displacement u is known all along the y axis, that is, we replace the boundary conditions (ii), Sec. 47.2, by the single condition

$$u = \begin{cases} w(y) & |y| \le c, \, x = 0 \\ 0 & |y| > c, \, x = 0 \end{cases}$$

where it is assumed that $w(y)$ is an even function of y, or, in other words, that the displacement is symmetrical about the x axis. We then have from equation (85)

$$\int_0^\infty \frac{\bar{p}(\xi)}{\xi} \cos (\xi y) d\xi = \begin{cases} \dfrac{\pi E}{4(1 - \sigma^2)} \, w(y) & 0 \le y \le c \\ 0 & y > c \end{cases}$$

Inverting this result by the Fourier cosine rule (Theorem 8), we have

$$\bar{p}(\xi) = \frac{\xi E}{2(1 - \sigma^2)} \int_0^c w(y) \cos (\xi y) dy \qquad (93)$$

With this value of $\bar{p}(\xi)$ in equations (34), (34a), and (34b) we obtain expressions for the components of stress in the interior of the solid. For example, if we take

$$w(y) = \epsilon \left(1 - \frac{y^2}{c^2} \right)$$

it follows from equation (93), as a result of integration by parts, that

$$\bar{p}(\xi) = \frac{E\epsilon}{c\xi(1 - \sigma^2)} \left[\frac{\sin (c\xi)}{c\xi} - \cos (c\xi) \right]$$

Substituting from this equation into equation (94), we obtain, for the normal component of stress along $x = 0$,

$$\sigma_x = - \frac{2E}{\pi(1 - \sigma^2)c} \left[1 - \frac{y}{c} \int_0^\infty \frac{\sin (u) \sin (yu/c)}{u} \, du \right]$$

Now,

$$\int_0^\infty \frac{\cos (qx) - \cos (px)}{x} \, dx = \frac{1}{2} \log \left(\frac{p^2}{q^2} \right)$$

so that, finally, we have

$$\sigma_x = -\frac{2E}{\pi(1-\sigma^2)c}\left[1-\frac{y}{2c}\log\left(\frac{c+y}{c-y}\right)\right] \quad 0 \le y < c \quad (94)$$

for the normal component of stress along the crack. This stress is compressive when $y = 0$ but becomes tensile for a value of y between 0 and c. Thus, if a crack of this shape is to be maintained, the applied stress must be tensile near the edges of the crack.

47.5 Crack opened up by uniform pressure. We now consider the distribution of stress in the solid when the crevice $-c \le y \le c$, $x = 0$, is opened up by the action of a uniform pressure p_0. Taking $a_0 = 1$, $a_n = 0$ $(n \ge 1)$ in equation (90) we find, after a little reduction, that

$$\bar{p}(\xi) = \tfrac{1}{2}\pi p_0 c J_1(c\xi) \tag{95}$$

Substituting from equation (95) into equations (34), (34a), and (34b), we obtain the expressions

$$\frac{1}{2}(\sigma_x + \sigma_y) = -p_0 c \int_0^\infty e^{-\xi x} \cos(\xi y) J_1(c\xi) d\xi \tag{96}$$

$$\frac{1}{2}(\sigma_y - \sigma_x) = p_0 c x \int_0^\infty \xi e^{-\xi x} \cos(\xi y) J_1(c\xi) d\xi \tag{97}$$

$$\tau_{xy} = -p_0 c x \int_0^\infty \xi e^{-\xi x} \sin(\xi y) J_1(c\xi) d\xi \tag{98}$$

for the components of stress. The maximum shearing stress across any plane through the point (x,y) can readily be found. It follows at once from equations (97) and (98) that

$$\frac{1}{2}(\sigma_y - \sigma_x) + i\tau_{xy} = p_0 c x \int_0^\infty \xi e^{-\xi z} J_1(c\xi) d\xi \tag{99}$$

where $z = x + iy = re^{i\theta}$. Now

$$\int_0^\infty \xi e^{-\xi z} J_1(c\xi) d\xi = c(c^2 + z^2)^{-\frac{3}{2}} = c(r_1 r_2)^{-\frac{3}{2}} e^{-\frac{3}{2}i(\theta_1 + \theta_2)} \tag{100}$$

if we write $z - ic = r_1 e^{i\theta_1}$ and $z + ic = r_2 e^{i\theta_2}$. But τ is the modulus of $\frac{1}{2}(\sigma_y - \sigma_x) + i\tau_{xy}$ so that we obtain from equation (100)

$$\tau = p_0 \frac{r}{c}\left(\frac{c^2}{r_1 r_2}\right)^{\frac{3}{2}} |\cos\theta| \tag{101}$$

If the components of stress are desired separately, then, equating real and imaginary parts of equations (99) and (100), we find that

$$\frac{1}{2}(\sigma_y - \sigma_x) = p_0 \frac{r}{c}\left(\frac{c^2}{r_1 r_2}\right)^{\frac{3}{2}} \cos\theta \cos\left[\frac{3}{2}(\theta_1 + \theta_2)\right] \tag{102}$$

$$\tau_{xy} = -p_0 \frac{r}{c}\left(\frac{c^2}{r_1 r_2}\right)^{\frac{3}{2}} \cos\theta \sin\left[\frac{3}{2}(\theta_1 + \theta_2)\right] \tag{103}$$

Similarly, we may write equation (96) in the form

$$\frac{1}{2}(\sigma_x + \sigma_y) = -p_0 c \mathsf{R}\int_0^\infty e^{-\xi z} J_1(c\xi)d\xi = -p_0 c \mathsf{R}\left[1 - \frac{z}{(z^2 + c^2)^{\frac{1}{2}}}\right]$$

which gives

$$\frac{1}{2}(\sigma_y + \sigma_x) = p_0\left[\frac{r}{(r_1 r_2)^{\frac{1}{2}}}\cos\left(\theta - \frac{1}{2}\theta_1 - \frac{1}{2}\theta_2\right) - 1\right] \tag{104}$$

The components of stress at any point in the solid are uniquely determined by the equations (102), (103), and (104).

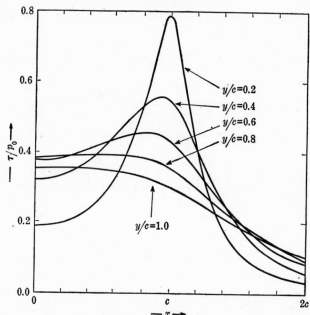

FIG. 84.   The variation of τ/p_0 with x and y.

It is readily verified from these equations that, when $x = 0$ and $|y| < c$, $\sigma_x = \sigma_y = -p_0$, $\tau_{xy} = 0$ and that, when $x = 0$ and $|y| > c$, $\tau_{xy} = 0$ and

$$\sigma_x = p_0\left[\frac{y}{(y^2 - c^2)^{\frac{1}{2}}} - 1\right]$$

Thus, if $(y - c)$ is small and positive, the normal component of the surface stress σ_x is given approximately by the formula

$$\sigma_x \simeq p_0 \left[\frac{c}{2(y - c)} \right]^{\frac{1}{2}} \tag{105}$$

To give some idea of the distribution of stress in the neighborhood of the crack, the maximum shearing stress τ was calculated for several values of x and y by means of equation (101). The results of these calculations are shown in Fig. 84. A convenient method of showing the

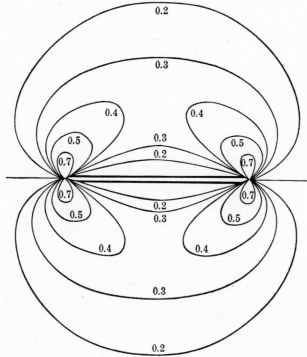

FIG. 85.   The isochromatic lines in the vicinity of a Griffith crack.

variation of the function and of visualizing the distribution of stress in the solid consists in plotting the isochromatic lines $\tau = const.$ If we write the constant as $p_0\alpha$, then the equation of this family of curves is seen from equation (101) to be

$$c^2 x^4 = \alpha [(y - c)^2 + x^2]^{\frac{3}{2}} [(y + c)^2 + x^2]^{\frac{3}{2}} \tag{106}$$

where α is a parameter. The isochromatic lines were constructed by determining the points in the vicinity of the crack at which the parameter α assumes the values 0.7, 0.5, 0.4, 0.3, and 0.2. The result is shown in Fig. 85. Although there would seem to be no photoelastic determinations of the stress distribution in the vicinity of a Griffith crack, there is a remarkable degree of similarity between the theoretical isochromatic lines of Fig. 85 and those in the vicinity of the lower straight edge of a railway tunnel as determined experimentally by Farquharson.[1]

47.6 Griffith's condition for rupture. Finally we make use of these results to derive Griffith's condition (82) for the rupture of the solid. When the semiminor axis of the ellipse is ϵ, it follows from equation (92a) that the internal pressure has the value $E\epsilon/2(1 - \sigma^2)c$. Considering an element of length of the crack, we find from equation (92) that the work done in increasing the semiminor axis to $\epsilon + d\epsilon$ is

$$2p \, dy \, dw = \frac{E}{(1 - \sigma^2)} \left(\frac{\epsilon + \frac{1}{2}d\epsilon}{c} \right) dy \left(1 - \frac{y^2}{c^2} \right)^{\frac{1}{2}} d\epsilon$$

so that the energy of the crack is

$$W = \frac{2E}{c(1 - \sigma^2)} \int_0^c \left(1 - \frac{y^2}{c^2} \right)^{\frac{1}{2}} dy \int_0^\epsilon d\epsilon = \frac{\pi(1 - \sigma^2)p_0^2 c^2}{E} \qquad (107)$$

where p_0 denotes the final pressure.

Let us now consider a crack in an elastic body of finite dimensions. If we assume that the length of the crack is very much less than the dimensions of the body, we may replace the finite elastic body by an infinite elastic body with a crack in its interior which is subjected to the stress system $\sigma_x = p_0$, when $x^2 + y^2$ is very large. Since the surface of the crack may be assumed to be free from external forces, the further boundary conditions $\sigma_x = \tau_{xy} = 0$ when $x = 0$ and $|y| < c$ follow. If the solution $\sigma_x = p_0$, $\sigma_y = p_1$, $\tau_{xy} = 0$ is added to equations (102) to (104), the expressions so obtained satisfy the equations of equilibrium and the new boundary conditions. The distribution of stress in the interior of the solid can then be determined from the results of Sec. 47.5 by a very simple calculation.

It follows immediately from equation (107) that, if a brittle body is acted upon by uniform stress $\sigma_x = p_0$, $\sigma_y = p_1$, the presence of a Griffith crack of length $2c$ lowers the potential energy of the medium by an amount $W = \pi(1 - \sigma^2)p_0^2 c^2/E$. The crack also has a surface energy $U = 4cT$, where T denotes the surface tension of the material. The condition that the crack may just begin to spread is that c should be such that

$$\frac{\partial}{\partial c} (W - U) = 0$$

[1] M. M. Frocht, "Photoelasticity" (Wiley, New York, 1941), Vol. 1, p. 347.

that is, that

$$c = \frac{2ET}{\pi(1 - \sigma^2)p_0^2}$$

which is equivalent to the Griffith condition (82).

48. Indentation Problems[1]

48.1 Introduction. In Sec. 45.2 we considered the distribution of stress in a semiinfinite elastic medium when its surface was deformed by the application of pressure. This analysis was based on the assumption that, along the surface, the shearing stress was zero and the normal component of stress was prescribed. If the surface is deformed by the pressure against it of a rigid body C, then by a suitable choice of coordinate system

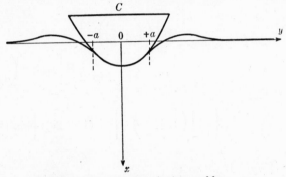

FIG. 86. The indentation problem.

we may assume, at least in first approximation, that the body C is in contact with the elastic solid along the band $x = 0$, $-a \leq y \leq a$ (cf. Fig. 86). In this case we may assume that the surface shearing stress is zero and that, within the band $|y| < a$, the normal component u of the surface displacement is prescribed but, outside $|y| < a$, we have, instead of a knowledge of u, the condition that the normal component of stress is zero. Along $x = 0$ we therefore have the conditions

$$\tau_{xy} = 0 \qquad -\infty < y < \infty \qquad (108)$$

and

$$\left. \begin{array}{ll} u = u_0(y) & |y| < a \\ \sigma_x = 0 & |y| > a \end{array} \right\} \qquad (108a)$$

where $u_0(y)$ is a prescribed function of y. One of the objects of the solution we then derive will be to yield the distribution of surface pressure within the band $|y| < a$ and the form of the displacement outside it.

[1] Cf. a paper by H. G. Hopkins to be published shortly. The author is indebted to Mr. Hopkins for communicating his results before publication.

We shall suppose that

$$u_0(y) = u_0^{(1)}(y) + u_0^{(2)}(y) \tag{109}$$

where $u_0^{(1)}(y)$, or simply $u_0^{(1)}$, is a constant and $u_0^{(2)}(y)$ corresponds to zero resultant applied force. In the following sections we shall discuss the solutions of this problem for the cases in which $u^{(2)}(y)$ is an even or an odd function of y. By combining these solutions we arrive at a solution of a more general kind.

48.2 Indentation of a semiinfinite solid by a rectangular block. The fundamental solution is that corresponding to the case in which the rigid body C is a rectangular block so that $u_0(y) = u_0^{(1)}$, a constant. It is readily shown, by the methods of Sec. 45.3, that the solution of this problem is given by[1]

$$u = u_0^{(1)} \left\{ 1 + \frac{x}{2a(1 - \sigma) \log_e 2} \, \mathsf{R}\left[\left(1 + \frac{z^2}{a^2} \right)^{-\frac{1}{2}} \right] \right.$$
$$\left. - \frac{1}{\log_e 2} \, \mathsf{R}\left[\sinh^{-1}\left(\frac{z}{a} \right) \right] \right\} \tag{110}$$

and

$$v = - \frac{u_0^{(1)}}{2(1 - \sigma) \log_e 2} \left\{ \frac{x}{a} \, \mathsf{I}\left[\left(1 + \frac{z^2}{a^2} \right)^{-\frac{1}{2}} \right] - (1 - 2\sigma) \, \mathsf{I}\left[\sinh^{-1}\left(\frac{z}{a} \right) \right] \right\} \tag{111}$$

where $z = x + iy$. If we write

$$k = \frac{u_0^{(1)}}{2a(1 - \sigma^2) \log_e 2} \tag{112}$$

and introduce the dimensionless variables $\xi = x/a$, $\eta = y/a$

$$s = z/a = (x + iy)/a$$

we find that the components of stress are given by the expressions

$$\left. \begin{aligned} \frac{\sigma_x}{E} &= - \frac{k}{\pi} \, \mathsf{R}[(1 + s^2 + \xi s)(1 + s^2)^{-\frac{3}{2}}] \\ \frac{\sigma_y}{E} &= - \frac{k}{\pi} \, \mathsf{R}[(1 + s^2 - \xi s)(1 + s^2)^{-\frac{3}{2}}] \\ \frac{\tau_{xy}}{E} &= \frac{k\xi}{\pi} \, \mathsf{R}[s(1 + s^2)^{-\frac{3}{2}}] \end{aligned} \right\} \tag{113}$$

It follows immediately from these equations that the stresses at the plane boundary are given by $\tau_{xy} = 0$, and

[1] Sadowsky, *loc. cit.*

$$\frac{\sigma_x}{E} = \frac{\sigma_y}{E} = \left\{ \begin{array}{ll} -\dfrac{u_0^{(1)}}{2a(1 - \sigma^2) \log_e 2} (1 - \eta^2)^{-\frac{1}{2}} & |\eta| < 1 \\ 0 & |\eta| > 1 \end{array} \right\} \quad (114)$$

The corresponding expression for the components of the surface displacement are

$$u = \left\{ \begin{array}{ll} u_0^{(1)} & |\eta| < 1 \\ u_0^{(1)} \left[1 - \dfrac{\log (2\eta^2 - 1)}{2 \log_e 2} \right] & |\eta| > 1 \end{array} \right\} \quad (115)$$

and

$$v = \left\{ \begin{array}{ll} -u_0^{(1)} \dfrac{1 - 2\sigma}{2(1 - \sigma)} \dfrac{\sin^{-1}(\eta)}{\log_e 2} & |\eta| < 1 \\ -u_0^{(1)} \dfrac{(1 - 2\sigma)}{4(1 - \sigma) \log_e 2} & |\eta| > 1 \end{array} \right\} \quad (116)$$

in agreement with the prescribed boundary conditions. A simple integration shows further that the total pressure P is given by the equation $E u_0^{(1)} \pi = 2(1 - \sigma^2) P \log_e 2$.

48.3 Symmetrical indentation. We shall now consider the case in which $u_0^{(1)}$ is zero and the function $u^{(2)}(y)$ is an even function. To simplify the final results we write $u_0^{(2)}(\eta) = u_0^{(2)}(y)/a$ and employ ξ and η as above. If we take E as the unit of stress, we may write $(\sigma_x, \sigma_y, \tau_{xy})$ in the dimensionless form $(\sigma_\xi, \sigma_\eta, \tau_{\xi\eta})$ and we see that we require a solution of the equilibrium equations which satisfies the boundary conditions

$$\tau_{\xi\eta} = 0, |\eta| < 1; \qquad u = \left\{ \begin{array}{ll} u_0^{(2)}(\eta) & 0 \leq \eta \leq 1 \\ u_0^{(2)}(-\eta) & -1 \leq \eta \leq 0 \end{array} \right\} \quad (117)$$
$$\sigma_\xi = \tau_{\xi\eta} = 0, \qquad |\eta| > 1 \quad \text{on } \xi = 0$$

It follows from equations (34) to (35a) that a suitable solution of the equations of equilibrium satisfying the condition that $\tau_{\xi\eta} = 0$ is given by the equations

$$\sigma_\xi = -\int_0^\infty \lambda^2 \alpha(\lambda)(1 + \xi\lambda)e^{-\xi\lambda} \cos(\lambda\eta)d\lambda$$
$$\sigma_\eta = -\int_0^\infty \lambda^2 \alpha(\lambda)(1 - \xi\lambda)e^{-\xi\lambda} \cos(\lambda\eta)d\lambda \quad \Biggr\} \quad (118)$$
$$\tau_{\xi\eta} = -\int_0^\infty \xi\lambda^3 \alpha(\lambda)e^{-\xi\lambda} \sin(\lambda\eta)d\lambda$$

and putting $U = u/a$, $W = v/a$,

$$\left.\begin{array}{l} \dfrac{U}{1+\sigma} = \displaystyle\int_0^\infty \lambda\alpha(\lambda)[2(1-\sigma)+\xi\lambda]e^{-\xi\lambda}\cos(\eta\lambda)d\lambda \\[3mm] \dfrac{V}{1+\sigma} = \displaystyle\int_0^\infty \lambda\alpha(\lambda)(2\sigma-1+\xi\lambda)e^{-\xi\lambda}\sin(\lambda\eta)d\lambda \end{array}\right\} \quad (119)$$

It follows from these expressions that the remaining boundary conditions in the set (117) are satisfied if $\alpha(\lambda)$ satisfies the dual integral equations

$$\left.\begin{array}{ll} \displaystyle\int_0^\infty \lambda\alpha(\lambda)\cos(\lambda\eta)d\lambda = \dfrac{u_0^{(2)}(\eta)}{2(1-\sigma^2)}, & 0 < \eta < 1 \\[3mm] \displaystyle\int_0^\infty \lambda^2\alpha(\lambda)\cos(\lambda\eta)d\lambda = 0 & \eta > 1 \end{array}\right\} \quad (120)$$

Because of the relation $J_{-\frac{1}{2}}(z) = (2/\pi z)^{\frac{1}{2}}\cos(z)$ we may write these equations in the form

$$\int_0^\infty [\lambda^{\frac{3}{2}}\alpha(\lambda)]\lambda^{-1}J_{-\frac{1}{2}}(\lambda\eta)d\lambda = \frac{1}{1-\sigma^2}(2\pi\eta)^{-\frac{1}{2}}u_0^{(2)}(\eta) \quad 0<\eta<1$$

$$\int_0^\infty [\lambda^{\frac{3}{2}}\alpha(\lambda)]J_{-\frac{1}{2}}(\lambda\eta)d\lambda = 0 \qquad \eta>1$$

whence from equation (47), Chap. 2, we obtain the solution

$$\alpha(\lambda) = \frac{1}{\pi(1-\sigma^2)}\left[-\frac{1}{\lambda}J_1(\lambda)\int_0^1 (1-\eta^2)^{-\frac{1}{2}}u_0^{(2)}(\eta)d\eta \right.$$
$$\left. +\int_0^1 (1-t^2)^{-\frac{1}{2}}dt\int_0^1 \eta u_0^{(2)}(\eta t)J_0(\eta\lambda)d\eta\right] \quad (121)$$

In particular, if we express $u_0^2(\eta)$ in the form of the power series

$$u_0^{(2)}(\eta) = \sum_{n=0}^{n} a_n\eta^n \quad (122)$$

we find that

$$\alpha(\lambda) = \frac{1}{\lambda}\sum_{n=0}^{n} A_n\int_0^1 t^n J_1(\lambda t)dt \quad (123)$$

where

$$A_n = -\frac{1}{\sqrt{\pi}}\frac{1}{(1-\sigma^2)}\frac{(\frac{1}{2}n-\frac{1}{2})!}{(\frac{1}{2}n-1)!}a_n \quad (124)$$

From equations (118), (119), (123), and (124) we find, on making use of well-known results[1] in the theory of Bessel functions, that the components of stress and displacement are given by the expressions

[1] Watson, *op. cit.*, formulas (5)–(8), Sec. 13.2.

$$\sigma_\xi = -\mathsf{R} \sum_{n=0}^{n} A_n \int_0^1 t^{n+1}[(s^2 + t^2)^{-\frac{3}{2}} + 3\xi s(s^2 + t^2)^{-\frac{5}{2}}]dt$$

$$\sigma_\eta = -\mathsf{R} \sum_{n=0}^{n} A_n \int_0^1 t^{n+1}[(s^2 + t^2)^{-\frac{3}{2}} - 3\xi s(s^2 + t^2)^{-\frac{5}{2}}]dt$$

$$\tau_{\xi\eta} = 3\mathsf{I} \sum_{n=0}^{n} A_n \xi s \int_0^1 t^{n+1}(s^2 + t^2)^{-\frac{5}{2}} dt$$

and

$$U = \mathsf{R} \sum_{n=0}^{n} (1+\sigma)A_n \int_0^1 t^{n-1}\{2(1-\sigma)[1 - s(s^2 + t^2)^{-\frac{1}{2}}]$$
$$- \xi t^2(s^2 + t^2)^{-\frac{3}{2}}\}dt$$

$$V = -\mathsf{I} \sum_{n=0}^{n} (1+\sigma)A_n \int_0^1 t^{n-1}[(1 - 2\sigma)s(s^2 + t^2)^{-\frac{1}{2}} + \xi t^2(s^2 + t^2)^{-\frac{3}{2}}]dt$$

When $\xi = 0$, these expressions reduce to $\tau_{\xi\eta} = 0$ and

$$\sigma_\xi = \sigma_\eta = \begin{cases} \sum_n A_n \left[(1 - \eta^2)^{-\frac{1}{2}} - n\eta^{n-1} \int_0^{1/\eta} t^{n-1}(t^2 - 1)^{-\frac{1}{2}} dt \right] & 0 < \eta < 1 \\ 0 & \eta > 1 \end{cases}$$

From this expression we may verify that the applied stress distribution has zero resultant; since

$$n \int_0^1 \eta^{n-1} d\eta \int_0^{1/\eta} t^{n-1}(t^2 - 1)^{-\frac{1}{2}} dt = n \int_1^\infty t^{n-1}(t^2 - 1)^{-\frac{1}{2}} dt \int_0^{1/t} \eta^{n-1} d\eta$$
$$= \int_1^\infty \frac{dt}{t}(t^2 - 1)^{-\frac{1}{2}} \equiv \int_0^1 (1 - t^2)^{-\frac{1}{2}} dt$$

the required result follows at once.

From the equations above and (114) it follows that, if

$$u_0(\eta) = u_0^{(1)} + \sum_{n=0}^{n} a_n \eta^n \qquad 0 < \eta < 1$$

then $\sigma_0(\eta)$, the value of σ_ξ and σ_η when $\xi = 0$ is given by

$$\sigma_0(\eta) = \frac{-u_0^{(1)}}{2(1 - \sigma^2) \log_e 2}(1 - \eta^2)^{-\frac{1}{2}} - \frac{1}{\pi^{\frac{1}{2}}(1 - \sigma^2)} \sum_{n=0}^{n} \frac{(\frac{1}{2}n - \frac{1}{2})!}{(\frac{1}{2}n - 1)!}$$
$$\times a_n \left[(1 - \eta^2)^{-\frac{1}{2}} - n\eta^{n-1} \int_0^{1/\eta} t^{n-1}(t^2 - 1)^{-\frac{1}{2}} dt \right]$$

with $0 < \eta < 1$, where

$$a_0 = -\sum_{n=1}^{n} \pi^{-\frac{1}{2}} \frac{(\frac{1}{2}n - \frac{1}{2})!}{(\frac{1}{2}n)!} a_n$$

and, in our system of units, the total applied pressure is

$$\pi u_0^{(1)}/2(1 - \sigma^2) \log_e 2$$

In general, therefore, there is an infinity in $\sigma_0(\eta)$ as $|\eta| \to 1$. This may be removed if we choose

$$u_0^{(1)} = -\frac{2}{\pi} \log_e 2 \sum_{n=1}^{n} \frac{(\frac{1}{2}n - \frac{1}{2})!}{(\frac{1}{2}n - 1)!} a_n \tag{125}$$

and then

$$\sigma_0(\eta) = \frac{1}{\pi^{\frac{1}{2}}(1 - \sigma^2)} \sum_{n=1}^{n} na_n \frac{(\frac{1}{2}n - \frac{1}{2})!}{(\frac{1}{2}n - 1)!} \eta^{n-1} \int_1^{1/\eta} \frac{t^{n-1} \, dt}{(t^2 - 1)^{\frac{1}{2}}} \tag{126}$$

The total applied pressure is then

$$-\pi^{\frac{1}{2}}(1 - \sigma^2)^{-1} \sum_{n=1}^{n} \frac{(\frac{1}{2}n - \frac{1}{2})!}{(\frac{1}{2}n - 1)!} a_n \tag{127}$$

In a similar way we find that the components of the surface displacement are

$$U = \left\{ \begin{array}{ll} \sum a_n \left[\eta^n - \pi^{-\frac{1}{2}} \frac{(\frac{1}{2}n - \frac{1}{2})!}{(\frac{1}{2}n)!} \right] & 0 < \eta < 1 \\ \sum 2(1 - \sigma^2) A_n \left[-\eta^n \int_0^{1/\eta} t^{n-1}(1 - t^2)^{-\frac{1}{2}} \, dt + \frac{1}{n} \right] & \eta > 1 \end{array} \right\} \tag{128}$$

and

$$V = \left\{ \begin{array}{ll} -\sum (1 + \sigma)(1 - 2\sigma) A_n \eta^n \int_0^{1/\eta} t^{n-1}(t^2 - 1)^{-\frac{1}{2}} dt & 0 < \eta < 1 \\ 0 & \eta > 1 \end{array} \right\} \tag{129}$$

48.4 Indentation by a wedge. The nature of the solution is illustrated sufficiently by confining our attention to some results in the particular case $a_n = 0$ if $n \geq 2$. In this instance we find that the surface stresses and displacements are given by the simple forms

$$\sigma_\xi = \sigma_\eta - \left\{ \begin{array}{ll} -\dfrac{a_1}{\pi(1 - \sigma^2)} \left[(1 - \eta^2)^{-\frac{1}{2}} - \cosh^{-1}\left(\dfrac{1}{\eta}\right) \right] & 0 < \eta < 1 \\ 0 & \eta > 1 \end{array} \right.$$

and

$$U = \begin{cases} a_1\left(\eta - \dfrac{2}{\pi}\right) & 0 < \eta < 1 \\[2mm] \dfrac{2a_1}{\pi}\left[\eta\,\sin^{-1}\left(\dfrac{1}{\eta}\right) - 1\right] & \eta > 1 \end{cases}$$

Adding the simple solution (114) and (115), we see that the surface stress corresponding to the surface displacement

$$U = u_0^{(1)} + a_1\left(\eta - \frac{2}{\pi}\right) \tag{130}$$

is

$$\sigma_0(\eta) = -\frac{a_1}{\pi(1 - \sigma^2)}\,(1 - \eta^2)^{-\frac{1}{2}}\left[1 + \frac{\pi}{2\log_e 2}\frac{u_0^{(1)}}{a_1}\right] \\ + \frac{a_1}{\pi(1 - \sigma^2)}\cosh^{-1}\left(\frac{1}{\eta}\right) \tag{131}$$

Hence, if the surface stress remains finite when $|\eta| = 1$, we have

$$1 + \frac{\pi}{2\log_e 2}\frac{u_0^{(1)}}{a_1} = 0 \tag{132}$$

Let us now consider the indentation of a semiinfinite elastic solid by a rigid wedge (cf. Fig. 87). Assuming that the axis of the wedge coincides

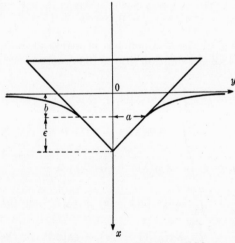

FIG. 87.   Indentation of a semiinfinite solid by a wedge.

with the x axis and that its vertex points downward into the interior of the medium, we see that the strained surface of the solid will fit the wedge over the length $-a \leq y \leq a$. For the x component of the displacement we may take

$$(u)_{x=0} = b + \epsilon \left(1 - \frac{y}{a} \right) \qquad 0 \leq y \leq a$$

which is equivalent to

$$U = \left(\frac{b}{a} + \frac{\epsilon}{a} \right) - \frac{\epsilon}{a} \eta \tag{133}$$

b being as yet unspecified. Identifying the equations (133) and (130) and making use of the relation (132), we find that

$$b = \epsilon \left[\frac{2}{\pi} (1 + \log_e 2) - 1 \right] \tag{134}$$

The corresponding distribution of stress on the surface immediately under the wedge is

$$\sigma_\xi = \sigma_\eta = - \frac{\epsilon}{\pi(1 - \sigma^2)} \cosh^{-1} \left(\frac{1}{\eta} \right)$$

48.5 Asymmetrical indentation. The asymmetrical indentation problem may be treated in a similar way, the boundary conditions being now

$$u = \left\{ \begin{array}{l} u_0^{(2)}(\eta),\ 0 < \eta < 1 \\ -u_0^{(2)}(-\eta),\ -1 < \eta < 0, \\ \sigma_\eta = \tau_{\xi\eta} = 0, \end{array} \right. \qquad \begin{array}{l} \tau_{\xi\eta} = 0,\ -1 < \eta < 1 \\ |\eta| > 1 \end{array} \right\} \tag{135}$$

and the vanishing of the components of stress at infinity. With the notation of Sec. 48.3 the solution (37) to (39a) may be written in the form

$$\sigma_\xi = - \int_0^\infty \lambda^2 \alpha(\lambda)(1 + \xi\lambda)e^{-\xi\lambda} \sin (\eta\lambda)d\lambda$$

$$\sigma_\eta = - \int_0^\infty \lambda^2 \alpha(\lambda)(1 - \xi\lambda)e^{-\xi\lambda} \sin (\eta\lambda)d\lambda$$

$$\tau_{\xi\eta} = \xi \int_0^\infty \lambda^3 \alpha(\lambda)e^{-\xi\lambda} \cos (\eta\lambda)d\lambda$$

$$\frac{U}{1 + \sigma} = \int_0^\infty \lambda\alpha(\lambda)[2(1 - \sigma) + \xi\lambda]e^{-\xi\lambda} \sin (\eta\lambda)d\lambda$$

$$\frac{V}{1 + \sigma} = \int_0^\infty \lambda\alpha(\lambda)[(1 - 2\sigma) - \xi\lambda]e^{-\xi\lambda} \cos (\lambda\eta)d\lambda$$

where, in view of the boundary conditions (135), it may readily be shown that $\alpha(\lambda)$ satisfies the dual integral equations

$$\int_0^\infty [\lambda^{\frac{3}{2}}\alpha(\lambda)]\lambda^{-1}J_{\frac{1}{2}}(\lambda\eta)d\lambda = \frac{(2\pi\eta)^{-\frac{1}{2}}}{(1-\sigma^2)}\, u_0^{(2)}(\eta) \quad 0 < \eta < 1$$

$$\int_0^\infty [\lambda^{\frac{3}{2}}\alpha(\lambda)]J_{\frac{1}{2}}(\lambda\eta)d\lambda = 0 \qquad \eta > 1$$

Hence, from equation (47), Chap. 2, we have

$$\alpha(\lambda) = \frac{1}{\pi(1-\sigma^2)}\left[\lambda^{-1}J_0(\lambda)\int_0^1 \eta(1-\eta^2)^{-\frac{1}{2}}u_0^{(2)}(\eta)d\eta \right.$$
$$\left. + \int_0^1 t(1-t^2)^{-\frac{1}{2}}\,dt \int_0^1 \eta u_0^{(2)}(t\eta)J_0(\lambda\eta)d\eta\right]$$

and in particular if

$$u_0^{(2)}(\eta) = \sum_n b_n\eta^n$$

then

$$\alpha(\lambda) = \frac{1}{\lambda}\sum_n B_n \int_0^1 t^n J_0(\lambda t)dt$$

$$B_n = \frac{b_n}{\pi^{\frac{1}{2}}(1-\sigma^2)}\frac{(\frac{1}{2}n)!}{(\frac{1}{2}n - \frac{1}{2})!}$$

The expressions for the components of stress and displacement may be found as in the symmetrical case. We find that, if

$$u_0(\eta) = u_0^{(1)}(\eta) + \Sigma b_n\eta^n \qquad 0 < \eta < 1$$

then the surface stress is given by

$$\sigma_0(\eta) = -\frac{u_0^{(1)}}{2(1-\sigma^2)\log_e 2}(1-\eta^2)^{-\frac{1}{2}} + \frac{1}{\pi^{\frac{1}{2}}(1-\sigma^2)}\sum \frac{(\frac{1}{2}n)!}{(\frac{1}{2}n - \frac{1}{2})!}$$
$$\times b_n\left[(1-\eta^2)^{-\frac{1}{2}} - (n-1)\eta^{n-2}\int_0^{1/\eta} t^{n-2}(t^2-1)^{-\frac{1}{2}}\,dt\right]$$

with $0 \leq \eta \leq 1$, so that if we wish to remove the infinity at the points $|\eta| = 1$ we must take

$$u_0^{(1)} = \frac{2}{\sqrt{\pi}}\log_e 2 \sum \frac{(\frac{1}{2}n)!}{(\frac{1}{2}n - \frac{1}{2})!}\, b_n$$

The analysis proceeds exactly as in the symmetrical case (Sec. 48.3) and is left as an exercise to the reader.

49. Two-dimensional Problems in Polar Coordinates

49.1 Introduction. In the determination of the distribution of stress in a wedge it is more convenient to make use of polar coordinates r and θ

instead of Cartesian coordinates.   In this section we shall illustrate the
use of Mellin transforms in the solution of problems of this kind.   The

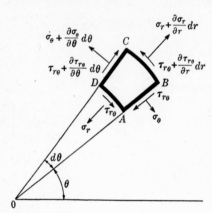

state of stress within the solid is, in
such problems, uniquely determined
by the three components $\sigma_r, \sigma_\theta, \tau_{r\theta}$,
which act in the manner shown in
Fig. 88.

If we consider the equilibrium of
the element $ABCD$, shown in Fig. 88,
in which $OA = OD = r$, $OB = OC$
$= r + dr$, $\angle xOA = \theta$, $\angle AOD = d\theta$,
then we find that the stresses $\sigma_r, \sigma_\theta, \tau_{r\theta}$
obey the relations

$$\frac{\partial \sigma_r}{\partial r} + \frac{1}{r}\frac{\partial \tau_{r\theta}}{\partial \theta} = 0,$$

FIG. 88.   Stresses acting on an element
of the solid.

$$\frac{\partial \tau_{r\theta}}{\partial r} + \frac{1}{r}\frac{\partial \sigma_\theta}{\partial \theta} = 0 \qquad (136)$$

If we express the components of stress in terms of an Airy stress function
χ by the relations

$$\sigma_r = \frac{1}{r}\frac{\partial \chi}{\partial r} + \frac{1}{r^2}\frac{\partial^2 \chi}{\partial \theta^2}, \qquad \sigma_\theta = \frac{\partial^2 \chi}{\partial r^2}, \qquad \tau_{r\theta} = -\frac{\partial}{\partial r}\left(\frac{1}{r}\frac{\partial \chi}{\partial \theta}\right) \quad (137)$$

it is readily verified that the equations of equilibrium (136) are satisfied
whatever the form of χ.   In order to satisfy the compatibility equations
we must, however, take χ to be a solution of the biharmonic equation

$$\left(\frac{\partial^2}{\partial r^2} + \frac{1}{r}\frac{\partial}{\partial r} + \frac{1}{r^2}\frac{\partial^2}{\partial \theta^2}\right)^2 \chi = 0 \qquad (138)$$

To solve this equation we introduce the Mellin transform[1]

$$\bar{\chi} = \int_0^\infty r^{s-1}\chi \, dr \qquad (139)$$

Making use of the result

$$\int_0^\infty \frac{\partial^n \chi}{\partial r^n} r^{s+n-1} \, dr = (-1)^n \frac{\Gamma(s+n)}{\Gamma(s)}\bar{\chi} \qquad (140)$$

which is readily established by integrating by parts, we see that equation
(138) is equivalent to the ordinary differential equation

$$\left(\frac{d^2}{d\theta^2} + s^2\right)\left[\frac{d^2}{d\theta^2} + (s+2)^2\right]\bar{\chi} = 0$$

[1] C. J. Tranter, *Quart. Jour. Mech. Applied Math. (Oxford)*, **1**, 125 (1948).

whose general solution is readily seen to be

$$\bar{\chi} = A \sin (s\theta) + B \cos (s\theta) + C \sin [(s + 2)\theta] + D \cos [(s + 2)\theta] \quad (141)$$

The arbitrary constants A,B,C,D occurring in this expression may be determined from the prescribed boundary conditions. To facilitate this determination, we shall determine the Mellin transforms of certain functions associated with the components of stress. If we multiply throughout the equations (137) by r^{s+1} and integrate with respect to r from 0 to ∞, we find, on making use of equation (140), that

$$\int_0^\infty (r^2 \sigma_r) r^{s-1} \, dr = \left(\frac{d^2}{d\theta^2} - s \right) \bar{\chi} \quad (142)$$

and

$$\int_0^\infty (r^2 \sigma_\theta) r^{s-1} \, dr = s(s + 1)\bar{\chi}, \qquad \int_0^\infty (r^2 \tau_{r\theta}) r^{s-1} \, dr = (s + 1) \frac{d\bar{\chi}}{d\theta} \quad (143)$$

Once the constants A,B,C,D have been determined from these equations, the function $\bar{\chi}$ may be written down from equation (141) and the components of stress determined by inverting equations (142) and (143), by means of Theorem 15, in the form

$$\left. \begin{aligned} \sigma_r &= \frac{1}{2\pi i} \int_{c-i\infty}^{c+i\infty} \left(\frac{d^2\bar{\chi}}{d\theta^2} - s\bar{\chi} \right) r^{-s-2} \, ds, \\ \sigma_\theta &= \frac{1}{2\pi i} \int_{c-i\infty}^{c+i\infty} s(s + 1)\bar{\chi} r^{-s-2} \, ds \\ \tau_{r\theta} &= \frac{1}{2\pi i} \int_{c-i\infty}^{c+i\infty} (s + 1) \frac{d\bar{\chi}}{d\theta} r^{-s-2} \, ds \end{aligned} \right\} \quad (144)$$

49.2 Distribution of stress in an infinite wedge. To illustrate the use of these formulas we shall consider the distribution of stress in an infinite wedge which is bounded by the lines $\theta = \pm\alpha$ (cf. Fig. 89). We shall suppose that the face $\theta = \alpha$ of the wedge is subjected to the surface stresses

$$\sigma_\theta = f_1(r), \qquad \tau_{r\theta} = g_1(r) \quad (145)$$

and the face $\theta = -\alpha$ to the stresses

$$\theta_\theta = f_2(r), \qquad \tau_{r\theta} = g_2(r) \quad (146)$$

Substituting these conditions into equations (143), we get, as the conditions on $\bar{\chi}$, the set of relations

$$\left. \begin{aligned} s(s + 1)\bar{\chi} = \bar{f}_1(s), \qquad (s + 1) \frac{d\bar{\chi}}{d\theta} = \bar{g}_1(s) \qquad \theta = \alpha \\ s(s + 1)\bar{\chi} = \bar{f}_2(s), \qquad (s + 1) \frac{d\bar{\chi}}{d\theta} = \bar{g}_2(s) \qquad \theta = -\alpha \end{aligned} \right\} \quad (147)$$

where $\bar{f}_i, \bar{g}_i$ $(i = 1,2)$ denote the Mellin transforms of $r^2 f_i(r)$ and $r^2 g_i(r)$, so that

$$(\bar{f}_i, \bar{g}_i) = \int_0^\infty (f_i, g_i) r^{s+1} \, dr \qquad i = 1,2 \quad (148)$$

If we take $\bar{\chi}$ in the form (141) and substitute in the equations (147), we obtain four simultaneous equations for the four constants A, B, C, D, whose solution may be written in the form

$$2s(s+1)G(\alpha,s)A = s(\bar{g}_1 + \bar{g}_2) \sin [(s+2)\alpha]$$
$$- (s+2)(\bar{f}_1 - \bar{f}_2) \cos [(s+2)\alpha] \quad (149)$$

$$2(s+1)G(\alpha,s)C = -(\bar{g}_1 + \bar{g}_2) \sin (s\alpha) + (\bar{f}_1 - \bar{f}_2) \cos (s\alpha) \quad (149a)$$

$$2s(s+1)H(\alpha,s)B = s(\bar{g}_1 - \bar{g}_2) \cos [(s+2)\alpha]$$
$$+ (s+2)(\bar{f}_1 + \bar{f}_2) \sin [(s+2)\alpha] \quad (149b)$$

$$2(s+1)H(\alpha,s)D = -(\bar{g}_1 - \bar{g}_2) \cos (s\alpha) - (\bar{f}_1 + \bar{f}_2) \sin (s\alpha) \quad (149c)$$

where

$$\left.\begin{array}{l} G(\alpha,s) = (s+1) \sin (2\alpha) - \sin [2(s+1)\alpha] \\ H(\alpha,s) = (s+1) \sin (2\alpha) + \sin [2(s+1)\alpha] \end{array}\right\} \quad (150)$$

The formal solution of the problem is now complete. $\bar{\chi}$ and its derivatives with respect to θ may be found from equations (149) to (149c)

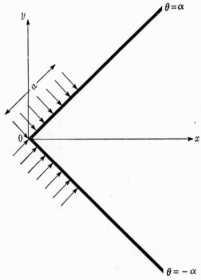

and (141). These expressions when substituted in equations (144) give line integrals which can be evaluated in terms of infinite integrals which may be calculated numerically. The calculations are straightforward but laborious, and therefore we shall illustrate the method by considering only a very special case.

49.3 Application of uniform pressure to the faces of an infinite wedge. As an example of the use of the general formulas derived in the last section we shall consider the distribution of stress in an infinite wedge of semiangle α (cf. Fig. 89) when its faces are each subjected to a uniform pressure p_0 for a dis-

FIG. 89. The loading of a wedge of angle 2α.

tance a measured from the vertex, the rest of the faces being free from normal stress. We shall further assume that both faces are entirely free from shearing stress.

In these circumstances it follows from equation (148) that

$$\bar{g}_1(s) = \bar{g}_2(s) = 0, \qquad \bar{f}_1(s) = \bar{f}_2(s) = -p_0 \int_0^a r^{s+1}\, dr = -\frac{p_0 a^{s+2}}{s+2}$$

Substituting these results in the equations (149) to (149c) we find that both A and C are zero and that B and D are given by the relations

$$\left.\begin{array}{c} s(s+1)H(\alpha,s)B = -p_0 a^{s+2} \sin\left[(s+2)\alpha\right] \\ (s+2)(s+1)H(\alpha,s) = p_0 a^{s+2} \sin(s\alpha) \end{array}\right\} \qquad (151)$$

$H(\alpha,s)$ being given by the second of equations (150). Substituting from equations (141) and (151) into equations (144), we obtain for the components of stress

$$\sigma_\theta = -\frac{p_0}{2\pi i} \int_{c-i\infty}^{c+i\infty} \left(\frac{a}{r}\right)^{s+2} \left\{\sin\left[(s+2)\alpha\right]\cos(s\theta)\right.$$
$$\left. -\frac{s}{s+2}\sin(s\alpha)\cos\left[(s+2)\theta\right]\right\} \frac{ds}{H(\alpha,s)} \quad (152)$$

$$\sigma_r = -\frac{p_0}{2\pi i} \int_{c-i\infty}^{c+i\infty} \left(\frac{a}{r}\right)^{s+2} \left\{\frac{s+4}{s+2}\sin(s\alpha)\cos\left[(s+2)\theta\right]\right.$$
$$\left. -\sin\left[(s+2)\alpha\right]\cos(s\alpha)\right\} \frac{ds}{H(\alpha,s)} \quad (152a)$$

$$\tau_{r\theta} = \frac{p_0}{2\pi i} \int_{c-i\infty}^{c+i\infty} \left(\frac{a}{r}\right)^{s+2} \left\{\sin\left[(s+2)\alpha\right]\sin(s\theta)\right.$$
$$\left. -\sin(s\alpha)\sin\left[(s+2)\theta\right]\right\} \frac{ds}{H(\alpha,s)} (152b)$$

If we restrict our attention to values of α between 0 and $\frac{1}{2}\pi$, it is readily shown that the only zero of the function $H(\alpha,s)$ in the strip for which $-2 < \mathsf{R}(s) < 0$ is $s = -1$. The contour integrals in the expressions (152) to (152b) can therefore be replaced by integrals from $-\infty$ to 0 and from 0 to ∞ along the line $\mathsf{R}(s) = -1$, minus πi times the residue at the point $s = -1$. In this way we find after a little reduction that

$$\frac{\pi r}{2p_0 a}(\sigma_\theta - \sigma_r) = \frac{\sin(\alpha)\cos(\theta)}{2\alpha + \sin(2\alpha)} - \int_0^\infty P(u)\sin\left[u\log\left(\frac{a}{r}\right)\right] du$$

$$\frac{\pi r}{2p_0 a}(\sigma_\theta + \sigma_r) = -\frac{\pi\sin(\alpha)\cos(\theta)}{2\alpha + \sin(2\alpha)}$$
$$+ \int_0^\infty \left\{(P - uQ)\sin\left[u\log\left(\frac{a}{r}\right)\right] - (Q + uP)\cos\left[u\log\left(\frac{a}{r}\right)\right]\right\}\frac{du}{1 + u^2}$$

$$\frac{\pi r}{p_0 a}\tau_{r\theta} = \int_0^\infty R(u)\cos\left[u\log\left(\frac{a}{r}\right)\right] du$$

where the functions P, Q, and R are given by

$$(u \sin 2\alpha + \sinh 2\alpha u)P(u) = \sin (\alpha - \theta) \cosh [(\alpha + \theta)u]$$
$$+ \sin (\alpha + \theta) \cosh [(\alpha - \theta)u]$$
$$(u \sin 2\alpha + \sinh 2\alpha u)Q(u) = \cos (\alpha - \theta) \sinh [(\alpha + \theta)u]$$
$$+ \cos (\alpha + \theta) \sinh [(\alpha - \theta)u]$$
$$(u \sin 2\alpha + \sinh 2\alpha u)R(u) = \sin (\alpha - \theta) \sinh [(\alpha + \theta)u]$$
$$- \sin (\alpha + \theta) \sinh [(\alpha - \theta)u]$$

For general values of α (between 0 and $\frac{1}{2}\pi$) the values of the stress component can be found only as a result of numerical integrations. For this purpose the method developed by Filon (see Appendix B) is the most convenient.

In the special case $\alpha = \frac{1}{2}\pi$ the wedge becomes a semiinfinite solid so that we should expect the solution derived above to reduce to the form (44). That this is so is readily verified if we make use of the well-known integrals[1]

$$\int_0^\infty \frac{\cosh (px)}{\sinh (\frac{1}{2}\pi x)} \sin (mx)dx = \frac{\sinh (2m)}{\cos (2p) + \cosh (2m)}$$
$$\int_0^\infty \frac{\sinh (px)}{\sinh (\frac{1}{2}\pi x)} \cos (mx)dx = \frac{\sin (2p)}{\cos (2p) + \cosh (2m)}$$

provided that $4p^2 \leq \pi^2$.

50. Dynamical Problems

50.1 Introduction. In the previous sections we have considered only problems of elastic equilibrium which are governed by the partial differential equations (2) and (6). We shall now consider briefly how the method of integral transforms can be applied to the solution of dynamical problems which are governed by the equations of motion (1).

For simplicity we shall assume that there are no body forces present so that the equations of motion (1) become simply

$$\frac{\partial \sigma_x}{\partial x} + \frac{\partial \tau_{xy}}{\partial y} = \rho \frac{\partial^2 u}{\partial t^2}, \qquad \frac{\partial \tau_{xy}}{\partial x} + \frac{\partial \sigma_y}{\partial y} = \rho \frac{\partial^2 v}{\partial t^2} \tag{153}$$

The relation between the components of stress and those of displacement, symbolized by equations (5), may be written in the alternative form

$$\sigma_x = \lambda \left(\frac{\partial u}{\partial x} + \frac{\partial v}{\partial y} \right) + 2\mu \frac{\partial u}{\partial x}, \qquad \sigma_y = \lambda \left(\frac{\partial u}{\partial x} + \frac{\partial v}{\partial y} \right) + 2\mu \frac{\partial v}{\partial y},$$
$$\tau_{xy} = \mu \left(\frac{\partial v}{\partial x} + \frac{\partial u}{\partial y} \right) \tag{154}$$

[1] J. Edwards, "A Treatise on the Integral Calculus" (Macmillan, London, 1922), Vol. 2, p. 276.

where $\lambda = E\sigma/(1 + \sigma)(1 - 2\sigma)$ and $\mu = E/2(1 + \sigma)$ are Lamé's elastic constants.

If we now introduce two functions $\phi(x,y,t)$ and $\psi(x,y,t)$ such that

$$u = \frac{\partial\phi}{\partial x} + \frac{\partial\psi}{\partial y}, \qquad v = \frac{\partial\phi}{\partial y} - \frac{\partial\psi}{\partial x} \tag{155}$$

the expressions (154) for the components of stress lead to the equations

$$\sigma_x = \lambda\nabla_1^2\phi + 2\mu\left(\frac{\partial^2\phi}{\partial x^2} + \frac{\partial^2\psi}{\partial x\,\partial y}\right), \quad \sigma_y = \lambda\nabla_1^2\phi + 2\mu\left(\frac{\partial^2\phi}{\partial y^2} - \frac{\partial^2\psi}{\partial x\,\partial y}\right) \Bigg\}$$
$$\tau_{xy} = \mu\left(2\frac{\partial^2\phi}{\partial x\,\partial y} - \frac{\partial^2\psi}{\partial x^2} + \frac{\partial^2\psi}{\partial y^2}\right) \tag{156}$$

If, now, we substitute from equations (155) and (156) into the equations of motion (153), we find that these equations are satisfied if the functions ϕ and ψ are chosen to be solutions of the wave equations

$$\frac{1}{c_1^2}\frac{\partial^2\phi}{\partial t^2} = \nabla_1^2\phi, \qquad \frac{1}{c_2^2}\frac{\partial^2\psi}{\partial t^2} = \nabla_1^2\psi \tag{157}$$

where we have written $c_1^2 = (\lambda + 2\mu)/\rho$ and $c_2^2 = \mu/\rho$. If, for convenience, we replace the time variable t by a spacelike variable τ defined by $\tau = c_1 t$, then we may write the equations (157) in the form

$$\frac{\partial^2\phi}{\partial\tau^2} = \nabla_1^2\phi, \qquad \beta^2\frac{\partial^2\psi}{\partial\tau^2} = \nabla_1^2\psi \tag{158}$$

where $\beta^2 = c_1^2/c_2^2 = (\lambda + 2\mu)/\mu$.

50.2 Solution of the equations of motion for a semiinfinite medium. To illustrate the procedure for the solution of dynamical problems we consider the distribution of stress in the semiinfinite elastic medium $y = 0$ when a variable pressure $p(x,\tau)$ is applied to the boundary $y = 0$. We take the x axis to be along the boundary and the y axis pointing *into* the medium. If we assume that the shearing stress is zero, the boundary conditions become simply

$$\sigma_y = -p(x,\tau), \qquad \tau_{xy} = 0 \qquad \text{on } y = 0 \tag{159}$$

Furthermore, the functions ϕ and ψ must be of such a nature that all the components of stress and displacement derived from them tend to zero as y tends to infinity. To find the solutions of the wave equations (158), we introduce the two-dimensional Fourier transforms

$$\bar{\phi}(\xi,y,\zeta) = \frac{1}{2\pi}\int_{-\infty}^{\infty}\int_{-\infty}^{\infty} \phi(x,y,\tau)e^{i(\xi x + \zeta\tau)}\,dx\,d\tau \Bigg\}$$
$$\bar{\psi}(\xi,y,\zeta) = \frac{1}{2\pi}\int_{-\infty}^{\infty}\int_{-\infty}^{\infty} \psi(x,y,\tau)e^{i(\xi x + \zeta\tau)}\,dx\,d\tau \tag{160}$$

of the functions $\phi(x,y,\tau)$ and $\psi(x,y,\tau)$. If, then, we multiply both sides of the equations (158) by $e^{i(\xi x + \zeta \tau)}$ and integrate over the entire x plane, we find that the functions $\bar{\phi}(\xi,y,\zeta)$ and $\bar{\psi}(\xi,y,\zeta)$ satisfy the ordinary differential equations

$$\frac{d^2\bar{\phi}}{dy^2} = (\xi^2 - \zeta^2)\bar{\phi}, \qquad \frac{d^2\bar{\psi}}{dy^2} = (\xi^2 - \beta^2\zeta^2)\bar{\psi} \qquad (161)$$

To satisfy the condition that the stresses tend to zero as $y \to \infty$, we take solutions of equations (161) of the forms

$$\bar{\phi}(\xi,y,\zeta) = A \exp\left[-(\xi^2 - \zeta^2)^{\frac{1}{2}}y\right], \qquad \begin{aligned}\bar{\psi}(\xi,y,\zeta)\\ = B \exp\left[-(\xi^2 - \beta^2\zeta^2)^{\frac{1}{2}}y\right]\end{aligned} \quad (162)$$

in which the arbitrary constants A and B are determined from the boundary conditions (159).

Once the functions $\bar{\phi}(\xi,y,\zeta)$ and $\bar{\psi}(\xi,y,\zeta)$ have been determined, the corresponding wave functions $\phi(x,y,\tau)$ and $\psi(x,y,\tau)$ are given by Fourier's inversion theorem (108), Chap. 1, for two-dimensional transforms. From these expressions we derive the equations

$$\frac{\sigma_x}{2\mu} = \frac{1}{2\pi} \int_{-\infty}^{\infty} \int_{-\infty}^{\infty} \left[i\xi(\xi^2 - \beta^2\zeta^2)^{\frac{1}{2}}\bar{\psi} - \left(\xi^2 + \frac{\lambda}{2\mu}\zeta^2\right)\bar{\phi} \right] e^{-i(\xi x + \zeta \tau)}\, d\xi\, d\zeta \tag{163}$$

$$\frac{\sigma_y}{2\mu} = \frac{-1}{2\pi} \int_{-\infty}^{\infty} \int_{-\infty}^{\infty} \left[i\xi(\xi^2 - \beta^2\zeta^2)^{\frac{1}{2}}\bar{\psi} - \left(\xi^2 - \frac{1}{2}\beta^2\zeta^2\right)\bar{\phi} \right] e^{-i(\xi x + \zeta \tau)}\, d\xi\, d\zeta \tag{164}$$

$$\frac{\tau_{xy}}{2\mu} = \frac{1}{2\pi} \int_{-\infty}^{\infty} \int_{-\infty}^{\infty} \left[i\xi(\xi^2 - \zeta^2)^{\frac{1}{2}}\bar{\phi} + \left(\xi^2 - \frac{1}{2}\beta^2\zeta^2\right)\bar{\psi} \right] e^{-i(\xi x + \zeta \tau)}\, d\xi\, d\zeta \tag{165}$$

for the determination of the components of stress, $\bar{\phi}$ and $\bar{\psi}$ being given by the equations (162). In a similar way we find for the components of the displacement vector

$$u = -\frac{1}{2\pi} \int_{-\infty}^{\infty} \int_{-\infty}^{\infty} [i\xi\bar{\phi} + (\xi^2 - \beta^2\zeta^2)^{\frac{1}{2}}\bar{\psi}]e^{-i(\xi x + \zeta \tau)}\, d\xi\, d\zeta \tag{166}$$

$$v = -\frac{1}{2\pi} \int_{-\infty}^{\infty} \int_{-\infty}^{\infty} [(\xi^2 - \zeta^2)^{\frac{1}{2}}\bar{\phi} - i\xi\bar{\psi}]e^{-i(\xi x + \zeta \tau)}\, d\xi\, d\zeta \tag{167}$$

It only remains to determine the constants A and B. Observing that, when $y = 0$, the functions $\bar{\phi}$ and $\bar{\psi}$ reduce to A and B, respectively, and substituting from equations (159) into the inverted forms of equations (164) and (165), we find that

$$\left(\xi^2 - \frac{1}{2}\beta^2\zeta^2\right) A - i\xi(\xi^2 - \beta^2\zeta^2)^{\frac{1}{2}}B = -\frac{\bar{p}(\xi,\zeta)}{2\mu}$$

$$i\xi(\xi^2 - \zeta^2)^{\frac{1}{2}}A + (\xi^2 - \frac{1}{2}\beta^2\zeta^2)B = 0$$

from which it follows immediately that

$$A = \frac{1}{2\mu}(\xi^2 - \frac{1}{2}\beta^2\zeta^2)\frac{\bar{p}(\xi,\zeta)}{f+g}, \qquad B = -\frac{i\xi}{2\mu}(\xi^2 - \zeta^2)^{\frac{1}{2}}\frac{\bar{p}(\xi,\zeta)}{f+g} \quad (168)$$

where $\bar{p}(\xi,\zeta)$ is the two-dimensional Fourier transform of $p(x,\tau)$ and f and g are functions of ξ and ζ defined by the equations

$$f(\xi^2,\zeta^2) = -(\xi^2 - \frac{1}{2}\beta^2\zeta^2)^2, \qquad g(\xi^2,\zeta^2) = \xi^2(\xi^2 - \zeta^2)(\xi^2 - \beta^2\zeta^2)^{\frac{1}{2}} \quad (169)$$

If we substitute from equations (168) and (169) into equations (163) to (165), we obtain, for the determination of the components of stress, the integral expressions

$$\sigma_y = \frac{-1}{2\pi}\int_{-\infty}^{\infty}\int_{-\infty}^{\infty}\frac{\bar{p}}{f+g}[fe^{-(\xi^2-\zeta^2)^{\frac{1}{2}}y} + ge^{-(\xi^2-\beta^2\zeta^2)^{\frac{1}{2}}y}]e^{-i(\xi x+\zeta\tau)}\,d\xi\,d\zeta \quad (170)$$

$$\sigma_x + \sigma_y = -\frac{\lambda+\mu}{2\mu\pi}\int_{-\infty}^{\infty}\int_{-\infty}^{\infty}\frac{\zeta^2\bar{p}}{f+g}\left(\xi^2 - \frac{1}{2}\beta^2\zeta^2\right)e^{-(\xi^2-\zeta^2)^{\frac{1}{2}}y-i(\xi x+\zeta\tau)}\,d\xi\,d\zeta \quad (171)$$

$$\tau_{xy} = \frac{1}{2\pi}\int_{-\infty}^{\infty}\int_{-\infty}^{\infty}\frac{i\xi\bar{p}}{f+g}(\xi^2 - \zeta^2)^{\frac{1}{2}}\left(\xi^2 - \frac{1}{2}\beta^2\zeta^2\right)[e^{-(\xi^2-\zeta^2)^{\frac{1}{2}}y} - e^{-(\xi^2-\beta^2\zeta^2)^{\frac{1}{2}}y}]$$
$$\times e^{-i(\xi x+\zeta\tau)}\,d\xi\,d\zeta \quad (172)$$

It may readily be verified from equations (170) and (172) that the boundary conditions on $y = 0$ are satisfied. In a similar way equations (166) and (167) give, for the components of the displacement vector,

$$u = \frac{1}{4\pi\mu}\int_{-\infty}^{\infty}\int_{-\infty}^{\infty}\frac{i\xi\bar{p}}{f+g}\left[\frac{g}{\xi^2}e^{-(\xi^2-\beta\zeta^2)^{\frac{1}{2}}y} - \left(\zeta^2 - \frac{1}{2}\beta^2\xi^2\right)e^{-(\xi^2-\zeta^2)^{\frac{1}{2}}y}\right]$$
$$\times e^{-i(\xi x+\zeta\tau)}\,d\xi\,d\zeta \quad (173)$$

and

$$v = -\frac{1}{4\pi\mu}\int_{-\infty}^{\infty}\int_{-\infty}^{\infty}\frac{(\xi^2-\zeta^2)^{\frac{1}{2}}\bar{p}}{f+g}\left[\left(\xi^2 - \frac{1}{2}\beta^2\zeta^2\right)e^{-(\xi^2-\zeta^2)^{\frac{1}{2}}y} - \xi^2 e^{-(\xi^2-\beta^2\zeta^2)^{\frac{1}{2}}y}\right]$$
$$\times e^{-i(\xi x+\zeta\tau)}\,d\xi\,d\zeta \quad (174)$$

so that the expressions for the components of stress and displacement may be evaluated once the Fourier transform $\bar{p}(\xi,\zeta)$ has been calculated from the prescribed form of $p(x,\tau)$.

50.3 Distribution of stress produced by a pulse of pressure moving uniformly along the boundary. We shall now make use of the general solution derived in the preceding section to determine the stress set up in the interior of the semiinfinite elastic medium when a pulse of pressure of "shape" $p = \chi(x)$ moves with uniform velocity v along the boundary $y = 0$. We then have $p(x,\tau) = \chi(x - vt) = \chi(x - \beta_1\tau)$, where $\beta_1 = v/c_1$, and it follows that

$$\bar{p}(\xi,\zeta) = \frac{1}{2\pi} \int_{-\infty}^{\infty} \int_{-\infty}^{\infty} \chi(x - \beta_1\tau)e^{i(\xi x + \zeta \tau)} \, dx \, d\tau$$

which by a trivial change of variable gives

$$\bar{p}(\xi,\zeta) = \frac{1}{2\pi} \int_{-\infty}^{\infty} \chi(u)e^{i\xi u} \, du \int_{-\infty}^{\infty} e^{i\tau(\zeta + \beta_1\xi)} \, d\tau = 2\bar{\chi}(\xi)\delta(\zeta + \beta_1\xi)$$

where, in general,

$$\bar{\chi}(\xi) = \frac{1}{2} \int_{-\infty}^{\infty} \chi(u)e^{i\xi u} \, du \tag{175}$$

and in cases in which $\chi(u)$ is an even function of u

$$\bar{\chi}(\xi) = \int_0^{\infty} \chi(u) \cos (\xi u) du \tag{176}$$

If we make use of the fact that, for any function $X(\xi^2,\zeta^2)$,

$$\int_{-\infty}^{\infty} X(\xi^2,\zeta^2)\delta(\zeta + \beta_1\xi)e^{-i\zeta\tau} \, d\zeta = X(\xi^2,\beta_1^2\xi^2)e^{-i\xi vt}$$

we find, for the components of stress, by substituting in the equations (170) to (172), the expressions

$$\sigma_y = -\frac{2}{\pi} \int_0^{\infty} \bar{\chi}(\xi) \cos [\xi(x - vt)]$$
$$\left[\frac{\theta}{\theta + \phi} e^{-(1-\beta_1{}^2)^{\frac{1}{2}}y\xi} + \frac{\phi}{\theta + \phi} e^{-(1-\beta_2{}^2)^{\frac{1}{2}}y\xi} \right] d\xi \tag{177}$$

$$\sigma_x + \sigma_y = -\frac{2\beta_1^2(\lambda + \mu)(1 - \frac{1}{2}\beta_2^2)}{\pi\mu(\theta + \phi)} \int_0^{\infty} \bar{\chi}(\xi)e^{-(1-\beta_1{}^2)^{\frac{1}{2}}y\xi} \cos [\xi(x - vt)]d\xi \tag{178}$$

$$\tau_{xy} = \frac{2(1 - \beta_1^2)^{\frac{1}{2}}(1 - \frac{1}{2}\beta_2^2)}{\pi(\theta + \phi)} \int_0^{\infty} \bar{\chi}(\xi)[e^{-(1-\beta_1{}^2)^{\frac{1}{2}}y\xi} - e^{-(1-\beta_2{}^2)^{\frac{1}{2}}y\xi}]$$
$$\times \sin [\xi(x - vt)]d\xi \tag{179}$$

The corresponding expressions for the displacement vector can be obtained from equations (173) and (174) in terms of $\beta_2 = v/c_2 = \beta\beta_1$ and the functions

$$\theta(\beta_2) = -(1 - \tfrac{1}{2}\beta_2^2)^2, \qquad \phi(\beta_1,\beta_2) = (1 - \beta_1^2)^{\frac{1}{2}}(1 - \beta_2^2)^{\frac{1}{2}} \tag{180}$$

The problem is thus reduced to a series of integrations—the calculation of $\bar{\chi}(\xi)$ and the integrations (177) to (179).

The simplest example of this kind is that in which the stress is produced by the application to the boundary of a point force of magnitude P whose point of application moves with uniform velocity v. The form of the pressure pulse in this case is $\chi(x) = P\,\delta(x)$, so that $\bar{\chi}(\xi) = \tfrac{1}{2}P$. The resulting integrals given by (177) to (179) are elementary and enable the components of stress to be expressed in terms of elementary functions. The details of such a calculation are left to the reader.

CHAPTER 10

AXIALLY SYMMETRICAL STRESS DISTRIBUTIONS

51. Equations of Equilibrium

51.1 Introduction. The class of boundary value problems in the mathematical theory of elasticity next in order of difficulty to the two-dimensional problems considered in the last chapter arises from the discussion of the distribution of stress in a solid of revolution which is

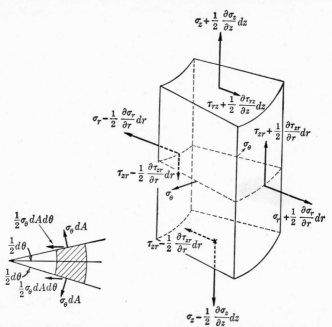

Fig. 90. Stresses acting on an element of a solid of revolution.

deformed symmetrically with respect to its axis of revolution. Such problems are also of great practical importance. The deformation being symmetrical with respect to the axis of revolution, it is most convenient to employ cylindrical coordinates r, θ, z and to take the z axis along the axis of symmetry. In these circumstances, the components of the displacement vector and of the stress tensor will all be independent of the angle θ, and the operator $\partial/\partial\theta$ will be a null operator. To derive the

450

equilibrium equations we consider an element of volume in a solid of revolution (cf. Fig. 90). As shown in Fig. 90 the state of stress at any point of the solid is uniquely specified by four components of stress $\sigma_r, \sigma_\theta, \sigma_z, \tau_{rz}$ in a notation similar to that used in Sec. 49. In the general case there would be two further components of shear stress $\tau_{r\theta}, \tau_{\theta z}$, but in the case of symmetrical deformations these two components are zero at every point of the solid. Similarly, in the general case the components of the displacement vector would be u_r in the radial direction, u_θ in the tangential direction, and u_z in the direction of the axis of symmetry, but in the case of symmetrical distortions the component u_θ vanishes identically at each point.

If we consider the total force in the radial direction, we must take into account the fact that the stress components σ_θ on each face of the element give rise to a force $-\sigma_\theta \, d\theta \, dr \, dz$ in the r direction as shown in the inset. We therefore obtain the equilibrium condition

$$\left(\sigma_r + \frac{1}{2}\frac{\partial \sigma_r}{\partial r}\, dr\right)\left(r + \frac{1}{2}\, dr\right) d\theta \, dz - \left(\sigma_r - \frac{1}{2}\frac{\partial \sigma_r}{\partial r}\, dr\right)\left(r - \frac{1}{2}\, dr\right) d\theta \, dz$$

$$- \sigma_\theta \, d\theta \, dz \, dr + \left(\tau_{rz} + \frac{1}{2}\frac{\partial \tau_{rz}}{\partial z}\, dz\right) r \, dr \, d\theta - \left(\tau_{rz} - \frac{1}{2}\frac{\partial \tau_{rz}}{\partial z}\, dz\right) r \, dr \, d\theta = 0$$

it being assumed that there are no body forces present and that the element, which is centered at the point (r,θ,z), has "edges" $(dr, d\theta, dz)$. In the limit as $dr, d\theta$, and dz tend to zero, we obtain the equation of equilibrium

$$\frac{\partial \sigma_r}{\partial r} + \frac{\partial \tau_{rz}}{\partial z} + \frac{\sigma_r - \sigma_\theta}{r} = 0 \tag{1}$$

Similarly, if we equate to zero the total force in the z direction, we obtain the second equation

$$\frac{\partial \tau_{rz}}{\partial r} + \frac{\partial \sigma_z}{\partial z} + \frac{\tau_{rz}}{r} = 0 \tag{2}$$

It may readily be shown[1] by a rotation of axes that the compatibility relations in cylindrical coordinates, in cases in which none of the components of stress depend on θ, may be written in the form

$$\nabla^2 \sigma_r - \frac{2}{r^2}(\sigma_r - \sigma_\theta) + \frac{1}{1+\sigma}\frac{\partial^2}{\partial r^2}(\sigma_r + \sigma_\theta + \sigma_z) = 0 \tag{3}$$

$$\nabla^2 \sigma_\theta + \frac{2}{r^2}(\sigma_r - \sigma_\theta) + \frac{1}{1+\sigma}\frac{1}{r}\frac{\partial}{\partial r}(\sigma_r + \sigma_\theta + \sigma_z) = 0 \tag{4}$$

[1] S. Timoshenko, "Theory of Elasticity" (McGraw-Hill, New York, 1934), p. 310.

where σ denotes Poisson's ratio and

$$\nabla^2 = \frac{\partial^2}{\partial r^2} + \frac{1}{r}\frac{\partial}{\partial r} + \frac{\partial^2}{\partial z^2} \tag{5}$$

is the Laplacian operator in cylindrical coordinates.

Furthermore, it is readily shown that, with axial symmetry, the relations between the components of the stress tensor and the nonvanishing components of the displacement vector may be written in the form

$$\sigma_r = \left[(\lambda + 2\mu)\frac{\partial}{\partial r} + \frac{\lambda}{r} \right] u_r + \lambda\frac{\partial u_z}{\partial z}, \qquad \sigma_\theta = \left[\lambda\frac{\partial}{\partial r} + \frac{\lambda + 2\mu}{r} \right] u_r + \lambda\frac{\partial u_z}{\partial z}$$

$$\sigma_z = \lambda\left(\frac{\partial}{\partial r} + \frac{1}{r}\right) u_r + (\lambda + 2\mu)\frac{\partial u_z}{\partial z}, \qquad \tau_{rz} = \mu\left(\frac{\partial u_r}{\partial z} + \frac{\partial u_z}{\partial r}\right)$$

If we now put[1]

$$u_r = -\frac{\lambda + \mu}{\mu}\Phi_{rz} \tag{6}$$

$$u_z = \frac{\lambda + 2\mu}{\mu}\nabla^2\Phi - \frac{\lambda + \mu}{\mu}\Phi_{zz} \tag{7}$$

in these equations, we obtain, for the components of stress,

$$\sigma_r = \lambda\,\nabla^2\Phi_z - 2(\lambda + \mu)\Phi_{rrz} \tag{8}$$

$$\sigma_z = (3\lambda + 4\mu)\nabla^2\Phi_z - 2(\lambda + \mu)\Phi_{zzz} \tag{9}$$

$$\sigma_\theta = \lambda\nabla^2\Phi_z - \frac{2}{r}(\lambda + \mu)\Phi_{zr} \tag{10}$$

$$\tau_{rz} = (\lambda + 2\mu)\frac{\partial}{\partial r}\nabla^2\Phi - 2(\lambda + \mu)\Phi_{zzr} \tag{11}$$

It may be verified by direct substitution that the equations of equilibrium (1) and (2) are satisfied by these expressions. If we substitute these expressions into the compatibility equations (3) and (4), we find that these equations are satisfied if the arbitrary function Φ is a solution of the biharmonic equation

$$\nabla^4\Phi = 0 \tag{12}$$

In this way the problem of determining the distribution of stress in a solid of revolution reduces to that of finding solutions of the biharmonic equation (12) satisfying certain boundary conditions.

51.2 Solution of the equations of equilibrium. By applying the theory of Hankel transforms we can reduce the biharmonic equation (12) in r and z to a fourth-order ordinary differential equation in z, the place of r

---

[1] It will be noted that Φ_{rz} denotes $\partial^2\Phi/\partial r\,\partial z$, etc.; no confusion should arise in the interpretation of u_r, σ_r, etc.

being taken by a parameter. The boundary conditions must then be treated in the same way, so that, instead of having relations concerning partial derivatives with respect to r and z, relations are obtained in terms of the derivatives with respect to z of an auxiliary function which depends on z alone.

Suppose that, in the problems under consideration, r ranges from 0 to ∞; then, as is shown in Sec. 10, we have

$$\int_0^\infty r \nabla^2 f J_0(\xi r) dr = \left(\frac{d^2}{dz^2} - \xi^2\right) \int_0^\infty rf J_0(\xi r) dr$$

Replacing f by $\nabla^2 \Phi$, and applying the result once more, we find that

$$\int_0^\infty r \nabla^4 \Phi J_0(\xi r) dr = \left(\frac{d^2}{dz^2} - \xi^2\right)^2 \int_0^\infty r\Phi J_0(\xi r) dr \tag{13}$$

Now, multiplying both sides of equation (12) by $rJ_0(\xi r)$ and integrating over the whole range of r, we see that it is equivalent to the ordinary differential equation

$$\left(\frac{d^2}{dz^2} - \xi^2\right)^2 G(\xi,z) = 0 \tag{14}$$

where $G(\xi,z)$ is the zero-order Hankel transform,

$$G(\xi,z) = \int_0^\infty r\Phi J_0(\xi r) dr$$

of the function $\Phi(r,z)$. The integration of equation (14) is elementary and leads to the expression

$$G(\xi,z) = (A + Bz)e^{-\xi z} + (C + Dz)e^{\xi z} \tag{15}$$

where $A, B, C,$ and D are determined from the boundary conditions.

The use of the Hankel transform $G(\xi,z)$ thus reduces the solution of the fourth-order partial differential equation (13) to that of the ordinary equation (14). The determination of the arbitrary constants occurring in (15) is further facilitated by transforming the expressions for the components of stress and displacement into relations involving G and its derivatives with respect to z.

For example, if we multiply both sides of equation (6) by $rJ_0'(\xi r)$ and integrate over r from 0 to ∞, we find, on integrating by parts, that

$$\int_0^\infty ru_r J_1(\xi r) dr = \frac{\lambda + \mu}{\mu} \xi \frac{dG}{dz}$$

Inverting this result by means of Theorem 19, we obtain the expression

$$u_r = \frac{\lambda + \mu}{\mu} \int_0^\infty \xi^2 \frac{dG}{dz} J_1(\xi r) d\xi \tag{16}$$

for the radial component of the displacement vector. Similarly from equation (7) we have

$$\int_0^\infty r u_z J_0(\xi r) dr = \frac{\lambda + 2\mu}{\mu} \left(\frac{d^2}{dz^2} - \xi^2 \right) G - \frac{\lambda + \mu}{\mu} \frac{d^2 G}{dz^2}$$

from which it follows by Theorem 19 that

$$u_z = \int_0^\infty \xi \left(\frac{d^2 G}{dz^2} - \frac{\lambda + 2\mu}{\mu} \xi^2 G \right) J_0(\xi r) d\xi \tag{17}$$

The corresponding expressions for the stresses σ_z and τ_{rz} can be derived simply. Multiplying equation (9) by $r J_0(\xi r)$, integrating over r, and inverting by means of Theorem 19, we find that

$$\sigma_z = \int_0^\infty \xi \left[(\lambda + 2\mu) \frac{d^3 G}{dz^3} - (3\lambda + 4\mu) \xi^2 \frac{dG}{dz} \right] J_0(\xi r) d\xi \tag{18}$$

and, multiplying equation (11) by $r J_1(\xi r)$, integrating over r, and inverting the result by means of Theorem 19, we have

$$\tau_{rz} = \int_0^\infty \xi^2 \left[\lambda \frac{d^2 G}{dz^2} + (\lambda + 2\mu) \xi^2 G \right] J_1(\xi r) d\xi \tag{19}$$

The expressions for σ_r and σ_θ are not obtained quite so easily. If, however, we add equations (8) and (10), we obtain

$$\sigma_r + \sigma_\theta = \left[2(\lambda + \mu) \frac{\partial^2}{\partial z^2} - 2\mu \nabla^2 \right] \Phi_z$$

Multiplying both sides of this equation by $r J_0(\xi r)$, and integrating with respect to r from 0 to ∞, we obtain

$$\int_0^\infty r(\sigma_r + \sigma_\theta) J_0(\xi r) dr = 2(\lambda + \mu) \frac{d^3 G}{dz^3} - 2\mu \left(\frac{d^2}{dz^2} - \xi^2 \right) \frac{dG}{dz}$$

Inverting this equation in the usual way, by Theorem 19, we obtain

$$\sigma_r + \sigma_\theta = 2 \int_0^\infty \xi \left(\lambda \frac{d^3 G}{dz^3} + \mu \xi^2 \frac{dG}{dz} \right) J_0(\xi r) d\xi \tag{20}$$

To obtain the expression for σ_r, we make use of the fact that the equation of equilibrium (1) may be written in the form

$$\frac{\partial}{\partial r} (r^2 \sigma_r) = r(\sigma_r + \sigma_\theta) - r^2 \frac{\partial \tau_{rz}}{\partial z}$$

from which it follows by substituting from equations (19) and (20) that

$$\frac{\partial}{\partial r}(r^2\sigma_r) = 2r \int_0^\infty \xi\left(\lambda\frac{d^3G}{dz^3} + \mu\xi^2\frac{dG}{dz}\right)J_0(\xi r)d\xi$$

$$- r^2 \int_0^\infty \xi^2\left[\lambda\frac{d^3G}{dz^3} + \xi^2(\lambda + 2\mu)\frac{dG}{dz}\right]J_1(\xi r)d\xi$$

Integrating with respect to r and interchanging the order of the integrations, we find that, by making use of the integrals

$$\int_0^r rJ_0(\xi r)dr = \frac{r}{\xi}J_1(\xi r), \qquad \int_0^r r^2J_1(\xi r)dr = \frac{2r}{\xi^2}J_1(\xi r) - \frac{r^2}{\xi}J_0(\xi r)$$

[equation (10), Appendix A], we obtain the result

$$\sigma_r = \int_0^\infty \xi\left[\lambda\frac{d^3G}{dz^3} + (\lambda + 2\mu)\xi^2\frac{dG}{dz}\right]J_0(\xi r)d\xi$$

$$- \frac{2(\lambda + \mu)}{r}\int_0^\infty \xi^2\frac{dG}{dz}J_1(\xi r)d\xi \quad (21)$$

it being assumed, on physical grounds for the problems we shall discuss later, that as $r \to 0$, $r^2\sigma_r \to 0$. Combining this result with equation (20), we have, finally,

$$\sigma_\theta = \lambda\int_0^\infty \xi\left(\frac{d^3G}{dz^3} - \xi^2\frac{dG}{dz}\right)J_0(\xi r)d\xi + \frac{2(\lambda + \mu)}{r}\int_0^\infty \xi^2\frac{dG}{dz}J_1(\xi r)d\xi$$

$$(22)$$

It is easily verified from these equations that all the components of stress tend to zero as r tends to infinity, a necessary condition if the medium is unbounded in the r direction.

52. Stresses Produced by the Indentation of the Plane Surface of a Semi-infinite Elastic Medium by a Rigid Punch[1]

52.1 Introduction. As a first application of these equations we shall apply them to determining the elastic stress distribution in a semiinfinite solid when the plane boundary is deformed by the pressure against it of a perfectly rigid body. In deriving the solution of this problem for the case in which the rigid punch is a solid of revolution it will be assumed that the normal displacement of a point within the area of contact between the elastic medium and the rigid body is specified and that the distribution of pressure over that area is then determined by calculation. The application of the analysis of the last section reduces the problem to that of solving a pair of dual integral equations belonging to the class con-

[1] J. W. Harding and I. N. Sneddon, *Proc. Cambridge Phil. Soc.*, **41**, 16 (1945).

sidered in Sec. 12. This procedure allows us to obtain the solution for an arbitrary shape of punch by a general method which avoids the rather troublesome procedure, adopted by Love[1] in the case of a conical punch, of guessing appropriate combinations of solutions which will satisfy the prescribed boundary conditions in any special case. Moreover, it can readily be appreciated that an attempt to apply Love's method to more complicated shapes of punch will lead to considerable mathematical difficulties. We shall begin by giving the general solution of the problem and then shall give a more detailed account of the calculations for the cases in which the rigid body is a flat-ended cylinder or a cone.

52.2 Boundary conditions and the corresponding integral equations. We shall consider the stresses produced in the semiinfinite elastic medium $z \leq 0$, bounded only by the plane $z = 0$. The solid will be supposed to be deformed by there being pressed against it a perfectly rigid solid of revolution of prescribed shape whose axis of revolution coincides with the z axis of the coordinate system (and hence is normal to the bounding plane). It is obvious from the axial symmetry that the strained surface of the elastic medium will fit the rigid body over the part between the lowest point and a certain circular section whose radius we shall denote by a (cf. Fig. 86).

In formulating the mixed boundary value problem we shall assume that the z component of the surface displacement is specified over the region $r < a$ of the surface $z = 0$, while outside that region is imposed the condition of zero normal stress. It will further be assumed that the shearing stress vanishes at all points of the boundary. Thus, for $z = 0$, the boundary conditions are

$$u_z = [u_z(r)]_{z=0} \qquad 0 \leq r \leq a \qquad (23)$$
$$\sigma_z = 0 \qquad\qquad r > a \qquad (24)$$
$$\tau_{rz} = 0 \qquad\qquad 0 \leq r < \infty \qquad (25)$$

Since the depth of the medium is infinite, we must also ensure that the solution of (12), and hence of (14), is of such a nature that all the components of stress and displacement tend to zero as $z \to \infty$. Thus we must take $A = B = 0$ in the solution (15), so that

$$G(\xi,z) = (C + Dz)e^{-\xi z} \qquad (26)$$

Substituting this value for the function G into equation (19) and setting $z = 0$, we see that the value of τ_{rz} on $z = 0$ is

$$[\tau_{rz}]_{z=0} = 2 \int_0^\infty \xi^2[(\lambda + \mu)\xi C - \lambda D]J_1(\xi r)d\xi$$

[1] A. E. H. Love, *Quart. Jour. Math. (Oxford)*, **10**, 161 (1939).

and since, by equation (25), this must be zero for all values of r, we must have $(\lambda + \mu)\xi C = \lambda D$, in which case $G(\xi,z)$ becomes

$$G(\xi,z) = \frac{D}{\xi}\left(\frac{\lambda}{\lambda + \mu} + \xi z\right)e^{-\xi z} \qquad (27)$$

where D is an arbitrary constant. Making use of this value for $G(\xi,z)$ and inserting the conditions (23) and (24) in equations (17) and (18), we obtain the relations

$$-\frac{\lambda + 2\mu}{\mu}\int_0^\infty \xi^2 D J_0(\xi r)d\xi = [u_z(r)]_{z=0} \qquad 0 \le r \le a$$

$$\int_0^\infty \xi^3 D J_0(\xi r)d\xi = 0 \qquad\qquad r > a$$

If we now make the substitutions

$$\xi a = p,\ r = a\rho,\ -\mu a^4[u_z(r)]_{z=0} = (\lambda + 2\mu)g(\rho),\ p^2 D = f(p) \quad (28)$$

in these equations, we find that the function $f(p)$ so defined is a solution of the dual integral equations

$$\int_0^\infty f(p)J_0(p\rho)dp = g(\rho),\ 0 < \rho < 1;$$

$$\int_0^\infty pf(p)J_0(p\rho)dp = 0,\ \rho > 1 \quad (29)$$

52.3 General solution of the equilibrium equations. Dual integral equations of the type (29) have been considered in Sec. 12, from the analysis of which it follows immediately by the substitutions $\alpha = -1$, $\nu = 0$ in equation (47), Chap. 2, that the solution of these equations may be put in the form

$$f(p) = \frac{2}{\pi}\cos(p)\int_0^1 y(1 - y^2)^{-\frac{1}{2}}g(y)dy$$

$$+ \frac{2}{\pi}\int_0^1 y(1 - y^2)^{-\frac{1}{2}}dy\int_0^1 g(yu)pu\sin(pu)du \quad (30)$$

In the particular case in which

$$g(\rho) = \sum_{n=0}^\infty A_n\rho^n \qquad 0 \le \rho \le 1 \quad (31)$$

the coefficients A_n being constant, it is easily seen that the solution (30) reduces to

$$f(p) = \frac{1}{\sqrt{\pi}}\sum_{n=0}^\infty \frac{\Gamma(1 + \frac{1}{2}n)}{\Gamma(\frac{3}{2} + \frac{1}{2}n)}A_n\left[\cos(p) + p\int_0^1 u^{n+1}\sin(pu)du\right] \quad (32)$$

If, in the general case, we adopt the notation

$$I_n^m(\rho,\zeta) = \int_0^\infty p^n f(p) e^{-p\zeta} J_m(p\rho) dp \tag{33}$$

where $\zeta = z/a$, we find from equations (16) to (22) that the components of the displacement vector and the stress tensor are given by the expressions

$$u_z = -\frac{1}{a^4}\left(\frac{\lambda + 2\mu}{\mu} I_0^0 + \frac{\lambda + \mu}{\mu} \zeta I_1^0\right) \tag{34}$$

$$u_r = \frac{1}{a^4}\left(I_0^1 - \frac{\lambda + \mu}{\mu} \zeta I_1^1\right) \tag{35}$$

$$\sigma_z = \frac{2(\lambda + \mu)}{a^5} (I_1^0 + \zeta I_2^0) \tag{36}$$

$$\tau_{rz} = \frac{2(\lambda + \mu)}{a^5} \zeta I_2^1 \tag{37}$$

$$\sigma_\theta = \frac{2}{a^5} I_1^0 + \frac{2\mu}{\rho a^5}\left(I_0^1 - \frac{\lambda + \mu}{\mu} \zeta I_1^1\right) \tag{38}$$

$$\sigma_r + \sigma_\theta = \frac{2}{a^5}[(2\lambda + \mu)I_1^0 - (\lambda + \mu)\zeta I_2^0] \tag{39}$$

so that, once the function $[u_z(r)]_{z=0}$ is specified, the components of stress and displacement can be determined at each point in the interior of the elastic body.   We shall illustrate the procedure by considering two special cases in a little more detail.

52.4 Indentation by a flat-ended cylinder.   The problem in which the rigid body is a flat-ended cylinder has important applications in soil mechanics,[1] especially in the theory of the safety of foundations.   In the latter instance the cylinder can be taken to represent a circular pillar and the elastic medium the soil upon which it rests.   The state of stress in the soil is likely to be more or less similar to that computed on the assumption that the soil is a perfectly elastic, isotropic, and homogeneous medium, at least if the factor of safety of a mass of soil with respect to failure by plastic flow exceeds a value of about 3.[2]   The distribution of stress in the interior of the medium due to a circular pillar has already been discussed by Love,[3] who makes the cruder assumption that both the extent of the pressed area and the distribution of the applied pressure over it are prescribed.   The solution corresponding to these boundary conditions can be derived easily by methods similar to those employed in this chapter.   The outline of this solution will be given later (Sec.

---

[1] D. P. Krynine, "Soil Mechanics," 1st ed. (McGraw-Hill, New York, 1941), Chap. IV.
[2] K. Terzaghi, "Theoretical Soil Mechanics" (Wiley, New York, 1943), p. 87.
[3] A. E. H. Love, *Phil. Trans.*, **A228**, 377 (1929).

53.2).   By the use of the type of solution developed in Sec. 52.3, the difficulty that the law of the distribution of pressure over the base of the pillar is not, in fact, known is overcome.

When the cylinder penetrates to a depth ϵ below the level of the undisturbed boundary, then, in the notation of equation (23),

$$[u_z(\rho)]_{z=0} = \epsilon \qquad 0 \leq \rho \leq 1 \qquad (40)$$

so that

$$g(\rho) = -\frac{\mu}{\lambda + 2\mu} a^4 \epsilon \qquad (41)$$

The solution of the dual integral equations is obtained immediately from equation (32) by putting $A_0 = -\mu a^4 \epsilon/(\lambda + 2\mu)$, $A_n = 0(n \neq 0)$.   We find in this way that

$$f(p) = -\frac{2\mu}{\lambda + \mu}\left(\frac{a^4 \epsilon}{\pi}\right)\frac{\sin (p)}{p} \qquad (42)$$

The expressions for the components of stress and displacement are then found from equations (34) to (39) to be

$$u_r = -\frac{2\mu}{\lambda + 2\mu}\left(\frac{\epsilon}{\pi}\right)\left(J_0^1 - \frac{\lambda + \mu}{\mu}\varsigma J_1^1\right) \qquad (43)$$

$$u_z = \frac{2\epsilon}{\pi}\left(J_0^0 + \frac{\lambda + \mu}{\lambda + 2\mu}\varsigma J_1^0\right) \qquad (44)$$

$$\sigma_z = -\frac{4\mu(\lambda + \mu)}{\lambda + 2\mu}\left(\frac{\epsilon}{\pi a}\right)(J_1^0 + \varsigma J_2^0) \qquad (45)$$

$$\tau_{rz} = -\frac{4\mu(\lambda + \mu)}{\lambda + 2\mu}\left(\frac{\epsilon}{\pi a}\right)\varsigma J_2^1 \qquad (46)$$

$$\sigma_\theta = -\frac{4\lambda\mu}{\lambda + 2\mu}\left(\frac{\epsilon}{\pi a}\right)J_1^0 - \frac{4\mu^2}{\rho(\lambda + 2\mu)}\left(\frac{\epsilon}{\pi a}\right)\left(J_0^1 - \frac{\lambda + \mu}{\mu}\varsigma J_1^1\right) \qquad (47)$$

$$\sigma_r + \sigma_\theta = -\frac{4\mu}{\lambda + 2\mu}\left(\frac{\epsilon}{\pi a}\right)[(2\lambda + \mu)J_1^0 - (\lambda + \mu)\varsigma J_2^0] \qquad (48)$$

where

$$J_n^m = \int_0^\infty p^{n-1} \sin (p)e^{-p\varsigma}J_m(p\rho)dp \qquad (49)$$

which is the imaginary part of the integral

$$\int_0^\infty p^{n-1}e^{-p(\varsigma-i)}J_m(p\rho)dp \qquad (50)$$

To evaluate the integral (50), we make use of equation (19), Appendix A, in the form

$$\int_0^\infty u^n e^{-\lambda u} J_m(\rho u)\,du = \frac{(n-m)!}{(\lambda^2 + \rho^2)^{\frac{1}{2}n + \frac{1}{2}}} P_n^m\left(\frac{\lambda}{(\lambda^2 + \rho^2)^{\frac{1}{2}}}\right) \tag{51}$$

where P_n^m denotes the associated Legendre function and $m \leq n$. For cases in which $m > n$ we must use the formula

$$\int_0^\infty u^n e^{-\lambda u} J_m(\rho u)\,du = \frac{(n+m)!}{(\lambda^2 + \rho^2)^{\frac{1}{2}n + \frac{1}{2}}} P_n^{-m}\left(\frac{\lambda}{(\lambda^2 + \rho^2)^{\frac{1}{2}}}\right) \tag{52}$$

To determine the distribution of stress across the base of the pillar, we put $\zeta = 0$ in (45). We then obtain

$$[\sigma_z]_{z=0} = -\frac{4\mu(\lambda + \mu)}{\lambda + 2\mu}\left(\frac{\epsilon}{\pi a}\right)\int_0^\infty J_0(p\rho)\sin (p)\,dp$$

The integral on the left is easily evaluated. It can be shown[1] that when $\rho > 1$ it has the value 0, confirming that σ_z vanishes across $z = 0$ when $r > a$. Similarly, when $r < a$, we find that

$$[\sigma_z]_{z=0} = -\frac{4\mu(\lambda + \mu)}{\lambda + 2\mu}\left(\frac{\epsilon}{\pi}\right)(a^2 - r^2)^{-\frac{1}{2}} \quad 0 \leq r \leq a \tag{53}$$

The total load which must be applied to the pillar to maintain the displacement ϵ is given by the formula

$$P = -2\pi \int_0^a [\sigma_z]_{z=0} r\,dr = \frac{8\mu(\lambda + \mu)}{\lambda + 2\mu} a\epsilon \tag{54}$$

If we write $p\pi a^2$ for this load P, we obtain, on substituting from equation (54) into (53), the relation

$$[\sigma_z]_{z=0} = -\frac{1}{2} p \frac{a}{(a^2 - r^2)^{\frac{1}{2}}} \quad 0 < r < a$$

showing that the contact pressure increases from $\frac{1}{2}p$ at the center of the punch to infinity round its edge. It appears, then, that, even for small loads, elastic conditions fail to hold round the edge of the punch and plastic flow occurs. If, however, the total load on the pillar is not large, the presence of a small region of plastic flow will not appreciably affect the distribution of stress.

To determine the nonvanishing components of stress on the axis of symmetry $r = 0$, we note that when $\rho = 0$ the integrals J_n^m assume a very simple form. For instance, since $J_0(p\rho) = 1$ when $\rho = 0$, we have

[1] G. N. Watson, "The Theory of Bessel Functions" (Cambridge, London, 1922), p. 405.

$$J_1^0 = \int_0^\infty \sin{(p)}e^{-p\zeta}\,dp = \frac{1}{1 + \zeta^2}$$

and, similarly, $J_2^0 = 2\zeta(1 + \zeta^2)^{-2}$. Also, since $J_1(p\rho)/\rho \to \frac{1}{2}p$ as $\rho \to 0$, it follows that

$$\frac{1}{\rho}J_0^1 = \frac{1}{2(1 + \zeta^2)}, \qquad \frac{1}{\rho}J_1^1 = \frac{\zeta}{(1 + \zeta^2)^2}$$

Substituting these values in the expressions for the components of stress, we obtain, for the nonvanishing components,

$$\sigma_z = -\frac{4\mu(\lambda + \mu)}{\lambda + 2\mu}\left(\frac{\epsilon}{\pi a}\right)\frac{1 + 3\zeta^2}{(1 + \zeta^2)^2}$$

$$\sigma_r = \sigma_\theta = -\frac{2\mu}{\lambda + 2\mu}\left(\frac{\epsilon}{\pi a}\right)\frac{(2\lambda + \mu) - \zeta^2}{(1 + \zeta^2)^2}$$

It is also of interest to determine the components of the displacement vector over the deformed surface when the punch has penetrated to a depth ϵ below the original level of the free surface. Putting $\zeta = 0$ in equation (44), we find that

$$[u_z(r)]_{z=0} = \frac{2\epsilon}{\pi}\int_0^\infty \frac{\sin{(p)}}{p}J_0\left(\frac{pr}{a}\right)dp = \begin{cases} \epsilon & 0 \le r \le a \\ \dfrac{2\epsilon}{\pi}\sin^{-1}\left(\dfrac{a}{r}\right) & r \le a \end{cases}$$

On the other hand, by substituting $\zeta = 0$ in equation (43) we find

$$[u_r(r)]_{z=0} = -\frac{2\mu}{\lambda + 2\mu}\left(\frac{\epsilon}{\pi}\right)\int_0^\infty \frac{\sin{(p)}}{p}J_1\left(\frac{pr}{a}\right)dp$$

$$= \begin{cases} -\dfrac{1 - 2\sigma}{1 - \sigma}\left(\dfrac{\epsilon}{\pi}\right)\dfrac{a - (a^2 - r^2)^{\frac{1}{2}}}{r} & 0 \le r \le a \\ -\dfrac{1 - 2\sigma}{1 - \sigma}\left(\dfrac{\epsilon a}{\pi r}\right) & r > a \end{cases}$$

We have transformed from the Lamé constants λ and μ to the Poisson ratio σ by means of the relation $\mu/\lambda = (1 - 2\sigma)/2\sigma$ to show that $[u_r(r)]_{z=0}$ vanishes when the medium is incompressible ($\sigma = \frac{1}{2}$).

Returning to the problem of determining the distribution of stress in the interior of the solid we make use of the results (20), Appendix A. Replacing p in these equations by $\zeta - i$ and adopting the notation

$$\left. \begin{array}{ll} r^2 = 1 + \zeta^2, & R^2 = (\rho^2 + \zeta^2 - 1)^2 + 4\zeta^2 \\ \zeta\tan{(\theta)} = 1, & (\rho^2 + \zeta^2 - 1)\tan{(\phi)} = 2\zeta \end{array} \right\} \qquad (55)$$

we find, on equating imaginary parts, that

$$
\left.
\begin{array}{l}
J_1^0 = R^{-\frac{1}{2}} \sin \left(\tfrac{1}{2}\phi\right), \qquad J_2^0 = rR^{-\frac{3}{2}} \sin \left(\dfrac{3}{2}\phi - \theta\right) \\[2mm]
J_0^1 = \dfrac{1}{\rho}\left(1 - R^{\frac{1}{2}} \sin \left(\tfrac{1}{2}\phi\right)\right),\ J_1^1 = r\rho^{-1}R^{-\frac{1}{2}} \sin \left(\theta - \dfrac{1}{2}\phi\right) \\[2mm]
\qquad\qquad\qquad\qquad J_2^1 = R^{-\frac{3}{2}} \sin \left(\dfrac{3}{2}\phi\right)
\end{array}
\right\} \qquad (56)
$$

with the notation of equation (49).

By means of the formulas (56) and equations (45) to (48) it is possible to compute the components of stress at any point $r = \rho a$, $z = \zeta a$ in the interior of the elastic medium.[1] The distribution of stress in the interior of the medium is shown, in the papers cited in the footnote, by drawing contours of equal maximum shearing stress—the three-dimensional analogue of the isochromatic lines of photoelasticity.

Since the shearing stress τ_{rz} is not, in general, zero, at any point the principal stresses are no longer given by σ_r, σ_θ, and σ_z. The principal stresses at any point are now determined by the roots of the discriminating cubic

$$
\begin{vmatrix}
\sigma - \sigma_r & 0 & \tau_{rz} \\
0 & \sigma - \sigma_\theta & 0 \\
\tau_{rz} & 0 & \sigma - \sigma_z
\end{vmatrix} = 0
$$

so that they are given by σ_θ, $\tfrac{1}{2}(\sigma_r + \sigma_z) \pm [(\tfrac{1}{2}\sigma_r - \tfrac{1}{2}\sigma_z)^2 + \tau_{rz}^2]^{\frac{1}{2}}$. Once the principal stresses at any point have been determined, the numerical value of the maximum shearing stress across a plane through the point under consideration may then be determined from the fact that it is equal to one-half of the algebraic difference between the maximum and minimum components of principal stress. Once the variation of this quantity, τ, with r and z has been studied it is a simple matter to draw out the family of curves $\tau = constant$, in the rz-plane. For details the reader is referred to the papers by Lodge and Sneddon cited above. These calculations have been used by Lodge to estimate the extent of any overstressed zone in the soil beneath a rigid structure and to consider the effect it may have on the stability of the structure.

52.5 Indentation by a rigid cone. The problem of the indentation of the plane surface of a semiinfinite elastic solid by a right circular cone whose axis is normal to the indented plane has been treated by Love.[2] Love's solution depends on the very fortunate circumstance that he was

---

[1] For details of the calculations see I. N. Sneddon, *Proc. Cambridge Phil. Soc.*, **42**, 29 (1946), and P. B. Lodge, M.Sc. thesis, Queen's University, Belfast, 1948.

[2] A. E. H. Love, *Quart. Jour. Math.* (Oxford), **10**, 161 (1939).

able to guess a combination of potentials which would satisfy the prescribed boundary conditions.   In this section we shall show that the use
of the theory of Hankel transforms leads to Love's solution in a more
direct way.   The analysis given here has another advantage over Love's:
his solution was in such a form that the actual computation of the distribution of stress in the interior of the elastic solid would have been a matter
of some difficulty—and was not, in fact, attempted by Love—whereas
the solution given below lends itself readily to numerical evaluation.

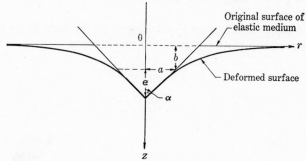

FIG. 91.   Indentation of a semiinfinite solid by a rigid cone.

Assuming that the axis of the cone coincides with the z axis and that
the vertex points downward into the interior of the medium, we see
that the strained surface of the elastic medium will fit the cone over the
area between the vertex and a circular section of radius a (cf. Fig. 91).
For the z component of the displacement we assume

$$[u_z(\rho)]_{z=0} = b + \epsilon(1 - \rho) \tag{57}$$

where, as before, $\rho = r/a$ and b is a parameter as yet unspecified.   In the
notation of equations (28) we may put

$$g(\rho) = A + B\rho$$

where A and B are given by the relations

$$A = - \frac{\mu}{\lambda + 2\mu} a^4(b + \epsilon), \qquad B = \frac{\mu}{\lambda + 2\mu} a^4\epsilon$$

Substituting $A_0 = A$, $A_1 = B$, $A_n = 0$ $(n \geq 2)$, in equation (32), we
obtain the solution

$$f(p) = 2 \left(\frac{A}{\pi} + \frac{B}{2} \right) \frac{\sin (p)}{p} + B \frac{\cos (p) - 1}{p^2} \tag{58}$$

We first of all consider the normal component σ_z of the surface stress.
Putting $z = 0$ in equation (36), we have

$$\frac{a^5}{2(\lambda + \mu)} [\sigma_z]_{z=0} = \int_0^\infty pf(p)J_0(p\rho)dp$$

Using the expression for $f(p)$ given above, we find that round the edge of the punch ($z = 0, \rho = 1$) the normal component of stress is given by

$$\frac{a^5}{2(\lambda + \mu)} \sigma_z$$

$$= 2\left(\frac{A}{\pi} + \frac{B}{2}\right) \int_0^\infty \sin (p)J_0(p)dp - B \int_0^\infty \frac{1 - \cos (p)}{p} J_0(p)dp$$

The normal stress σ_z must, on physical grounds, remain finite round the edge of the punch. On the other hand the integral

$$\int_0^\infty \sin (p)J_0(p)dp$$

is divergent, so that, if σ_z is to remain finite, we must take $B = -2A/\pi$. Inserting the values of A and B as defined above, we find that this relation is equivalent to the condition

$$b = \epsilon(\tfrac{1}{2}\pi - 1) \tag{59}$$

which fixes the parameter b. This is in agreement with the value obtained by Love. We therefore obtain finally, for the function f,

$$f(p) = \frac{\mu}{\lambda + 2\mu} a^4\epsilon \frac{\cos (p) - 1}{p} \tag{60}$$

We now obtain the expressions for the z component of the displacement of the boundary for $r > a$. From equations (44) and (60) we obtain the expression

$$[u_z(\rho)]_{z=0} = \epsilon \int_0^\infty \frac{1 - \cos (p)}{p^2} J_0(p\rho)dp$$

Now

$$\int_0^\infty \frac{\sin (\lambda p)}{p} J_0(p\rho)dp = \sin^{-1}\left(\frac{\lambda}{\rho}\right) \qquad \rho > \lambda$$

so that if we integrate both sides of this equation with respect to λ over the range (0,1) we find an expression for the integral involved, which leads to the formula

$$[u_z(\rho)]_{z=0} = \epsilon\left[\sin^{-1}\left(\frac{1}{\rho}\right) + (\rho^2 - 1)^{\frac{1}{2}} - \rho\right] \qquad \rho > 1 \tag{61}$$

If we remember that $\rho = r/a$ and write $a \cot \alpha$ for ϵ, we see that this expression is identical with that given by Love.[1]

[1] *Quart. Jour. Math. (Oxford)*, **10**, 171 (1939).

Similarly, for the radial component of the surface displacement, we have, from equation (43),

$$[u_r(\rho)]_{z=0} = \frac{\mu}{\lambda + 2\mu} \epsilon \int_0^\infty \frac{\cos(p) - 1}{p^2} J_1(p\rho)dp$$

In order to evaluate the integral on the right when $0 \leq \rho \leq 1$ we make use of the known integral [deducible from the first of equations (20), Appendix A]

$$\int_0^\infty \frac{\sin(p)}{\rho} J_1(p\rho)dp = \begin{cases} \dfrac{b}{\rho} & \rho \geq b \\[2ex] \dfrac{\rho}{b + \sqrt{(b^2 - \rho^2)}} & \rho \leq b \end{cases}$$

Integrating both sides of this relation with respect to b over the range $(0,1)$, we obtain the relation

$$\int_0^\infty \frac{1 - \cos(p)}{p^2} J_1(p\rho)dp = \frac{1}{\rho} \int_0^\rho b\, db + \rho \int_0^1 \frac{db}{b + \sqrt{(b^2 - \rho^2)}} \quad \rho < 1$$

When the integrations have been carried out, we find that

$$[u_r(\rho)]_{z=0} = \frac{\mu\epsilon\rho}{2(\lambda + 2\mu)} \left(\log \frac{\rho}{1 + \sqrt{1 - \rho^2}} - \frac{1 - \sqrt{1 - \rho^2}}{\rho^2} \right) \rho < 1 \quad (62)$$

On the other hand, when $\rho > 1$ we have

$$\int_0^\infty \frac{\cos(p) - 1}{\rho^2} J_1(p\rho)dp = -\frac{1}{\rho} \int_0^1 b\, db = -\frac{1}{2\rho}$$

so that

$$[u_r(\rho)]_{z=0} = -\frac{\mu\epsilon a}{2r(\lambda + 2\mu)} \qquad r \geq a \qquad (63)$$

Further, from equation (36) we have the relation

$$\frac{\lambda + 2\mu}{2\mu(\lambda + \mu)} [\sigma_z]_{z=0} = \frac{\epsilon}{a} \int_0^\infty \frac{\cos(p) - 1}{p} J_0(p\rho)dp \qquad (64)$$

To evaluate this integral, we integrate both sides of the equation

$$\int_0^\infty e^{-iap} J_0(p\rho)dp = \begin{cases} (\rho^2 - a^2)^{-\frac{1}{2}} & \rho > a \\ -i(a^2 - \rho^2)^{-\frac{1}{2}} & 0 < \rho < a \end{cases}$$

with respect to the parameter a over the interval $(0,1)$ to obtain

$$i \int_0^\infty \frac{e^{-ip} - 1}{p} J_0(p\rho)dp = \int_0^\rho \frac{da}{\sqrt{\rho^2 - a^2}} + \frac{1}{i} \int_\rho^1 \frac{da}{\sqrt{a^2 - \rho^2}}$$

from which it follows, on equating real and imaginary parts, that

$$\int_0^\infty \frac{\cos(p) - 1}{p} J_0(p\rho) dp = -\cosh^{-1}\left(\frac{1}{\rho}\right) \quad 0 < \rho < 1 \quad (65)$$

and that

$$\int_0^\infty \frac{\sin(p)}{p} J_0(p\rho) dp = \frac{1}{2}\pi \quad 0 < \rho < 1 \quad (66)$$

Substituting the value given by equation (65) into equation (64) and replacing the Lamé constants by their values in terms of E and σ we obtain the expression

$$[\sigma_z]_{z=0} = -\frac{E}{2(1 - \sigma^2)}\left(\frac{\epsilon}{a}\right)\cosh^{-1}\left(\frac{a}{r}\right) \quad 0 \leq r \leq a \quad (67)$$

Making use of the formula

$$P = -2\pi \int_0^a [\sigma_z]_{z=0} r \, dr$$

for determining the total force P on the pressed area $0 \leq r \leq a$, we find from equation (67) that

$$P = \frac{\pi E}{(1 - \sigma^2)}\left(\frac{\epsilon}{a}\right) \int^a \cosh^{-1}\left(\frac{a}{r}\right) dr = \frac{\pi a \epsilon E}{2(1 - \sigma^2)} \quad (68)$$

For the determination of the components of stress at an interior point of the medium we have, from equations (36) to (39), the set of relations

$$\frac{a\sigma_z}{\epsilon E} = -\frac{1}{2(1 - \sigma^2)}(K_1^0 + \zeta K_2^0) \quad (69)$$

$$\frac{a\sigma_\theta}{\epsilon E} = -\frac{1}{2(1 - \sigma^2)}\left(2\sigma K_1^0 + \frac{1 - 2\sigma}{\rho}K_0^1 - \frac{\zeta}{\rho}K_1^1\right) \quad (70)$$

$$\frac{a(\sigma_r + \sigma_\theta + \sigma_z)}{\epsilon E} = -\frac{1}{1 - \sigma}K_1^0 \quad (71)$$

$$\frac{a\tau_{rz}}{\epsilon E} = -\frac{\zeta}{2(1 - \sigma^2)}K_2^1 \quad (72)$$

where $K_n^m(\rho,\zeta)$ denotes the integral

$$K_n^m(\rho,\zeta) = Z_n^m(\rho,\zeta) - C_n^m(\rho,\zeta) \quad (73)$$

with

$$Z_n^m(\rho,\zeta) = \int_0^\infty p^{n-2} J_m(p\rho) e^{-p\zeta} \, dp \quad (74)$$

and

$$C_n^m(\rho,\zeta) = \int_0^\infty p^{n-2} \cos(p) J_m(p\rho) e^{-p\zeta} \, dp \quad (75)$$

The value of $Z_n^m(\rho,\zeta)$ is given by equations (51) and (52), while that of $C_n^m(\rho,\zeta)$ may be obtained from the same equations by replacing λ by $\zeta + i$ and equating real parts. In this way we obtain the formulas

$$K_2^0(\rho,\zeta) = \frac{1}{\sqrt{\rho^2 + \zeta^2}} - \frac{\cos(\phi)}{R} \tag{76}$$

$$K_1^1(\rho,\zeta) = \frac{1}{\rho}[\sqrt{\rho^2 + \zeta^2} - R\cos(\phi)] \tag{77}$$

$$K_2^1(\rho,\zeta) = \frac{1}{\rho}\left[\frac{r}{R}\cos(\theta - \phi) - \frac{\zeta}{\sqrt{\rho^2 + \zeta^2}}\right] \tag{78}$$

where the quantities $r, R, \theta,$ and ϕ are defined by the relations (55).

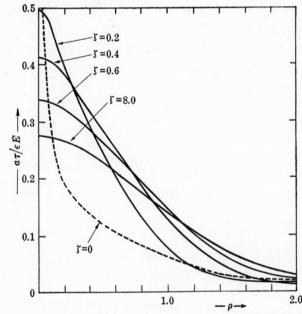

Fig. 92. Variation with ρ and ζ of the maximum shearing stress τ.

To determine the stress completely, it remains only to evaluate K_1^0 and K_0^1. For the former we integrate both sides of the equation

$$Z_2^0(\rho,w) = \int_0^\infty e^{-wp}J_0(p\rho)dp = (\rho^2 + w^2)^{-\frac{1}{2}}$$

with respect to w from ζ to $\zeta + i$ and then separate real parts. In this way we obtain the result

$$K_1^0(\rho,\zeta) = \frac{1}{2}\log_e \frac{R^2 + 2Rr\cos(\theta - \phi) + r^2}{(\zeta + \sqrt{\rho^2 + \zeta^2})^2} \tag{79}$$

Similarly, from the result

$$Z_1^1(\rho,w) = \int_0^\infty e^{-wp} J_1(p\rho) \frac{dp}{p} = \frac{1}{\rho}(\sqrt{\rho^2 + w^2}^{\frac{1}{2}} - w) \qquad (80)$$

we obtain

$$K_0^1(\rho,\zeta) = \frac{1}{2}\left[\rho K_1^0(\rho,\zeta) - \zeta K_1^1(\rho,\zeta) + \frac{1}{\rho}(1 - R\sin\phi)\right] \qquad (81)$$

The above formulas for the integrals K_n^m and the equations (69) to (72) are sufficient for the computation of the components of stress at any point in the interior of the medium.[1]   The principal stresses may then

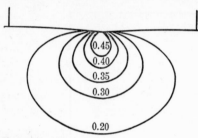

be calculated and the value of the maximum shearing stress τ found at each point. The variation of $a\tau/\epsilon E$ with ρ and ζ in the case $\sigma = \frac{1}{4}$ is shown in Fig. 92. The contours of equal maximum shearing stress calculated by means of the curves of Fig. 92 are shown in Fig. 93. The shape of these curves shows clearly the high concentration of stress in the neighborhood of the

Fig. 93.   Contours of equal maximum shearing stress.

apex of the cone.   The semivertical angle of the cone is shown in this diagram to be nearly a right angle, merely to obtain a sufficiently large value of a to show the detail of the distribution of stress under the punch.

53. Application of Pressure to the Faces of a Thick Plate

53.1 Introduction.   In the preceding sections an analysis was given of the distribution of stress in a semiinfinite elastic medium deformed by the pressure of a rigid body on part of the plane boundary, the remainder of the plane being free.   In that form of the problem the normal displacement of a point within the pressed area was prescribed, and the distribution of stress over that area was determined.   In this section we shall consider the case in which the pressed area and the distribution of pressure over it are both prescribed and the normal displacement of a point on the free surface is determined.

A formal solution of this problem for the case of a semiinfinite medium was given by Boussinesq[2] by means of the theory of the logarithmic

---

[1] For tables of the stress components see I. N. Sneddon, *Proc. Cambridge Phil. Soc.*, **44**, 492 (1948).

[2] J. Boussinesq, "Applications des potentiels" (Paris, 1885).

potential, but the difficulty of evaluating the double integral involved has hindered the application of the general solution to special problems. Boussinesq's method has been developed by Love,[1] who gave the first complete discussion of the cases in which the pressure is distributed over a circle or a rectangle. An alternative method, applicable to circular boundaries only and to cases in which the pressure is distributed symmetrically with respect to the center of the circle, was developed by Lamb and Terezawa.[2]

In this section the problem of the semiinfinite solid is solved by the method of Hankel transforms, and Terezawa's solution is obtained as a special case of a more general theory.[3] This general theory is then applied to the case where the elastic medium is bounded by two parallel planes a finite distance apart; *i.e.*, we are considering the deformation of a thick plate by pressure applied to its surfaces. Again we are restricted to the consideration of those cases in which the pressures on the boundaries of the plate are distributed symmetrically about an axis normal to the surfaces. By the further assumption that there is symmetry about a central plane the analysis is considerably simplified, and we obtain the solution of a three-dimensional problem analogous to one in two dimensions considered in Sec. 45.4.

53.2 Terezawa's solution for a semiinfinite medium. Consider, in the first instance, an elastic medium bounded by the infinite plane $z = 0$ and otherwise unlimited. Choose the z axis normal to this plane and pointing *into* the medium. The elastic solid will be supposed to be deformed by the application of the pressure $p(r)$ distributed symmetrically with respect to the z axis and acting normal to the boundary. The boundary conditions on the plane $z = 0$ then become

$$\sigma_z = -p(r), \qquad \tau_{rz} = 0 \tag{82}$$

In addition the solution must be such that the components of stress and displacement all tend to zero as r and z tend to infinity. The solutions given in Sec. 51.2 satisfy the former of these two conditions. To ensure the latter, we must assume a function of the form

$$G(\xi,z) = (A + Bz)e^{-\xi z} \tag{83}$$

for G occurring in the equations of Sec. 51.2.

From equations (83), (18), and (19) we have

[1] A. E. H. Love, *Phil. Trans.*, **A228**, 377 (1929).

[2] H. Lamb, *Proc. London Math. Soc.*, **34**, 276 (1902); K. Terezawa, *Jour. Coll. Sci. Imp. Univ. Tokyo*, **37**, Art. 7 (1916).

[3] I. N. Sneddon, *Proc. Cambridge Phil. Soc.*, **42**, 260 (1946).

$$\int_0^\infty r\sigma_z J_0(\xi r)dr = \xi^2 e^{-\xi z}[\lambda\xi A + (2\mu + \lambda\xi z)B]$$

$$\int_0^\infty r\tau_{rz} J_1(\xi r)dr = 2\xi^2 e^{-\xi z}\{(\lambda + \mu)\xi A + [(\lambda + \mu)\xi z - \lambda]B\}$$

Thus, if we put $z = 0$ and write

$$Z(\xi) = -\xi\bar{p}(\xi) = -\xi\int_0^\infty rp(r)J_0(\xi r)dr$$

we find, on inserting the conditions (82), the equations

$$\xi^{-3}Z(\xi) = \lambda\xi A + 2\mu B, \qquad 0 = (\lambda + \mu)\xi A - \lambda B$$

Solving these equations for A and B and substituting the results in the expression for $G(\xi,z)$, we obtain finally

$$G(\xi,z) = \frac{\lambda}{(\lambda + \mu)^2}\frac{Z(\xi)}{\xi^4}\left(1 + \frac{\lambda + \mu}{\lambda}\xi z\right)e^{-\xi z} \tag{84}$$

Substituting from equation (84) into equations (16) to (22), we obtain the expressions

$$u_r = -\frac{z}{2\mu}\int_0^\infty Z(\xi)e^{-\xi z}J_1(\xi r)d\xi + \frac{1}{2(\lambda + \mu)}\int_0^\infty Z(\xi)e^{-\xi z}J_1(\xi r)\frac{d\xi}{\xi} \tag{85}$$

$$u_z = -\frac{z}{2\mu}\int_0^\infty Z(\xi)e^{-\xi z}J_0(\xi r)d\xi - \frac{\lambda + 2\mu}{2\mu(\lambda + \mu)}\int_0^\infty Z(\xi)e^{-\xi z}J_0(\xi r)\frac{d\xi}{\xi} \tag{85a}$$

$$\sigma_z = z\int_0^\infty \xi Z(\xi)e^{-\xi z}J_0(\xi r)d\xi + \int_0^\infty Z(\xi)e^{-\xi z}J_0(\xi r)d\xi \tag{85b}$$

$$\tau_{rz} = z\int_0^\infty Z(\xi)e^{-\xi z}J_1(\xi r)\xi\,d\xi \tag{85c}$$

$$\sigma_r + \sigma_\theta + \sigma_z = \frac{3\lambda + 2\mu}{\lambda + \mu}\int_0^\infty Z(\xi)e^{-\xi z}J_0(\xi r)d\xi \tag{85d}$$

$$\sigma_r = \int_0^\infty (1 - \xi z)Z(\xi)e^{-\xi z}J_0(\xi r)d\xi + \frac{1}{r}\int_0^\infty Z(\xi)\left[z - \frac{\mu}{(\lambda + \mu)\xi}\right]$$
$$\times J_1(\xi r)\frac{d\xi}{\xi} \tag{85e}$$

which constitute Terezawa's solution of the problem.

For example, if a uniform normal pressure acts on the surface within a circular area of radius a, outside of which the surface is free from traction, then $p(r) = P/\pi a^2$ when $0 \le r \le a$ and zero when $r > a$, P being the total force applied to the surface, and, as a result of equation (11), Appendix A, $Z(\xi) = -PJ_1(\xi a)/\pi a$. The expressions for the stress components may then be obtained by substituting this value of $Z(\xi)$ in equations (85) to (85e). The integrals occurring in these expressions cannot be evaluated in a very simple way;[1] hence we shall consider only the simplest case, that of a point force, for which

$$Z(\xi) = -\frac{P}{\pi} \lim_{a \to 0} \frac{J_1(\xi a)}{a} = -\frac{P\xi}{2\pi}$$

Inserting this value for $Z(\xi)$ into equations (85) to (85e), we obtain, on evaluating the integrals by the formulas (51) and (52), for the components of stress in a medium deformed by the application of a point force to the boundary,

$$\sigma_z = -\left(\frac{P}{2\pi}\right)\frac{3z^3}{(r^2+z^2)^{\frac{5}{2}}}, \qquad \tau_{rz} = -\left(\frac{P}{2\pi}\right)\frac{3rz^2}{(r^2+z^2)^{\frac{5}{2}}}$$

$$\sigma_r = -\left(\frac{P}{2\pi}\right)\left\{\frac{3r^2z}{(r^2+z^2)^{\frac{5}{2}}} - \frac{\mu}{\lambda+\mu}\left[\frac{1}{r^2} - \frac{z}{r^2(r^2+z^2)^{\frac{1}{2}}}\right]\right\}$$

$$\sigma_\theta = \left(\frac{P}{2\pi}\right)\left(\frac{\mu}{\lambda+\mu}\right)\left[\frac{z(2r^2+z^2)}{r^2(r^2+z^2)^{\frac{3}{2}}} - \frac{1}{r^2}\right]$$

On the surface $z = 0$, these expressions reduce simply to

$$\sigma_z = \tau_{rz} = 0, \qquad \sigma_r = \frac{P\mu}{2\pi(\lambda+\mu)}\frac{1}{r^2}, \qquad \sigma_\theta = -\frac{P\mu}{2\pi(\lambda+\mu)}\frac{1}{r^2}$$

In a similar way we may obtain expressions for the components of the displacement vector from equations (85) and (85a), namely,

$$u_r = -\frac{P}{4\pi(\lambda+\mu)}\int_0^\infty\left(1 - \frac{\lambda+\mu}{\mu}\xi z\right)e^{-\xi z}J_1(\xi r)d\xi = \frac{P}{4\pi\mu}\left\{\frac{rz}{(r^2+z^2)^{\frac{3}{2}}}\right.$$
$$\left. -\frac{\mu}{\lambda+\mu}\left[\frac{1}{r} - \frac{z}{r(r^2+z^2)^{\frac{1}{2}}}\right]\right\}$$

and

$$u_z = \frac{(\lambda+2\mu)P}{4\pi\mu(\lambda+\mu)}\int_0^\infty\left(1 + \frac{\lambda+\mu}{\lambda+2\mu}\xi z\right)e^{-\xi z}J_0(\xi r)d\xi$$
$$= \frac{P}{4\pi\mu}\left[\frac{z^2}{(r^2+z^2)^{\frac{3}{2}}} + \left(\frac{\lambda+2\mu}{\lambda+\mu}\right)\frac{1}{(r^2+z^2)^{\frac{1}{2}}}\right]$$

On the boundary we obtain $u_r = -P/4\pi(\lambda+\mu)r$,

$$u_z = (\lambda+2\mu)P/4\pi\mu(\lambda+\mu)r$$

It is of interest to show graphically the state of deformation at different depths below the surface. For the sake of simplicity we assume that $\sigma = \frac{1}{4}$ (that is, $\lambda = \mu$), and we take only one component of displacement,

---

[1] For details of the integrations the reader is referred to Terezawa, *op. cit.*

u_z say, for reference.   With $\lambda = \mu$ we have

$$\frac{4\pi\mu u_z}{P} = \frac{z^2}{(r^2 + z^2)^{\frac{3}{2}}} + \frac{3}{2(r^2 + z^2)^{\frac{1}{2}}}$$

The variation of $4\pi\mu u_z/P$ with r and z is shown in Fig. 94.

As seen from this diagram the state of affairs in the neighborhood of the origin, and even at a finite distance from it, is an impossible one, and the mathematical theory of elasticity is inapplicable to such a case.   The above argument must, if possible, be amended by a suitable process of

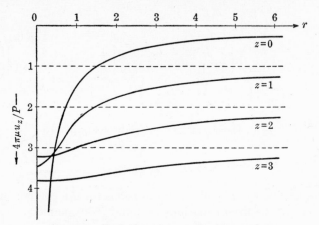

FIG. 94.   Variation of $4\pi\mu u_z/P$ with r and z.

analysis.   What follows from the assumption of point concentration of the given pressure may, however, be considered, except locally, as the limiting case of the effect of a pressure which acts on a slightly extended area of the boundary.   We could have left $a > 0$, but, as we have noted, this would lead to the evaluation of integrals of the type

$$\int_0^\infty e^{-\xi z} J_m(\xi r) J_1(\xi a) \xi^p \, d\xi$$

which leads to elliptic functions.   Instead of this, we might suppose the point force to be the limiting case of the normal pressure

$$p(r) = \left(\frac{P}{2\pi}\right) \frac{a}{(a^2 + r^2)^{\frac{3}{2}}} \qquad a > 0$$

P being its total amount.

Now applying the Hankel inversion theorem 19 to the result

$$\int_0^\infty e^{-a\xi} J_0(\xi r) d\xi = a(a^2 + r^2)^{-\frac{3}{2}}$$

which is a simple case of equation (51), we obtain the formula

$$\int_0^\infty J_0(\xi r)\,\frac{ar\,dr}{(a^2+r^2)^{\frac{3}{2}}} = e^{-a\xi}$$

so that $Z(\xi) = -P\xi e^{-a\xi}/2\pi$. Substituting this expression in equation (85b), we obtain for the normal component of stress

$$\sigma_z = -\frac{P}{2\pi}\int_0^\infty \xi(1-\xi z)e^{-\xi(z+a)}J_0(\xi r)d\xi = -\left(\frac{P}{2\pi}\right)\frac{(3z+a)(z+a)^2+ar^2}{[r^2+(a+z)^2]^{\frac{5}{2}}}.$$

The other components of stress may be evaluated similarly.

For the normal component of displacement we find

$$u_z = \frac{P}{4\pi\mu}\int_0^\infty \left(\frac{\lambda+2\mu}{\lambda+\mu}+\xi z\right)e^{-\xi(z+a)}J_0(\xi r)d\xi$$

from which it follows from equation (51)—or equations (20), Appendix A—that

$$u_z = \frac{P}{4\pi\mu}\left\{\frac{z(z+a)}{[r^2+(a+z)^2]^{\frac{3}{2}}}+\left(\frac{\lambda+2\mu}{\lambda+\mu}\right)\frac{1}{[r^2+(a+z)^2]^{\frac{1}{2}}}\right\}$$

The variation of u_z with r and z on the hypothesis that $\lambda = \mu$ is shown in

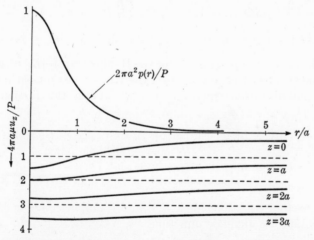

FIG. 95.   Variation of $4\pi\mu a u_z/P$ with r and z. The upper curve shows the form of $p(r)$.

Fig. 95. It will be observed that, in this instance, u_z does not become infinitely large in the vicinity of the origin.

53.3 Solution for a thick plate.[1]   We shall now extend the analysis to the case in which the elastic solid is bounded by the parallel planes

[1] I. N. Sneddon, *Proc. Cambridge Phil. Soc.*, **42**, 260 (1946).

$z = \pm d$, to form a thick plate of finite radius. The plate will be considered to be deformed by the application of normal pressures to these free surfaces. The boundary conditions then assume the form

(i) $\qquad\qquad\qquad \sigma_z = -p_1(r), \qquad \tau_{rz} = 0 \qquad$ on $z = +d$

(ii) $\qquad\qquad\qquad \sigma_z = -p_2(r), \qquad \tau_{rz} = 0 \qquad$ on $z = -d$

Then, either we have the relation

$$\int_0^\infty r p_1(r) dr = \int_0^\infty r p_2(r) dr$$

or the plate must be held "at infinity" in such a way as to preserve its equilibrium as a whole.

Assuming a solution of equation (14) in the form

$$G(\xi,z) = (A + Bz) \cosh (\xi z) + (C + Dz) \sinh (\xi z) \qquad (86)$$

inverting equation (18), and inserting the boundary conditions relating to σ_z, we obtain the two equations

$$\frac{(1 + \sigma)(1 - 2\sigma)}{E} \bar{p}_1(\xi) = A \xi^3 \sinh (\xi d) + B\xi^2[\xi d \sinh (\xi d) - (1 - 2\sigma)$$

$$\times \cosh (\xi d)] + C\xi^3 \cosh (\xi d) + D\xi^2[\xi d \cosh (\xi d) - (1 - 2\sigma) \sinh (\xi d)]$$

$$\frac{(1 + \sigma)(1 - 2\sigma)}{E} \bar{p}_2(\xi) = -A \xi^3 \sinh (\xi d) + B\xi^2[\xi d \sinh (\xi d) - (1 - 2\sigma)$$

$$\times \cosh (\xi d)] + C\xi^3 \cosh (\xi d) - D\xi^2[\xi d \cosh (\xi d) - (1 - 2\sigma) \sinh (\xi d)]$$

where we have written $\bar{p}_1(\xi)$, $\bar{p}_2(\xi)$ for the Hankel transforms of zero order of $p_1(r)$ and $p_2(r)$ and have expressed the Lamé constants in terms of E and σ. Similarly from equation (19) we obtain the further pair of equations

$$0 = A \xi \cosh (\xi d) + B[\xi d \cosh (\xi d) + 2\sigma \sinh (\xi d)] + C\xi \sinh (\xi d)$$
$$+ D[\xi d \sinh (\xi d) + 2\sigma \cosh (\xi d)]$$

$$0 = A \xi \cosh (\xi d) - B[\xi d \cosh (\xi d) + 2\sigma \sinh (\xi d)] - C\xi \sinh (\xi d)$$
$$+ D[\xi d \sinh (\xi d) + 2\sigma \cosh (\xi d)]$$

Solving these four equations for $A, B, C,$ and D and inserting in expression (86), we obtain the auxiliary function

$$\frac{E}{(1 + \sigma)(1 - 2\sigma)} G(\xi,z) = \left(\frac{\bar{p}_1 - \bar{p}_2}{\xi^3} \right)$$

$$\times \frac{[\xi d \sinh (\xi d) \cosh (\xi z) + 2\sigma \cosh (\xi d) \cosh (\xi z) - \xi z \sinh (\xi z) \cosh (\xi d)]}{\sinh (2\xi d) - 2\xi d}$$

$$+ \left(\frac{\bar{p}_1 + \bar{p}_2}{\xi^3} \right) \frac{\{[\xi d \cosh (\xi d) + 2\sigma \sinh (\xi d)] \sinh (\xi z) - \xi z \cosh (\xi z) \sinh (\xi d)\}}{\sinh (2\xi d) + 2\xi d}$$

Substituting this value for $G(\xi,z)$ in the formulas (16) to (22), we obtain integral expressions for the components of stress and displacement so that the problem is solved formally if we are given the applied pressures $p_1(r)$ and $p_2(r)$.

53.4 Symmetrical deformation of a thick plate. We shall consider in more detail the case in which the applied pressures are symmetrical about the plane $z = 0$ as well as about the z axis. This greatly simplifies the analysis, which, however, proceeds in a similar fashion when no such symmetry exists. In the symmetrical case we may write

$$p_1(r) = p_2(r) = p(r)$$

say, so that $G(\xi,z)$ reduces to

$$\frac{2(1 + \sigma)(1 - 2\sigma)\bar{p}(\xi)}{E\xi^3}$$

$$\times \frac{\{[\xi d \cosh(\xi d) + 2\sigma \sinh(\xi d)] \sinh(\xi z) - \xi z \sinh(\xi d) \cosh(\xi z)\}}{2\xi d + \sinh(2\xi d)} \quad (87)$$

Substituting the expression (87) into equations (16) to (21), we obtain expressions for the components of stress and displacement. For example, from equation (18) we obtain, on transforming from λ and μ to E and σ, the relation

$$\sigma_z = -2 \int_0^\infty$$

$$\times \frac{\xi d \cosh(\xi z) \cosh(\xi d) - \xi z \sinh(\xi z) \sinh(\xi d) + 2\sigma \sinh(\xi d) \cosh(\xi z)}{2\xi d + \sinh(2\xi d)}$$

$$\times \xi \bar{p}(\xi) J_0(\xi r) d\xi \quad (88)$$

It is easily verified from this equation, and the Hankel inversion theorem 19, that, when $z = \pm d$, $\sigma_z = -p(r)$, while in the central plane $z = 0$,

$$\sigma_z = -\frac{2}{d^2} \int_0^\infty u\bar{p}\left(\frac{u}{d}\right) \frac{u \cosh(u) + \sinh(u)}{2u + \sinh(2u)} J_0(\rho u) du \quad (89)$$

where $\rho = r/d$. Equation (88), together with the corresponding formulas for the other components of stress, gives a solution exactly similar to the Fourier integral solution obtained by Filon[1] in the analogous problem in two dimensions.

Some of the integrals in the expressions for the components of stress can, if $\bar{p}(\xi)$ satisfies certain conditions, be written in the form

$$\int_0^\infty \phi(\xi) J_0(\xi r) d\xi$$

[1] See Sec. 45.4 above.

where $\phi(\xi)$ is an odd function of ξ. Integrals of this type have been treated by Dougall[1] by the methods of the calculus of residues. In our problem $\phi(\xi) \to 0$ as $\xi \to \infty$ and also as $\xi \to 0$. Suppose that, in addition, $\phi(\xi)$ is, in fact, odd. Then by considering the integral

$$\int \phi(\zeta) H_0^{(1)}(\zeta r) d\zeta$$

taken round a rectangle, in the ζ plane, with vertices at the points $(\pm \alpha, 0)$, $(\pm \alpha, \beta)$ and indented at the origin, it can readily be established that the value of the integral is πi times the sum of the residues of the function $\phi(\zeta) H_0^{(1)}(\zeta r)$ in the upper half plane. But the advantages of evaluating the integral in this way are not very substantial since the result is then presented in the form of a sum of a rather complicated function over all those roots of the transcendental equation

$$2\zeta + \sinh (2\zeta) = 0$$

whose imaginary parts are positive, and such expressions do not lend themselves readily to computation. In any practical example it would probably be more convenient to retain the integrals in their real variable form and to evaluate them by numerical or mechanical methods.

It is the occurrence of the factor $[2\xi d + \sinh (2\xi d)]^{-1}$ in the integrand which renders integration by analytical methods troublesome. In an approximate calculation this difficulty may be overcome by employing an approximate expression of the form

$$f_1(u) = (\alpha u + \tfrac{1}{2})e^{-\nu u} + 2ue^{-u} \tag{90}$$

to represent the function

$$f(u) = \frac{u}{u + \sinh (u)} \tag{91}$$

over the entire range of integration. It is obvious from equation (90) that $f_1(u) \to \tfrac{1}{2}$ as $u \to 0$ and that $f_1(u) \sim 2ue^{-u}$ as $u \to \infty$ (provided that $\nu > 1$) as is required by equation (91). The values of α and ν may be chosen in several ways, but as we have to evaluate integrals in which the integrand is the product of $f(u)$ and an exponential factor, it is more important to ensure that the fit is close for large values of u than to aim at a good approximation near the origin. As $f(u)$ will occur solely as an integrand, any variations in $f_1(u)$ near the origin may be compensated for by choosing α and ν in such a way that the area under the curve $v = f_1(u) - f(u)$ is as small as possible. It is found that these conditions are satisfied to a large degree by choosing

$$\alpha = -1.55, \qquad \nu = 1.40 \tag{92}$$

[1] J. Dougall, *Trans. Roy. Soc. Edinburgh*, **41**, 129 (1904).

The variation with u of the functions $f(u)$ and $f_1(u)$ is shown in Fig. 96, from which it will be observed that the fit is reasonably close. Further evidence as to the closeness of the approximation will be adduced later (cf. Table 3).

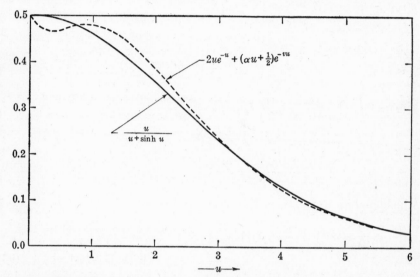

Fig. 96.   Comparison of the functions $u/[u + \sinh (u)]$ and $2ue^{-u} + (\alpha u + \frac{1}{2})e^{-\nu u}$.

The approximation could doubtless be improved by representing $f_1(u) - f(u)$ as a sum of terms of the form $c_n u^n e^{-\nu_n u}$, but this would complicate the analysis unduly and is omitted here since the present approximation appears to be sufficiently accurate for most practical purposes.[1]

53.5 Symmetrical deformation of a thick plate by concentrated forces. As an example of the use of the formulas derived in the last section we shall now consider the case in which the deformation is produced by concentrated forces of magnitude P acting on the plate at the points $z = \pm d, r = 0$. If we take $p(r) = \delta(r)/2\pi r$, we have

$$\bar{p}(\xi) = \frac{P}{2\pi} \tag{93}$$

Substituting from equation (93) into equation (89), we see that σ_z may be expressed in terms of integrals of the type

$$\int_0^\infty \frac{u^n}{2u + \sinh (2u)} J_0(\rho u) \frac{\sinh}{\cosh} (xu)du \tag{94}$$

[1] This view is confirmed by A. E. Green and T. J. Willmore, *Proc. Roy. Soc. (London)*, **A193**, 229 (1948).

We can then approximate to the value of integrals of this type by substituting from equations (90) and (92) and making use of equations (51) and (52). By this method we obtain the approximate results

$$I_1(x) \equiv \int_0^\infty \frac{u \sinh (xu)}{2u + \sinh (2u)} J_0(\rho u)du = \frac{2 - x}{[\rho^2 + (2 - x)^2]^{\frac{3}{2}}}$$
$$- \frac{2 + x}{[\rho^2 + (2 + x)^2]^{\frac{3}{2}}} + \frac{0.125\rho^2 + (2\nu - x)[\frac{1}{2}\alpha + 0.125(2\nu - x)]}{[\rho^2 + (2\nu - x)^2]^{\frac{3}{2}}}$$
$$- \frac{0.125\rho^2 + (2\nu + x)[\frac{1}{2}\alpha + 0.125(2\nu + x)]}{[\rho^2 + (2\nu + x)^2]^{\frac{3}{2}}}$$

$$I_2(x) \equiv \int_0^\infty \frac{u^2 \cosh (xu)}{2u + \sinh (2u)} J_0(\rho u)du = \frac{2(2 - x^2) - \rho^2}{[\rho^2 + (2 - x)^2]^{\frac{3}{2}}} - \frac{2(2 + x)^2 - \rho^2}{[\rho^2 + (2 + x)^2]^{\frac{3}{2}}}$$
$$+ \frac{[0.125(2\nu - x) - \frac{1}{2}\alpha]\rho^2 + (2\nu - x)^2[0.125(2\nu - x) + \alpha]}{[\rho^2 + (2\nu - x)^2]^{\frac{3}{2}}}$$
$$+ \frac{[0.125(2\nu + x) - \frac{1}{2}\alpha]\rho^2 + (2\nu + x)^2[0.125(2\nu + x) + \alpha]}{[\rho^2 + (2\nu + x)^2]^{\frac{3}{2}}}$$

which enables us to find σ_z from the formula

$$\sigma_z = -\frac{P}{2\pi d^2}[I_1(1 + \zeta) + I_1(1 - \zeta) + (1 - \zeta)I_2(1 + \zeta)$$
$$+ (1 + \zeta)I_2(1 - \zeta)] \quad (95)$$

where $\zeta = z/d$. Similar expressions can be written down to give the other components of stress in terms of integrals of the form (94).

To estimate the accuracy of formulas (90) and (92) in calculating stresses of this kind, the integral

$$- \frac{\pi d^2}{P}[\sigma_z]_{z=0} = \int_0^\infty \frac{u^2 \cosh (u) + u \sinh (u)}{2u + \sinh (2u)} J_0(\rho u)du \quad (96)$$

was computed for five values of ρ and the results compared with those obtained by the approximate method outlined above. The results are given in Table 3.

TABLE 3

ρ	0.0	0.2	0.4	0.5	1.0
Numerical integration	2.5842	2.3118	1.6858	1.0422	0.2997
Approximate formula	2.5672	2.2997	1.6847	1.0549	0.3020
Error	−0.66 %	−0.52 %	−0.07 %	1.22 %	0.77 %

given in Table 3. It will be observed that the error incurred by the use of the approximate method is of the order of 1 per cent in the cases examined.

To illustrate the variation in stress through the thickness of the plate, the stress component σ_z was calculated in some noncentral planes by means of equation (95). The results are shown in Fig. 97 for four planes parallel to the faces of the plate. It will be observed that the magnitude of this stress increases greatly as we approach the free surface $z = d$,

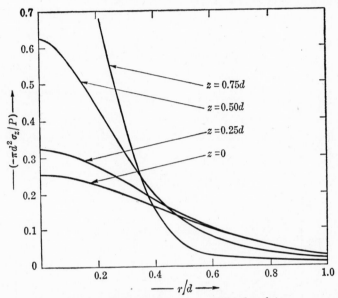

FIG. 97.   The variation of σ_z within the plate.

becoming very large in the neighborhood of $r = 0$. This is just what we should expect when we recall that in the plane $z = d$ this component of stress is everywhere zero except at the point $r = 0$, where it is infinitely large.

53.6 Symmetrical deformation of a thick plate by pressure applied to circular areas. We may readily extend the calculations of the preceding section to the case in which the applied pressure acts over the circles $z = \pm d$, $r \leq a$. In the case where $a \neq 0$ but the pressure is still distributed uniformly over the circular area the various components of stress are given by equations (16) to (22) with $G(\xi,z)$ given by equation (87) with $\bar{p}(\xi) = PJ_1(\xi a)/\pi \xi a$. If we again approximate to the integrals by replacing the function $f(u)$ by its approximate form $f_1(u)$, we find that the problem reduces to that of calculating integrals of the type

$$\int_0^\infty e^{-\lambda u} u^m J_\mu(\rho u) J_\nu(\alpha u)\, du$$

which can be expanded in series in certain cases. The arithmetical work is naturally more cumbersome in this case, but no new principle is involved.   To give some idea of the effect of varying the radius of the circles of application of the external pressure, the normal stress σ_z was calculated in the central plane $z = 0$ for the values 0.5 and 1.0 of $\alpha = a/d$, on the assumption that the total force P remains constant.   In this case instead of equation (51) we use

$$\int_0^\infty e^{-\lambda u} u^m J_0(\rho u) J_1(\alpha u)\,du = \sum_{s=0}^{\infty} \frac{(-1)^s (m + 2s + 1)!(\alpha/2)^{2s+1}}{s!(s + 1)!(\lambda^2 + \rho^2)^{m+2s+\frac{3}{2}}}$$

$$\times P_{m+2s+1}\left(\frac{\lambda}{(\lambda^2 + \rho^2)^{\frac{1}{2}}}\right)$$

which is derived from (51) by expanding $J_1(\alpha u)$ in ascending powers of αu and by means of which all the integrals involved in the expression for σ_z can be calculated.   The results of these calculations are embodied in

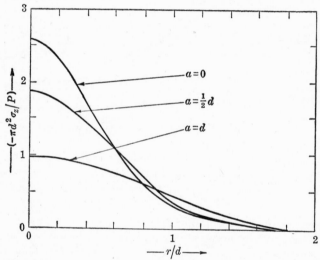

Fig. 98.   The effect on $(\sigma_z)_{z=0}$ of distributing the force uniformly over a circle.

Fig. 98, in which the curve for a concentrated force is also included for reference.   It will be seen that the *form* of the curve is roughly the same in the three cases, except that the stress at the center of the plate is greater the smaller the area to which the external force is applied.

53.7 Effect of an internal force on the stress distribution in a semi-infinite elastic solid.   In the previous sections we discussed the distribution of stress in a semiinfinite elastic solid when its surface is subjected to applied pressure.   We shall now consider the conditions at the surface of a semiinfinite elastic body when an external force is applied to the interior of the body, in a direction at right angles to the boundary. The conditions in the interior of the solid can be studied in precisely the same way, but the analysis is rather more complicated and will not be reproduced here since most interest in problems of this type is focused on conditions at the surface.

In the case where the external force is applied to a single internal force ("concentrated force") the solution was first derived by Mindlin,[1] and later by Dean, Parsons, and Sneddon.[2]   The same solution will be derived here by a method strictly analogous to the two-dimensional case (Sec. 46), the Fourier transform being replaced by a Hankel transform.

The displacement of an *infinite* elastic body caused by the application of an external force of magnitude $8\pi\mu(\lambda + 2\mu)/(\lambda + \mu)$ to the origin of coordinates has components[3]

$$u_r = \frac{rz}{\rho^3}, \qquad u_z = \frac{z^2}{\rho^3} + \frac{(\lambda + 3\mu)}{\rho(\lambda + \mu)} \tag{97}$$

if the positive z direction is chosen along the direction of the force and $\rho^2 = r^2 + z^2$ with the usual notation r, θ, z for cylindrical polars.   The components of stress associated with the z direction are then

$$\sigma_z = -\frac{2\mu^2 z}{(\lambda + \mu)\rho^3} - \frac{6\mu z^3}{\rho^5}, \qquad \tau_{rz} = -\frac{2\mu^2 r}{\rho^3(\lambda + \mu)} - \frac{6\mu r z^2}{\rho^5} \tag{98}$$

Consider next the equilibrium of a semiinfinite elastic body, $z \leq 0$, if a force of magnitude $8\pi\mu(\lambda + 2\mu)/(\lambda + \mu)$ acts at the point $(0,0,-h)$ in the positive z direction.   The components of the displacement vector must have the same singularity at the point $(0,0,-h)$ as the components of equation (97) have at the origin and must further be such that

$$\sigma_z = \tau_{rz} = 0 \qquad\qquad \text{on } z = 0 \tag{99}$$

the boundary being supposed free from stress.   These conditions can be partially satisfied by modifying the previous solution.   Let

$$\left. \begin{aligned} u_r &= \frac{r(z + h)}{\rho_1^3} - \frac{r(z - h)}{\rho_2^3} \\ u_z &= \frac{(z + h)^2}{\rho_1^3} - \frac{(z - h)^2}{\rho_2^3} + \frac{\lambda + 3\mu}{\lambda + \mu}\left(\frac{1}{\rho_1} - \frac{1}{\rho_2}\right) \end{aligned} \right\} \tag{100}$$

[1] R. D. Mindlin, *Physics*, **7**, 195 (1936).

[2] W. R. Dean, H. W. Parsons, and I. N. Sneddon, *Proc. Cambridge Phil. Soc.*, **40**, 5 (1944).

[3] A. E. H. Love, "The Mathematical Theory of Elasticity," 4th ed. (Cambridge, London, 1934), p. 185.   This solution can also be derived by a method similar to that employed in Sec. 44.

where $\rho_1^2 = r^2 + (z + h)^2$ and $\rho_2^2 = r^2 + (z - h)^2$. This is the displacement of an infinite solid due to the application of two equal and opposite forces at the points $(0,0,\pm h)$. The displacement given by equations (100) therefore satisfies the conditions of equilibrium and gives the correct singularity at the point $(0,0,-h)$, but it can be seen by applying equations (98) that, while $\tau_{rz} = 0$ if $z = 0$, the normal component of stress does not vanish on the boundary but is of magnitude

$$[\sigma_z]_{z=0} = - \frac{12\mu h^3}{(r^2 + h^2)^{\frac{5}{2}}} - \frac{4\mu^2 h}{(\lambda + \mu)(r^2 + h^2)^{\frac{3}{2}}}$$

We must therefore add to the components given by equations (100) another set which satisfy the equations of equilibrium, have no singularity for negative values of z, and are such that, on $z = 0$,

$$\sigma_z = \frac{12\mu h^3}{(r^2 + h^2)^{\frac{5}{2}}} + \frac{4\mu^2 h}{(\lambda + \mu)(r^2 + h^2)^{\frac{3}{2}}}, \qquad \tau_{rz} = 0 \qquad (101)$$

This second set of components can be found by the method of Sec. 53.2, the only difference being that here we are dealing with the half space $z \leq 0$, not $z \geq 0$, as in Sec. 53.2. The analysis is similar, and we obtain

$$G(\xi,z) = - \frac{\lambda}{(\lambda + \mu)^2} \frac{Z(\xi)}{2\xi^4} \left(1 - \frac{\lambda + \mu}{\lambda} \xi z\right) e^{\xi z} \qquad (102)$$

where

$$\frac{Z(\xi)}{\xi} = 12\mu h^3 \int_0^\infty \frac{rJ_0(\xi r)dr}{(r^2 + h^2)^{\frac{5}{2}}} + \frac{4\mu^2 h}{\lambda + \mu} \int_0^\infty \frac{rJ_0(\xi r)dr}{(r^2 + h^2)^{\frac{3}{2}}}$$

Making use of the integral

$$h \int_0^\infty \frac{rJ_0(\xi r)dr}{(r^2 + h^2)^{\frac{3}{2}}} = e^{-h\xi}$$

and the result

$$3h^3 \int_0^\infty \frac{rJ_0(\xi r)dr}{(r^2 + h^2)^{\frac{5}{2}}} = (1 + h\xi)e^{-h\xi}$$

which is derived from it by differentiating with respect to h, we obtain

$$Z(\xi) = 4\mu\xi \left(\frac{\lambda + 2\mu}{\lambda + \mu} + h\xi\right) e^{-h\xi} \qquad (103)$$

Substituting from equations (102) and (103) into equations (16) and (17), we obtain, for the displacement components corresponding to this solution,

$$u_r = \frac{2\mu r}{(\lambda + \mu)\rho_2} \left[\frac{\lambda + 2\mu}{(\lambda + \mu)(h - z + \rho_2)} + \frac{h}{\rho_2^2} \right]$$

$$+ \frac{2rz}{\rho_2^3} \left[\frac{\lambda + 2\mu}{\lambda + \mu} - \frac{3h(z - h)}{\rho_2^2} \right] \quad (104)$$

$$u_z = \frac{2(\lambda + 2\mu)}{(\lambda + \mu)\rho_2} \left[\frac{\lambda + 2\mu}{\lambda + \mu} - \frac{h(z - h)}{\rho_2^2} \right]$$

$$- \frac{2z}{\rho_2^3} \left[\frac{\mu h - (\lambda + 2\mu)z}{\lambda + \mu} + \frac{3h(z - h)^2}{\rho_2^2} \right] \quad (105)$$

Combining the components given by equations (104) and (105) with those given by equations (100), we have, finally,

$$u_r = \frac{r(z + h)}{\rho_1^3} - \frac{r(z - h)}{\rho_2^3} + \frac{2\mu r}{(\lambda + \mu)\rho_2} \left[\frac{\lambda + 2\mu}{(\lambda + \mu)(h - z + \rho_2)} + \frac{h}{\rho_2^2} \right]$$

$$+ \frac{2rz}{\rho_2^3} \left[\frac{\lambda + 2\mu}{\lambda + \mu} - \frac{3h(z - h)}{\rho_2^2} \right] \quad (106)$$

$$u_z = \frac{(z + h)^2}{\rho_1^3} - \frac{(z - h)^2}{\rho_2^3} + \frac{\lambda + 3\mu}{\lambda + \mu} \left(\frac{1}{\rho_1} - \frac{1}{\rho_2} \right) + \frac{2(\lambda + 2\mu)}{\rho_2(\lambda + \mu)} \left[\frac{\lambda + 2\mu}{\lambda + \mu} \right.$$

$$\left. - \frac{h(z - h)}{\rho_2^2} \right] - \frac{2z}{\rho_2^3} \left[\frac{\mu h - (\lambda + 2\mu)z}{\lambda + \mu} + \frac{3h(z - h)^2}{\rho_2^2} \right] \quad (107)$$

as the displacement of the semiinfinite body $z \leq 0$ caused by a force of magnitude $8\pi\mu(\lambda + 2\mu)/(\lambda + \mu)$ acting at the point $(0,0,-h)$ in the positive z direction, the boundary $z = 0$ being supposed free from external forces.

The conditions at the surface of the body are of most interest, and we therefore confine our attention to the surface displacement and stress in what follows. For the surface stress and displacement due to a force of magnitude F acting at $(0,0,-h)$ in the positive z direction we have, therefore, the equations

$$u_r = \frac{F}{4\pi\mu} \left\{ \frac{rh}{(r^2 + h^2)^{\frac{3}{2}}} + \frac{\mu}{\lambda + \mu} \frac{r}{[h + (r^2 + h^2)^{\frac{1}{2}}](r^2 + h^2)^{\frac{1}{2}}} \right\} \quad (108)$$

$$u_z = \frac{F}{4\pi\mu} \left[\frac{r^2 + 2h^2}{(r^2 + h^2)^{\frac{3}{2}}} + \frac{\mu}{(\lambda + \mu)(r^2 + h^2)^{\frac{1}{2}}} \right] \quad (109)$$

$$\sigma_r + \sigma_\theta = \frac{(3\lambda + 2\mu)F}{2\pi(\lambda + 2\mu)} \left[\frac{h(2h^2 - r^2)}{(r^2 + h^2)^{\frac{5}{2}}} + \frac{h}{(\lambda + \mu)(r^2 + h^2)^{\frac{3}{2}}} \right] \quad (110)$$

$$\sigma_r - \sigma_\theta = \frac{F}{2\pi} \left\{ \frac{-3r^2 h}{(r^2 + h^2)^{\frac{5}{2}}} + \frac{\mu}{\lambda + \mu} \left[-\frac{2}{r^2} + \frac{2h}{r^2(r^2 + h^2)^{\frac{1}{2}}} \right. \right.$$

$$\left. \left. + \frac{h}{(r^2 + h^2)^{\frac{3}{2}}} \right] \right\} \quad (111)$$

If, instead of being concentrated at a point, the force is uniformly distributed over the area of a circle of radius a and center $(0,0,-h)$, lying wholly in the plane $z = -h$, we may calculate the surface values of the components of stress and displacement by straightforward integrations. Since there is symmetry about $0z$ we need only consider the point $A(R,0,0)$ on the x axis (cf. Fig. 99). The displacement at the point A due to the elementary force $Fr \, dr \, d\theta/\pi a^2$, acting at the point $Q(r,\theta,-h)$, can be deduced from equations (108) and (109). There is a normal displacement and a displacement in the direction $Q'A$, where Q' is the projection of Q on the plane $z = 0$, and the magnitude of these displacements can be found from

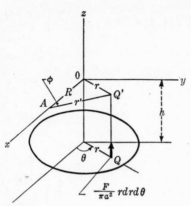

Fig. 99. Internal force distributed uniformly over a circle.

equations (108) and (109) by substituting $r' = AQ'$ for r and multiplying by a numerical factor. We therefore have for the radial component of the displacement, due to a distributed force,

$$u_r = \frac{F}{2\pi^2 a^2 \mu} \int_0^\pi d\theta \int_0^a \left\{ \frac{r'h}{(r'^2 + h^2)^{\frac{3}{2}}} + \frac{r'}{(\lambda + \mu)[(r^2 + h^2)^{\frac{1}{2}}h + r'^2 + h^2]} \right\} \\ \times \cos(\phi) r \, dr \quad (112)$$

where $r'^2 = R^2 - 2Rr \cos(\theta) + r^2$, $r' \cos(\phi) = R - r \cos(\phi)$. The problem of determining the effect of the distributed force is very much simplified by the assumption that the elastic body is incompressible $(\mu/\lambda \to 0)$. It follows from equation (112) that, in this case, the radial component of the displacement at the point $(R,0,0)$ is given by

$$u_r = \frac{F}{2\pi^2 a^2 \mu} \int_0^\pi d\theta \int_0^a \frac{r'h \cos(\phi)}{(r'^2 + h^2)^{\frac{3}{2}}} r \, dr \quad (113)$$

Similarly, it follows that the normal component of displacement of the surface is given by the equation

$$u_z = \frac{F}{2\pi^2 a^2 \mu} \cdot \int_0^\pi d\theta \int_0^a \frac{r'^2 + 2h^2}{(r'^2 + h^2)^{\frac{3}{2}}} r \, dr \quad (114)$$

The evaluation of these integrals is elementary.[1] It turns out that

[1] For details, see Dean, Parsons, and Sneddon, *op. cit.*

$$u_r = \frac{Fh}{2\pi^2 a^2 \mu} \left[\frac{(a+r)^2 + h^2}{r^2} \right]^{\frac{1}{2}} \left[\frac{r^2 + a^2 + h^2}{(r+a)^2 + h^2} F\left(k, \frac{1}{2}\pi\right) - E\left(k, \frac{1}{2}\pi\right) \right] \Big\rbrace$$

$$u_z = \frac{F}{2\pi^2 a^2 \mu} \left[(a+r)^2 + h^2\right]^{\frac{1}{2}} \left[\frac{a^2 - r^2 - h^2}{(r+a)^2 + h^2} F\left(k, \frac{1}{2}\pi\right) + E\left(k, \frac{1}{2}\pi\right) \right] \Big\rbrace$$

$$(115)$$

where, in the usual notation,

$$F\left(k, \frac{1}{2}\pi\right) = \int_0^{\frac{1}{2}\pi} \frac{d\phi}{(1 - k^2 \sin^2 \phi)^{\frac{1}{2}}},$$

$$E\left(k, \frac{1}{2}\pi\right) = \int_0^{\frac{1}{2}\pi} (1 - k^2 \sin^2 \phi)^{\frac{1}{2}} \, d\phi$$

and $k^2 = 4ar/[(r+a)^2 + h^2]$. Now it is obvious from equations (110) and (111) that, on the surface $z = 0$ (in the incompressible case),

$$\sigma_r + \sigma_\theta = 6\mu \left(\frac{\partial u_r}{\partial r} + \frac{u_r}{r} \right), \qquad \sigma_r - \sigma_\theta = 2\mu \left(\frac{\partial u_r}{\partial r} - \frac{u_r}{r} \right)$$

The surface stresses can readily be deduced from these formulas and equations (115). We obtain, finally,

$$\sigma_r = \frac{Fh}{\pi^2 r^2 a^2 [(r+a)^2 + h^2]^{\frac{1}{2}}} \left[(r^2 - a^2 - h^2) F\left(k, \frac{1}{2}\pi\right) \right.$$
$$\left. - \frac{r^4 - (a^2 + h^2)^2}{(r-a)^2 + h^2} E\left(k, \frac{1}{2}\pi\right) \right]$$

$$\sigma_\theta = \frac{Fh}{\pi^2 r^2 a^2 [(r+a)^2 + h^2]^{\frac{1}{2}}} \left[(2r^2 + a^2 + h^2) F\left(k, \frac{1}{2}\pi\right) \right.$$
$$\left. - \frac{(r^2 + a^2 + h^2)^2 + r^2(r^2 - 5a^2 + h^2)}{(r-a)^2 + h^2} E\left(k, \frac{1}{2}\pi\right) \right]$$

As a check on these equations it may easily be shown that in the limit $a = 0$ they reduce to the corresponding equations for a concentrated force.

Values of the stress components σ_r and σ_θ can be calculated from these equations. The variation of these components with r and h (a being regarded as fixed) is shown in Fig. 100. Outside the circle $r = a$ there is little surface stress, σ_r being small and σ_θ very much smaller, but, with the smallest value 0.2 of h/a, there is a localized region of relatively high radial stress, the whole effect being due to the proximity of the circle to which the external force is applied. Another point of interest is that the central value of σ_r regarded as a function of h, F and a being constant, does not increase steadily as h decreases but increases to a maximum and then decreases.

The solution of the problem of a uniform surface load distributed over a circle may be obtained by letting $h \to 0$ in the above equations and is

left to the reader (cf. the paper by Dean, Parsons, and Sneddon referred
to above).

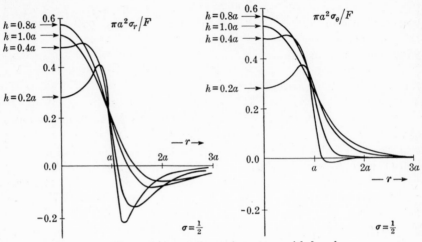

FIG. 100.   The variation of the surface stress with h and r.

54. Distribution of Stress in the Neighborhood of a Circular Crack in an Elastic Body

54.1 Introduction. We saw in Sec. 47 that the theory of Fourier
transforms could be employed to obtain the distribution of stress in the
neighborhood of a Griffith crack.   We shall now make use of the theory
of Hankel transforms to discuss the distribution of stress in the neighborhood of a circular crack of the type introduced by Sack in his extension[1]
of Griffith's theory of rupture to three dimensions.   Observing that the
length of internal cracks does not greatly exceed their width, Sack cal-
culates the conditions of rupture for a solid containing a plane crack
bounded by a circle—a "penny-shaped" crack—when one of the principal
stresses is acting normally to the plane of the crack.   By treating the
crack as a limiting case of an oblate spheroid Sack established that rupture
occurs when the tensile stress P, normal to the crack, exceeds the critical
value P_c given by the equation

$$P_c = \left[\frac{\pi E T}{2c(1 - \sigma^2)} \right]^{\frac{1}{2}} \tag{116}$$

where c is the radius of the crack and T denotes the surface tension of the
material of the body and E its Young's modulus.

Sack's calculations are based on Neuber's solution[2] of the equations

[1] R. A. Sack, *Proc. Phys. Soc.* (*London*), **58**, 729, (1946).
[2] H. Neuber, *Z. angew. Math. u. Mech.*, **14**, 203 (1934).

of elastic equilibrium in oblate spheroidal coordinates. This method could, no doubt, be adopted to the case of a variable internal pressure, but the calculations would probably be rather laborious. Even in the case of a constant pressure being applied to the inner surfaces of the crack the expressions obtained by Sack for the components of stress do not yield numerical results easily. In addition, the choice of coordinate system makes the interpretation of the results somewhat difficult. In the analysis given below, cylindrical polar coordinates are used. The solution of the elastic equations in these coordinates is reduced, by the method of Hankel transforms developed above, to that of a pair of dual integral equations.[1] As is usual, it is assumed that the crack is of such dimensions that its depth exceeds the radius of molecular action at all points not very near its edges. The theory of elasticity then gives the stress components accurately at all points other than those in the immediate vicinity of the edges of the crack. If the crack is sufficiently large, the error incurred in the calculation of the strain energy is then negligible, for the stress near the edge of the crack is proportional to $r^{-\frac{1}{2}}$ so that the strain energy in any small sphere whose center lies on the edge of the crack is finite and negligible in comparison with the strain energy of the rest of the solid. The elastic body is assumed to consist of homogeneous isotropic material and to be so large that its linear dimensions are very much greater than the radius of the crack. When this last condition is satisfied, we may consider the crack to be situated in the interior of an infinite elastic medium. In the first instance we shall consider the elastic body to be deformed by an internal pressure acting on the surfaces of the crack, the effect of tensile stress applied to a body with an internal crack free from stress being deduced later.

54.2 Deduction of the dual integral equations from the boundary conditions. In the three-dimensional case we assume that the crack is created in the interior of an infinite medium and that it is "penny-shaped," occupying the circle $r^2 \equiv x^2 + y^2 = c^2$ in the plane $z = 0$. If we assume that the crack is deformed by the application of an axially symmetrical pressure, then we see that, when $z = 0$, $\sigma_z = -p(r)$ $(r < c)$. Just as in the two-dimensional case (Sec. 47) we see that we may assume that the distribution of stress in the neighborhood of the crack is the same as that produced in a semiinfinite elastic medium $z \geq 0$ when its free surface $z = 0$ is subjected to the boundary conditions

(i) $\tau_{rz} = 0$ for all values of r

(ii) $\sigma_z = -p(r), 0 \leq r \leq c;$ $u_z = 0, r > c$

In the first instance we assume that the applied pressure p is a function

[1] I. N. Sneddon, *Proc. Roy. Soc. (London)*, **A187**, 229 (1946).

of r. The only restriction on the function $p(r)$, imposed by the subsequent analysis, is that it is such that the integral

$$\int_0^c rp(r)J_0(\xi r)dr$$

exists for all values of the parameter ξ. The conditions (ii) do not correspond accurately to a hydrostatic pressure in the crack in all cases. In the analyses of Griffith and Sack the crack is assumed to be of very small depth so that the surface of the crack may be taken to be coincident with the plane $z = 0$. In this case the pressure across the surface of the crack is $-\sigma_z$, and the conditions (ii) are exact. Even in cases in which the depth of the crack is taken into account the distribution of stress given by these boundary conditions will not differ much from that given by a hydrostatic pressure inside the crack, except, possibly, near the boundary of the crack.

Now we know from equation (27) that a solution of the equilibrium equations which makes $\tau_{rz} = 0$ when $z = 0$ is given by inserting

$$G(\xi,z) = \frac{B(c\xi)}{\xi}(2\sigma + \xi z)e^{-\xi z} \tag{117}$$

in equations (16) to (22). Substituting the function (117) into equations (17) and (18) and putting $z = 0$, we obtain

$$[\sigma_z]_{z=0} = \frac{E}{(1 + \sigma)(1 - 2\sigma)}\int_0^\infty \xi^3 B(c\xi)J_0(\xi r)d\xi$$

$$[u_z]_{z=0} = -\frac{2(1 - \sigma)}{1 - 2\sigma}\int_0^\infty \xi^2 B(c\xi)J_0(\xi r)d\xi$$

Inserting the boundary conditions (ii) and making the substitutions

$$\eta = c\xi,\ f(\eta) = \eta^2 B(\eta),\ \rho = \frac{r}{c},\ g(\rho) = -\frac{(1 + \sigma)(1 - 2\sigma)}{E}c^4 p(c\rho) \tag{118}$$

we see that the problem reduces to that of solving the dual integral equations

$$\int_0^\infty \eta f(\eta)J_0(\rho\eta)d\eta = g(\rho),\ 0 < \rho < 1;$$

$$\int_0^\infty f(\eta)J_0(\rho\eta)d\eta = 0,\ \rho > 1 \tag{119}$$

for the unknown function $f(\eta)$ and hence of the constant $B(c\xi)$. Once $B(c\xi)$ has been determined, the components of stress and displacement are readily found by substituting from equation (117) into equations (16) to (22).

54.3 Solution of the dual integral equations. Dual integral equations of the type (119) have been considered in Sec. 12. The solution of the pair (119) can be derived easily from equation (47), Chap. 2, in the form

$$f(\eta) = \frac{2}{\pi} \int_0^1 \mu \sin (\mu\eta) d\mu \int_0^1 \frac{\rho g(\rho\mu) d\rho}{(1 - \rho^2)^{\frac{1}{2}}} \tag{120}$$

Substituting from (120) into the expression for $[u_z]_{z=0}$ and interchanging the order of the integrations, we find that

$$[u_z]_{z=0} = - \frac{4(1 - \sigma)}{\pi c^3 (1 - 2\sigma)} \int_0^1 \mu \, d\mu \int_0^1 \frac{\rho g(\rho\mu) d\rho}{(1 - \rho^2)^{\frac{1}{2}}} \int_0^\infty \sin (\mu\eta) J_0(\rho\eta) d\eta$$

Making use of the result

$$\int_0^\infty \sin (\mu\eta) J_0(\rho\eta) d\eta = \begin{cases} 0 & \rho > \mu \\ (\mu^2 - \rho^2)^{-\frac{1}{2}} & 0 < \rho < \mu \end{cases}$$

we find that, when the applied pressure is $p(r)$, the value of the normal component of the surface displacement is given by the equation

$$[u_z]_{z=0} = \frac{4(1 - \sigma^2)c}{\pi E} \int_\rho^1 \frac{\mu \, d\mu}{(\mu^2 - \rho^2)^{\frac{1}{2}}} \int_0^1 \frac{x p(x\mu c) dx}{(1 - x^2)^{\frac{1}{2}}} \tag{121}$$

If, for example, the applied pressure is given by the power series

$$p(r) = p_0 \sum_{n=0}^\infty \alpha_n \left(\frac{r}{c}\right)^n \qquad 0 \le r \le c \tag{122}$$

then, substituting into equation (121), we obtain

$$[u_z]_{z=0} = \frac{4(1 - \sigma^2)p_0 c}{\pi E} \sum_{n=0}^\infty \alpha_n \int_\rho^1 \frac{\mu \, d\mu}{(\mu^2 - \rho^2)^{\frac{1}{2}}} \int_0^1 \frac{x(x\mu c)^n \, dx}{c^n (1 - x^2)^{\frac{1}{2}}}$$

Now

$$\int_0^1 x^{n+1}(1 - x^2)^{-\frac{1}{2}} \, dx = \frac{1}{2} \frac{\Gamma(\frac{1}{2})\Gamma(1 + \frac{1}{2}n)}{\Gamma(\frac{3}{2} + \frac{1}{2}n)}$$

so that the normal component of the surface displacement now has the value

$$[u_z]_{z=0} = \frac{2(1 - \sigma^2)p_0}{\pi^{\frac{1}{2}}E} \sum_{n=0}^\infty \frac{\Gamma(1 + \frac{1}{2}n)}{\Gamma(\frac{3}{2} + \frac{1}{2}n)} \alpha_n I_n \left(\frac{r}{c}\right)^{n+1} \qquad 0 \le r \le c \tag{123}$$

where I_n denotes the integral

$$I_n = c \int_1^{c/r} \frac{u^{n+1} \, du}{(u^2 - 1)^{\frac{1}{2}}} \qquad 0 \le r \le c \tag{124}$$

Integrating by parts, we may readily show that I_n satisfies the recurrence relation

$$I_n = \frac{n}{n+1} I_{n-2} + \frac{1}{n+1} \left(\frac{c}{r}\right)^{n+1} (c^2 - r^2)^{\frac{1}{2}} \qquad (125)$$

By means of these equations we can calculate the value of the normal component of the surface displacement when the law of variation of the applied pressure is known.

The value of the radial component of the surface displacement is found from equations (117) and (16) to be

$$[u_r]_{z=0} = \frac{1}{c^3} \int_0^\infty f(\eta) J_1(\rho\eta) d\eta \qquad (126)$$

whence by equation (120) and the result

$$\int_0^\infty J_1(\rho\eta) \sin(\mu\eta) d\eta = \begin{cases} \dfrac{\mu}{\rho(\rho^2 - \mu^2)^{\frac{1}{2}}} & \mu < \rho \\ 0 & \mu > \rho \end{cases}$$

we obtain, in the general case,

$$[u_r]_{z=0} = -\frac{2(1+\sigma)(1-2\sigma)}{\pi E} \int_0^1 \mu^2 \, d\mu \int_\mu^1 \frac{p(\rho\mu c) d\rho}{[(1-\rho^2)(\rho^2 - \mu^2)]^{\frac{1}{2}}} \qquad (127)$$

It will be observed from this equation that the radial component of the surface displacement is zero when the medium is incompressible ($\sigma = \frac{1}{2}$).

54.4 Shape of a crack opened by constant internal pressure. If we suppose that the applied pressure $p(r)$ is constant over the circle $0 \leq r \leq c$, then we have $p(r) = p_0(0 \leq r \leq c)$. Substituting this value for $p(r)$ into equation (121), we obtain the expression

$$w = \frac{4p_0(1-\sigma^2)}{\pi E} (c^2 - r^2)^{\frac{1}{2}} \qquad (128)$$

for the normal component of the surface displacement, $w = [u_z]_{z=0}$. If $w = \epsilon$ when $r = 0$, then

$$\epsilon = \frac{4p_0(1-\sigma^2)c}{\pi E} \qquad (129)$$

and we may write equation (128) in the form

$$\frac{r^2}{c^2} + \frac{w^2}{\epsilon^2} = 1$$

showing that the crack resulting from the application of an internal pressure is ellipsoidal in shape, provided that the pressure is constant. It follows from equation (129) that

$$p_0 = \frac{E}{4(1 - \sigma^2)} \left(\frac{\epsilon}{c}\right) \tag{130}$$

from which it follows that p_0 is constant for constant values of the ratio ϵ/c.

We shall now consider the work done in forming an ellipsoidal depression of circular section, of radius c, and of depth ϵ. When the depth of the depression is ϵ, the pressure is given by equation (130). When the depth of the depression has increased to $\epsilon + d\epsilon$, the pressure will have increased to $\pi E(\epsilon + d\epsilon)/4c(1 - \sigma^2)$ so that in bringing about a change $d\epsilon$ in the depth of the depression the average pressure is

$$\pi E(\epsilon + \tfrac{1}{2}d\epsilon)/4c(1 - \sigma^2)$$

Considering a ring element of surface intersecting the plane $\theta = 0$ at the

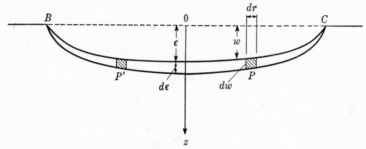

FIG. 101.   The work done in opening a circular crack.

points P, P' (see Fig. 101), we find that the work done in making a small normal displacement dw is

$$2\pi r p_0 \, dr \, dw = \frac{\pi E(\epsilon + \tfrac{1}{2}d\epsilon)}{4c(1 - \sigma^2)} 2\pi r \, dr \, d\epsilon \left(1 - \frac{r^2}{c^2}\right)^{\tfrac{1}{2}}$$

by equation (128). Thus the total work done in forming the ellipsoidal depression on the surface of a semiinfinite elastic solid is

$$W_1 = \frac{\pi^2 E}{2(1 - \sigma^2)c} \int_0^c r \left(1 - \frac{r^2}{c^2}\right)^{\tfrac{1}{2}} dr \int_0^\epsilon d\epsilon = \frac{\pi^2 E c \epsilon^2}{12(1 - \sigma^2)}$$

The energy of a crack formed by internal pressure is twice this energy. Multiplying the result by 2 and substituting the value of ϵ in terms of the final pressure p_0, we obtain for the energy of a crack of radius c the formula

$$W = \frac{8(1 - \sigma^2)}{3E} p_0^2 c^3 \tag{131}$$

54.5 Distribution of pressure necessary to produce a crack of prescribed shape. We have just shown that as long as the internal pressure is constant the crack will be ellipsoidal in shape, whatever the radius of the crack. It is natural then to try to determine whether cracks of a shape other than ellipsoidal are possible and, if they are, to determine the distribution of internal pressure necessary to preserve their shape. This is equivalent to assuming that we know the value of $[u_z]_{z=0}$ when $r < c$ but that the function $p(r)$ is unknown. We might then regard equation (121) as an integral equation determining $p(r)$ when $[u_z]_{z=0}$ is known. It is, however, simpler to consider the problem as that of determining the distribution of stress in a semiinfinite elastic medium, bounded by the plane $z = 0$, when the surface value of u_z is prescribed for all values of r. The analysis proceeds along similar lines except that, now, the boundary conditions assume the form

(i) $\qquad\qquad\qquad \tau_{rz} = 0 \qquad\qquad z = 0, r > 0$

(ii) $\qquad\qquad\qquad u_z = \begin{cases} w(r) & z = 0, r < c \\ 0 & z = 0, r > c \end{cases}$

Substituting the condition (ii) into the expression for $[u_z]_{z=0}$, we obtain the relation

$$\int_0^\infty \xi^2 B J_0(\xi r) d\xi = \begin{cases} -\dfrac{1 - 2\sigma}{2(1 - \sigma)} w(r) & 0 < r < c \\ 0 & r > c \end{cases}$$

for the determination of the unknown function B. Inverting this result by means of the Hankel inversion theorem, we obtain

$$\xi B = -\frac{1 - 2\sigma}{2(1 - \sigma)} \int_0^c r w(r) J_0(\xi r) dr \qquad\qquad (132)$$

If we denote the integral on the right-hand side of this equation by $\bar{w}(\xi)$, then we find that

$$[\sigma_z]_{z=0} = -\frac{E}{2(1 - \sigma^2)} \int_0^\infty \xi^2 \bar{w}(\xi) J_0(\xi r) d\xi \qquad\qquad (133)$$

This equation gives the value of the applied pressure $p(r) = -\sigma_z$ on the circle $z = 0, r < c$ which must be applied to maintain the prescribed surface displacement.

For example, if we assume that

$$w(r) = \epsilon \left(1 - \frac{r^2}{c^2}\right) \qquad\qquad (134)$$

we find that $\bar{w}(\xi) = 2\epsilon J_2(c\xi)/\xi^2$ and so, by equation (133), that the normal component of the surface stress is given by the expression

$$[\sigma_z]_{z=0} = -\frac{E\epsilon}{1-\sigma^2} \int_0^\infty J_2(c\xi)J_0(r\xi)d\xi$$

Using the recurrence relation [obtained by combining equations (5) and (7), Appendix A],

$$J_2(c\xi) = J_0(c\xi) - \frac{2}{c}\frac{\partial}{\partial\xi}J_1(c\xi)$$

we find, after an integration by parts, that

$$\int_0^\infty J_2(c\xi)J_0(r\xi)d\xi = \int_0^\infty J_0(c\xi)J_0(r\xi)d\xi - \frac{2r}{c}\int_0^\infty J_1(r\xi)J_1(c\xi)d\xi$$

Now, by Gübler's formula,[1] the value of the first integral is found to be $c^{-1}{}_2F_1(\frac{1}{2},\frac{1}{2};1;r^2/c^2) = \frac{2}{\pi}K(r/c)(r<c)$ in the usual notation,

$$K(k) = F(k,\tfrac{1}{2}\pi)$$

for elliptic integrals. The second integral could also be evaluated by the Gübler formula but the hypergeometric series involved in this instance is not readily summed. The integration can be carried out more easily by making use of Neumann's result

$$J_1(\xi r)J_1(\xi c) = \frac{1}{\pi}\int_0^\pi J_0(\xi R)\cos\theta\,d\theta$$

where $R^2 = c^2 + r^2 - 2cr\cos\theta$. Multiplying both sides of this equation by $e^{-\xi z}$ and integrating with respect to ξ from 0 to ∞, we find that

$$\int_0^\infty e^{-\xi z}J_1(\xi r)J_1(\xi c)d\xi = \frac{1}{\pi}\int_0^\pi \cos(\theta)d\theta\int_0^\infty e^{-\xi z}J_0(\xi R)d\xi$$
$$= \frac{1}{\pi}\int_0^\pi \frac{\cos\theta\,d\theta}{(R^2+z^2)^{\frac{1}{2}}}$$

the inner integration being readily performed by means of equation (51). Letting z tend to zero, we find that

$$\int_0^\infty J_1(\xi r)J_1(\xi c)d\xi = \frac{1}{\pi}\int_0^\pi \frac{\cos(\theta)d\theta}{R}$$

in which the integral on the right can be evaluated in terms of elliptic integrals. With the usual notation for complete elliptic integrals we find that

$$\frac{2r}{c}\int_0^\infty J_1(\xi r)J_1(\xi c)d\xi = \frac{2[1+(r/c)^2]}{\pi(c+r)}K(k) - \frac{2(c+r)}{\pi c^2}E(k)$$

[1] Watson, *op. cit.*, p. 410.

where $k^2 = 4rc/(r + c)^2$. Thus the displacement (134) is maintained by an applied pressure

$$p(r) = -[\sigma_z]_{z=0} = \frac{2E\epsilon}{\pi c(1 - \sigma^2)} f(\rho)$$

where the function $f(\rho)$ is defined by the equation

$$f(\rho) = \frac{1 + \rho^2}{1 + \rho} K(k) - K(\rho) - (1 + \rho)E(k)$$

and $\rho = r/c$, $k^2 = 4\rho/(1 + \rho^2)$. The variation with ρ of $f(\rho)$ is shown in Fig. 102. From this curve it follows that the applied internal force is *compressive* in the body of the crack but that near the circular edge of the crack the applied force becomes *tensile* until round the edge of the crack

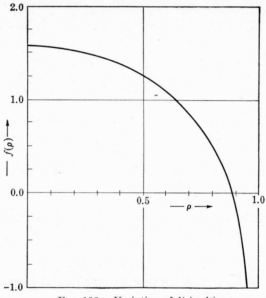

FIG. 102. Variation of $f(\rho)$ with ρ.

it is both infinite and tensile. This is precisely the kind of variation which would be predicted on physical grounds for a crack of this shape.

54.6 Distribution of stress in the solid. We now return to the problem of determining the distribution of stress in the interior of the medium, in the case where the applied pressure is a constant. Putting $p(\rho c) = p_0$ in equation (118) and substituting the expression for $g(\rho)$, so found, in equation (120), we find that

$$f(\eta) = \frac{2p_0 c^4}{\pi E} (1 + \sigma)(1 - 2\sigma) \frac{d}{d\eta} \left(\frac{\sin \eta}{\eta} \right) \tag{135}$$

Substituting this value for $f(\eta)$ into the expression for $[\sigma_z]_{z=0}$ we obtain, after an integration by parts,

$$[\sigma_z]_{z=0} = \frac{2p_0}{\pi}\left[\rho \int_0^\infty \sin(\eta)J_1(\rho\eta)d\eta - \int_0^\infty \frac{\sin(\eta)}{\eta}J_0(\rho\eta)d\eta\right] \quad (136)$$

By means of the results

$$\int_0^\infty \frac{\sin(\eta)}{\eta}J_0(\rho\eta)d\eta = \begin{cases} \sin^{-1}\left(\dfrac{1}{\rho}\right) & \rho \geq 1 \\ \dfrac{1}{2}\pi & \rho \leq 1 \end{cases}$$

$$\rho \int_0^\infty \sin(\eta)J_1(\rho\eta)d\eta = \begin{cases} (\rho^2 - 1)^{-\frac{1}{2}} & \rho > 1 \\ 0 & \rho < 1 \end{cases}$$

it is easily verified that $[\sigma_z]_{z=0} = -p_0$, when $\rho < 1$, and we find that, when $\rho > 1$,

$$[\sigma_z]_{z=0} = -\frac{2p_0}{\pi}\left[\sin^{-1}\left(\frac{1}{\rho}\right) - \frac{1}{(\rho^2 - 1)^{\frac{1}{2}}}\right] \quad (137)$$

For the values of the other components of stress on the plane $z = 0$ we obtain, from equations (20) and (21) with G given by equations (117) and (135),

$$[\sigma_r + \sigma_\theta]_{z=0} = (1 + 2\sigma)[\sigma_z]_{z=0}$$

$$[\sigma_r - \sigma_\theta]_{z=0} = \frac{2(1 - 2\sigma)p_0}{\pi}\int_0^\infty J_2(\rho\eta)\cos(\eta)d\eta - \int_0^\infty J_2(\rho\eta)\frac{\sin(\eta)}{\eta}d\eta$$

Evaluating the integrals in the brackets, it is found that the bracket vanishes when $\rho < 1$ and has the value $-(\rho^2 - 1)^{-\frac{1}{2}}$ when $\rho > 1$. Thus, if $z = 0$ and $\rho < 1$, $\sigma_\theta = \sigma_r = -(\sigma + \frac{1}{2})p_0$, $\sigma_z = -p_0$. It will be observed that, in the incompressible case ($\sigma = \frac{1}{2}$), $\sigma_r = \sigma_z = \sigma_\theta = -p_0$, so that, in this instance, the internal pressure is truly hydrostatic.

When $z = 0$ and $\rho > 1$,

$$\sigma_r = \frac{2p_0}{\pi}\left[\frac{1}{(\rho^2 - 1)^{\frac{1}{2}}} - \left(\sigma + \frac{1}{2}\right)\sin^{-1}\left(\frac{1}{\rho}\right)\right]$$

$$\sigma_\theta = \frac{2p_0}{\pi}\left[\frac{2\sigma}{(\rho^2 - 1)^{\frac{1}{2}}} - \left(\sigma + \frac{1}{2}\right)\sin^{-1}\left(\frac{1}{\rho}\right)\right]$$

The evaluation of the stress components in the interior of the medium is similar to that involved in the solution of the punching problems for a flat-ended cylinder and a right circular cone (Secs. 52.4 and 52.5). Obtaining the value of $B(c\xi)$ from equations (118) and (135) and substituting from equation (117) into equations (18), (19), and (20), we obtain for the components of stress at a general point in the interior of the elastic solid

$$\sigma_z = \frac{2p_0}{\pi} [C_2^0(\rho,\zeta) - S_1^0(\rho,\zeta) + \zeta C_3^0(\rho,\zeta) - \zeta S_2^0(\rho,\zeta)] \tag{138}$$

$$\tau_{rz} = \frac{2p_0}{\pi} [C_3^1(\rho,\zeta) - S_2^1(\rho,\zeta)] \tag{139}$$

$$\sigma_r + \sigma_\theta + \sigma_z = \frac{4(1 + \sigma)p_0}{\pi} [C_2^0(\rho,\zeta) - S_1^0(\rho,\zeta)] \tag{140}$$

$$\sigma_r - \sigma_\theta = -\frac{2p_0}{\pi} \{(1 - 2\sigma)[C_2^2(\rho,\zeta) - S_1^2(\rho,\zeta)] - \zeta[C_3^2(\rho,\zeta) - S_2^2(\rho,\zeta)]\} \tag{141}$$

where $C_n^m(\rho,\zeta)$ is defined by equation (75) and

$$S_n^m(\rho,\zeta) = \int_0^\infty p^{n-2} \sin(p) J_m(p\rho) e^{-p\zeta} dp \tag{142}$$

so that

$$C_n^m(\rho,\zeta) - iS_n^m(\rho,\zeta) = Z_n^m(\rho,\zeta + i) \tag{143}$$

where $Z_n^m(\rho,\zeta)$ is defined by equation (74). Therefore, once we have evaluated $Z_n^m(\rho,\zeta + i)$ the expressions for $C_n^m(\rho,\zeta)$ and $S_n^m(\rho,\zeta)$ can be obtained from the separation of real and imaginary parts.

It follows immediately from equations (20), Appendix A, by this procedure that

$$C_2^0 = R^{-\frac{1}{2}} \cos(\tfrac{1}{2}\phi), \qquad S_2^0 = R^{-\frac{1}{2}} \sin(\tfrac{1}{2}\phi)$$
$$C_3^0 = rR^{-\frac{3}{2}} \cos(\tfrac{3}{2}\phi - \theta), \qquad S_3^0 = rR^{-\frac{3}{2}} \sin(\tfrac{3}{2}\phi - \theta)$$
$$C_1^1 = \frac{1}{\rho}\left(R^{\frac{1}{2}} \cos\frac{1}{2}\phi - \zeta\right), \qquad S_1^1 = \frac{1}{\rho}\left(1 - R^{\frac{1}{2}} \sin\frac{1}{2}\phi\right)$$
$$C_2^1 = \frac{1}{\rho} - \frac{r}{\rho} R^{-\frac{1}{2}} \cos\left(\theta - \frac{1}{2}\phi\right), \qquad S_2^1 = \frac{r}{\rho} R^{-\frac{1}{2}} \sin\left(\theta - \frac{1}{2}\phi\right)$$
$$C_3^1 = \rho R^{-\frac{3}{2}} \cos\tfrac{3}{2}\phi, \qquad S_3^1 = \rho R^{-\frac{3}{2}} \sin\tfrac{3}{2}\phi$$

and from the recurrence relation $J_2(\xi r) = 2J_1(\xi r)/\xi r - J_0(\xi r)$,

$$C_2^2 = \frac{2}{\rho} C_1^1 - C_2^0, \qquad S_2^2 = \frac{2}{\rho} S_1^1 - S_2^0, \qquad C_3^2 = \frac{2}{\rho} C_2^1 - C_3^0$$

The quantities r, R, θ, and ϕ which occur in these equations are defined by the relations (55).

It remains only to evaluate S_1^0 and S_1^2. Integrating the expressions for $Z_2^0(\rho,w)$ and $Z_1^1(\rho,w)$ with respect to w, we obtain

$$\int_0^\infty \frac{1 - e^{-wx}}{x} J_0(\rho x) dx = \log \frac{(\rho^2 + w^2)^{\frac{1}{2}} + w}{\rho} \tag{144}$$

$$\int_0^\infty \frac{1 - e^{-wx}}{x^2} J_1(\rho x) dx = \frac{1}{2\rho}\left[w(w^2 + \rho^2)^{\frac{1}{2}} - w^2 + \rho^2 \log \frac{(\rho^2 + w^2)^{\frac{1}{2}} + w}{\rho}\right]$$

it being assumed in both cases that $\rho \neq 0$.   Expressing $J_2(\rho x)$ in terms of $J_1(\rho x)$ and $J_0(\rho x)$ by equation (7), Appendix A, we obtain

$$\int_0^\infty \frac{1 - e^{-wx}}{x} J_2(\rho x)dx = \frac{1}{\rho^2}[w(w^2 + \rho^2) - w^2] = \frac{w}{\rho} Z_1^1$$

Putting $w = \zeta + i$, $Z_1^1 = C_1^1 - iS_1^1$ in this equation and equating imaginary parts, we find

$$S_1^2 = \frac{1}{\rho}(C_1^1 - \zeta S_1^1)$$

so that S_1^2 is readily calculated.   Similarly, substituting $w = \zeta + i$ in equation (144) and equating imaginary parts, we find that

$$S_1^0 = \tan^{-1}\left(\frac{r \sin \theta + R^{\frac{1}{2}} \sin \frac{1}{2}\phi}{r \cos \theta + R^{\frac{1}{2}} \cos \frac{1}{2}\phi}\right) \qquad \rho \neq 0$$

By means of these expressions for the integrals S_n^m, C_n^m and equations (138) to (141) the stress components can be calculated at any point in the interior of the elastic body.   In the case $\sigma = \frac{1}{4}$ tables are available[1] by means of which the stress components at any point may be obtained by interpolation.   From these values of σ_r, σ_θ, σ_z, and τ_{rz} it is a simple matter to calculate the principal stresses σ_θ,

$$\tfrac{1}{2}(\sigma_r + \sigma_z) \pm [(\tfrac{1}{2}\sigma_r - \tfrac{1}{2}\sigma_z)^2 + \tau_{rz}^2]^{\frac{1}{2}}$$

and from them to deduce the numerical value of the maximum shearing stress τ which is equal to one-half of the algebraic difference between the maximum and the minimum components of the principal stress. The results of such a calculation are shown in Fig. 103, which exhibits the variation of the maximum shearing stress in planes parallel to the plane of the crack.   In general outline this variation is similar to that of the maximum shearing stress in the two-dimensional case (Fig. 84).

If we again wish to employ contours of equal maximum shearing stress to visualize the distribution of stress in the vicinity of the circular crack, we may use Fig. 103 and the table of values from which it is constructed to determine the points in the rz plane at which the maximum shearing stress reaches the values $0.25p_0$, $0.30p_0$, $0.35p_0$, and $0.40p_0$.   Drawing the curves through corresponding values, we obtain the contours of equal maximum shearing stress—Fig. 104.   It will be observed that, except in the vicinity of the edges of the crack—and apart from numerical values —these contours of equal maximum shearing stress are very like the isochromatic lines in the two-dimensional case (Fig. 85).   The main difference between the two systems of curves lies in their behavior near the

[1] I. N. Sneddon, *Proc. Roy. Soc. (London)*, **A187**, 252–253 (1946).

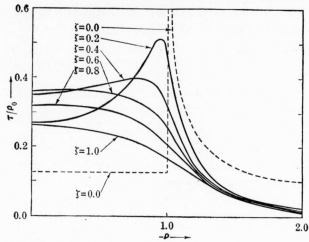

FIG. 103.   Variation of the maximum shearing stress τ with ρ and ζ.   The broken curve shows the variation of τ in the plane of the crack.

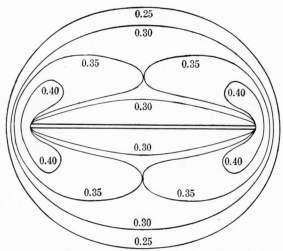

FIG. 104.   The contours of equal maximum shearing stress in the vicinity of a circular crack.

edges of the crack.   In the two-dimensional case the points $x = \pm c$ are nodes separating two loops of the curves (cf. the curves corresponding to the values $\tau/p_0 = 0.4, 0.5, 0.7$ in Fig. 85), but in the three-dimensional case the point $r = c$ is a simple point of the curve.   Each branch which passes through $r = c$ cuts the z axis again at a point for which $r = c$.

54.7 Variation of the displacement near a crack.   Similar expressions may be derived for the components of the displacement vector at any point in the solid.   Substituting for $B(c\xi)$ from equations (118) and (135) and making use of the form (117) for $G(\xi,z)$, we find from equations (16) and (17) that the components of displacement are given by the equations

$$u_r = \frac{2p_0c}{\pi E}(1+\sigma)\int_0^\infty (1-2\sigma-\zeta\eta)\frac{d}{d\eta}\left[\frac{\sin(\eta)}{\eta}\right]e^{-\zeta\eta}J_1(\rho\eta)d\eta$$

$$u_z = -\frac{4p_0c(1-\sigma^2)}{\pi E}\int_0^\infty \left[1+\frac{\zeta\eta}{2(1-\sigma)}\right]\frac{d}{d\eta}\left[\frac{\sin(\eta)}{\eta}\right]e^{-\zeta\eta}J_0(\rho\eta)d\eta$$

Inserting the value (129) for the half depth ϵ of the crack and adopting the notation of equations (75) and (142), we have, as a result of an integration by parts,

$$u_z = \epsilon\left[1 - \rho S_1^1 - \zeta S_1^0 - \frac{\zeta}{2(1-\sigma)}(\zeta S_2^0 + \rho S_2^1 + S_0^0)\right] \qquad (145)$$

and similarly

$$u_r = \epsilon\left[\frac{1-2\sigma}{2(1-\sigma)}(C_1^1 - S_0^1) - \frac{\zeta}{2(1-\sigma)}(C_2^1 - S_1^1)\right]$$

The state of strain in the vicinity of a crack can be illustrated by calculating the normal component of the displacement vector for points in

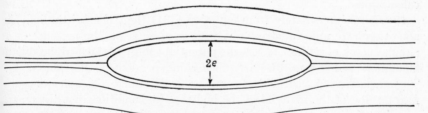

Fig. 105.   The normal displacement of planes parallel to the plane of an ellipsoidal crack of small depth.   The depth of the crack, 2ϵ, has been greatly exaggerated to show more clearly the variation of the normal displacement.

the body and then drawing the normal displacement of planes which were originally parallel to the plane of the crack.   Since the normal component of stress σ_z is infinitely large at the edge of the crack, it might at first sight appear that u_z should also be infinite there.   That this is *not* so is immediately obvious from an examination of equation (145).   Putting $\zeta = 0$, $\rho = 1$ in that equation, we obtain

$$u_z = \epsilon\left[1 - \int_0^\infty \frac{\sin(\eta)}{\eta}J_1(\eta)d\eta\right]$$

and the integral is convergent.

By means of the formula (145) the variation of the normal component of the displacement along the planes $z/c = 0.05, 0.2, 0.4$ was calculated. The results are shown in Fig. 105, which shows the position of the planes $z/c = 0.05, 0.2, 0.4$ after the crack has been opened out to a depth 2ϵ, by a uniform pressure. In this diagram the ratio ϵ/c has been very much exaggerated to show more clearly the variation of the normal displacement in planes near to the crack.

54.8 Condition for rupture. The condition for rupture can be derived as in the two-dimensional case. Assume that the radius c of the crack is considerably smaller than the dimensions of the elastic body. Then we may replace the finite elastic body by an infinite body with a crack in its interior which is subjected to the stress system $\sigma_z = p_0$, $\sigma_r = \sigma_\theta = p_1$, when r is very large. Since the surface of the crack may be assumed to be free from external forces, the further boundary conditions $\sigma_z = \tau_{rz} = 0$ follow when $z = 0$ and $r \leq c$. If the solution

$$\sigma_z = p_0, \qquad \tau_{rz} = 0, \qquad \sigma_r = \sigma_\theta = p_1$$

be added to equations (138) to (141), the expressions so obtained for the components of stress satisfy the new boundary conditions and the equations of equilibrium. The distribution of stress in the interior of the solid can then be determined from the results of Sec. 54.6 by a very simple calculation.

It follows immediately from equation (131) that, if a brittle body is acted upon by uniform stresses $\sigma_r = \sigma_\theta = p_1$, $\sigma_z = p_0$, the presence of a circular crack of radius c lowers the potential energy of the medium by an amount $W = 8(1 - \sigma^2)p_0^2 c^3/3E$ which is independent of the value of p_1. The crack also has a surface energy $U = 2\pi c^2 T$, where T denotes the surface tension of the material of the body. The condition that the crack may just begin to spread is that c should be such that

$$\frac{\partial}{\partial c}(W - U) = 0$$

that is, that

$$c = \frac{\pi E T}{2p_0^2(1 - \sigma^2)}$$

In other words the crack will become unstable and spread if p_0 exceeds the critical value $[\pi E T/2c(1 - \sigma^2)]^{\frac{1}{2}}$. This is the criterion derived by Sack—equation (116).

55. Distribution of Stress in a Semiinfinite Elastic Medium Due to a Torsional Displacement of the Surface

55.1 Reissner-Sagoci problem. In their investigation of the torsional oscillations produced in a semiinfinite, homogeneous, isotropic medium by a periodic shear stress applied in an axially symmetrical manner to a circular area of the plane surface of the medium, Reissner and Sagoci[1] began by considering a boundary value problem in the mathematical theory of elasticity. The distribution of stress in the interior of a semi-infinite elastic medium is determined when a load is applied to the surface by means of a rigid disk; the torsional displacement is prescribed immediately under the disk, and it is assumed that that part of the boundary which lies beyond the edge of the disk is free from stress. The solution of this mixed boundary value problem is obtained by Reissner and Sagoci through the introduction of a certain system of oblate spheroidal coordinates.

We shall now show that this boundary value problem may be reduced by the use of Hankel transforms to the solution of a pair of dual integrals, of the type already shown to arise in a number of mixed boundary value problems in elasticity, and whose solution was discussed in Sec. 12. Only the static problem is discussed in detail, but a possible approach to the dynamic problem will be outlined.[2]

The problem is that of determining the components of stress and displacement in the interior of the semiinfinite solid $z \geq 0$ when a circular area $r = r_0$ of the surface is forced to rotate through an angle Φ about an axis which is normal to the undeformed surface of the medium. It is assumed that the region of the surface lying outside the circle $r \leq r_0$ is free from stress. It has been shown by Reissner[3] that in this case only the circumferential component u_θ of the displacement vector is different from zero and that all the stress components vanish except $\tau_{z\theta}$ and $\tau_{r\theta}$, which are given by the relations

$$\tau_{z\theta} = \mu\,\frac{\partial u_\theta}{\partial z}, \qquad \tau_{r\theta} = \frac{\partial u_\theta}{\partial r} - \frac{u_\theta}{r} \tag{146}$$

where, in the absence of internal damping, u_θ satisfies the partial differential equation

$$\frac{\partial^2 u_\theta}{\partial r^2} + \frac{1}{r}\frac{\partial u_\theta}{\partial r} - \frac{u_\theta}{r^2} + \frac{\partial^2 u_\theta}{\partial z^2} = \frac{1}{c^2}\frac{\partial^2 u_\theta}{\partial t^2} \tag{147}$$

where $c^2 = \mu/\rho$. The boundary conditions of the problem are

$$u_\theta = f(r,t) \qquad\qquad z = 0,\ r \leq r_0 \tag{148}$$
$$\tau_{z\theta} = 0 \qquad\qquad z = 0,\ r > r_0 \tag{148a}$$

[1] E. Reissner and H. F. Sagoci, *Jour. Applied Phys.*, **15**, 652 (1944); H. F. Sagoci, *Jour. Applied Phys.*, **15**, 655 (1944).

[2] I. N. Sneddon, *Jour. Applied Phys.*, **18**, 130 (1947).

[3] E. Reissner, *Ing. Archiv.*, **8**, 229 (1937).

In the case considered by Reissner and Sagoci the surface displacement $f(r,t)$ is of the form

$$f(r,t) = r\Phi(t) \tag{149}$$

A relation between the angle Φ and the applied torque T may be derived from the equation

$$T = 2\pi \int_0^{r_0} \tau_{z\theta}(r,0)r^2\, dr \tag{150}$$

55.2 Reduction of the partial differential equation by means of a Hankel transform. To solve the partial differential equation (147), we introduce the Hankel transform

$$U = \int_0^\infty r u_\theta J_1(\xi r) dr$$

of the circumferential component u_θ. Multiplying both sides of equation (147) by $rJ_1(\xi r)$, integrating with respect to r from 0 to ∞, and making use of equation (32), Chap. 2, we find that U satisfies the partial differential equation

$$\left(\frac{1}{c^2}\frac{\partial^2}{\partial t^2} - \frac{\partial^2}{\partial z^2} + \xi^2\right) U = 0 \tag{151}$$

For the determination of u_θ in terms of the solution U of this equation we have the formula

$$u_\theta = \int_0^\infty \xi U(z,t,\xi) J_1(\xi r) d\xi \tag{152}$$

which is a special case of Theorem 19.

Making use of the recurrence relation (7), Appendix A—with $n = 1$— we have, for the nonvanishing components of stress,

$$\tau_{r\theta} = \frac{1}{2}\mu \int_0^\infty \xi^2 U(z,t,\xi)[J_0(\xi r) - J_2(\xi r)]d\xi \tag{153}$$

$$\tau_{z\theta} = \mu \int_0^\infty \xi \frac{\partial U(z,t,\xi)}{\partial z} J_1(\xi r) d\xi \tag{154}$$

The arbitrary functions introduced in the solution of equation (151) are determined by the boundary conditions. The solution must be such that the displacement and both components of stress tend to zero as $z \to \infty$. When $z = 0$, the conditions (148) and (148a) must be satisfied. Substituting these relations into the expressions (152) and (154) for u_θ and $\tau_{\theta z}$, we obtain the dual integral equations

$$\int_0^\infty \xi U(0,t,\xi) J_1(\xi r) d\xi = f(r,t) \qquad r \le r_0 \tag{155}$$

$$\int_0^\infty \xi \frac{\partial U(0,t,\xi)}{\partial z} J_1(\xi r) d\xi = 0 \qquad r > r_0 \tag{156}$$

for the determination of the remaining arbitrary part of the function $U(z,t,\xi)$.

55.3 Solution for the static case.   In the static case, the function $\Phi(t)$ of equation (149) is a constant, or, in the general case, the function $f(r,t)$ of equation (148) is a function of r alone—say $f(r)$.   We therefore take $\partial/\partial t$ to be identically zero in equation (151) so that it reduces to the ordinary linear differential equation

$$\left(\frac{d^2}{dz^2} - \xi^2\right) U = 0$$

whose solution

$$U = A(\xi)e^{-\xi z} + B(\xi)e^{\xi z} \tag{157}$$

is immediate.   Since u_θ, and hence U, tends to zero as $z \to \infty$, we must take $B(\xi)$ to be identically zero in equation (157).   Substituting this value for U into the equations (155) and (156), we obtain the dual integral equations

$$\int_0^\infty \eta^{-1}F(\eta)J_1(\rho\eta)d\eta = g(\rho) \qquad 0 \le \rho \le 1 \tag{158}$$

$$\int_0^\infty F(\eta)J_1(\rho\eta)d\eta = 0 \qquad \rho > 1 \tag{159}$$

in which we have written $r = \rho r_0$, $\xi = \eta/r_0$, $f(r) = r_0 g(\rho)$,

$$\eta^2 A(\eta/r_0) = r_0^3 F(\eta)$$

This pair of dual integral equations belong to the class considered in Sec. 12.   Putting $\alpha = -1$, $\nu = 1$ in equation (47), Chap. 2, we obtain the solution

$$F(\eta) = \left(\frac{2}{\pi}\right)^{\frac{1}{2}} \eta \left[\eta^{\frac{1}{2}}J_{\frac{1}{2}}(\eta) \int_0^1 (1 - y^2)^{-\frac{1}{2}}y^2 g(y)dy \right.$$
$$\left. + \int_0^1 u^2(1 - u^2)^{-\frac{1}{2}} du \int_0^1 g(yu)(\eta y)^{\frac{1}{2}}J_{\frac{1}{2}}(\eta y)dy \right]$$

In the case considered by Reissner and Sagoci, $g(\rho) = \Phi\rho$ so that

$$F(\eta) = \frac{4\Phi}{\pi}\left[\frac{\sin(\eta)}{\eta} - \cos(\eta)\right] \tag{160}$$

giving finally

$$u_\theta = \frac{4\pi r_0}{\pi} \int_0^\infty \frac{\sin\eta - \eta\cos\eta}{\eta^2} e^{-\zeta\eta}J_1(\rho\eta)d\eta$$

where $\zeta = z/r_0$.

Now it was shown in Sec. 54.6 that the integrals S_0^1, S_1^1, C_1^1, and C_2^1 defined by equations (75) and (142) may be evaluated simply in terms of the quantities defined by the equations (55). With this notation we see that

$$u_\theta = \frac{4\Phi r_0}{\pi}(S_0^1 - C_1^1), \qquad \tau_{z\theta} = -\frac{4\Phi\mu}{\pi}(S_{\frac{1}{2}}^1 - C_2^1)$$

with a similar expression for the other shearing stress $\tau_{r\theta}$.

When $z = 0$, it is easily shown that

$$S_0^1 = \frac{1}{2\rho}\left\{(\rho^2 - 1)^{\frac{1}{2}} + \rho^2\left[\frac{1}{2}\pi - \tan^{-1}(\rho - 1)^{\frac{1}{2}}\right]\right\}, \qquad C_1^1 = \frac{(\rho^2 - 1)^{\frac{1}{2}}}{\rho}$$

with $\rho > 1$

$$S_{\frac{1}{2}}^1 = \frac{1}{\rho}[1 - (1 - \rho^2)^{\frac{1}{2}}], \qquad C_2^1 = \frac{1}{\rho}\left[1 - \frac{1}{(1 - \rho^2)^{\frac{1}{2}}}\right] \qquad \rho < 1$$

so that when $z = 0$ we have

$$u_\theta = \Phi r_0\left\{\rho[1 - 2\tan^{-1}(\rho^2 - 1)^{\frac{1}{2}}] - \frac{2}{\pi}\left(1 - \frac{1}{\rho^2}\right)^{\frac{1}{2}}\right\} \qquad \rho > 1$$

$$\tau_{z\theta} = -\frac{4\Phi\mu}{\pi}\left(\frac{1}{\rho^2} - 1\right)^{-\frac{1}{2}} \qquad \rho < 1$$

in agreement with the expressions found by Reissner and Sagoci.

56. Stress Distribution in a Long Circular Cylinder when a Discontinuous Pressure Is Applied to the Curved Surface

In the preceding sections we have solved problems in the equilibrium of axially symmetrical elastic solids by means of Hankel transform theory. In this way the partial differential equation (12) is reduced to an ordinary differential equation in z as a result of an integration over r. A similar solution, appropriate to the discussion of problems involving long circular cylinders, has been given by Tranter and Craggs.[1] The method employed by them consists in the reduction of the partial differential equation to an ordinary equation in r by means of a Fourier transform. In the particular problem treated by Tranter and Craggs the surface of the cylinder $r = a$ is deformed by the application of unit pressure to the part $z > 0$, while the remainder, $z < 0$, of the boundary is unloaded. The shear stress over the curved surface is taken to be zero for the whole length of the cylinder. Generalizing this slightly, we shall consider the case in which

$$\tau_{rz} = 0 \qquad r = a, \ -\infty < z < \infty$$

$$\sigma_r = \begin{cases} -f(z), & 0 < z < \infty \\ 0 & -\infty < z < 0 \end{cases}$$

[1] C. J. Tranter and J. W. Craggs, *Phil. Mag.* (vii), **36**, 241 (1945).

To solve the equations of equilibrium we note that if we write

$$\chi = 2(\lambda + \mu)\Phi$$

the solutions (6) to (11) become

$$\sigma_r = \frac{\partial}{\partial z}\left(\sigma \nabla^2 - \frac{\partial^2}{\partial r^2}\right)\chi \tag{161}$$

$$\tau_{rz} = \frac{\partial}{\partial r}\left[(1 - \sigma)\nabla^2 - \frac{\partial^2}{\partial z^2}\right]\chi \tag{162}$$

$$\sigma_\theta = \frac{\partial}{\partial z}\left(\sigma \nabla^2 - \frac{1}{r}\frac{\partial}{\partial r}\right)\chi \tag{163}$$

$$\sigma_z = \frac{\partial}{\partial z}\left[(2 - \sigma)\nabla^2 - \frac{\partial^2}{\partial z^2}\right]\chi \tag{164}$$

$$u_r = -\frac{1 + \sigma}{E}\frac{\partial^2\chi}{\partial r\,\partial z} \tag{165}$$

$$u_z = \frac{1 + \sigma}{E}\left[(1 - 2\sigma)\nabla^2 + \frac{\partial^2}{\partial r^2} + \frac{1}{r}\frac{\partial}{\partial r}\right]\chi \tag{166}$$

where σ, E are Poisson's ratio and Young's modulus of the material. The equation governing χ obviously reduces to

$$\nabla^4\chi = 0 \tag{167}$$

and the boundary conditions become

$$\frac{\partial}{\partial z}\left(\sigma \nabla^2 - \frac{\partial^2}{\partial r^2}\right) = \left\{\begin{array}{ll} -f(z) & 0 < z < \infty, \; r = a \\ 0 & -\infty < z < 0, \; r = a \end{array}\right\} \tag{168}$$

and

$$\frac{\partial}{\partial r}\left[(1 - \sigma)\nabla^2 - \frac{\partial^2}{\partial z^2}\right]\chi = 0 \quad -\infty < z < \infty, \; r = a \tag{169}$$

To solve the biharmonic equation (167), we multiply both sides of it by $e^{i\xi z}$ and integrate with respect to z from $-\infty$ to ∞, having a positive imaginary part. Then writing

$$X = \int_{-\infty}^{\infty} \chi e^{i\xi z}\,dz \tag{170}$$

and integrating by parts, we find that equation (167) is equivalent to

$$\overline{\nabla}^4 X = 0 \tag{171}$$

where

$$\overline{\nabla}^2 = \frac{d^2}{dr^2} + \frac{1}{r}\frac{d}{dr} - \xi^2$$

Similarly, denoting by $F(\xi)$ the integral

$$\int_0^\infty f(z)e^{i\xi z}\, dz$$

we find that equation (168) may be written as

$$\left(\sigma\,\overline{\nabla}^2 - \frac{d^2}{dr^2}\right)X = -\frac{iF(\xi)}{\xi}\qquad r = a\qquad(172)$$

and equation (169) as

$$\frac{d}{dr}[(1-\sigma)\overline{\nabla}^2 + \xi^2]X = 0\qquad r = a\qquad(173)$$

The solution of equation (171), which remains finite at $r = 0$, is

$$X = A(\xi)I_0(\xi r) + B(\xi)\xi r I_1(\xi r)\qquad(174)$$

Using standard recurrence formulas for Bessel functions, we find

$$\overline{\nabla}^2 X = 2\xi^2 B(\xi)I_0(\xi r)\qquad(175)$$

Substituting this relation in the boundary conditions (172) and (173), we then obtain the equations

$$A\left[I_0(\xi a) - \frac{1}{\xi a}I_1(\xi a)\right] + B[(1-2\sigma)I_0(\xi a) + \xi a I_1(\xi a)] = -\frac{iF(\xi)}{\xi^3}$$

$$A I_1(\xi a) + B[2(1-\sigma)I_1(\xi a) + \xi a I_0(\xi a)] = 0$$

for the determination of the constants A and B. Solving these equations we find that

$$A(\xi) = \frac{ai}{\xi^3 D(\xi a)}[2(1-\sigma)I_1(\xi a) + \xi a I_0(\xi a)]F(\xi)\qquad(176)$$

$$B(\xi) = -\frac{ai}{\xi^3 D(\xi a)}I_1(\xi a)F(\xi)\qquad(177)$$

in which

$$D(z) = [z^2 + 2(1-\sigma)]I_1^2(z) - z^2 I_0^2(z)\qquad(178)$$

The components of stress are readily determined once the auxiliary function X has been determined. For example, if we multiply equation (161) by $e^{i\xi z}$ and integrate with respect to z from $-\infty$ to ∞, we obtain

$$\Sigma_r = \int_0^\infty \sigma_r e^{i\xi z}\, dz = -i\xi\left(\sigma\,\overline{\nabla}^2 - \frac{d^2}{dr^2}\right)X$$

Substituting for X in this equation from equations (176), (177), (178), and (174), we obtain, for the transform Σ_r of the radial stress σ_r,

$$\Sigma_r = \frac{aF(\xi)}{r\,D(\xi a)} \{ ar\xi^2 I_0(a\xi)I_0(r\xi) + \xi r I_0(r\xi)I_1(a\xi) - a\xi I_0(a\xi)I_1(r\xi)$$
$$- [r^2\xi^2 + 2(1-\sigma)]I_1(a\xi)I_1(r\xi) \}$$

The stress σ_r is then obtained from its Fourier transform by Theorem 10, namely,

$$\sigma_r = \frac{1}{2\pi} \int_{-\infty}^{\infty} \Sigma_r e^{-i\xi z} \, d\xi \qquad (179)$$

In the case in which $f(z) = 1$ it follows from Example 1 of Sec. 45.2 that $F(\xi) = 2\pi\,\delta_+(\xi)$, where $\delta_+(\xi)$ is defined by equation (41). Substituting this value for $F(\xi)$ and changing the variable from ξ to $\eta = \xi a$, we find that

$$\sigma_r = -\frac{1}{2} + \frac{a}{\pi r} \int_0^\infty \left\{ \frac{r}{a}\eta^2 I_0(\eta) I_0\left(\frac{r\eta}{a}\right) + \left(\frac{r}{a}\right)\eta I_0\left(\frac{r\eta}{a}\right)I_1(\eta) \right.$$
$$\left. - I_0(\eta)I_1\left(\frac{r\eta}{a}\right) - \left[\left(\frac{r^2}{a^2}\right)\eta^2 + 2(1-\sigma)\right]I_1(\eta)I_1\left(\frac{r\eta}{a}\right) \right\}$$
$$\times \frac{\sin(z\eta/a)d\eta}{\eta\,D(\eta)} \qquad (180)$$

Similarly from equations (162) to (164) we find on multiplying by $e^{i\xi z}$ and integrating from $-\infty$ to ∞ that the transforms of the other components of stress are, in an obvious notation,[1]

$$\Sigma_\theta = 2\pi\,\delta_+(\xi)\frac{a}{r}\frac{1}{D(\xi a)}[a\xi I_0(a\xi)I_1(r\xi) + 2(1-\sigma)I_1(a\xi)I_1(r\xi)$$
$$+ (2\sigma - 1)\xi r I_1(a\xi)I_1(r\xi)]$$

$$\Sigma_z = \frac{1}{i\xi}\frac{a\xi}{D(\xi a)}[a\xi I_0(a\xi)I_0(r\xi) - \xi r I_1(a\xi)I_1(r\xi) - 2I_0(r\xi)I_1(a\xi)]$$

$$T_{rz} = \frac{1}{\xi}\frac{a}{D(\xi a)}[a\xi I_1(\xi r)I_0(\xi a) - \xi r I_1(\xi a)I_0(\xi r)]$$

Inverting these equations by means of Theorem 10, we obtain for the components of stress

$$\sigma_\theta = -\frac{1}{2} + \frac{a}{\pi r}\int_0^\infty \left[\eta I_0(\eta)I_1\left(\frac{\eta r}{a}\right) + 2(1-\sigma)I_1(\eta)I_1\left(\frac{\eta r}{a}\right) \right.$$
$$\left. + (2\sigma - 1)\frac{r}{a}\eta I_1(\eta)I_0\left(\frac{\eta r}{a}\right) \right]\frac{\sin(\eta z/a)d\eta}{\eta\,D(\eta)} \qquad (181)$$

$$\sigma_z = \frac{1}{\pi}\int_0^\infty \left[2I_0\left(\frac{\eta r}{a}\right)I_1(\eta) + \frac{r}{a}\eta I_1(\eta)I_1\left(\frac{\eta r}{a}\right) - \eta I_0(\eta)I_0\left(\frac{\eta r}{a}\right) \right]$$
$$\times \frac{\sin(\eta z/a)d\eta}{D(\eta)} \qquad (182)$$

[1] Here we make use of the result that $\xi\,\delta(\xi) \equiv 0$.

$$\tau_{rz} = \frac{1}{\pi} \int_0^\infty \left[\eta I_1 \left(\frac{\eta r}{a} \right) I_0(\eta) - \frac{r}{a} \eta I_1(\eta) I_0 \left(\frac{\eta r}{a} \right) \right] \frac{\cos{(\eta z/a)} d\eta}{D(\eta)} \quad (183)$$

It does not seem possible to evaluate these integrals explicitly; hence recourse to numerical computation is necessary. To illustrate the method employed by Tranter and Craggs, we shall show how they computed the value of σ_θ on the surface $r = a$ when $\sigma = \frac{1}{4}$.

When $r = a$ and $\sigma = \frac{1}{4}$, equation (181) becomes

$$\sigma_\theta = -\frac{1}{2} - \frac{1}{2\pi} \int_0^\infty \psi(\eta) \sin \left(\frac{\eta z}{a} \right) d\eta \quad (184)$$

where

$$\psi(\eta) = \frac{[\eta I_0(\eta)/I_1(\eta)] + 3}{\eta \left\{ \left[\frac{\eta I_0(\eta)}{I_1(\eta)} \right]^2 - \eta^2 - 1.5 \right\}} \quad (185)$$

When $\eta \geq 12$, $\psi(\eta)$ can be represented, with sufficient accuracy for numerical calculation, by making use of the asymptotic expansions for the Bessel functions as far as the term in η^{-4}. In this way we find

$$-\sigma_\theta = \frac{1}{2} + \frac{1}{2\pi} \int_0^{12} \psi(\eta) \sin \left(\frac{\eta z}{a} \right) d\eta + \frac{1}{2\pi} \int_{12}^\infty \left(\frac{1}{\eta} + \frac{4}{\eta^2} + \frac{5}{4\eta^3} - \frac{5}{\eta^4} \right)$$

$$\times \sin \left(\frac{\eta z}{a} \right) d\eta$$

By successive integrations by parts we may readily establish that the second integral has the value

$$\left[1 - \frac{5}{8} \left(\frac{z}{a} \right)^2 \right] \left[\frac{\pi}{2} - \text{Si} \left(\frac{12z}{a} \right) \right] - \frac{z}{a} \left[4 + \frac{5}{6} \left(\frac{z}{a} \right)^2 \right] \text{Ci} \left(\frac{12z}{a} \right)$$

$$+ \left[\frac{3,491}{10,368} + \frac{5}{72} \left(\frac{z}{a} \right)^2 \right] \sin \left(\frac{12z}{a} \right) + \frac{5}{108} \left(\frac{z}{a} \right) \cos \left(\frac{12z}{a} \right)$$

where, as before

$$\text{Si}(x) = \int_0^x \frac{\sin{(u)}}{u} du, \qquad \text{Ci}(x) = - \int_x^\infty \frac{\cos{(u)}}{u} du$$

To evaluate the first integral a method due to Filon (cf. Appendix B) is employed.

Using this method Tranter and Craggs[1] have drawn up a table of values of the stress components for various values of r/a and z/a. The variation of the radial stress σ_r and the shearing stress τ_{rz} with r and z is shown in Figs. 106 and 107, respectively.

[1] Op. cit., p. 249.

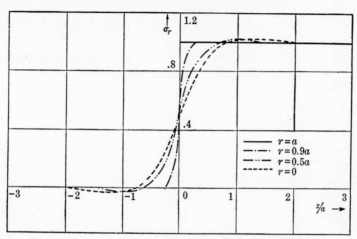

Fig. 106.   The variation with z and r of the radial stress σ_r.

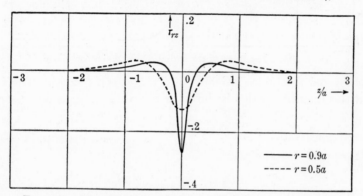

Fig. 107.   The variation with z and r of the shearing stress τ_{rz}.

The components of the displacement vector may be calculated in the same way.   If we multiply equations (165) and (166) by $e^{i\xi z}$ and integrate with respect to z from $-\infty$ to ∞, we find that

$$\frac{EU_r}{a} = \frac{i\xi}{a}\frac{dX}{dr} \qquad \frac{EU_z}{a} = \frac{1+\sigma}{a}\left[(1-2\sigma)\bar{\nabla}^2 + \frac{d^2}{dr^2} + \frac{1}{r}\frac{d}{dr}\right]X$$

for the transforms U_r and U_z of the displacement components u_r and u_z, respectively.   Integral expressions for the components of displacement can therefore be obtained easily by inverting these expressions by Theorem 10.

Alternatively, we may compute u_r from the expression for the circumferential strain

$$\frac{u_r}{r} = \frac{1}{E}\left[\sigma_\theta - \sigma(\sigma_r + \sigma_z)\right]$$ (186)

The value of Eu_r/a, on the surface $r = a$, may be computed from equa-

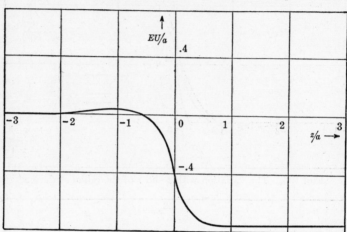

FIG. 108.   The form of the radial displacement on $r = a$.

tion (186) and the tables provided by Tranter and Craggs. The variation of this quantity with z is shown in Fig. 108.

APPENDIX A

SOME PROPERTIES OF BESSEL FUNCTIONS

We shall derive here some of the properties of Bessel functions which are of most frequent use in the theory of integral transforms. The subject is, of course, too vast to be treated adequately in so short a space, so that only the more important properties can be considered. For a fuller discussion of the topics touched upon here the reader is referred to the standard treatises.[1]

A.1. Bessel's Differential Equation. The differential equation

$$\frac{d^2y}{dx^2} + \frac{1}{x}\frac{dy}{dx} + \left(1 - \frac{n^2}{x^2}\right) y = 0 \tag{1}$$

which arises with great frequency in mathematical physics, as, for example, when Laplace's equation is separated in cylindrical coordinates, is called *Bessel's equation*. To find a solution of this equation, regular near the origin, we assume a power series solution of the type

$$y = \sum_{\nu=0}^{\infty} a_\nu x^{\nu+\rho}$$

and substitute in equation (1) to obtain a recurrence relation for the determination of the constants a_ν and an indicial equation giving possible values of ρ. A series solution of this type carried through in the usual way shows that the function defined by the infinite series

$$J_n(x) = \sum_{\nu=0}^{\infty} \frac{(-1)^\nu (x/2)^{n+2\nu}}{\nu! \Gamma(\nu + n + 1)} \tag{2}$$

is a solution of the differential equation (1). If n is not an integer, the function $J_{-n}(x)$ is linearly independent of $J_n(x)$ so that the complete solution of equation (1) may be written

$$y = AJ_n(x) + BJ_{-n}(x)$$

where A and B are arbitrary constants. If n is an integer, a second independent solution of equation (1) may be shown to be

$$G_n(x) = \tfrac{1}{2}\pi \operatorname{cosec} (n\pi)[J_{-n}(x) - e^{-in\pi}J_n(x)] \tag{3}$$

This expression is indeterminate for integral values of n but may be evaluated by the usual methods. We may therefore write the solution of equation (1) in the form

$$y = AJ_n(x) + BG_n(x)$$

whether n is an integer or not.

[1] G. N. Watson, "The Theory of Bessel Functions" (Cambridge, London, 1922); A. Gray, G. B. Matthews, and T. M. MacRobert, "Bessel Functions" (Macmillan, London, 1922).

The function $J_n(x)$, defined by equation (2), is called a *Bessel function of the first kind of order n* and the function $G_n(x)$ a *Bessel function of the second kind of order n*.

A.2. Recurrence Relations for Bessel Functions of the First Kind. If we differentiate both sides of equation (2) with respect to x and then multiply throughout by x, we obtain the equation

$$x \frac{dJ_n(x)}{dx} = \sum_{\nu=0}^{\infty} \frac{(-1)^{\nu}}{\nu!} \frac{n + 2\nu}{\Gamma(n + \nu + 1)} \left(\frac{x}{2}\right)^{n+2\nu} \tag{4}$$

Now, we may write

$$\frac{n + 2\nu}{\Gamma(n + \nu + 1)} = \frac{2}{\Gamma(n + \nu)} - \frac{n}{\Gamma(n + \nu + 1)}$$

so that

$$x \frac{dJ_n(x)}{dx} = x \sum_{\nu=0}^{\infty} \frac{(-1)^{\nu}}{\nu!} \frac{1}{\Gamma(n + \nu)} \left(\frac{x}{2}\right)^{n+2\nu-1} - n \sum_{\nu=0}^{\infty} \frac{(-1)^{\nu}}{\nu!} \frac{1}{\Gamma(n + \nu + 1)} \left(\frac{x}{2}\right)^{n+2\nu}$$

Appealing again to equation (2), we may identify each of the series on the right with a Bessel function of the first kind to obtain

$$xJ_n'(x) = xJ_{n-1}(x) - nJ_n(x) \tag{5}$$

Alternatively, we could use the result

$$\frac{(-1)^{\nu}}{\nu!} \frac{n + 2\nu}{\Gamma(n + \nu + 1)} = \frac{(-1)^{\nu}}{\nu!} \frac{n}{\Gamma(n + \nu + 1)} + \frac{(-1)^{\nu}}{(\nu - 1)!} \frac{2}{\Gamma(n + \nu + 1)}$$

in equation (4) to obtain the relation

$$xJ_n'(x) = nJ_n(x) - xJ_{n+1}(x) \tag{6}$$

Eliminating $J_n'(x)$ between equations (5) and (6), we obtain the further recurrence relation

$$J_{n-1}(x) - \frac{2n}{x} J_n(x) + J_{n+1}(x) = 0 \tag{7}$$

Similarly, from equation (2), we have that

$$x^n J_n(x) = \sum_{\nu=0}^{\infty} \frac{(-1)^{\nu} x^{2n+2\nu}}{\nu! \Gamma(\nu + n + 1)} \left(\frac{1}{2}\right)^{n+2\nu}$$

Differentiating both sides of this equation with respect to x and making use of the fact that $(2n + 2\nu)/\Gamma(\nu + n + 1) = 2/\Gamma(\nu + n)$, we have

$$\frac{d}{dx} [x^n J_n(x)] = \sum_{\nu=0}^{\infty} \frac{(-1)^{\nu} x^{2n+2\nu-1}}{\nu! \Gamma(\nu + n)} \left(\frac{1}{2}\right)^{n+2\nu-1} = x^n J_{n-1}(x) \tag{8}$$

Similarly we can establish that

$$\frac{d}{dx} [x^{-n} J_n(x)] = -x^{-n} J_{n+1}(x) \tag{9}$$

A.3. Definite Integrals Involving Bessel Functions. The recurrence relations derived above may be written in the form of definite integrals. For example, it follows immediately from equation (8) that

$$\int_0^\alpha x^n J_{n-1}(x)\,dx = \left[x^n J_n(x) \right]_0^\alpha = \alpha^n J_n(\alpha) \qquad n > 0 \qquad (10)$$

since $x^n J_n(x) \to 0$ as $x \to 0$. Putting $n = 1$ in this result and writing $x = \xi r$, $\alpha = \xi a$ in the integral on the left, we obtain the integral

$$\int_0^a r J_0(\xi r)\,dr = \frac{a}{\xi} J_1(a\xi) \qquad (11)$$

which is used repeatedly in the application of the theory of Hankel transforms to special problems.

Further we can write

$$\int_0^a r^3 J_0(\xi r)\,dr = \int_0^a r^2 \frac{1}{\xi} \frac{\partial}{\partial r}[r J_1(\xi r)]\,dr$$

$$= \left[\frac{r^3}{\xi} J_1(\xi r) \right]_0^a - \frac{2}{\xi} \int_0^a r^2 J_1(\xi r)\,dr$$

Now the integral on the right can be evaluated from equation (10) by the simple substitution $n = 2$, $x = \xi r$, $\alpha = \xi a$, and we obtain, with the use of equation (7) with $n = 1$,

$$\int_0^a r^3 J_0(\xi r)\,dr = \frac{a^2}{\xi^2}\left[2 J_0(\xi a) + \left(a\xi - \frac{4}{a\xi}\right) J_1(\xi a) \right] \qquad (12)$$

Combining equations (11) and (12), we obtain

$$\int_0^a r(a^2 - r^2) J_0(\xi r)\,dr = \frac{4a}{\xi^3} J_1(\xi a) - \frac{2a^2}{\xi^2} J_0(\xi a) \qquad (13)$$

A.4. Infinite Integrals Involving Bessel Functions. An integral which occurs in the application of Hankel transforms to the vibrations of a thin plate is $I(\nu,p,\mu)$ defined by the equation

$$I(\nu,p,\mu) = \int_0^\infty J_\nu(at) e^{-pt^2} t^{\mu-1}\,dt$$

Substituting for $J_\nu(at)$ from equation (2), we obtain

$$I(\nu,p,\mu) = \sum_{r=0}^\infty \frac{(-1)^r (a/2)^{\nu+2r}}{r!\,\Gamma(\nu + r + 1)} \int_0^\infty e^{-pt^2} t^{\nu+2r+\mu-1}\,dt$$

$$= \frac{a^\nu}{2^{\nu+1} p^{\frac{1}{2}\mu+\frac{1}{2}\nu}} \sum_{r=0}^\infty \frac{\Gamma(\frac{1}{2}\nu + \frac{1}{2}\mu + r)}{\Gamma(\nu + 1 + r)} \left(-\frac{a^2}{4p}\right)^r$$

If we adopt the usual notation

$$\,_1F_1(a;b;x) = 1 + \frac{a}{b}x + \frac{a(a+1)}{b(b+1)} \frac{x^2}{2!} + \cdots = \sum_{r=0}^\infty \frac{\Gamma(a + r)\Gamma(b) x^r}{\Gamma(a)\Gamma(b + r) r!} \qquad (14)$$

for a confluent hypergeometric function, we may write

$$I(\nu,p,\mu) = \frac{a^\nu \Gamma(\frac{1}{2}\nu + \frac{1}{2}\mu)}{2^{\nu+1} p^{\frac{1}{2}\mu+\frac{1}{2}\nu} \Gamma(1 + \nu)} \,_1F_1\left(\frac{1}{2}\nu + \frac{1}{2}\mu;\nu + 1;\, -\frac{a^2}{4p}\right) \qquad (15)$$

a result due to Hankel.

It follows at once from equation (14) that $\,_1F_1(a;a;x) = e^x$, so that, putting

$$\tfrac{1}{2}\nu + \tfrac{1}{2}\mu = \nu + 1$$

in equation (15), we obtain the simple result

$$I(\nu,p,\nu + 2) = \frac{a^\nu}{(2p)^{\nu+1}} e^{-a^2/4p} \tag{16}$$

In a similar way we can evaluate the integral

$$J(\nu,p,\mu) = \int_0^\infty J_\nu(at)e^{-pt}t^\mu \, dt$$

We find that

$$J(\nu,p,\mu) = \frac{2^\mu a^\nu}{p^{\mu+\nu+1}} \frac{\Gamma(\tfrac{1}{2}\mu + \tfrac{1}{2}\nu + \tfrac{1}{2})\Gamma(1 + \tfrac{1}{2}\mu + \tfrac{1}{2}\nu)}{\Gamma(\tfrac{1}{2})\Gamma(\nu + 1)} \,\, {}_2F_1\left(\frac{1}{2}\mu + \frac{1}{2}\nu + \frac{1}{2}; 1 + \frac{1}{2}\mu + \frac{1}{2}\nu;\right.$$
$$\left. 1 + \nu; -\frac{a^2}{p^2}\right)$$

where, as is usual, ${}_2F_1(a,b;c;x)$ is defined by the equation

$${}_2F_1(a;b;c;x) = 1 + \frac{ab}{c}\frac{x}{1!} + \frac{a(a + 1)b(b + 1)}{c(c + 1)}\frac{x^2}{2!} + \cdots$$

and satisfies the relation

$${}_2F_1(a;b;c;x) = (1 - x)^{-a}{}_2F_1\left(a;c - b;c;\frac{x}{x - 1}\right)$$

Making use of this relation, we have

$$J(\nu,p,\mu) = \frac{2^\mu a^\nu}{(a^2 + p^2)^{\tfrac{1}{2}\mu+\tfrac{1}{2}\nu+\tfrac{1}{2}}} \frac{\Gamma(\tfrac{1}{2}\mu + \tfrac{1}{2}\nu + \tfrac{1}{2})\Gamma(1 + \tfrac{1}{2}\mu + \tfrac{1}{2}\nu)}{\Gamma(\nu + 1)\Gamma(\tfrac{1}{2})}$$
$$\times \,\, {}_2F_1\left(\frac{1}{2}\mu + \frac{1}{2}\nu + \frac{1}{2},\frac{1}{2}\nu - \frac{1}{2}\mu;1 + \nu;\frac{a^2}{a^2 + p^2}\right) \tag{17}$$

Letting $p = 0$ in this expression and making use of the formula[1]

$${}_2F_1(a,b;c;1) = \frac{\Gamma(c)\Gamma(c - a - b)}{\Gamma(c - a)\Gamma(c - b)}$$

we obtain the formula

$$\int_0^\infty J_\nu(at)t^\mu \, dt = \frac{2^\mu\Gamma(\tfrac{1}{2} + \tfrac{1}{2}\mu + \tfrac{1}{2}\nu)}{a^{\mu+1}\Gamma(\tfrac{1}{2} - \tfrac{1}{2}\mu + \tfrac{1}{2}\nu)} \tag{18}$$

It may also be shown that equation (17) can be written in the form

$$J(\nu,p,\mu) = \frac{\Gamma(\mu - \nu + 1)}{(a^2 + p^2)^{\tfrac{1}{2}\mu+\tfrac{1}{2}}} P_\mu^\nu\left[\frac{p}{(a^2 + p^2)^{\tfrac{1}{2}}}\right] \tag{19}$$

where $P_\mu^\nu(z)$ denotes the associated Legendre function of argument z.

From either equation (17) or (19) we have the special results

$$\left.\begin{array}{ll}
\displaystyle\int_0^\infty e^{-px}J_1(ax)\frac{dx}{x} = \frac{(a^2 + p^2)^{\tfrac{1}{2}} - p}{a}, & \displaystyle\int_0^\infty e^{-px}J_0(ax)dx = (a^2 + p^2)^{-\tfrac{1}{2}} \\[2ex]
\displaystyle\int_0^\infty e^{-px}J_1(ax)dx = \frac{1}{a} - \frac{p}{a(a^2 + p^2)^{\tfrac{1}{2}}}, & \displaystyle\int_0^\infty xe^{-px}J_0(ax)dx = p(a^2 + p^2)^{-\tfrac{3}{2}} \\[2ex]
\displaystyle\int_0^\infty xe^{-px}J_1(ax)dx = a(a^2 + p^2)^{-\tfrac{3}{2}} &
\end{array}\right\} \tag{20}$$

A.5. Relation between the Bessel Functions and Circular Functions. If we let $n = \tfrac{1}{2}$ in equation (2) and make use of the duplication formula for the gamma function in the form

[1] T. M. MacRobert, "Spherical Harmonics" (Methuen, London, 1927), p. 28.

$$2^{2\nu}\Gamma(\nu + 1)\Gamma(\nu + \tfrac{3}{2}) = \Gamma(\tfrac{1}{2})\Gamma(2\nu + 2) = \pi^{\frac{1}{2}}(2\nu + 1)!$$

we obtain

$$\left(\frac{\pi x}{2}\right)^{\frac{1}{2}} J_{\frac{1}{2}}(x) = \sum_{\nu=0}^{\infty} (-1)^{\nu} \frac{x^{2\nu+1}}{(2\nu + 1)!} = \sin x$$

showing that

$$J_{\frac{1}{2}}(x) = \left(\frac{2}{\pi x}\right)^{\frac{1}{2}} \sin(x) \tag{21}$$

Again, if we put $n = -\tfrac{1}{2}$ in equation (2) and make use of the duplication formula for the gamma function, we obtain the relation

$$J_{-\frac{1}{2}}(x) = \left(\frac{2}{\pi x}\right)^{\frac{1}{2}} \cos(x) \tag{22}$$

A.6. Integral Expression for the Bessel Function $J_n(x)$. Let us now consider the value of the integral

$$I(\mu) = \int_0^{2\pi} \cos(\mu \cos \varphi) d\varphi$$

Using the cosine expansion, we obtain the series

$$I(\mu) = \sum_{n=0}^{\infty} \frac{(-1)^n \mu^{2n}}{(2n)!} \int_0^{2\pi} \cos^{2n}\varphi \, d\varphi$$

Now it is readily shown that

$$\frac{1}{(2n)!} \int_0^{2\pi} \cos^{2n} \varphi \, d\varphi = 2\pi \left(\frac{1}{2}\right)^{2n} \frac{1}{(n!)^2}$$

so that

$$I(\mu) = 2\pi \sum_{n=0}^{\infty} \left(-\frac{\mu^2}{4}\right)^n \frac{1}{(n!)^2}.$$

If we compare the series on the right with that occurring in equation (2), we see that

$$\int_0^{2\pi} \cos(\mu \cos \varphi) d\varphi = 2\pi J_0(\mu) \tag{23}$$

Also

$$\int_0^{2\pi} \sin(\mu \cos \varphi) d\varphi = 0$$

so we may write equation (23) in the form

$$\int_0^{2\pi} e^{i\mu \cos \varphi} \, d\varphi = 2\pi J_0(\mu) \tag{24}$$

These results may readily be generalized by considering the integral

$$I_n = \int_0^{\pi} \sin^{2n} \varphi \cos(\mu \cos \varphi) d\varphi$$

Expanding the cosine factor in ascending powers of $\cos \varphi$ and making use of the duplication formula for the gamma function, it is readily shown that

$$I_n(\mu) = \left(\frac{2}{\mu}\right)^n \pi^{\frac{1}{2}} \Gamma\left(n + \frac{1}{2}\right) J_n(\mu) \tag{25}$$

APPENDIX B

APPROXIMATE METHODS OF CALCULATING INTEGRAL TRANSFORMS

In the application of the theory of integral transforms to boundary value problems we saw that it was often possible to determine the integral transform $I_f(\alpha)$ of the physical quantity $f(x)$ whose behavior we are investigating. It sometimes happens that, by the use of the appropriate inversion theorem, an analytical expression for $f(x)$ can be obtained. In other instances the form of $I_f(\alpha)$ is so complicated that the evaluation of the integral for $f(x)$ is a matter of great difficulty. Though the precise form of $f(x)$ is not readily obtainable, it is often of interest to know the asymptotic form of $f(x)$ as $x \to \infty$. When values of $f(x)$, for general values of x, are desired, recourse may have to be made to numerical methods. Certain methods of evaluating $f(x)$ in these circumstances will now be considered briefly.

B.1. Method of Steepest Descents for Contour Integrals. In the first instance we consider the asymptotic behavior of the Laplace transform

$$\phi(p) = \int_0^\infty e^{-px} f(x) \, dx$$

for large values of p. The result, which is of extensive use in the theory of asymptotic expansions of functions defined by integrals, particularly in the method of steepest descents, is contained in

Watson's Lemma:[1] *If $f(x)$ is an analytical function of x, regular when $|x| < R + \delta$ $(R, \delta > 0)$ and if*

$$f(x) = \sum_{\nu=1}^\infty \alpha_\nu x^{\nu-1} \qquad |x| < R$$

and $|f(x)| < K e^{bx}$, K and b being positive and independent of x, then the Laplace transform $\phi(p)$ has the asymptotic expansion

$$\phi(p) \sim \sum_{\nu=1}^\infty \alpha_\nu \Gamma(\nu) p^{-\nu}$$

where $|p|$ is large and $|\arg (p)| < \frac{1}{2}\pi - \epsilon$, where ϵ is an arbitrary positive number.
For example, in the case of the function

$$J_\mu(x) = \sum_{\nu=0}^\infty \frac{(-1)^\nu x^{\mu+2\nu}}{2^{\mu+2\nu} \nu! \Gamma(\mu + 1 + \nu)}$$

we have $\alpha_\nu = 0 (\nu < \mu + 1)$, $\alpha_{\mu+1} = \frac{1}{2}^\mu \Gamma(1 + \mu)$, $\alpha_{\nu+2} = 0$, $\alpha_{\mu+3} = -\frac{1}{2}^{\mu+2}\Gamma(\mu + 2)$, so that

[1] For a proof of this theorem, see G. N. Watson, *Proc. London Math. Soc.*, **17**, 33 (1918).

$$\phi(p) \sim \frac{1}{2^\mu p^{\mu+1}} \left(1 - \frac{\mu + 2}{4p^2} + \cdots \right)$$

in agreement with the expansion obtained from the exact formula

$$\phi(p) = (1 + p^2)^{-\frac{1}{2}}[p + (1 + p^2)^{\frac{1}{2}}]^{-\mu}$$

The converse problem of determining the asymptotic form of the function $f(x)$ when its Laplace transform $\phi(p)$ is known is included in Debye's discussion[1] of the behavior of the integral

$$I = \int f(\zeta) e^{zg(\zeta)} \, d\zeta$$

as $|z| \to \infty$, the path of integration being an arc or a closed curve in the ζ plane. This path may be deformed continuously without affecting the value of I provided that the path of integration does not, during the deformation, pass through a singularity of the integrand. The method of steepest descents devised by Debye consists essentially in taking a path of integration which has a special geometrical property giving the method its name. The path of integration is chosen to pass through a point ζ_0 such that $g'(\zeta_0) = 0$ and, if possible, so that $\mathrm{I}[g(\zeta)]$ is constant on it. We shall consider the case $z \to +\infty$ and write $\zeta = \xi + i\eta$, $g(\zeta) = \theta(\xi,\eta) + i\phi(\xi,\eta)$. The equation of the Debye path of integration is

$$\phi(\xi,\eta) = \phi(\xi_0,\eta_0)$$

and the integrand becomes

$$f(\xi + i\eta) e^{iz\phi(\xi_0,\eta_0)} e^{z\theta(\xi,\eta)}$$

Now $f(\zeta)$ does not depend on z so that, since z and θ are both real, the integrand is not a rapidly oscillating function for large values of z.

At the point ζ_0, $g' = 0$, which is equivalent to the equations

$$\frac{\partial \theta}{\partial \xi} = \frac{\partial \theta}{\partial \eta} = 0$$

and since the function $\theta + i\phi$ is a holomorphic function of $\xi + i\eta$,

$$\frac{\partial^2 \theta}{\partial \xi^2} + \frac{\partial^2 \theta}{\partial \eta^2} = 0$$

so that the point (ξ_0,η_0,θ_0) is a stationary point on the surface S, $\theta = \theta(\xi,\eta)$, at which θ is neither a maximum nor a minimum. Such a point is called a *saddle point* or *col*. Mapping the surface S on the $\xi\eta$ plane by drawing the level curves $\theta(\xi,\eta) = \text{const.}$ we see that a saddle point is the intersection of four or more level curves. The curves $\phi(\xi,\eta) = \text{const.}$, being the orthogonal trajectories of the level curves, are therefore maps of the curves of steepest descent or ascent on S. The path of integration we have chosen is therefore a path of steepest descent through a saddle point.

Now on a steepest path through a saddle point (ξ_0,η_0) we have

$$\theta(\xi,\eta) = \theta(\xi_0,\eta_0) - \tau, \qquad \phi(\xi,\eta) = \phi(\xi_0,\eta_0)$$

or, what is the same thing,

$$g(\zeta) = g(\zeta_0) - \tau$$

[1] P. Debye, *Math. Ann.*, **67**, 535 (1909); *Münch. Ber.*, **40**, No. 5 (1910).

where τ is real. Hence $d\tau/d\sigma = \pm|g'(\zeta)|$, where σ is the arc length of this steepest path, and is of constant sign along the path unless the path passes through another saddle point or a singularity of $g'(\zeta)$. Hence τ is, in general, a monotonic function of σ and either decreases steadily to $-\infty$ or increases steadily to $+\infty$. In choosing the path of integration we must choose a path on S through the given saddle point which descends on both sides of the saddle point, for if we do not, τ will tend to $+\infty$ and the integral will diverge since z is positive. The path of integration is therefore obtained by joining together paths of steepest descent from a saddle point, the parameter τ varying from 0 to ∞. Thus the integral I can be expressed as a sum of integrals of the type

$$e^{zg(\zeta_0)} \int_0^\infty e^{-z\tau} f(\zeta) \frac{d\zeta}{d\tau} \, d\tau$$

whose asymptotic expansions for large values of z may be obtained by the application of Watson's lemma.

The difficulty in applying the method of steepest descents is that it is often a troublesome process to express ζ in terms of the parameter τ when ζ moves along a curve of steepest descent. In such cases, a simpler procedure, known as the *saddle-point method*, may be used. The essence of this method lies in the fact that if z is large the dominant contribution to the integral I is made by the part of the path of integration in the immediate neighborhood of the highest saddle point. If this saddle point is ζ_0 and ζ_0 is a simple zero of $g'(\zeta)$, we may write

$$g(\zeta) = g(\zeta_0) + \frac{1}{2!} (\zeta - \zeta_0)^2 g''(\zeta_0) + \cdots$$

for ζ in the neighborhood of ζ_0. The path of integration is now chosen to be in such a direction that the second term in this series is real and negative for ζ near to ζ_0 and hence is the direction of the two paths of steepest descent from the saddle point. Putting $u^2 = -\frac{1}{2}(\zeta - \zeta_0)^2 g''(\zeta_0)$, we see that

$$I = f(\zeta_0) e^{zg(\zeta_0)} \int_{\zeta_0 - \alpha}^{\zeta_0 + \alpha} e^{\frac{1}{2} z (\zeta - \zeta_0)^2 g''(\zeta_0)} \, d\zeta$$

$$= f(\zeta_0) e^{zg(\zeta_0)} \int_{-\lambda}^{\lambda} e^{-u^2} \, du \left[- \frac{2}{zg''(\zeta_0)} \right]^{\frac{1}{2}}$$

where $\lambda \to \infty$ as $z \to \infty$. Hence, for large values of z, we have approximately

$$I = e^{zg(\zeta_0)} f(\zeta_0) \left[- \frac{2}{zg''(\zeta_0)} \right]^{\frac{1}{2}}$$

If there are two or more saddle points at which the values of ζ_0 are greatest, each makes a contribution to the required asymptotic expression.

As an example of the use of this method let us consider the evaluation of the expression for the density of the energy levels of a heavy nucleus

$$\rho(Q) = \frac{1}{2\pi i} \int_{\gamma - i\infty}^{\gamma + i\infty} e^{(Q\zeta + \alpha/\zeta)} \, d\zeta$$

obtained by applying the theory of Laplace transforms to Bethe's theory of the nucleus.[1] In this case $f(\zeta) = 1$ and $g(\zeta) = \zeta + (\alpha/Q\zeta)$ so that $\zeta_0^2 = \alpha/Q$. The highest saddle point is then $\zeta_0 = \alpha^{\frac{1}{2}} Q^{-\frac{1}{2}}$ so that, since $e^{Qg(\zeta_0)} = e^{2\alpha^{\frac{1}{2}} Q^{\frac{1}{2}}}$ and

---

[1] I. N. Sneddon and B. F. Touschek, *Proc. Cambridge Phil. Soc.*, **44**, 391 (1948).

$$- \left(\frac{2\pi}{Qg''}\right)^{\frac{1}{2}} = i\pi^{\frac{1}{2}}\alpha^{\frac{1}{4}}Q^{-\frac{3}{4}}$$

we find that, for large values of Q,

$$\rho(Q) \sim \frac{\alpha^{\frac{1}{4}}}{2\pi^{\frac{1}{2}}Q^{\frac{3}{4}}} e^{2\alpha^{\frac{1}{2}}Q^{\frac{1}{2}}}$$

However, making use of the result

$$\int_0^\infty e^{-x^2/4\alpha\tau} I_1(x)dx = e^{\alpha\tau} - 1$$

we see that the exact expression for $\rho(Q)$ is

$$\rho(Q) = \delta(Q) + \left(\frac{\alpha}{Q}\right)^{\frac{1}{2}} I_1(2\alpha^{\frac{1}{2}}Q^{\frac{1}{2}})$$

The Dirac delta function makes no contribution to the asymptotic formula, but, since for $z \to \infty$

$$I_1(z) \sim \frac{e^z}{(2\pi z)^{\frac{1}{2}}} \left[1 - \frac{3}{8z} + \frac{3}{2(8z)^2} + \cdots \right]$$

we find, for large values of Q,

$$\rho(Q) \sim \frac{\alpha^{\frac{1}{4}}}{2\pi^{\frac{1}{2}}Q^{\frac{3}{4}}} e^{2\alpha^{\frac{1}{2}}Q^{\frac{1}{2}}} \left[1 - \frac{3}{16\alpha^{\frac{1}{2}}Q^{\frac{1}{2}}} + \cdots \right]$$

so that the error involved in the use of the saddle-point method is of order $(\alpha Q)^{-\frac{1}{2}}$, which is small if both α and Q are large.

B.2. Numerical Calculations of Fourier Integrals. The calculation of Fourier sine transforms can often, as we have seen in Sec. 56, be reduced to the numerical computation of integrals of the type

$$I_1 = \int_a^b f(x) \sin (kx)dx$$

When k is large, but not infinite, the actual computation of integrals of this type is a matter of great difficulty since, because of the violent oscillations of the function $\sin (kx)$, the ordinary quadrature formulas require for their application the division of the range of integration into such minute steps that the labor of computation is prohibitive.

It has been shown by Filon[1] that if we divide the interval (a,b) into $2n$ intervals, each of length h, and compute the sums

$$S_{2r} = \sum_{r=0}^\infty f(a + 2rh) \sin [k(a + 2rh)] - \frac{1}{2} [f(a) \sin (ka) + f(b) \sin (kb)]$$

$$S_{2r-1} = \sum_{r=1}^\infty f(a + \overline{2r-1}h) \sin [k(a + \overline{2r-1}h)]$$

then, approximately,

$$I_1 = h\{\alpha[f(a) \cos (ka) - f(b) \cos (kb)] + \beta S_{2r} + \gamma S_{2r-1}\}$$

where, in terms of the parameter $\theta = hk$,

[1] L. N. G. Filon, *Proc. Roy. Soc. Edinburgh*, **49**, 38 (1928–1929).

$$\alpha = \frac{1}{\theta} + \frac{\sin{(2\theta)}}{2\theta^2} - \frac{2\sin^2\theta}{\theta^3}, \qquad \beta = 2\left[\frac{1 + \cos^2\theta}{\theta^2} - \frac{\sin{(2\theta)}}{\theta^3}\right]$$

$$\gamma = 4\left(\frac{\sin\theta}{\theta^3} - \frac{\cos\theta}{\theta^2}\right)$$

The error involved in the use of this formula is less than $\frac{2}{3}(b - a)M\sin\left(\frac{1}{2}\theta\right)$ $\left[1 - \frac{\sec{(\frac{1}{4}\theta)}}{16}\right]$, where M is the maximum numerical value of $\Delta_{\frac{1}{2}}^2 f$, the $\frac{1}{2}$ denoting that differences are calculated for the interval $\frac{1}{2}h$.

When θ is small, we find that $I_1 = \frac{1}{3}h(2S_{2r} + 4S_{2r-1})$, which is simply Simpson's formula.

A special case of the integral I_1 is

$$I_2 = \int_0^\infty g(x)\,\frac{\sin{(kx)}}{x}\,dx$$

in which $g(x)$ does *not* vanish at $x = 0$. In this instance

$$I_2 = \frac{1}{4}g(0)[(2 - \beta - \gamma)\pi + 2\beta\theta] + h[\alpha g'(0) + \beta T_{2n} + \gamma T_{2n+1}]$$

where α, β, and γ are defined as before and

$$T_{2n} = \sum_{n=1}^\infty \frac{g(2nh)}{2nh}\sin{(2n\theta)}, \qquad T_{2n+1} = \sum_{n=0}^\infty \frac{g(\overline{2n+1}h)}{(2n+1)h}\sin{(2n+1)\theta}$$

Provided that $g(x)$ diminishes rapidly as x increases, the series T_{2n} and T_{2n+1} are rapidly convergent and can be computed easily.

In order that they may be available for immediate application Filon's values of α, β, and γ for a sequence of values of θ are given in Table I.

TABLE I†

θ, deg	α	β	γ
0	0.000 0000	0.666 6667	1.333 3333
1	0.000 0002	0.666 7073	1.333 2927
2	0.000 0019	0.666 8291	1.333 1709
3	0.000 0064	0.667 0319	1.332 9678
4	0.000 0151	0.667 3156	1.332 6836
5	0.000 0295	0.667 6798	1.332 3182
6	0.000 0510	0.668 1243	1.331 8717
7	0.000 0809	0.668 6484	1.331 3442
8	0.000 1206	0.669 2516	1.330 7357
9	0.000 1717	0.669 9334	1.330 0464
10	0.000 2353	0.670 6930	1.329 2762
11	0.000 3129	0.671 5296	1.328 4253
12	0.000 4058	0.672 4423	1.327 4938
13	0.000 5153	0.673 4302	1.326 4819
14	0.000 6429	0.674 4923	1.325 3896
15	0.000 7897	0.675 6274	1.324 2172
16	0.000 9571	0.676 8343	1.322 9646
17	0.001 1464	0.678 1117	1.321 6323
18	0.001 3588	0.679 4584	1.320 2202
19	0.001 5955	0.680 8729	1.318 7285
20	0.001 8577	0.682 3537	1.317 1577
25	0.003 5929	0.690 6947	1.308 1206
30	0.006 1345	0.700 4291	1.297 1353
35	0.009 6042	0.711 2961	1.284 2377
40	0.014 1033	0.723 0007	1.269 4693
45	0.019 7108	0.735 2204	1.252 8780

† Reproduced by kind permission of the Council of the Royal Society of Edinburgh.

APPENDIX C

TABLES OF INTEGRAL TRANSFORMS

In order to facilitate the solution of particular problems, we gather together in this appendix the integral transforms of the functions which occur most frequently in physical applications. In these tables no attempt is made to give complete lists of transforms; only those which are used in the text are cited. For exhaustive lists of transforms the reader should consult G. A. Campbell and R. M. Foster, "Fourier Integrals for Practical Applications," *Bell Telephone-System, Tech. Pub.*, 1931; N. W. McLachlan and P. Humbert, "Formulaire pour le calcul symbolique" (Gauthier-Villars, Paris, 1941); W. Magnus and F. Oberhettinger, "Formeln und Satze fur die speziellen Funktionen der mathematischen Physik" (Springer, Berlin, 1948); R. V. Churchill, "Modern Operational Mathematics in Engineering" (McGraw-Hill, New York, 1944); G. G. Macfarlane, *Phil. Mag.*, **40**, 194 (1949); I. Roettinger, *Quart. Applied Math.*, **5**, 298 (1947).

TABLE II. FOURIER TRANSFORMS

$$f(x) = \frac{1}{\sqrt{2\pi}} \int_{-\infty}^{\infty} F(\xi)e^{-i\xi x}\, d\xi \qquad F(\xi) = \frac{1}{\sqrt{2\pi}} \int_{-\infty}^{\infty} f(x)e^{i\xi x}\, dx$$

$f(x)$	$F(\xi)$
$\dfrac{\sin\,(ax)}{x}$	$\left(\dfrac{\pi}{2}\right)^{\frac{1}{2}} \quad \lvert\xi\rvert < a$ $0 \qquad\quad \lvert\xi\rvert > a$
$e^{i\omega x} \quad p < x < q$ $0 \qquad x < p,\, x > q$	$\dfrac{i}{(2\pi)^{\frac{1}{2}}} \dfrac{e^{ip(\omega+\xi)} - e^{iq(\omega+\xi)}}{\xi}$
$e^{-cx+i\omega x} \quad x > 0$ $0 \qquad\qquad x < 0$	$\dfrac{i}{(2\pi)^{\frac{1}{2}}(\omega + \xi + ic)}$
$e^{-px^2} \quad \mathsf{R}(p) > 0$	$(2p)^{-\frac{1}{2}}e^{-\xi^2/4p}$
$\cos\,(px^2)$	$(2p)^{-\frac{1}{2}} \cos\left(\dfrac{\xi^2}{4p} - \dfrac{1}{4}\pi\right)$
$\sin\,(px^2)$	$(2p)^{-\frac{1}{2}} \sin\left(\dfrac{\xi^2}{4p} + \dfrac{1}{4}\pi\right)$
$\lvert x\rvert^{-s} \quad 0 < \mathsf{R}(s) < 1$	$\dfrac{2^{\frac{1}{2}}\Gamma(1-s)\sin\left(\frac{1}{2}s\pi\right)}{\pi^{\frac{1}{2}}\lvert\xi\rvert^{1-s}}$
$\dfrac{1}{\lvert x\rvert^{\frac{1}{2}}}$	$\dfrac{1}{\lvert\xi\rvert^{\frac{1}{2}}}$
$\dfrac{e^{-a\lvert x\rvert}}{\lvert x\rvert^{\frac{1}{2}}}$	$\dfrac{[(a^2+\xi^2)^{\frac{1}{2}} + a]^{\frac{1}{2}}}{(a^2+\xi^2)^{\frac{1}{2}}}$
$\dfrac{\cosh\,(ax)}{\cosh\,(\pi x)} \quad -\pi < a < \pi$	$\left(\dfrac{2}{\pi}\right)^{\frac{1}{2}} \dfrac{\cos\left(\frac{1}{2}a\right)\cosh\left(\frac{1}{2}\xi\right)}{\cosh\,(\xi) + \cos\,(a)}$
$\dfrac{\sinh\,(ax)}{\sinh\,(\pi x)} \quad -\pi < a < \pi$	$\left(\dfrac{1}{2\pi}\right)^{\frac{1}{2}} \dfrac{\sin\,(a)}{\cosh\,(\xi) + \cos\,(a)}$
$(a^2 - x^2)^{-\frac{1}{2}} \quad \lvert x\rvert < a$ $0 \qquad\qquad\quad \lvert x\rvert > a$	$\left(\frac{1}{2}\pi\right)^{\frac{1}{2}}J_0(a\xi)$
$\dfrac{\sin\,[b(a^2+x^2)^{\frac{1}{2}}]}{(a^2+x^2)^{\frac{1}{2}}}$	$0 \qquad\qquad\qquad\quad \lvert\xi\rvert > b$ $\left(\frac{1}{2}\pi\right)^{\frac{1}{2}}J_0(a\sqrt{b^2-\xi^2}) \quad \lvert\xi\rvert < b$
$P_n(x) \quad \lvert x\rvert < 1$ $0 \qquad\quad \lvert x\rvert > 1$	$i^n\pi^{-\frac{1}{2}}J_{n+\frac{1}{2}}(\xi)$
$\dfrac{\cos\,(b\sqrt{a^2-x^2})}{(a^2-x^2)^{\frac{1}{2}}} \quad \lvert x\rvert < a$ $0 \qquad\qquad\qquad\quad \lvert x\rvert > a$	$\left(\frac{1}{2}\pi\right)^{\frac{1}{2}}J_0(a\sqrt{\xi^2+b^2})$
$\dfrac{\cosh\,(b\sqrt{a^2-x^2})}{(a^2-x^2)^{\frac{1}{2}}} \quad \lvert x\rvert < a$ $0 \qquad\qquad\qquad\quad \lvert x\rvert > a$	$\left(\frac{1}{2}\pi\right)^{\frac{1}{2}}J_0(a\sqrt{\xi^2-b^2})$

TABLE III. FOURIER COSINE TRANSFORMS*

$$f(x) = \sqrt{\frac{2}{\pi}} \int_0^\infty F_c(\xi) \cos(\xi x) d\xi \qquad F_c(\xi) = \sqrt{\frac{2}{\pi}} \int_0^\infty f(x) \cos(\xi x) dx$$

$f(x)$	$F_c(\xi)$
$\begin{array}{ll}1 & 0 < x < a \\ 0 & x > a\end{array}$	$\left(\frac{2}{\pi}\right)^{\frac{1}{2}} \dfrac{\sin(\xi a)}{\xi}$
$x^{p-1} \quad 0 < p < 1$	$\left(\frac{2}{\pi}\right)^{\frac{1}{2}} \Gamma(p)\xi^{-p} \sin\left(\frac{1}{2} p\pi\right)$
$\begin{array}{ll}\cos(x) & 0 < x < a \\ 0 & x > a\end{array}$	$\left(\frac{1}{2\pi}\right)^{\frac{1}{2}} \left\{\dfrac{\sin[a(1-\xi)]}{1-\xi} + \dfrac{\sin[a(1+\xi)]}{1+\xi}\right\}$
e^{-x}	$\left(\frac{2}{\pi}\right)^{\frac{1}{2}} \dfrac{1}{1+\xi^2}$
$\operatorname{sech}(\pi x)$	$\dfrac{1}{1+\xi^4}$
e^{-x^2}	$e^{-\xi^2}$
$\cos(\frac{1}{2}x^2)$	$\dfrac{1}{\sqrt{2}} \left[\cos\left(\frac{1}{2}\xi^2\right) + \sin\left(\frac{1}{2}\xi^2\right)\right]$
$\sin(\frac{1}{2}x^2)$	$\dfrac{1}{\sqrt{2}} \left[\cos\left(\frac{1}{2}\xi^2\right) - \sin\left(\frac{1}{2}\xi^2\right)\right]$
$\begin{array}{ll}(1-x^2)^\nu & 0 < x < 1 \\ 0 & x > 1, \\ & \nu > -\frac{3}{2}\end{array}$	$2^\nu \Gamma(\nu+1)\xi^{-\nu-\frac{1}{2}} J_{\nu+\frac{1}{2}}(\xi)$

* Three general rules are worthy of notice:
1. If $F_c(\xi)$ is the Fourier cosine transform of $f(x)$, then $f(\xi)$ is the Fourier cosine transform of $F_c(x)$.
2. If $f(x)$ is an even function of x in $(-\infty, \infty)$, then the Fourier cosine transform of $f(x)$ $(0 \leq x < \infty)$ is $F(\xi)$.
3. The Fourier cosine transform of $f(x/a)$ is $aF_c(\xi a)$.

TABLE IV. FOURIER SINE TRANSFORMS*

$$f(x) = \sqrt{\frac{2}{\pi}} \int_0^\infty F_s(\xi) \sin (\xi x) d\xi \qquad F_s(\xi) = \sqrt{\frac{2}{\pi}} \int_0^\infty f(x) \sin (\xi x) dx$$

$f(x)$	$F_s(\xi)$
e^{-x}	$\left(\frac{2}{\pi}\right)^{\frac{1}{2}} \frac{1}{1 + \xi^2}$
$xe^{-\frac{1}{2}x^2}$	$e^{-\frac{1}{2}\xi^2}$
$\dfrac{\sin (x)}{x}$	$\dfrac{1}{(2\pi)^{\frac{1}{2}}} \log \left|\dfrac{1 + \xi}{1 - \xi}\right|$
$x(1 - x^2)^\nu \quad 0 < x < 1, \nu > -1$ $0 \qquad\qquad x > 1$	$2^\nu \Gamma(\nu + 1)\xi^{-\frac{1}{2}-\nu} J_{\nu+\frac{3}{2}}(\xi)$
$x^{p-1} \quad 0 < p < 1$	$\left(\frac{2}{\pi}\right)^{\frac{1}{2}} \Gamma(p) \sin \left(\frac{1}{2} p\pi\right) \xi^{-p}$
$x^n e^{-px}$	$\dfrac{2^{n+\frac{1}{2}}p^n n!\xi}{\pi^{\frac{1}{2}}(p^2 + \xi^2)^{n+1}}$
$\cos (ax^2)$	$-a^{-\frac{1}{2}}\left[\cos\left(\dfrac{\xi^2}{4a}\right) S\left(\dfrac{\xi}{\sqrt{2\pi a}}\right)\right.$ $\left. - \sin\left(\dfrac{\xi^2}{4a}\right) C\left(\dfrac{\xi}{\sqrt{2\pi a}}\right)\right]$
$x^{-\frac{1}{2}}e^{-ax^{-\frac{1}{2}}}$	$\xi^{-\frac{1}{2}}[\cos (2a\xi)^{\frac{1}{2}} - \sin (2a\xi)^{\frac{1}{2}}]$
$0 \qquad\qquad 0 < x < a$ $(x^2 - a^2)^{-\frac{1}{2}} \quad x > a$	$\left(\dfrac{\pi}{2}\right)^{\frac{1}{2}} J_0(a\xi)$

* In the calculation of Fourier sine transforms we may make use of the rules:
1. If $F_s(\xi)$ is the Fourier sine transform of $f(x)$ then $f(\xi)$ is the Fourier sine transform of $F_s(x)$.
2. If $f(x)$ is an odd function of x in $(-\infty, \infty)$, then the Fourier sine transform of $f(x)$ $(0 < x < \infty)$ is $-iF(\xi)$.
3. The Fourier sine transform of $f(x/a)$ is $aF_s(a\xi)$.

TABLE V. LAPLACE TRANSFORMS

$$f(t) = \frac{1}{2\pi i} \int_{c-i\infty}^{c+i\infty} \phi(p) e^{pt}\, dp \qquad \phi(p) = \int_0^\infty f(t) e^{-pt}\, dt$$

$f(t)$	$\phi(p)$
t^n	$\Gamma(n+1) p^{-n-1}$
$t^n e^{-qt}$	$\Gamma(n+1)(p+q)^{-n-1}$
$\cos(at)$	$\dfrac{p}{(p^2+a^2)}$
$\sin(at)$	$\dfrac{a}{(p^2+a^2)}$
$t\cos(at)$	$\dfrac{(p^2-a^2)}{(p^2+a^2)^2}$
$t\sin(at)$	$\dfrac{2ap}{(p^2+a^2)^2}$
$t^{-\frac{1}{2}}\cos(2at^{\frac{1}{2}})$	$\left(\dfrac{\pi}{p}\right)^{\frac{1}{2}} e^{-a^2/p}$
$\sin(2at^{\frac{1}{2}})$	$a\left(\dfrac{\pi}{p^3}\right)^{\frac{1}{2}} e^{-a^2/p}$
$t^{-\frac{1}{2}} e^{-a/t} \quad \arg(a) < \frac{1}{2}\pi$	$\left(\dfrac{\pi}{p}\right)^{\frac{1}{2}} e^{-2(ap)^{\frac{1}{2}}}$
$J_\nu(at) \quad \mathsf{R}(\nu) > -1$	$\dfrac{1}{r}\left(\dfrac{a}{p+r}\right)^\nu \quad r = (a^2+p^2)^{\frac{1}{2}}$
$t^\nu J_\nu(at) \quad \mathsf{R}(\nu) > -\frac{1}{2}$	$\pi^{-\frac{1}{2}}\Gamma(\nu+\frac{1}{2})(2a)^\nu (p^2+a^2)^{-\nu-\frac{1}{2}}$

TABLE VI. MELLIN TRANSFORMS

$$f(x) = \frac{1}{2\pi i} \int_{c-i\infty}^{c+i\infty} F(s)x^{-s}\, ds \qquad\qquad \mathsf{F}(s) = \int_0^\infty f(x)x^{s-1}\, dx$$

$f(x)$	$\mathsf{F}(s)$
e^{-px}	$p^{-s}\Gamma(s)$ $\mathsf{R}(s) > 0$
$x^{\frac{1}{2}}J_\nu(x)$	$\dfrac{2^{s-\frac{1}{2}}\Gamma(\frac{1}{2}s + \frac{1}{2}\nu + \frac{1}{4})}{\Gamma(\frac{1}{2}\nu - \frac{1}{2}s + \frac{3}{4})}$
e^{-x^2}	$\frac{1}{2}\Gamma(\frac{1}{2}s)$
$\sin(x)$	$\Gamma(s)\sin(\frac{1}{2}s\pi)$
$\cos(x)$	$\Gamma(s)\cos(\frac{1}{2}s\pi)$
$\cos(x)J_\nu(x)$ $\mathsf{R}(\nu) > -\frac{1}{2}$	$\dfrac{2^{s-1}\pi^{\frac{1}{2}}\Gamma(\frac{1}{2}s + \frac{1}{2}\nu)\Gamma(\frac{1}{2} - s)}{\Gamma(1 + \frac{1}{2}\nu - \frac{1}{2}s)\Gamma(\frac{1}{2} - \frac{1}{2}\nu - \frac{1}{2}s)\Gamma(\frac{1}{2} + \frac{1}{2}\nu - \frac{1}{2}s)}$
$\sin(x)J_\nu(x)$ $\mathsf{R}(\nu) > -\frac{1}{2}$	$\dfrac{2^{s-1}\pi^{\frac{1}{2}}\Gamma(\frac{1}{2}s + \frac{1}{2}\nu + \frac{1}{2})\Gamma(\frac{1}{2} - s)}{\Gamma(1 + \frac{1}{2}\nu - \frac{1}{2}s)\Gamma(1 - \frac{1}{2}\nu - \frac{1}{2}s)\Gamma(\frac{1}{2} + \frac{1}{2}\nu - \frac{1}{2}s)}$
$(1 + x)^{-1}$	$\pi\operatorname{cosec}(\pi s)$
$(1 + x)^{-p}$ $\mathsf{R}(p) > 0$	$\dfrac{\Gamma(s)\Gamma(p - s)}{\Gamma(p)}$
$(1 + x^2)^{-1}$	$\frac{1}{2}\pi\operatorname{cosec}(\frac{1}{2}\pi s)$
$\begin{array}{ll}1 & 0 \le x \le a \\ 0 & x > a\end{array}$	$\dfrac{a^s}{s}$
$\begin{array}{ll}(1-x)^{p-1} & 0 \le x < 1 \\ 0 & x > 1,\ \mathsf{R}(p) > 0\end{array}$	$\dfrac{\Gamma(s)\Gamma(p)}{\Gamma(s + p)}$
$\begin{array}{ll}0 & 0 \le x \le 1 \\ (x-1)^{-p} & x > 1,\ \ 0 < \mathsf{R}(p) < 1\end{array}$	$\dfrac{\Gamma(p - s)\Gamma(1 - p)}{\Gamma(1 - s)}$
$\log_e(1 + x)$	$\dfrac{\pi}{s}\operatorname{cosec}(s\pi)$
$_2F_1(a,b;c;-x)$ $\mathsf{R}(a,b) > 0$	$\dfrac{\Gamma(s)\Gamma(a - s)\Gamma(b - s)\Gamma(c)}{\Gamma(c - s)\Gamma(a)\Gamma(b)}$
$J_\nu(ax)e^{-p^2x^2}$	$\dfrac{\Gamma(\frac{1}{2}\nu + \frac{1}{2}s)(a/2p)^\nu}{2p^s\Gamma(1 + s)}\,{_1F_1}\left(\frac{1}{2}\nu + \frac{1}{2}s;\ \nu + 1;\ \frac{-a^2}{p^2}\right)$
$J_\nu(ax)e^{-px}$	$\dfrac{\Gamma(s + \nu)(a/2p)^\nu}{p^s\Gamma(1 + \nu)}\,{_2F_1}\left(\frac{1}{2}s + \frac{1}{2}\nu,\ \frac{1}{2}s + \frac{1}{2}\nu + \frac{1}{2};\right.$ $\left. \nu + 1;\ \frac{-a^2}{p^2}\right)$
$\operatorname{Ci}(x)$	$s^{-1}\Gamma(s)\cos(\frac{1}{2}s\pi)$
$\operatorname{Si}(x) - \frac{1}{2}\pi$	$s^{-1}\Gamma(s)\sin(\frac{1}{2}s\pi)$
$\frac{1}{2}\pi - \tan^{-1}(x)$	$\frac{1}{2}\pi s^{-1}\sec(\frac{1}{2}s)$

TABLE VII. HANKEL TRANSFORMS

$$f(x) = \int_0^\infty \xi \bar{f}(\xi) J_\nu(\xi x) d\xi \qquad\qquad \bar{f}(\xi) = \int_0^\infty x f(x) J_\nu(\xi x) dx$$

$f(x)$	ν	$\bar{f}(\xi)$
x^ν $\;0 < x < a$ $0\quad x > a$	> -1	$\dfrac{a^{\nu+1}}{\xi} J_{\nu+1}(\xi a)$
$1\;\;0 < x < a$ $0\;\;\;x > a$	0	$\dfrac{a}{\xi} J_1(a\xi)$
$(a^2 - x^2)\;\;0 < x < a,$ $0,\qquad\quad x > a$	0	$\dfrac{4a}{\xi^3} J_1(\xi a) - \dfrac{2a^2}{\xi^2} J_0(\xi a)$
$x^{\mu-2} e^{-px^2}$	> -1	$\dfrac{\xi^\nu \Gamma(\frac{1}{2}\nu + \frac{1}{2}\mu)}{2^{\nu+1} p^{\frac{1}{2}\mu + \frac{1}{2}\nu} \Gamma(1 + \nu)}\, {}_1F_1\left(\dfrac{1}{2}\nu + \dfrac{1}{2}\mu;\, \nu + 1;\, -\dfrac{\xi^2}{4p}\right)$
$x^\nu e^{-px^2}$	> -1	$\dfrac{\xi}{(2p)^{\nu+1}}\, e^{-\xi^2/4p}$
$x^{\mu-1} e^{-px}$	> -1	$\dfrac{2^\mu \xi^\nu \Gamma(\frac{1}{2}\mu + \frac{1}{2}\nu + \frac{1}{2}) \Gamma(1 + \frac{1}{2}\mu + \frac{1}{2}\nu)}{(\xi^2 + p^2)^{\frac{1}{2}\mu + \frac{1}{2}\nu + \frac{1}{2}} \Gamma(\nu + 1) \Gamma(\frac{1}{2})}$ $\times\, {}_2F_1\left(\dfrac{1}{2}\mu + \dfrac{1}{2}\nu + \dfrac{1}{2};\, \dfrac{1}{2}\nu - \dfrac{1}{2}\mu;\, 1 + \nu;\, \dfrac{\xi^2}{\xi^2 + p^2}\right)$
$x^{\mu-1}$	> -1	$\dfrac{2^\mu \Gamma(\frac{1}{2} + \frac{1}{2}\mu + \frac{1}{2}\nu)}{\xi^{\mu+1} \Gamma(\frac{1}{2} - \frac{1}{2}\mu + \frac{1}{2}\nu)}$
$\dfrac{e^{-px}}{x}$	0	$(\xi^2 + p^2)^{-\frac{1}{2}}$
e^{-px}	0	$p(\xi^2 + p^2)^{-\frac{3}{2}}$
$x^{-2} e^{-px}$	1	$\dfrac{(\xi^2 + p^2)^{\frac{1}{2}} - p}{\xi}$
$\dfrac{e^{-px}}{x}$	1	$\dfrac{1}{\xi} - \dfrac{p}{\xi(\xi^2 + p^2)^{\frac{1}{2}}}$
e^{-px}	1	$\xi(\xi^2 + p^2)^{-\frac{3}{2}}$
$\dfrac{a}{(a^2 + x^2)^{\frac{3}{2}}}$	0	$e^{-a\xi}$
$\dfrac{\sin (ax)}{x}$	0	$0 \qquad\qquad\quad \xi > a$ $(a^2 - \xi^2)^{-\frac{1}{2}}\;\; 0 < \xi < a$
$\dfrac{\sin (ax)}{x}$	1	$\dfrac{a}{\xi(\xi^2 - a^2)^{\frac{1}{2}}}\;\; \xi > a$ $0 \qquad\qquad\quad \xi < a$
$\dfrac{\sin (x)}{x^2}$	0	$\sin^{-1}\left(\dfrac{1}{\xi}\right)\;\; \xi > 1$ $\dfrac{1}{2}\pi \qquad\qquad \xi < 1$

TABLE VIII. FINITE FOURIER COSINE TRANSFORMS

$$f(x) = \frac{1}{a}\bar{f}_c(0) + \frac{2}{a}\sum_{n=1}^{\infty}\bar{f}_c(n)\cos\left(\frac{n\pi x}{a}\right) \qquad \bar{f}_c(n) = \int_0^a f(x)\cos\left(\frac{n\pi x}{a}\right)dx$$

$f(x)$	$\bar{f}_c(n)$
1	$a \quad n = 0$ $0 \quad n = 1,2,3,\ldots$
$1 \quad 0 < x < \frac{1}{2}a$ $-1 \quad \frac{1}{2}a < x < a$	$0 \qquad\qquad n = 0$ $\dfrac{2a}{\pi n}\sin\left(\dfrac{1}{2}n\pi\right) \quad n = 1,2,\ldots$
x	$\frac{1}{2}a^2 \qquad\qquad n = 0$ $\left(\dfrac{a}{\pi n}\right)^2[(-1)^n - 1] \quad n = 1,2,\ldots$
x^2	$\frac{1}{3}a^3 \qquad n = 0$ $\dfrac{2a^3}{\pi^2 n^2}(-1)^n \quad n = 1,2,\ldots$
$\left(1 - \dfrac{x}{a}\right)^2$	$\frac{1}{3}a \quad n = 0$ $\dfrac{2a}{\pi^2 n^2} \quad n = 1,2,\ldots$
x^3	$\frac{1}{4}a^4 \qquad\qquad n = 0$ $\dfrac{3a^4(-1)^n}{\pi^2 n^2} + \dfrac{6a^4}{\pi^4 n^4}[(-1)^n - 1], \quad n = 1,2,\ldots$
e^{kx}	$\dfrac{a^2 k}{k^2 a^2 + n^2\pi^2}[(-1)^n e^{ka} - 1]$
$\dfrac{\cosh[c(a - x)]}{\sinh(ca)}$	$\dfrac{a^2 c}{c^2 a^2 + n^2\pi^2}$
$\sin(kx)$	$\dfrac{a^2 k}{n^2\pi^2 - a^2 k^2}[(-1)^n\cos(ka) - 1] \quad n \neq \dfrac{ka}{\pi}$
$\sin\left(\dfrac{m\pi x}{a}\right) \quad m$ an integer	$0 \qquad\qquad n = m$ $\dfrac{ma}{\pi(n^2 - m^2)}[(-1)^{n+m} - 1] \quad n \neq m$

TABLE IX. FINITE FOURIER SINE TRANSFORMS

$$f(x) = \frac{2}{a} \sum_{n=1}^{\infty} \bar{f}_s(n) \sin\left(\frac{n\pi x}{a}\right) \qquad \bar{f}_s(n) = \int_0^a f(x) \sin\left(\frac{n\pi x}{a}\right) dx$$

$f(x)$	$\bar{f}_s(n)$
1	$\dfrac{a}{\pi n}[1 + (-1)^{n+1}]$
x	$(-1)^{n+1}\dfrac{a^2}{\pi n}$
$1 - \dfrac{x}{a}$	$\dfrac{a}{\pi n}$
$\begin{array}{ll} x & 0 \leq x \leq \frac{1}{2}a \\ a - x & \frac{1}{2}a \leq x \leq a \end{array}$	$\dfrac{2a^2}{\pi^2 n^2} \sin\left(\dfrac{1}{2} n\pi\right)$
x^2	$\dfrac{a^3(-1)^{n-1}}{\pi n} - \dfrac{2a^3[1 - (-1)^n]}{\pi^3 n^3}$
x^3	$(-1)^n \dfrac{a^4}{\pi^5}\left(\dfrac{6}{n^3} - \dfrac{\pi^2}{n}\right)$
$x(a^2 - x^2)$	$(-1)^{n+1}\dfrac{6a^4}{\pi^3 n^3}$
$x(a - x)$	$\dfrac{2a^3}{\pi^3 n^3}[1 - (-1)^n]$
e^{kx}	$\dfrac{n\pi a}{n^2\pi^2 + k^2 a^2}[1 - (-1)^n e^{ka}]$
$\cos(kx)$	$\dfrac{n\pi a}{n^2\pi^2 - k^2 a^2}[1 - (-1)^n \cos(ka)] \quad n \neq \dfrac{ka}{\pi}$
$\cos\left(\dfrac{m\pi x}{a}\right) \quad m$ an integer	$\begin{array}{ll} \dfrac{na}{\pi(n^2 - m^2)}[1 - (-1)^{n+m}] & n \neq m \\ 0 & n = m \end{array}$
$\sin\left(\dfrac{m\pi x}{a}\right) \quad m$ an integer	$\begin{array}{ll} 0 & n \neq m \\ \frac{1}{2}a & n = m \end{array}$

TABLE X. FINITE HANKEL TRANSFORMS

$$f(x) = \frac{2}{a^2} \sum \bar{f}_J(\xi_i) \frac{J_\mu(x\xi_i)}{[J'_\mu(a\xi_i)]^2} \qquad \bar{f}_J(\xi_i) = \int_0^a xf(x)J_\mu(x\xi_i)dx$$

where the sum is taken over all the positive zeros of $J_\mu(a\xi_i)$

$f(x)$	μ	$\bar{f}_J(\xi_i)$
x^μ	> -1	$\dfrac{a^{\mu+1}}{\xi_i} J_{\mu+1}(a\xi_i)$
c	0	$\dfrac{ac}{\xi_i} J_1(a\xi_i)$
$a^2 - x^2$	0	$\dfrac{4a}{\xi_i^3} J_1(a\xi_i)$
$\dfrac{J_\mu(\alpha x)}{J_\mu(\alpha a)}$	> -1	$\dfrac{\xi_i a}{\alpha^2 - \xi_i^2} J'_\mu(\xi_i a)$
$\dfrac{J_0(\alpha x)}{J_0(\alpha a)}$	0	$\dfrac{\xi_i a}{\alpha^2 - \xi_i^2} J_1(\xi_i a)$

INDEX